Christmas 2014

Love, ☐ Sand

# THE
# AMERICAN SONGBOOK

Ella Fitzgerald

# THE AMERICAN SONGBOOK

## THE SINGERS, THE SONGWRITERS, AND THE SONGS

KEN BLOOM

FOREWORD BY MICHAEL FEINSTEIN

BLACK DOG
& LEVENTHAL
PUBLISHERS
NEW YORK

ISBN 1-57912-448-8
Library of Congress Cataloging-in-Publication Data is on file
at the offices of Black Dog & Leventhal Publishers.

Book design: Scott Citron
Manufactured in China

Published by
Black Dog & Leventhal Publishers, Inc.
151 West 19th Street
New York, NY 10011

Distributed by
Workman Publishing Company
708 Broadway
New York, NY 10003

h g f e d c b a

**ABOVE:** Lonely at the top. Irving Berlin in his office.
**OPPOSITE:** Harry Revel and Mack Gordon seek inspiration.

# ACKNOWLEDGMENTS

IT'S NEVER EASY, BUT THIS BOOK WAS AN ESPECIALLY COMPLEX ONE TO PULL OFF. Luckily, a bunch of wonderful people banded together to make it happen despite daunting odds, and I'm especially grateful for their assistance, support, and talents. Michael Feinstein was an early booster, opening up his extensive collection, lending tapes of many interviews, and reviewing the pages. Who else could have possibly written the Foreword? Michael is a good person and a good friend, in addition to his many other talents. Black Dog's publisher, J. P. Leventhal, contributed many useful suggestions in the conceptual stage of the book and provided a world of support and encouragement. My editor at Black Dog, Laura Ross, is the perfect editor: smart, sensitive, stern, and savvy. She did an amazing job of pulling this project together with good humor and aplomb (and just edited this sentence down to half its original length while adding twice the meaning).

Designer Scott Citron is the team's great closer, and he performed miracles in a timeframe that was beyond challenging. Scott's lieutenant designers, Nici von Alvensleben and Richard Shearer, were indefatigable in turning out seamlessly beautiful work. Frank Vlastnik, my collaborator on *Broadway Musicals: The 101 Greatest Shows of All Time*, proved himself a great friend by giving up every minute of his time not performing in Broadway-bound workshops and at resident theater companies.

Will Friedwald, David Torresen, Robert Sixsmith, and the aforementioned Michael Feinstein graciously vetted the manuscript and saved me from many embarrassing mistakes. Their knowledge, suggestions, and support are a major reason for any success this book might have. Will's brilliant book, *Jazz Singing*, provided me with many ideas that I appropriated as my own. Naturally, any mistakes are entirely my fault. If you find any, my publishers and I would be very grateful if you would send any corrections to Black Dog and Leventhal, so future editions might be corrected.

This book features more than 500 photos, many of which have never before been published. The vast majority came from Photofest. Howard Mandelbaum and Ron Mandelbaum were, as usual, knowledgeable and professional while maintaining their inimitable humor and seemingly limitless patience. Though Photofest is a business, Howard and Ron are true collaborators, making it a joy to undertake such an ambitious enterprise. Many of the Broadway photos came from the vast collection of the New York Public Library, Billy Rose Theatre Collection at Lincoln Center. Robert Taylor, Curator of the Theatre Collection, and his colleagues Jeremy Megraw and Louise Martzinek were unfailingly patient and helpful. Some of the rarer early photos of Tin Pan Alley and its habitués (and sons of habitués) came from the remarkable collection of expert David Jasen. David's own book, *Tin Pan Alley*, published by Routledge Press, was a seminal source for this one, and remains a remarkable history of the early days of American popular song. Thanks, too, to the always supportive Manoah Bowman for his photographic assistance. Some additional photos came from Michael Kerker and Jim Steinblatt of ASCAP, George Zeno, and Ben Carbonetto.

Many of the rare pieces of sheet music came from the collection of Barry Kleinbort, a brilliant songwriter and brilliant friend. Help on the Career Highlights and Great Songs sections was given by Robert Sixsmith and David Schmittou, two experts in all things musical. Thanks, too, to Dana Trombley of Black Dog and Leventhal for production assistance and organizational abilities, and True Sims, also of that outfit, for her production genius; to Iris Bass, a stern but wise textmistress; to Cory Plowman for his computer savvy and advanced state of logic; and to Stephen Mosher for being on call for when the going got really, really rough.

Thanks, finally, to Adrian Bryan-Brown of Boneau/Bryan Brown, Ellen Donaldson, Mark Trent Goldberg of the Ira and Leonore Gershwin Trusts, Lynn Lane, Stanley Mills, Pat Plowman, and Donald Smith of the Mabel Mercer Foundation.

# CONTENTS

# FOREWORD

This book is important.

There is so much that is changing in our world and somehow, we need music—great music—more than ever. I've pretty much dedicated my life to that idea, and I have a feeling that you agree, as you have gone as far as taking this marvelous volume down off the shelf for at least a peek. Sadly, with all of the upheaval surrounding us, the assaults on culture and the constant barrage of sounds and images, much of our precious musical heritage is fast disappearing. More accurately, our musical history is becoming largely unknown to most people—even those who buy CDs, download music, spend half of their lives plugged into their iPods, and profess an avid attachment to music. While I'd never consider it a requirement that everyone be a walking syllabus of popular standards, I feel that we are in danger of losing something essential when our past is not celebrated and appreciated by today's audiences.

It is only through the efforts of such passionate and committed individuals as Ken Bloom that the Great American Songbook (as this wide range of music has been rather glibly dubbed) is being preserved and fittingly celebrated. This book, clearly a labor of love as well as a mission, serves the important purpose of chronicling and commenting on an incredible body of work created over many decades. And, just as important, it gathers into one place hundreds of precious photographs, including many that even I've never seen, that help bring the artists and their work to life as never before. What is more, it includes many first-person reminiscences and comments by the artists themselves, culled from hundreds of hours of interviews (some conducted by me). This very personal material, most of it never-before published, preserves the words and thoughts of a generation of artists who were part of the golden era of the art form. Seeing all of these words and images in one place, it's very clear (to quote Ira Gershwin) that when we talk about the American Songbook we're not just talking about an assortment of great songs—we are setting down a history, and it is *our* history.

Irving Berlin once said, "History makes music and music makes history." It's true. American popular song is our country's invention and its great gift—it has become, to quote Burton Lane, "our greatest export." People all over the world have images and opinions of America that are filtered through thirty-two bars of such disparate songs as "White Christmas," "What the World Needs Now," "Hooray for Hollywood," and "Great Balls of Fire." Songs express our inner feelings and elevate the mundane to the magnificent, and I think it is safe to say that we could not exist as a civilized society without music and the interpreters who bring them to life.

The beauty of what lies in the pages ahead is that there is a great deal of information carefully distilled into a compact and entertaining form. It is a daunting prospect to try and encapsulate so many aspects of American popular music into a single volume while retaining the flavor, fun, and fervor of the form. Happily, that is exactly the miracle that has been achieved. The anecdotes contained here are fresh and illuminating, the song lists imposing, and the biographies of the performers and writers models of economy. There is a lot to savor in these pages.

Like I said, this book is important—but don't let that frighten you. It is a sheer joy, as well.

—Michael Feinstein

# INTRODUCTION

Welcome to a look back at 100 years of American popular song, a celebration of our greatest singers, songwriters, and songs. All of my favorites are here—and I can only hope that I didn't leave out too many of yours. But please understand that this book is supposed to be fun—not homework—and any nondefinitive list is subjective. Perhaps I included some people and songs that you find unworthy, or I barely mentioned someone who you feel towers above the rest. All I can say in defense of this rather crazy enterprise is that maybe, in perusing these pages, you will come across someone you are meeting for the first time, about whom you might want to learn more. The world of popular music is so rich and various—it shouldn't surprise you that I learned many new things in putting this book together. Now its your turn to take the journey.

With only a few exceptions, the artists I included are those whom I most admire for creating the marvelous and enduring songs and recordings that comprise the soundtrack of our lives. It's a cliché, maybe—but that doesn't mean it ain't true. We love these artists and their work because of the sheer joy they continue to bring us, even as decades pass and musical tastes change. No matter what state of mind you're in, there's an American popular standard that can express your emotions in words and music, elevate your mood (or help you wallow in it), and cement the memory of the moment for all time. No scientist has come up with a useful theory as to why music has such a profound and lasting effect on us, but we all know it's true. And for many of us, this is the music about which it is *most* true.

This book is very Tin Pan Alley–centric, so some of our finest composers, including Leonard Bernstein, Stephen Sond-

Who else but Kate Smith could possibly provide a warm enough welcome to *The American Songbook?*

heim, Jerry Bock and Sheldon Harnick, and Charles Strouse and Lee Adams, are not included. Although they wrote brilliant songs, they were primarily Broadway composers and not central to the Tin Pan Alley tradition. Their work is celebrated in loving detail in my previous book, *Broadway Musicals.* The same goes for many singers who took a stroll through Tin Pan Alley but were mainly associated with country, classical, or other forms of songwriting.

There are many fine biographies of the major singers, composers, and lyricists featured here, as well as many encyclopedias of jazz and popular song. On the Internet you can find more information on virtually any one of these artists. This book is meant to be both more and less than those other sources—while less encyclopedic, it is more opinionated, more lively, more anecdotal—and much more visual than anything yet published on this vast subject. I've tried to hit the highlights of each career, complete with song lists and capsule biographies, though, of necessity, not every recording or appearance is included. There are other books you can turn to for that. These singers, bandleaders, and composers sang, played, or composed thousands of songs, but I have attempted to select for you the most significant of these, as a starting point for appreciating the artists. Feel free to write any of your favorites that I've overlooked in the book's margins, or—better yet—write to me care of the publisher, and let me know what you feel I've omitted. As I said, I live and learn.

As I did when putting together *Broadway Musicals: The 101 Greatest Shows of All Time,* on which I collaborated with Frank Vlastnik, I feel that photos are a great way to tell the story of song. Frank kindly helped out on that aspect of this book, too. With the help of Photofest, the Billy Rose Theatre Collection at Lincoln Center, and many private collectors, we uncovered a wealth of striking images that have never before been published. We are especially gratified to include so many rare and excellent color photos here.

I hope that reading this book brings back happy memories, or even bittersweet ones. Above all, I hope it leads you to a greater passion for the wonderful singers and songwriters of Broadway, Hollywood, and Tin Pan Alley, those artists who have created and propagated our Great American Songbook.

—Ken Bloom

a's historic appearance at the New York Paramount.

# THE SINGERS

# Louis Armstrong

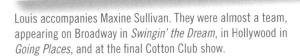

Louis accompanies Maxine Sullivan. They were almost a team, appearing on Broadway in *Swingin' the Dream*, in Hollywood in *Going Places*, and at the final Cotton Club show.

America in the first years of the new century could be a harsh place, but despite racism and poverty, urban blacks formed a strong society built of lodges, parades, street bands, unions, a caste system within narrow boundaries, and a unique kind of music. New Orleans was a more liberal town than most, especially when compared to other Southern cities, and while blacks weren't exactly welcomed into white society, they were mostly left alone and, in certain areas, encouraged to excel. Music was one such area.

Black music in America began with slavery, employing found instruments such as washboards, jugs, homemade banjos, and the like. With the optimism brought on by the century's turning, the rapid growth of the city, and the beginnings of the industrial revolution, blacks had more opportunities and a slightly better standard of living. For the first time they could afford manufactured instruments, which were cheap and plentiful.

Blacks in New Orleans grew up surrounded by the music of street bands, riverboat concerts, parades, and any number of society events, both black and white. In 1881, at the funeral procession for President Garfield, there were more than a dozen black bands. Storyville, the city's black ghetto, had its own clubs including Pete Lala's, the Palm Gardens, the 101 Ranch, and Tom Anderson's Annex. Bordellos always had at least a pianist in the parlor. White society often hired black musicians for parties and balls.

White do-gooders' attempts to help their poorer brethren often included cultural encouragement. And, since blacks were thought to have a fine natural sense of rhythm, music seemed an obvious way to help poor blacks improve their lot. It turns out that, in spite of the racist logic behind this initiative, it helped to launch the musical careers of many black artists.

Louis Armstrong was one such miscreant whose lot in life was changed through music. After getting arrested for shooting off a pistol during a New Year's Eve celebration, Armstrong was thrown into the Colored Waifs' Home. He was given a cornet by Peter Davis, the band leader at the home, and his natural abilities catapulted him to success relatively quickly.

At the time, local popular music was based on an amalgam of styles. Ragtime (its strict structure based on the French quadrille) slave songs, the harmonies of the black church, blues-tones, the rhythms of the street band, melodic lines from popular ballads, syncopation from street dancers all merged in New Orleans and jazz was born. White bands merged the styles into Dixieland, with the cornet and clarinet carrying the melody, while black musicians created a brand of jazz in which the cornet and trumpet carried the melody.

By the time the army closed down Storyville in 1917, the music had already begun its journey up the Mississippi to Kansas City, St. Louis, and Chicago. With every stop along the way there were local variations and side trips to Detroit, Memphis, and New York.

When he arrived in Chicago in 1923, Armstrong found a community of blacks and whites shaping the new music to new talents. Though Jelly Roll Morton claimed to have "invented" jazz, Armstrong was able to draw upon all of these influences and adapt them into his own idiom. In 1925, Armstrong founded the Hot Fives and over the next three years he invented a new way to play jazz, a style that has remained the standard up to today. Armstrong played in the 4/4 time structure, injecting the previously popular fox trot rhythm with a bit of swing. He sandwiched solos between more straight-ahead renditions of the melody and encouraged long improvisations, always within the rhythmic framework already set up. He codified a form of jazz improvisation wherein he would state the melody, loosen it up with variations, and then go on to make further variations on the variations.

Armstrong moved from jazz into popular music, bringing a jazz influence right with him. Not for him the staid ballads and square songs of the last century or the European-influenced music of the operetta. Armstrong's vocals freed the popular song and his early experiments with scatting sealed the bargain, as he jazzed the words as well as the music.

Armstrong's performance style was endearing and unforgettable: the gravelly voice, the wide grin, the handkerchief constantly mopping his mouth and face, the laughter, the "oh, yeaaaah!" at the end of a number—it's no surprise that both whites and blacks adored him. But make no mistake—he wasn't a clown, he was that rarest of beings: an accessible jazz musician, never employing the strange chords and rhythms or arcane musical lines of the more "serious" players. Early on, Armstrong appeared alongside such popular entertainers as Crosby (practically a partner) on radio and was a regular feature at the local movie theatre. And once the television era dawned, Armstrong's fame exploded. By that time his repertoire included more popular songs and he became a staple of such variety shows as *Ed Sullivan*. It was at this point that he broke through the barriers of simple celebrity to become an icon.

Armstrong's style suited him well throughout his career. Even when criticized for becoming cartoonish in his later years, his musicianship was as solid as ever. The lessons he taught, the techniques he commanded, and the forms he created have become the bedrock of all popular song styling. Not only does he head the list of greats alphabetically, he leads them chronologically and in importance. Satchmo was the beginning, the middle, and the end, the first and last word in jazz and popular music performance. ◆

## THE GREAT SONGS

| | |
|---|---|
| 1925 | St. Louis Blues (with Bessie Smith) |
| 1926 | Heebie Jeebies; Muskrat Ramble |
| 1927 | Struttin' with Some Barbecue; Wild Man Blues |
| 1928 | I Can't Give You Anything but Love; West End Blues |
| 1929 | After You've Gone; Ain't Misbehavin' |
| 1931 | When It's Sleepytime Down South |
| 1932 | All of Me; Chinatown, My Chinatown |
| 1933 | Baby, Won't You Please Come Home |
| 1936 | Swing That Music |
| 1938 | Jeepers Creepers |
| 1945 | I Wonder; You Won't Be Satisfied (Until You Break My Heart) |
| 1947 | Do You Know What It Means to Miss New Orleans? |
| 1951 | A Kiss to Build a Dream On |
| 1956 | Mack the Knife; Now You Has Jazz |
| 1964 | Hello, Dolly! |
| 1968 | What a Wonderful World |

## Song and Story

### WHEN IT'S SLEEPYTIME DOWN SOUTH

This bucolic view of the South became a signature tune for Armstrong, who added a spoken introduction in which two Northern blacks realize they've been away from the South for a long time. The song recounts their shared nostalgia for a South that never existed.

### JEEPERS CREEPERS

Sung in the film *Going Places*, "Jeepers Creepers" is the name of a racehorse who refuses to run unless Louis is singing to him! Johnny Mercer, the lyricist, recalled its inspiration: "My wife and I went to see a movie one night at Grauman's Chinese Theater and Henry Fonda played a farm boy in it…. And in the movie he saw something, something impressed him, and he said, 'Jeepers creepers,' and that just rang a little bell in my head, and I wrote it down when I got out of the movie."

### HELLO, DOLLY!

Songwriter Jerry Herman never believed that this song could possibly be a popular hit. Imagine his surprise when the Louis Armstrong recording hit the top of the charts.

### WHAT A WONDERFUL WORLD

Bob Thiele of ABC Records gave Armstrong the song to consider. Armstrong loved it and recorded it with an orchestra but as a vocal only—he didn't play the trumpet on the recording. Larry Newman, then the head of ABC, hated the song and didn't want to release it. He finally agreed to put it out but without any publicity whatsoever. What should have been a glorious follow-up to "Hello, Dolly!" was a complete failure. In England, the record hit the top of the charts but in America, nothing. It wasn't until the song was featured on the soundtrack of the film *Good Morning, America* that it became a success in the States.

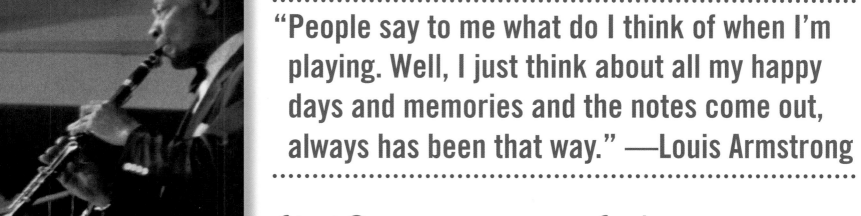

"People say to me what do I think of when I'm playing. Well, I just think about all my happy days and memories and the notes come out, always has been that way." —Louis Armstrong

### First Person

Guitarist Danny Barker described the typical dressing room scene in the 1950s: And in the room, you see maybe two nuns. You see a streetwalker dressed all up in flaming clothes. You see a guy come out of a penitentiary. You see a blind man sitting there. You see a rabbi. You see a priest. Liable to see maybe two policemen or detectives. You see a judge. All of them different levels of society in the dressing room and he's talking to all of 'em.

### Asides

The first widespread adoption of electric recording came in 1925, supplanting the inferior acoustic recording. It was also the year that Louis Armstrong first sang on a recording.

Louis Armstrong was nicknamed "Satchmo," an abbreviation of the earlier nickname "Satchel Mouth."

Armstrong with Trummy Young on trombone and Ed Hall on clarinet.

# Fred Astaire

The greatest dancer of the twentieth century was also one of the best interpreters of American popular song. Notice the word "interpreter" rather than singer. Astaire, like many other great singers, understood the confines of his own range and compensated through an emphasis on performance, interpretation, and the rhythms of a song. It's been stated that limitations make great art—and so it is with singers. The challenge of escaping the margins of one's natural talents can bring creativity to the fore, and great artists find new ways to communicate without relying on gimmicks.

In fact, many mediocre singers rely on the nice sounds they can make while never actually connecting with the meaning of a song. Others, especially of recent vintage, rely solely on lung power and clichéd techniques and end up making every song sound exactly the same.

Astaire was smart and talented enough to find strengths that obviated his weaknesses. While some singers use their voices like horns (or so the saying goes), he used the rhythms in songs to create a form of jazz singing all his own. In a way it makes sense that his singing, like his sublime dancing, relied on rhythms and accents as much as melody and tone.

Astaire always shared an affinity with jazz performers, preferring the jazzy feel of a Gershwin tune to the square operetta composers of his early career. He appeared in the otherwise dismal *Second Chorus* because Artie Shaw was in the film. When he turned to television he collaborated with such greats as Jonah Jones and Count Basie. And his recording *The Fred Astaire Story* features accompaniment by Oscar Peterson.

He made singing seem natural, conversational, and effortless, yet his listeners could always sense and appreciate the thought behind the performance. It all seemed so unforced, just like his dancing. Dance on the walls and ceiling? Why not? Use a trench coat as a matador's cape? No problem. Take a hat stand as a dancing partner? Absolutely. Clarify the trickiest of rhythms in a song, build variations on them, make the connections between notes seem inevitable? All done with aplomb.

Never showing off but communicating in the simplest of ways the happiness and heartbreak of popular song, Astaire made the hardest phrase—or the hardest dance step—seem easy. When we dance around the living room, lost in the fantasy that we are lighter than air, we aren't imagining ourselves as Gene Kelly or Mikhail Baryshnikov—it's Fred Astaire we have in mind. And when we sing in the shower or while mowing the lawn, it isn't Ella Fitzgerald or Luciano Pavarotti we emulate—it's the incomparable Astaire.

Astaire made it all sound good. Can you think of an Astaire performance that was bad, or even slightly below par? Doubtful. Considering he didn't even think of himself as a singer, it must be noted that he introduced and made his own some of the greatest standards in the American repertoire. Like Bob Hope, Astaire brought humanity to his singing. Like Mabel Mercer, he took his limitations and made them secondary. Like Bing Crosby, he emphasized through understatement. Above all, he was uniquely Fred Astaire. ◆

## *Fred's Partners*

| | |
|---|---|
| Adele Astaire | Joan Leslie |
| Tilly Losch | Lucille Bremer |
| Claire Luce | Joan Caulfield |
| Dorothy Stone | Olga San Juan |
| Joan Crawford | Judy Garland |
| Ginger Rogers | Ann Miller |
| Harriet Hoctor | Vera-Ellen |
| Joan Fontaine | Betty Hutton |
| George Burns and | Jane Powell |
| Gracie Allen | Cyd Charisse |
| Eleanor Powell | Leslie Caron |
| Paulette Goddard | Audrey Hepburn |
| Rita Hayworth | Barrie Chase |
| Marjorie Reynolds | Lilli Palmer |
| Virginia Dale | Debbie Reynolds |

## CAREER HIGHLIGHTS

**1899** Born in Omaha, Nebraska, on May 10.

**1905** Mother and children move to New York City in January to develop sister Adele's talents; premiere of act in Keyport, New Jersey, in November.

**1906** Travel on the Orpheum Circuit for $150 a week plus train fare.

**1909** Appear in vaudeville with Eduardo Cansino, father of Rita Hayworth; break from performing until children come of age.

**1912** Minor vaudeville engagements.

**1917** Debut on Broadway in *Over the Top* on November 28.

**1918** Second Broadway show, *The Passing Show of 1918*.

**1919** Father comes from Omaha to rejoin family in spacious new apartment that kids pay for.

**1924** Father dies; *Lady, Be Good!* opens on Broadway.

**1928** *Funny Face* opens on Broadway.

**1930** Meets Ginger Rogers while choreographing "Embraceable You" for *Girl Crazy*.

**1931** *The Band Wagon* opens on Broadway.

**1932** Adele leaves tour of *The Band Wagon* on March 5 to marry Sir Charles Cavendish and quits show business; *Gay Divorce* opens on Broadway on November 29, marking Astaire's debut as a solo performer.

**1933** Marries Phyllis Potter on July 12 and they leave for California and the movies on July 14; film debut dancing with Joan Crawford in *Dancing Lady*; *Flying Down to Rio* opens marking beginning of screen pairing with Ginger Rogers as well as choreographer Hermes Pan.

**1934** *The Gay Divorcee* opens—star billing and a percentage of the profits.

**1940** Begins MGM contract with *Broadway Melody of 1940* with Eleanor Powell.

**1944** Entertains troops in Europe.

**1946** Retires from show business in October with end of filming of *Blue Skies*.

**1947** Opens first Fred Astaire Dance Studio.

**1948** Replaces Gene Kelly in *Easter Parade*.

**1949** *The Barkleys of Broadway* reunites him with Ginger Rogers.

**1950** Awarded an honorary Oscar.

**1953** Film *The Band Wagon* opens; *The Astaire Story* recording released with Oscar Peterson's backup.

**1954** Phyllis Astaire dies on September 13.

**1955** Television debut on *Toast of the Town*, *What's My Line?*, and *I've Got a Secret* promoting film *Daddy Long Legs*.

**1958** First dramatic television role in *Imp on a Cardboard Leash*; Television special, *An Evening with Fred Astaire*.

**1959** Autobiography, *Steps in Time*; films dramatic debut in *On the Beach*.

**1968** Last film musical, *Finian's Rainbow*.

**1975** Records album in London with Bing Crosby.

**1976** Breaks wrist after falling from skateboard.

**1980** Marries Robyn Smith.

**1981** Adele Astaire dies on January 25.

**1987** Dies on June 12.

# Asides

For a long time, Astaire refused to kiss the heroine in his pictures. This was duly noted by the press and fans, so in *Carefree*, Astaire put in a slow-motion kiss that lasted about four minutes. In *Swing Time*'s "A Fine Romance," Dorothy Fields wrote the lyric "with no kisses" as a reference to the lack of mouth-to-mouth action in the Astaire-Rogers films.

The public and the critics were obsessed with Astaire's partners, comparing each one to Adele or to Ginger Rogers. In Belgium, where he was entertaining for the USO, a young boy stopped him saying in broken English, "I...know...you." "You do?" Astaire responded, "Who am I?" The boy thought and then proclaimed, "Ginger Rogers!"

While in Bridgeport, Connecticut, for the 1922 show *For Goodness Sake,* Fred bought a fourteen-dollar green bathrobe. That night he stopped the show and ascribed his luck to the new bathrobe. From then on he wore the robe on the day of every opening night or film premiere until the robe wore out.

Fred Astaire performing "If Swing Goes I Go Too," cut from the MGM spectacular *Ziegfeld Follies.*

# Song and Story

### CHEEK TO CHEEK

This is the longest song written by Irving Berlin.

### THE CARIOCA

This number was danced by Fred Astaire and Ginger Rogers in their first movie as a team, *Flying Down to Rio*. In his autobiography, Astaire wrote, "I was under the impression that we weren't doing anything particularly outstanding in 'The Carioca'. I had thrown in a few solos, too, in the limited time given me, but I never expected that they would register so well. However, everything clicked."

### NIGHT AND DAY

Cole Porter was nonplused when Astaire worried about singing the song because of the range. Porter replied, "Sure you can. I wrote it especially for your voice."

### OH, LADY, BE GOOD!

Astaire didn't sing the song in *Lady, Be Good!*, Walter Catlett sang it. Fred recalled in his autobiography, "Walter was a funny man, and, like a lot of comedians, even his voice was funny—in fact, it was terrible. And what he did to 'Lady, Be Good!' was nobody's business." Fred did record the song and it was long associated with him.

# Mildred Bailey

S cientists and creationists agree, the story of American popular song is a story of evolution. In both performance and composition, each generation has slowly built upon the strides of previous artists. Among the most influential singers, despite her relatively short twenty-year career, was Mildred Bailey.

The illustrious Jack Kapp recorded Bailey and the Casa Loma Orchestra in 1931. Her high (but not operatic) and girlish voice cut through the orchestra, and her relaxed singing style and self-confidence set her apart from the boop-boop-a-doopers then enjoying a vogue. Sweet, girlish voice, yes—but she was no flapper. Nor was she just the girl singer breaking up the band's instrumentals with a quick vocal chorus. Somehow, Bailey became the focus and the band became the accompaniment.

Bailey's easy going vocals gave her a faintly Southern sound, though she was born on February 27, 1903, in Tekoa, Washington. Her first big hit, Hoagy Carmichael's "Rockin' Chair," certainly possessed a Dixie feeling. In fact, the unity of song and performance provided Bailey with the nickname "The Rockin' Chair Lady." Bailey's easy-swinging style was her own personal twist on the style of Ethel Waters, who had given up rough-and-ready blues for more refined musical interests.

Just as Bailey was influenced by Waters and others, including a blues legend named Bessie Smith, she set the stage for the next generation of such singers as Frank Sinatra. But before the next generation took the stage, Bailey had a more important, more influential role to play in the history of American popular song.

Like most good girls of the period, Mildred played the piano. Unlike most good girls of the period, Mildred was married three times before she was thirty-five. She played piano for silent movies and demonstrated sheet music. Just like in the movies, while she was singing in a five-and-dime, a smalltime club owner from Vancouver hired her for his club. That first break set her on her way and she was smart enough to realize just how lucky she was. Mildred clearly appreciated the break she got and would, in a few years, give a break to a couple of guys and change music history.

But first she moved to Los Angeles, where she hooked up with a Fanchon and Marco tab show and with them made her screen debut (and her screen farewell, too).

She also appeared on radio station KMTR, singing the latest hit songs. At the same time she encouraged her brother Al to come to LA and to bring along his cohort, Bing Crosby—and that's when the sound of American music changed forever. In LA at the time was bandleader Paul Whiteman who hired Al and Bing and put them together with Harry Barris to create the Rhythm Boys. In 1929, Al and Bing returned the favor and allowed Whiteman to "discover" Mildred and make her his band's featured vocalist.

She became the first girl singer to enjoy steady employment as part of a band's entourage.

After she left Whiteman, Jack Kapp snapped Bailey up and had her record over two hundred sides for his Vocalion label. The success with Whiteman and her burgeoning recording career shot Bailey to the top of her profession. She enjoyed her own radio show and married xylophonist Red Norvo in 1933, having met him in Whiteman's ensemble. The recordings they made together, including an excellent redo of "Rocking Chair" in 1937, were the some of the finest of her career. Norvo

Mildred Bailey admiring the pianistic genius of Art Tatum.

and Bailey put their own band together and were soon dubbed "Mr. and Mrs. Swing." The Bailey/Norvo band lasted only three years and the marriage broke up soon thereafter.

Bailey went on to enjoy a successful solo career that included dabbling with the Benny Goodman band on his *Camel Caravan* radio show as well as a few recordings and a performance relationship with Alec Wilder's semiclassical chamber octet. She continued recording for Kapp's Decca label and made a splash in 1944 on CBS radio as the lead in her own show. By now she was regarded as perhaps the best singer around, and many notables guested on the show. Barney Josephson, the legendary impresario of Café Society, booked Bailey in Manhattan, and she reached the pinnacle of her success.

Bailey had suffered injuries in an auto accident in the thirties, and while recuperating gained a lot of weight that she was never able to take off. Her weight problem led to other medical ills and, after stints in the hospital in 1938, 1943, and 1949, she decided to retire to a farm! Unable to keep away from performing, she recorded her last sides and appeared with Bing Crosby in 1950. The next year, she performed in Detroit but her health was rapidly declining. She died penniless in a Poughkeepsie Hospital on December 12, 1951. Throughout her many bouts with diabetes and heart ailments, Bing Crosby, Frank Sinatra, and Jimmy Van Heusen split her medical bills.

In addition to influencing Bing Crosby, Bailey also inspired Tony Bennett and Billie Holiday, whom she discovered along with John Hammond while they were clubbing together in New York. Often cantankerous and occasionally sweet, Bailey's ease with lyrics, emotional purity, simplicity of style, and gentle swinging made her one of the first great female singers of American popular song. ◆

# Tony Bennett

**H**ere are some generalizations for you: People love a regular guy who has made it big. Women like a good-looking guy with a hint of sex. Men like a guy they can have a beer with, who doesn't threaten their own masculinity. Tony Bennett fills the bill for everyone—and the added bonus is, he's a great singer.

Bennett isn't what you'd call a "soft singer"; rather he puts across his songs with power and conviction. No wispy ballads or affected, swingy tunes for Tony—he attacks each song straight on, at full volume, without ever sounding as if he's shouting or showing off. As he builds in volume through the course of a song, he increases the dramatic intensity. In an age when popular singers tend to go for audience adulation via the emotionless belt and ear-splitting ending, Bennett earns his props by believing in the song, respecting it, and making audiences feel at ease with his genuine artistry.

It wasn't always this way. Bennett explains, "Before I recorded 'San Francisco,' I was advised to try out all sorts of tricks and gimmicks. Songs were offered to me which were supposed to be surefire, but they weren't my style." Bennett's style is decidedly middle-of-the-road and that's where he shines. Luckily, Columbia had faith in him and allowed him to find his niche during the first few years of his career.

True, he was forced to record some of the typical repertoire of gimmicky, catchy songs with no depth—but luckily, these were released only as singles (still a lucrative category at the time). Singles were meant for kids to stack up on their changers so they could hop around their rec rooms. On albums, which were meant for adults sitting in front of the hi-fi with a martini in one hand and a cigarette in the other, Bennett recorded new show tunes, Broadway standards and other choice cuts from the American songbook. Bennett recorded more new show tunes than any other singer.

Those Broadway songs served Bennett well: more of his repertoire is devoted to songs by the masters of Broadway than any other performer save, perhaps, Ella Fitzgerald with her Songbooks. Bennett prefers jazz-oriented writers, such as Harold Arlen, Cy Coleman, and Burt Bacharach, who wrote songs with depth but also with a catchy beat. There aren't many male pop singers who are much jazzier

Bennett isn't one of those soulful, intimate singers who makes each listener believe he's singing especially to him or her. Instead, he simply pours his heart out (without the histrionics of many singers) while we happen to be looking on. Just look at his song list: there are a lot of songs about "I" and not many about "we." He isn't a master of the love song. His signature song, "I Left My Heart in San Francisco," may be a song of loss—but it's not a plea to the girl who done him wrong. Songs of loss make up a big part of his catalog: besides "San Francisco," there's "When the Sun Comes Out," "Boulevard of Broken Dreams," "When Joanna Loved Me," and on and on. With Tony Bennett, the best is always yet to come.

Although "San Francisco" may be the song most associated with him, it's hardly his best recording, a fact that prompted Columbia to move him further and further away from jazz and into the easy-listening genre, featuring a strong foundation of strings underpinning his voice. And although he had many hit songs, Bennett seldom scored a hit album in his mid-career period. Not for him, the concept album. His later Columbia albums have plenty of swell stuff on them but there doesn't seem any rhyme or reason to the song choices or the order of tracks. It's as if he spent the majority of his career on shuffle play.

In 1972, left Columbia. "I wouldn't sing the garbage they were peddling," he stated at the time. "The record companies were forcing artists to take a dive and I resisted. I thought the only important thing was to be trusted. And I made a stink about it. I still do. Naturally, they don't like me; I consider it a compliment. Remember, we're talking about law-yers, accountants, and marketing guys; they're in charge of the business. Imagine an industry run by people who don't know anything about the product?

"There's a tremendous business injustice going on. The record companies have been saying for years that people like me can't sell, but we keep selling out wherever we go. To me, it's twenty times harder to get people out on the town—and and at least that much more expensive—than to get them to buy a record. The truth is, the industry won't sell the records, not that we can't sell 'em."

His marriage kaput, Bennett lapsed into a self-admitted booze-and-drug-induced lull. But just in time (as the song goes), his son Danny took over his career. Together they worked tirelessly to build a new fan base. The segment of the popularion that had bought his records got out of the habit. They didn't love Bennett any less, but they just didn't go into stores or clubs.

Bennett successfully made the transition from nightclubs to concert halls and even MTV! He soon re-signed with Columbia Records and entered a fertile new period. He was finally making exactly the albums he wanted to make, very personal compilations that won a lot of Grammy Awards in a field with little competition. While his old fans still weren't flocking to buy his albums, at least Bennett had his artistic integrity back and, with his voice diminished very little by time, he could still sell out Radio City Music Hall, the seats filled with a brand-new, younger set of fans.

So, fifty years after his debut, Tony Bennett is on the road to living legend status. He might just get there—all the while remaining a regular Joe, just doing his job the best he knows how. ◆

## CAREER HIGHLIGHTS

**1926** Born Anthony Bennedeto on August 3 in Astoria, Queens, New York.

**1936** Sings at opening of Triboro Bridge.

**1944** Drafted into army.

**1946** Attends American Theatre Wing on GI Bill; first nightclub engagement at Shangri-La in Astoria.

**1948** Auditions for High Martin for a part in the new musical *Look Ma, I'm Dancin'*. Hugh likes his voice but doesn't think it's right for the stage. Hugh writes a letter to Columbia Records recommending him for a contract.

**1949** Opens for Pearl Bailey; Bob Hope attends the show and gives him the name Tony Bennett (he'd been going by "Joe Bari").

**1950** Signed to Columbia Records by Mitch Miller; first released recording, "The Boulevard of Broken Dreams," becomes a hit.

**1951** "Because of You" becomes first gold record, followed by "Cold, Cold Heart."

**1952** 10" album *Because of You* first hit compilation album.

**1955** First album , *Cloud 7* released.

**1956** Chosen by NBC as summer replacement host for *The Perry Como Show* TV variety show.

**1957** Teams up with pianist Ralph Sharon; records *The Best of My Heart*.

**1959** Records *In Person with Count Basie*.

**1962** Records "I Left My Heart in San Francisco"; plays Carnegie Hall and wins first Grammy.

**1972** Leaves Columbia for MGM Records.

**1973** Creates own label, Improv.

**1977** Improv goes out of business.

**1979** Danny Bennett becomes manager.

**1986** Signs with Columbia Records again; records album *Art of the Excellence*.

**1992** *Perfectly Frank*.

**1993** *Steppin' Out*.

**1994** Appears on *MTV Unplugged*, album wins "Album of the Year" Grammy.

**1995** *Here's to the Ladies*.

**1996** *On Holiday: A Tribute to Billie Holiday*.

**2001** *Playin' with My Friends: Bennett Sings the Blues*.

**2003** Twelfth Grammy for *A Wonderful World* with k.d. lang.

> "I don't like saying I'm a jazz singer or a pop singer; I don't like categories. I just like to sing."—Tony Bennett

## Bennett on Bennett

I imitated Al Jolson and Eddie Cantor and it used to break my relatives up every Sunday. I had an aunt that adored Bing Crosby. After supper I'd go over, my uncle was a tap dancer in vaudeville, and we'd listen to Bing Crosby.

I call myself a "Bing Crosby singer." I was very influenced by Bing. I liked the essence of Bing. He made us all a living; he showed us all how to communicate as popular singers by relaxing. He was blessed by the fact he liked to sing. It had nothing to do with fame or ambition. You could feel him being transformed as soon as he got into a tune, and he got carried away until it was finished. He was shy of any category, because he just sang whatever he liked. And I like that. I don't like saying I'm a jazz singer or a pop singer; I don't like categories. I just like to sing, and I like Bing for that reason. Country, pop, classical, jazz, whatever—if he liked the melody, he did it.

What I try to do is find a song that tells a story. The melody hits the audience and then the words tell a story and the more you can tell a story, I think it connects with everybody. The way young people are treated by producers is frustrating. They hit them quick and then if the next album doesn't make it they go with the next new thing. It wasn't that way when people like Rosemary Clooney and I started. They gave us five or six years to develop. We were able to work with and learn from people like Count Basie and Woody Herman—they show you the way to do things better.

There are certain albums you can put on all day long. My favorites are probably Frank Sinatra, *In the Wee Small Hours of the Morning*; Billie Holiday, *Lady in Satin*, and anything by Louis Armstrong. I also listen to classical music, especially Delius, Ravel, and Tchaikovsky.

## Song and Story

### I LEFT MY HEART IN SAN FRANCISCO

Tony Bennett once told an interviewer: Rock-and-roll all but ruined me. It seemed that any singer over twenty-five who couldn't play a steel guitar was in trouble. The Sinatras and the Crosbys had become institutions, but I wasn't anchored yet. Also, I lacked poise and experience. Then I had a date at the Fairmont Hotel in San Francisco, and I thought this may be my last. I wanted some special material and against the advice of my cohorts took a ten-year-old song that had new lyrics about San Francisco. I recorded the song—also against managerial advice—and the last I heard it had sold more than three million, and I'm still working.

### BLUE VELVET

Bennett had one of hs earliest hits with "Blue Velvet" in 1951, over a decade before Bobby Vinton's better known version. Ella Fitzgerald told Bennett it was one of her favorite recordings when the two met for the first time in 1962.

# Connee Boswell

Singers who come out of vocal groups swinging and singing solo tend to retain their identities as members of the group. Think of Ed Ames, Andy Williams, and June Hutton. Fine singers all, with lots of hits, but none had much personality on his or her own. There are exceptions, of course, most notably Bing Crosby, who left Paul Whiteman's Rhythm Boys and developed his own persona and style. (Truth is, though, the Rhythm Boys had always sounded more like Crosby than vice versa.) Another notable exception to the rule is Connee Boswell of the legendary Boswell Sisters. The sisters were hot as pistols as a close harmony group, but the only one with real individual personality was Connee, when she sang lead. Her sisters really functioned as her backup group, much like the Supremes did for Diana Ross. And like Diana Ross, Connee made solo records while also recording as a member of the trio.

Connee was raised in New Orleans, which was her first break, as she emerged as a kind of feminized Louis Armstrong. She, too, sang like a musical instrument, the growls and spikes softened into a feminine sound that still had plenty of strength. Her New Orleans childhood might account for the Armstrong connection, but she was also influenced by the likes of Bessie Smith and Bing Crosby. (You could say that Crosby, too, was a kind of feminized Armstrong.)

Connee could sing straight, gently swing, or twist the melody around her chords with abandon—often on the same recording. She and the songs she sang fit perfectly, and there are two reasons for that: she picked her own material (though Jack Kapp never really approved of her choices or jazz interpretations) and she wrote her own arrangements. The fact that she played saxophone, cello, piano, and trombone accounts for

**LEFT:** Connee Boswell with Victor Young.

her arranging skills. She understood the strengths and weaknesses of each component of the band and, while her arrangements were sometimes complex in rhythm and harmony, they were never show-offy or muddy. There was always an idea behind the arrangement and everything grew out of that core concept.

Although Connee was an adept jazz singer who loved to play around with a song, she never adopted that detached singing style that plagues a lot of improvisers like Ethel Waters. If she didn't always sing the lyric verbatim, she certainly sang the meaning of a song—and the warmth of her voice gave her singing an intimacy.

Connee Boswell's career ranged from the twenties through the breakup of the Boswell Sisters act in 1935, and into the 1960s as a soloist. She appeared in nightclubs and on radio, television, film, and record. And all the while, she was confined to a wheelchair due to childhood polio. (Have fun watching how filmmakers disguised her disability much as they disguised singers' pregnancies.) Her talents influenced the careers of such artists as Ella Fitzgerald, as Ella herself admitted. The history of jazz singing is evolutionary, with each succeeding generation building on the talents and techniques that came before. In that way, Connee Boswell remains one of our most influential jazz singers. ◆

**June Christy**

The majors (as the major record companies are called) are stuck in a bind. Most of their newer talent is expensive and tends to flop, while the back catalogue generates the day-to-day income for the labels. Each technological advancement generates additional sales for the back catalogue. Recordings on 78s made way for 45s, then 10-inch LPs, 12-inch LPs, cassettes and eight-track tapes, and now CDs. That's a whole lot of trips to the well—and hold on to your bonnets for the era of the "download."

The "misty Miss Christy" might just hold the record for the most incarnations of a single recording. Her album, *Something Cool*, began life on August 14, 1953, when the title number was recorded and released as a single. It achieved widespread acclaim and the cautious Capitol Records had June Christy and her arranger, Pete Rugolo, record another six songs to make a 10-inch LP and a 45-rpm box set. But wait, there's more. In 1955, the album was released again as a 12-inch LP with the addition of four songs. When stereo came in, Christy and Rugolo rerecorded the entire proceedings and the record was released in stereo.

Obviously, audiences considered the compilation worth purchasing again and again. And they were right—it's a marvelous album, with Christy half singing, half speaking a long title song that's as much a monologue as a piece of music. One can picture her on the bar stool, ceiling fans whirring overhead, as she dabs her brow with a lace handkerchief. Funny that more such experiments weren't undertaken—but of course large bureaucracies aren't known for taking chances.

Though Christy is more than cool in her rendition, she could also swing and get plenty hot. Her up-tempo songs were every bit as effective as the sultry ballads, and she hid her intonation problems and small range with inventiveness, great arrangements, and a sense of fun and drama. During her years with Stan Kenton she had many hits, both ballad and up tempo, including "Across the Alley from the Alamo," "It's Been a Long, Long Time," "Shoo Fly Pie and Apple Pan Dowdy," "Tampico," and "Willow Weep for Me."

When the Beatles took over America and the world of pop music fell apart in the middle 1960s, it was over for all but a few singers (Sinatra, seeing the writing on the proverbial wall, sold Reprise in 1964 but managed to keep his career going until 1971, when he entered his first retirement). Capitol, who happened to have the Beatles on its roster, pulled the plug on its singers. The house that Johnny Mercer built turned its attention to rock. In her forced retirement, Christy drank a little too much, appeared on an album with Stan Kenton, and died in 1990. ❖

## Song and Story

### SOMETHING COOL

At a BMI workshop, Billy Barnes created "Something Cool" as an exercise for a musical version of *A Streetcar Named Desire!*

# Russ Columbo

"Crosby, Columbo, and Vallee" went the old refrain from Joe Burke and Al Dubin's popular song of the 1930s. The lyric should have gone "Vallee, Crosby, and Columbo," chronologically speaking — but it's so much harder to rhyme "Columbo" than "Vallee." Vallee was a nasal crooner firmly ensconced in the world of "Boola Boola" and "Poor little lambs that have lost their way." His style of megaphone-assisted crooning went the way of the dodo when Crosby showed up.

Columbo was a more earnest Crosby with darker, more romantic looks and little of the all-American boyishness of the early Crosby. He grew up in California and found fame as a violin prodigy, first in pit orchestras and then accompanying silent movies. Columbo also dubbed vocals for such stars as Gary Cooper (*Wolf Song*, 1929) and Lewis Stone, and even dubbed Betty Compson on the violin in the film *Street Girl*. He made the jump onto the screen in the Cecil B. De Mille film *Dynamite* in 1929, though he was not credited (he played a Mexican prisoner).

In 1927, Gus Arnheim hired Columbo to play violin in his orchestra (he already had the Rhythm Boys on board as vocalists) and in 1930, when Crosby left Arnheim for greener fields, Columbo replaced him. With his slicked back hair, white suit, and smoldering good looks, Columbo was quickly touted as Crosby's successor in what would be dubbed "the battle of the baritones." Columbo soon left Arnheim and formed his own band in 1931.

Composer and manager Con Conrad ("The Continental," "Way Down Yonder in New Orleans," "Ma, He's Makin' Eyes at Me") took a liking to Columbo. On a coast-to-coast train trip the two wrote the song "You Call It Madness (But I Call It Love)," the first big hit for the singer. The song became the radio theme for Columbo when NBC tapped him as "the Romeo of Radio." Columbo, Clarence Gaskill, and Leo Robin wrote another big hit for the singer, "Prisoner of Love."

In late 1932, when Conrad dropped Columbo, the singer's career took a temporary nosedive. In 1933, he made a Vitaphone short entitled "That Goes Double" that brought him back to Hollywood, where he signed a contract with Darryl Zanuck's Twentieth Century Pictures. He made the features *Broadway Through a Keyhole* (1933) and *Moulin Rouge* (1934), and was lent out to Universal for *Wake Up and Dream*, in which he introduced "Too Beautiful for Words." Columbo re-signed with NBC and revived his recording career with a session on August 31, 1934.

Columbo's life and career came to an abrupt end on September 2, 1934. The singer's friend, portrait photographer Lansing Brown, Jr., owned a pair of antique dueling pistols, which he used as paperweights. The two were fooling around, pretending to duel, when Brown lighted the fuse on one of the pistols and it went off, the bullet ricocheting and hitting Columbo in the head, fatally wounding him.

Though he left only a handful of recordings and a few film appearances, Columbo's influence was felt for decades afterwards. Some historians say his Italian good looks (he was born Eugenio Ruggerio de Rudolpho Columbo) and suave manner paved the way for other Italian crooners like Frank Sinatra, Dean Martin, and Perry Como. That's doubtful—but his repertoire was adopted by a number of later singers, most notably Billy Eckstine. ◆

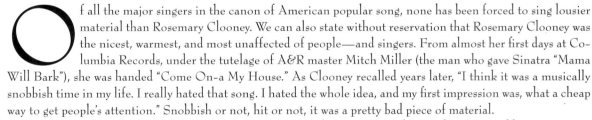

O f all the major singers in the canon of American popular song, none has been forced to sing lousier material than Rosemary Clooney. We can also state without reservation that Rosemary Clooney was the nicest, warmest, and most unaffected of people—and singers. From almost her first days at Columbia Records, under the tutelage of A&R master Mitch Miller (the man who gave Sinatra "Mama Will Bark"), she was handed "Come On-a My House." As Clooney recalled years later, "I think it was a musically snobbish time in my life. I really hated that song. I hated the whole idea, and my first impression was, what a cheap way to get people's attention." Snobbish or not, hit or not, it was a pretty bad piece of material.

Let's take a closer look at Clooney's repertoire. On March 9, 1950, at the very beginning of her association with Columbia, she sang five songs, including "The Canasta Song," "I Found My Mamma," and "Me and My Teddy Bear." She was then assigned to sing a number of children's songs. After managing to record three adult songs, she was given "Punky Punkin (The Happy Punkin)" and "The Wobblin' Goblin." More children's songs and Christmas covers followed, but it was after "Come On-a My House" that she was really saddled with novelty numbers, including "I Wish I Wuz (Hi, Ho, Fiddle Dee Dee)," "Botch-a-Me," "Lovely Weather for Ducks," "Cheegah, Choonem," "Dot's Nice, Donna Fight," and "Sailor Boys Have to Talk to Me in English."

> "Do you know what? In a year from now nobody's even going to be talking about me." —Rosemary Clooney to Dante DiPaolo on the set of her second movie, *Here Come the Girls*, in 1952

Clooney continued to beg Miller to let her record quality material. Occasionally he relented, but he always put the better-known songs on the B sides of the records.

The MGM years featured a slightly better repertoire, but, of the few covers she made of Broadway show tunes over the course of her career, the ones she recorded for Columbia tended to be better since that label owned rights to the more prestigious shows. Leave it to MGM to give her a cover album (with husband Jose Ferrer) of Livingston and Evans's *Oh, Captain!*

Clooney's marriage to Jose Ferrer dissolved, although they parted amicably, and she fell in love with arranger Nelson Riddle, who was married at the time. She turned to drugs and developed a dependency that complicated her emotional state. Her unhappiness with her career and private life came to a head in 1968 when she was present at the Ambassador Hotel where Robert Kennedy was assassinated.

Through counseling and medication she was able to put her life back in order, and with her newfound stability came a new depth and emotional connection to the songs she sang. She resolved to take greater control of her life and get in touch with her emotions on a daily basis.

Upon her return to singing in the early seventies, she seemed more at peace with who she was—and that translated into more heartfelt and vulnerable performances. Rosie began to let her natural sense of humor come to the fore as well as the anger and hurt that she had kept bottled up. This gave her ballads a greater poignancy. With her newfound self-confidence and ability to open up emotionally she no longer needed to resort to any tricks or clichés in her interpretations. Her work was simpler and more direct, and thus more personal. Left to her own devices, she chose songs that meant something to her and she was able to act the lyrics more convincingly. She tended to pick songs that were positive, told a good story, or taught a good lesson. Her voice had mellowed and deepened but had lost none of its luster or slightly smoky quality. Her maternal qualities came out in her singing, too, and it was impossible to listen to her, on disc or live, without feeling her love and kindness.

Rosemary Clooney's glory years, from 1977 until her death, were spent at Concord Records. She was able to pick her own songs, oversee her own arrangements, and hone her own way of singing. Her performances deepened (though many sound underrehearsed—a common problem with Concord) All told, she made around thirty albums of great songs for Concord.

Many singers have fantastic first acts and then either lose their vitality, become parodies of themselves, or stand by as the business deserts them. Rosemary Clooney was the opposite. She (very much) enjoyed the second act of her career and lived to achieve more success than almost any other singer of her generation. She fought off her personal and professional demons and endured long enough to become a great singer and a great human being—and she could never have been one without being the other. ◈

Rosie Clooney and one-time hubby Jose Ferrer.

## CAREER HIGHLIGHTS

**1928** Born May 23 in Maysville, Kentucky.

**1931** Sings "When You're Hair Has Turned to Silver" first public appearance (at age three!); mother leaves for California with brother Nick.

**1933** Appears in high school revue *Little Tots on Parade*.

**1945** Father deserts Betty and Rosemary; the sisters audition for WLW in Cleveland, singing "Hawaiian War Chant," win, and are offered $20 per week.

**1946** Betty and Rosemary discovered by Tony Pastor's road manager.

**1947** Begins touring with Pastor for $125 per week after debuting at Steel Pier in Atlantic City; sisters record for Columbia Records in Hollywood; Rosemary's first solo, "I'm Sorry I Didn't Say I'm Sorry When I Made You Cry Last Night."

**1948** Betty returns to Cincinnati.

**1949** Last recording with Pastor Band—"Bargain Day"; Rosemary decides to quit Pastor and moves to New York; signs solo contract with Columbia at $50 per week; competes on Arthur Godfrey's *Talent Scouts* singing "Golden Earrings," wins first prize, beating Tony Bennett.

**1951** Meets Jose Ferrer; records first hit singles "Beautiful Brown Eyes." "Mixed Emotions," "Half as Much," and "Come On-a My House."

**1952** Meets Bing Crosby; signs with Paramount; makes first film, *The Stars Are Singing*; meets dancer Dante DiPaolo.

**1953** Second film, *Here Come the Girls* released; marries Ferrer.

**1954** Cameos in Ferrer's Romberg biopic, *Deep in My Heart*; records number one hit "Hey There"; film *White Christmas* is released and becomes hit.

**1955** Son Miguel Ferrer born.

**1956** Daughter Maria born; meets Nelson Riddle; first appears on television on *The Rosemary Clooney Show* for 39 half-hour episodes.

**1957** Son Gabriel born.

**1958** Monsita born; Album *Fancy Meeting You Here* with Bing Crosby released.

**1960** Son Rafael born

**1966** Separates from Ferrer and files for divorce.

**1967** Riddle divorces his wife but marries his secretary; Ferrer remarries.

**1968** Present at assassination of Robert F. Kennedy; hospitalized for drug-induced psychosis; announces retirement from show business.

**1972** Returns to show business at Copenhagen's Tivoli Gardens.

**1974** Reconnects with Dante DiPaolo, who moves in.

**1976** Crosby asks her to tour with him in celebration of his fifty years in show business; tours *4 GIRLS 4* with Margaret Whiting, Barbara McNair (replaced by Helen O'Connell), and Rose Marie; tours heavily, sometimes 40 out of 52 weeks through 1981.

**1976** Betty Clooney dies.

**1977** Signs with Concord Records.

**1991** Carnegie Hall concert.

**1996** Marries Dante DiPaolo.

**1998** Second Carnegie Hall concert; Ella Lifetime Achievement Award from the Society of Singers.

**1999** Writes autobiography, *Girl Singer*.

**2001** Last performance at the Count Basie Theatre, Redbank, New Jersey, December 15.

**2002** Dies on June 29.

# Song and Story

## COME ON-A MY HOUSE

The quintessential novelty number was written by the unlikely pair of songwriter Ross Bagdasarian (creator of the Chipmunks) and playwright William Saroyan (they were cousins). To keep themselves awake while driving across New Mexico in 1949 they made up this little ditty. Saroyan put it into the Off-Broadway production of his play, *Son*, and it was recorded by Kay Armen. Mitch Miller, always attracted to gimmicky songs, persuaded Rosemary Clooney to sing it against her better judgment. It became her first big hit.

## ME AND MY TEDDY BEAR

J. Fred Coots: The title was suggested to me by Leo Talent, chief executive for Mutual Music Society. He suggested I try writing a song about a teddy bear, since all children have a strong attachment for such objects. I played around with the idea for a few weeks and with the help of Talent, finally completed the song. We showed it to Hecky Karasnow, head man at Columbia Records' children's division. He thought it would be suitable for a young singer named Rosemary Clooney, just making her record debut at that time. The record was released and became an immediate hit— Rosemary Clooney's springboard to prominence.

## TENDERLY

Jack Lawrence on writing the lyric: The tune haunted me and the lyric practically wrote itself during my waking and sleeping hours. Words came so easily that I decided to wait a while before calling Walter for fear that he might think I'd written an off-the-cuff lyric. Literally, I waited about ten days. Then feigning great excitement, I called Walter and said, "I've got it, Walter! I've got it!" In a rather dead-pan tone, he asked, "What's the title?"

I took a deep breath and practically sang out, "TEN-der-LY!" There was a long pause at his end. Then he sneered, "That's no title! That's what you put at the top of the sheet music: Play Tenderly!"

Rosemary Clooney wanted to sing the song but Mitch Miller refused to let her. Finally she did sing it on the B side of a 45. It became a smash hit despite Miller (and Walter Gross) and the misaccent of the title word.

# First Person

Rosemary Clooney on working with Billy Straythorn on *Blue Rose*: We became friends. He had a key to my back door; he'd come in and bring me soda crackers from the kitchen when I was having morning sickness. Once he brought an apple pie and carried it straight up to my room. We saw it on the bed and dug right in, ate the whole thing while we looked at the music, picking songs and laughing. Eventually we went downstairs for more focused work on the tunes; standards like "I Let a Song Go Out of My Heart" and "Mood Indigo"… and a new number Billy had written especially for me, an instrumental called "Blue Rose." I had no lyrics to sing, just vocalizing along with the melody. "I want you to imagine you're living in New York and you've got a really hot date and you're getting ready to to go out," Bill said, looking at me through his big square glasses. "You're a beautiful woman, looking into the mirror and combing your hair and there's no Duke Ellington and there's no band. The radio is playing the record, and you just sing along with the orchestra and we overhear it."

Michael Feinstein: It was her voice after all that made her beloved, even by those who never even knew her. The voice carried a resonance that caressed you completely. It had humor, honesty, life lessons, heartbreak, a smile in spite of the tears, joy, candor, abandon, and grace. And holding it all together was an innate musicianship that effortlessly expressed everything she felt and lived. We were there with her through it all.

Rosemary Clooney at Rainbow and Stars nightclub in New York City: I'm gonna do one of my songs from the fifties so you'll know who I am. People often mistake me for other singers and ask mvve to sing songs by Doris Day, Patti Page, even Johnnie Ray. I suppose they think, "She's recorded so much crap that she must've done it."

# Perry Como

Como with long-time musical director Nick Perito.

When the Second World War ended, so did the era of the big band. It seems everyone just wanted to sit in their suburban homes and take a break from saving the world. When Perry first joined the Ted Weems orchestra, he tried some vocal gymnastics, and the performances weren't well received. Weems taught him to enunciate clearly, sing with strength, and let the arrangements do the work. It was a lesson Perry learned very well, discovering how to trust the minimalist approach that worked for him. He had a beautiful voice, good looks, and a pleasant personality, so he made an easy transition from the big-band era to the age of the singer without ever changing. He still kept his personality to a minimum, kept his crooning smooth and simple, and kept up the discipline that singing with a band had demanded.

Those of us who grew up in the fifties have a soft spot in our hearts for Perry Como and Dinah Shore, mainstays of the network variety shows. Yes, Perry (never Mr. Como) was relaxed—really, really relaxed—but this was an antidote to the manic comedy of Milton Berle, Jerry Lewis, and Jackie Gleason, who shared the airwaves. Perry seemed to be having a good time, so we did, too. He could be mildly reflective with a ballad and jovially upbeat when singing one of those silly novelty songs like "Hot Diggity Dog Diggity." He always seemed to have a chorus around to back him up, giving him just enough of a lift to support his lighter-than-air vocals. In his ubiquitous cardigan sweaters, he prefigured Mr. Rogers—but with a wonderful voice.

Perry seemed happy to be on a show where he didn't have to do too much. He sang all the gentler new hit songs and let his guest stars do the heavy lifting. He made his audiences feel happy and safe, often reminding them that his first job had been as a barber. If he had remained true to that profession, he would have been terrific as one-fourth of a barbershop quartet. Women liked his good humor and men could picture themselves in exactly his position, throwing off a song now and then. He was truly an everyman singer. ❖

Nat King Cole

Nat King Cole
Ballads of the Day

Art imitates life, especially when it comes to popular singers and the movies. Many an artist has taken a film role that was very close to his or her own life, with only the names changed to protect the not-so-innocent.

There's Judy Garland in *I Could Go on Singing*, Fred Astaire in both *Royal Wedding* and *The Band Wagon*—and then there's Nat King Cole in *St. Louis Blues*. In this classic biopic, Cole stars as the great composer W. C. Handy, author of the title song and other great blues numbers.

As the film unfolds, Handy's father, a preacher, disapproves of his son's interest in the devil's music. He rants and raves about the perils of a life given over to such debauchery. Nat King Cole's real life followed the same path. His father, Edward Coles, was a Baptist minister who expected his children to follow in his footseps. Nat gravitated toward the piano and by age four began picking out tunes he heard in church. As he got older, he secretly listened to secular music on the radio, particularly jazz and blues. While playing piano and organ in his father's church, he would occasionally throw in a hot jazz lick or blues note. He usually got a whipping for his mischief but he didn't mind; he enjoyed the music too much.

> "My voice is nothing to be proud of. It runs maybe two octaves in range. I guess it's the hoarse, breathy noise that some like."—Nat King Cole, 1954

Edward Coles expected his boys to follow in his footsteps and devote their lives to the ministry. They had other ideas. Nat began a small group called the Rogues of Rhythm. He quit school to devote time to the band and played many engagements. Nat's brother Eddie, a pianist and bass player, played with several groups and toured the country before returning to Chicago to join the Rogues of Rhythm. For his troubles, the group soon became known as Eddie Cole's Band (much to Nat's disappointment) and then Eddie Cole's Solid Swingers. Under that name, they recorded for Decca's Sepia Label, devoted to what were called "race records."

The band was folded into the orchestra of a revival of Sissle and Blake's famous musical, *Shuffle Along*, which was making a run for Broadway. It didn't quite get that far—in fact, the show closed about as far from Broadway as a show can get, Los Angeles. The producers ran out of money, and the cast and orchestra found themselves stranded on the West Coast.

Nat, by this time married to a woman of whom his father disapproved, decided to play it safe by playing piano in Los Angeles. When Bob Lewis, owner of the Swanee Inn, heard Nat at the Century Club, he proposed that he put together a small group and make the Swanee Inn their base.

Nat contacted guitarist Oscar Moore, bassist Wesley Prince, and drummer Lee Young to join the new group. Young failed to appear on opening night, experiencing doubt about the new group and Cole's leadership. At the time, small combos were often used for intimate functions where the size of a big band was inappropriate, but a trio or quartet was considered inadequate for serious jazz. Young just didn't believe that a small group had suitable instrumentation to make effective music. Nat had no choice: the group went on as a drumless trio—and made history.

It was Nat's talents as a superior player that made the trio work so well. He could keep the rhythms usually supplied by the drums with his left hand while his right described delicious variations on the melody. Cole combined the jazz techniques of Earl Hines, his major influence, with the melodic training he had gained working at his father's church.

The trio became the most influential small group of its day, especially after they started recording for Decca in 1943. Not surprisingly, it was also the most commercially successful. The King Cole Trio started a new trend in jazz and, suddenly, the music scene was loaded with trios and quintets. They might not have been imitations, but they certainly owed their existence to the King Cole Trio's popularity. Among the small groups that followed in King Cole's footsteps were the Barbara Carroll Trio, the George Shearing Quintet, the Erroll Garner Trio, the Page Cavanaugh Trio, and the Art Van Damme Quintet.

From the beginning of his career, Nat occasionally sang along with his own piano playing. He would sit on the bench with his torso cocked toward the audience while his hands roamed the keys. Sitting ramrod straight and beaming a wide smile, Cole would serenade his listeners, lending another musical line to the trio's instrumentation. He didn't make a big deal of his singing, nor did he often contribute vocals at first, but gradually his singing became an integral part of the act.

By 1944, Nat had begun performing apart from the trio on occasion. In the 1946 smash hit, "The Christmas Song," his vocal was the dominant sound on the recording, proving once and for all that he could carry a song with his voice. By the time he married his second wife, Maria, in 1948, the trio was starting to fall apart. The original members of the trio were gone, replacements were coming and going, strings entered the arrangements, and the writing was on the wall: in 1955 the trio was kaput. Nat was already making solo recordings for Capitol and, more and more, was stepping away from the piano to sing standing in front of a mike.

And for his newfound solo career, Nat veered away from jazz and into pop. The talent was all still there but he found himself caught up in the schlock of the sixties, as did many of his contemporaries. If he hadn't died in 1965, would he have suffered the fate of so many other greats? We'll never know—but the mark he made on jazz in the forties is enough to ensure his legacy in the history of jazz vocals. ◆

## *Asides*

Cole's biggest influence was pianist Earl Hines.

Cole moonlighted while he was under an exclusive contract with Capitol Records, using the pseudonyms "Eddie Laguna," "Shorty Nadine," "Sam Schmaltz," and others, for a variety of jazz legends including Buddy Rich, Willie Smith, and Lester Young. Whether Capitol Records knew or not, they never said a word.

## THE GREAT SONGS

**1940** Sweet Lorraine

**1943** Gee, Baby, Ain't I Good to You?; Straighten Up and Fly Right; It's Only a Paper Moon

**1944** Body and Soul; The Man I Love

**1945** The Frim Fram Sauce; Errand Boy for Rhythm

**1946** The Christmas Song; I Love You (For Sentimental Reasons); You're the Cream in My Coffee; Route 66; Baby, Baby All the Time

**1947** Too Marvelous for Words; If I Had You; I Miss You So; When I Take My Sugar to Tea

**1948** Nature Boy

**1949** For All We Know; Lush Life; Calypso Blues

**1950** Mona Lisa; Lost April

**1951** Too Young, Unforgettable

**1952** When I Fall in Love

**1953** Nat King Cole Sings for Two

**1955** There Goes My Heart; Let's Fall in Love; This Can't Be Love; You Stepped Out of a Dream; There Will Never Be Another You; Tenderly

**1956** Just You, Just Me; Blame It on My Youth; You're Looking at Me; I Know That You Know; When I Grow Too Old to Dream; Caravan

**1957** Send for Me; When I Fall in Love; Stardust; Stay as Sweet as You Are; Love Letters; At Last; Where Can I Go Without You?

**1958** To Whom It May Concern; The Party's Over; When Your Lover Has Gone; Once in a While; These Foolish Things; The Song Is Ended

**1960** The Touch of Your Lips

**1961** Let There Be Love; I Got It Bad; I'm Lost; Fly Me to the Moon; There's a Lull in My Life

**1962** Ramblin' Rose

**1963** Those Lazy-Hazy-Crazy Days of Summer

**1964** L-O-V-E

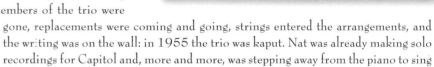

"MINE IS A CASUAL APPROACH TO A SONG; I LEAN HEAVILY ON THE LYRICS. BY THAT I MEAN I TRY TO TELL A STORY WITH THE MELODY AS BACKGROUND."
—NAT KING COLE

# Song and Story

### NATURE BOY

This odd popular song was written by eden ahbez (he didn't believe humans were deserving of capital letters). The writer gave the manuscript of the song to the stage doorman at a theater in which Cole was performing. Taken with the strange melody and lyrics, Cole recorded the song and its release squeaked by just before the infamous recording ban of 1948.

### STRAIGHTEN UP AND FLY RIGHT

As a child, Nat King Cole heard a sermon and never forgot it. He wrote the song (and there's the king of the cut-in, Irving Mills, credited as lyricist) but as was the practice of the day, he sold the rights for $50.

### SWEET LORRAINE

During an engagement at the Swanee Inn nightclub in Los Angeles, a drunk in the audience insisted that Cole sing "Sweet Lorraine." Cole had never sung in public before but, to keep the guy quiet, acquiesced and thus started his singing career.

### MONA LISA

Veteran songwriters Jay Livingston and Ray Evans wrote a song titled "Prima Donna" and sent the music to Cole. He rejected the song, as had Frank Sinatra before him. The songwriters asked if they could come to his house and perform the song for him and he agreed out of respect for the writers' reputation. They arrived to sing the song, now titled "Mona Lisa," with a few changes in the music and lyrics. Cole asked, "What kind of a song is that?" But when he heard it he changed his mind. Cole's wife was convinced the song was all wrong for him and asked, "Why are you doing an Italian song?" "Mona Lisa" ended up winning an Academy Award and became the best-selling song of Cole's career.

Mel Tormé with Nat King Cole.

# Singing Instrumentalists

There are those aficionados of American popular song who truly believe that instrumentalists make the best singers. They may not possess the most pleasant voices or the ability to interpret a lyric in a unique way but they do know music and, if there's anything Louis Armstrong taught us, musicianship can carry a performer a long way.

We could list many a singer whose range spans the octaves but who doesn't have any sense of swing or dynamics or just plain musicality. Some of these are great stars. Charlotte Church and Jane Monheit take note: a broad range and a sweet voice alone do not a great singer make. Pitch is important, but so is a deep understanding of the lyrics. We've all heard those barely pubescent young men who think they're Frank Sinatra. They've got the big record companies behind them and they sell millions of discs (especially in Europe)—but honestly, do you think they know what they are singing about?

Jack Teagarden, Chet Baker, and Barbara Carroll understood, perhaps through a combination of instinct and experience, the subtle art of singing and playing. Their superior grasp of music distinguished their singing from vocalists such as Betty Hutton, who could swing a song with the best of them but was always a bit square. Martha Raye, on the other hand, applied real musicianship to her swinging style and came out a great jazz singer.

Trombonist Jack Teagarden's career started in the 1920s, when he began appearing with Eddie Condon, Red Nichols, and Louis Armstrong, among others. He joined the Paul Whiteman Orchestra in 1933 and played out his five-year contract, leaving in 1939 to start his own group. In 1947, he joined the Louis Armstrong All-Stars and stayed with the group for four years. Teagarden and Armstrong loved performing live and embraced their music and their fans. Armstrong may have been the more expansive performer but they were equally beloved in their day. Teagarden then formed a Dixieland sextet that was extremely successful. His singing had a lot in common with Johnny Mercer and Maxine Sullivan, a relaxed, almost offhand sound that belied the solid musicianship and invention in his playing and vocals. Teagarden's great recordings include an arrangement of "Basin Street Blues" with a patter section of "Won't You Come Along with Me"—written by none other than Glenn Miller; "Red Wing"; "The Sheik of Araby"; Makin' Friends"; "Aunt Hagar's Blues"; and "Peg o' My Heart."

Chet Baker applied his own distinctive style of trumpet-playing to his singing, and the result was a seamless blend of instrument and vocals. His music was a reflection of who he was—soulful, tortured, and honest. Listening to Baker today, one has the impression that he knew exactly what he was doing as he slid further and further into his addiction to heroin. He made no apologies and didn't demand sympathy. He lived the life he wanted and sang the way he felt. "Performance" is the wrong word to describe Baker's appearances, as he made no attempt at anything resembling production values. He simply blew his horn and sang, and whether the audience was there or not was somehow incidental. Listening to him was like peering into a man's battered psyche—disturbing and exhilarating and somewhat uncomfortable.

A lot of pianists also sing, but none is better than Barbara Carroll. Classy, swinging, smart, and charming, Carroll draws in the audience with her artistry. Many pianists hunker down over the keys, lost in a reverie of inspiration. The audience sits admiring but detached from the musical proceedings. Carroll, on the other hand, improvises with the best of them but includes the audience in the dialogue between artist and composer.

Carroll was trained classically at the New England Conservatory of Music (at the time the term was rather redundant—it was a very conservative conservatory). She wanted to play jazz, though, and was influenced by Nat King Cole, Art Tatum, Thelonious Monk, Bud Powell, and Charlie Parker. Faced with sexism in hiring, she came up with the name Bobbie Carroll and landed a debut gig at the Downbeat Club on 52nd Street. When a woman showed up instead of the expected man, it was too late to renege, and she played the engagement. She appeared in Rodgers and Hammerstein's *Me and Juliet*, playing piano in a trio, and has recorded for RCA, Atlantic, Verve, Blue Note, and Harbinger.

Other major instrumentalist singers include the famous—Fats Waller, Nat King Cole, and Louis Armstrong; the near-famous—Bunny Berigan and Matt Dennis; and the should-be famous—Marky Markowitz and Major Holley. ◆

**ABOVE LEFT:** Chet Baker. **ABOVE RIGHT:** Barbara Carroll.
**BOTTOM LEFT:** Jack Teagarden.

# Barbara Cook

Very few pop singers start in musical theater and move on to successful careers as interpreters of the American songbook. Barbara Cook is the most notable exception, having begun as one of the leading Broadway ingenues of the 1950s and developed into perhaps the finest interpreter of classic American songs of our lifetime.

Among the theatrical performers who have created characters that will be forever associated with them are Rex Harrison in *My Fair Lady*, Robert Preston in *The Music Man*, Richard Kiley in *Man of La Mancha*, and Barbra Streisand in *Funny Girl*. Very rare are the actors who have created more than one character-defining performance: Carol Channing in *Gentlemen Prefer Blondes* and *Hello, Dolly!*; Mary Martin in *South Pacific* and *The Sound of Music*; Ethel Merman in *Annie Get Your Gun* and *Gypsy*; and Barbara Cook—with the hat trick—as Marian the Librarian in *The Music Man*, Cunegonde in *Candide*, and Amalia Balish in *She Loves Me*.

Actually, it's not so much that Cook was identified with the roles as that particular songs from the shows became hers alone. Her interpretations of "My White Knight," "Glitter and Be Gay," and "Ice Cream" remain American musical theater classics.

Beyond Cook's rich soprano voice and excellent diction, it's her acting that makes the songs memorable. Whether she's playing an innocent Amish farm girl or the lonely shopgirl of *She Loves Me*, she remains a woman with a mind of her own and a touch of fire behind her eyes. She has an affinity for the characters she plays, never winking at the audience, and her warmth and humanity shine through her performances. And whether she's singing a song from a show or from Tin Pan Alley, Cook always creates a character with true emotions, making every song into a kind of play in itself.

After performing in *The Grass Harp*, tired of being an ingenue—and no longer quite suited to the role, what with her burgeoning weight—she quit musicals to concentrate on concertizing, beginning with an evening at Carnegie Hall that has become legendary. In recent years, she has focused on the works of America's greatest composers and lyricists in a series of cabaret and concert appearances that have also been captured on CD.

Barbara Cook's status owes more than a little to the contributions of her longtime collaborator, accompanist, arranger, and musical soul mate, Wally Harper. Also a veteran of Broadway, Harper, who died in the fall of 2004, was an accomplished dance and vocal arranger, pianist, conductor, record producer, and even songwriter.

Cook and Harper's collaboration was in the great tradition of such cabaret teams as Sophie Tucker and Ted Shapiro, Frank Sinatra and Bill Miller, Tony Bennett and Ralph Sharon, Julie Wilson and William Roy, and Kaye Ballard and Arthur Siegel. Upon Harper's death, Cook was forced to consider other pianists, a painful experience after thirty years with the same musical partner—but she'd be wise to settle on a worthy candidate: The death of another dear colleague, Bobby Short, leaves Cook poised to take over the intimate little stage at the Hotel Carlyle. ❖

## *Song and Story*

### GOODNIGHT MY SOMEONE
Sung by Marian the Librarian in *The Music Man*, this song is based on the same notes as "Seventy-six Trombones." Author Meredith Willson wanted to subliminally indicate the strong connection between the two characters.

### GLITTER AND BE GAY
Whenever he needed a high note in *Candide*, Leonard Bernstein gave it to Cunegonde. Her showiest song, "Glitter and Be Gay," is a parody of the "Jewel Song" from Gounod's *Faust*. The original production of *Candide* came before the era of ubiquitous microphones on Broadway, and Cook's bravura rendition wasn't miked. By the end of each performance, Cook had no voice left and would mouth the words to "Make Our Garden Grow."

· · · · · · · · · · · · · · · · · · · · · · · · · · · · · ·

"If you're able to be yourself, then you have no competition. All you have to do is get closer and closer to that essence."
—Barbara Cook

· · · · · · · · · · · · · · · · · · · · · · · · · · · · · ·

## CAREER HIGHLIGHTS

**1927** Born in Atlanta.

**1941** Wins amateur night contest at the Roxy Theater, singing "My Devotion."

**1948** Moves to NYC with mother to pursue musical theater career.

**1950** Performs at Camp Tamiment in Poconos, seen by Max Gordon, owner of the Blue Angel.

**1950** Opens in first Broadway show, *Flahooley*. Big flop.

**1952** Stars in *Oklahoma!* at City Center.

**1955** First success on Broadway, *Plain and Fancy*.

**1956** Creates role of Cunegonde in *Candide*.

**1957** Creates role of Marian the Librarian in *The Music Man*.

**1958** Records first album, *Songs of Perfect Propriety*, on Urania label; birth of son, Adam LeGant.

**1963** Creates role of Amalia Balish in *She Loves Me*.

**1965** Makes dramatic play debut as cast replacement in comedy *Any Wednesday*.

**1971** Opens in flop, *The Grass Harp*, last Broadway musical appearance.

**1972** Opens in last Broadway dramatic appearance, Gorky's *Enemies* at Lincoln Center; cabaret debut at Brothers and Sisters with Wally Harper as musical director.

**1973** Carnegie Hall debut.

**1981** Returns to Carnegie Hall.

**1985** Appears in *Follies in Concert* at Lincoln Center.

**1986** London concert debut.

**1988** Opens in musical *Carrie* at the Royal Shakespeare Company, last dramatic role to date.

**2003** Metropolitan Opera debut in production of *The Merry Widow*.

**2004** Longtime accompanist and arranger Wally Harper dies.

**OPPOSITE PAGE:** Barbara looking especially girlish in Howard Dietz and Arthur Schwartz's *The Gay Life*.

**NEAR RIGHT:** Barbara wonders "Will He Like Me" in Jerry Bock and Sheldon Harnick's *She Loves Me*.

**FAR RIGHT:** Cook is enjoying a second career as the greatest living interpreter of American popular song.

# Chris Connor

What makes someone a jazz singer? Is it the need to bend notes, improvise, scat? No popular singer is all the way to the left (square as square can be) or so jazzy as to be off the charts (though there are some that are out of this world). Many singers inhabit the middle, and they can be described as "jazz-influenced." This is a good description of Chris Connor: tightly controlled, understated, cool.

Connor seemed fated from birth to be a jazz singer. She was born in the jazz hot spot of Kansas City, on November 8, 1927. Her father, an amateur violinist, took her to hear the great bands as they came through town, and she spent hours listening to jazz on the radio. Prophetically, the first record she bought was Stan Kenton's *And Her Tears Flowed Like Wine*, featuring a vocal by Anita O'Day.

In 1945, while in college in Missouri, Connor began singing with a band. Among their charts were several Kenton pieces, and Connor dared to dream that one day she would sing with him. In the spring of 1949, she moved to New York, starved for seven weeks, then was hired as a member of the Snowflakes, Claude Thornhill's vocal group. She quit to join Herbie Fields but soon rejoined Thornhill for eighteen months of one-night stands.

Connor developed her chops and began earning a small reputation among musicians. Orchestra leader Jerry Wald (fated to be compared, not always favorably, to Artie Shaw) hired Connor. Their engagements at the Roosevelt Hotel in New Orleans were broadcast on radio, and singer June Christy, a Connor favorite (and ready to quit Stan Kenton's band), heard her and recommended her to Kenton. Six months later, he hired her and Connor's dream came true. Surprisingly, she left after less than a year, in July 1953, to launch a solo career.

Bethlehem Records signed her and she made some records that were well received critically and commercially. She wasn't happy though, and Bethlehem dropped her in 1955. Atlantic Records was happy to pick her up.

The Atlantic years are considered to be the highpoint of her recording career. Backed by such greats as John Lewis and Ralph Burns, Connor sang in a straight-ahead style, made the audience come to her, kept her vibrato under wraps, and used her husky voice to further the mood of the song. Her Atlantic albums were smash successes; by the end of the decade, she was selling more than 100,000 copies a title.

But by 1962, the recording industry had changed drastically and Atlantic dropped her. She cut a few albums on other labels and finally decamped to Europe. Connor recorded as late as 1995 (for the Japanese label Alfa) and as the century turned, she was turning out an album a year on the HighNote label.

Looking back, Connor recently commented, "When you're young, you overplay as a musician and you oversing as a singer because you're trying all these ideas. And I was throwing in everything but the kitchen sink. I've eliminated a great deal of the things I used to do. The simpler it is, the better it works for me." The truth is, simplicity and clarity have always been the hallmarks of Chris Connor. ◆

# Keepers of the Flame

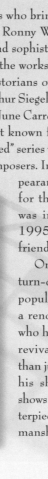

American popular song lives on through the talents of a few contemporary artists whose careers are devoted to preserving and reinterpreting the well known as well as the arcane, the indisputably great and the mere curiosities of the canon. These singers and musicians, as devoted to research and preservation as they are to performing, each have amassed extensive personal collections of sheet music, arrangements, books, and rare recordings—as well as interviews, stories, and lore. Meet them and be prepared to hear fantastic tales of the glory days of Tin Pan Alley. (Their encyclopedic brains might well be preserved until such time that science can extract knowledge directly from their gray matter.) These artists aren't nostalgists—they make songs live every night for their own discerning audiences. But their performances aren't tricked up with clichéd instrumentation or ironic commentary—they don't have to be. What these artists are delivering is musical history, filtered through their own particular talents.

The most popular of these performers by far is Michael Feinstein. He performs in intimate cabarets—including the one in New York with his own name on it—as well as in huge halls before symphony orchestras. In addition, the seemingly indefatigable singer/pianist writes books, liner notes, and articles; supplies commentary on DVDs; records a series of popular songbooks with the songwriters providing accompaniment; has the premier private collection of all things relating to popular song; hosts a subscription series at Carnegie Hall; tours incessantly; and even has a real life! Feinstein jumped in full-force while still a teenager: his letters to Ira Gershwin resulted in his becoming the lyricist's assistant. Liza Minnelli helped him early on, and he soon graduated from obscure piano bars to headlining concerts and cabaret performances. The mystery is: why is Feinstein's profile so much higher than those of his very worthy fellow practitioners? Part of it has to do with his relaxed, friendly performance style and his easy good looks. The joy he finds in his repertoire has a lot to do with it, too.

Three other pianist-singers who bring this rarefied repertoire to the masses are Steve Ross, Ronny Whyte, and Peter Mintun. Ross and Mintun are smart and sophisticated—Ross most often appears in a tuxedo and sings the works of Porter or Coward.

All these pianist/singer/historians owe a debt of gratitude to the amazingly ingratiating Arthur Siegel. Siegel wrote the hit song "Love Is a Simple Thing" with June Carroll for the Broadway show *New Faces of 1952*. He is best known for a series of recordings made for Ben Bagley's "Revisited" series that celebrated the lesser-known songs of Broadway composers. In his frequent cabaret appearances, Siegel's enthusiasm for the songs and songwriters was infectious. His death in 1995 was a blow to his fans, friends and to songwriters.

One of the world's experts on turn-of-the-century American popular song is Max Morath, a renowned pianist and singer who helped inspire the ragtime revival of the 1970s. Rather than just concert performances, his shows are true one-man shows with ragtime as the centerpiece. With his mix of showmanship and pedagogy, Morath

**ABOVE:** Max Morath. **RIGHT:** Arthur Siegel.
**TOP RIGHT:** Michael Feinstein.

has entranced audiences for almost fifty years. His performance style is in a direct line from Jolson, Cantor, Williams, and other greats, and he has recorded many LPs and CDs. His Epic recording, *Living a Ragtime Life*, is a classic that deserves to be reissued on CD.

Ian Whitcomb, briefly a pop/rock singer in his native England, is himself a distinguished author of several insightful and entertaining books on American popular song. He hosted a long-running radio show in southern California that was informative and entertaining. Whitcomb's many albums feature songs of the teens and twenties, with, unfortunately, additional lyrics by Whitcomb himself. It's too bad that he doesn't limit his songwriting to his own compositions, which brilliantly capture and comment upon early American popular song.

The sole bandleader amongst the keepers of the flame is the extraordinary Vince Giordano. Outfitted in a tuxedo he leads a band composed of the country's premier practitioners of twenties, thirties, and forties music. Using all original orchestrations and transcriptions, Giordano's entourage is unforgettable—and invaluable in bringing great music to new audiences. Hollywood calls when they need an authentic looking and sounding band, and Giordano and company have appeared in such films as *The Aviator* and *Radio Days*, and on many soundtracks. Where else could you hear a phonofiddle, an aluminum bass, or a bass saxophone except in Giordano's expert ensemble?

Many pop singers—and a few rock stars, most recently Bryan Ferry, Rod Stewart (ugh), and Cyndi Lauper—have dabbled in the Songbook. The best examples include k.d. lang, Janis Siegel, and Harry Connick, Jr. ◆

# Bing Crosby

## THE GREAT SONGS

**1926** I've Got the Girl; Wistful and Blue; Pretty Lips

**1927** I'm Coming Virginia; My Blue Heaven

**1928** Ol' Man River; You Took Advantage of Me; Let's Do It; Makin' Whoopee; I'll Get By

**1929** Great Day; My Kinda Love; Can't We Be Friends; If I Had a Talking Picture of You; S'posin

**1930** A Bench in the Park; Three Little Words; Happy Feet; Them There Eyes; Song of the Dawn; You Brought a New Kind of Love to Me

**1931** I Surrender Dear; Just One More Chance; Out of Nowhere; Temptation; Sweet and Lovely; Where the Blue of the Night; Just a Gigolo

**1932** Dinah (with the Mills Brothers); Here Lies Love; St. Louis Blues; Lawd, You Made the Night Too Long (with the Boswell Sisters), Please; Shine (with the Mills Brothers); Sweet Georgia Brown; Some of These Days; Just an Echo in the Valley; Sweet Sue; Just You

**1933** Learn to Croon; Shadow Waltz; Moonstruck; Did You Ever See a Dream Walking?; Thanks; I've Got the World on a String; Temptation

**1934** June in January; Little Dutch Mill; With Every Breath I Take; Someday Sweetheart; Love Is Just Around the Corner; Love in Bloom

**1935** It's Easy to Remember; Red Sails in the Sunset; Soon; I Wished on the Moon; Moonburn

**1936** I'm an Old Cowhand; Pennies from Heaven; The Way You Look Tonight; A Fine Romance

**1937** Bob White; It's the Natural Thing to Do; The Moon Got in My Eyes; Basin Street Blues; Too Marvelous for Words; Sweet Leilani

**1938** Alexander's Ragtime Band Small Fry; I've Got a Pocketful of Dreams; I Cried For You; Mr. Gallagher and Mr. Shean (with Johnny Mercer); Moon of Manakoora; You Must Have Been a Beautiful Baby (with Bob Crosby)

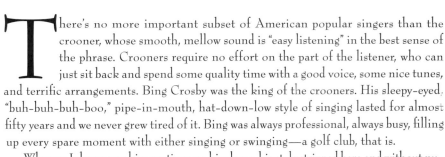

There's no more important subset of American popular singers than the crooner, whose smooth, mellow sound is "easy listening" in the best sense of the phrase. Crooners require no effort on the part of the listener, who can just sit back and spend some quality time with a good voice, some nice tunes, and terrific arrangements. Bing Crosby was the king of the crooners. His sleepy-eyed, "buh-buh-buh-boo," pipe-in-mouth, hat-down-low style of singing lasted for almost fifty years and we never grew tired of it. Bing was always professional, always busy, filling up every spare moment with either singing or swinging—a golf club, that is.

Whereas Jolson wore his emotions on his sleeve, his style stripped bare and without nuance, the next great singer, Bing Crosby, kept his personality in check. He gave us nothing to make us cry, nothing to make us laugh—but he could draw a big smile, a pang of nostalgia, a wistfulness. Crosby dealt in emotions lite, keeping the audience entertained, singing as if he were singing just for us, and all without offering a clue as to who he was or what he thought. We bought it all. He asked little of us and we asked little of him.

Even Bing's friends and family couldn't tell what was going on behind his facade. Dogs wag their tails when happy, snarl when they're mad. Cats flick their tails when they're annoyed. Bing had his own set of signals and we were forced to look for them in order to discover the person underneath the performance.

For Maxene Andrews, it was his hat: "He could be very moody, and when he came into the recording studio we could always tell what mood he was in by looking at his hat. If his hat was square on his head, you didn't kid around with him. But if it was back a little bit, sort of jaunty, then you could have a ball."

His own wife, Kathryn, searched for clues in his dress: "People who didn't know thought Bing had difficulty expressing affection. Not at all. As I was to learn much later, the secret was in that top button on the pajamas. If it was fastened, it was going to be a quiet read-in-bed and lights-out-at-10 p.m.-after-chaste-prayers [night]. If it was unbuttoned, however, watch out."

Hats and pajamas as the windows to a man's soul? Some claimed he was self-absorbed but perhaps he was just introspective. That's why Johnny Burke was the perfect lyricist for Crosby, his work full of down-home homilies, the joys of living simply and simply living, the notion that money can't buy happiness.

Though Crosby was one of the richest men in Hollywood, and certainly enjoyed his wealth, he was never pretentious. As Wilfred Hyde-White reported, "Sinatra would turn up with three or four Karmann Ghias. The doors would open and bodyguards would march down. But Bing would turn up in a little car, stop at the gate for his dressing-room key, and then park it himself! The difference was rather marvelous."

His image, relaxed and easy-going, was

carefully controlled. James Cagney noted, "Here he had been to all appearances perfectly loose and relaxed, but not at all. He was giving everything he had in every note he sang, and the apparent effortlessness was a part of his very hard work."

Here was a man who hated being in crowds but was one of the kindest to his fans. He enjoyed being seen as the nice guy, gave millions to charity, raised millions more, and was truly selfless. However, as his brother, Bob Crosby, noted, "I think probably the one trait that would concern me about brother Bing would be his lack of responsibility. He is a loner; he likes to take care of Harry Lillis Crosby and he does take care of Harry Lillis Crosby." If taking care of Harry Lillis Crosby was burnishing his image and sticking to the plan, so be it.

We all know about the great friendship between Bob Hope and Bing Crosby. They mock-feuded, appeared on each other's radio and television broadcasts, enjoyed a long relationship on film in the "road" movies, and popped up in cameos in each other's film and stage vehicles. They honestly enjoyed each other's company. Linda Hope, Bob's daughter, says it was during the filming that of *Road to Hong Kong* (1962) that they really began to spend a great deal of time together and became quite close.

Perhaps he was the only one to truly know himself, but that's true of most of us. Still, it doesn't diminish one of the greatest singers of the twentieth century. A man who brought us out of the acoustic age and into the electronic. Jolson could take or leave a microphone, his actions meant everything. Crosby embraced the microphone and used it to draw us into the music. He refined Jolson's emotional peaks and smoothed out the edges on Jolson's need for approval. He led the way to Frank Sinatra, a complex man who let us into his id. Crosby was a transitional figure but also his own man and most of all, a great talent. ◆

## CAREER HIGHLIGHTS

**1903** Born in Tacoma, Washington, May 3 (Bob Hope born May 29 in England).

**1906** Family buys phonograph.

**1910** Neighbor, Valentine Hobart, dubs him "Bingo" after "The Bingville Bugle" newspaper comic.

**1916** First public performance singing at the Parish Hall.

**1917** Bing works backstage when Al Jolson appears in Spokane.

**1919** Sings in high school jazz band.

**1921** Attends Gonzaga College; works backstage at another Jolson appearance, begins thinking about show business.

**1922** Starts junior year as a pre-law major.

**1924** Meets Al Rinker when he joins band the Musicaladers; drops out of college to make money as a performer.

**1925** Moves to Los Angeles with Al Rinker; they land jobs with a tab show, *The Syncopation Idea*.

**1926** Crosby and Rinker watch Paul Whiteman's band arrive by train to Los Angeles; Crosby and Rinker sign with the Paramount-Publix vaudeville circuit as "Crosby and Rinker—Two Boys and a Piano—Singing Songs Their Own Way"; hired by Paul Whiteman for $125 a week but first must finish vaudeville bookings; records first uncredited single, "I've Got the Girl," with Don Clark's Biltmore Hotel Orchestra on the Columbia label; joins Whiteman in Chicago on December 6 and begins performing with the orchestra; Bing sees Louis Armstrong in Chicago at the Sunset Café; Crosby and Rinker's second record is released, "Wistful and Blue," produced by Whiteman for the Victor Talking Machine Company.

**1927** Opens to good reviews at the Paramount Theater in New York; records "Muddy Waters" with Bing's first (uncredited) solo; makes Broadway debut in show *Lucky*, along with the Whiteman orchestra; Harry Barris joins the duo and they become "Rhythm Boys" in June with their first record, "Mississippi Mud."

**1928** Radio debut with Whiteman troupe on NBC's Victory Hour; Rhythm Boys go on tour without Whiteman band.

**1929** Rhythm Boys rejoin Whiteman Band for *Old Gold* radio show; on March 14, Bing records "My Kinda Love" and "Till We Meet Again" and is credited for first time!; Bing meets Dixie Lee in Los Angeles while waiting for shooting to commence on *King of Jazz*; takes up golf with a passion; makes screen test for MGM.

**1930** Rhythm Boys find great success at Cocoanut Grove nightclub in LA; Bing marries Dixie Lee on September 29; makes "Them There Eyes," the last recording by the Rhythm Boys.

**1931** Records demo with George Gershwin for Fox film *Delicious*; signs with Mack Sennett for four two-reel comedies; records "I Surrender Dear," first recording under new, solo Brunswick Records contract; signs with CBS for first solo radio program; begins long engagement at the Paramount Theater in New York, costarring with the Mills Brothers, Kate Smith, the Boswell Sisters, Cab Calloway, and Lillian Roth.

**1932** Signs with Paramount Pictures and begins filming *The Big Broadcast*; meets Bob Hope at New York's Friars Club.

## *Song and Story*

### WHITE CHRISTMAS

One of the top 25 holiday songs of all time, "White Christmas" was written in New York City by Irving Berlin who was inspired by thinking back to his years in Hollywood and how he would long to be in New York for the holidays. He wrote the song in one day, plus a few more hours for polishing the melody and lyric. Introduced by Crosby in the film *Holiday Inn*, the song continues to be a remarkable success, boasting over 500 recordings that have sold over 30 million copies. More than 21 million of those were Crosby's version.

### SWINGING ON A STAR

Der Bingle inadvertently inspired this song during a dinner party that included Johnny Burke and Jimmy Van Heusen. One of Bing's children acted up and he berated the boy, comparing him to a mule. Burke fashioned that idea into a song the next day and the phrase "…or would you rather be a mule?" was born.

### TEMPTATION

Crosby sang this Nacio Herb Brown song in the film, *Going Hollywood*. He remembered it as "my first attempt at presenting a song dramatically." It became a huge hit and allowed him to expand his repertoire.

# First Person

Rudy Vallee: Suddenly, the room was as quiet as a grave. Out in the middle of the floor was one of this trio, singing. The crowd was quiet, very quiet, and when he finished the place went into ecstasy. They applauded like mad and this young man walked right off the floor with no expression whatsoever on his face. No triumph! No elation! No conquest!

Frank Sinatra: Bing's death is almost more than I can take. He was the father of my career, the idol of my youth, and a dear friend of my maturity. His passing leaves a gaping hole in our music and in the lives of everybody who ever loved him. And that's just about everybody. Thank God we have his films and his records providing us with his warmth and talent forever.

Sonny Burke: I don't think there's anybody better in the studio than Bing. He and Sinatra are two of the finest people I've ever worked with from that standpoint. When Bing comes into the studio, he's there to perform and nothing else. He's a pure professional and is that much of a pro that he doesn't tolerate anyone else who isn't. Bing is probably one of the fastest studies I've ever seen. He's got great ears. He has something approaching total recall, in that it doesn't take him long to get the feeling of a piece and learn it.

Maxene Andrews: Even if he came in and he was, for whatever reason, in a sour mood, he was always great with us. We always had a wonderful time. Bing was the perfection artist to work with—at least with us. We worked with so many artists that left you wanting. Bing never did.

Will Friedwald: It was as though he were deaf like Beethoven and couldn't hear that the audience had liked what he did. I think that the whole of popular music before Sinatra can be described as a gradual building toward Sinatra. First, there was Jolson, who was great at what he did, and then Bing Crosby built on what Jolson had done. Then along comes Sinatra who brings what they did together and builds on it. Crosby was the first singer to really explore the idea of lyric interpretation, but Sinatra did it on a deeper and much more emotional level than Crosby had been able to do. Obviously, Crosby was a major influence on Sinatra. He was the one who inspired Sinatra to take up a singing career. Sinatra also recorded something like a hundred songs or more that had earlier been sung by Crosby.

# Bobby Darin

Energy, personality, a terrific sense of swing—and absolutely no depth—mark Bobby Darin's brief rise to the top of the middle of pop singers. Darin's style owes a lot to the worst qualities of the late Sinatra—the smugness, the finger-snapping coolness, the interpolated "hip" lyrics that drove songwriters crazy.

Darin was born on May 14, 1936, in the Bronx as Robert Walden Cassotto. After graduating from Bronx High School, Darin, who already knew how to play piano, guitar, and drums (barely), started a band and acquired a manager who got him a contract with Decca Records. Decca was trying to enter the newly emerging teen market but didn't quite know how to use Darin (who had at this point acquired his new last name, supposedly randomly selected from a phone book). After a year, Darin moved to Atlantic Records' Atco label as a songwriter/arranger, with a minor in performing.

With the release of "Splish, Splash," Darin enjoyed his first million-seller. His next hit, "Dream Lover," sported a calypso beat and was another hugh smash. But Darin wasn't satisfied with being a rock-and-roll star—he wanted to follow in the footsteps of his idol, Frank Sinatra, so he hooked up with older, more established performers, including George Burns and Jimmy Durante.

Darin's recording of "Mack the Knife" was an immediate hit and established him as an adult singer. Darin parlayed the recording into a brief film career, including the title role in *Captain Newman, M.D.*, for which he received an Oscar nomination. He appeared in ten films in all.

When he was offered a contract with Sinatra's Reprise Records, Darin balked and signed with Capitol instead, the label at which Sinatra ultimately made his comeback. Darin had been heard boasting that he wanted to be "bigger than Sinatra."

His personal life was just as frantic and needy as his professional life. Most infamously, he dated Sandra Dee's mother—then married Sandra herself. They were divorced in 1967. Darin campaigned for Robert F. Kennedy and, like Rosemary Clooney, felt his life change dramatically upon Kennedy's tragic assassination. At Kennedy's funeral, Darin experienced an epiphany. He sold his possessions and began living in a trailer at Big Sur. A year later, transformed into a folk singer, he started Dimension Records. The new label was a failure, and in the early 1970s Darin signed with Motown—but he never managed to achieve the momentum of his glory years. On December 20, 1973, he died during heart surgery.

Whether he was performing the ultra-hip "Mack the Knife" or the supremely stupid "Splish Splash," Darin's self-confidence made him the first genius of style over substance. In that way, he was the godfather of all those *American Idol* wannabes. Bobby Darin came along just as America was ceding popular song to kids, so perhaps it's not surprising that we bought his act lock, stock, and finger snaps. As sales of televisions and Lazy Boys soared, American pop settled into its own recliner-with-cup-holder. Let the entertainer do all the work, we seemed to be saying, while we sit back, semi-conscious, and let the music splish-splash over us. ◆

## Song and Story

### MACK THE KNIFE

This song was written in 1928 by Kurt Weill and Bertolt Brecht for *Die Dreigroschenoper* (*The Threepenny Opera*), and Weill said the song was inspired by the sound of Berlin's traffic. When the show made its way to New York in 1933, it had lyrics by Gifford Cochran and Jerrold Krimsky, and was called "The Legend of Mackie Messer." Nothing came of the song until 1954, when a revival of *The Threepenny Opera* opened Off-Broadway with lyrics by Marc Blitzstein, who titled it "Mack the Knife."

Like Liz and Dick or Debbie and Eddie, Bobby Darin and Sandra Dee were America's perfect couple. And like the aforementioned, it didn't last.

## Blossom Dearie

Soft, childlike Blossom Dearie (her given name was clearly her destiny) has taken the June Christy school of cool to its extreme. Her voice barely hovers over her piano self-accompaniment. She's a little fey (her CD company's name is Daffodil, for heaven's sake) but she certainly has her fans, who still pack her performances in New York City *in her seventh decade*. No less an expert than Johnny Mercer loved her singing, and wrote "My New Celebrity Is You" for her.

She started recording in France in 1954, forming the Blue Stars and performing in supper clubs and lounges. In 1956, she returned to America and inked a contract with Verve Records. During the Verve years she was jazzy, accompanied by such jazz artists as Ray Brown, and she developed a following among sophisticates. Although her playing is expert, her singing really reveals her personality, cool but wonderfully playful. On her album of Comden and Green songs for Verve, she had a chance to act the songs in her inimitable style—and the acting is important. She always does better with a tune that has a point.

In 1964, Dearie made one album for Capitol. They surrounded her with an orchestra, strings, the whole shebang, but they missed the point of Blossom Dearie, who fares best using a spare, simple approach and an almost hypnotic delivery that emphasizes the basics of words and music. As pop music lost its foothold in the mid-sixties, Dearie, like many other singers, went to Europe, where rock had not yet trampled the popular song. She appeared at Ronnie Scott's legendary jazz club in Soho and cropped up regularly on British television. She also made two records for the Fontana label, the latter of which featured self-penned haikulike, stream-of-consciousness songs about Dusty Springfield, John Lennon, Georgie Fame, and others.

Then it was back to the United States, where she's carved out a niche for herself in cabaret, the poor man's supper clubs. (There are no supper clubs left in New York City, more's the pity.) She continues to hold her fans enthralled, though newcomers are sometimes puzzled as to her attractions. ◆

Sammy Davis, Jr.

## THE GREAT SONGS

The need to be loved has scuttled many a performer's career. Jolson was the first great star who became obsessed with the sound of applause, to the point where he would seemingly go to any extreme to get it, including singing the same tried-and-true repertoire for almost forty years and working himself to death—literally. Bob Hope had this burning need for adulation, too, and though it was masked by a veneer of relaxation, an examination of his career reveals a man incessantly onstage or in front of a microphone or camera—someone who eventually lost touch with the real world and became increasingly anachronistic. Sammy Davis, Jr., too, spent his entire life in front of audiences. His world seemed to stop at the footlights and his neediness grew so extreme that, late in his career, he became a sort of monstrous caricature of himself. There's desperation in these men's performances, a sense of extreme exertion that comes from the gross need to be loved *or else*.

Sammy Davis, Jr., was certainly one of the great multiple talents of popular history. He started performing at the age of three and, without the influence of a mother or any formal schooling, spent his early life moving from theater to theater along with his father, Sammy, Sr., and his nominal uncle, Will Mastin.

The two men saw to it that Davis was protected from the racism that pervaded America in the 1920s and '30s. He was too busy performing to get into trouble and, although you could never call his childhood "traditional," it wasn't so bad. He grew self-confident in the company of his guardians and in front of the thousands of name-

> "Being a star has made it possible for me to get insulted in places where the average Negro could never hope to get insulted." —Sammy Davis, Jr.

less faces in the audience every day. The racism and intolerance he faced was all to come later, in the army and beyond.

In his private life he seemed to be goading the racists. He dated the ultrawhite Kim Novak and married May Britt, a blond, Swedish beauty. When he appeared on Broadway in *Golden Boy*, his love interest was Paula Wayne, another blonde. Bullets were fired into the marquee of the theater.

When Davis hugged Richard Nixon, the liberal establishment howled and Davis was branded an Uncle Tom. (Duke Ellington and Nat King Cole suffered a similar fate because they wouldn't take a more radical role in the burgeoning civil rights movement—but the three were quietly doing their part in their own ways.)

Davis was a deeply instinctual singer. There's not a genre in which he didn't excel, and he seldom missed a beat in his choice of material or his treatment of a song. In fact, he made it look almost too easy. With a brilliant sense of rhythm and fine acting, he could perform any kind of song. His delivery was energetic but focused. The skinny little singer was wound as tight as a spring and, when he hit the stage, all of that kinetic energy burst forth in a geyser of talent. He could sing a ballad as well as Bennett, swing as well as Sinatra, and dance rings around any other performer. He loved to work hard, needed that audience approval, and gave his all. By the end of a set, both he and the audience were exhilarated but exhausted.

Davis needed to remain on top; he was hooked on success as if it were a drug. So, in the 1960s he set to work incorporating the new, mod culture into his life and art. It wasn't enough for him to be hip—he had to be hipper than hip. And thus, the master of impersonation became the subject of impersonations himself. The self-reverential, slang-slinging, Rat Pack character had sunk into self-parody.

Davis started losing his credibility after *Golden Boy* and his divorce from May Britt, the missteps of the late '60s, '70s, and '80s overshadowing the heights he'd achieved in his first thirty years. The songs he chose were light pop dross, many of them covers of hits originated by artists young enough to be his children. There were some rewards to this approach, of course: "The Candy Man," and "Mr. Bojanges" became best-selling records. With his guest appearances on sit-coms and his sycophantic photo-ops with Richard Nixon, Davis became as much a punchline as an artist, and people soon forgot what a brilliant talent he had proved himself to be.

It was a sad end to a truly remarkable career, and there are still those who think Davis was the greatest singer of them all. Certainly he wins the prize for all-around talent. And, if nothing else, he never stopped attracting the attention he wanted and needed—and deserved. It's just a pity that he had to work so hard to earn it. ◈

She could do it, she wanted to do it, but she didn't often do it. That's the story of Doris Day, who, though she was one of our finest singers and actresses, seldom seemed able to show off her talent because of the image that had been created for her—and because of the influence of some bad, bad men.

Day didn't want to be known as the eternal virgin she portrayed in film after film. That was the idea of her husband, Marty Melcher, the same man who wasted more than twenty million dollars of his wife's money, sunk her into debt, and signed her for a CBS television show without consulting her. She found out all of the above when he died. Day didn't want to sing the increasingly lightweight songs that she specialized in during her years with Columbia Records.

Day started out as an excellent band singer with poise and pluck, a direct descendant of Connee Boswell. She could sing sweetly and rhythmically but she also had a backbone and could handle the most bluesy of ballads (including her number one hit, "Sentimental Journey") while keeping up with whatever swinging the Les Brown Band of Renown could dish out. If you want to hear just how jazzy Day could be, have a listen to her collaboration with Harry James on the album *Young Man with a Horn*; or check her out on the soundtrack of *Love Me or Leave Me* and on her best albums from the Columbia years, *Day By Day* and *Day By Night*, both with Paul Weston. The latter show her proficiency at ballad-singing.

It might surprise you, but more than a few actors and directors named Day their favorite actress of all. She could hold her own in musicals, dramas, suspensers, light comedies—the works. Day was the rare individual who could sing and act in equal measure. She sang with depth and intimacy, making each listener believe she was singing especially to him or her. She produced a wonderful tone and possessed a great sense of rhythm. She had it all.

There are some fine singers who grow better with age, such as Margaret Whiting, Mabel Mercer, Maxine Sullivan, Rosemary Clooney, Mimi Hines, and Alberta Hunter. Then there are singers of promise who go off on tangents and end up in the musical unknown. Still others get stuck in a rut, repeating their mantra till it becomes a cliché. That's the story of Sammy Davis, Jr., Bette Midler, and—sadly—Doris Day.

Perhaps it was because she started as a big band singer, a job that was considered just below the third trumpet in importance in some early bands, that she was willing to follow orders rather than call the shots. At least three of her husbands abused her, either physically, mentally, or financially. (And that's not counting Mitch Miller's career abuse.) By the time she was well rid of both Melcher and Miller, she had become more worried about maintaining her physical image (just try actually focusing your eyes when viewing her through the Vaseline-coated lens on her later TV work) than on the material she performed.

She did have the guts to stand up to America on her talk show *Doris Day's Best Friends* when, on the very first episode, she had a loving reunion with an obviously ill Rock Hudson. This act of bravery and friendship on Day's part exemplifies her fine character, steadfastness, and integrity. Her work on behalf of animal rights is worthy and serious. She gave up a business that had never really given her much pleasure and created a life for herself filled with meaning and satisfaction.

Yet to us, it doesn't seem fair. The slings Day suffered in show business hurt us more than they hurt her, as we were denied the talents of someone who might have had a remarkable career rebirth, much as Rosemary Clooney did. What's even worse is the fact that Day actually did go back into the studio in the 1980s and was, by all reports, in excellent voice. Two notable record producers approached Day through her son, Terry Melcher, to make a record again. Melcher was all for it, Day's friend Kaye Ballard encouraged her, but she refused even when the producers offered to give all monies to Day's animal charities.

Perhaps it was the fear of not being the singer she was, or maybe she was simply sick and tired of show business. No matter. In order to right this inequity, we propose a Constitutional amendment forcing the genuinely talented to work until their abilities dim. A nonpartisan committee will decide when an artist can retire. After all, laws are made for the greater good. Day's return to singing would have benefited humanity as well as many members of the animal kingdom. Everyone would have been happy—with the possible exception of Doris Day. But what is sacrifice when there is so much to gain? ◈

Doris sings "It's Magic" in *Romance on the High Seas.*

## CAREER HIGHLIGHTS

**1922** Born Doris Kappelhoff in Evanston, Ohio on April 3.

**1935** Wins grand prize dancing as part of amateur team, Doris and Jerry (Doherty).

**1937** Serious accident to legs forces end to dancing career; listens to singers on radio while bedridden and on jukebox in tavern downstairs.

**1939** Joins Barney Rapp's band.

**1940** Joins Bob Crosby's band; joins Les Brown's band.

**1941** Marries Al Jorden; quits Les Brown's band.

**1942** Birth of Terry Melcher.

**1943** Divorces Al Jorden; back with Les Brown.

**1946** Leaves Les Brown to become a solo act; marries George Weidler.

**1947** Joins Frank Sinatra on *Hit Parade* radio show; begins recording for Columbia Records.

**1948** First film for Warner Brothers, *Romance on the High Seas* with first solo hit "It's Magic."

**1949** First album *You're My Thrill* released on Columbia Records; divorces George Weidler.

**1950** Premiere of film *Young Man with a Horn*; soundtrack album released with Harry James.

**1953** Number one hit record "Secret Love" released.

**1955** Portrays Ruth Etting in dramatic film *Love Me or Leave Me* with James Cagney.

**1956** Records album *Day By Day* with Paul Weston for Columbia Records; co-stars with James Stewart in Alfred Hitchcock's *The Man Who Knew Too Much* with hit song "Que Sera Sera."

**1957** Records album *Day By Night* with Paul Weston for Columbia Records.

**1959** Paired with Rock Hudson on film *Pillow Talk.*

**1962** Last musical film, *Jumbo*; records album *Duet* with Andre Previn for Columbia Records.

**1967** Turns down role of Mrs. Robinson in *The Graduate.*

**1968** Retires from films after opening of *With Six You Get Eggroll*; husband Marty Melcher dies; TV sitcom, *The Doris Day Show* (runs until 1972).

**1976** Marries Barry Comden.

**1981** Divorces Barry Comden; retires from show business.

**1985** Talk show, *Doris Day's Best Friends.*

**1987** Founds Doris Day Animal League.

**2004** Terry Melcher dies.

"All my life, I have never felt lonely with a dog I loved at my side. I love people and animals, though not necessarily in that order."
—Doris Day

# Song and Story

### DAY AFTER DAY

This song, written by Dietz and Schwartz for the show *Flying Colors*, was sung by Doris Kappelhoff in an audition for bandleader Barney Rapp. Rapp suggested the singer change her name to something more suitable and the singer chose the name "Day," having just sung the song.

### IT'S MAGIC

Sammy Cahn: The song was written for Doris Day, then still unknown. Jule Styne and I brought her to the attention of Mike Curtiz at Warner's, who gave her her first important chance in the movies which catapulted her to stardom. Another interesting fact about this song is that Jule Styne had played the melody for me for two years, and I kept passing it by because it had a slightly Spanish flavor. Only after I had seen the script for *Romance on the High Seas*, and saw the song as a number for Doris Day and Jack Carson in a Latin nightclub scene, did the song come into focus for me and I was able to do the lyrics.

# Asides

Judy Garland was unavailable and Betty Hutton read and rejected the script to *Romance on the High Seas*. Jule Styne heard Doris Day singing in The Little Club in New York City and was impressed with the girl singer he remembered from the Les Brown band. He thought she would make a good lead for the film, not knowing that Jack Warner himself had rejected her as being sexless. Sammy Cahn set up an interview with director Michael Curtiz and Day sang "Embraceable You,"

then burst into tears. Distraught over her recent divorce with George Weidler, Day tried to pull herself together. She sang "What Do You Do on a Rainy Night in Rio?" while Curtiz tried to get her to do more than just stand there by taking her hips into his hands and pushing her side to side. Day commented, "I don't bounce around, I just sing." Curtiz was suitably impressed and ordered a screen test. Marion Hutton (sister of Betty) also tested, but Curtiz chose Day and her movie career was born.

Despite her years singing in bands, After her first film, Day wouldn't sing in a personal appearance. She never gave concerts, never played benefits, and refused all offers from Broadway.

Vernon Duke and Sammy Cahn auditioned their score for *April in Paris* for Day, who squealed with delight over the songs. A few days later they found out she actually hated them all. Years later, when Cahn went to Day and asked if he could produce the film *Three Sailors and a Girl* with her for Warner, Day smiled and said, "Of course. Are you kidding?" When Cahn went to tell Steve Trilling, Jack Warner's assistant the good news, Trilling informed Cahn that Day didn't want Cahn to produce the picture. Day just couldn't say no to anyone to this face.

# First Person

Doris Day to Ralph Gleason: I really sing the lyrics rather than the music. I try to sing the words the way you speak them.

Doris Day on her name: I never liked it. Still don't—I think it's a phony name.

# Billy Eckstine

**B**illy Eckstine's rich baritone, wide vibrato, and outsize interpretations made him a popular balladeer of the 1950s. He was also known as the leader of a preeminent big band with bebop at its core and the always natty Eckstine out front. His good looks and sophistication distinguished him among black vocalists of his day.

Mr. B, as he was dubbed (Perry Como was Mr. C), was born in Pittsburgh on July 8, 1914. His given name was "Eckstein," but a helpful booker suggested it looked too Jewish—and this in the days before Sammy Davis, Jr., converted! In 1930, Eckstine won a local talent contest with an imitation of Cab Calloway, but he was equally interested in sports and might have become a pro football player if he hadn't broken his collarbone—something that seldom happened in front of a mike. He joined Tommy Myles's big band but soon left it to complete his studies. After a year at Howard University, he quit to become a singer full-time.

In 1939, Chicago big band leader Earl Hines hired Eckstine as a singer and trumpeter. Possessed of a good ear, Eckstine suggested that Hines hire Charlie Parker and Sarah Vaughan. Eckstine set off in 1943 to explore a solo career but the era of the solo singer hadn't quite matured enough for the young man to make a go of it, so in 1944, at the suggestion of fellow Hinesian Dizzy Gillespie, Eckstine started his own big band, one that was devoted to bebop. Eckstine recruited Gillespie and Budd Johnson from the Hines unit and they were joined by Dexter Gordon, Art Blakey, Miles Davis, Charlie and Leo Parker, Gene Ammons, Kenny Dorham, Lucky Thompson, and Fats Navarro. Sarah Vaughan signed on as a vocalist. It was a mighty group, but the band's records struck out, probably because of the poor quality of the pressings and bad engineering. Even Eckstine's singing seemed out of whack, which he explained by saying, "My band was on a bebop kick, and you can't sing with that so well."

The band folded and Eckstine seemed relieved, stating, "You feel so much freer singing by yourself. You're not constantly singing in tempo; you get a chance to express yourself more fully. I like it better than singing with my own band. They wanted me to get a commercial band, to be a background for my singing. So what happens when I'm not singing? They'd be playing some old-time stuff, and *I* wouldn't be on the stand. I decided the best thing was to do a single and go hear Dizzy for kicks."

In 1945, before he broke up the band, Eckstine scored hits with "Cottage for Sale" and "Prisoner of Love"—enough to entice the new MGM Records label into signing him in 1947, the year the band folded. That year he had a big hit with the Burton Lane/Harold Adamson standard, "Everything I Have Is Yours" and the next year with "Blue Moon." In 1949, Eckstine scored again with "Caravan" and the following year with "My Foolish Heart" and "I Apologize."

As his career continued, Eckstine's singing became more about sound than meaning, his interpretations becoming more and more ethereal. Fans weren't buying it and his popularity waned, though he did have a hit in 1957, joining Sarah Vaughan on "Passing Strangers." For the rest of his career, Eckstine went from label to label and subsisted mainly on live appearances, where his velvety voice and longevity attracted his diehard fans. He died on March 8, 1993. ◆

# Ruth Etting

Plaintive singing and a soupçon of depression, even in rhythm numbers like "Sam the Old Accordion Man," made Ruth Etting a star. Most other performers of her era depended on energy and lung power to sell their songs. They came from minstrel, vaudeville, and musical comedy backgrounds, where being heard over the orchestra was the most important thing. But the introduction of the microphone allowed such performers as Etting and Bing Crosby to shine. She wasn't really a jazz singer but she gave that impression due to the jazz backing on her recordings and her trick of changing tempi in order to vary the recordings.

She was variously called the "Sweetheart of Columbia Records," "Chicago's Sweetheart," not to mention "America's Radio Sweetheart" and "America's Sweetheart of Song," but her fans would have been shocked to learn that their sweetheart was married to the mobster Martin "Moe the Gimp" Snyder. Snyder managed Etting's career and Etting herself, through bullying and intimidation.

Though she didn't have a classically beautiful face, Etting was considered a sexy woman. She appeared in six Broadway shows introducing an impressive number of hit songs. For her first appearance, in the Ziegfeld Follies of 1027, she sang "Shaking the Blues Away." In Whoopee, she was given the gift of "Love Me or Leave Me," and in the 9:15 Revue she sang Harold Arlen's first hit, "Get Happy." It was in Simple Simon that she introduced her most famous song, Rodgers and Hart's "Ten Cents a Dance." In her last show, the Ziegfeld Follies of 1931, the famed producer gave her a song made famous by Nora Bayes, "Shine on Harvest Moon." Etting made it a hit all over again.

"Love Me or Leave Me" and "Ten Cents a Dance" seemed perfectly suited to Etting's personality. She went on to make thirty-five mostly sub-par short films in New York and Los Angeles, finally ending her screen career with three features: Roman Scandals, in which she appeared in a horrible blond wig and emoted all of two lines (and one song); Hips, Hips, Hooray (they don't make titles like that anymore!); and Gift of Gab.

Etting finally wised up, divorced her gangster husband, and began concentrating on her radio career. Not one to take rejection in stride, Moe the Gimp shot Etting's boyfriend and accompanist, Myrl Alderman, in October 1938 (he lived). And so ended the career of Ruth Etting. A brief attempt at a comeback in 1947 came to naught. She might have disappeared entirely from the memories of all but a few collectors of 78s if it wasn't for the 1955 MGM biopic Love Me or Leave Me, starring Doris Day as Etting and film gangster James Cagney as real-life gangster Moe Snyder. ◆

# Cliff Edwards

sang, made sound effects with his voice, and scatted—or as Edwards then called it, "eefin." When eefin, Edwards would make trumpetlike sounds that soon developed into a sort of scatting.

Edwards found work in Chicago in 1917, singing at the Ansonia Café. The engagement would prove a turning point in his career. He developed the persona of "Ukulele Ike," a collegiate, jazzy uke player. He met Bob Carleton, who had written a little nonsense tune titled "Ja Da." Edwards soon teamed up with stuttering comic Joe Frisco (reputed by those who knew him to be the funniest human on earth) to create a hugely successful vaudeville act.

Edwards incorporated scatting into his early recordings beginning in 1922. By the late '20s, he had recorded with such greats as Miff Mole, Adrian links Rollini, and Red Nichols. Edwards was one of the greatest jazz singers of his day, but was never given his due for two important reasons. First, his personal life was as untidy as his vocalizing (actually his singing, unlike his life, could be called "controlled anarchy"). His bouts with alcohol, drugs, gambling, and women (vices that brought down many a stronger man) kept putting the breaks on a career that not only had a second act but a third, fourth, and fifth. Edwards's second problem, believe it or not, was his lack of sex appeal. He was having too much fun as a singer to be a matinee idol. He was the kind of guy women wanted to mother.

God knows Edwards had his chances at stardom. After some early recording successes (which predated Louis Armstrong's jazz explosion), Edwards was cast in the Gershwins' smash hit show, *Lady Be Good!*, where he introduced "Fascinating Rhythm." After a slow decline, he restarted his career at MGM studios in *The Hollywood Revue of 1929*, in which he introduced the song "Singing in the Rain." This was followed by many lesser pictures. He then made a triumphant return as the voice of Jiminy Cricket in Walt Disney's *Pinocchio*, once more introducing a future standard, "When You Wish Upon a Star." Edwards made a number of children's records for the Golden label and drifted into obscurity once more, until he was rediscovered in the 1950s for a brief television career.

Though he lived until 1971, Cliff Edwards was never recognized as the early jazz master he was. ◆

Scattin' started right there, because we dropped the music and the man in the booth said, 'Go ahead! Go ahead!'—Louis Armstrong, recalling the 1926 recording of "Heebie Jeebies."

Well, that wasn't exactly true. Scatting started early and, like much of jazz, its origins are lost—but we do know that before Armstrong's scatting, way back in 1911, there was Gene Greene's recording of "King of the Bungaloos." Jelly Roll Morton, the supreme egotist of all time (unsurpassed even by the mightily self-involved Al Jolson), who claimed to invent jazz, boasted that he invented scatting as well. Our money, though, is on the white (though he sounded mighty black), Cliff Edwards.

Running away to join the circus or carnival seems to be a common modus operandi for performers and songwriters (even Anne Brown of Porgy and Bess fame tried to join the circus), and Cliff Edwards answered the call in 1913. He began his singing career in the orchestra pit of silent movie houses, where he played his ukulele,

# Darlene Edwards

Darlene Edwards is a true anomaly of show business. A woman with a fairly extensive output of recordings—always accompanied on the piano by her equally talented husband, Jonathan Edwards—she may come across to the neophyte listener as painfully talent-free. But closer and repeated listenings reveal true genius in the duo's intelligent altering of the cliché forms of popular music and jazz. Their experiments with pitch, meter, and rhythm break all the rules but show an innate intelligence and design. Timing means nothing to them; Darlene can back phrase with the best of them, often leaving Jonathan entirely on his own (and on an entirely different page in the songbook).

Jonathan's loose piano technique shows little regard for the notes, per se. It is as if he feels that the keys to the left or right of the "correct" note are close enough. Darlene takes advantage of sharpws and flats, often missing the note as written. Yet, despite it all, the songs come through clearly, their integrity reflected through a prism of distortion and misrepresentation. A testament to their talents is the large number of professionals who have followed in their footsteps. (Though some disagree— arranger Paul Weston told author/critic Will Friedwald that Edwards was "a pain in the ass.") These brave innovators totally ignore the shape and intent of the original composers; and some treat pitch as a bothersome obstacle to interpretation. The true impact of visionaries Jonathan and Darlene Edwards has yet to be felt as we poor listeners struggle inside the cage of our own musical expectations. ◆

# Sister Acts & Brother Acts

## THE ANDREWS SISTERS

**1937**  Bei Mir du Schoen

**1938**  Hold Tight

**1939**  Boogie Woogie Bugle Boy

**1940**  Ferryboat Serenade

**1941**  I'll Be with You in Apple Blossom Time

**1942**  Strip Polka

**1943**  Shoo-Shoo Baby

**1945**  Rum and Coca-Cola

**1946**  Rumors Are Flying (with Les Paul)

**1947**  Civilization (with Danny Kaye); Near You

**1948**  Cuanto Le Gusta (with Carmen Miranda); Toolie Oolie Doolie; Underneath the Arches; Woody Woodpecker (with Danny Kaye); You Call Everybody Darling

**1949**  I Can Dream, Can't I?; Now! Now! Now! Is the Time; She Wore a Yellow Ribbon (both with Russ Morgan)

**1950**  I Wanna Be Loved; The Wedding Samba (with Carmen Miranda)

## THE BOSWELL SISTERS

**1930**  Heebie Jeebies

**1931**  I Found a Million Dollar Baby (In a Five-and-Ten-Cent Store); It's the Girl; River, Stay Away from My Door; Roll On, Mississippi, Roll On; Shout, Sister, Shout; When I Take My Sugar to Tea

**1932**  Between the Devil and the Deep Blue Sea; Down Among the Sheltering Palms; Everybody Loves My Baby; If It Ain't Love; Louisiana Hayride, Minnie Moocher's Wedding Day; There'll Be Some Changes Made; Was That the Human Thing to Do

**1933**  Forty-second Street; Mood Indigo; Shuffle Off to Buffalo; Sophisticated Lady; That's How Rhythm Was Born

**1934**  Alexander's Ragtime Band; Dinah

**1935**  I'm Putting All My Eggs in One Basket; Let Yourself Go

There's something about sister acts. Somehow they become a unified whole with a closer connection than even brother acts have. Is it sexist to think that it's quintessentially female to be able to maintain an individual personality while becoming totally integrated into a group? Most fans of popular music can identify the different Andrews Sisters by sight, but we probably couldn't distinguish one Mills Brother from another. Yet, the Andrews Sisters were certainly a more cohesive organism than the Mills Brothers, who, for all their technical expertise, were quite limited in style and repertoire. The Andrews Sisters could sing ballads, comic songs, novelty numbers, and imbue them all with the appropriate emotions. They were beloved for showy numbers like "Boogie Woogie Bugle Boy" that conveyed nothing more profound than the joy of singing—but they could also sing deeper songs, altering the mood of the moment at the drop of a chord.

Less emotional but definitely the most inventive, and the tightest of all vocal groups (male, female, or other), was the Boswell Sisters. Connee, Vet, and Martha played a variety of instruments and began as an instrumental trio, but it was when they started singing that they really broke through. No one before or since has been able to replicate their intricate vocal gymnastics and intelligent, emotional harmonies. Rhythm, though sometimes underestimated, was as important an element of their excellence as were their tight harmonies. They could switch rhythms with ease, draw out notes in a low-down drawl, or go off on New Orleans's blues riffs, stretching and growling one moment and purring the next.

The sisters interpolated one song into another, sang slow songs quickly and fast songs slowly, and even sang in their own made-up language sometimes, a sort of pig Latin with a Boswell twist. The intimacy that empowered them to invent their own language is a key to the Boswells' success. They were a tight-knit trio both on stage and off, combining equal parts solid rehearsing and intuition. Other groups haven't been as copasetic and that's hurt their singing. Stories of the Andrews Sisters's bickering are legendary, but the Boswells never had a bad word to say about one another.

There have been other sister groups of course, the Dinnings, McGuires, Lennons, and Kings, but none of them ever reached the artistic or professional heights of the Andrews and especially the Boswell Sisters. ◇

**TOP:** The Andrews Sisters with Sholom Secunda, composer of "Bei Mir Bist du Schoen." **ABOVE LEFT:** The Andrews Sisters (two anyway) reunite. Patti and Maxene in the hit show *Over Here!* (1974). **OPPOSITE TOP:** The McGuire Sisters. **OPPOSITE MIDDLE:** The Boswell Sisters with their fan Bing Crosby. **OPPOSITE BOTTOM:** The Mills Brothers in the 1935 film *Broadway Gondolier*.

## Song and Story

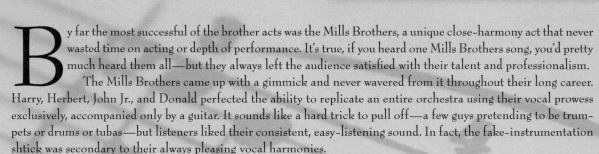

### BEI MIR BIST DU SCHOEN

"Bei Mir Bist du Schoen" was written by Sholom Secunda and Jacob Jacobs for the 1935 Yiddish musical comedy, *I Would If I Could*. Sammy Cahn fell in love with the song and added English lyrics—but Secunda and Jacobs weren't told. Imagine their surprise when they heard the Andrews Sisters' recording.

### DON'T SIT UNDER THE APPLE TREE

The music was originally written for a song titled "Anywhere the Bluebird Goes."

By far the most successful of the brother acts was the Mills Brothers, a unique close-harmony act that never wasted time on acting or depth of performance. It's true, if you heard one Mills Brothers song, you'd pretty much heard them all—but they always left the audience satisfied with their talent and professionalism.

The Mills Brothers came up with a gimmick and never wavered from it throughout their long career. Harry, Herbert, John Jr., and Donald perfected the ability to replicate an entire orchestra using their vocal prowess exclusively, accompanied only by a guitar. It sounds like a hard trick to pull off—a few guys pretending to be trumpets or drums or tubas—but listeners liked their consistent, easy-listening sound. In fact, the fake-instrumentation shtick was secondary to their always pleasing vocal harmonies.

Following the 1931 splash of their up-tempo hit "Tiger Rag," they specialized in moderate-tempo ballads with lyrics that were less than pithy. Their rendition of "You Always Hurt the One You Love," never a great tune to begin with, was about as deep as they got, and it was eminently open to parody—Spike Jones answered the call to memorable effect.

The Mills Brothers' legacy is not a noble one. Following the laws of devolution of music, each succeeding vocal group in their lineage was lower on the artistic scale. The Ink Spots (not even brothers) were scraping the bottom of the gene pool. The Ames Brothers had their share of fame in the 1950s, specializing in Mills Brothers–type songs. Ed Ames wisely broke away from the group and, although he had a fine voice and excellent sense of humor, he continued in the vein of his brothers with two hits, "Try to Remember" from *The Fantasticks* and "My Cup Runneth Over with Love" from *I Do! I Do!*, Ames never could find a personality of his own—a problem shared by many veterans of brother or sister acts.

Another brother act that spawned a successful solo career was the Williams Brothers. They were a minor act out of which came the 1960s superstar Andy Williams. It's telling that Andy Williams was an early booster of the whitest and blandest of all the brother acts, the Osmond Brothers, who began by singing a mixture of gospel and barbershop quartet.

Generally speaking, the history of brother groups is a kind of downward spiral into the bland and soulless. Just as big bands devolved into the lush miasma of Lawrence Welk, the brother act found itself at its presumed low point with the Osmonds (not to mention their Motown co-conspirators, the Jackson Five). And who came out of the Osmonds, none other than brother Donny, leader of a pretty-boy, nonthreatening substrata of rock-and-roll that included such artists as Shaun Cassidy and Bobby Sherman. ◇

## THE MILLS BROTHERS

| | |
|---|---|
| 1932 | Tiger Rag |
| 1932 | Coney Island Washboard; I Ain't Got Nobody; Old Rockin' Chair |
| 1933 | Dinah; When Yuba Plays the Rhumba on His Tuba |
| 1934 | Jungle Fever; Put on Your Old Gray Bonnet |
| 1943 | Paper Doll |
| 1944 | Till Then; You Always Hurt the One You Love |
| 1945 | I Wish |
| 1947 | Across the Alley from the Alamo |
| 1948 | Gloria |
| 1949 | I Love You So Much It Hurts; I've Got My Love to Keep Me Warm; Someday (You'll Want Me to Want You) |
| 1950 | Daddy's Little Girl; Nevertheless |
| 1952 | Be My Life's Companion; Glow Worm; The Jones Boy |
| 1955 | Suddenly There's a Valley |
| 1956 | All the Way 'Round the World; Standing on the Corner |
| 1957 | Queen of the Senior Prom |
| 1958 | Get a Job |
| 1959 | Yellow Cab |
| 1968 | Cab Driver; My Shy Violet; The Ol' Race Track |

# Ella Fitzgerald

Ella Fitzgerald is, quite simply, the most popular jazz singer of all time. While Sarah Vaughan is dismissed by some for her excesses, Billie Holiday chastised for her lack of variety, and Anita O'Day chided for her quirky interpretations, no one, including this writer, disputes the all-around excellence of Ella Fitzgerald. But, for all of her peerless perfection, Fitzgerald lacked the air of danger possessed by Vaughan, Holiday, and O'Day. Maybe she was just a little too perfect. Ella's recordings are luminescent, clean, orderly.

Perhaps it is the drama in their own lives that informs the style of the great blues and torch singers. Her young years were dismal, by her teens she was practically living on the street. Luckily, she achieved fame early and, from there, her star continued to rise. Perhaps this was reflected in her evenhanded, almost superficial song interpretations and her reliance on her astounding voice rather than her ability to act a lyric. Sarah Vaughan had a magnificent instrument, too, but she was constantly pushing the envelope, sometimes going too far. Holiday seemed almost to

## "I never knew how good our songs were until I heard Ella Fitzgerald sing them." —Ira Gershwin

be having a breakdown while singing a ballad, and, as with Judy Garland, the drama was partially voyeuristic: Will she survive intact to the end of the song? Will we? O'Day was a loose cannon vocally, leaving audiences open-mouthed at her more audacious flights of vocaleise. Fitzgerald was nothing if not steady.

But then there were those occasions when Fitzgerald let loose and scatted, surprising the audience with her mad invention. When "the first lady of song" let down her guard and went loopy, her free associations carried listeners up, down, inside, and around a song. She imitated instruments, climbed high up the scale only to drop down low, and threw in references to other songs, nursery rhymes, and doggerel.

A less talented singer who attempts to scat (meaning practically all of them—Diane Schuur, we're talking to you) goes off the chart, out of the world, and can't bring us back naturally to the flow of the song. Fitzgerald's scatting was structured, almost mathematical. Her return to the melody and lyric was a smooth landing that wrapped itself up neatly before returning us to reality.

Louis Armstrong, Cab Calloway, Johnny Scat Davis, and Ella Fitzgerald (not to mention the little-known Leo Watson) were the kings and queen of scat. In their capable hands, scatting sounded easy—but in fact it is extremely difficult work. So, we recommend an amendment to the jazz constitution that forbids scatting from now on. It's too painful to the ears of those of us who revere its past masters. Hey, we love Sammy Davis, Jr., but even he couldn't handle great scatting. He had the attitude but not the instinct, which is strange since he was such an instinctual singer. Cleo Laine flutters around like a balloon when the air is let out. Mel Torme had the technique down pat but never captured the emotion. Scatting calls for emotion—the joy of carrying a song (and an audience) beyond the confines of melody, time, rhythm, and meaning.

The true genius of Ella Fitzgerald came out when she transcended her own honeyed voice, impeccable diction, and superb timing. On the average song, she relied on the composer, lyricist, and arranger to provide the foundation for her work, bringing nothing to the party beyond great sound and technique. Sure, the icing she provided was sweet and smooth but the cake was baked by others. However, sometimes Ella's scatting was truly improvised, as when she forgot the lyrics to "Mack the Knife" on her *Ella in Berlin* album. When inspired, she approached up-tempo songs with abandon or simply sped up the timing of a song into a tongue-twisting tour de force. On ballads she took the opposite tack, slowing them down into a creamy river of words and music. Charm songs stayed right in the middle. She peppered her sets with all of these variations, along with an occasional bop number. Fitzgerald could do everything

and all of it bore her individual stamp.

Her joy truly emerged when she was scatting, but she always exhibited a strong sense of humor. Her emotional detachment worked well in humorous songs, where her interpretations verged on irony. She was categorized as a happy singer even when she sang sad ballads. One reviewer wrote in 1951 that she was a "large cheerful child. Her smile is as entrancing as her cherubic face; her eyes twinkle with more than a touch of mischief."

Fitzgerald had more than just a great set of pipes and crisp delivery. She was an amalgam of all the best of the singers who came before her—but with the rough edges smoothed out. She admitted to stealing from everyone, and her spot-on impressions of her contemporaries proved it. She programmed her mind with all of the ideas, techniques, and approaches of the greats and spun herself into Ella the Über-singer.

Throughout her career, Fitzgerald was committed to performing excellent songs, as exemplified by her Verve recordings, especially the series of "songbooks" devoted to single composers. Not surprisingly, her Decca years included the recording of a lot of novelty tunes along with a few important ballads. (Ella was probably assigned more novelties than most because of the wild success of "A-Tisket, A-Tasket," which she'd released in 1938.)

She built up to the songbooks with the Decca album *Ella Sings Gershwin*, an eight-song, ten-inch LP with piano by the incomparable Ellis Larkins (possibly the greatest of accompanists, who also did yeoman's work on an Anita Ellis LP). In 1956 Fitzgerald moved to Verve, where she leaned away from jazz and bop and ventured into the Broadway catalog. She explored the works of most of the great tunesmiths, Porter, Mercer, Kern, and others, usually with string accompaniment. Her fame grew and, as she became associated with

# CAREER HIGHLIGHTS

**1917** Born in Newport News, Virginia, on April 25.

**1934** Enters Apollo Theater amateur contest singing "Judy" in style of idol Connee Boswell, encores with "The Object of My Affection"; wins, gets to sing with Tiny Bradshaw for one week at Harlem Opera House; one-nighter with Chick Webb at Yale University dance leads to contract for $12.50 a week.

**1935** First Decca recording date with Chick Webb and his orchestra.

**1936** Records three songs with Benny Goodman and his orchestra for Victor.

**1937** Writes and records first song "You Showed Me The Way" with Chick Webb.

**1938** Writes and records number-one novelty hit, "A-Tisket, A-Tasket," with Chick Webb.

**1939** Records hit "Undecided"; Webb dies on June 16; Fitzgerald leads band as "Ella Fitzgerald and Her Famous Orchestra."

**1941** Disbands orchestra and starts solo career.

**1944** Records "Into Each Life Some Rain Must Fall" with The Ink Spots.

**1945** "Flying Home," first scat recording.

**1946** Marries Ray Brown; begins relationship with Norman Granz and Jazz at the Philharmonic.

**1947** Records "Oh, Lady Be Good."

**1950** Sings with Ellis Larkins accompaniment on Cole Porter songs; records *Ella Sings Gershwin*.

**1952** Amicable divorce from Ray Brown.

**1955** Films *Pete Kelly's Blues*; signs with Norman Granz's Verve label; makes the cover of *Life*.

**1956** First songbook albums released, *The Cole Porter Songbook* and *The Rodgers and Hart Songbook* with Buddy Bregman; *Ella and Louis* with Louis Armstrong.

**1957** Records *Like Someone in Love* with Frank Devol and Stan Getz; *The Duke Ellington Songbook* with Duke Ellington.

**1958** Records *The Irving Berlin Songbook* with Paul Weston.

**1959** Records *The George and Ira Gershwin Songbook* with Nelson Riddle.

**1960** Records *The Harold Arlen Songbook* with Billy May.

**1963** Records *The Jerome Kern Songbook*; *Ella and Basie* with Count Basie; and *Swings Lightly, Swings Gently* with Nelson Riddle.

**1964** Records *The Johnny Mercer Songbook*.

**1966** Leaves Verve.

**1972** Signs with Norman Granz's new Pablo label.

**1974** Appears in New York with Frank Sinatra and Count Basie.

**1986** Quintuple coronary bypass surgery and diagnosis of diabetes.

**1991** Final concert given at Carnegie Hall.

**1994** Retires from performing.

**1996** Dies on June 15 in Beverly Hills.

ELLA*swings brightly* with NELSON*

*Fitzgerald-Riddle

If her peak years were those with Verve, the last third of her career, when she recorded for Capitol, Reprise, and then Pablo, marked a decline in both her repertoire and vocal powers. Obviously, age affects all singers, but Fitzgerald's loss of range and the slowing of her mental reflexes showed up more than it might on a less pristine singer. She could no longer take breathtaking chances with scatting and her inventiveness grew less sure-footed. Still, she remained better than a great deal of singers and she was, nevertheless, always a privilege to hear.

Ella Fitzgerald at her peak, of course, remains available for all to hear and enjoy. A singer who devoted herself to the music first, Fitzgerald's stories in song could be as thrilling as Sarah Vaughan's, Billie Holiday's, or Anita O'Day's—but she told them in a different way. ❖

"I want to be a star like Ethel Waters with a Broadway show. I doubt it, though. Maybe I got an inferiority complex. Maybe I'm saying I doubt it because I'm hoping it will be just the opposite."

—Ella Fitzgerald

## Song and Story

### A-TISKET, A-TASKET

Swinging classics were the rage beginning with Maxine Sullivan's version of "Loch Lomand." The fifteen-year old Ella Fitzgerald and Van Alexander (sing his real name, Al Feldman) took the 1879 children's tune "I Sent a Letter to My Love" and swung it. The result was "A-Tisket A-Tasket." Its success was significant. It ws the first time a vocalist with a major big band rose above the band in popularity. From its release in 1938 to Webb's death in 1939, the band recorded far less instrumental sides and far more vocals with Ella, trying to have another success with the popularity of "A-Tisket A-Tasket." With every success comes problems and from then till her contract ended in 1955, Decca foisted inferior novelties on her.

> "Honey, in this business you've always got to get there the firstest with the mostest and the newest." —Chick Webb

### OH, LADY BE GOOD!

One of Fitzgerald's earliest and most famous scat vocals almost never happened. The 1947 Decca recording session with Bob Haggart needed another tune so this arrangement was made up on the spot. It was the hit of the date.

### BASIN STREET BLUES

Ella Fitzgerald recorded many times with Louis Armstrong, first in the late 1940s for Decca with a recording of duets and later for Verve in the late 1950s. Her 1949 recording for Decca of "Basin Street Blues" is the only instance where, on the second chorus, she impersonates Armstrong, a gimmick she performed many times in concert.

### GOODNIGHT MY LOVE

Benny Goodman wanted Billie Holiday to join his orchestra in 1933. Three years later he also wanted Fitzgerald to join him. She was offered $5,000 to join Goodman's band, but she remained loyal to Chick Webb until his death in 1939. However, in 1936, Goodman and Fitzgerald saw no harm in recording three tunes together. What they did not know is that the singer's Decca contract forbade her from recording with another label. The records were out for only a few months before being recalled. They were finally released in the 1950s by RCA and have been available ever since.

Ella's first champion, the great Chick Webb.

> "Man, woman, or child, Ella is the greatest." —Bing Crosby

## First Person

Ella on Marilyn Monroe: I owe Marilyn Monroe a real debt. It was because of her that I played the Mocambo, a very popular nightclub in the '50s. She personally called the owner of the Mocambo and told him she wanted me booked immediately, and if he would do it, she would take a front table every night. She told him—and it was true, due to Marilyn's superstar status—that the press would go wild. The owner said yes, and Marilyn was there, front table, every night. The press went overboard.

Tommy Flanagan to author Ernest Dunbar: Sometimes Ella comes up with a tune that she's heard somewhere, or I may send her a song that I feel is especially for her. Then we get together to find the key she's comfortable in. She tells me how she feels this piece should be done—serious or playful or humorous—the kind of mood it communicates to her. I then work up an orchestration that embodies her ideas and my own and we try it together. But an arrangement for Ella if only a framework within which to move. She will still do all kinds of things within that framework. Often, she'll add a new twist or improvisation, even when we're actually onstage performing. She may lag behind the beat a bit or move ahead of it, but she always knows exactly what she is doing. What would be musically risky for some singers, she pulls off easily. She rarely sings a song exactly the same way she did it last. But we've all played together for so long that no matter what she does, we are all right there together.

Helen Forrest

Helen Forrest was a chameleon—which perhaps explains why she sang under a variety of names over the course of her career, including Bonnie Blue and the Blue Lady. Her particular talent was her ability to adapt her style to match whatever band she sang with, though she never quite found her identity as a soloist.

When she sang with Artie Shaw, replacing Billie Holiday, she mimicked his heat, and her singing was daring and emotionally complex. When it was rumored that Shaw intended to split up the band, she decamped and joined Benny Goodman's entourage in 1939. That same year, arranger extraordinaire Eddie Sauter jointed Goodman, and Forrest went along with the change in sound that Sauter inspired, always the dutiful band singer. Goodman had been experiencing bad luck with singers—Louise Tobin left to have a baby; Kay Foster didn't please him—and Forrest provided a new stability along with her talent and star quality.

At the same time, Forrest was sitting in with the King Cole Trio and Lionel Hampton, gaining a variety of experience in preparation for moving on. Goodman was a hard band leader to work for—he tended to hog the spotlight, always noodling around behind the singer's solos. In August 1941, Forrest abruptly left him "to avoid having a nervous breakdown," as she recalled.

"Then, just on a hunch, I decided to contact Harry [James]. I loved the way he played that trumpet with that Jewish phrasing, and I thought I'd fit right in with the band. But Harry didn't seem to want me because he already had Dick Haymes to sing all the ballads and he was looking for a rhythm singer. Then Peewee Monte, his manager, had me come over to rehearsal, and after that the guys in the band took a vote and they decided they wanted me with them. So Harry agreed."

James and Forrest were well suited to each other, and Forrest also found a soulmate in Dick Haymes, her male counterpart on the bandstand. James's romantic crooning on the trumpet was counterbalanced by the cooler, less emotional style Forrest adopted. It was a wonderfully symbiotic relationship and the hits started coming fast and furious. Forrest loved Haymes despite his personal peccadilloes, and matched his creamy vocals note for note.

The artistic generosity that James had shown toward Sinatra, he extended to Forrest, as well. James realized that Forrest was a major talent and a big draw, so he allowed her to start a song, rest during an instrumental interlude, then pick up the lyric again. This was in direct opposition to what most big band singers were asked to do: they tended to fill in the middle refrain while the band took over the rest. When Forrest came on, the audience actually listened to the vocal for a minute or two, rather than just following the beat as they danced across the polished wood floors. ◆

The Haymes/Forrest pairing was a success and she followed him to radio, where they continued to collaborate. With the big band era all but over in the 1950s, Forrest's career slowed down—for all her talent, she'd never figured out the fine art of the soloist. Without a band leader and arranger to lead the way, she lost her direction. Ironically, perhaps the greatest showcase for her talents came in 1955, when she reunited with Harry James for the album *Harry James in Hi-Fi*, on Capitol Records. In the '60s, she briefly joined Tommy Dorsey's ensemble, under the baton of Sam Donahue, but she wasn't happy performing the nostalgia-filled engagements. She sang in some clubs over the next few decades and made her impressive final album for Bernie Brightman's Stash label in 1983. Helen Forrest died in Los Angeles in 1999.

## Song and Story

### SKYLARK

Late in 1944, Harry James decided to add the Hoagy Carmichael and Johnny Mercer classic "Skylark" to his repertoire. When rehearsing it, Helen Forrest just couldn't pick up the melody line. She asked if James would consider making the song an instrumental but he refused. It was decided that Forrest would stand right in front of James while he quietly played the melody. If you listen to the original recording very closely you can still hear James giving Forrest her notes in the background.

**ABOVE LEFT:** Helen and Johnny McAfee on the air with Harry James and His Music Makers.

**CENTER:** Helen Forrest and her duet partner Dick Haymes.

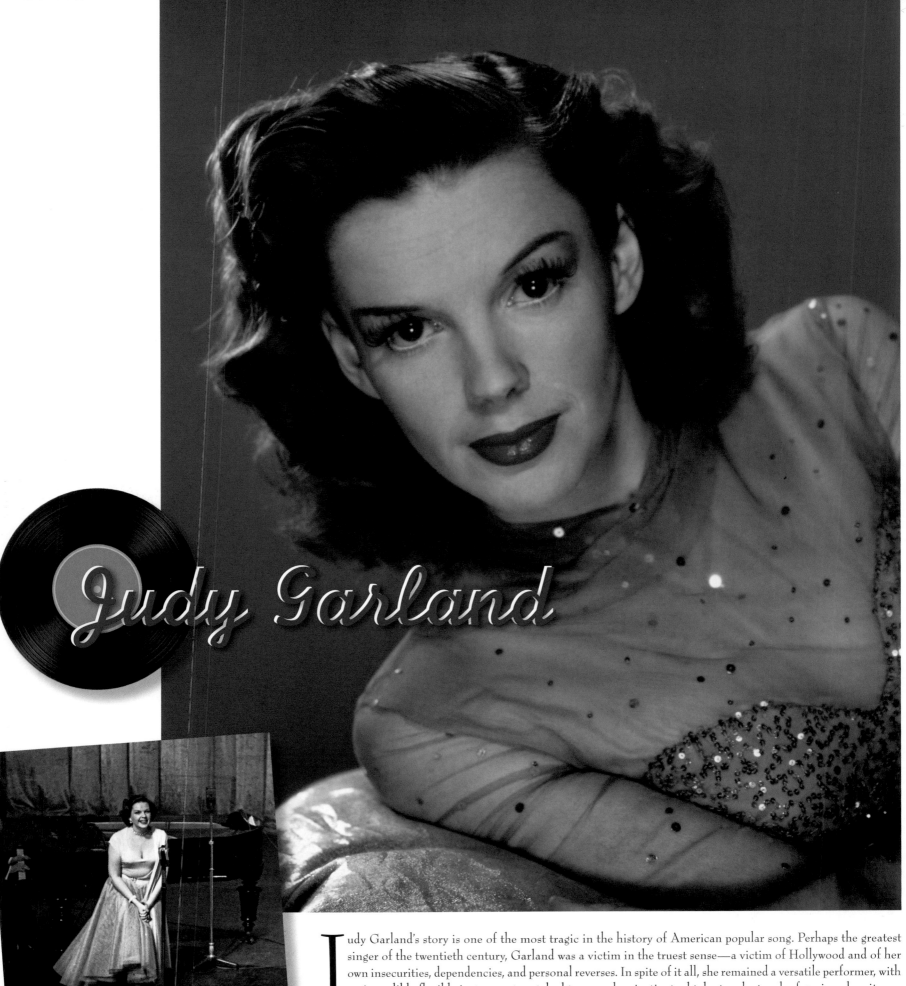

# Judy Garland

Judy Garland's story is one of the most tragic in the history of American popular song. Perhaps the greatest singer of the twentieth century, Garland was a victim in the truest sense—a victim of Hollywood and of her own insecurities, dependencies, and personal reverses. In spite of it all, she remained a versatile performer, with an incredibly flexible instrument matched to a peerless instinctual talent and a touch of genius when it came to interpreting a song.

Though she lived only forty-seven years, she spent forty-five of them in show business, and in that almost half-century of performing, she did it all, beginning with hundreds of vaudeville and radio appearances as a member of the Gumm Sisters. From there, it was on to short films; more than thirty feature films; more than one thousand live performances in concert halls, nightclubs, and theaters (including three appearances on Broadway); a special Oscar, a special Tony Award, and five Grammy Awards; dozens of bestselling record albums; and more than one hundred singles.

# "She can do everything better than anybody else."
## —Hugh Martin

Judy Garland was born Frances Ethel Gumm in Grand Rapids, Minnesota, on June 10, 1922. At her parents' urging, she got her feet wet in the family act, and by 1930 she'd won a contest and a screen test at Paramount Pictures. She soon tested at Twentieth Century-Fox and Columbia as well, but, although the studios were drawn to her precocity and her remarkably mature singing voice, none of them knew quite what to do with her.

She was finally discovered by someone at MGM, though exactly who that visionary was is lost in the fog of the past. Composer Burton Lane claimed to have spotted her talents and brought her to the attention of Louis B. Mayer. Joseph Mankiewicz heard her sing at a party given by Marcus Rabwin and recommended the young girl to Mayer's executive assistant, Ida Koverman. However it happened, Louis B. Mayer himself attended her audition, at which Garland sang "Zing Went the Strings of My Heart." A few days later came a screen test, and within a few weeks, she'd signed a contract with the studio.

With the exception of a few pictures, Garland spent her Hollywood years at MGM. When she arrived, she was immediately given lessons in how to be a star. The brilliant Roger Edens, who had accompanied her at her fateful MGM audition, helped her capitalize on her natural vocal talents; Kay Thompson worked with her on carriage and deportment; she was made up by the finest cosmeticians and dressed by brilliant designers. And of course, when she suffered from inevitable exhaustion or experienced inconvenient weight gain, there was always someone standing by with a miraculous chemical concoction to keep her going.

Garland was no fragile flower. Her pluck, sense of humor, and inner strength pulled her through her share of troubles, and she was a consummate pro: on film, she never showed a sign of inner turmoil or insecurity. Vulnerability, yes—but that only served to deepen her performances. Even at the very end of her career with MGM, in the few scenes she filmed for *Annie Get Your Gun*, she showed us the brave and open Judy Garland we'd always known and loved.

Garland's earliest recordings are marked by her natural voice, sense of humor, and willingness to try anything. As her career progressed, she learned to swing in a contemporary jazz sense, and to let her emotions emerge through song. Perhaps because of her remarkable vocal maturity, she started right out with a large

## THE GREAT SONGS

| Year | Songs |
|------|-------|
| 1937 | (Dear Mr. Gable) You Made Me Love You |
| 1938 | On the Bumpy Road to Love; Zing! Went the Strings of My Heart |
| 1939 | Over the Rainbow |
| 1940 | Embraceable You; Friendship (with Johnny Mercer); I'm Nobody's Baby; In-Between; It's a Great Day for the Irish; Our Love Affair; A Pretty Girl Milking a Cow |
| 1941 | F.D.R. Jones; How About You?; I'm Always Chasing Rainbows |
| 1942 | For Me and My Gal (with Gene Kelly); Poor Little Rich Girl; When You Wore a Tulip (with Gene Kelly) |
| 1943 | But Not for Me; Embraceable You; I Got Rhythm |
| 1944 | The Boy Next Door; Boys and Girls Like You and Me; Have Yourself a Merry Little Christmas; Meet Me in St. Louis, Louis; The Trolley Song; Under the Bamboo Tree (with Margaret O'Brien) |
| 1945 | On the Atchison, Topeka and the Santa Fe; |
| 1946 | Look for the Silver Lining; Love; Who |
| 1948 | Be a Clown (with Gene Kelly); A Couple of Swells (with Fred Astaire); I Wish I Were in Love Again; Johnny One Note; Love of My Life; You Can Do No Wrong |
| 1949 | Meet Me Tonight In Dreamland |
| 1950 | Get Happy; If You Feel Like Singing, Sing |
| 1951 | Last Night When We Were Young |
| 1954 | Born in a Trunk; Here's What I'm Here For; It's a New World; The Man That Got Away |
| 1955 | Rock-a-Bye Your Baby with a Dixie Melody |
| 1956 | Dirty Hands, Dirty Face; Just Imagine |
| 1962 | Paris Is a Lonely Town |
| 1963 | I Could Go On Singing |

For those who have been living in caves, here's Judy with the brainless, the heartless, and the courage-deficient.

## CAREER HIGHLIGHTS

---

### "She was the most sympathetic, the funniest, the sharpest, and the most stimulating woman I ever knew." —James Mason

repertoire of older songs such as "You Made Me Love You," I Cried for You," "I'm Nobody's Baby," "Under the Bamboo Tree," and "For Me and My Gal." Her signature song, Arlen and Harburg's "Over the Rainbow," came early and ripened right along with her throughout her life. It was written for the film that made her a star (and continues to introduce her to new generations), *The Wizard of Oz*. If "Over the Rainbow" provided one bookend to Garland's film career, perhaps the other was "The Man That Got Away," written for her by Arlen and Ira Gershwin at the end of her Hollywood period. She continued to sing both those songs until the end.

Garland's emotional interpretations are viewed by detractors as overacting, but it's almost impossible not to be swept up by her technique. She is so committed to each performance that we rarely get a glimpse of the singer behind the song. It is Garland who perfected the ability to build a ballad inexorably toward a no-holds-barred finale. Tony Bennett learned this lesson well. Barbra Streisand, though a powerful interpreter in her own right, seems to lack the patience for it, often starting a song at a level of intensity where others end. But it was Garland who set the pace for all who came after, with her carefully calibrated and mesmerizing performances, both on screen and onstage.

When the cameras were on, Garland was every inch a star, but away from the spotlight, her insecurities reigned. MGM had kept her so busy as a teenager (and well into her twenties) that she had little time to develop a full-blown off-screen identity. Having had virtually no childhood in the traditional sense, she was never savvy when it came to relationships, plunging headlong into affairs and marriages as if desperate to escape the roles she played onscreen. Ironically, she didn't really know how to be herself, so she always seemed to be "on"—which is understandable, given that all of the love she'd ever felt had come when she sang or told stories. Since the studio publicity machine played fast and loose with the facts of her life, why should she be any different? According to her

**BELOW:** Judy performing "The Black Bottom" in the "Born in a Trunk" section of *A Star Is Born*.

"She was a tremendous musician, Judy. I guess that's the greatest talent I've ever encountered in my life." —Hugh Martin

mood, she either loved being in pictures or despised every minute. She constantly cast herself as a victim until this became a self-fulfilling prophecy. The line between the Judy Garland story and the real Judy Garland melted away.

But perhaps the real Judy Garland was right here all the time, right in our own backyard. She was here in her films, her radio and television broadcasts, her recordings, and in her electrifying stage appearances. Out of the spotlight, she was done in by a combination of external forces and internal demons; but behind a microphone, sitting on the edge of a stage, as if inviting an entire audience into her home and heart, her own best qualities came through every time: her vulnerability, her sense of humor, her intelligence, and her consummate artistry. Onstage, Garland was at home, and for all of the pain she may have experienced in her life, there was no mistaking the pure joy she brought to her work.

We're lucky to live in an age when we can call up the entire breadth of a brilliant career with the touch of a button; Judy Garland will be with us forever, continuing to set the standard for all who aspire to follow her. ◆

## First Person

Virginia Gumm, to biographer Christopher Finch: The studio doctor gave her Dexedrine, I believe it was, to keep her weight down. Nobody thought it was bad. My mother didn't think it was bad—if she had, she wouldn't have let Judy take it. But nobody knew anything about it then.

## Asides

Judy Garland, larger than life, brilliant, and misunderstood, has always been a kind of patron saint of the gay community. Her death helped provoke the Stonewall Riots in New York's Greenwich Village, marking the beginning of the modern gay rights movement.

Some 22,000 people viewed Judy Garland's body at Campbell's funeral home in Los Angeles.

## Song and Story

### THE MAN THAT GOT AWAY

Hugh Martin on working on 1954's *A Star Is Born*: I wanted her to sing it moodily, quietly, and so did Harold Arlen, I found out later. When I went back to New York, he called me and said, "What happened?" I told him that she had belted it. He said, "Oh no! It shouldn't be belted. It's an introspective song." Both Harold and George Cukor thought I was right. The day of the recording, George said, "Can you do anything to stop her from yelling that song and making it such a tour de force? If she does that, I don't have a movie." I said, "What do you mean?" He said, "Well, if you know she's a star in the first fifteen minutes, you don't have any place to go."

### THAT OLD BLACK MAGIC

Johnny Mercer meant his 1942 lyric, set to Havrold Arlen's tune, to refer specifically to Judy Garland, with whom he was having an affair. The song includes the famous line: "I should stay away, but what can I do?"

Living proof of the maxim "Like mother like daughter," Liza and mom.

# Hildegarde

The question we pose to you now is how a little girl from the sticks became one of the most sophisticated singers in New York and London. Don't try to answer the question —it's a mystery that may never be solved. Perhaps it was her background in vaudeville. Like many artists who came out of that tradition, she invented a persona for herself.

Hildegarde Sell was born in dairy country—Adell, Wisconsin, to be exact. She moved soon to the aptly named New Holstein, Wisconsin, where her dad played in a local band and her mom directed the church choir. She was a member of Gus Edwards's *School Days* act in vaudeville, where such future stars as Eddie Cantor, Georgie Jessel, Groucho Marx, Walter Winchell, Sally Rand, Ray Bolger, Elsie Janis, and a host of others made their professional debuts. The Incomparable Hildegarde (as she was billed) went on to play at the Café de Paris in London, with subsequent engagements in Paris and

elsewhere in Europe. She appeared in the West End musical *Seeing Stars*, and was the first non-English person signed by the BBC.

Upon returning to New York, she became the top society singer, with her trademark elbow-length white gloves, hair piled high on her head, vase of roses (which she handed out to her audience), and handkerchiefs that she used to great effect. She accompanied herself on the piano through a series of literate, sophisticated songs from the Broadway songbook, including songs by her friend Gladys Shelley and Cole Porter's "Ev'ry Time We Say Goodbye," which she helped popularize. She recorded albums for Decca Records and introduced many show songs on record. In fact, her album of songs from *Lady in the Dark* was released before the cast album, prompting its star, Gertrude Lawrence, to threaten to back out of recording the cast album. Hildegarde's career lasted into the 1990s with appearances at whatever top rooms were left in what became an increasingly less sophisticated city. She died on July 29, 2005 at the age of 99.

# Shirley Horn

Shirley Horn is another singing pianist, but she's as opposite from Hildegarde as a girl can get. Horn was brought up and still lives in Washington, D.C. She never really wanted the limelight though she ended up with such fans as Miles Davis and Quincy Jones.

After attending Howard University, she began her career as a lounge pianist in D.C. clubs. She started her first trio in 1954, limiting herself to playing the piano. That is, until one day, while she was still only seventeen, a steady customer came in with a great big teddy bear and told her that if she sang "Melancholy Baby" she could have the bear. She did and she did.

She recorded a little in the 1960s and, like Maxine Sullivan, retired to raise her family. She came back in the 1980s and in 1987 began a long

relationship with Verve Records. Among her biggest boosters was Washington jazz critic and producer Joel E. Siegel. He got her to perform as much as possible in New York, London, Paris, and Tokyo, to name a few of the cities where she is revered.

Unlike a lot of virtuoso pianist/singers, Horn's strength lies in her simplicity, which only adds to her emotional impact. She's neither a great pianist nor a great singer, but her depth of feeling comes through, in both her singing and playing. She can be a surprisingly dramatic singer, and maybe it's the very lack of pyrotechnics that makes the audience come to her. There's not a lot of talking in the room when Shirley Horn is performing. Naysayers call her slow (and thus boring), but Shirley believes in taking her time with a song and discovering its essence through minimalism.

Another fine singer who retired briefly to attend to family matters is the upbeat Helen Humes. Surprisingly, given her sunny (but never saccharine) performances, she started her career as a blues singer, cutting ten sides at the tender age of thirteen! The year was 1927 and young Helen was typecast, as were many of her black, female contemporaries, into singing in the vein of Ethel Waters and Bessie Smith. At that early age, Humes professed not to understand what all the double entendres were really about. And that gave her an innocence that she carried with her even when she darn well knew what she was singing about! Then it was back to school for Helen, following her recording debut.

When the music business loosened up (a little) in the '30s, Helen switched genres and sang pop songs for the likes of saxophone player Al Sears and Stuff Smith and later for Harry James and Count Basie (replacing Billie Holiday). In the 1940s, after a stint at Barney Josephson's swank Café Society (where Holiday also performed), Humes discovered rhythm and blues, which clearly suited her talents: she had a big hit with "E-Baba-Le-Ba."

Then came a new decade and a new style. In the 1950s, she tackled jazz with a five-year stint with Norman Granz's Jazz at the Philharmonic troupe, followed by years as a solo act. In the 1960s, she moved to Australia after touring there with Red Norvo, not coming back until 1967 to nurse her mother (and find work in a muni-

# Helen Humes

tions factory). But those who had helped her in the past wouldn't let her stay out of the limelight for long. In the 1970s, John Hammond (who had conspired with Basie to get her to join the band) brought her out of retirement, and Barney Josephson booked her at his new club, the Cookery, in 1975. That's when Hammond recorded her for Columbia, and the resulting album, *It's the Talk of the Town*, remains one of her best, though she broke no new ground.

The *New York Times* responded with the headline "HELEN HUMES DISCOVERED AGAIN AT 63" and her career was off and running. Over the next ten years, she recorded for several foreign labels and a couple of small American ones, including the highly respected Audiophile. By the time she died in 1981, Helen Humes was regarded as one of the best singers in any genre.

# The Younger Generation

It seems as if the garage of every male baby boomer has a guitar moldering behind an unused exercise machine. In the 1950s and '60s, whether you were a folkie or rocked out, learning a few simple chords was the key to fame and fortune—or at least high school popularity. Nowadays, teens don't need any accoutrements save a loose-fitting T-shirt and a pair of baggy pants sans a belt (not Sansabelt—that's for the aforementioned '50s pop stars on the Florida condo circuit).

Against all odds, there remain a select few young singers who prefer M & M (McRae and Mercer) to Eminem. These are the younger generation of pop standard-bearers, and by younger I mean in their forties or fifties. None of them has broken through like keeper-of-the-flame Michael Feinstein, but they all make a living performing and recording the American songbook, and their CDs are snatched up by a few thousand jazz and pop lovers who appreciate fresh new takes on old favorites.

Ann Hampton Callaway is the most successful of the bunch, performing around the country in concerts and nightclubs, and at private parties. She's a marvelous pianist and her wonderful sense of humor makes her a delight. One of her gimmicks is to make up jazzy songs on the spot and, surprisingly, they're great. It's a wonderful party trick but apart from her facility with the idiom, she's a musician with real heart who clearly enjoys performing and brings the audience along on the joy ride.

Eric Comstock is a singer and pianist who has played the top rooms around the country, not that there are many left. He plays New York's Algonquin on a semi-regular basis, usually with intelligent, well-researched theme shows spotlighting a particular composer or singer. His sense of humor and drama carry him far when interpreting the Tin Pan Alley catalog, and he has parlayed his knowledge into a few musical revues, really glorified cabaret shows, which have proved successful in New York and around the country. *Our Sinatra* was the first and most famous of these, followed by *Made for the Movies: A Hollywood Songbook* and *Singing Astaire*.

Daryl Sherman is one of our most accomplished younger performers. She's just as good a singer as pianist, which makes sense since she comes from a musical family: her mother and sister are both pianists; her brother, a drummer; and her father, Sammy Sherman, a big-band trombonist and fiddler. She holds court at the Waldorf Astoria, playing Cole Porter's piano and doing it proud. Maybe its her natural modesty that's kept her from becoming better known, but the more discerning devotees of the genre hold her in high esteem.

Mary Cleere Haran is the one nonpianist in this bunch. Her warm intelligence and quick wit are hallmarks of her performances, which feel more like wonderful parties than concerts. Like Feinstein, Haran treats her audiences like old friends, her natural, unforced, and, dare we say honest delivery placing equal weight on lyric and music. Maybe the fact that she started her career on Broadway accounts for her exquisite diction, respect for her material, and rapport with her listeners. And though an evening with her is sheer entertainment, somehow you always walk away having learned something new and fascinating about a composer, a song, or Haran herself.

Heather MacRae is the least known of this group, in cabaret circles, anyway. The daughter of Sheila and Gordon MacRae, she has logged a lot of hours on Broadway but has recently begun performing more frequently in clubs and at private parties, which is fortunate for us. Her voice is reminiscent of Barbara Cook's, with clear tones and and a warm soprano, and her easy sense of humor and gentle nature (not to say she can't be a dame on occasion) are wonderfully evident when she sings ballads. In fact, there's no better ballad-singer around, and her joy in performing is palpable.

These five artists aren't as well known as their predecessors, but it's a harder climb to the top when the songs you love are marginalized in the entertainment firmament. Aficionados of American popular song still exist, and the more perceptive among them have discovered the varied talents of these marvelous performers. ◆

**TOP LEFT:** Daryl Sherman. **BOTTOM LEFT:** Eric Comstock. **TOP RIGHT:** Mary Cleere Haran. **BOTTOM RIGHT:** Heather MacRae's CD.

# Billie Holiday

God Bless' The Child

A swing-spiritual based on the authentic proverb
"GOD BLESSED THE CHILD THAT'S GOT HIS OWN"

Words and Music by
ARTHUR HERZOG, Jr.
and
BILLIE HOLIDAY

BILLIE HOLIDAY
on Decca Record No. 3-0729

EDWARD B. MARKS MUSIC CORPORATION · 136 WEST 52nd STREET · NEW YORK 19, N. Y.

Billie Holiday, considered by many to be one of our best blues singers, was actually not a blues singer in the traditional sense. She sang only a handful of authentic twelve-bar blues in her entire career. Perhaps she was dubbed a blues singer because of her autobiography, which was called *Lady Sings the Blues* (a title chosen by her publisher, who thought the word "blues" would sell books). Holiday did bring a bluesy feel to her material, though her repertoire consisted almost exclusively of American popular songs.

She presented her life and music without apology—drugs, raspy voice, and all—and she didn't sound like anyone who came before or after her. Holiday was the first singer after Bing Crosby to realize the potential of the microphone—but she took her technique a step further even than Crosby. "Lady Day" made a listener feel she was singing directly to him or her. In this regard, she had a major influence on the likes of Frank Sinatra (whom Billie taught how to phrase) and Peggy Lee. Sinatra has often cited her as his biggest influence. (According to Holiday, her own biggest influences were Louis Armstrong and Bessie Smith. She never admitted to the role Ethel Waters played.)

Before Holiday, male pop singers were crooners in the Crosby mode and women were either '20s flappers like Annette Hanshaw and Ruth Etting, or sopranos like Jeanette MacDonald. Helen Morgan was the bluesiest of the singers of the late '20s and early '30s, a soprano who could also put across a "Negro" song like "Can't Help Lovin' Dat Man" or a white blues number like "Why Was I Born?"

Her natural good humor led to lots of recordings of terrific B songs (and keep in mind that good B songs by the Tin Pan Alley masters are better than so-called A songs by hacks). Song-pluggers gave Holiday second-class numbers knowing that she could make them into hits. After all, Holiday never sang a song as written, always adding her own jazz variations. "One, Two, Button Your Shoe," for example, is a charming, gimmicky, rhythmic number that will never be mistaken for Gershwin or Berlin, but it provided Holiday with an excuse to swing with personality.

When Holiday got hold of a song with depth, even if she swung it, she could impart a richness of emotion that has never been equaled. Into every performance she wove her past, present, and future, creating personal monologues rich in character. And of course we always assumed the character was Holiday herself.

Lots of great singers, Doris Day for one, can act a song but we never forget it's a performance. Holiday seemed to show us her soul. She was gutsy in her song choices and she wrote some of her most effective songs. Her achingly vulnerable "Good Morning, Heartache" couldn't seem a more honest revelation of her personal demons. A lesser singer might turn the song into kitsch and it wouldn't take much. Even Holiday's somewhat overacted "Strange Fruit" (the bluesier corollary to Irving Berlin's "Supper Time") is deeply affecting because of the sense of conviction she brings to every line.

Holiday's was an intensity without histrionics. There was no screaming, no gospel-infused, multisyllabic wailing, no blues shouting. She conveyed the song's meaning with the twist of a word, a bit of back phrasing, a particular emphasis on a note. She was a minimalist, using her ultra precise technique to hypnotize us.

One or two songs with the dramatic intensity of "Strange Fruit" are all right but a whole career they don't make. Unfortunately for Holiday, that's what people think of when they remember her, along with the long, downhill slide into drug addiction, prison, heartache, and death. Holiday is the perfect companion when you're in a blue mood yourself, feeling dark and smoky and alone. At least that seems to be the prevailing opinion.

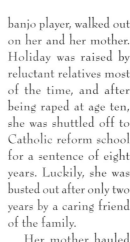

Holiday clowns around with Louis Armstrong.

Billie Holiday could never be confused with "easy listening," Muzak, or jazz lite. Her singing was meant to elicit a reaction, whether joy or sorrow. Her brilliant technique and smoky voice underpin the life she celebrated to the fullest, whether in her upbeat, joyful songs (which are always a surprise) or her blues numbers, which exhibit a sort of masochistic joy in feeling bad. It's the full-blown life she injected into her art that makes her unique. She recognized the value in Tin Pan Alley fluff. She never stooped to performing the nonsense songs or really bad pop ditties that many of her colleagues found themselves saddled with. She was lucky enough to have John Hammond, Milt Gabler, and Norman Granz in her corner.

She certainly had a right to sing the blues. The miracle is that she didn't exploit the terrible events of her life. Nor did she become angry like Lena Horne, who had relatively little to be angry about. She was born out of wedlock and her father, a jazz guitarist and

banjo player, walked out on her and her mother. Holiday was raised by reluctant relatives most of the time, and after being raped at age ten, she was shuttled off to Catholic reform school for a sentence of eight years. Luckily, she was busted out after only two years by a caring friend of the family.

Her mother hauled her to New Jersey and then closer to civilization, Brooklyn. She worked as a maid alongside her mother and turned to prostitution to make a little spending money. It was singing that got her off the streets and into the clubs at the beginning of the 1930s. A few years later, John Hammond found her and her recording career began in earnest in 1935, accompanied by no less than the brilliant pianist, Teddy Wilson. Holiday defined small jazz combo singing with now legendary recordings with her collaborators in rhythm Cozy Cole, Ben Webster, Lester Young, Roy Eldridge, and Wilson. Solid, unpretentious songs that lent themselves to jazz riffs and improvisation formed a foundation for their interpretations.

During the last half of the thirties, Holiday sang with Jimmie Lunceford, Fletcher Henderson, Count Basie, and Artie Shaw's bands. It was the brilliant club owner Barney Jacobson who booked her into Café Society, a rare integrated club populated by the crème de la crème of New York society. Audiences went to hear Holiday exactly because she didn't sound the same as every other band singer.

## THE GREAT SONGS

**1933** You're Mother's Son In Law; Riffin' the Scotch

**1935** Miss Brown to You; I Wished on The Moon; What a Little Moonlight Can Do; If You Were Mine; A Sunbonnet Blue; What a Night; What a Moon; What a Girl

**1936** I Cried for You; Billie's Blues; Summertime; Easy to Love; Pennies from Heaven; The Way You Look Tonight

**1937** He's Funny That Way; I Must Have That Man; Easy Living; I Can't Give You Anything But Love; Me Myself and I; This Year's Kisses; Mean to Me; Nice Work If You Can Get It; One Never Knows

**1938** Any Old Time; You Go to My Head; They Say; I'm Gonna Lock My Heart; Say It with a Kiss

**1939** Strange Fruit; Fine and Mellow; Them There Eyes;Yesterdays; Some Other Spring; Sugar

**1940** The Man I Love; Body and Soul; I Hear Music; St. Louis Blues; Loveless Love

**1941** Gloomy Sunday; God Bless the Child; Solitude; All of Me; Georgia on My Mind; Am I Blue?; Love Me or Leave Me; Solitude; Jim

**1942** Until The Real Thing Comes Along; Trav'lin' Light

**1944** I Cover the Waterfront; Lover Come Back to Me; Embraceable You; As Time Goes By; I'll Get By; My Old Flame; Lover Man; I'll Be Seeing You; On the Sunny Side of The Street

**1945** Don't Explain; You Better Go Now; No More; That Ole Devil Called Love

**1946** Good Morning; Heartache; Guilty; No Good Man; I'll Look Around; The Blues Are Brewin'

**1947** There Is No Greater Love; Deep Song

**1948** My Man; Porgy

**1949** You're My Thrill; Crazy He Calls Me; Ain't Nobody's Business If I Do; Do Your Duty; Now or Never; Baby Get Lost

**1951** Detour Ahead; Blue Turning Grey Over You

**1952** East of the Sun; Love for Sale; These Foolish Things; Autumn In New York; Moonglow; Stormy Weather; I Only have Eyes for You; Tenderly; Everything I Have Is Yours

**1955** What's New; I Get a Kick out of You; Prelude to a Kiss; When Your Lover Has Gone; It Had to Be You; A Ghost of a Chance;Come Rain or Come Shine; Ain't Misbehavin'; Do Nothing Till You Hear from Me

**1956** Willow Weep for Me; I Thought about You; Too Marvelous for Words; Lady Sings the Blues

**1957** Day In; Day Out; A Foggy Day; One for My Baby; I Didn't Know What Time It Was; Speak Low; Love Is Here to Stay; April in Paris; Comes Love; Cheek to Cheek; Darn That Dream; Ill Wind; But Not for Me; All or Nothing at All

**1958** I'm A Fool to Want You; You've Changed; Violets for Your Furs; Easy to Remember; I Get Along without You Very Well; I'll Be Around; The End of a Love Affair

**1959** Don't Worry 'Bout Me

## CAREER HIGHLIGHTS

**1915** Born Eleanor Fagan Gough in Philadelphia, April 7; later settles in Baltimore.

**1930** Moves from Baltimore to New York; first singing jobs in Harlem.

**1933** Discovered by John Hammond at Monette Moore's speakeasy; introduced by Hammond to Benny Goodman; recording debut with Goodman "Your Mother's Son in Law."

**1934** Debut at Apollo Theater, billed as "Billy Halliday,"makes one-reeler *Symphony in Black* with Duke Ellington, singing "Saddest Tale."

**1935** First recordings with Teddy Wilson, "What a Little Moonlight Can Do" for Brunswick.

**1936** First hit record "I Cried For You" with Teddy Wilson; makes first solo records on Vocalion with own composition, "Billie's Blues."

**1937** First records with Lester Young; tours with Count Basie band.

**1938** Tours with Artie Shaw; first performer to play Barney Josephson's Café Society in New York.

**1939** Records "Strange Fruit" and own composition, "Fine and Mellow" for Commodore. The latter becomes a commercial hit.

**1941** Composes and records "God Bless The Child"; marries Jimmy Monroe.

**1942** After 153 titles leaves Columbia Records; records with Paul Whiteman at Capitol Records as "Lady Day"; begins club residency on New York's 52nd Street, starting at the Famous Door.

**1944** First black artist to sing at Metropolitan Opera House in *Esquire All-American Jazz Concert*; begins using heroin; records sixteen titles with Commodore; begins contract with Decca Records; records hit "Lover Man," her first record with string backing.

**1945** Divorces Jimmy Monroe and marries trumpeter Joe Guy. Composes and records "Don't Explain."

**1946** Records "Good Morning, Heartache"; Town Hall Concert on February 16.

**1947** Only major film role, *New Orleans*, with Louis Armstrong; checks into rehab for addiction; FBI arrests for possession on May 19; sentenced to year prison term in Alderson, West Virginia .

**1948** Released from prison; first solo concert at Carnegie Hall April 17; denied Cabaret Card due to prison record, cannot perform in New York clubs; opens "Holiday on Broadway" at Strand Theater, New York with Count Basie.

**1949** Records "You're My Thrill" and duets with Louis Armstrong for Decca.

**1950** Decca recording contract not renewed; appears in film short with Count Basie.

**1951** Plays Storyville Club, Boston; records four songs for Aladdin Records with Tiny Grimes.

**1952** Trial for possession of opium, not guilty; signs with Norman Granz's Clef, Norgran, and Verve labels; returns to Storyville Club.

**1953** First tour of Europe with Norman Granz's *Jazz at the Philharmonic*.

**1955** *Music for Torching* and *Velvet Mood* released.

**1956** Arrested for narcotic possession and use; autobiography *Lady Sings the Blues* published; Carnegie Hall concert; appears in first Newport Jazz Festival.

---

While Columbia rejected "Strange Fruit," with its wrenching lyric depicting a Southern lynching, as being too explicit, they allowed Holiday to make a recording of it for Milt Gabler's tiny Commodore label. It became a big hit without the help of radio, from which it was banned. Gabler signed Holiday to Decca in 1944 and took close control of her career, having her record the song "Lover Man." That success led Decca to grant her request to record with strings, a first for a jazz singer but a move that would catch on to the point of cliché.

Holiday's addictions to alcohol and marijuana didn't distinguish her from many musicians but in the early forties she began smoking opium with the encouragement of her then husband, Jimmy Monroe. She soon divorced Monroe and traded up to heroin during her marriage to trumpeter Joe Guy. That led to her arrest for possession in 1947, and an eight-month jail sentence. Her arrest nearly destroyed her career, depriving her of the cabaret license she needed to work in clubs. She was dropped from Decca, supposedly because of her drug use but in fact, with the death of founder Jack Kapp, those in charge decided that black singers didn't have a place on the label. Along with Holiday, out went Louis Jordan and Buddy Johnson, among others.

In the mid-Forties she began appearing in concerts produced by Norman Granz, owner of the Clef label and then at Verve. He recorded on his label beginning in 1952 with small ensembles and she seemed to be rejuvenated artistically even as her health deteriorated. She toured Europe, appeared at Carnegie Hall and on television, and continued to use drugs. Her autobiography, equal parts fact and imagination, created the off-record legend of Billie Holiday. In 1959, suffering from heart and liver ailments, she was hospitalized. She died on July 17.

With her autobiography and the recordings of "Strange Fruit" and "Good Morning, Heartache," her legend grew. The film *Lady Sings the Blues*, starring Diana Ross and Richard Pryor, was even less accurate than her book and the play *Lady Day at the Emerson Bar and Grill* further served to accentuate the negative. It is her recordings that reveal the real Billie Holiday, uncompromising, complex, and the complete musician. ◆

## *Song and Story*

### STRANGE FRUIT

"Strange Fruit" was written by Abel Meeropol, a Jewish schoolteacher and union activist living in the Bronx, after he saw a photo of a lynching. Using the pseudonym Lewis Allen, he decided to put music to the song. He debuted the song at a teacher's union meeting where it was received with an ovation. Barney Jacobson, owner of Café Society, was told about the song and gave it to Billie Holiday. Columbia refused to let Holiday record because they thought their Southern singers would complain so they let her out of her contract for one day so she could sing it on Milt Gabler's Commodore label. Meeropol later wrote "The House I Live In" which was performed by Frank Sinatra in an Oscar-winning short. Later, Meeropol and his wife Anne adopted Robert and Michael Rosenberg, the children of Julius and Ethel Rosenberg.

### DON'T EXPLAIN

Billie Holiday: One of the songs I wrote and recorded has my marriage to Jimmy Monroe written all over it. One night he came in with lipstick on his collar. He saw I saw it and started explaining and explaining. I cut him off, just like that. "Take a bath, man," I said, "don't explain." The more I thought about it, it changed from an ugly scene to a sad song. This is one song I couldn't sing without feeling every minute of it.

> ## "I always wanted Bessie's big sound and Pop's feeling, but I didn't have a real big voice, so out of the two, I sort of got Billie Holiday." —Billie Holiday

## First Person

Billie Holiday: No two people on earth are alike. It's got to be that way in music or it isn't music. I can't stand to sing the same song the same way two nights in succession, let alone two years or ten years. If you can, then it ain't music. It's calisthenics, exercise, yodeling or something, but not music.

Teddy Wilson: I would get together with Billie first, and we would take a stack of music, maybe thirty, forty songs, and go through them, and pick out the ones that would appeal to her—the lyric, the melody. And after we picked them we'd concentrate on the ones we were going to record. And we rehearsed them until she had a very good idea of them in her mind, in her ear... Her ear was phenomenal, but she had to get the song into her ear so she could do her own style on it. She would invent different little phrases that would be different melody notes from the ones that were written. All great singers do that, do variations on the melody. Of course they have to know the melody inside out in order to do that. We did this at my apartment because I had a piano.... We'd do it in the afternoons, after two, because we were working at night and slept during the day.

Count Basie: She was something. I was really turned on by her. She knocked me out. I thought she was so pretty. A very, very attractive lady. And when she sang, it was an altogether different style. I hadn't heard anything like it, and I was all for it and I told John [Hammond] I sure would like to have her come and work with the band if it could be arranged. And naturally John agreed, because he already had the same idea before he took me to see her.

## Asides

Holiday gave Lester Young his nickname, "Pres," and he returned the favor, dubbing her "Lady Day."

**ABOVE:** Teddy Wilson and Billie Holiday.

# Lena Horne

When Lena Horne made her triumphant return to Broadway in 1981, in *Lena Horne: The Lady and Her Music*, she sang the great Harold Arlen and Ted Koehler song, "Stormy Weather," as she had performed it in the Twentieth Century-Fox film of the same name in 1943. It was heartfelt, moving, and melodic. Then the sixty-four-year-old Horne sang it again, the way she would have performed it had the studio bosses allowed her to express herself as she wished. The second rendition was angry, melodramatic, and unlike any performance from the '40s. The crowd went wild at the histrionics and energy. But some in the audience wondered what Lena Horne was so angry about.

Plenty, as it turned out. Horne was born in 1917 in Brooklyn into a middle-class black family. Her father worked for the New York Department of Labor and was a numbers runner; her mother was a would-be actress; her grandfather was a teacher and newspaper editor; and her grandmother was a prominent member of the NAACP. Horne inherited her sense of right and wrong from her grandparents and, thanks to them, at two years old she was the youngest member of the NAACP.

Horne's father left for Seattle in 1920, leaving her mother free to pursue her acting. Surprisingly, she was somewhat successful, working with Harlem's Lafayette Stock Company and touring the country in black productions of previously white shows, including *Madame X*, in which young Lena appeared onstage for the first time.

After several years on the road, with occasional stops at the homes of friends and relatives, Horne moved back in with her grandparents in 1929. When her grandmother died three years later, Horne lived with a friend. When her mother returned to New York, she took Lena from Brooklyn to the Bronx and eventually to Harlem, where, at age sixteen, she was hired for the chorus at the Cotton Club.

The Cotton Club was the most notable of the great jazz clubs in Harlem, and a favorite spot for white folk to go "slumming." The club had a strict whites-only policy, and even the friends and family of its performers were barred from the shows. This offended Horne's sensibilities, and she eventually quit the club in 1935.

She took a job with Noble Sissle's band and recorded two sides for the Decca label. And though her career was starting to take off, when she met Pittsburgh politician Louis Jordan Jones she quit show business and married him, eventually having two children. The marriage was rocky, and in 1938, when Horne was offered a small role in *The Duke Is Tops*, she went back to work. She made her Broadway debut as "A Quadroon Girl" in *Dance with Your Gods* and followed it with a short-lived appearance in *Lew Leslie's Blackbirds of 1939*.

After another try at her marriage, she left again, this time to join Charlie Barnet's Orchestra as the first black singer in an all-white band. Audiences had a hard time accepting a beautiful black singer at the mike, and at certain bookings Horne waited on the bus while the band performed. Worried about dragging her daughter on band dates (her husband had custody of their son) and tired of the problems brought on by the racism of audiences, hotels, and bookers, she returned to New York City.

In early 1941, Barney Josephson booked her into his Café Society Downtown. Six months later, she quit and moved to California to open a new club. Because of the war, building materials were scarce and Horne's Los Angeles debut was postponed. She finally opened in February 1942 at the Little Troc and was scouted by Roger Edens of MGM. Horne signed with the studio, but not until she had her contract vetted by the NAACP to make sure that she wouldn't have to play maids or other parts she deemed demeaning. Instead, she was relegated to performing a number or two in movie musicals starring white performers. These interludes could easily be excised for showings in southern theatres. Her appearances may have been brief, but her excellence was noted and she gained a much wider fan base. She was always dressed and lit in the best Hollywood style and treated like an exotic screen goddess. Clearly, she left audiences hungry for more.

In 1943, she did appear in full-fledged acting roles in two pictures, MGM's *Cabin in the Sky*, acting opposite the quite jealous Ethel Waters, and Twentieth Century-Fox's *Stormy Weather*, costarring Bill "Bojangles" Robinson, whom Horne considered an "Uncle Tom" performer. She was, by this time, the highest-paid black actor in the country but she felt estranged from the white community, whom she felt only invited her to parties if she would perform. (Since most Hollywood parties of the day included performances by the guests, this might not have been such an insult.)

Horne devoted herself to entertaining troops as part of the USO. She refused to perform in front of segregated audiences and, once, when German POWs were seated closer to the stage than black soldiers, she declined to go on. Just as Betty Grable was the pinup girl for white servicemen, Lena Horne became the black soldier's dream of perfection.

After the war, Horne performed in England, France, and Belgium, where she was greeted with acclaim. In December 1947, she married Lennie Hayton, a white man, in Paris (it was illegal then for them to marry in California). She once claimed that she married Hayton not out of love but because he could open doors for her.

Horne returned to the United States to find herself blacklisted as a communist sympathizer, her performing limited to nightclubs and recordings. She spent much of the next seven years in Europe, avoiding the blacklist and racism of America. She returned to the States in September 1950 for an appearance at the Sands Hotel in Las Vegas but then it was back to Europe. With the blacklist finally lifted, Horne returned in 1954, signed a new contract with RCA, and did some television guest spots. Her career was in full swing, with bookings at key nightclubs and hotels, hit records, and, in 1957, a starring role in the Broadway show, *Jamaica*, by Harold Arlen and E. Y. Harburg.

She spent the 1960s in clubs and recording studios. As the civil rights movement heated up, Horne threw herself into the battle, marching with Medgar Evers in Mississippi and Dr. King in Washington, D.C. She received wide publicity after publishing an article in *Show* magazine titled "I Just Want to Be Myself." Songwriters Arlen and Harburg took the hint and wrote her the song "Silent Spring," taking a cue from the title of Rachel Carson's groundbreaking book about the pillaging of the environment. Jule Styne, Betty Comden, and Adolph Green wrote her the song, "Now," a civil rights anthem (based on "Chava Nagila." The team, with librettist Arthur Laurents, would later write the show *Hallelujah, Baby!* with her in mind, though the lead eventually went to Leslie Uggams.

Horne's career continued unabated through the '60s though her recording career, like those of many of her contemporaries, was spotty. She appeared on a number of television specials, including one with Harry Belafonte based on their Caesar's Palace appearance in 1969. She slowed down a bit in the seventies, appearing with Tony Bennett in Europe and the States, including an engagement at Broadway's Minskoff Theater.

## THE GREAT SONGS

**1936** I Take to You; That's What Love Did to Me

**1939** You're So Indifferent

**1941** Don't Take Your Love from Me; Good for Nothin' Joe; Ill Wind; Mad About the Boy; The Man I Love; Moanin' Low; Prisoner of Love; St. Louis Blues; Stormy Weather; You're My Thrill; I Gotta Right to Sing the Blues; Out of Nowhere

**1942** Ain't It the Truth; Just One of Those Things

**1943** Honeysuckle Rose; I Can't Give You Anything but Love

**1944** As Long As I Live; One for My Baby; Paper Doll; Somebody Loves Me; I Didn't Know About You

**1945** How Long Has This Been Going On?

**1946** Can't Help Lovin' Dat Man; Frankie & Johnny; Why Was I Born?; Whispering Love; More Than You Know; Squeeze Me; You Go to My Head; At Long Last Love; I've Got the World on a String

**1948** The Lady Is a Tramp; Where or When; Sometimes I'm Happy; Love of My Life; Deed I Do

**1955** Love Me or Leave Me

**1956** At Long Last Love; It's All Right with Me; Let Me Love You; It's Love; Then I'll Be Tired of You; Fun to Be Fooled

**1957** Any Place I Hang My Hat Is Home; I'll Be Around; Coconut Sweet; Push de Button; Day In-Day Out

**1958** Give the Lady What She Wants; Diamonds Are a Girl's Best Friend; Bewitched; Speak Low; Baubles, Bangles and Beads; Just in Time; People Will Say We're in Love

**1961** Surrey with the Fringe on Top

**1962** I Concentrate on You; I'm Confessin'; I Get the Blues When It Rains; I Surrender, Dear; I've Grown Accustomed to His Face; I Let a Song Go Out of My Heart; I Understand

**1963** Now!; Silent Spring; By Myself; Night and Day; Old Devil Moon; Meditation; Take Me

**1974** Watch What Happens

**1976** My Funny Valentine; Someone to Watch Over Me; I Have Dreamed; A Flower Is a Lovesome Thing

**1978** Believe in Yourself

**1988** September Song; Everytime We Say Goodbye; When I Fall in Love; Look to the Rainbow

**1994** Something to Live For; Prelude to a Kiss; My Buddy; We'll Be Together Again

## CAREER HIGHLIGHTS

**1917** Born on June 30 in Brooklyn.

**1919** Youngest member of the NAACP, her grandmother was an activist with the organization.

**1920** Parents separate in August.

**1933** Makes professional debut in the chorus of the Cotton Club.

**1935** Leaves Cotton Club to join Noble Sissle's Orchestra billed as Helen Horne.

**1936** March 11, release of first recordings with Noble Sissle's band on Decca; sings on "That's What Love Means to Me" and "I Take to You;" Broadway debut on October 6 in play, *Dance with Your Gods*.

**1937** Marries Louis Jordan Jones, Pittsburgh politician; daughter Gail born on December 21, 1937.

**1938** Film debut in *The Duke Is Tops*.

**1939** *Lew Leslie's Blackbirds of 1939* opens on Broadway on February 11.

**1940** Son, Edwin Fletcher, born; separates from husband; joins Charlie Barnet's band.

**1941** Records with Barnet for Bluebird label; quits band to create home for children and because of racial problems singing with white band; begins singing as Helen Horne at Barney Josephson's Café Society Downtown in March accompanied by Teddy Wilson, radio work with Chamber Music Society of Lower Basin Street; records with Henry Levine and the Dixieland Jazz Group, Artie Shaw, and Teddy Wilson; moves to Los Angeles for club engagement.

**1942** Opens at the Little Troc nightclub in LA in February; records for RCA Records; signs with MGM and begins prerecordings for *Panama Hattie*; Moves to Mocambo nightclub; appears in *Cabin in the Sky*; November 26 return to New York for engagement at the Café Lounge in the Savoy-Plaza Hotel.

**1943** Films *Cabin in the Sky*, *Stormy Weather*, *As Thousands Cheer* open.

**1944** Films *Swing Fever* and *Two Girls and a Sailor* open; records with Horace Henderson and his orchestra; divorces husband.

**1946** Quits RCA Records and signs with Black and White label; appears on MGM's soundtrack of *Till the Clouds Roll By*, the first soundtrack recording.

**1947** Signs with MGM Records; appears in London, France, and Belgium; falls in love and marries Lennie Hayton in December (a secret for 2½ years).

**1950** *The Duchess of Idaho* released marking end of MGM contract; name appears in *Red Channels* as sympathizer to communists in the performing arts; publishes first autobiography, *In Person*; begins annual Vegas appearances at Sands Hotel; major work in Europe otherwise.

**1955** Re-signs with RCA; first LP, *It's Love*.

**1956** Back to MGM for *Meet Me in Las Vegas*.

**1957** February 20th release of *Lena Horne Live at the Waldorf Astoria*; first and last Broadway musical, *Jamaica*, opens on October 31.

**1958** *Give the Lady What She Wants* released to great acclaim.

**1959** RCA releases *Porgy and Bess* LP with Horne and Belafonte though Horne sues to bar its release; *Songs by Burke and Van Heusen* released.

**1960** Second autobiography, *Lena*, is published.

**1961** *Lena at the Sands* released; *Lena Horne in Her Nine O'Clock Revue* closes in New Haven before Broadway.

In 1981, she appeared in her record-breaking one-woman show, *Lena Horne: The Lady and Her Music*, which might have been better titled, *Lena Horne: A Lady and Her Anger*. The entire evening was a rant against those whom she perceived had held her back. Audiences accepted Horne's blame with liberal guilt and she was awarded a special Tony Award, which she grudgingly accepted. Her righteous indignation also won her two Grammy Awards and a Kennedy Center Honor following the tour, in 1982.

More awards and a few recordings followed in the 1990s, including a cut on Sinatra's *Duets* album. She did some of her best understated singing on *An Evening with Lena Horne* on her new label, Blue Note. In 2000, she came out of retirement to record three songs for a Duke Ellington tribute album, *Classic Ellington*.

Lena Horne was a classy, beautiful interpreter of jazz-oriented popular song. She underwent the all-too-usual degradations of her race and emerged a great star of nightclubs and recordings with a few film and Broadway appearances in the mix. ❖

## Song and Story

### SHOO SHOO, BABY

Songwriter Phil Moore habitually used the words "shoo shoo" in conversation. Once, when rehearsing Lena Horne at MGM, he said, "Shoo, shoo, Lena, take it easy, shoo, shoo." He made up a little song to go with the phrase and Lena Horne was so taken with the number, she sang it in nightclubs and at parties. When the sheet music was eventually published, it sold over 300,000 copies and hit *Your Hit Parade* a total of seventeen times. Georgia Gibbs was another champion of the number.

### AIN'T IT DE TRUTH

"Ain't It de Truth" was an early hit for Horne which she performed in the film *Cabin in the Sky* only to have the number cut, supposedly at the request of a jealous Ethel Waters, but possibly because she sang the number in a bathtub and it was considered too risqué for its time. Arlen and Harburg later interpolated the song into *Jamaica*.

## First Person

Lena Horne: In my early days I was a sepia Hedy Lamarr. Now I'm black and a woman, singing my own way.

## Asides

Harold Arlen and E. Y. Harburg were disappointed that their musical, *Jamaica*, was changed so much that it became virtually "the Lena Horne show." Harry Belafonte was originally set to costar, and when he dropped out Horne became the single big name in the show. (Her love interest, Ricardo Montalban, wasn't in the same league.) She started throwing her weight around and demanded saxophones in the pit band. They had to build a new microphone sound system, the beginning of floor mikes, because she couldn't be heard over the orchestra, it was so brassy.

Horne hated air-conditioning and insisted that it be turned off during her summertime engagement of *Lena Horne: The Lady and Her Music* at the Nederlander Theater.

# Classical Crossovers

Mario Lanza

A fair number of classical singers have tried to break into the popular song market, usually after their voices are no longer suitable for the demands of opera. Few succeed. The most successful stick to a straight-ahead pop format while a few of the distaff singers have attempted to swing it—usually to disasterous results.

Three opera singers who actually made the jump successfully (to the amazement of all involved, and probably themselves, too) are Eileen Farrell, Sylvia McNair, and Dawn Upshaw. Farrell made a few popular recordings for Columbia, abetted by sensitive and wholly suitable orchestrations by Luther Henderson. McNair turned out to be marvelous interpreter of American popular song, particularly when paired with pianist Andre Previn on the Philips label. She also recorded a delightful album devoted to the songs of P. G. Wodehouse (along with Hal Cazalet) on the Harbinger Records label. Upshaw recorded albums paying tribute to the songs of Rodgers and Hart, Sondheim, Blitzstein, and Vernon Duke, to great effect, and has become one of our most compelling interpreters of the popular canon.

The crossover artists who really delivered the goods on Broadway were Ezio Pinza in *South Pacific* and *Fanny*, Helen Traubel in *Pipe Dream*, Robert Weede in *The Most Happy Fella* and *Milk and Honey*, and Teresa Stratas in *Rags* (though not, alas, on the cast album).

Hollywood also endured its share of opera singers trying their luck at popular melodies. They usually had the sense to confine themselves to semi-operatic ballads in the vein of "Be My Love," sung by Mario Lanza in *The Toast of New Orleans*. This was just one of the many opera and operetta standards he warbled in a series of mostly forgettable Hollywood musicals. James Melton and Lawrence Tibbett also hit Hollywood and pulled off successful crossover careers.

We must mention the horrendous subcategory of studio cast recordings featuring opera singers in roles previously sung by the likes of Mary Martin, Larry Kert, and Alfred Drake. Here are some of these members of the Crossover Hall of Shame: Dame Kiri Te Kanawa and Jose Carreras in *South Pacific* and *West Side Story* (actually condoned by Bernstein!); Dame Kiri in *My Fair Lady* with, God help us, Jeremy Irons; Placido Domingo in *Man of La Mancha*; Frederica Von Stade in *The Sound of Music* and *Show Boat* (which also featured Teresa Stratas as a quite effective Julie La Verne); and Samuel Ramey in *Carousel* and *Kismet*. Bryn Terfel may be a remarkable singer but his interpretations of Rodgers and Hammerstein are, shall we gently put it, not one of our favorite things. ◊

DAWN UPSHAW *sings* VERNON DUKE

Eileen Farrell

MY LOVE AN' MY MULE

Lyric by DOROTHY FIELDS        Music by HAROLD ARLEN

M-G-M PRESENTS

LANA TURNER · EZIO PINZA

IN "Mr. Imperium"

M-G-M SINGING TECHNICOLOR ROMANCE

MARJORIE MAIN · BARRY SULLIVAN

SIR CEDRIC HARDWICKE

SCREEN PLAY BY
EDWIN H. KNOPF and DON HARTMAN

A METRO-GOLDWYN-MAYER PICTURE

EDWIN H. MO

# Dick Haymes

Dick Haymes had everything going for him: he was talented, handsome—but he still managed to screw up his career. He was a superstar but he couldn't sustain it. Considered by many of the cognoscenti the best ballad singer of all, the creamy baritone enjoyed immense success in the 1940s. The Decca years, 1943–1951, were his richest, with such hits as "You'll Never Know," "'Till the End of Time," "It Can't Be Wrong," "Little White Lies," and "Mam'selle."

Haymes began his career in 1940 with Harry James. He tried peddling his songs to the bandleader who turned around and hired him as a singer. In 1942, he hooked up with Benny Goodman and the next year moved over to Tommy Dorsey's group—just in time for the recording ban.

Haymes also enjoyed a successful radio and film career, landing fine showcases in Twentieth Century-Fox's *State Fair*, *Diamond Horseshoe*, *The Shocking Miss Pilgrim*, *Irish Eyes Are Smiling*, *Four Jills in a Jeep*, and a few that were less notable. The movie years were good to him, and he introduced the standards "The More I See You," "It's a Grand Night for Singing," "I Wish I Knew," "Aren't You Kinda Glad We Did," and "For You, for Me, Forevermore." He starred on radio beginning with his own show in the mid-40s and continued his broadcasting career on the *Lucky Strike Hit Parade*, *Club 15*, and most importantly, *The Auto-Lite Hour*.

Despite his success on screen, recordings, and in live performances, his personal life was rather messy. Born in Argentina, he was brought to the States as a baby but somehow never got U.S. citizenship. In 1944, he avoided the draft by registering as a resident alien, which backfired on him when he went to Hawaii (not yet a state) in pursuit of Rita Hayworth. The government refused to let him re-enter the country, pointing out that he wasn't a citizen.

Haymes always blamed Columbia Pictures owner Harry Cohn for tipping off the Feds. The dispute was settled but the publicity surrounding it and his draft dodging didn't do his career any good. Haymes was all set to go on a European tour with Billie Holiday in the early 1950s but the Internal Revenue Service forbade him to leave the country. In 1955 and 1956, he recorded two classic Capitol albums: *Moondreams* and *Rain or Shine*.

Haymes had six wives, four of whom were actresses (Joanne Dru, Nora Eddington, Rita Hayworth, and Fran Jeffries). He had a long bout with alcoholism and was deeply in debt (all that alimony!). Finally, he went abroad in the 1960s, like many of his singing brethren. He returned to the States in 1971 and enjoyed mild success touring in nostalgia big band packages before his death in 1980 from lung cancer. ◆

# Al Jolson

et's not even talk about blackface. In these politically correct times, blackface is unimaginable. That's the problem in trying to assess Jolson. By far the greatest singer of the teens and twenties, Jolson was truly a man of his time. It takes a leap of faith on our part, and a sensitivity to the past, to appreciate Jolson's persona and style.

The strides he made, the doors he opened, were elemental and necessary, but his need to be adored could put people off. Through his efforts, the sound of popular music changed—but the changes ended up leaving him in the past. Just as today's clichés were once original ideas, Jolson's style now seems out of date.

His performance style, the way he belted his songs, rolled his eyes (this was all the more visible in contrast to his blackened face), his overemphatic hand gestures, the falling on one knee, were all developed to carry his sound and image to the furthest reaches of the theater. In the days before microphones, Jolson could be heard in the last rows of the second balconies. Even someone sitting in the very back of the house could appreciate the emotion of the song from Jolson's face and gestures. Emotions were worn on the sleeve, and depth of feeling was indicated in performance (rather than simply by climbing the scale, as it is now). One hundred years ago, a singer employed a catch in the throat, a sob, a wiped-away tear.

Popular songs of the period developed, as did Jolson, out of the minstrel tradition. Jolson sang a fair amount of lachrymose ballads as well as overly sentimental paeans to motherhood and the sunny Southland. He also sang a whole lot of comedy songs but, unfortunately, these are mostly forgotten.

Jolson was pivotal in the transition from the square ballad of the 1900s to the syncopated, ragtime, and jazz-influenced rhythms of the new century. Like Elvis Presley (yes Elvis!) and Irving Berlin, Jolson made black music palatable to white audiences.

Jolson also led the way into new technologies, unafraid to take chances. He recorded his first sides at the end of 1911. He appeared in what is generally considered the first talkie (or at least the first to get noticed), *The Jazz Singer*. Another film of his, *The Singing Fool*, was the most profitable picture of all time until *Gone with the Wind*. Jolson wasn't afraid to be heard on radio in an era when many of his Broadway contemporaries considered it beneath them in the same way movie stars shunned early television.

Jolson was also a hit-maker. When he interpolated a song into one of his shows, sheet music sales (with Jolson's picture on the cover) soared. Publishers vied for the right to print "As performed by Al Jolson at the Winter Garden Theater."

Jolson wasn't one to leave the profits to others—so he became the king of the cut-in. If you wanted Jolie to introduce your song on the stage, you had to give him credit (and royalties) as coauthor. He'd then sing the song on Broadway, tour the show and the song all around the nation, sing it on records, and later introduce it on radio. And when Decca signed, him he'd sing the same repertoire again. The songs would be featured in the two Jolson biopics, *The Jolson Story* (1946) and *Jolson Sings Again* (1949), both smash successes. Writers and publishers got their money's worth by cutting in Jolson.

Jolson introduced more hit songs than any other performer, with the possible exception of Bing Crosby. Whether he cut himself in is immaterial in that he had fantastic taste. He knew exactly what kind of a song suited his talents and exactly how to put the song over.

Jolson adopted his blackface character around 1899, as a member of the vaudeville act Jolson, Palmer, and Palmer. To Jolson, the blackface was simply a gimmick added to what would otherwise be simply another singing act. Somewhat shy, he also found it easier to portray a character other than himself. He most certainly did not adopt blackface in order to make fun of blacks, nor did he indulge in the stereotypes most often connected with the blackface comic. Jolson simply used the conceit as a means to stand out from other singers. And the blackface and white gloves emphasized Jolson's eyes, mouth, and hands, especially in the glare of the spotlight. Later in his career, when he had become inextricably linked to the character, he used the makeup to signal that a highlight of the performance was coming up.

Jolson's ego, selfishness, and disregard for his fellow performers and for the creators of his material are the stuff of legend. With an almost insatiable need to be loved, Jolson was always "on." He defined himself through his performances and seemed to be alive only when he was the center of attention. But his personal shortcomings pale in comparison to his immense legacy. He was the greatest performer of his time—and just when his popularity would begin to wane, newer generations would find themselves entranced by the Jolson mystique. It's hard for us now to appreciate fully Jolson's impact on popular song, through the haze of old movies, scratchy recordings, and faded photographs. We can only take the word of those who were there.

Robert Benchley, writing in the old *Life* magazine, captured Jolson's unique effect on audiences: "The word 'personality' isn't quite strong enough for the thing that Jolson has. Unimpressive as the comparison may be to Mr. Jolson, we should say that John the Baptist was the last man to have such power. There is something supernatural at the back of it, or we miss our guess. When Jolson enters, it is as if an electric current has been run along the wires under the seats where the hats are stuck. The house comes to a tumultuous attention. He speaks, rolls his eyes, compresses his lips, and it is all over. You are a member of the Al Jolson Association." ◆

# *Song and Story*

## AVALON

When lawyers for G. Ricordi, music publishers of Puccini, heard Vincent Rose and Al Jolson's "Avalon," they accused the composer of plagiarism. They alleged that the music was based on the aria "*E lucevan le stelle*" from Puccini's *Tosca*. Ricordi's attorney's brought a piano, violin, and trumpet into the courtroom on January 28, 1921. Instrumentalists played the popular song and the attorneys played a phonograph record of the aria. Ricordi won the lawsuit and was awarded $25,000 in damages as well as all future royalties from "Avalon."

## MA BLUSHIN' ROSIE (MA POSIE SWEET)

John Stromberg wrote this tune for Bessie Clayton but she never performed it. Later, when Stromberg and Edgar Smith were writing the score for Fay Templeton's show, *Fiddle Dee Dee*, they replaced a song with it. With Smith's lyrics, the song was a great hit at Weber and Fields Music Hall. Jolson picked up the song and sang it at Sunday concerts at the Winter Garden, then went on to record it in 1946. The Decca record sold over a million copies. The song was then featured in *Jolson Sings Again* with Jolson providing the soundtrack.

## MY MAMMY

This song was introduced by none other than William Frawley, best known as Fred Mertz on the television series *I Love Lucy*. (Frawley also introduced "Melancholy Baby," among other songs!) Publisher Saul Bourne brought it to Jolson, who interpolated it into the musical *Bombo* in 1921 and also sang it in *The Jazz Singer* and then in *The Jolson Story*. That same year, he recorded it for Decca and sold over a million copies. Jolson famously sang the song down on one knee, launching a million imitations.

## SONNY BOY

The song was written overnight by De Sylva, Brown, and Henderson at the behest of Jolson, who was about to film *The Singing Fool*. The producers needed a song fast to replace one dropped from the score. Rumor has it that the songwriters meant it as a parody of the heartstring-pulling ballads for which Jolson was known. Whatever the intention, it was a smash hit.

## SWANEE

George Gershwin and Irving Caesar were lunching at Dinty Moore's restaurant, trying to come up with a surefire hit. "Hindustan" was popular at the time and Caesar suggested marrying the one-step rhythms of that song to another locale. The team continued discussing the song while riding on the upper level of a double-decker bus to Gershwin's apartment. By the time they reached the piano, the song had been sketched out.

## WAITING FOR THE ROBERT E. LEE

Lyricist L. Wolfe Gilbert got the idea for this song while actually watching the steamboat *Robert E. Lee* unloading its cargo in Baton Rouge. When composer Lewis F. Muir took the song to publisher F. A. Mills, it made no impression and was rejected. A while later, Gilbert came by to pick up the music and Mills told him that the song would be published. Song plugger Tubby Garron showed the number to Al Jolson, who interpolated it into a Winter Garden Sunday concert.

## YOU MADE ME LOVE YOU

Jolson was performing in *The Honeymoon Express* at the Winter Garden when he dropped down on one knee to ease the pain from an ingrown toenail. Finding himself in this awkward position, he spread his arms as if to envelop the audience—and a cliché was born. The song subsequently proved popular for Fannie Brice, Ruth Etting, Judy Garland, and Harry James.

# Eartha Kitt

"**S**ex kitten" is the adjective most often applied to Eartha Kitt, a self-invented star with a unique persona. Many performers with so distinctive (some would say eccentric) a style last only a few years, but Kitt's underlying talent has carried her through fifty years of fame.

She burst on to the scene fully formed in Leonard Sillman's *New Faces of 1952*, in which she performed alongside such future stars as Paul Lynde, Carol Lawrence, Alice Ghostley, and Robert Clary. Sillman helped develop Kitt's catlike persona, and it fit her to a tee. She honed this drawling, hissing, rapid-vibrato style of sexiness over many years of nightclub and Broadway appearances, recordings, and television and film roles,.

Singing in several languages, speaking with an undefinable accent, and affecting a refined, soignée demeanor, she fooled people into thinking she was a sophisticate born in some vaguely European country. In fact, she was raised on a cotton farm in North Carolina, and dubbed "Eartha" to commemorate a good crop the year she was born.

Kitt's parents (a white father and black mother) divorced soon after she came along and she was virtually abandoned by her mother, who died soon thereafter. Kitt was shuttled from one family member to another, ending up with an aunt in Harlem at age eight,

## THE GREAT SONGS

1952 **Monotonous**

1953 **Uska Dara (A Turkish Tale)**

1954 **C'est Si Bon; I Want To Be Evil; Let's Do It; Lilac Wine; My Heart Belongs To Daddy; Santa Baby; Smoke Gets In Your Eyes; Somebody Bad Stole The Wedding Bell; Under the Bridges of Paris**

1954 **Apres Moi; (If I Love Ya, Then I Need Ya) I Wantcha Around**

1955 **Je Cherche un Homme; Just An Old Fashioned Girl**

1956 **Lazy Afternoon; Lullaby of Birdland; Thursday's Child**

1995 **Where Is My Man?**

at which point her situation improved. She was able to take music and dance lessons and entered the High School for the Performing Arts, but had to drop out when her aunt kicked her out of the house. At sixteen, she was asked directions by a young member of Katherine Dunham's dance company. Kitt decided to try out for the troupe, and received a scholarship. She toured with the company throughout the United States, Mexico, and South America, before landing in Europe.

While in Paris with Dunham, she replaced an ill singer at a performance, and a nightclub owner who happened to be in the audience signed Kitt to perform in his club. She was then discovered by Orson Welles, who put her into his European production of *Time Runs*, a Wellsian version of *Faust* in which she played Helen of Troy. (Hey, it's Orson Welles, folks!)

Following her return to the U.S., Kitt played the Blue Angel and Village Vanguard before being discovered yet again, this time by Leonard Sillman. Following her Broadway debut in *New Faces*, she starred in *Shinbone Alley* (1957), a musicalization of Don Marquis's archy and mehitibel stories, and in *Timbuktu* (1978), an all-black version of *Kismet*.

Kitt's intelligence and sense of justice put her in a league with Lena Horne. At the height of her fame, appearing as Catwoman on the *Batman* television series, Kitt stood up to President Lyndon Johnson and his wife Lady Bird during a 1968 White House event, criticizing the Vietnam War and its effect on inner-city adolescents. Lady Bird was reduced to tears and Kitt's bookings dried up. Apart from a few television variety show appearances, she spent most of the next decade in Europe.

Kitt also performed for white-only audiences in South Africa, inspiring much criticism and bewilderment, in that she had always refused to appear in front of segregated audiences previously. To her credit, she did make sure her act was integrated. She also sold her autograph at appearances in department stores, eventually raising enough money to build two schools for black children.

Kitt's mixed-race features and coloring were sometimes a hindrance to her career. Like Lena Horne, she could pass for white but refused to do so, and found herself relegated to black films. She made the most of her appearances, showing herself to be an excellent actress in the style of Pearl Bailey: sexy, outspoken, sly—but more subtle than Bailey. She appeared opposite Nat King Cole (along with Bailey) in *St. Louis Blues*, the story of W. C. Handy, and opposite Sammy Davis, Jr., in *Anna Lucasta*.

In recent times, Kitt has appeared in the less-than-stellar films *Erik the Viking*, *Ernest Scared Stupid*, *Boomerang*, and *The Emperor's New Groove*. In 1996, she played Billie Holiday in the Chicago production of *Lady Day at the Emerson Bar and Grill*. Kitt returned to Broadway in 2000 in *The Wild Party* and in 2004 in the New York City Opera production of *Cinderella*. She stopped both shows cold, flaunting her status as an icon (or was it a parody of herself?) to the delight of audiences. ◆

## Asides

## First Person

"'C'est Si Bon,' people would say when they saw me walking down the street or in the restaurant. I felt wanted. I was getting the love I wanted…. I was getting it the hard way, for I had to constantly prove myself in order to maintain it." –Eartha Kitt, in her autobiography, *Thursday's Child*.

# Julie London

Blasé, beautiful Julie London had a double life as a pop singer and an actress. She enjoyed a surprisingly long career in film and television and on record, remarkable for its consistency. (If you heard one Julie London record, you had heard them all, which is exactly what her fans wanted.)

London was born to vaudevillian parents, and when vaudeville died, they made the switch to radio — providing an important lesson for their daughter: if one business doesn't work out, switch careers. The family moved to Los Angeles and Julie began singing with Matty Malneck's orchestra.

She attended Hollywood Professional High School, from which she graduated in 1944. Alan Ladd's wife, Sue Carol, spotted London working as an elevator operator that same year and soon she was featured in the forgettable film *Nabonga* (also known as *Gorilla*, *Nabonga Gorilla*, *The Girl and the Gorilla*, and *The Jungle Woman*). She followed up whatever-its-name-was with more B pictures.

London met actor/producer/director Jack Webb, who was then in the marines, and married him in 1947, giving up the business to become a wife and the mother of two daughters. When she divorced Webb in November 1953 (apparently, with no hard feelings—see below), she resumed her career.

She met songwriter Bobby Troup ("Route 66") in 1955, and he became her producer and occasional songwriter. He honed her image as a sexy siren draped in the finest jewelry and furs. She was cool (but not in the June Christy way), detached, and ready for pleasure—if the price was right.

Her first recording was 1955's "Cry Me a River," written by Hollywood Professional High School classmate Arthur Hamilton. Following its immense success (3 million albums and singles), she recorded thirty-one more LPs, all for the Liberty label. Troup and London were married on New Year's Eve, 1959. With her singing career in high gear, she picked up her film career, making a number of movies for MGM and United Artists, none of them memorable. After Liberty closed up shop in 1968, a victim of changing musical tastes, London stopped recording.

When club work and recordings dried up in the '60s, she switched to television, appearing on *The Big Valley* and achieving fame and fortune on the 1970s series *Emergency*, produced by her first husband and costarring her second. It seems she did get what she wanted out of men.

London described herself in *Life* magazine this way: "It's only a thimbleful of a voice, and I have to use it close to the microphone. But it is a kind of oversmoked voice and it automatically sounds intimate." She certainly made the most of her resources, creating an indelible impression on many a man. ◆

# Husband & Wife Teams

HOW HIGH THE MOON

WORDS BY
NANCY HAMILTON

MUSIC BY
MORGAN LEWIS

PRICE 60c

RECORDED BY LES PAUL AND MARY FORD ON CAPITOL RECORD #1451

CHAPPELL

**M**embers of husband-and-wife teams may be individually talented but, like other performing arts teams, they gain a dimension when appearing together. Audiences enjoy the couple's special rapport and joy in performing as a unit.

Sometimes audiences like to see themselves reflected in the artists. Les Paul and Mary Ford were your clean-cut, all-American couple, always operating on the same wavelength with an even-tempered conviviality. Paul had first come to the public's attention as a master of the guitar. In 1948, he recorded the popular song, "Brazil," overdubbing his guitar part five times in the studio, resulting in a kind of "wall of music" never before heard. An early masterpiece of multitracking, the recording and Paul became famous. Though rhythm guitar had long been a component of popular arrangements, especially in country-and-western music, guitar wasn't thought of as a solo instrument. There were a few exceptions: Nick Lucas, a guitar player and singer, had enjoyed a big hit with "Tiptoe Through the Tulips" in 1929, and Roy Smeck had also earned some acclaim on the instrument. But blues players like Charlie Christian would have to wait until the 1960s for their rare recordings to achieve success.

Mary Ford, born Iris Colleen Summers (it's a familiar story: Paul picked her name out of a telephone book), started her career as a western singer in the late 1940s. She performed with Gene Autry, who introduced her to

Les Paul. The couple was married in 1949. In 1951, Paul and Ford had two number one hits, "How High the Moon" and "Mockin' Bird Hill." Other hits of the 1950s included "Tennessee Waltz," "The World Is Waiting for the Sunrise," "My Baby's Coming Home," "Bye Bye Blues," and "Vaya Con Dios."

Audiences also love it when slight cracks in the couple-singers' relationships come to the surface. Keely Smith took it on the chin from Louis Prima but maintained her trademark deadpan. We know now that Prima meticulously choreographed all the mayhem surrounding their high-octane numbers, but we also know that the team broke up—so perhaps it wasn't all in good fun after all. Prima had enjoyed a long career as a big band leader and performer as well as composer. Among the popular songs he composed were "Sing, Sing, Sing," "Robin Hood," "Angelina," and "A Sunday Kind of Love."

Prima discovered Smith and brought her into his newly pared-down band in 1949, along with musician Sam Butera. Prima molded the act, emphasizing the talents of Smith and creating a particular relationship on stage. During their time together Smith also recorded solo for Capitol, though she was better known for her work with Prima. "That Old Black Magic" was a hit for the duo in 1958. They broke up in 1961 and each continued with solo careers. Prima died in 1978 but Smith is still going strong, performing regularly in New York, Las Vegas, and elsewhere.

Throughout the '50s and '60s, Steve Lawrence and Eydie Gorme enjoyed needling each other in a much more good-natured way. Steve would throw a zinger at Eydie (it's impossible to refer to them as anything but Steve and Eydie) and she'd come right back with a quip, and they'd both laugh. But that's not what makes Steve and Eydie the greatest husband-and-wife act of all time. Their solo talents alone would have made them stars at some level, but it is their special rap-

port and shared energy that have made them beloved. Their singing styles complement each other, each one singing every song in full voice with knockout energy. Lawrence never actually inspires any emotion—rather, he's sort of personification of the Count Basie band: a little mechanical, a little slick, but, wow, what a thrill when he swings. Gorme, on the other hand, is all about unbridled emotion, which she socks over the footlights in a way that we'd hazard to call Mermanesque. Gorme's solo hits include "If He Walked Into My Life" from Jerry Herman's and "What Did I Have That I Don't Have?" from Burton Lane and Alan Jay Lerner's *On a Clear Day*. Lawrence and Gorme have spent the early part of this century on a continuing series of farewell tours, still exhibiting all of the power and professionalism of their heyday. ◈

## *Asides*

When Eydie Gorme had a hit song from *Mame,* Steve Lawrence decided he wanted his own Jerry Herman hit—so when Herman's next show, *Dear World,* opened, Lawrence recorded the show's "I Never Said I Loved You."

**OPPOSITE**: Steve Lawrence and Eydie Gorme, the longest lasting husband and wife team. **LEFT**: The 1950s ideal couple, the genial Les Paul and Mary Ford. **ABOVE**: The Bickersons, or as they were otherwise known, Louis Prima and Keely Smith.

# Peggy Lee

## SONGS BY PEGGY LEE

**1941** Little Fool

**1945** You Was Right, Baby (Dave Barbour); What More Can a Woman Do? (Dave Barbour)

**1946** Don't Be So Mean to Baby; I Don't Know Enough About You; It's a Good Day (all Dave Barbour)

**1947** Everything's Movin' Too Fast; Lonesome for Love; Just an Old Love of Mine (all Dave Barbour)

**1948** Let It Bother Me; Mañana (Is Soon Enough for Me); If I Can Live My Life with You; North Dakota(Dave Barbour); Confusion Says; Lullaby for a Wee One; Nice to Be Small; Take a Little Time to Smile; Could You Love Somebody Like Me? (all Dave Barbour)

**1949** Blum, Blum (I Wonder Who I Am); Neon Signs (Gonna Shine Like Neon, Too); My Small Señor (all Dave Barbour); Bless You (For the Good That's in You) (Mel Torme)

**1950** Happy Music; I'm in the Mood for Music; Please Treat Her Nicer (all Dave Barbour); When You Speak with Your Eyes (Dave Barbour, Rene Touzet); When It Rains, It Pours (Dave Barbour, Woody Herman)

**1951** If I Had a Chance with You; That Ol' Devil (Won't Get Me) (both Dave Barbour); I Gotta Do Something Fast; Wife, Go Home and Mind Your Cleanin'; The White Birch and the Sycamore (Willard Robison, Hubert Wheeler); A Straw Hat Full of Lilacs (Willard Robison); I Love You But I Don't Like You (Henry Beau)

**1952** Sans Souci (Sonny Burke); How Strange; Goodbye, My Love (both Victor Young)

**1953** This Is a Very Special Day (from *The Jazz Singer*); Who's Gonna Pay the Check?; Don't Make Believe; O, Baby, Come Home; New York City Ghost (Victor Young); Whee, Baby (Alice Larson)

**1954** The Joy of Easter; Your Last Adios; Funny Little Ole Bluebird; Where Can I Go without You?; Johnny Guitar; I Love You So (all Victor Young); With Joy Shall Ye Drink; It's Because We're in Love; The Gypsy with the Fire in His Shoes (Laurindo Almeida); (I Love Your) Gypsy Heart (Harry Sukman); I Don't Want to Walk in the Dark; This Is a Brand New Day

**1955** Peace on Earth; Bella Notte; What Is a Baby?; The Siamese Cat Song; La La Lu; He's a Tramp (all Sonny Burke); Straight Ahead; It Must Be So; It's a Funny Old World; Mr. Magoo Does the Cha Cha Cha (Gene di Novi); We (Stella Castellucci); The Gold Wedding Ring (Harry Sukman)

**OPPOSITE PAGE:** Peggy holds up Dean Martin on his television series.

Our vote for the most intelligent, most all-around talented of all the singers in this book is Peggy Lee. In fact, we'll state it now, she was our greatest popular female singer. She was sultry but she could put across a song with real power. She knew just how to control a song, an arrangement, and an audience. She was quick-witted enough to assert her own talents and never knuckled under to anyone else's notion of what was best for her career. (She even sued Disney!) A great singer and songwriter (actually, the first genuine singer/songwriter), a brilliant actress and an author, Lee could do it all—and it all came out of the mind and heart of Norma Egstrom, who was smart enough and talented enough to invent Peggy Lee. There were three faces to Peggy Lee, the persona, the voice, and the repertoire.

Lee believed her image was all-important. The platinum wig, the oversized sunglasses, the choreographed hand gestures, the gowns, and the excitement as she made her entrance, these were all part of the creation. As Lee herself admitted, "I wanted to make it as close to a Broadway performance as I could. Dave Barbour [Lee's first husband and frequent songwriting partner from 1943 to 1951] said, 'Why do you have to do all that stuff? Go out there and sing. You could wear a twelve-dollar dress and swing.' Yes, I could, but the audience wouldn't be getting a show."

Lee was the first to insist on hiring her own lighting designer as well as paying close attention to costume changes, song order, and sound design. She felt better when she was dressed up. As she recalled about her Capitol sessions, "I

## "The song dictates what it is." —Peggy Lee

used to dress up to go to a recording session because it made me feel good and I wanted to sing like that." Remember that scandalous appearance by Marilyn Monroe at President John F. Kennedy's birthday party? Well, blame it at least partly on Lee, whose lighting scheme was used to light Marilyn from behind, making her dress all but invisible.

As for Lee's singing, let's be upfront about it: she was a jazz singer throughout her career. She never flaunted her singing—she was quite secure in her work and didn't rely on the approbation of others. And if audiences didn't really appreciate her jazz chops, she said, "I don't mind that. I'm just glad when they do. I don't think I fit any hole....I can sing pop things or folk songs or whatever. It doesn't bother me. I know when it's jazz." Lee refused to categorize music, or, rather, felt there were only two kinds: good and bad.

Much has been made of Lee's vocal technique of singing softly and saving her energy for when it mattered. Prior to Crosby and Lee, music came out of the belting, theatrical tradition, where voices had to be heard in the second balcony of huge theatres. Jolson, Cantor, Sophie Tucker, and their ilk practically shouted their songs. Lee commented, "I noticed that I always liked that Maxine Sullivan sang quietly. I noticed when I was singing myself, when I sang quietly I felt more emotion. Try saying, 'I love you' real loud. Unless you're being funny it's almost anger or calling after someone in the distance. For a while, there were a lot of people who thought that belting was really the sign of a great singer. That may hold true in opera; they could reach the balcony, but when an opera singer comes down to double pianissimo it really cuts into your heart."

In fact, Maxine Sullivan was a major influence on Lee, though Billie Holiday is more often credited as her inspiration. As Lee explained, "I never heard Billie Holiday until I was with Benny Goodman. She was wonderful. I've been told that I copied her but I didn't copy anyone, I just sang...I think you're supposed to develop your talent. I've tried to work on that always. mainly to keep interested."

Lee created the same intimacy that Bing Crosby did. He was first singer to really usze the microphone, and his singing had an immediacy that was previously unheard of. "I learned a lot about microphones," said Lee, "and I've noticed that particularly with today's high technology, you have to be more careful. They can do terrible things to your voice or wonderful things. My voice seems to have a central core surrounded by rings of overtones and when I sing loud, I lose some of those overtones. When I sing softly they're all there."

Richard Rodgers was known for composing the "wrong note," that is, the note that the audience doesn't expect to come next. Lee would also sing the "wrong note," that is just to the left or right of the note as written. She's so superior a musician that she can get away with things that the ordinary singer couldn't even dream of. As Will Friedwald points out in his book, *Jazz Singing*, "She sings over, ahead of, or behind the beat, like Sinatra or Tony Bennett, as opposed to on top of it like Cole or Torme."

Lee has been accused of being difficult and irrational, but isn't this the fate of many a perfectionist? "It can look like it's fun and games, which it is," Lee explained. "So you can play with it and be more relaxed, you have to be ready to be able to do that....You have to know where to come back in there. and hit it right on the note." She was seldom less than brilliant, until the very end that is, when insensitive record producers didn't protect her, releasing less than stellar performances on badly orchestrated and poorly produced product. She was very unhappy with her releases on DRG and Chesky.

Her choice of songs was as important as her interpretations. She would work with producers like Dave Cavanaugh at Capitol and make lists of songs. Since she didn't limit herself to any one genre of music, she could choose from a wealth of great tunes, from early blues to sixties rock-and- roll. Sometimes she went out on a limb, as on her LP *Sea Shells* (1955) where she sang translations of Chinese poetry. She sometimes shocked people but she always won them over. She even sang Japanese songs—in in Japanese.

Once the songs had been chosen, Lee would explore how to perform them. "I seem to feel the rhythmic pattern. It's just a question of knowning that within 2 and 3:4 and 4:4 and 6:8 you can find all the combinations, and by looking at the lyric, that's the key." The arrangement had to suit the lyric, and finding a character was an important element of the performance, for it helped

## THE GREAT SONGS

her illuminate and dramatize the words and music. "I'm a singer. I use words. The melody is extremely important but it's not as important as the lyric. Then, what mood is it in? Should it stay as it is or should it be changed? Then comes a discussion with the arranger, telling him what you want to accomplish. And tempo is very important, because some songs improve by going faster or slower but some should stay where they are. The song dictates what it is."

We'd like to conclude by talking about Peggy Lee's sheer strength of character. She wasn't always so sure of herself and how her world and her music should be. "Once I was sent out on the road by myself," she related. "This is during the time we were recording a lot of different things in all different ways, orchestras, small groups, whatever. David [Barbour] wasn't well so my manager and David sent me out by myself. I think that it was a dirty trick but it turned out to be a good one. They sent me out with arrangements for "Golden Earrings" with big strings. I

get down there to St. Louis and there was a society band; three tenor saxophones! I thought, what do I do now? The guitarist Mike Bryant, formerly with Benny Goodman, called me and I said, 'Mike, how are you and where are you?' He said, 'I'm right here in St. Louis.' I said, 'Come down here and bring the guitar.' He said, 'I sold it.' I said, 'Borrow one and bring a bass player.' And so he did. He was there within an hour and the rest of that afternoon we put together a whole show of things with a quartet and it was a big success and it was thrilling to do it. We could do anything we wanted. We weren't restricted in any way. So you see, they did me a good turn. Threw me in the water and let me sing or swim."

The quotes in this piece come from an interview Bill Rudman and I had with Lee after producing her album *Love Held Lightly*. She told us something that could stand as her legacy, as the last word on her life and career: "The way I've gone is the way I had to go." ◆

## Asides

Peggy Lee sang on Mel Torme's *California Suite* album (1949) billed as Susan Melton.

In the original version of *Lady and the Tramp*, Trusty dies. Peggy Lee convinced Disney to let him live.

Peggy Lee was a taskmistress when it came to her household staff. As the years went by it became more and more difficult to find employees, since agencies refused to send prospective staff members over. Once, her staff locked her out of the house And she had to have the police come and

let her in. One of the policemen went to the kitchen to look for any staff members who were left, and Lee heard him laughing. When she got to the kitchen to see what was so funny she found him reading this note: "Dear Miss Lee, Fuck you. The Staff. P.S. There's a turkey in the oven."

When she was rehearsing for the *Ed Sullivan Show*, Lee stopped the fifty-piece orchestra because she could tell that, amid all the instruments, the fender bass wasn't there.

Though friends and coworkers called her Peggy when they were alone with her, in front of others she was always addressed as "Miss Lee."

## Song and Story

### DON'T SMOKE IN BED

Peggy Lee: Dave [Barbour] and I wrote that song, but we didn't write it all, because Willard Robison had the title and the first line, and then he had a drink, dear Willard. I used to lock him in a room and try to get him to work, and I'd say, "When you get all through I'll give you a beer," because he had a drinking problem. So he came to us with the title "Goodbye, Old Sleepyhead." And from there on, I wrote the rest. Since his daughter didn't have anything of her father's, or so she said, I gave her that copyright.

### I DON'T KNOW ENOUGH ABOUT YOU

Peggy Lee: Johnny Mercer helped me when I was writing it. He said, "You have a really good idea there, but I think you should rewrite this and that. I tore it up and rewrote and it made all the difference.

### THE SHINING SEA

Peggy Lee: I like "The Shining Sea." That was an interesting experience because Johnny [Mandel] played it for me and said I want you to write a lyric for it. It just came out like water. He said, "How do you do that? I'm going to take you down to the director's theater and show you what you wrote." It's the scene where the Russian boy and the girl are sitting on the sand and the sun is shining on the sea and it was like the song. But I heard it in his music. You see?"

### I'M GONNA GO FISHING

Peggy Lee: It's a whole story. Ellington brought me, "Do do do do do do." [The first six notes of the song]. Basically that. Max Bennett pointed out that I wrote the melody on that, but I don't know. It's an interesting construction. I heard the melody

in there, loud and clear. It suited the character of Jimmy Stewart [the lawyer in the film *Anatomy of a Murder*. The lawyer was looking for the murderer and he used to go out and go fishing when he wanted to think. That's what took me away from the ugliness of murder itself and still left the feeling in it. It was an interesting project, one of the most interesting.

### PEACE ON EARTH

Peggy Lee on, this song from *Lady and the Tramp*: It wasn't easy. Because it's a counter melody of "Silent Night" and I had to make the lyric come out so that the key words fit in the right place. So it wasn't just a matter of writing a plain lyric, it was a matter of writing a counter lyric. I don't think that's done too often.

### LOVER

Peggy Lee: I had seen a French movie about a man that had joined the French Foreign Legion because he had been treated very badly by his lady love. He became the head of a platoon and they would take off at a full gallop but for a while they would trot, they would canter, then zam! If you listen to "Lover" that's what happens. We'd start in the original key, then we'd go up a half or a whole step, and then another step, and the rhythm would increase underneath us by using all of the percussion possible—we had eight percussionists—and I was paying for it! It was especially noticeable to me when one whole session they couldn't pick up my voice and I went home crying. I didn't cry till I got home, I cried then. In the middle of the night Marty Paich called me up and said, "We've figured it out." That must have been one of the first multi-separation recordings. I was away from the orchestra and wearing headsets. It was at Liederkranz Hall, an especially live and great recording hall—not with all those horses in it! When we went back in to do the whole thing over again it had to come out right. So it did.

### IS THAT ALL THERE IS?

Peggy Lee: The decision on how to approach this song is the longest I ever went through. I couldn't figure out whether it was negative or positive, and until I could feel it was positive I didn't want to sing it. But I couldn't get it out of my mind, it just stayed there, night and day. And I thought, this song is really telling me something. So that was the answer. I think the subconscious shows you the way all the time, especially if you ask it for direction.

# Vocal Groups

ocal groups have always been a part of the American popular music scene. Barbershop quartets gave way to brother-and-sister acts, and when vaudeville came along, loose conglomerations of singers pretended to be brothers or sisters because they thought it looked better on the bill. By the 1930s there were actual vocal groups touring the country and singing with big bands. The Merry Macs, the Debutantes, the Modernaires, the Rhythm Boys, the Biltmore Rhythm Boys, the Charioteers, the Mel-Tones, and the Bob-o-Links (God help us), were all harmonizing away. Special mention should be made of Horace Heidt's group Donna and Her Don Juans (cute, eh?), that at various points included Gordon MacRae and, believe it or not, Art Carney.

One of the top vocal groups of the 1940s was the Pied Pipers. Along with Jo Stafford the group included Chuck Lowry, John Huddleston, and guitarist Clark Yocum. Michael Feinstein sat down with Jo Stafford and discussed the Pied Pipers.

"That's my first love, group singing. I loved singing with them and hated leaving them. They were fun. There's something very satisfying in singing lead in group singing, it's a kick.

"We met on *Alexander's Ragtime Band*. There was a group called the Four Esquires and the Three Rhythm Kings. And the Four Esquires and the Three Rhythm Kings and Jo Stafford used to pass their time singing together between takes. There were eight of us in the beginning.

"I guess we starved to death for about a year and then one of the King Sisters said, 'we're going to a big singers' jam session on Sunday and you guys are invited. And the jam session turned out to be at the house that Paul Weston and Axel Stordahl had rented for the summer while the band was playing the old Palomar Ballroom. So we went to their little rented house and I think every singer in town was there. That was the first that Paul and Axel heard us. Eventually they recommended us to Tommy Dorsey and Tommy had us on as guest stars without ever having heard us. We drove to New York to do one guest shot. Can you imagine, eight silly people driving 3,000 miles for the promise of one guest shot?

"That was our first acquaintance with Tom and we did about nine or ten radio shows. The tenth guest shot was the first time the sponsor had ever been in this country (he was from London) and the song that the Pipers were doing that day was 'Hold Tight', which got us fired. The sponsor said, 'Get those people off my show.' He didn't understand 'foo-de-le yaki saki.' So we got fired and walked the streets of New York for six months until we ran out of money.

"Everybody came home and four of the guys quit, they had families to support. We hadn't worked in months. I had gone down to get my last unemployment check, looking starvation in the face, and I got home and there was a message to call Operator Something in Chicago and I was very puzzled, knowing no one in Chicago—but it was free, so why not? I returned the call and it was Tom and he said, 'I want a quartet, I can't take eight of you, and with you singing lead.' And I said, 'As a matter of fact, that's what we are at this point.' And so in 1939 we joined the Dorsey band, which was a real good opening for us and we were with him for three years."

After the Pipers left the band, along with Sinatra in mid-1942, John Huddleston was drafted and replaced in the Pipers with Hal Hopper. In 1944, Stafford was replaced by June Hutton. They continued with their Capitol contract and, also in 1944, appeared regularly on Johnny Mercer's radio show, *Music Shop*. The group rejoined Frank Sinatra on his Lucky Strike radio show from 1944 to 1947.

With various personnel changes, the group has continued to perform to this day, and can be spotted on cruise ships and at conventions and fairs. ◈

## ANNIE ROSS

A most remarkable woman with a most remarkable career, Annie Ross has been in show business since the age of three. She was born in 1930, in Mitcham, Surrey, though there was some confusion about the exact date, Saturday July 25 or Sunday the twenty-sixth. She knew she was born right after her parents' matinee performance and, many years later determined that she was born on the Saturday not the Sunday because, as her father told her, there was a big football game that day. At about two, Annie joined her parents' act. A year later she and her mother came to America to live with Ella Logan, Ross's aunt and later the star of *Finian's Rainbow*. Logan took the three-year-old Annie to Hollywood after the tot won a radio talent contest carrying a prize of a six-month contract with MGM. At age seven she performed "Loch Lomond" in the *Our Gang Follies of 1938*. That one screen appearance was it for Annie Ross until 1942 and *Presenting Lily Mars*.

In the late forties she rejoined the family's act back in Scotland, and in 1948 she made her solo singing debut at the Orchard Room in London. Hugh Martin heard her and took her to Paris. When songwriting duties called him back to Hollywood, Ross stayed on and made her first recording, vocalizing on "Le Vent Vert," with James Moody and pianist Jacques Duval.

She came to New York and made her first recordings in America on April 1, 1952, for Dizzy Gillespie's DeeGee label. Fellow expatriates Blossom Dearie, Kenny Clarke, Milt Jackson, and Percy Heath also played the session. On October 9 of that year she recorded on the Prestige label with pianist George Wallington and drummer Art Blakey. Prestige owner Bob Weinstock suggested that Ross write lyrics to some instrumentals and the results included "Twisted," with her own lyrics to Wardell Gray's music.

As the 1950s dawned, Ross toured with a number of bands in England, America, and France including those of Ronnie Scott, Jack Parnell, and Lionel Hampton. She played in the musical *Cranks* in London and New York, then, in 1958, she joined Dave Lambert and Jon Hendricks to form the trio Lambert, Hendricks, and Ross. Their six albums were the hippest things going and they played all the great festivals. Ross quit in 1962 to concentrate on acting and singing in London. She came back to the States in 1985 and continued to pursue both disciplines. Her appearance in the 1993 film *Short Cuts*, and her contributions to the soundtrack, introduced her to a new generation of fans—and proved that she still had chops and then some.

Annie Ross lives in New York City and is still performing.

## Asides

Jon Hendricks had recorded some earlier albums backed by a choir but he felt it was too expensive and besides, times were changing so why not put together a vocal quartet? He and Dave Lambert auditioned women to fill the other two slots. Annie Ross and Georgia Brown were roommates in New York at the time and they both auditioned. Afterward, Hendricks told Ross that he and Lambert liked them both—but Ross wanted to be the only female in the group. She went back to the apartment and told Brown that she wasn't wanted, and it wasn't until years later that Brown found out she'd been duped. By then she'd starred in *Oliver!* and other shows on Broadway and in the West End.

## LAMBERT, HENDRICKS, AND ROSS

Just as the big bands had their vocal groups, jazz and pop were populated with trios, quartets, and quintets of singers, many of whom dressed exactly alike to retain a kind of uniform anonymity. The Four Freshmen (great), the Ink Spots (great backup singers), the Hi-Los (cool), the Brothers Four (ugh!), the Four Aces, the Four Lads (unmemorable), and the Kirby Stone Four (shiver) were the best and worst of them. Let's not even discuss the Ray Charles, Anita Kerr, or Johnny Mann singers. Over in France, where they embraced jazz with a fervor equal to our own, there were the Double Six and Les Blue Stars (featuring Blossom Dearie!). More recently, we've endured the Swingle Singers and Manhattan Transfer, the former too square and the latter too cool for their own good.

The ultimate in jazz vocal groups was Lambert, Hendricks, and Ross. Dave Lambert wrote the arrangements, Jon Hendricks supplied lyrics to jazz standards, and Annie Ross contributed lyrics as well. It all added up to one of the most innovative, exhilarating, and unique musical groups in jazz. They weren't together very long, from 1957 to 1962, but the mark they made was impressive. Annie Ross left the group in 1962 and was replaced by Yolande Bavan, but the trio wasn't the same. Ross, however, went on to a long, successful career.

**OPPOSITE PAGE:** Johnny Mercer (center) and the Pied Pipers. **TOP LEFT:** Annie Ross. **TOP RIGHT:** Mel Tormé and the Mel-Tones. **ABOVE:** Dave Lambert, Annie Ross, and Jon Hendricks.

# Dean Martin

I talian-Americans make up an interesting subcategory of popular singer. Male Italians, that is. Women never entered the men's club of crooners of Italian ancestry (with the distaff exceptions of Joni James and Connie Francis). Russ Columbo was the first on the scene, and he led the way for Frank Sinatra, the godfather of them all. Sinatra begat Como, Damone, Bennett, Roselli, La Rosa, Martino, Vale, Laine, and Darin.

Martin was a relaxed singer in the vein of Perry Como, but with more sex appeal and humor. His gimmick, at least later in his career, was to behave as if he was drunk most of the time, and his slightly slurred diction made it believable.; but early in his career, he was just another Italian pop singer. Following an aborted career as a welterweight boxer called Kid Crochet (his real name was Dino Crocetti), he sang with the Sammy Watkins band in 1941 and cut a few sides for the Diamond and Apollo labels. He didn't make much of a splash until 1946, when he worked for the first time with an up-and-coming comic, Jerry Lewis, at the 500 Club in Atlantic City.

The pairing would prove propitious for both. Martin's laid-back style and Lewis's manic energy, along with Martin's bemusement at Lewis's childish antics, made them a good match. By 1949, they were popular enough to be called to Hollywood to make a series of pictures. After two tryout films, the team starred in fourteen comedies.

Martin had signed with Capitol Records in 1948 and balanced his film career with his recording duties. Songs like "You Belong to Me," "Love Me, Love Me," "That's Amore," "Memories Are Made of This," "Innamorata," "Standing on the Corner," and "Volare" took him to the top of the charts.

Perhaps it was Martin's success as a singer that led to the eventual split with Lewis. Lewis fancied himself a singer (he even made a few records) but his popular success was confined to comedy. In 1956, the team made its last films, the ironically titled *Pardners* and *Hollywood or Bust*, and then broke up acrimoniously. Pundits predicted that Martin would have a harder time than Lewis establishing himself as a single act, but he actually blossomed as an actor, taking on dramatic parts as well as the occasional musical film; in addition, his singing career continued unabated for many years.

Luckily for him, he was a member of Sinatra's Rat Pack. Sinatra started his own label, Reprise Records, in 1961 and took Martin with him. Martin remained as popular in the '60s as he'd been in the '50s, with such hits as "Everybody Loves Somebody Sometime," which replaced the Beatles' "A Hard Day's Night" on the charts; "You're Nobody Till Somebody Loves You"; "Houston"; and "In the Chapel in the Moonlight."

Martin's continued success in the 1960s was due in part to his popular NBC television variety show. For nine years, beginning in 1964, it provided Martin with a weekly showcase for his talents.

Martin's singing style never changed much, though his style became more and more laid back, and he steadfastly refused to take himself seriously. In his recordings, too, Martin's easygoing style, in which he seldom attempted to swing or enter the perilous world of jazz, put the "easy" in easy listening. His voice was pleasant, solid, and highly listenable, if that is your idea of good music. Clearly, for many, it was. ◆

Martin, pictured here with Jerry Lewis prior to a television taping, is best remembered as a member of the Rat Pack and partner to Lewis.

# Johnny Mathis

Few parents raise their children to be pop singers (though this may be changing in the era of *Star Search* and *American Idol*), so most singers start out life in a different career entirely. Johnny Mathis had to choose between singing and training for the Olympic high jump. Some critics think he made the wrong choice—but thousands of devoted listeners thrill to Mathis's ultra-pasteurized baritone. You think Johnny Hartman sounded white? Listen to Mathis's earnest ballad interpretations. He has enjoyed remarkable success, lodged just behind Frank Sinatra, Nat King Cole, and Elvis Presley on the most successful recording artists list. No doubt with an aging painting in his closet, Mathis has presented an ever-youthful, clean-cut, nonthreatening image to millions for almost fifty years.

In 1955, when Mathis was only nineteen years old, producer George Avakian heard him at Ann Dee's 440 Club, a small room in San Francisco, and quickly signed him to Columbia records. For his first album, Columbia placed Mathis in a jazz setting, backed by the likes of Gil Evans and Teo Macero. It was not a success, so the label handed him over to Mitch Miller, king of pop. While the Miller touch may have been disastrous for Sinatra, he was great for Mathis. The soft pop songs Miller favored suited the young boy's voice and image, and Mathis quickly established himself as a hit with teenage girls and their mothers. His recording of "Wonderful! Wonderful!" cemented his success, and he went on to score a phenomenal number of hits in America as well as in England. Among the best loved are, "Chances Are," "The Twelfth of Never," "A Certain Smile," "It's Not for Me to Say," "Misty," "Winter Wonderland," "My Love for You," and "Someone." It's quite a roster, all the more impressive considering that, at the time, pop music and its singers were being cut from record company rosters as fast as their contracts expired.

Mathis's consistency has been a hallmark of his career. He seems to have been always part of the popular music scene, never

## Song and Story

### IT'S NOT FOR ME TO SAY

"It's Not for Me to Say" was so popular, Columbia issued a 78 RPM record of the song, the last 78 issued by a major label.

. . . . . . . . . . . . . . . . . . . . . . . . . . . . . . . . . . . . . . . . . . . . . .

**"Have found phenomenal 19-year-old boy who could go all the way. Send blank contracts." —George Avakian, Columbia Records producer**

. . . . . . . . . . . . . . . . . . . . . . . . . . . . . . . . . . . . . . . . . . . . . .

suffering the ups and downs—or the experiments with varying styles—of his contemporaries. This staying power is anathema to his detractors and validation to his millions of fans. He still records, tours regularly, and seems to be gliding into his fiftieth year of show business with the ease and charm he has always displayed. ❖

One of the greatest interpreters of American popular song wasn't widely known, nor did she possess a remarkable instrument, but Mabel Mercer's understanding of her own vocal limitations, her brilliant acting, crisp diction, sense of humor, precise phrasing, and emotional depth put her in the top five greatest singers.

Born on February 3, 1900, in Staffordshire, England, to a Welsh mother who entertained in music halls and a black father who performed gymnastics, Mercer was raised by her mother's parents. Her own parents had never bothered to tie the knot, and in fact, she didn't even know her father's name until age fourteen. She was eventually sent to a Catholic convent school, where she was bullied because of her mixed heritage and her left-handedness.

Her mother's parental involvement was limited to bringing Mabel to an abandoned music hall, instructing her to sing loudly and clearly—and then leaving on a grand theatrical tour from which she never returned. From then on, Mabel was basically on her own and, with the theater in her blood, she auditioned for variety, the English form of vaudeville. Her aunt and uncle, who were also in the business, included her in an act they called the Five Romanys, in which they performed as gypsies.

When the war came, Mercer, along with a friend named Kay, traveled through Europe scaring up jobs. Having never met a black person, she met actual Negroes from America and joined them in a revue titled *Coloured Society*. When the conductor came down with the flu during the 1918 pandemic, young Mercer conducted the orchestra dressed in white tie and tails and sporting a monocle.

Her professional stock rose when she was cast in the London company of *Lew Leslie's Blackbirds of 1926*. When the show moved to Paris, Mercer supplemented her income with cabaret performances, singing at the legendary Bricktop's. Strolling among the tables and singing sweetly into a tiny megaphone, she learned how to communicate a song in an intimate setting. When she sang in bigger halls later in her career, she carried with her the lessons she had learned at Bricktop's, and always drew the audience in as if serenading them in a small boite.

As she became the toast of Paris, Mercer met the haut monde and the stars of the theater and jazz worlds. In 1938, with war looming, she fled Europe for the safety of New York's Harlem. Her fame preceded her and she was quickly booked into Le Ruban Bleu, New York's most sophisticated nightclub. After a tonsillectomy, her voice became husky, but it didn't matter: it was secondary to her skills of interpretation and phrasing. She spent much of 1939 in the Bahamas before returning triumphantly to Le Ruban Bleu in 1941. A remarkable seven-year engagement at Tony's began in 1942, and in 1949 she moved her music and the highbacked chair in which she sat and sang—to the Byline Room. In 1955 she opened the New Byline Room, where she remained until 1957. Mercer was firmly established on the cabaret scene, symbolizing sophisticated New York at its best in much the same way that her protégé, Bobby Short, would do a few decades later.

During the 1950s, Mercer enjoyed a long relationship with Atlantic Records, making some of the most unique and timeless albums of the era. She championed the famous and the unknown alike, treating the works of Cole Porter and Bart Howard with equal importance. Her friend Alec Wilder was also a benefactor of Mercer's unique interpretations.

New York changed in the late sixties as discos replaced nightclubs, and Mercer's fortunes faltered. She still enjoyed occasional engagements at the Café Carlyle and Julius Monk's Downstairs at the Upstairs, but Mercer bought a farm in upstate New York on the proceeds from a winning lottery ticket, and was prepared to enter a forced retirement. In the 1970s, Donald Smith, a cabaret fan and agent, booked her across the country, in the few spots available to those of her ilk. She distinguished herself all over again, and began to make fans of younger audiences. A booking at the prestigious St. Regis Room in New York City was the capstone to her cabaret career. She performed two sold-out concerts in New York's Town Hall with Bobby Short. Atlantic Records, also home to Short, recorded both evenings to great acclaim. Mercer also appeared with Eileen Farrell, the queen of opera crossover artists, at a concert in Lincoln Center's Alice Tully Hall.

Following her death on April 20, 1984, Donald Smith created the Mabel Mercer Foundation, whose goal is to keep the art of cabaret alive. ◈

## THE GREAT SONGS

**1952** While We're Young; You Are Not My First Love; By Myself; Charm; First Warm Day in May; Let Me Love You; Remind Me; Some Fine Day; It Was Worth It; Goodbye John; Little Girl Blue; Did You Ever Cross Over to Sneeden's?; The End of a Love Affair; The Riviera

**1955** Ev'ry Time We Say Goodbye; Down in the Depths; Experiment; Looking at You; After You; So in Love; Use Your Imagination; Ace in the Hole;

**1956** Is It Always Like This?; Some Other Time; It Was Worth It; Wait Till You See Her; Walk Up; Lazy Afternoon; Young and Foolish; Blame it on My Youth; Wouldn't It Be Lovely?

**1958** The Twelve Days of Christmas; Look at Him; If Love Were All; Sunday in New York; Guess I'll Go Back Home; Once in a Blue Moon; My Shining Hour; Isn't It a Pity?

**1960** Fascinate Me So; Let's Begin; All in Fun; Merely Marvelous; Nobody Else but Me

**1964** Year After Year; Hello My Lover, Goodbye; More I Cannot Wish You; Once Upon a Time

**1968** Isn't He Adorable?; Why Did I Chose Him?

**1969** Not a Moment Too Soon; Wait Till We're Sixty-five

**1976** Christopher Robin; When the World was Young; Fun to be Fooled

**BELOW:** Mabel Mercer perusing music with the Eddie South Orchestra in Amsterdam, 1938.

# Carmen McRae

Carmen McRae's consummate musicianship and intelligence served her well over the course of her fifty-year career. She knew what she wanted and refused to be classified. By turns cool, swinging, intimate, and brassy, McRae tailored each performance to the requirements of the song, always singing the meaning and using the music to help tell the story. She could be funny, she could be intense, always ably navigating the tightrope between words and music. She never showed off with extended scatting, vocal pyrotechnics, or wild improvisation—though she was certainly capable of all those things. Rather, she preferred to rely on technique rather than ego.

It was Carmen McRae's absolute belief in herself that saw her through the hills and valleys of her career. She was insistent, but never a diva, and for that she earned the respect of her fellow musicians. Though her parents pushed her toward a career as a classical pianist, McRae preferred jazz and Tin Pan Alley tunes, and—given her respect for lyrics—it's telling that McRae's first success came as a songwriter. She was born in Harlem on April 8, 1920, to Jamaican parents. A win at the Apollo Theater's amateur contest brought her to the attention of Teddy Wilson's wife, Irene Wilson Kitchings, herself a songwriter. Kitchings helped McRae place her song "Dream of Life" with Wilson and singer Billie Holiday, who recorded the song, thus kicking off McRae's career.

McRae soon turned to singing, and spent the 1940s singing with the bands of Benny Carter (1944), Count Basie, Earl Hines, and Mercer Ellington (1946–47). She made her recording debut with Ellington's band under the name Carmen Clarke, as she was then married to drummer Kenny Clarke. In spite of her obvious talent, fame came slowly. Clarke got her a gig as the intermission pianist and singer at Minton's Playhouse in Harlem, where she picked up new ideas from the performers (especially Thelonius Monk) and expanded her range as a musician. During an engagement in Brooklyn, she was spotted by a small record label and, on May 17, 1946, she was hired to sing four sides with Mercer Ellington. One of them, "Pass Me By," was issued on the Musicraft label. Recordings she made in 1953 with Matt Matthews (when she was a member of the band), Larry Elgart, and Sy Oliver were issued by the Stardust label. But the most important recording session of her life came in 1954, for Bethlehem—because it was heard by Milt Gabler, the inspiration behind Decca Records. McRae signed with Decca and released her first album that same year, and after that her career took off.

McRae made twelve excellent albums with Decca and Kapp, a label owned by Decca—and she did it

all. She sometimes accompanied herself, or she sang with trios, big bands, or orchestras. Not willing to be pigeonholed, she mixed up her arrangements and repertoire, too. McRae was given free rein, and that artistic freedom served her well. Given her personality, it would have been foolish to confine her to one style or type of song. (She never would have lasted under the iron hand of Mitch Miller over at Columbia Records.)

For Decca, she ran the gamut, from accordion accompaniment on *By Special Request* to cello on *Carmen for the Cool Ones*. She made an album of Noel Coward songs called *Mad About the Man*; an album of songs with birds in the title called *Birds of a Feather*; and a remarkable collection of duets with Sammy Davis, Jr., first on 45 and then collected under the title *Boy Meets Girl*. In 1958, Davis and McRae recorded an album of songs from *Porgy and Bess*.

The Decca and Kapp albums were the best of her career, though she continued to record for a variety of labels, including Columbia, Mercury, Mainstream, Atlantic, Blue Note, Concord, Novus, and Verve. She toured the world playing jazz festivals and the occasional concert, and always the lyrics remained of the utmost importance, even as she aged and her singing became more detached. In 1988, nearing the age of seventy, she recorded a tribute to Thelonius Monk on RCA. *Carmen Sings Monk* recalled her early days at Minton's Playhouse, for years the most important jazz club in Harlem.

In May 1991, she collapsed after a performance at the Blue Note in New York City and retired, suffering from emphysema. ◆

## First Person

Carmen McRae: The popular song is slight in scope compared to drama or opera, but it can be a high form of melodic poetry.

"If Billie Holiday hadn't existed, I probably wouldn't have, either."
—Carmen McRae

# Singing Stars from the Movies

**OPPOSITE PAGE TOP:** Trigger and Roy Rogers, who together introduced Cole Porter's "Don't Fence Me In." **OPPOSITE PAGE BOTTOM:** Dorothy Lamour, Bing Crosby, Bob Hope, and Dona Drake in Burke and Van Heusen's *Road to Morocco.* **CLOCKWISE FROM TOP LEFT:** Deanna Durbin, Carmen Miranda, Betty Grable, and Betty Hutton.

**TOP:** Warner Brothers Studio's Ruby Keeler and Samuel Goldwyn's Eddie Cantor. **BOTTOM LEFT:** The sweetheart of 20th Century-Fox, Alice Faye. **BOTTOM RIGHT:** You may not have seen her but you heard her all right. Dubber to the stars Anita Ellis—a great singer in her own right whose severe stage fright curtailed what might have been a brilliant career. **OPPOSITE PAGE:** A rare photo of Judy Garland on the set of *A Star Is Born*.

# Anita O'Day

A nita O'Day's singing is like a tossed boomerang: the melody soars up and around and almost out of sight, but always returns to its starting place. Other vocal improvisers, Cleo Laine for example, similarly perform vocal gymnastics without a net—but all too often they trail off into the ether. O'Day's flights of musical fancy may threaten to veer into the blue, but her audiences rightly trust her to come back to earth safely—and oh so satisfyingly.

As O'Day herself put it, "I'm not a singer, I'm a song stylist. I made my own style and that's even better. That's why I got into rephrasing and songs with a lot of words." According to O'Day, she had a hard time sustaining notes because a doctor accidentally sliced off her uvula. This was her excuse to eschew ballads, with their long lines, in favor of upbeat, swinging numbers. So it's no surprise that her two main influences were Billie Holiday and, especially, Martha Raye. (Raye was a consummate jazz singer, sort of a Betty Hutton with the manic edge taken off, who introduced such rhythmic numbers as "Mr. Paganini" and "Public Enemy No. 1.") O'Day included novelty numbers in her repertoire as well, though never as winningly as had Hutton and Raye.

O'Day led the way for white jazz singers who didn't sound black. In her years with the Stan Kenton orchestra, she developed a cool style, aloof, sexy, with a wry sense of humor. Her spontaneity lent her singing a breathless excitement and her use of dynamics, moving from softness to growls, enabled her to project emotions while never exactly acting the lyrics.

If anything held O'Day back, it was her personal weaknesses. The addictions that fueled her highs eventually caught up with her, and she stayed too long at the fair, long after her powers had left her. She laid out all the madness in her mesmerizing 1981 autobiography, *High Times, Hard Times*, in which she was honest to a fault. Her approach to telling her own story was quite in keeping with her approach to a song: reckless, unapologetic, and self-aware.

O'Day was born Anita Belle Colton in Chicago on October 18, 1919, and changed her name when she began competing in dance marathons or "Walkathons." At one of these, Erskine Tate's orchestra accompanied the contestants and O'Day had plenty of time to consider a career in singing. As she tells it, when she was fifteen, Jesus came to her during a Walkathon, and asked her what she wanted to be. She told Jesus she wanted to sing, and her wish was granted.

She got her start in 1939 at the Off-Beat Club, singing with Max Miller's combo. It was there that she came to the attention of drummer extraordinaire Gene Krupa, whom she joined in 1941 after short stints with Benny Goodman (who didn't like her improvisation) and Raymond Scott (who didn't like her scatting). Krupa then hired trumpeter Roy Eldridge, and the three of them clicked.

O'Day described touring with the Krupa ensemble as follows: "I didn't play girl on a bus with 27 men. I don't want to be the den mother. I drank with them, we played poker together. Just a swinging group of people and they played that way because it was from the heart." O'Day made it clear from day one that her onstage image would be neither virginal nor asexual—rather, she was one of the boys on the bandstand, even wearing the same outfit they wore. Though she went off on a brief interlude with Woody Herman's band, she soon joined Krupa again. When the band broke up in 1943, she looked at her options and met Stan Kenton.

Over the eleven sometimes tumultuous months she sang with Kenton, beginning in 1944, O'Day really hit her stride and perfected the cool sound—but ultimately, she decided to quit. As she put it, "After one year I says, 'I got to get out of here, it don't swing'. He didn't know where the upbeats were. He didn't even know where to stop the upbeats at the end of the song." So O'Day told Kenton, "It's been real nice and bye. Man, I've been on the road all my life, I'm not going back."

After leaving Kenton, O'Day again returned to Krupa, but in 1946 she decided to take her chances as a solo performer, bringing along drummer John Poole as an accompanist. He stayed with her for thirty-two years. O'Day's solo career stalled after a 1953 conviction for heroin possession. It's ironic, since O'Day claimed she was framed—but shortly after that, she did become hooked and never really kicked the habit.

Norman Granz signed O'Day to his Clef label in 1952, and after her release from prison, she began the uphill climb to reestablish herself. In 1955, she recorded the album "*Anita*" for Granz's new Verve label (it was Verve's first LP)—and just like that, she was back on top.

In 1958, a stoned O'Day performed at the Newport Jazz Festival alongside such masters as George Shearing, Thelonius Monk, Dinah Washington, and Louis Armstrong. The event was filmed and released as *Jazz on a Summer's Day*, a huge success in America and Europe.

The Verve years were O'Day's heyday, during which she released a series of breathtaking albums. Among the best were *Anita O'Day Swings Cole Porter with Billy May*; *Cool Heat*; *Anita Sings the Most*; *Time for Two*; and *Pick Yourself Up, Anita*. As the Verve years progressed, O'Day's voice and stamina declined. In 1964 she quit Verve (or did Verve quit her?), and in 1967 she suffered a physical breakdown from which she never truly recovered. She overdosed in 1969, barely escaping death.

The 1970s were productive years spent recording and touring overseas. O'Day continued performing into the 1990s, realizing diminishing artistic returns. Still, her technique never deserted her and she remained surprisingly resilient, even as she began forgetting her lyrics toward the end of the century. ◆

> ## "The stage, that's my life. I come alive when I have that going." —Anita O'Day

## THE GREAT SONGS

| Year | Songs |
|---|---|
| 1941 | Boogie Blues; Just a Little Bit South of North Carolina; Let Me Off Uptown |
| 1942 | That's What You think; Skylark; Massachusetts; Murder He Says; Boloero at the Savoy |
| 1944 | And Her Tears Flowed Like Wine, The Lady in Red |
| 1945 | Boogie Blues; Chickery Chick; Opus No. 1; Tea for Two |
| 1947 | Key Largo |
| 1952 | Love for Sale; Lover Come Back to Me |
| 1954 | From This Moment On; I Cover the Waterfront; You're Getting to be a Habit with Me |
| 1955 | You're the Top; I'll See You in My Dreams; Honeysuckle Rose; A Nightingale Sang in Berkeley Square; Time After Time |
| 1956 | Stompin' at the Savoy; There's a Lull in My Life; Don't Be That Way; Pick yourself Up; Tenderly; S'Wonderful; Old Devil Moon; Bewitched |
| 1958 | Sweet Georgia Brown;Four Brothers; Frenesi; The Peanut Vendor; Sing Sing Sing |
| 1959 | Come Rain or Shine; Get Out of Town; I Get a Kick Out of You; Night and Day |
| 1960 | Have You Met Miss Jones?; Ten Cents a Dance; That Old Feeling; Stella  by Starlight; Angel Eyes; The Thrill is Gone |
| 1961 | Night Bird; Alone with the Blues |
| 1962 | You and the Night and the Music; The Party's Over |

> ## "It's like a high-wire act." —Chris Connor

## *First Person*

O'Day on O'Day: It gets a little dumb singing melody every night. I have a lot of rhythm, not much voice.

O'Day on money: I made $100,000 a year for nine years with Verve. My partner took it, my manager took it, my husbands took it, my road manager took it, the government got it, and I helped spend some of it.

O'Day in 1998: Four years ago, I had $200 to my name. Now I have $300, but I don't owe anyone.

Chris Connor: Kenton wanted that low sound with all the high brass. He preferred singers with lower voices. I would study her timing and everything. But, of course, nobody could ever duplicate anything Anita does, she's completely original.

Marian McPartland: I find what she does defies description.

# Dinah Shore

Proving that nice guys (or gals) can sometimes finish first, Dinah Shore, a truly kind, upbeat performer, brought her sunny disposition, optimism, and Southern drawl to radio, films, recordings, and television over the course of a fifty-year career. Her style was the very definition of pop singing for its day, with few jazz embellishments. Even when she sang a jazz-influenced, bluesy tune like the Arlen-Koehler "Tess' Torch Song," which she introduced in *Up in Arms*, she delivered it straight-on and uninflected, with her trademark lilt. Shore didn't insert her own point of view into a song, preferring to serve the songwriter by performing a song directly, making it as accessible as possible.

Born in Winchester, Tennessee, on February 29, 1916, Frances Shore grew up in one of the few Jewish families in that neck of the woods. Just before her second birthday she contracted polio but made a full recovery, save a slight limp. When the family moved to Nashville she began performing, making her nightclub debut at age fourteen and singing on local radio station WSM. After the death of her mother, Shore moved in with older sister Bessie and Bessie's husband. Shore attended Vanderbilt University, graduating in 1938 with a degree in sociology.

She decided to try to make it as a singer and moved to New York. Shore was eventually hired (along with the young Frank Sinatra) at station WNEW, as a staff singer. DJ Martin Block called her "that 'Dinah' girl" after she sang the song of the same name. Never liking the name Frances, she changed her name to Dinah.

Xavier Cugat hired her, and she made her first popular recordings with his band. RCA then signed her to their inexpensive Bluebird label, and she had her first hit in 1940, "Yes, My Darling Daughter." She was a member of NBC's Chamber Music Society of Lower Basin Street for a while before auditioning for Eddie Cantor's *Time to Smile* later that year. Cantor became a mentor to Shore (if not more than that—he had a reputation for having affairs with his female discoveries).

Cantor brought her to Hollywood for her first film appearance, in *Thank Your Lucky Stars* in 1943. Shore took a leading role in the war effort, traveling to Europe to entertain the troops, even having a bridge named after her. Her "Command Performances" on Armed Forces Radio were big hits and her recordings of "Blues in the Night" and "I'll Walk Alone" were soon hitting the top of the charts.

While entertaining at the Hollywood Canteen, Shore met actor George Montgomery, who was about to be inducted into the service, and they were married

on December 5, 1943. Shore's sweet, direct way with a song led to more hits, "Shoofly Pie and Apple Pan Dowdy," "Dear Hearts and Gentle People," "It's So Nice to Have a Man Around the House," "The Gypsy," and "Buttons and Bows." She appeared on the radio shows *Birds-Eye Open House*, the *Ford Radio Show*, and with Jack Smith three times weekly on CBS radio.

Columbia Records signed her in 1949. Ed Wynn tapped her for her television debut in 1950, and Bob Hope asked her to appear on his first TV show. She began her long association with Chevrolet on NBC on November 27, 1951. The show began as a fifteen-minute program, twice a week. The next year she appeared in two hour-long shows for Chevrolet and finally the weekly, Sunday evening variety show, *The Dinah Shore Chevy Show*, premiered in October 1956. She was the first female host of a variety series, and her easy-going attitude (she was a sort of female Perry Como, but with a bit more energy) carried the show into 1961 for Chevrolet and for an additional two years for other sponsors. Her trademarks were the jingle, "See the USA in Your Chevrolet" and throwing a big kiss to the audience at the end of every show, accompanied by a sound that can only be described as "M'wah!"

Just as her television show was winding down, she signed with Capitol Records. She appeared in nightclubs and gave concerts and, to the surprise of her fans, she and George Montgomery divorced in 1962. Around that time, many singers found themselves abandoned by record companies and record buyers. Like many of her peers, Dinah began recording for Frank Sinatra's Reprise Records.

In 1970, Shore returned to the small screen with the NBC daytime show, *Dinah's Place*, which featured Dinah the conversationalist, cook, and homemaker more than Dinah the singer. The show lasted until 1974, at which point Shore moved almost immediately to a ninety-minute daily talk show on CBS called *Dinah!* That ran for six successful years and was followed by *Dinah and Friends* which ran until 1984, and finally *A Conversation with Dinah*, which went off the air in 1991. There are many today who know Dinah Shore only as an affable daytime TV hostess.

In 1972, Shore, an avid tennis player, was approached by Colgate to host a women's golf tournament. She didn't actually play the game but took a crash course and began hosting the popular Women's PGA tournament.

Throughout her long television career, audiences never tired of spending time with her. Her cheery demeanor, quick sense of humor, and 1940s singing style, which remained consistent, made her a household favorite for over fifty years. Shore won more Emmys than any other television performer. Dinah Shore died on February 24, 1994. ◆

## Asides

When Eddie Cantor auditioned Shore for his radio series, he asked her to sing song after song. When she asked why she had to sing so many songs he replied, "You'll forgive me…but I figure it's the last time I'm going to hear you for nothing."

# Carol Sloane

Carol Morvan was born on March 5, 1937, in Providence, Rhode Island. At age fourteen she began singing professionally with Ed Drew's band in her home town. In 1958, she sang with the Larry Elgart orchestra (he suggested she change her name to Sloane). She subbed for Annie Ross at the Village Vanguard as a member of Lambert, Hendricks, and Ross in 1961. Hendricks arranged for her to appear at the 1961 Newport Jazz Festival, which led to a contract with Columbia Records. They promptly set about molding her into another Barbra Streisand. Just look at the artwork on her albums and you'll see the effort to shoehorn her into a style that didn't suit her warm jazz phrasing at all.

Sloane performed around the country for a while, opening for top acts and appearing on Johnny Carson's *Tonight Show* and Arthur Godfrey's radio program. She quickly gained a devoted coterie of fans and made records for Audiophile, Progressive, two for Contemporary, six recordings for Concord, and recently, two for HighNote. She's a star in Japan, where they still appreciate great singing, and performs throughout the Northeast including New York City, to as much acclaim as it is possible to find nowadays for singing great jazz. ◆

# Kay Starr

the Glenn Miller Orchestra, got sick and Starr sat in for a two-week engagement at the Glen Island Casino. She made her first recordings with the Miller band, but singing in Hutton's keys.

After graduating from high school, Starr rejoined Venuti, but the band broke up one year later, in 1941. She went on to Wingy Manone's New Orleans Jazz Band in 1943, and later that year replaced Lena Horne with Charlie Barnet's group. She made some V-Discs (recorded for use by the armed forces) as well as some Decca Records with Barnet. In 1945 a bout with pneumonia forced Starr to take a break—she was forbidden by her doctors from singing or even talking for six months.

By 1947, her voice was back but huskier, and Starr signed with Capitol, where she recorded such hits as "I'm the Lonesomest Gal in Town," "So Tired," "Hoop-Dee-Doo," and "Bonaparte's Retreat," the last of which sold nearly a million copies. Her repertoire started inching toward the country canon, and she even recorded some duets with Tennessee Ernie Ford. On January 17, 1952, she recorded "Wheel of Fortune," the biggest hit of her career.

Starr moved to RCA in 1955 and recorded "The Rock and Roll Waltz" the following year. She returned to Capitol in 1959 and cut several LPs, and then cut "a series of recordings" including *Movin'* (1959), *Losers, Weepers* (1960), and *I Cry by Night* (1962). By 1966, Starr and a lot of her fellow singers found themselves marginalized by radio and the recording industry. Capitol dropped her and she began concentrating on her live act, pleasing her large Las Vegas fan base by appearing in nightclubs and giving concerts.

In 1968, Starr made an album with Count Basie, followed by a few more on successively smaller labels. She toured with fellow songbirds Helen O'Connell and Margaret Whiting in the late 1980s and continued performing through the '90s.

Starr remains one of our most versatile singers, comfortable with jazz, blues, pop, R & B, and country music. She started early, she could sing it all—and she did, over the course of a jam-packed sixty-year career. ◆

Kay Starr was born in Dougherty, Oklahoma, on July 21, 1922. Her family moved to Dallas when she was nine and her Aunt Nora entered her in radio station WWR's weekly talent contest. She kept winning—and finally, the station let her have a weekly fifteen-minute program. The family soon moved to Memphis and Starr joined WREC's *Saturday Night Jubilee*.

Joe Venuti heard the youngster and hired her for an engagement at the Peabody Hotel, where she joined the band during her summer vacations (bringing her mother along as chaperon). Venuti recommended her to Bob Crosby's agent and in 1939 she appeared on the *Camel Caravan*. Later that same year, Marion Hutton, then with

What accounts for a sustained, successful career? Talent might be the most important thing but there are other elements involved, including brains, timing, friends, the ability to evolve with the times, sex appeal, a bit of danger and risk, and sometimes just plain, dumb luck. Sinatra was smart enough, talented enough, and lucky enough to incorporate all of them into his remarkable career.

His rise came just as the country was going to war and our musical taste was slowly evolving from an infatuation with the instrumental sounds of the big bands (and their straight-ahead vocalists) to an interest in individual singers. Many of the best band singers were striking out on their own, taking center stage without the crutch (or the hindrance) of an orchestra. It was a brave act to step out but an artistically fulfilling one, as Sinatra himself proved. His whole career was guided by his innate desire to stretch as an artist, and he demanded a great deal from himself and all of those with whom he worked. He was unafraid to walk away from a gig or a contract, even during periods when his artistic or financial future was unsure; his self-confidence and drive rendered him unafraid of taking risks. This certainty would pay off spectacularly, until the very end of his career.

## Sinatra's nicknames included the Sultan of Swoon, the Voice, the Chairman of the Board, and Ol' Blue Eyes.

Sinatra's big move came when he left Tommy Dorsey in 1942 (owing Dorsey thousands on his contract), and, from that point on, his career soared. He launched his solo career in a spectacular way, with a week of appearances with Benny Goodman's orchestra at New York's Paramount Theater on Times Square. We know now that some of the fans may have been paid to scream—but thousands of girls swooned for free during the weeklong engagement that anointed Sinatra the greatest popular singer of the day. His sense of humor, sex appeal, slight whiff of danger, and those mesmerizing blue eyes—not to mention the carefully chosen songs that resonated with his audience—made him an instant favorite of the bobby-soxers.

Sinatra's decision to go it alone coincided with America's entrance into the Second World War. Disqualified from service, Sinatra was still on the scene while much of the competition was occupied elsewhere, and the public's interest in lyrics had never been stronger. "I'll Be Seeing You," a song Sinatra had recorded in 1940, took on new meaning for a female population unsure that they might ever see their boyfriends, brothers, sons, or husbands again. In 1944, the Sammy Fain and Irving Kahal song became a number one hit.

Sinatra had the good sense and taste to pick songs that suited him and that were perfect for the moment, and this carried him along brilliantly through the '40s—but when that task was taken from him in the 1950s, when Mitch Miller was calling the shots for Columbia Records, Sinatra's career plummeted to its lowest point. Ultimately, brains and technology saved

the day. Sinatra broke his contract with Columbia and set out on his own, just when he was generally considered washed up both professionally and personally (His highly publicized marriage to Ava Gardner was kaput). He may have been down and out but he still had his intelligence and his high standards, and he spotted his next golden opportunity and took a leap that could be summed up by the quintessential Sinatra title, "All or Nothing at All."

If his singing career was at a standstill, he reasoned, he should concentrate on his film career. The first half of Sinatra's career started when he was signed by MGM after making his acting debut at RKO. His early screen roles featured him as a sort of grown-up Bowery Boy, rough around the edges but eager to please. *Anchors Aweigh* (1945) found him paired with Gene Kelly and singing songs written by Jule Styne and Sammy Cahn, thereafter his favorite songwriters. *It Happened in Brooklyn* (1947) and *Take Me Out to the Ball Game* (1949) were among his MGM films. After 1949's *On the Town*, Sinatra's films became less and less successful both artistically and at the box office. He needed a change.

After reading James Jones's bestseller *From Here to Eternity*, Sinatra lobbied hard for the part of Maggio and got it. The film came out in 1953 and soon he had an

**BOTTOM:** Bob "Bazooka" Burns, Cass Daley, and Frank Sinatra.

## THE GREAT SONGS

**1939** All or Nothing At All

**1940** I'll Never Smile Again; Imagination; Stardust; I'll Be Seeing You; East of the Sun

**1941** Polka Dots and Moonbeams; This Love of Mine; Oh, Look At Me Now; How About You?; Everything Happens To Me; Violets for Your Furs; It's Always You; Let's Get Away from It All

**1942** Night and Day; There Are Such Things; Street of Dreams; It Started All Over Again; The Song Is You; Be Careful It's My Heart

**1943** You'll Never Know; The Music Stopped; Sunday, Monday or Always; Close to You; People Will Say We're In Love

**1944** Saturday Night; Ol' Man River; I Dream of You; If You Are But a Dream; I Fall In Love Too Easily; Stormy Weather; White Christmas

**1945** Dream; Nancy; Oh What It Seemed to Be; These Foolish Things; I Should Care; Day by Day; The House I Live In; If I Loved You; Put Your Dreams Away; You Go to My Head

**1946** They Say It's Wonderful; Five Minutes More; The Coffee Song; Blue Skies; Time After Time; That Old Black Magic; September Song

Proud Papa serenades "Nancy with the Laughing Face."

Oscar to join his Gold Records. Sinatra became a hot commodity in Hollywood and followed his stunning comeback with a remarkably diverse series of film roles. His 1955 output illustrates his high artistic goals as well as his refusal to be typecast: in that one year he took on lead roles in two dramas (*The Man with the Golden Arm* and *Not As a Stranger*), a musical (*Guys and Dolls*), and a comedy (*The Tender Trap*). But Sinatra knew his real claim to fame was his voice, and reviving his dormant recording career remained a priority. He signed with the newly formed Capitol Records and developed an entirely new singing style, a total departure from the formal, "square" techniques of the '40s. He adopted a kind of loose, jazz-influenced style that was much more in tune with the '50s. An army of arrangers kept him au courant, beginning with Axel Stordahl and continuing most notably with Nelson Riddle and Billy May. Many consider Sinatra's Capitol period the greatest of his career.

Propitiously, the 33 1/3 rpm record was just coming into vogue, replacing the 78 rpm disc. On 78s, the choice of songs and their order hadn't been so important, as individual songs could be easily purchased and played. As the 10-inch 78 was replaced by the LP, Sinatra and his producers were able to imbue these long playing records with concepts, carefully choosing the songs and their order. Once he was back on top, riding the popularity of such carefully crafted and enduring discs as *In the Wee Small Hours* and *Songs for Swinging Lovers*, Sinatra stayed there.

At the same time as his film and recording career were succeeding anew, Sinatra went to Las Vegas. His reputed mob ties came in handy, and Sinatra opened at the Desert Inn in September of 1951. His pioneering efforts in Vegas are credited with the city's success. In the 1960s, Sinatra made Vegas the clubhouse for the Rat Pack, an ultra-cool club of which he was the chairman. Members Sammy Davis, Jr., Joey Bishop, Peter Lawford, and Dean Martin followed their leader, and they held court onstage and in such films as *Ocean's Eleven* (1960) and *Sergeants Three* (1962). Sinatra brought a sense of sophistication to the Strip, which had been a glorified cowboy town before his arrival, and during his reign, entertainment grew into an attraction on a par with gambling for many visitors.

Sinatra's hip persona was a natural extension of his street smarts. His swagger, tilted hat, raincoat-over-the-shoulder style spawned a whole trend in attitude and became a blueprint for thousands young men. Some of Sinatra's acolytes like Sammy Davis, Jr., perhaps went too far in the ring-a-ding-ding lifestyle but Sinatra sailed through the years being true to himself.

Sinatra's career faltered only at the very end, when his ego and boredom kept him performing and recording long past his prime. Still, audiences never stopped adoring him and even his horrific *Duets* albums (on which he teamed [in separate recording sessions] with contemporary pop stars many years his junior for indifferently recorded numbers), became bestsellers. It was a strange ending to a career marked by the highest artistic ideals—but nothing could erase the musical legacy of the man most consider the greatest singer of the twentieth century. ◆

# Song and Story

### THREE COINS IN THE FOUNTAIN

Fox thought they had a bomb on their hands with the picture *We Believe in Love*, when producer Sol Siegel approached composer Jule Styne and lyricist Sammy Cahn to write a title tune for the film. Styne asked Siegel why the film wasn't titled after the book on which it was based, *Three Coins in the Fountain*. Siegel asked if it would be easier to write for that title and Cahn replied, "It's a helluva lot easier than 'We Believe in Love.'" The team worked all night and the next day played the new song for Siegel and Zanuck. Spyro Skouras, then the studio chief, didn't like it and commented, "the other title had 'love' in it and that's a good thing." It seemed that the song was dead, but Zanuck told Styne that if he could get a big name to sing it, he could get it into the movie.

## "Frank's musical taste was developed at Tommy's elbow."
### —Tommy Dorsey arranger Dick Jones

Styne had written several hits for Frank Sinatra and he was determined to extract a return favor. Learning that Sinatra was returning to LA from Europe with a stopover in New York, Styne booked himself on the same flight and got a seat next to him. He implored Sinatra for help and, worn down, the singer agreed to record the song the very next morning—but he didn't want to be paid. Rather, there was a certain painting in a gallery that he admired. Sinatra got his painting, and both the record and the film were smash hits. PS: the song won the Academy Award. As Jule Styne said, "The difference was Frank Sinatra. Without him, it wouldn't have gotten off the ground."

## First Person

Jule Styne: I says, Frank, we have to split. I'm no good for you, Frank. Cause I'm writing for you. You have to sing other things. It's not good for me. Every song I write is a Sinatra song. I gotta go write for some other people, I have another dimension for me. And that's when he got angry at me. He thought I'm dismissing him. He didn't understand it. I play him "Just in Time," I tell him I'm writing a Sinatra song. I didn't want to tell him it was a Fred Astaire song. I met Fred Astaire at a party once. I said "Gee, it's too bad I didn't write some of the songs when you were dancing away. You know I've been writing Fred Astaire songs my whole life. Don't tell Sinatra, he thinks they were his songs."

Jule Styne: When I write music I hear the orchestra, I don't hear a piano. I play piano orchestrally, too. I hear the brass, I hear the woodwind. George Gershwin made a sound at the piano that he learned from a player piano he heard on the corner. He was playing the orchestra all the time. He felt more than he knew and that's a wonderful thing. Feelings is the whole ball game. If you don't have feelings you can't compose you can't sing. You can act feelings. I think that when Sinatra in the 40s sang I think he was getting feelings that he hasn't got. He was falling in love when he sang, he was talking to somebody. He just didn't sing the words. He was inside the song. Sinatra always made the song his song. He took that song.

## Sinatra on Sinatra

On his influence: It is Billie Holiday, whom I first heard in Fifty-second Street clubs in the early thirties, who was and still remains the single greatest musical influence on me.

After seeing a Bing Crosby movie: That's what I'm going to do.

On how he chose a song: I'll leave the music to somebody else. I pick the lyrics.

## Asides

Sinatra joined the Tommy Dorsey band and sang with the Pied Pipers. They had great success with the song, "I'll Never Smile Again." Jo Stafford explained to George Simon how much they loved working with him: "Most solo singers don't fit too well into a group, but Frank never stopped working at it and, of course, as you know, he blended beautifully with us. He was meticulous about his phrasing and dynamics. He worked very hard so that his vibrato would match ours. And he was always conscientious about learning his parts."

Sinatra with Ava Gardner (left) and Nat King Cole (below).

# Kate Smith

I f there were a Mount Rushmore of popular song, Kate Smith's formidable profile would undoubtedly be featured there. Possessed of a big, rich, booming voice and a physique to match, she must be considered one of the most popular singers of the twentieth century. She knew exactly how to control the power of her voice and made sure never to rely on big sound alone; she was an excellent interpreter of lyrics, always delivered with perfect diction.

Smith concentrated on songs with mass appeal, the kind that spoke to the regular guy on the street or the farm. She was never a great interpreter of Broadway's more sophisticated output, concentrating instead on wholesome songs with straightforward lyrics. Although she was never a particularly nuanced singer, Smith excelled at putting over a song cleanly and succinctly, without vocal mannerisms. When she's described as a craftsman, it's a compliment.

Smith was born on May 1, 1907, in Washington, D.C. She broke into show business by entertaining troops during World War I, and made her first splash on Broadway in *Honeymoon Lane*, *Hit the Deck*, and *Flying High*. In 1926 she began recording, and her successes included "River, Stay 'Way from My Door" (1931), "The Woodpecker Song" (1940), "The White Cliffs of Dover" (1941), "I Don't Want to Walk Without You" (1942), "There Goes That Song Again" (1944), "Seems Like Old Times"(1946), and "Now Is the Hour" (1947). Nineteen of her recordings sold over a million copies. Her later LPs on the RCA label were also immense bestsellers.

Columbia Records vice president Ted Collins saw her potential and signed on as her manager. He got her a radio contract in 1930 and booked her into the Palace Theater, where she broke the record for longest engagement. In 1933, she was voted the most popular woman on radio.

In 1931, Smith got her own radio show, *Kate Smith Sings*, and adopted "When the Moon Comes Over the Mountain" as her theme song. The show ran until 1947, and simultaneously she had a daytime talk and news show, *Kate Smith Speaks*, making her the most ubiquitous and successful woman in radio.

She made her debut in 1932's *The Big Broadcast* in a cameo spot. She starred in 1933's *Hello, Everybody!*, the title of which was how she began her radio broadcasts (she ended them with "Thanks for listening"). President Franklin Delano Roosevelt introduced Smith to King George VI of England after a command performance at the White House by saying, "Your majesties, this is Kate

Smith. This is America." Three years later, in 1942, Kate was voted one of the three most popular women in America, alongside Mrs. Roosevelt and Helen Hayes.

In 1950 Smith made the transition to television with an afternoon variety show, *The Kate Smith Hour*. She soon added an additional show, *The Kate Smith Evening Hour*. The afternoon show left the air in 1954. Her final radio show was broadcast on the Mutual network in 1958. She switched to CBS in 1960 in a half-hour format called *The Kate Smith Show*. She made her Carnegie Hall debut in 1963.

In the 1970s, Smith concentrated on nightclub and concert appearances. In 1976 she was named Grand Marshal of the Tournament of Roses Parade. The Bicentennial year was her last in show business. Kate Smith died in Raleigh, North Carolina, on June 17, 1986—but she lives on as the only voice that is likely ever to be associated with "God Bless America." ◆

## Song and Story

### GOD BLESS AMERICA

"God Bless America" was written in 1918 for Irving Berlin's army show, *Yip, Yip, Yaphank*, but he decided that it was too patriotic and put it in

the proverbial trunk. In the fall of 1938, with the demise of the Munich Pact, Berlin returned from Europe knowing there would be a war. He remembered "God Bless America." Kate Smith's manager seized on it as the perfect patriotic song for her Armistice Day broadcast. Smith wanted to sing it with a marshal beat, but Berlin prevailed upon her to sing it more lyrically. Smith sang the song per Berlin's instructions and it went over fantastically. Berlin was so excited, he went down to the network to hear Smith sing it again for the West Coast feed.

Hearing Kate Smith sing the song, Congress was urged by thousands of citizens to make the song the new national anthem. Berlin and Smith said no.

Smith sang the song on December 11, 1969, before a Philadelphia Flyers game. She was made an unofficial mascot of the team with a career record of 64-15-3.

"God Bless America" was the last song she sang, on a Bicentennial special.

"I just couldn't sing it straight," was Maxine Sullivan's reaction when handed the song "Trees" to perform for members of Pittsburgh's Benjamin Harrison Literary Club in 1934. We should state that the club catered to those gentlemen who enjoyed drinking more than coffee from their coffee cups.

Maxine, like Peggy Lee, a singer she influenced greatly, had the power to belt a swinging song. But Maxine, also like Peggy, preferred to keep her power in check, to save it up so that it made a greater impact when she called upon it. In a way, that also explains Maxine's personality. Her singing style was often described as "gently swinging" and that described Maxine, too. She never made too much of a fuss, even about things that others might have raised hell about. As a young black performer, she suffered her share of indignities but refused to let them stop her.

She got on the road to fame—if not fortune—with Claude Thornhill's band, on the recommendation of a pianist with Ina Rae Hutton's all-girl band. Thornhill borrowed a gimmick from the Sullivan songbook, pairing the young black girl's sense of swing with Olde English airs. They had a massive hit with "Loch Lomond" and played the catalog for all it was worth. From the Hebrides, they moved on to Russian folk tunes, pseudo-Yiddish ditties, Shakespearean sonnets, and other incongruities before the gimmick wore thin.

Sullivan married John Kirby and made some excellent recordings with his group, a classically-influenced, chamber jazz ensemble. In 1940, they became the first black jazz stars to have a regular radio program. She appeared in *Going Places* and also *St. Louis Blues;* at the Cotton Club with Louis Armstrong; on Broadway, with Armstrong again, in *Swinging the Dream,* in which she introduced "Darn That Dream"; and back on Broadway decades later in *My Old Friends,* which earned her a Tony nomination. When her career began to wane, she retired to raise her two children, pursue a nursing career, learn the flugelhorn, and do community work in the South Bronx.

When she made her "comeback" in 1967, by that time married to pianist Cliff Jackson, the world of music had changed and so had she. The great nostalgia wave was about to break and Maxine connected more with her lyrics. She grew bolder and more willing to act

her songs, perhaps to make up for the natural deterioration of her voice that had come with age.

Which brings us to one of Sullivan's great strengths as an older performer: she knew her limitations and always sang within them. Employing a looser style, fine acting, and a renewed sense of fun, she did her best work in the last twenty-or-so years of her life. In fact, she recorded more than ever, received Grammy nominations, made annual trips to Japan and Sweden, and generally had a ball. She devoted lots of time to the House That Jazz Built in the South Bronx, where she supported programs encouraging young talent and introducing children to the world of jazz. Among those she influenced was the wonderful tenor saxophonist Harry Allen.

Maxine's last recordings revealed a vulnerability that must have always lurked beneath the surface. Leader Bob Wilber and arranger Keith Ingham recognized Maxine's strengths and offered her the opportunity to stretch her talents in both voice and repertoire. When called upon to perform purely swinging songs that didn't

call for acting, she could still perform on autopilot, reverting to such chestnuts as "We Just Couldn't Say Goodbye." Teamed with Wilber, Ingham, and Dick Hyman, though, she was at her best—and that was the best there was. ◆

THE LADY'S IN LOVE WITH YOU
MAXINE SULLIVAN
Sings the Music of Burton Lane
Musical Direction and Arrangements by Keith Ingham

*Maxine Sullivan*

# Singing Stars from Broadway

Everyone loves a mystery and here's one for you. Anyone's list of the musical theater stars with the best voices would have to include Ethel Merman, Julie Andrews, Mary Martin, John Raitt, Richard Kiley, Barbara Cook, and Alfred Drake. So, why didn't any of these greats have extensive recording careers during their heyday on Broadway? All while we're pondering the cosmos, why didn't the greatest recording stars—Peggy Lee, Judy Garland, Ella Fitzgerald, etc.—ever appear in book musicals on Broadway? Lena Horne appeared in one, *Jamaica,* but that's about it.

The answer, we suppose, is that the stage and the microphone require different talents. Voice alone does not make the star, whether on stage or on record. The Broadway performer is an actor first and a singer second, and many a magnificent singer has failed to cut it on Broadway, for lack of stage presence or a sense of theatrical timing. The stage performer must collaborate with the director, arranger, conductor, and cast, working to play a part within an artistic whole. Conversely, the recording star must be first and foremost a musician, and the interpretation follows.

It is interesting that, all through the heyday of popular song, while the greats of the stage were usually the first to put their stamp on a number, their original-cast recordings rarely achieved success on the singles charts. Rather, it tended to be a cover version (or more than one) that made the grade with the public and turned a good song into a standard.

Nonetheless, it is worth mentioning a few of the greatest singers in musical theater history, some well known today, others not. These were the theatrical performers who broke through and put an indelible stamp on the great songs they introduced. They are justly remembered by musical theater aficionados, not just as actors but as peerless interpreters of the musical theater repertoire. ◆

**ABOVE:** Julie Andrews was the sophisticated lass from England. She first made a splash in *The Boy Friend* and then surprised everybody, including herself, with her brilliant portrayal of Eliza Doolittle in Alan Jay Lerner and Frederick Loewe's *My Fair Lady.* Here, she sings one of the show's standards, "Wouldn't It Be Loverly?" Others that she sang in this show included "The Rain in Spain" and "I Could Have Danced All Night." She next starred in Lerner and Loewe's *Camelot,* which included "If Ever I Would Leave You" among the hits in its brilliant score. **TOP:** Kaye Ballard utilized her clarion voice to great comic effect, most notably here, in *Carnival!* The Bob Merrill score gave us "Love Makes the World Go 'Round." Ballard introduced a future standard, "Lazy Afternoon," in the unjustly neglected *The Golden Apple*, with a score by John Latouche and Jerome Moross.

## First Person

Ira Gershwin: Merman had a no-nonsense voice that could reach not only standees but ticket-takers in the lobby.

Jule Styne: I came up to coach Merman in *Red, Hot and Blue*. She had taken out two songs and Cole Porter had argued with her. He said to me, "Do you know Merman?" I said no. He said, "You haven't missed anything." I taught her the song ["It's De-lovely"] on the road.

## Asides

Frank Loesser always demanded that his singers project to the back of the last row of the top balcony. "Sing louder!" was his mantra. He knew that paying customers wanted to hear the actors on-stage and deserved to. During rehearsals of *Guys and Dolls* he would walk up the aisle to the back of the house while the cast was singing. Once he actually opened the lobby doors and walked out through them, then opened the doors to the street. He could still hear the cast belting out the song. He then went to an ice-cream store and bought a cone and walked to his hotel. All the while, the cast kept singing at the top of their lungs. It's not clear at what point he moved out of earshot.

**ABOVE:** John Raitt, seen here with his *Pajama Game* costar Janis Paige, possessed one of Broadway's finest voices. He exhibited the perfect blend of machismo and insecurity as Billy Bigelow in Rodgers and Hammerstein's *Carousel*. In *The Pajama Game* he introduced "Hey There."

**LEFT:** Ethel Merman's name was synonymous with Broadway. She introduced more standards than any other Broadway performer, save, perhaps, Al Jolson. Merman introduced such great songs as George and Ira Gershwin's "I Got Rhythm," De Sylva, Brown, and Henderson's "Life Is Just a Bowl of Cherries," De Sylva, Richard A. Whiting, and Brown's "Eadie Was a Lady," and Jule Styne and Stephen Sondheim's "Everything's Coming Up Roses" and "Together." She also launched a slew of standards by Cole Porter, including "Anything Goes," "You're the Top," "I Get a Kick Out of You," "It's De-Lovely," "Ridin' High," and "Friendship." She put her stamp on nearly as many songs by Irving Berlin including, "They Say It's Wonderful," "I Got the Sun in the Morning," "There's No Business Like Show Business," and "You're Just in Love." She even pulled hits out of her few flop shows: here she is in *Happy Hunting*, which brought forth "Mutual Admiration Society" by Matt Dubey and Harold Karr.

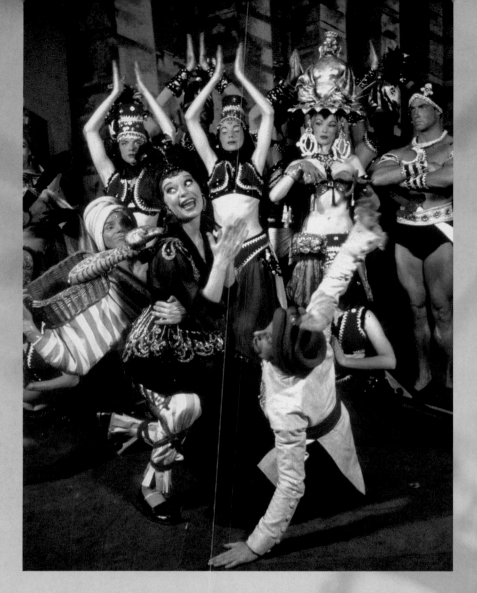

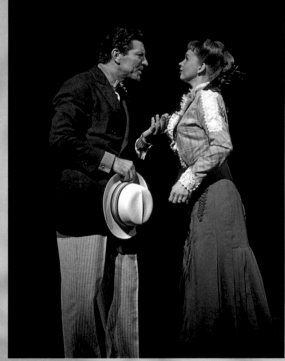

**LEFT:** Robert Preston and Barbara Cook discover that opposites attract in Meredith Willson's classic musical, *The Music Man*. With "Till There Was You," "Seventy-six Trombones," "Trouble," "My White Knight," and "Lida Rose," *The Music Man* boasts one of Broadway's finest scores. Preston teamed with Mary Martin in Tom Jones and Harvey Schmidt's *I Do! I Do!* and with Bernadette Peters in Jerry Herman's troubled *Mack and Mabel*—a great score married to an impossible libretto.

**RIGHT:** Richard Kiley and Diahann Carroll starred in Richard Rodgers's first foray into lyric writing, *No Strings*. "The Sweetest Sounds" was the hit of the score. Carroll had made an auspicious debut in the Harold Arlen and Truman Capote flop, *House of Flowers*, which did have an extraordinary score, nonetheless. Kiley was one of Broadway's finest singers and actors, a rare combination. He made a success in *Kismet*, *Redhead*, and, most notably, *Man of La Mancha*.

**ABOVE:** Susan Johnson (left) was the very definition of a belter, a good strong voice that could handle upbeat numbers as well as ballads. Johnson appeared in only one hit, *The Most Happy Fella*, but her voice was among Broadway's greatest. Here she is with Abbe Lane in *Oh, Captain*.

**FAR LEFT:** Liza Minnelli was a true Broadway star who mirrored her mother's vulnerability, feistiness, and joy of living. Here, she makes her Broadway debut in John Kander and Fred Ebb's *Flora, the Red Menace* **LEFT:** Elizabeth Allen and Sergio Franchi make a perfectly charming couple in Richard Rodgers and Stephen Sondheim's *Do I Hear a Waltz?* Franchi possessed an impressively versatile voice and acting chops, to boot, making him that rare recording star who made a successful transition to Broadway. **BELOW:** Vivian Blaine hoofs it with the girls in *Say, Darling.* She made her biggest Broadway splash as Miss Adelaide in *Guys and Dolls.* A character voice is just as important as a beautiful soprano, and it's perhaps even rarer. Blaine used hers with intelligence and, more important, restraint, placing her in a category with fellow character greats Judy Holliday, Shirley Booth, Fanny Brice, and Gwen Verdon.

# Bobby Short

Bobby Short's life was built on a contradiction: he was a man who so believed in himself that nothing stood in the way of his greatest invention—himself. Born in Danville, Illinois, a hick town in the middle of nowhere, he became the ultimate symbol of sophistication in New York, the most sophisticated city in the world. He was a black man who eschewed blues and soul in favor of the songs of the great songwriters; a cabaret artist who was a master jazz arranger; a fine jazz pianist who put the lyrics on an equal plane with the music; and his career gained momentum just when others were sliding into obscurity under the onslaught of rock-and-roll.

The ninth in a family of ten children (of which only six survived into adulthood), Short was a child prodigy, performing professionally by the age of nine. Two years later, a couple of booking agents put him in a white tie and tails and advertised him as "the miniature king of swing."

Some folks resented the youngster. "Back then," Short recalled, "it never once occurred to me what the problem was, though it was pointed out to me much later on: here I was, a young black boy at the piano, who had the audacity to wear evening clothes and sing Cole Porter and Rodgers and Hart. I never thought there was anything wrong with that, but it must have bothered a lot of people."

At age twelve, he left home and soon arrived in the Big Apple. New York and Bobby Short seemed to be waiting for each other to be complete. Still, he returned home to finish high school and afterward began touring, a journey upon which he met the performers who would serve as his real teachers. In Omaha, he heard Nat King Cole and learned new ways to play piano,

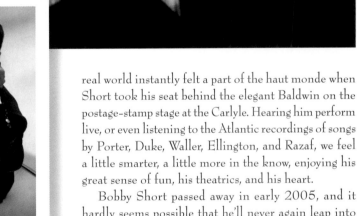

sing, and present himself with style and dignity. He learned more piano technique from Art Tatum on a gig in Milwaukee, and in St. Louis, he learned about performance from the "Incomparable Hildegarde." "She had the slickest nightclub act of all time," recalled Short, "produced down to the last sigh. Even down to a blue spotlight that brought out the color in the red roses that invariably stood by her piano."

Hildegarde wasn't the only woman who influenced Short's life and performing style. Torch singer Helen Morgan, jazz documentarian Jean Bach, pianist/singer Barbara Carroll, fashion doyenne Jean Muir, and, most of all, Mabel Mercer each did their bit to shape the young man into an expert performer. Mercer, a fellow toiler in the fields of the obscure, taught Short the art of understatement, of acting, of composure. When she died in 1984, Short was heartbroken: "Half of the legacy is gone. I don't know if I can carry the whole burden alone. These shoulders are elegant, but very narrow."

Short did survive, and for thirty-five years he held court at the Carlyle Hotel, creating a world that thousands were happy to be a part of, if only for an evening. "Supper club life, if you're a protagonist in it as I seem to be, well, there's nothing can replace it. While all the rest of the world is going to hell, there it is, a reserved, quiet, enchanted corner of existence with civilized people sipping lyrics and wine." Even those who weren't particularly sophisticated in the

real world instantly felt a part of the haut monde when Short took his seat behind the elegant Baldwin on the postage-stamp stage at the Carlyle. Hearing him perform live, or even listening to the Atlantic recordings of songs by Porter, Duke, Waller, Ellington, and Razaf, we feel a little smarter, a little more in the know, enjoying his great sense of fun, his theatrics, and his heart.

Bobby Short passed away in early 2005, and it hardly seems possible that he'll never again leap into his seat at the big piano in the glamorous little supper club on Madison Avenue. ◆

## Song and Story

### BYE BYE BLACKBIRD

Nesuhi Ertegun of Atlantic Records: I'll never forget when he did "Bye Bye Blackbird." I think we did only one take. It was so perfect, so right, although it was a totally new approach to this standard. Bobby chose a much slower tempo than usual and he imbued the song with melancholy and despair. When he finished, I was speechless. It was a triumph, one of the greatest moments of music I had ever heard.

Jeri Southern became a singer out of sheer practicality: she knew that she could earn more money singing than she could as simply a pianist. However, she suffered through the repertoire choices of a variety of A&R men, and made no bones about her reluctance to sing for her supper. At the same time, her detached quality and refusal to be the perky girl singer set her apart from her contemporaries and gave an edge to her singing.

Southern was born on August 5, 1926, in Royal, Nebraska. She attended Notre Dame University, where she studied classical piano—but her evenings were spent listening to the stars of jazz and pop on radio and recordings. She soon gave up her classical aspirations and set her sights on a career playing jazz piano.

In 1943, she began playing in night spots around Omaha, including a gig in 1944 at the Blackstone Hotel. After a stint touring with a navy recruiting show, she started singing while she played, apparently at the urging of her agent. She moved to Chicago and in 1949 landed a gig at the Hi Note Club, where she accompanied Anita O'Day, Carmen McRae, and Edie Adams, among other jazz greats and not-so-greats. In 1950, she became a regular on local television's *Marty Stevens Show*.

Monte Kay, the booker at New York's legendary Birdland, offered Southern $150 a week to play intermissions at the club, and the move was a smart one. She met a bevy of great singers who played the club, and attracted the attention of Decca Records. In 1950, she signed with Decca and enjoyed her first hit song, "You Better Go Now" (given to her by Billie Holiday), the following year. In 1954, Southern scored hits with "Joey" and "When I Fall in Love," and in 1957, she scored another with the title tune from the film *Fire Down Below*, which she sang on the soundtrack. In fact,

most of the Decca years were marked by an above-average repertoire reflecting Southern's intelligence and good taste.

In the late fifties, she moved to Capitol Records, and in 1959 her album, *Jeri Southern Sings Cole Porter*, featuring Billy May arrangements, became a best seller. She then moved to Roulette Records, but she was clearly losing interest in performing. Southern began missing performances and openly expressed her restlessness. She moved to Los Angeles in the early 1960s, and in 1962 gave up her career as a performer, preferring to work behind the scenes as a vocal and piano coach for

Steve Allen, Charlie Cochran, Jack Lemmon, and others. Throughout this period, she worked and lived with composer Hugo Friedhofer.

In addition to writing the occasional song, in 1972 Southern wrote a book, *Interpreting Popular Music at the Keyboard*. She appeared once more on stage, in 1991, at the Vine Street Bar and Grill. It was Anita O'Day who convinced her to take the stage and perform a medley of Jerome Kern songs. She died later that year, on August 4, 1991. ◆

## *Aside*

Jeri Southern was most influenced by Frank Sinatra. She was especially drawn to the way he "considered a lyric above all, with a sensitivity to the individual words, phrases, and the total song."

# Jo Stafford

In a hard-to-believe story that made the rounds for years, it was said that inmates in mental institutions couldn't listen to Jo Stafford recordings because her lack of vibrato sent them into fits. Like we said, improbable. But the fact remains that Stafford, who got her start with the Pied Pipers, remained a group singer even when she wasn't surrounded by a group. Very straight-ahead, very exacting in her pitch and intonation—but removed from the meaning of the songs. She comments, "What attracts me to a song is the harmonic structure. I'm a big fan of chords and bass notes. The lyrics have something to do with it too. There's some words that are unsingable. I like the idea of the lyrics being singable."

Stafford's excellent sense of music, as precise as one could be without having perfect pitch, and the smoky quality of her voice were a perfect match for the creamy ballads of her heyday in the 1940s and '50s. On her *Jo + Jazz* album she proved she could hold her own with hot jazz musicians, not just the lush, thick string arrangements of her husband, Paul Weston. Yet Stafford crossed the line from light swinging to easy listening, a road her husband traveled to its dead end. She had her integrity, refusing to sing songs she wasn't interested in (especially in the Columbia/Mitch Miller years) because, as she said, "I'm not very good at hiding the fact that I don't like what I'm singing. It shows, somehow."

Stafford began her career right after high school. She told Michael Feinstein about her early years breaking into the business: "We all took piano lessons, my mother insisted on it. I guess I was the one that was most interested in it, and that's when I learned to read music. My two older sisters, Chris and Pauline, were already in radio when I was still in school. They had moved up to Hollywood by the time I graduated from high school, which my mother insisted upon. I graduated on Friday afternoon, and I was up with them by Monday and started singing with them, which made it a lot easier. They had already knocked on the doors. I just joined them, and we worked a lot in town on radio and a lot of background music in movies. I had a vacation over the weekend, and then I was a working girl.

"My first coast-to-coast show was *California Melodies*; David Broekman was the conductor. He was a real hard conductor, but I learned a lot from him. We had our own little fifteen-minute show on KHJ when they were still downtown in LA, three days a week. I'll never forget, there was a big cattle call audition at KHJ and this man came out and said, 'Any act here have their own accompaniment?' And my sister Chris said, 'We do!' and I almost fainted because I was the piano player and I had no idea of playing the piano except just to rehearse us. We ended up with our own fifteen-minute show, with me pounding away at the piano very badly. I was too busy to be frightened, both singing and playing at the same time."

The Staffords also provided background vocals for several movies, including *Alexander's Ragtime Band,* and in *Damsel in Distress,* dubbing the on screen singers of "Nice Work If You Can Get It."

After joining the Pied Pipers (see Vocal Groups for Stafford's reminiscences of those days), they joined the Tommy Dorsey orchestra. Stafford continues, "I did some solo singing with Dorsey. After we left Tom that's when we started working with Johnny Mercer. Mercer had been a fan of the band and had told us, 'If you ever leave Tommy please get in touch with me, because I'm starting a record company.' When we first went with Capitol it was basically the Pied Pipers, but John Mercer was a good fan of mine. He recorded me solo for the first time and I stayed with the Pipers until we finally were doing a radio show five nights a week and I couldn't do both—sing the lead with the Pipers and do solo work too. I guess it was 1944."

Dubbed "GI Jo" by servicemen, Stafford was "the voice of home." She had a distinguished and popular career in the 1940s and '50s, selling more recordings than any other female artist (a claim shared with Joni James and Patti Page). Among her greatest hits were, "Embraceable You," "The Night We Called It a Day," "Long Ago and Far Away," "It Could Happen to You," "No Other Love," "Some Enchanted Evening," "Star Dust," "Jambalaya," and her biggest hit, "You Belong to Me."

With her husband, Paul Weston, Stafford continued her career through the mid-1960s, with a brief mini-career as the incomparable Darlene Edwards who, with her husband Jonathan, were a smash comedic hit on Columbia recordings. Stafford then decided to curtail her career to raise her family. "When I think of my life, I think I'm probably one of the luckiest people to come down the pike. To spend your life doing what you like, boy, it's a gift and I appreciate it [to] no end. I had a great life." ❖

## First Person

Jo Stafford on meeting her husband and collaborator, Paul Weston: We knew each other since the year one and about twenty years later, it's like, hey, I think there's a boy there. Really, we'd known each other since 1938 when we first met, going back to that afternoon at Paul and Axel's house. I went to NY in 1944 to do my first nightclub which was the Martinique. Paul came back for that. We were very good friends and had been for a very long time. On opening night, he came to the nightclub and after the last show, my sisters and Paul and I went back to our hotel to relax and have some coffee. My sisters were over in one corner talking away, and Paul and I suddenly found each other kissing like mad on the other side of the room. And that was the beginning. It was like out of the blue. It was like wow! It was great, it was very romantic. I liked it. It's like we discovered each other all of a sudden. Paul and I had our song, which is "All the Things You Are," the epitome of the American pop song.

Jo Stafford reminisces about the beginnings of Jonathan and Darlene Edwards: Paul for years had a special chorus of "Star Dust" which was Jonathan—it was awful. It was just pitiful. When some Columbia executives went to a record convention in Key West, they went to this little bar after the meetings were finished and there was a cocktail pianist there who, as Paul says, "What more could you ask for from a pianist playing in Key West?" He was pretty much Jonathan. After he left and went home for the evening, Paul got up and played "Star Dust" and a couple of the guys from Columbia said, "You've got to record that!" Paul thought they were joking. They said, "You should do an album." So he started thinking about it and he thought, "I cannot do an album all by myself like this." So that's when he enlisted me. I

had never done Darlene, I had done Cinderella D. Stump. So we kind of got a kind of mental picture of Jonathan and Darlene and we even found out where they came from and where they lived. And I got the idea for the name Darlene, which I thought fit the character beautifully. So we went from there and made the album. And we wound up making five albums of these two people, nice people.

Jo Stafford remembers Matt Dennis: I introduced Matt Dennis to Tommy Dorsey. At that time Tommy had this music publishing firm and we were coming for one of our first trips out to California since we joined the band. And I told Tom, "I know a couple of guys who write tremendous songs and I wish you'd listen to them." And he said, "Sure." So we had a record date. I called Matt and Tom Adair and said, "Come down and sing some of your stuff for Tommy Dorsey." And Tom hired them after one song and they were part of his organization for several years. I was a big fan of Matt's even before I was with Dorsey. I don't know if he ever knew how good he was.

The first solo record I ever made was a Matt Dennis song, "The Little Man with a Candy Cigar." That was my favorite, and it was the only time I went to Tom and said, "I've never done this before in my life and I'll probably never do it again but if you record that song, could I please do it?" Because I wasn't a solo singer in the band at that time. And he said, "sure," and he let me have it.

**OPPOSITE PAGE:** Paul Weston directs Jo and the orchestra.
**TOP:** Jo and Peggy Lee.
**LEFT:** Jo Stafford with the original Pied Pipers. Heads would soon roll!

# Barbra Streisand

Barbra Streisand came out of the small Greenwich Village clubs fully formed, bursting upon the worlds of Broadway, Hollywood, television, and recordings in a totally unique, sometimes controversial, way. She first achieved fame in the 1960s, just when a previous generation of singers and songwriters found their careers on the wane—an anomaly in the era of rock-and-roll, folk music, the British invasion, and the first stirrings of world music. There was something about Streisand's voice, her approach to a song, her power and intensity, her quirky personality, her striking looks—even the spelling of her first name—that made the jaded and uninitiated alike take notice and embrace her as nothing less than the future of American popular song. This one impossible-to-categorize singer seemed to embody a respect for the past, a contemporary sensibility, and a hope for the future that would safeguard traditional music in the new era.

Controversy has dogged her from the beginning. When she was playing her first starring role on Broadway, Fanny Brice in *Funny Girl*, rumors began swirling about her outrageous behavior offstage. If she stood up for what

**"Barbra Streisand is nine-teen, was born in Mada-gascar and reared in Rangoon."** —opening lines of Streisand's first *Playbill* biography

she believed in, she was labeled a perfectionist and micromanager. If she disagreed with a director, she was a bitch. If she wanted privacy, she was a prima donna. Everything about her seemed somehow larger than life—her ego as well as her talent.

But, if sometimes Streisand seemed out of control she most certainly wasn't—she was shrewd and street smart, and could handle the controversy surrounding her with aplomb. When greeted with criticism, she could joke her way around it, slipping into the role of nice little awkward Jewish girl from Brooklyn. When it was called for, she could be elegant and sophisticated. She could also be tough and demanding—but she was seldom mean or irresponsible. Only later in her career did she begin to live up to the personal criticism of her detractors, but by that time she had become an institution.

Streisand has the intensity of Lena Horne but without Horne's kinetic energy. One has always gotten the feeling that emotions burst forth from Horne—but Streisand's lyrical voice and emotions flow out of her naturally. Audiences are often overwhelmed by the ease and joy of her singing, even when she delivers a torch song. She has few mannerisms that get in the way of the music, unlike many artists who stretch and bend a song to fit their talents. Streisand's facility at switching from ballads to novelty numbers is uncanny and leaves the audience slightly off balance, building suspense about what might be coming next on the bill or the record. It's like riding a roller coaster blindfolded. You don't know where the hills and curves are but you know you're safe taking the journey.

From her earliest days Streisand developed a rabid coterie of fans who hung on her every release, col-lected photos, memorabilia, programs, screenplays, and other ephemera. Yet, even as her career progressed brilliantly, Streisand pulled a moderate Garbo, all but disappearing from the screen and recording studio for awhile—which only made her fans need her and want her more. She had begun her career at such a high level artistically that—perfectionist that she is—perhaps she found the thought of living up to it crushing. But the truth is, her fans have continued to love her no matter what her output.

She even had the nerve to desert the American popular song catalog and change her image, singing light rock and new pop ballads with the same inten-sity that she'd brought to standards in her glory days. Stars with long careers, such as Crosby, Sinatra, and Peggy Lee, also moved away from the microphone into

film and television with great success. But Crosby and Sinatra stayed within the somewhat strict confines of the popular song until very late in their careers—and they never really managed to pull off the transition to Beatles songs. Lee did venture successfully into a num-ber of different genres, but still, you'd never characterize her as a rock star. Streisand was most successful at this, switching successfully from film roles to contemporary pop recordings and back again. Her pop hits have in-cluded everything from duets with the Bee Gees' Barry Gibb to ballads by Paul Williams. Her films have run the gamut from slapstick comedies like *What's Up Doc?* and *Meet the Fockers* to traditional musicals like *Funny Lady* and modern ones like *A Star Is Born* and *Yentl*. She's made her share of great soap (*The Way We Were*) and terrible suds (*The Mirror Has Two Faces*), along the way remaining somehow unscathed by mixed reviews and the ups and downs of the box office.

The films she's directed, including *Yentl* and *The Mirror Has Two Faces*, have fared indifferently at the box office and with reviewers. Still, Streisand is admired as a female director in a male-dominated medium, and her films certainly reflect her perfectionism. In fact, a little looseness and spontaneity might serve her pictures well. She chooses scripts with a distinctive point of view and a compelling reason to be made; for that she should be commended.

Beneath Streisand's self-confident exterior is a shy, sensitive person who covers up her insecurities with a brusque, sometimes imperious facade. In this way she resembles Judy Garland, another great singer who ap-proached her work with intelligence and gut instinct. Where Garland could trade on her vulnerability, Strei-sand has used her quirkiness as a big part of her act, both on and off the stage. Streisand has always wanted it both ways, to be a glamorous torch singer as well as a screwball comedian, and she has succeeded.

It's telling that she wanted to be an actress before she took up singing. She learned to interpret songs rather than just sing the notes and rely on her remarkable instrument to carry her along. Streisand always knows what she's singing about and creates a persona to put it

Isn't this the height of nonchalance? Barbra Streisand and Sydney Chaplin in *Funny Girl*.

across. While others rely on their beautiful voices but have little clue as to the lyrics, Streisand ingests a song and lets it out as an integral part of her personality. So, if she picks her material well, she can sing brilliantly.

In recent decades, her rare concerts are treated like worldwide events—but performing has become secondary to Streisand's political activism. She has been an outspoken proponent of liberal causes and candidates, human rights issues, AIDS, and the environment. She started the Barbra Streisand Foundation, which has given away millions, and has hosted numerous political fund-raisers.

Streisand has always been a lightning rod, and she deserves much of the acclaim as well as the brickbats that have been thrown her way. She's a complex artist—smart, talented, and unconventional. Throughout her long career she's been more demanding of herself than of others, constantly attempting to expand her horizons personally and artistically. Everything everyone says about her has a grain of truth and a bit of hyperbole, and that's part of what makes Barbra Barbra. ◆

## Song and Story

### FUNNY GIRL

After *Hello, Dolly!* people thought every show needed a hit title song. Producers wouldn't open the Jones and Schmidt show *110 in the Shade* in England unless there was a title song. The first version of the song "Funny Girl" was written to be sung on roller skates, but this proved too dangerous to stage. When they cut the skating, they also cut the number. Styne and Merrill then wrote a second version, then a third one for the movie, hoping finally to pull off a hit title song and grab an Oscar. It was nominated—but alas, lost out to Michel Legrand's "The Windmills of Your Mind."

### LOVER COME BACK TO ME

Barbra Streisand: When I was a kid I had this wonderful bathrobe. I always used to love to come home from school and read movie magazines and listen to the radio or watch TV wearing this bathrobe. One day I came home from a terrible day at school, and like Linus' blanket, I couldn't wait till I got into that bathrobe. I looked around and I couldn't find it. My mother came home from work and I said, "Where's the bathrobe?" She said, "Oh, I took it to the thrift shop." Now, every time I sing that song, I think of that bathrobe.

## Asides

Streisand got hit recordings out of shows that ran a week or less. Columbia was one of the investors in *The Yearling* (which ran only three performances) and arranged for Streisand to record five of its songs, "The Kind of Man a Woman Needs," "My Pa," "I'm All Smiles," "Why Did I Choose You," and a single, "My Love." The writers, Michael Leonard and Herbert Martin, lived for many years

on the royalties from those songs. Streisand also got a share of the publishing revenue.

When her then husband, Elliott Gould, was starring in the show *Drat! The Cat!*, Streisand recorded the Ira Levin and Milton Schafer songs "I Like Him" for a single, and "He Touched Me" on an album. It says something about her power and her success that the latter song became a big hit.

Her singing of a series of Harold Arlen songs on her albums introduced a whole generation to such Arlen songs as "A Sleepin' Bee" and "Down with Love." She later guested on a Columbia album, *Harold Sings Arlen with Friend*.

When Streisand returned to New York in 1967 to perform a concert in Central Park, she didn't know that *Funny Girl* was still running on Broadway. She assumed the show had closed after she left.

## First Person

Jule Styne: Streisand was a terrible yenta when I first met her. She used to want to talk to the audience. I said, "I'm bringing some people down, don't open your mouth, just sing." Barbra's a one-of-a-kinder. She makes a sound, it's her sound. There's a lot of people who want to phrase like her. The sound goes with the phrasing. You have to have your own identification, your own sound. It's an amazing thing, her concept of singing. She sings the words all the time, she's a great word singer. I wrote *Funny Girl* for Anne Bancroft. She didn't do it so we went out and Barbra did it. She didn't want to sing "Don't Rain on My Parade." I said, "Listen, let her quit, the score is set." I told Robbins, he said, "Oh, don't listen to her." Robbins used to say, "She better get an acting coach and learn how to act. She doesn't know anything about it."

# Dakota Staton

The amazing thing about the careers of the greats like Peggy Lee, Frank Sinatra, Bing Crosby, and their ilk isn't their vocal accomplishments. The miracle is that they remained at the top of their game for such a long period. Many a fine singer has had his or her day in the sun, only to fade from public acceptance after a decade or so. Some singers, like Maxine Sullivan, retired to take care of families. Some got married and left the business. Some changed styles and the public decided not to go along for the ride. The best singers kept their basic personae intact even as they experimented with new forms.

Dakota Staton performed until recently but she left her fame behind. Most often compared to Dinah Washington (an early influence), Staton enjoyed a nice, slow climb to fame during which she honed her chops and found her voice. She began performing at Pittsburgh's Filion School of Music. Joe Wespray, a leading bandleader in Pittsburgh, hired her to sing with the band for a couple of years. She subsequently played show rooms from Detroit to Toronto.

It was while she was singing at the Harlem club known as the Baby Grand that the Apollo Theater's Willie Bryant brought her to the attention of Dave Cavenaugh, one of Capitol Records' top producers. Back then, record companies knew how to protect and market the singers on their roster. She sang on a few singles before Capitol was ready to launch her on LP. Cavenaugh played to Staton's strengths, pairing her with Jonah Jones on her first album, *The Late, Late Show*, in 1957. The title tune would become her biggest hit. Later that year Capitol put her together with the George Shearing Quintet (they made sure she hitched her wagon to an established star) for the album, *In the Night*. The late fifties were the tail end of the glory days of the female jazz singer, as rock-and-roll began to capture the public's imagination. Only Peggy Lee, Dinah Shore, and a few other female singers would successfully stay in place at the top of the charts into the sixties. When Staton's sales slumped, she decamped to where jazz was still king, Europe, not returning to America until the 1970s. Staton hopped from label to label and still performed, albeit in a less mainstream style, exploring R & B along with a smattering of soul and gospel.

As good a singer as she is, she never really found her own unique identity. Her style remained too close to that of Dinah Washington. When Staton tried to branch out, audiences wouldn't go along with her, preferring to hear her sing jazz rather than R & B. ◆

Sylvia Syms, like Mabel Mercer, is considered to have been a singer's singer. Both were known for their precise phrasing and attention to lyrics. Both were adored by their more famous brethren, especially Frank Sinatra. And Syms enjoyed a most remarkable career marked by ups, downs, and unusual alliances.

In 1951, she joined pianist/singer Barbara Carroll on a terrific record for Atlantic. Syms and Carroll started the recording session at three in the morning, after their regular gigs were over. The piano was out of tune and a tuner had to be dragged out of bed and brought down to the studio. But after that initial glitch, the session went swimmingly and the whole record was finished in that one session.

Syms was good friends with both Frank Sinatra and Billie Holiday. One evening, Sinatra and Syms went backstage to visit Holiday. They found the singer distraught over having just burned her hair with a curling iron. Syms rushed down to the hatcheck girl and bought a gardenia for Holiday to wear, to cover up the burned spot—and thus an indelible trademark was born.

Mae West spotted Syms singing at the Cinderella Club in Greenwich Village and cast her in a the 1949 Broadway revival of *Diamond Lil*, which marked the beginning of her acting career. She returned to Broadway in the mega-flop *Whoop-Up* in 1958, followed in 1961 by *13 Daughters* (a Hawaiian musical!), another huge failure without even the camp factor that makes a flop worth loving. In 1970, Syms played a supporting role in Tennessee Williams's *Camino Real* at the Repertory Theatre of Lincoln Center.

Syms's life was marked by interesting associations. Her husband at one time was Brett Morrison, the voice of radio's Lamont Cranston, "The Shadow." Their houseboy for a time was Marlon Brando.

She managed only one big hit record: "I Could Have Danced All Night" in 1956. It turned out to be the best-selling version ever of that tune—yet Syms never repeated the success. After two albums, she went to Columbia and made some uninspired 45s and one album. Then she let go of her dream of pop stardom to concentrate on saloon singing.

Frank Sinatra dubbed her "Buddha" because of her short, squat physique. He also called her "the best saloon singer in the world." Syms even went out with a flourish, dropping dead of a heart attack while performing a tribute to Sinatra in the Oak Room of the Algonquin Hotel in New York.

A huge hit song, a strategic fashion choice for Billie Holiday, adoration by Sinatra, a houseboy named Marlon Brando, a legendary Broadway flop, talent forever, and topping it all off, sudden death in the middle of a number at the most prestigious club in New York. What a life! ◆

# Sylvia Syms

and gets pregnant. Naturally, the boss won't answer her phone calls. Hence the lyric, "Mr. Siegel, please make it legal." Racy but witty. Bette Midler performs explicitly sexual (call them dirty) jokes in her act that she claims are Sophie Tucker's—but Tucker never resorted to such crass material, nor could she have gotten away with it. Tucker returned from a 1925 engagement in Berlin wearing pants. It was shocking at the time but pants for women soon caught on, in part due to Tucker.

Ted Shapiro was Tucker's accompanist for decades and, when Tucker died, she left him $50,000. She also left a good deal of her estate to the black maid who had traveled with her throughout her career..

Tucker enjoyed a long career in vaudeville, on radio, and on television, and she made eight films. In the 1950s, she signed with Mercury Records and made a series of hit albums. She never stopped working, and only a few months before her death from lung cancer in 1966, she completed an engagement at the Latin Quarter nightclub. ◆

## Song and Story

### SOME OF THESE DAYS

In 1910, Sophie Tucker was appearing at the White City Park in Chicago when an unknown black songwriter, Shelton Brooks, approached her. She didn't want to meet with him but her maid, Mollie Elkins, convinced her to give the guy a break. As Tucker remembers, "The minute I heard 'Some of These Days,' I could have kicked myself for almost losing it.... It had everything. Hasn't it proved it? I've been singing it for thirty years, made it my theme. I've turned it inside out, singing it every way imaginable, as a dramatic song, as a novelty number, as a sentimental ballad, and always audiences have loved it and asked for it."

### MY YIDDISCHE MAMA

Jack Yellen: On an impulse, I called up Sophie Tucker at the Claridge Hotel in New York. She bawled me out for spoiling her sleeping pill, but she listened, and when I finished singing, she was weeping. Between gulps, she asked me to send her a copy. She wrote me that her agents and friends suggested the title be changed to "Jewish'"or "Hebrew Mama'" being afraid of the word "Yiddish." I told her that if she sang it, it would be 'Yiddische Mama' or nothing at all; and what is more, I insisted that she sing the chorus in Yiddish, the way I had written it.

## Sophie Tucker

The Last of the Red-Hot Mamas and the First Lady of Show Business, Sophie Tucker was an aggressive, hilarious, self-assured singer/comedienne who was fat and proud of it. She made fun of her weight and was delightfully open about her interest in sex, in such songs as "He Hadn't Up Till Yesterday, But I Bet He Will Tonight," "I May Be Getting Older Every Day, But Getting Younger Every Night," "Nobody Loves a Fat Girl," and "You've Got to See Mama Every Night." Tucker claimed, "I've never sung a single song in my whole life on purpose to shock anyone. My 'hot numbers' are all, if you will notice, written about something that is real in the lives of millions of people."

Tucker was born Sonia Kalish in 1884 in Russia. The family immigrated to Hartford, Connecticut. She married Louis Tuck, a beer wagon driver, in 1903. One day, Willie and Eugene Howard walked in. Sophie sang some songs for them and they suggested she should be on the stage. In 1906, she showed up in New York having divorced her husband and left her son with her parents. The Howard brothers told her they had been kidding.

She found work at the German Village Club, where she made $15 a week singing and holding the "bank" for the prostitutes that worked the restaurant. She sang in such clubs as Kid McCoy's Saloon, Kelly's, and Nigger Mike's, where Irving Berlin got his start as a singing waiter. Berlin taught her the value of lyrics. She went into burlesque and then vaudeville.

Tucker performed in blackface, because manager Chris Brown told her she had a funny face, and she should hide it. When she played the Boston Atheneum in 1907, her makeup kit didn't arrive with the rest of her luggage. She went on stage and told the audience, "You all can see I'm a white girl. Well, I'll tell you something more: I'm not Southern. I'm a Jewish girl, and I just learned this Southern accent doing a blackface act for two years. And now, Mr. leader, please play my song." She sang "That Lovin' Rag" to thunderous applause. She exclaimed as she came offstage, "I can hold an audience without it. I've got them eating out of my hand. I'm through with blackface. I'll never black up again."

Ziegfeld put her into the *Follies of 1910*. Jack Yellen gave her the famous nickname "Last of the Red-Hot Mamas" and was instrumental in forming her persona. He wrote most of Tucker's special material, usually in collaboration with Milton Ager. In 1910, she introduced what would become her most famous number, "Some of These Days."

She performed some pretty controversial songs, including "Mr. Siegel," the story of a girl who sleeps with her boss

# Mel Tormé

Mel Tormé was the Renaissance man of American popular song—singing was only one aspect of his amazing repertoire of talents. He had an acting career beginning at RKO (his first film, *Higher and Higher*, was also Sinatra's first); wrote fiction and nonfiction books, countless articles, and television scripts; arranged his own music; wrote songs including one of the top Christmas standards of all time, "The Christmas Song"; was an excellent drummer. Yet Tormé's reputation has suffered in comparison with such contemporaries as Sinatra and Tony Bennett.

This might be due in part to his ego, which is legendary, and to the apparent ease with which he went about his many accomplishments. As a singer, perhaps he's not as highly regarded as those other guys because, although he claimed that the lyric was 99 percent of a song, he never put across the meaning and emotional depth of a song the way they did. Make no mistake, Tormé was an excellent actor when he sang a song—but he didn't convey the vulnerability of Sinatra. (Sinatra's vulnerability was all the more effective given his cocksure persona most of the time.)

Tormé was certainly the jazziest of singers, and jazz calls for a discerning listener. It's hard to vacuum the floor or do the dishes with Tormé scatting in the background. His seemingly endless inventions and interpretations demand a little brainpower and concentration. Jazz can be emotional but it's also cerebral, and part of the fun of twisting tempi and melody is knowing the source and marveling at the invention. It's not quite the same experience as, say, listening to Andy Williams crooning "Moon River."

When Tormé took off from the printed page he wasn't, like many of his contemporaries in cool, just winging it, counting on his talent and subconscious to carry him along. He actually planned his "improvisations" up, around, in, and out of the printed score. His experience in writing and singing close, elaborate harmonies with the Meltones formed the foundation of his talent for musical embroidery. As he gained experience and confidence, he ventured further and further off the musical line, exploring the many ways that traditional popular song could be bent, molded, and expanded upon, both lyrically and musically.

Peggy Lee would become the closest equivalent to Tormé in his intellectual examination of every aspect of a piece of music. They both sat down and deconstructed a song before deciding what to change and, equally important, what to keep as written. Amazingly, no one has ever accused either Lee or Tormé of not respecting a songwriter's intentions. They both exhibited respect for the songs they sang, never considering their work an improvement on the original. Sometimes, popular singers change songs for the wrong reasons—for ego, for mistrust of the lyric or music, for ironic commentary on the original. Lee and Tormé wanted to enhance and expand the possibilities of the song, to bring out new aspects for the benefit of the listener. Their expansions on the music and lyrics paid homage to the songwriters' talents.

Tormé, like Lee, felt comfortable tackling all genres of music. They both attacked Latin rhythms, Lee with *Latin à la Lee* and Tormé with *Olé Tormé*. They didn't always swing—sometimes they even slowed ballads down. While Lee sang Chinese poetry on *Sea Shells*, Tormé ruminated on Gordon Jenkins' *California Suite*, a series of eleven non–32-bar songs examining Jenkins' home state. Where the two singers differed was that while Lee believed she needed a solid foundation of sound under her vocal, Tormé insisted that his voice become one with the backup. The careers of the two did overlap at times: Lee sat in on the *California Suite* album (under a pseudonym); they duetted in 1950 on "The Old Master Painter"; they cohosted a fifteen-minute, thrice-weekly television show, *TV's Top Tunes*, in 1951; and they appeared together in 1995, toward the end of their careers, at the Hollywood Bowl.

Tormé was a unique figure in the world of American popular song. No one understood songs better than he and nobody explored them as completely. He could sing anything with intelligence and daring, put together a medley that was like a brilliant crash course in popular music, and he could write a mean song, too. He wouldn't compromise his style or his repertoire—and for all of that, he isn't given his due today. Mel Tormé lived and performed his own way and left behind a recorded legacy that is unsurpassed in taste, class, and talent. ◆

# Sarah Vaughan

We've repeatedly noted in these pages how a parent's devotion to music could at one time spark an interest in a budding genius. Times have changed and today's singers don't get their starts sitting around the parlor piano or singing in the church choir. The Apollo Theater's amateur shows, long a springboard to fame, don't have the cachet or influence they once enjoyed.

Once bop had usurped traditional jazz singing, the lyric began to lose its centrality and vocalese ruled the day. The queen of the vocal singers (though she could act, too) was Sarah Vaughan. She bridged the gap between the old-style singing of Billie Holiday, who had been greatly influenced by the black church, and the new bop traditions.

Vaughan was born in Newark, New Jersey, on March 27, 1924. She grew up in a musical family (do these exist anymore?) with her father playing guitar and her mother singing in the church choir. Vaughan herself started off playing the organ and singing at the Mount Zion Baptist Church. She took piano lessons for eight years, beginning in 1931. It was clear from the start that she had a great vocal instrument as well as a strong will to succeed. Plus, she loved singing. All her life Vaughan suffered from nerves when she first took the stage, but once the music started she lost herself in her performance. She'd seldom talk to the audience and sometimes forgot lyrics, so thoroughly was she concentrating on the music.

Sarah Sings Soulfully

As a girl, Vaughan toured Newark with trumpeter Jabbo Smith, and at age fifteen he encouraged her to compete in the Apollo Theater Amateur Night contest. She won, impressing singer Billy Eckstine who was in the audience. Ella Fitzgerald was there also, and stopped Vaughan from signing with the agents hanging around backstage. Soon, she was working with Eckstine in the Earl Hines band. She took to life on the road and followed Eckstine, who had a big influence on her style during this period, when he formed his own big band. Vaughan mimicked Eckstine's silken-smooth stylings as well as his precise diction and emphasis on the middle and low range of his voice. She also adopted bop stylings, too, mirroring the experiments of Dizzy Gillespie and Charlie Parker, both players in Eckstine's band. It was at this time she made her first recordings, as there had been a recording ban during her years with the Hines ensemble.

Vaughan met her future husband and Svengali, George Treadwell, in 1945, while he was playing the trumpet at Barney Josephson's Café Society. Treadwell decided to take hold of her career and took $8,000 out of the bank to give her a makeover, both personally and professionally. They married in 1946 and divorced a decade later, at which point she married Clyde Atkins, a former professional football player. It was to be another ten-year hitch—they divorced in 1966. (She would endure a couple more marriages that closed out of town.) After a brief stint with John Kirby in the mid-forties, Vaughan went out on her own as a solo singer and hit pay dirt with her recording of the weirdly accented "Tenderly" in 1947.

Just as Louis Armstrong used his voice as a trumpet, Vaughan employed her two- to three-octave range as if playing a church organ, favoring its bass notes and modulations. She once said that she "always wanted to imitate the horns" of Gillespie and Parker. In her ◆

"Is that child singing or am I dreaming?"
—Earl Hines on hearing Vaughan sing for the first time

## THE GREAT SONGS

1944   Interlude (A Night in Tunesia)
1946   If You Could See Me Now
1947   Tenderly
1948   It's Magic
1950   Sassy
1954   All of Me; Make Yourself Comfortable
1955   C'est la Vie; Experience Unnecessary; How Important Can It Be?; Whatever Lola Wants
1956   The Banana Boat Song; Fabulous Character; It Happened Again; Hot and Cold Running Tears; Mr. Wonderful; The Other Woman
1957   Leave It to Love; Passing Strangers (with Billy Eckstine)
1958   Broken-Hearted Melody
1959   Separate Ways; Smooth Operator
1960   Eternally; Serenata; You're My Baby
1966   A Lover's Concerto
1973   Send in the Clowns

**In addition to her nickname "Sassy," Sarah Vaughan was sometimes called "the divine one."**

personal life she liked to shop and read comic books, "especially the weird kind that feature witches and vampires."

As Vaughan's career proceeded she gained confidence musically and expanded her skills, though she never got over her stage fright She became more adventurous in her improvisations, moving toward pop songs while becoming jazzier in her singing. Vaughan preferred to sing with a trio but occasionally fronted a symphony orchestra. She began to blur the lines between jazz and pop, her magnificent instrument conquering new ground as she gained the respect and admiration of her peers and influenced countless younger singers. Funnily enough, as she became more skilled, she became better known within jazz circles and her popular base started to erode, general audiences preferring the more accessible jazz of Ella Fitzgerald and her ilk. One reason

> **"He can count good, and he likes chili and so do I."**
> **—Vaughan explaining why she married George Treadwell**

for this was Vaughan's dearth of successful studio LPs, the exception being her two-LP Gershwin set. In the 1960s she became an out-and-out jazz singer.

As the decades wore on, Vaughan grew wilder and more daring in her flights of musical fancy, embroidering impressive if soulless riffs far removed from the composers' original intent. She replaced "Misty" as her theme song with Sondheim's "Send in the Clowns," and her rendition reflected the changes in her approach to music. Her performances of "Misty" had reflected her pop influences, while her "Clowns" was a wry and humorous observation of a life fully lived. Trust us, she didn't sing "Send in the Clowns" in any sort of a traditional manner.

"Sassy," as she was aptly dubbed early in her career, recorded with Continental Records in 1944 and 1945, then with Musicraft from 1946 to '48. Columbia grabbed her in 1949 and kept her until 1953, during which time she earned more than a million dollars a year. She then moved through a series of labels including Mercury, EmArcy, Roulette (1960–64), Mercury (1963–67), Mainstream (1971–74), and Pablo (1977–1982). One of her last recordings was the Columbia album of Rodgers and Hammerstein's *South Pacific*. She sang the part of Bloody Mary.

Vaughan never had to modify her singing due to the deterioration of her instrument; it remained clean and true to the end, though she employed it for more and more far-out purposes. Sarah Vaughan died on April 3, 1990. ◆

**OPPOSITE PAGE TOP:** Stan Kenton, Sarah Vaughan, and Nat King Cole.

# Dinah Washington

Here's a singer you wouldn't have wanted to meet in a dark alley—she could've whipped the tar out of you. Yet, as is so often the case, her brusque personality was a front for a mass of insecurities. Her lifelong battle with her weight was the main issue, and perhaps it accounted for her seven marriages—or was it nine? It was certainly the cause of her death.

If Lena Horne's signifying characteristic was her intensity, Washington's was her toughness. She began as a blues singer in the vein of the early Ethel Waters, full of piss and vinegar. When she moved on to jazz, R & B, and pop, she kept that aggressive posture even when singing a tender love song, and her high-pitched vocals and tremendous energy translated into exciting recordings. Unlike such masters of the microphone as Bing Crosby, Dinah Washington always sang full out, using her own power to project her voice onto the disc. She tended to prefer her first takes, which were energetic, fresh, and spontaneous.

**DINAH WASHINGTON**

*In Love*

ARRANGED & CONDUCTED BY
**DON COSTA**

Washington was born Ruth Lee Jones in Tuscaloosa, Alabama, on August 9, 1924. When she was three, her family moved to Chicago and she began singing in the St. Luke's Baptist Church choir. She joined Salle Martin's gospel choir, which toured the neighborhoods of Chicago, and when she was fifteen, she won an amateur contest at the Regal Theater and that spurred her on to pursue a career as a singer. For many years, her musical life was divided between directing the church choir and playing piano in clubs. In 1942 she opened at the Garrick Stage Bar in Chicago.

Manager Joe Glaser heard her and recommended her to Lionel Hampton, who hired her in 1943. Hampton claimed he named her Dinah Washington—though she might have been so dubbed by the manager of the Garrick Stage Bar or by Glaser. Whatever the origin of the name, the Dinah Washington persona soon took hold and her star began its rise. Jazz critic and historian Leonard Feather was the unlikely writer of her first R & B successes. He wrote her first hit, "Evil Gal Blues," and arranged for her to sing it on the Keynote label in 1943, accompanied by a sextet drawn from Hampton's ensemble. Washington stayed with Hampton and Keynote until 1946, and her singing grew ever jazzier. By the time she signed with Mercury and its sister label, Emarcy, she was firmly in the jazz camp, but she continued to record whatever she wanted, refusing to be pigeonholed.

Once Washington recorded "What a Difference a Day Makes" in 1959, she tended to concentrate on ballads with lush string accompaniment. In this way, she mirrored the careers of Nat King Cole and Ray Charles, whose choice of material and accompaniment grew more and more mainstream. It's notable that her jazz material prior to her first pop success remains her most accomplished work, and her singing on the Mercury label has influenced succeeding generations of R & B and soul singers, including Nancy Wilson and Diane Schuur, among many other lesser talents. Washington certainly deserved her titles, Queen of the Blues and Queen of the Jukebox.

Jazz critics and aficionados bemoaned the fact that Washington went popular. She fell prey to the "Muzak" style arrangements of the time, but she did occasionally make a recording that succeeded by commercially and critically, especially when she worked with Quincy Jones and arranger Ernie Wilkins. Washington didn't care about the critics, of course—the money was rolling in and she was spending it as fast as she could, buying clothes, furs, cars, and other luxuries. But in spite of her success, she remained sensitive, always, about her weight. She began taking the diet pills that were all the rage at the time, and at the age of thirty-nine, Dinah Washington died of an accidental overdose of the pills, perhaps mixed with alcohol. She died in Detroit, Michigan, on December 14, 1963. ❖

"She could take the melody in her hand, hold it like an egg, crack it open, fry it, let it sizzle, reconstruct it, put the egg back in the box and back in the refrigerator and you would've still understood every single syllable." —Quincy Jones

## CAREER HIGHLIGHTS

**1924** Born Ruth Lee Jones on August 9.

**1927** Moves to Chicago with family.

**1939** Wins amateur contest at Regal Theater.

**1942** Plays piano at Three Deuces; plays Garrick Stage Bar.

**1943** Joins Lionel Hampton's band.

**1946** Becomes a single act; records for the Apollo label with Lucky Thompson All-Stars.

**1948** Signs with Mercury label when Mercury buys Keynote.

**1957** Appears at the Newport Jazz Festival.

**1959** Records "What a Diff'rence a Day Makes."

**1962** Joins Roulette label.

**1963** Dies on December 14.

> "Dinah was strong-willed and forceful. Her personality was such that whenever she was around, performing or not, you knew it."—Betty Carter

## Song and Story

### WHAT A DIFF'RENCE A DAY MAKES

Actually titled "What a Difference a Day Made," this song was originally a tango, written by Mexican lyricist and composer Maria Grever and titled, "Cuando Vuelva a tu Lado." Stanley Adams wrote the English lyrics and the Dorsey Brothers first made it a hit, with Bob Crosby supplying the vocal.

## Asides

Keynote Records, Dinah Washington's first label, was founded in 1940 by Eric Bernay, a treasurer of the magazine New Masses. The label's first release was a reissue of Soviet recordings, *Six Songs for Democracy*, which had been sung during the Spanish Civil War. In 1943, producer Harry Lim came on board and began recording jazz. In addition to Washington, Keynote recorded Lester Young, Coleman Hawkins, and Benny Carter. In 1948, Keynote went bankrupt and Mercury assumed its catalogue.

# Celebrity "Singers"

Here's a salute to all those stouthearted souls who managed to make recordings without the slightest notion of how, actually, to sing. These…let's call them reciters… capitalized on their television and film fame to make some strange, usually quite pretentious albums.

What exactly did the public do to deserve Lorne Greene's *On the Ponderosa* (1964)? One of the cuts on this album, the spoken (or intoned) "Ringo," actually knocked "Leader of the Pack" off the top spot on the *Billboard* charts. It didn't last long, though, as Bobby Vinton's "Mr. Lonely" arrived a week later to replace it. Dan "Hoss" Blocker joins Greene on "Skip to My Lou" (the image it evokes is soul shattering).

Hubris is perhaps what drives some stars into the recording studio. That fine actor William Shatner, star of *The World of Suzie Wong* on Broadway in addition to his captaining duties on the Starship Enterprise, always had a self-deprecating sense of humor and knew enough not to attempt to sing on his recordings. *Transformed Man* (1968) featured very serious readings of "Lucy in the Sky with Diamonds" and "Tambourine Man" along with some Shakespeare monologues to class up the act. All kidding aside (which ain't easy), there's actually an intelligence behind the choices on this concept album. Shatner returned to the studio in 2004 to record *Has Been*, produced by Ben Folds. Surprisingly, the spoken-word album worked. Shatner's self-mocking remains but he managed to unleash some very personal revelations and introspection.

There was always some friendly rivalry between Shatner and his *Star Trek* costar, Leonard Nimoy, so it was no surprise when Nimoy showed up on vinyl, too. While Shatner chose a soliloquy from *Hamlet*, Nimoy opted to interpret "If I Had a Hammer." Ouch.

So, it's on to Jack Webb of *Dragnet* fame. Webb's voice was fine for briskly admonishing, "Just the facts, ma'am." Singing, however, proved to be something else. His *You're My Girl* (1958) employed wonderful arrangements by Billy May but over them, Webb speaks (rather than sings, thank God) a variety of pop tunes from "Try a Little Tenderness" to "When Sunny Gets Blue."

Tony Randall (who really could sing) and Jack Klugman (who really couldn't) paired up for *The Odd Couple Sings*, on which Klugman gamely gave his all to "Johnny One Note" while Randall sang "While Banana Skins Are Falling"—whatever that is. They duetted on, get this, "You're So Vain." Luckily, both were clearly having a ball, and their enthusiasm and lack of pretension carried the day.

Another sitcommer, Bill Cosby, made *Bill Cosby Sings—Silver Throat* for Warner Brothers in 1967. It was his first LP, and featured sometimes tongue-in-cheek versions of rock hits. It even spawned a #40 hit: Stevie Wonder's "Uptight," with slightly amended lyrics. Cosby then attempted to crack the *Billboard* 5,000 with the strangely named *Hooray for the Salvation Army Band!* Given his reputation as a comedian perhaps he wasn't really serious—he appears on the album jacket shirtless, with an orange tie and a studded orange vest. The Beatles (who seem to be the favorite targets of the pseudo-singers) have the dubious honor of having *Sergeant Pepper's Lonely Hearts Club Band*, um, interpreted by Coz and he also tries his best with the Rolling Stones' "I Can't Get No Satisfaction." Backing him is the excellent Watts 103rd Street Rhythm Band, the truth is, Cosby, a huge jazz fan, acquits himself honorably. ◆

**TOP:** Lorne Greene at Tower Records, "suggesting" that people buy his album.
**LEFT:** William Shatner in deep thought after recording his album.

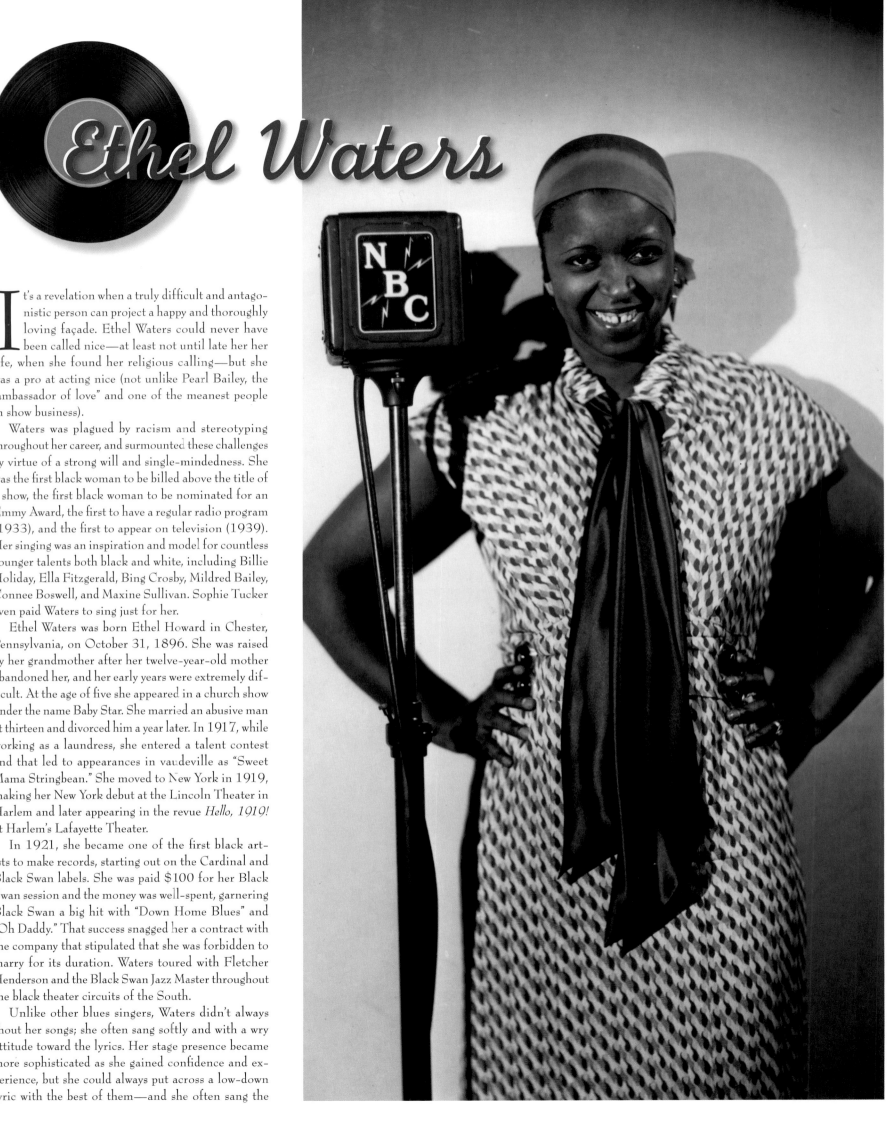

# 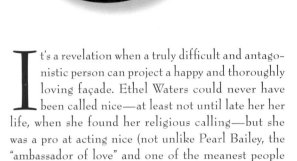 Ethel Waters

I t's a revelation when a truly difficult and antagonistic person can project a happy and thoroughly loving façade. Ethel Waters could never have been called nice—at least not until late her her life, when she found her religious calling—but she was a pro at acting nice (not unlike Pearl Bailey, the "ambassador of love" and one of the meanest people in show business).

Waters was plagued by racism and stereotyping throughout her career, and surmounted these challenges by virtue of a strong will and single-mindedness. She was the first black woman to be billed above the title of a show, the first black woman to be nominated for an Emmy Award, the first to have a regular radio program (1933), and the first to appear on television (1939). Her singing was an inspiration and model for countless younger talents both black and white, including Billie Holiday, Ella Fitzgerald, Bing Crosby, Mildred Bailey, Connee Boswell, and Maxine Sullivan. Sophie Tucker even paid Waters to sing just for her.

Ethel Waters was born Ethel Howard in Chester, Pennsylvania, on October 31, 1896. She was raised by her grandmother after her twelve-year-old mother abandoned her, and her early years were extremely difficult. At the age of five she appeared in a church show under the name Baby Star. She married an abusive man at thirteen and divorced him a year later. In 1917, while working as a laundress, she entered a talent contest and that led to appearances in vaudeville as "Sweet Mama Stringbean." She moved to New York in 1919, making her New York debut at the Lincoln Theater in Harlem and later appearing in the revue *Hello, 1919!* at Harlem's Lafayette Theater.

In 1921, she became one of the first black artists to make records, starting out on the Cardinal and Black Swan labels. She was paid $100 for her Black Swan session and the money was well-spent, garnering Black Swan a big hit with "Down Home Blues" and "Oh Daddy." That success snagged her a contract with the company that stipulated that she was forbidden to marry for its duration. Waters toured with Fletcher Henderson and the Black Swan Jazz Master throughout the black theater circuits of the South.

Unlike other blues singers, Waters didn't always shout her songs; she often sang softly and with a wry attitude toward the lyrics. Her stage presence became more sophisticated as she gained confidence and experience, but she could always put across a low-down lyric with the best of them—and she often sang the

## "I'm not concerned with civil rights. I'm concerned with God-given rights, and they are available to everyone!" —Ethel Waters

requisite double-entendre songs of the time to great effect. Even when she growled out a lyric, you could always understand every word. Waters's intelligence shone in her performances and she was a better actress than many of her contemporaries, which served her well as she graduated to better and more dramatically rich material. Her early blues renditions were tinged with jazz, and she was able to make the transition from blues to jazz to Tin Pan Alley standards with ease.

Black Swan folded in 1923 and in 1925, after Waters appeared at the Plantation Club in Times Square singing "Dinah," Columbia Records signed her. She continued moving forward in her career, spending more and more time on stages rather than in clubs. She made her Broadway debut in the revue *Africana* (1927), in which she sang "Dinah" and "I'm Coming Virginia." When producer Lew Leslie's revue *Blackbirds of 1928* turned out to be a smash on Broadway, it heralded a second wave of black revues and musicals, just as Waters was ready to leave the road completely and conquer Broadway. She appeared in Leslie's follow-up, the sensibly named *Blackbirds of 1930*. That same year she made her first appearance in Europe.

Three years later, Waters appeared at the Cotton Club, where she introduced the Harold Arlen and Ted Koehler standard, "Stormy Weather." It would be associated with her for the rest of her career. That same year she made Broadway history in the cast of Irving Berlin's *As Thousands Cheer*, singing the searing "Supper Time," heady material for a Broadway largely confined to presenting musical fluff for the weary masses. Her costars,

Marilyn Miller and Clifton Webb, resented the fact that her name was above the title and didn't want to share their curtain call, but Waters clearly stole the show.

She played Carnegie Hall in 1938 and, in 1939, she appeared in the straight play *Mamba's Daughters*, becoming a sensation all over again and racking up seventeen curtain calls opening night. That play would be broadcast by NBC-TV as part of an experimental broadcast. They followed it up with *The Ethel Waters Show*, probably the first television revue.

Throughout her Broadway career, Waters recorded her stage hits as well as a number of other tunes. On these recordings she was backed by such greats as Benny Goodman, Jack Teagarden, Duke Ellington, and Bunny Berigan. She recorded for Decca in the late '30s, to great success.

Her 1940 triumph in Vernon Duke's *Cabin in the Sky* was repeated on film for MGM in 1943, though in the film she was forced to perform with Lena Horne, whom she resented as a member of the younger, prettier generation of black performers. Horne would end up taking "Stormy Weather" and making it her own. Waters had made her film debut more than a decade earlier, in 1929's *On with the Show*, and had also appeared in *Check and Double Check* (1930) with Amos 'n' Andy and Duke Ellington's Orchestra. She soon graduated to dramatic parts in such films as *Gift of Gab* (1934), *Tales of Manhattan*, and *Cairo* (both 1940).

Between 1942 and 1949, Waters was absent from Broadway. Her bad temper had finally overtaken her drive, and she was considered too difficult to work with.

## CAREER HIGHLIGHTS

| | |
|---|---|
| **1896** | Born on October 31. |
| **1910** | Marries Merritt Pernsley. |
| **1917** | Begins career in vaudeville. |
| **1919** | Moves to New York and begins acting in musicals and revues. |
| **1921** | Begins recording career. |
| **1927** | Broadway debut in *Africana*. |
| **1928** | Marries Clyde Matthews. |
| **1930** | Appears on Broadway in *Lew Leslie's Blackbirds of 1930*. |
| **1930** | Appears in revue *Rhapsody in Black*. |
| **1933** | Featured in Cotton Club singing "Stormy Weather;" becomes first black performer given equal billing with white costars in *As Thousands Cheer*; introduces "Supper Time;" first black woman to have her own network radio show. |
| **1935** | Appears in Dietz and Schwartz's *At Home Abroad*; tours with then husband, Eddie Mallory, until 1939. |
| **1939** | Appears on Broadway in *Mamba's Daughters*; appears in early television broadcasts of *Mamba's Daughters* and *The Ethel Waters Show* on NBC. |
| **1940** | Appears on stage in *Cabin in the Sky*. |
| **1943** | Film version of *Cabin in the Sky* released. |
| **1948** | Tours with Fletcher Henderson. |
| **1949** | Acts in film *Pinky*. |
| **1950** | Last Broadway appearance in *Member of the Wedding*; appears in *Beulah* television show. |
| **1951** | Pens autobiography, *His Eye Is on the Sparrow*. |
| **1952** | Film version of *Member of the Wedding* released. |
| **1972** | Writes second autobiography, *To Me It's Wonderful*. |
| **1977** | Dies on September 1. |
| **1994** | United States Postal Service issues a commemorative stamp. |

But she returned triumphantly in 1950, in *Member of the Wedding*, winning the New York Drama Critics Award for Best Actress and scoring her second Oscar nomination when she reprised the role on screen in 1952. (She had once before been nominated for an Oscar, for her performance in *Pinky* in 1949.)

Waters starred in a television series, *Beulah*, from 1950 to '52, in which she played—what else?—a maid. She made frequent guest appearances on television as late as 1972. She became a devout Christian and follower of Reverend Billy Graham, appearing at several of his crusades from 1957 to 1976.

Ethel Waters died on September 1, 1977. ❖

**OPPOSITE PAGE:** Ethel Waters in March 1933

**THIS PAGE:** Tommy Dorsey conducts while Ethel Waters sings, circa 1935.

## Song and Story

### AM I BLUE?

Ethel Waters discussed the writing of this, one of her biggest hits, in her autobiography, *His Eye Is on the Sparrow*: Harry Akst came to my dressing room. He said he was working on the score for a new musical Warner's wanted from him. They needed a song hit, and Harry thought he had it. He had brought the lead sheet to me so I could work on it…. So we worked on it, and the song was "Am I Blue?"…. Mr. Zanuck listened to my interpretation [and exclaimed,] "This is it!"

### STORMY WEATHER

Ethel Waters knew she had a great song to sing the minute she heard this tune. "When I got out there in the middle of the Cotton Club floor…I was singing the story of my misery and confusion…the story of the wrongs and outrages done to me by people I had loved and trusted…. I sang 'Stormy Weather' from the depths of my private hell in which I was being crushed and suffocated."

## Asides

Black Swan records was named after the nickname of soprano Elizabeth Taylor Greenfield. The label, owned by the Pace Phonograph Company, began in 1921 under the auspices of Harry Pace, a renowned music publisher who was once a partner to W. C. Handy. The company was black owned and run and made recordings for the black audience featuring black artists. When it folded in 1923, Paramount Records acquired the catalog and began issuing the sides in 1924.

"I can't sing on the beat, that's white."
—Ethel Waters to conductor Georgie Stoll, during recording sessions for the film *Cairo*

Vincent Price told Michael Feinstein that when he toured with Waters in *Mamba's Daughters* she would call him only by his character's name. In one very angry scene they shared, she would either speak in a very low tone or shout the dialogue at the top of her lungs. Price never knew which she would do. Perhaps her erratic behavior was due in part to the fact that Waters was forced to stay at black hotels, apart from the rest of the company.

Waters loved composer Harold Arlen and referred to him as her son.

## First Person

When she appeared in the black musical comedy *Miss Calico* in 1927, Jimmy McPartland saw her. He told Nat Hentoff and Nat Shapiro, "We were enthralled with her. We liked Bessie Smith very much, too, but Waters had more polish, I guess you'd say. She phrased so wonderfully, the natural quality of her voice was so fine."

# Lee Wiley

**M**any singers have had successful careers as songwriters. Mel Torme is best known for his collaboration with Robert Wells on "The Christmas Song"; Billie Holiday supposedly collaborated on "Don't Explain" and "God Bless the Child"; and the queen of singer/songwriters was Peggy Lee, whose many, many hit songs are listed elsewhere in this book. Lee Wiley, though less well known, was also a successful tunesmith, usually in collaboration with composer Victor Young, with whom she also enjoyed a personal relationship. Among Wiley's most successful songs are "Anytime, Any Day, Anywhere" and "Got the South in My Soul."

She appreciated the masters and recorded the first albums ever devoted to the output of a single composer. These "songbooks" were released by Columbia Records, starting in 1939 with a set of discs devoted to the music of George Gershwin. Subsequent recordings spotlighted the music of Cole Porter, Rodgers and Hart, and Harold Arlen. Four ten-inch 78s comprised each set. The concept was soon adopted by a variety of other artists, most notably Ella Fitzgerald under the direction of producer Norman Granz.

Wiley was probably born on October 9, 1910—or was it 1915, or even 1908? One can't be sure as she changed the details of her life at whim. She was born in Fort Gibson, Oklahoma, and claimed to be a Cherokee princess. (Musicians nicknamed her "Pocahontas.") After studying in Tulsa, Wiley moved to New York to pursue a singing career. Her throaty, sultry, tender style was directly influenced by Mildred Bailey and Ethel Waters (whose style Wiley said she "adapted" and "softened"). Never a showoff, Wiley employed a wry, sophisticated approach to a lyric and made the words as important as the music.

After appearing in clubs and on radio, she had her first breakthrough with Leo Reisman's orchestra in 1931. Her first hit was the Vincent Youmans tune "Time on My Hands," which she put forth in a gently swinging manner. She claimed to have been temporarily blinded when thrown by a horse in the middle of her engagement with Reisman. She returned to Reisman's band, but finally quit in 1933. She subsequently worked with Paul Whiteman, the Casa Loma Orchestra, with whom she recorded "A Hundred Years from Today" in 1934, the Dorsey Brothers, and Johnny Green, making appearances and recordings.

After a year spent away from performing, fighting what she claimed was tuberculosis (but that's doubtful, too), Wiley returned in 1939 to record the songbooks. She found her perfect accompanists on those recordings—musicians such as Eddie Condon, Pee Wee Russell, Jess Stacy (whom she married), and Bunny Berigan (with whom she had an affair). In the forties, she appeared with Stacy in person and on radio, and also appeared with Eddie Condon's crew on radio in a series of broadcasts emanating from New York's Town Hall.

In 1950, Wiley joined Columbia for a year and made some wonderful recordings. She recorded one album for Storyville in 1954 (the same year she played the first Newport Jazz Festival) and then signed with RCA Victor, where she made only two records, "West of the Moon" (1956) and "A Touch of the Blues" (1957), both excellent. Sadly, she disappeared in 1957 and didn't re-emerge until 1971, when she released "Back Home Again" on Monmouth-Evergreen. It showed her at the top of her form, which made her fourteen years away from the studio all the more poignant to her fans. It's surmised that Wiley went into seclusion out of vanity, choosing not to perform in less than perfect fitness. In 1972, she made a triumphant appearance at Carnegie Hall as part of the New York Jazz Festival, and was not heard from again. She died on December 11, 1975. ◆

## Song and Story

**I'VE GOT A CRUSH ON YOU**
A number of songs have been rediscovered by the great singers of American popular song. Lee Wiley resurrected this number from oblivion when she recorded it in a slow tempo (it was an upbeat number when originally written). Wiley also changed the lyric slightly at the end, to "I have got a crush, my baby, on you."

## Asides

New York's Liberty Music Shop opened in 1927. In 1933, it began selling its own label recordings of cabaret artists, Broadway show stars, jazz combos, and dance recordings. In all, Liberty recorded more than two hundred 78s, plus a few ten-inch LPs. The company petered out in the late 1940s. Among the stars recorded by Liberty were Cy Walter, Beatrice Lillie, Ethel Merman, Gracie Fields, and Lee Wiley.

# THE
# BIG BANDS

The Count Basie band was like a machine, so tight, so together, with no wasted notes, no clams, no hesitation. To sit in the first rows of a club with the Basie horns facing you like a firing squad was to feel the power of music. Basie's band was a consistently high-energy, powerhouse group, the hippest, swingingest congregation going. This isn't to say that they couldn't play softly or with feeling, but, whatever the tune, it was delivered with intensity and feeling. And at the helm (sometimes even wearing a captain's cap) was William "Count" Basie.

While his band blasted away, Basie would chime in with a piano note here and there, the minimalist in the midst of the maximumist. He could play piano with the best of them but he saw his role as a pointillist, contributing here or there to accent the melody, set the rhythm, cap a phrase, or contrast with the horns. It might not always have been obvious but he was an excellent jazz player, having studied with none other than Fats Waller and studied the techniques of such masters as James P. Johnson and Willie "the Lion" Smith.

Singers loved to be backed by Basie's band, which offered them musical support and energy while letting them have a rollicking time. Basie, for his part, loved to accompany singers and could easily join forces with his old friend Jimmy Rushing on a blues tune or back the latest pop ballad sung by Helen Humes. Joe Williams performed with the band as did the irrepressible Thelma Carpenter.

Basie's arrangers, Eddie Durham, Neal Hefti, Ernie Wilkins, and Quincy Jones, loved to write for the band and for the singers, too. Basie recorded a series of magnificent—yes , that's the word—albums with Tony Bennett (just listen to the joy of "Are You Havin' Any Fun"), Sammy Davis, Jr. (including the utterly masculine arrangement of a feminine tune, "April in Paris"), Frank Sinatra (on the fantastic *It Might As Well Be Swing*), Joe Williams (the perfect pairing on *Count Basie Swings—Joe Williams Sings*), Ella Fitzgerald, Arthur Prysock, Sarah Vaughan, Teresa Brewer, the Mills Brothers, and Big Joe Turner.

Basie was a secure, generous man. His band paired up with Duke Ellington's orchestra for a recording and he devoted another disc to the music of Ellington. It's hard to think of another band leader who would devote two albums to his ostensible competition.

Basie started his band in 1935 and kept it going until his death in 1984, expanding and contracting as musical tastes changed. It was quite a feat of legerdemain, and one reason for his success was that he didn't see his music as rooted in any one era or style. When swing was in, he swung (well, he always swung); he was an early proponent of bebop, played blues and Beatles, and recorded an avant-garde exercise with arranger Oliver Nelson and instrumentalists Albert Ayler and Pharoah Sanders. He used head arrangements when it suited him and written arrangements, too. Above all, he was Basie and he kept the music going, made sure everyone had a good time, kept a sense of humor in his music, and really, really meant it when he played. With Basie, you never heard a false note or sensed a false emotion. He was true to his music and to himself—and that's what long careers are made of. ◆

## THE GREAT SONGS

1947   Open the Door Richard
1955   Every Day (I Have the Blues)
1956   April in Paris
1957   Li'l Darlin'
1958   Going to Chicago Blues
1962   The Basie Twist
1963   I Can't Stop Loving You
1968   Chain Gang; For Your Precious Love

## Asides

The creation of Basie's band was evolutionary. He sat in with the Walter Page Blue Devils in 1938 at the suggestion of blues shouter Jimmy Rushing. When the band broke up, some of the personnel joined Bennie Moten's band. When Moten died in 1935, Basie started his own ensemble with members of Moten's group.

Basie appeared at the Waldorf-Astoria Hotel in Manhattan for four months in June 1957, the first black performer to appear there. His success opened the way for Lena Horne and other blacks to play the Waldorf and other big rooms in New York.

Billie Holiday sang with Basie in 1937, but her recording contract was with Brunswick while Basie's was with Decca. (You can hear her on two air checks, though.)

Basie was discovered by Hollywood in 1938 and the band appeared in the short *Policy Man* and such feature films as *Reveille with Beverly, Hit Parade of 1943, Top Man,* and *Stage Door Canteen* (all in 1943) and *Cinderfella* (1960). They could be seen on screen as recently as 1974, in the Mel Brooks comedy, *Blazing Saddles.*

## First Person

George T. Simon, in the January 1937 *Metronome*: True, the band does swing, but that sax section is so invariably out of tune. And if you think that sax section is out of tune, catch the brass! And if you think the brass by itself is out of tune, catch the intonation of the band as a whole!!

Two of the greatest singers with or without a band. **LEFT**: Joe Williams. **RIGHT**: Joe Turner.

# Cab Calloway

**W**hether Cab Calloway was a better singer or band leader is sometimes debated, but truthfully he was the same energetic hipster whether facing the band or the microphone. Calloway's band was a reflection of his personality rather than having its own unique sound, as did those of Glenn Miller and Harry James. He was definitely the star of the show, though he spared little expense in backing his vocals with the finest musicians. Calloway had no illusions about the importance of the band, stating, "I'm up front there doing my act, but it's the guys themselves who are making this band what it is." In truth he hired the musicians, shaped their playing, and gave them their identity.

As a swing band his group had just as much punch as Count Basie's but they employed a somewhat looser style. Buster Harding directed the band and wrote its arrangements, and he knew how to showcase such excellent musicians as Doc Cheatham, Jonah Jones, Ben Webster, Hilton Jefferson, Milt Hinton, Shad Collins, Tyree Glenn, Cozy Cole, Dizzy Gillespie, and Chu Berry, as well as Calloway himself. Unfortunately, the recording ban hit just as the band was at its peak.

## THE GREAT SONGS

**1930** Gotta Darn Good Reason Now; St James Infirmary; St. Louis Blues

**1931** Between the Devil and the Deep Blue Sea; Minnie the Moocher; Trickeration

**1933** Jitterbug; The Scat Song; Zah Zuh Zah

**1938** April in My Heart; Blue Interlude; Deep in a Dream; FDR Jones; Scrontch; There's a Sunny Side to Everything

**1939** Abei Gezundt

**1940** Are You Hep to This Jive; Chicken Ain't Nothin' but a Bird; Cupid's Dream; Feelin Tip Top; 15 Minute Intermission; The Lone Arranger; Silly Old Moon; Who's Yehoodi?; Yo Eta Cansa

**1941** Jumpin Jive; My Coo Coo Bird

**1942** Eadie Was a Lady; Minnie the Moocher's Wedding Day; Nagasaki; That Old Black Magic; Reefer Man

**1944** We the Cats Shall Hep You

**1946** How Big Can You Get?

**1947** Everybody Eats When They Come to My House; Jungle King

**1949** Rooming House Boogie

In live appearances, Calloway encouraged his musicians to take solos and improvise freely, but he was always front and center on his recordings, with the band blowing up a storm between his vocal flights. Calloway's vocals were hot, hot, hot—but he could also match Jolson for sentimentality. He sang about drug addicts and sex and got away with it by using slang that was unrecognizable to white record company executives and audiences. Harold Arlen and Ted Koehler wrote "Kicking the Gong Around," a paean to opium, which Calloway sang at the Cotton Club. "Minnie the Moocher," his best-known number, was also about a dope fiend—bet you didn't know that. (Calloway's coauthors on "Minnie" were Clarence Gaskill and Irving Mills, the latter the king of the cut-in.) Calloway sang freely though cryptically about sex in such songs as Arlen and Koehler's "Trickeration" and Fats Waller's "Six or Seven Times."

It's quite apt to compare Calloway to Jolson, though Calloway was not nearly as lachrymose. He was, however, practically Hebraic in some of his intonation—in fact, he sang a number of songs in Yiddish! This mixture of blues, jazz, and cantorial crooning made Calloway one of the most eclectic singers in popular song.

His fearless performances translated well to both stage and screen. While still in his teens he appeared in Chicago in the *Plantation Revue*; in 1929, he appeared on Broadway in *Hot Chocolates*; and he returned to the stage in an historic 1953 revival of *Porgy and Bess* and then, almost forty years after his Broadway debut, played opposite Pearl Bailey in *Hello, Dolly!* Following a role in an unfortunate revival of *The Pajama Game*, he was featured in *Bubbling Brown Sugar* in 1980 and made his last Broadway appearance in *Uptown…It's Hot!* in 1986. He made his film debut as a voice in a series of surrealistic Betty Boop cartoons in the early 1930s, going on to perform in a series of films with and without his band up to 1980's *The Blues Brothers*.

Even in his final appearances Calloway retained all the irrepressible wit and energy of his early years. Today people still recognize and adore "The Hi-De-Ho Man" in the sparkling zoot suit, through his film appearances and recordings. ◆

# The Dorsey Brothers

Jimmy Dorsey

my Dorsey

The brothers joined forces and in 1906 formed Dorsey's Novelty Six. They changed the name to Dorsey's Wild Canaries a few years later, and then Jimmy left for the Scranton Sirens (they certainly don't name bands the way they used to). In 1924, Jimmy joined the California Ramblers (where he played alongside Fred MacMurray) and brother Tommy followed. The next year, Jimmy joined the Jean Goldkette Orchestra and brother Tommy followed. In 1926, Jimmy joined Paul Whiteman's ensemble and—you guessed it—brother Tommy followed.

In 1927, figuring if you can't beat 'em, join 'em, the brothers formed the Dorsey Brothers Orchestra and recorded on the Okeh label. The band was a success and in 1934 they decided to tour for the first time. That same year they signed with Decca Records, a wise decision that would prove propitious later in their careers.

On May 30, 1935, the brothers were playing the Glen Island Casino. Tommy was conducting and gave the downbeat for "I'll Never Say Never Again." Jimmy yelled to his brother, "Isn't that a little too fast, Mac? Let's do it right or not at all." Tommy responded, "All right! We won't do it at all!" and stormed off the bandstand.

Jimmy assumed leadership of the band, and though he took his work seriously, he could never be called driven. A withdrawn man, his happiest moments were playing his instruments and golfing. He found that running a band was a lot of work, but he surrounded himself with wonderful musicians who were also friends. The group thrived as Jimmy led it with humor and a relaxed attitude. At the end of 1935, he officially changed the name from the Dorsey Brothers Orchestra to Jimmy Dorsey and His Orchestra (not quite as catchy as the Wild Canaries). When the opportunity arose to become the house band for Bing Crosby's radio show, *The Kraft Music Hall*, Jimmy jumped at the chance to stay in one place for a while, remaining with the program for a year and a half.

S ibling rivalry is an odd thing. It drove Jimmy and Tommy Dorsey apart before finally bringing them back together. Jimmy was the older of the two brothers, and, after taking trumpet lessons from his music teacher father, he made his debut in his father's marching band when he was only seven years old. Two years later, in 1913, he became a pro, playing with J. Carson McGee's King Trumpeters. Tommy also took lessons from dad and decided to play trombone and trumpet, so Jimmy switched to alto saxophone and clarinet.

One of the mainstays of the Jimmy Dorsey band was vocalist Bob Eberly, brother of Ray Eberle (yes, they spelled it differently). Eberly was a great friend to Jimmy: they shared a house and stayed together through thick and thin, wives or not, until Jimmy's death. Eberly was considered one of the top singers in the business, influencing many including Dick Haymes. He might have gone far—Warner even offered him a film contract hoping he'd replace Dick Powell. He had offers to record as a single act or to head a band of his own. But the fame and money didn't matter to him, he liked where he was and stayed put. As he recalled to George T. Simon, "I didn't want to leave, and I told Jimmy so. I was very happy making my four hundred dollars a week and twelve hundred and fifty dollars extra when we made movies." Eberly even refused to sign a contract with Jimmy, preferring to operate on mutual trust.

Eberly's partner in the band was Helen O'Connell, and they made a number of successful recordings together. Their duets were unusual in that they tended to take alternate verses rather than singing together, but they clicked and America loved them. O'Connell had come to Jimmy straight from Larry Funk and his Band of a Thousand Melodies, which performed at the Village Barn in New York City. She punched out her vocals and sang hard, specializing in torchy ballads and novelty songs. Both genres were ideally suited to her style of oversinging.

When the war came Eberly went into the service. With his departure, December 1943 marked the end of the golden era of Jimmy Dorsey and His Orchestra.

Tommy, after he left Jimmy with the band, needed to start his own group and he accomplished the task in one fell swoop by taking over the band of Joe Haymes, then playing at the McAlpin Hotel in New York City and going nowhere slowly. After a few adjustments in personnel and a change from nondescript dance music to the smooth, sentimental, creamy style that would serve him well for the next thirty-odd years, the band hit its stride. Dorsey made an important decision to bring in Axel Stordahl as an arranger and the difference in sound was immediate and historic, for when Frank Sinatra joined the band, Stordahl's arrangements helped rocket him to the top of the charts with his own unique style.

If Jimmy was laid back and relaxed, Tommy was a taskmaster with a very, very short fuse. His musicians admitted that he was a brilliant musician who knew exactly what he wanted, but his temper and belittling attitude led to constant personnel changes, until the leader learned to relax a little and support his players. Luckily for Tommy, after he erupted he tended to realize the error of his ways and make fun of himself. Tenor sax great Bud Freeman reported that he quit the band twice—and was fired three times!

Tommy's first important vocalist was Jack Leonard, a favorite with the band and with audiences. But after five years of placidity, Tommy's natural sense of competition grew and grew and he fired Leonard for no concrete reason. After a brief stint with Allan DeWitt, Tommy found the perfect replacement: The band was playing at the Palmer House in Chicago while Harry James was playing the Sherman Hotel. Tommy went to check out "that skinny kid with James." His name was Frank Sinatra and Tommy made him an offer to join the band. With his wife Nancy pregnant, Sinatra needed more money so James let him out of his contract.

Sinatra was an immediate sensation but he had a lot to learn and Tommy Dorsey was there teaching him. Sinatra was serious about singing and practiced all the time, perfecting his phrasing, dynamics, and

even his vibrato, all learned at the knee of Tommy. He worked closely with Jo Stafford and the rest of the Pied Pipers on achieving just the right blend of voice and style. Ambitious and intelligent, Sinatra and the band had a marvelously symbiotic relationship. But in 1942 Sinatra left to go it alone, just as the war years and the recording ban were about to change the face of music forever. Members of the band were drafted and Jo Stafford quit the Pied Pipers to spend more time with her husband, Paul Weston.

In 1944, it appeared that the Dorsey brothers might be getting back together. Tommy bought the Casino Gardens ballroom in Ocean Park, California, and Jimmy became a partner in the venture (as was Harry James). His band played there to great success. The two bands even joined up to record a "victory disc" or V-Disc for the troops. But the time was not right for the brothers to join forces permanently.

After the war, audiences were abandoning the big bands in favor of vocalists like Frank Sinatra. Bookings were harder to come by and the competition was fierce. America's suburbs were growing and the cities were largely abandoned in the evenings, so many of the great music venues folded and even the musicians themselves preferred to stay near home, declining to tour.

Dorsey announced the breakup of his band in December 1946. It would prove to be a premature announcement. Two years later he put together another ensemble and found work where he could, self-producing records that he licensed to various companies.

By 1953, Jimmy had shut down his band and Tommy convinced him to join a newly renamed Dorsey Brothers Orchestra. Jimmy was happy to play in the band while his still-more-driven brother led the ensemble. In a typical performance, Tommy would lead the band for the first half while Jimmy played some solos. After intermission, Jimmy would conduct his hits, giving Tommy a chance to solo. They played a few songs together at the end.

For two seasons beginning in 1954, the brothers had their own television series, Stage Show, a summer replacement for Tommy's friend Jackie Gleason, who also produced it. Stage Show marked the first appearances by a young Elvis Presley and a younger Connie Francis.

In November 1956, Tommy Dorsey died. Jimmy followed in June 1957. ◆

## Song and Story

### MARIE

Tommy Dorsey wrote in the June 1938 Metronome, "We were playing a theatre in Philly once upon a time, and there was a colored band playing the same show called the Sunset Royal Serenaders [led by Doc Wheeler]. They had this arrangement of 'Marie' and all of us in the band liked it; in fact, after a couple of days we all knew it by heart. I figured that we could do more with it

than they could, and so I traded them about eight of our arrangements for one of theirs.

"The funny part of it is that I tried to get Eli Oberstein to let us record it. Eli couldn't see it, and so I tried it out on our studio audience after one of our commercials. It went over so big that I tried it out on the program. We got so many requests that we had to repeat it the next week. It was then that Oberstein let us record it." The song was a huge hit for Victor.

### SONG OF INDIA

The flip side of "Marie," this tune was suggested to Tommy Dorsey by Victor recording chief, Eli Oberstein. "The funny part of it was that for months, driving home at night, I had been singing to myself that lick that we used on the introduction—you know: DUH—duh deed a dee duh duh duh duh duh—DA DA—but I could never get a tune to follow that figure. As soon as Eli suggested 'Song of India' I saw the connection."

### I'LL NEVER SMILE AGAIN

In the summer of 1939, the Tommy Dorsey band flew to Toronto (the first time a band flew to an engagement) to play at the Canadian National Exhibition. Every evening a young girl named Ruth Lowe waited by the stage door in order to meet Tommy. This went on for most of the engagement. Band members noticed the girl, and finally guitarist and arranger Carmen Mastren asked her what she was there for. She explained she had a demo of a new song that she considered perfect for the band. Mastren loved the demo and played it for Cliff Leeman, who also loved the number—but for months no one could get Tommy to give it a hearing. Songwriter Ray Henderson listened to the demo and gave the song his approval. Once Henderson had listened to the song, Tommy relented, but wasn't bowled over. In fact, he offered it to Glenn Miller, who recorded it at a relatively fast tempo.

Finally, eight months after the Toronto engagement, Dorsey decided to record the song. Frank Sinatra and the Pied Pipers were looking for a way to perform it that would set it apart from the Miller version. They slowed it down and made it more intimate and conversational. They couldn't get it quite right until Tommy suggested that they sing it as if they were just getting together informally at someone's house. It worked—the song became one of their biggest hits.

Tommy Dorsey at the Astor Hotel on Times Square (what the heck is that bird doing there?) on July 15, 1950.

# Duke Ellington

**W**hat made Ellington so great? His musicianship was unsurpassed, yes. He hired the finest musicians and encouraged them to express themselves through their instruments. His art never appeared phony or premeditated or facile. But Ellington's success had other components as well.

When Glenn Miller went looking for replacements, the candidates had to be great musicians able to play charts perfectly—their own personalities and talents had to remain secondary. Miller wanted his band to sound exactly the same no matter who was playing in it. Benny Goodman put himself out front-and-center, always the focal point of the music. Sweet bandleader Sammy Kaye went after a sound that was unsurprising and unemotional—mood was everything.

Ellington, to a greater extent than any other bandleader of his day, revered the individuality of his players. When replacing a member of the band, he found himself facing a problem. Should he force the newcomer to play the arrangements as written—arrangements that had been concocted to capitalize on the special talents of a previous player? Or should the arrangements be changed to take advantage of the skills of the new band member? Ultimately, Ellington always chose to nurture the individual personalities and talents of his members. He also revered his singers, and the queen of them all was Ivie Anderson, his first permanent band singer. She joined him in Chicago in 1931, and Ellington considered Anderson to be a good luck symbol for the band. She was equally adept at singing ballads and swinging. Ellington felt that when she sang "Stormy Weather" she outperformed the great Ethel Waters, for whom the song had been written. (Ellington had accompanied Waters at the Cotton Club when she sang the song so he knew whereof he spoke.) According to Ellington, when Anderson sang the song, "the audience and all the management brass broke down crying and applauding....Tears streaming down her cheeks, Ivie did the most believable performance ever." She could also outswing most other singers. Her recording

**LEFT:** Ellington appreciates the sound of lovely Joya Sherrill.

**OPPOSITE PAGE BOTTOM:** The magnificent and underappreciated Ivie Anderson.

debut with the band in 1932 was on "It Don't Mean a Thing (If It Ain't Got that Swing)" and her renditions of "Rose of the Rio Grande," "Swingtime in Honolulu," "Rocks in My Bed," "Solitude," and "Raisin' the Rent" were brilliant even when the songs were not.

Anderson had sung with a variety of bands in Los Angeles and with Earl Hines, but with Ellington she found her true match. She was more than the "girl singer,"—she became an integral member of the ensemble, as important as any of the musicians. Because Ellington valued lyrics so much, she became, literally, the voice of the band. Anderson can be seen in the Marx Brothers film *A Day at the Races,* singing and swinging "All God's Chillun Got Rhythm." Perhaps the greatest band singer of all time, she became the standard to which all future Ellington singers aspired.

Joya Sherrill was another Ellington favorite, discovered by the leader when she came to sing him a lyric she had written for "Take the 'A' Train." What Ellington thought of the lyric is unknown, but he called up Sherrill a few weeks later and asked her to join the band. She was in school at the time and couldn't join

him until June 1942, at the end of the school year. Ellington loved her diction and credited the success of "I'm Beginning to See the Light" to her presentation of the song.

Ellington also employed Kay Davis, a well-trained musician who could sight read and had perfect pitch. Because of this, Ellington decided that, in addition to asking her to sing lyrics, he would use her voice as an instrument. In January 1946 at Carnegie Hall, she sang the brand-new (really, really new) tune "Transbluency" in front of the band with the music on a stand. She was joined by the featured musicians, Jimmy Hamilton and Lawrence Brown, who also required music stands. The performance was a huge hit. In the late 1920s, Adelaide Hall had made a career out of growling vocalese on such numbers as "Creole Love Call" with Ellington's band, and Davis was a kind of soprano version of Hall.

Ellington also employed male singers from time to time, chief among them Al Hibbler. As Ellington himself wrote, "He had so many sounds that even without words he could tell of fantasy beyond fantasy. Hib's great dramatic devices and the variety of his tonal changes give him almost unlimited range." As he did with all his singers, Ellington greatly valued Hibbler's enunciation. The ability to create something in the minds of audiences, whether a mood, an emotion, or a story, was key to Ellington's philosophy of music.

As a performer, Ellington put communication with the audience foremost. Other bands might be easier to dance to, or evoke an easy emotion, or create a romantic mood, but he and his band created a dialogue with the audience; the musicians spoke through their instruments, the audience listened, felt, and responded. It was this great communion that made the Ellington band absolutely unique. ◆

## Asides

At the end of 1936, Ellington remarked that the British bands had a certain resonance when they recorded. He and his engineers experimented and finally found the sound they were looking for—in the men's room. Ellington credits this as the first echo chamber.

## Song and Story

### TAKE THE "A" TRAIN

Duke Ellington on Billy Strayhorn's tune: At one point, he was having some sort of trouble and I pulled a piece of his out of the garbage. I said, "What's wrong with this?" And he said, "That's an old thing I was trying to do something with, but it's too much like Fletcher Henderson." I looked it over—it was "'A' Train"—and I said, "You're right." It was written in sections, like Fletcher Henderson. But I flattened it out anyway and put it in the pile with the rest of the stuff.

# Lounge Songs

No, we don't mean songs like Cole Porter's "Make It Another Old-Fashioned, Please." Cocktail or lounge songs occupy that particular niche in the repertoire that makes them best suited to hotel bars where they are played on synthesizers and interpreted by women with big hair and men with their shirts open and gold chains around their necks. Okay, that's a little harsh. Well, actually it isn't—but even these tunes had mothers and fathers once, and some of them aren't half bad. Something has to set the mood at the local Holiday Inn or the occasional Bar Mitzvah, after all.

What makes a good lounge song? A catchy melody that is devoid of depth; a beat that can be programmed into a drum machine; and self-important, pseudo-poetic lyrics all help. (Think of Barry Manilow's "I Write the Songs" or Neil Diamond's "I Am, I Said" and you're in lounge heaven.) Let us state again, though, that some of these songs were at one point very good and creditable, until they were sung to death or mangled beyond recognition by many less than stellar Sinatra or Streisand wannabes.

Since this book concerns itself with the golden era of popular song, i.e., pre-1970, there's no point in discussing some of the best (meaning worst) lounge songs, including "We Built This City" by Dennis Lambert, Martin Page, Bernie Taupin, and Peter Wolf (four people had to collaborate on this Jefferson Starship tune!); "Afternoon Delight" by William Danoff, "Margaritaville" (Dey Martin); "Everybody Have Fun Tonight" by Nicholas Feldman, Jeremy Ryder, and "We Built This City co-author Peter Wolf, and Paul McCartney's "Ebony and Ivory." We're even skipping over the most often performed lounge song of all time, 1975's "Feelings" (Peter Pepini, Jane Schwartz). Pity. No "The Way We Were" (Marvin Hamlisch and Marilyn and Alan Bergman), no "You Light Up My Life" (Carole King). Broadway gave us "Memories" by Sir Andrew Lloyd Webber and Trevor Nunn; "Send in the Clowns" by Stephen Sondheim; and Marvin Hamlisch and Edward Kleban's "What I Did for Love." Not eligible.

If we wanted to pick from the last three decades we could make this a whole chapter, but we're concentrating on the classics—so we'll start with "The Girl from Ipanema" (Antonio Carlos Jobim and Norman Gimbal), a really great song that has been ruined by close association with drinks served with little umbrellas. Oh, wait—that's a foreign song. Not eligible.

The original lounge song was (cheesy drum roll and fake cymbal crash) "My Melancholy Baby," a sweet song from 1912, by George A. Norton and Ernie Burnett, whcih has been a favorite of drunks for close to a century. "Sing 'Melancholy Baby'," the drunk in A Star Is Born's "Born in a Trunk" number yells out to Judy Garland. Slow, lachrymose, self-pitying songs are always favorites when you've had a few too many highballs. "In the Wee Small Hours of the Morning" is an especially favorite feel-bad song. Why Frank Loesser's "My Time of Day" didn't make it in places that smell of dried booze is a mystery.

Then there are the songs that actually have to do with bars and drinks. "Something Cool" (Billy Barnes) and "Black Coffee" (Francis Burke and Paul Francis Webster) are but two favorites. "Scotch and Soda" (Richard Maltby) never had a life beyond bars and Vegas lounges. If your waitress is wearing a skimpy yet impenetrable outfit, "Lush Life" by Billy Strayhorn is the song for you, whether or not the lyric actually refers to drunks. (It does and it doesn't.) "Why Try to Change Me Now?" might be an anthem for people who blow their noses with cocktail napkins.

There are also the songs that pianists plunk out from fake books as instrumentals, songs like "Star Dust" by Hoagy Carmichael and Mitchell Parish and "I'll Be Around" (Alec Wilder). Nobody seems to know the lyrics past the first line (in the case of "Star Dust" they don't even know the first word) but it doesn't matter.

So, let's have "one more for the road" (hey, that's from our favorite, "One for My Baby" by Harold Arlen and Johnny Mercer) and start wiping down the bar. Then we'll put a buck in the brandy snifter for the pianist and go home to sleep in our clothes. ◆

IN THE
## WEE SMALL HOURS
Lyrics by BOB HILLIARD  OF THE MORNING  Music by DAVID MANN
PRICE 50 CENTS

FRANK SINATRA
in the wee small hours

## Song and Story

### FLY ME TO THE MOON

This song's original title was "In Other Words" but nobody could remember it. They kept calling it "Fly Me to the Moon," its first line. Mabel Mercer introduced it and Kaye Ballard also sang it, and Peggy Lee finally told its writer, Bart Howard, he had no choice but to change the title. A few other songs endured the same fate, including Lerner and Loewe's "I'm Getting Married in the Morning," originally "Get Me to the Church on Time," and another song from My Fair Lady, "Wouldn't It Be Lovely?" or as it is commonly known, "All I Want Is a Room Somewhere." When Howard Dietz heard about the great success of Arthur Schwartz and his "Blue Pajamas" song, a favorite of the Duke of Windsor, he was confused, having written the song as "I Guess I'll Have to Change My Plans." but for some reason it was actually issued on record as "The Blue Pajama Song." Try stumping the band with that one.

# Benny Goodman

Perseverance usually pays off—that is, if you can stay alive until you hit the big time. Clarinetist/band leader Benny Goodman made many false moves before ascending to the role of the "King of Swing," beginning with the caliber of musicians he chose for his band. Early on, they just weren't very good.

The Goodman band's first hotel engagement was in May 1935 at New York's Roosevelt Hotel, usually home to the sweet sounds of Guy Lombardo and His Royal Canadians. Goodman's attempts at swinging didn't go over well with the twelve members of the audience. He was hardly a household name at that point and he was certainly no Guy Lombardo. Not surprisingly, Goodman was given his two weeks' notice on opening night. Lucky for him he had two formidable men championing his talents: John Hammond, the legendary record producer, and MCA booking agent Willard Alexander. Together, they pushed Goodman to improve the band's roster and persevered in finding work for the young leader.

In July 1935, Goodman sat in with Teddy Wilson's Orchestra and they recorded three classic songs with vocals by Billie Holiday, "I Wished on the Moon," "What a Little Moonlight Can Do," and "Miss Brown to You." Wilson returned the favor on July 13 when he joined Goodman and drummer Gene Krupa on four sides for Victor Records. Though Wilson wouldn't actually join Goodman's band for a year, these first recordings by the Benny Goodman Trio were the start of a historic relationship.

Goodman went on tour with little success until August 21, when he played the Palomar Ballroom in Los Angeles. The band opened with some dance arrangements, and the audience was definitely not amused. Krupa told Goodman, "If we're gonna die, Benny, let's die playing our own thing." Out came the band's swing arrangements, written especially for them by such greats as Fletcher Henderson, and the audience cheered. They rushed the bandstand, not dancing but content to stand and listen to this exciting music. It was a personal revelation to Goodman. No more would he try to conform to the tried and true. He began to trust his instincts and from then on, he vowed to play only music in which he believed. The band was held over for a second month. Radio broadcasts from Los Angeles helped spread the word nationwide, and the band began to build a national reputation.

When the band reached Chicago they were received with mild interest. Their first performance, at the Joseph Urban room at the Congress Hotel, took place on November 6, 1935. While in the Windy City, they participated in what is generally agreed to be the first jazz concert in the United States. Helen Oakley, a Chicago socialite interested in jazz, started the Rhythm Club, a group of jazz lovers in Chicago. She hired Goodman and members of Fletcher Henderson's band (also in Chicago to play at the Urban Room)

**LEFT:** Helen Wardin in 1934, at the time of the *Let's Dance* radio program on NBC Radio.

**OPPOSITE PAGE BOTTOM:** Goodman and his Sextet at the Basin Street Club, 51st Street and Broadway in New York City.

in what she advertised as a "Tea Dance." It was so successful that *Time* magazine reported on the event. As Goodman's engagement at the Urban Room was extended, Oakley produced two more Sunday concerts for the Rhythm Club.

The second concert took place at the Grand Terrace Ballroom, where Fletcher Henderson's band was holding forth. Goodman and Krupa played along with Henderson's outfit, marking what was probably the first time that black and white jazz musicians played together before a paying audience. But there was more to come. The third concert took place on Easter Sunday, March 29, 1936, back at the Congress Hotel. Oakley arranged for Teddy Wilson to come from New York and sit in with Goodman. Hammond, Kaufman, and Goodman decided that Wilson would join Goodman and Krupa and play as a trio during intermissions. They were such a success that Wilson stayed with Goodman, creating the first racially integrated band. Goodman was held over at the Urban Room for six months. His radio broadcasts from the hotel and the hit recordings he made while in Chicago raised his national profile considerably. Goodman was definitely in the groove—he won the 1935 Metronome poll as Best Swing Band.

In 1936, after a detour to Hollywood to make the Big Broadcast of 1937, Goodman returned to New York and the *Madhattan* Room of the Hotel Pennsylvania. Vibraphonist Lionel Hampton joined the band, and the Benny Goodman Quartet was formed. Though they had all of the earmarks of success, it wasn't until March 3, 1937, that the band officially "made it." They were playing the Madhattan Room to large and polite audiences when they landed a booking at the Paramount Theater on Times Square. The theater was showing a lackluster film, *Maid of Salem* with Claudette Colbert and Fred MacMurray, so that certainly wasn't what drew the thousands of fans to the immense cinema. As soon as the band rose into view on the hydraulic orchestra pit elevator, the audience went wild. In scenes that presaged Sinatra's later triumphant appearance at the same venue, fans crowded the stage, jitterbugged in the aisles, and fainted at their seats. There had never been such a frenzy created by live performers, yet here, in the midst of the Depression, was an emotional outlet for anyone who could afford the thirty-five-cent admission. The privation on the streets and somber mood of the times were forgotten for a few hours inside the gilded movie palace, as hordes jived to their favorite

Two great Bennys: Jack and Goodman.

band, live and in person—not on radio or records or in a stuffy hotel ballroom.

In the days before television, fans could only glimpse their favorite performers in fan magazines or an occasional film appearance. They were starved for the real-life experience of their recording idols. With the advent of TV, these stars were suddenly accessible—but imagine being able to see the band of your dreams for less than half a dollar. Audiences immediately felt the power of the music much more palpably than they had when it came from the horn of a Victrola. They saw their idols moving right in front of them (though they might have been almost a city block away from the upper-tier seats). The excitement grew into a kind of mass hysteria, and it was that energy that propelled the Goodman band into the stratosphere.

Goodman's band was the most thrilling of them all, and when they swung they really swung, Goodman's clarinet cutting through the driving sound of the band, embroidering the melody against a brilliant background. The trumpet section was certainly the strongest of any, with Chris Griffin, Ziggy Elman, and, perhaps most important, Harry James, blowing hard. Vibraphonist Hampton filled in the holes with élan and drummer Krupa kept it all in the groove—and it was that special groove that made the Goodman band so successful. While not as much of a machine as the Count Basie organization, the Goodman group managed to convey emotion with its precision—whether the longing of "It Never Entered My Mind" or the pure joy of "Swing, Swing, Swing." Despite their reputation as a hard-driving swing band, a look at the Great Songs section reveals plenty of ballads. And some of the swing tunes, like "Bob White," "Elmer's Tune," and "Oh! Look at Me Now," were gentle and easy to dance to.

One barometer of exactly how great the Goodman ensemble was is the number of members who left to start their own conglomerations of musicians. Krupa, Hampton, James, even Count Basie. In a land full of Counts, Kings, and at least one Duke, Benny Goodman definitely lived up to his royal moniker. ◆

## First Person

Peggy Lee: The biggest thing I noticed from my standpoint was the value of rehearsing. He would go over it and over it and over it. There is such a thing as overrehearsing something but not in his case because he was rehearsing the section pieces, then leaving the choruses open for free form extemporizing. And also Benny had a tremendous amount of discipline. I've used all those things.

Harry James on Goodman's clarinet: I think he takes the damn thing to bed with him.

Benny Goodman to George T. Simon: I'll never be satisfied with any band. I guess I just expect too much from my musicians and when they do things wrong I get brought down.

## Asides

In 1937, Benny Goodman joined Teddy Wilson and His Orchestra on some Brunswick Records sides. Since Goodman was under contract to Victor he was billed as "John Jackson" on the Wilson recordings.

The first recording of a live event ever issued was the historic 1938 *Carnegie Hall Jazz Concert*. Singer Helen Ward's husband, Albert Marks, placed a single microphone over the band. The recording that resulted was issued in 1950 on LP and has sold millions of copies. Suddenly, live recordings were all the rage.

Goodman recorded the *Quintet for Clarinet and Strings* with the Budapest String Quartet in 1938, the first of his many classical recordings.

When Goodman was upset with a band member he would give him what was dubbed "the Goodman ray"—a straight-faced stare that looked right through him.

# Harry James

**W**hy do people start bands? Some bandleaders are driven by ego or a deep need to express their musical ideas on a large canvas; others are figureheads for business conglomerates; and some step to the front just for the thrill of it.

When Harry James left the Goodman organization to start his own band, they were on such good terms that Goodman actually gave him money for the start-up. Goodman then owned a piece of the James band and made a healthy profit from his investment. James was a real showman, having grown up in a circus family, and he played a pretty mean trumpet—but he'll go down in history as the man who first recognized the talents of Frank Sinatra.

In 1939, Sinatra was acting as emcee at the Rustic Cabin in Englewood, New Jersey—about as far off the musical trail as one could get—when James happened to catch a broadcast of the house band, Harold Arden's ensemble. He liked the singer's voice and took a trip over to Englewood to see the young soloist in person. When he arrived he was told there was no singer but the emcee did occasionally warble a tune.

James was suitably impressed and signed the neophyte, becoming a kind of mentor to him. The James band was heartily received at Roseland in New York but elsewhere, the response was cool. Sinatra got an offer from Tommy Dorsey and needed the money as his wife was pregnant. James kindly let him out of his contract five months early. At that point James needed a new singer and, one day, while rehearsing at the World Transcription studios on Fifth Avenue, music publisher Larry Shayne brought along a new songwriter to demonstrate his songs. James didn't like the songs too much but he did like the singer and soon signed Dick Haymes.

The band floundered in spite of receiving some excellent reviews, but their luck changed in 1941, when James recorded "I'll Get By" featuring his new string section. With the addition of band veteran Helen Forrest on vocals, the James band seemed to know no limits. James's white-hot playing, utilizing what Forrest called his "Jewish phrasing," along with the vocals of Haymes and Forrest and the string section smoothing it all out, caused a sensation.

But the high times would be short-lived. With the draft decimating his roster and the musicians' strike standing in the way of any new recordings, James was frustrated. His interest in the band was waning, and it seemed that he was just going through the motions. In 1945, his string section totaled twenty-four, and the hot band grew sweeter and sweeter. Jazz was shunted to the sidelines.

James began drinking and reportedly abusing his wife. In December 1946, the same month that Benny Goodman threw in the towel, James broke up the band—but somehow the James story wasn't quite over. He pulled himself together and formed a new ensemble less than half the size of the old. "I've settled a few problems in my mind," James admitted in 1947, "problems nobody ever knew I had and which I didn't bother telling anyone about. But when you're worried and upset, you don't feel like playing and you certainly can't relax enough to play anything like good jazz." The new, sleeker group certainly satisfied the musical cognoscenti and, in one permutation or another, the James group kept playing great jazz until nine days before the bandleader's death in 1983. James might be remembered first and foremost for his part in the Sinatra legacy, but any number of his recordings reveal what a consummate player and bandleader he was. ◆

> **"I wanted him to change his name because I thought people couldn't remember it. But he didn't want to."**
> **—Harry James on Frank Sinatra**

## THE GREAT SONGS

**1939** All or Nothing at All; Flash

**1941** Lament to Love; Music Makers; A Sinner Kissed an Angel; You Made Me Love You

**1942** He's My Guy; I Don't Want to Walk Without You; I Don't Want to Walk Without You; I Had the Craziest Dream; Manhattan Serenade; Mister Five By Five; One Dozen Roses; Sleepy Lagoon; Strictly Instrumental

**1943** I Heard You Cried Last Night; I've Heard That Song Before; Velvet Moon

**1944** Cherry; I'll Get By (with Dick Haymes)

**1945** 11:60 P.M.; I'll Buy that Dream; I'm Beginning to See the Light; It's Been a Long, Long Time; Waitin' for the Train to Come In (all with Kitty Kallen); I Can't Begin to Tell You

**1947** Heartaches

# The Start of the Big Band Era

Bands have always been a part of the American psyche. Throughout our history they have celebrated elections, provided communal entertainment, led us into battle, and formed the soundtrack for our most significant social occasions—and for our lives. In the '20s, with the development of the fox-trot rhythm, popular bands took off. These new, jazz-age groups left the martial sounds of Sousa, Creatore, and their ilk in the dust. Jazz became a part of the lexicon and bands evolved to provide audiences with what they wanted: energetic, mood-elevating dance music. Even Prohibition and the Depression couldn't keep people off their feet. Remote broadcasts and recordings made bandleaders and musicians into household names throughout the country, even in places they never visited in person. Movies featured bands in short subjects and then in features. Swing music came along and excited a new generation, further propelling the big bands and bandleaders to a level of fame previously reserved for radio and film stars. With their rise from dance hall to nightclub to hotel ballroom and movie palace, bands became ubiquitous.

Paul Whiteman, Leo Reisman, Coon-Sanders Nighthawks, and George Olsen were among the best bands of the twenties. Duke Ellington made black musicians safe for white audiences, paving the way for other black bands, including those of Cab Calloway and Count Basie. Ellington also turned the bandleader into a personality. Before Ellington, only Paul Whiteman had forged a unique persona.

Early bands, such as those led by Fletcher Henderson, Ben Pollack, Glen Gray, and Jean Goldkette, were among the most influential in the twenties, providing many future leaders with a foothold in the business as they revved up the music. On the other side of the musical coin were a number of sweet bands, such as those of Guy Lombardo, Ozzie Nelson, Hal Kemp, and Wayne King—but, perhaps fortunately, their style of music remained a sideline to the jazz-oriented big bands.

Benny Goodman's 1935 success at the Palomar Ballroom in Los Angeles really started the ball rolling. The next few years saw a burgeoning of bands, and by 1939, the country was poised for a musical explosion. The event that lit the fuse wasn't musical at all, it was chemical. In 1938, Doctor Wallace Hume Carothers, a chemist working at DuPont, invented nylon. The synthetic fabric was specifically invented to replace silk in women's hosiery. Women who had previously been forced to draw lines up the back of their legs to simulate the seams in silk hose could afford inexpensive, durable stockings and they wanted to show them off. Skirts became shorter, Harry James's wife, Betty Grable, had her legs insured for a cool million, and where was the best place to show off? Not while sitting in movie theaters or strolling up Main Street. Dancing was the answer! Sporting a pair of heels and a twirly skirt, every woman felt good about how she looked—and the men certainly noticed. By 1941, 64 million pairs of nylons had been sold.

It was a happy juxtaposition of culture and science that set the stage for the musical mania that swept the country in the forties. Though the big-band era wouldn't last very long, its impact on the history of twentieth-century music is incalculable. ◈

**TOP:** Betty Grable exhibits her assets.

**OPPOSITE PAGE:** Cab Calloway. His career spanned the twentieth century, surviving changes in popular taste and the emergence of new media.

# The End of the Big Band Era

The Big Band era came to a crashing halt in the space of only a few years, due in large part to greed and intractability on all fronts—surprising in that this was an era in which Americans were pulling together as never before to help win the Second World War. Of course the war itself helped hasten the end of the big bands as a cultural force, as they were made up almost exclusively of male musicians and found their ranks decimated by the draft. In some cases, an entire band enlisted as a whole and spent their service time entertaining the troops.

A blow came in 1940 when the music licensing society known as ASCAP (American Society of Composers, Authors and Publishers), decided to double the fees radio stations had to pay for playing records on the air. The stations rebelled and began their own society, BMI (Broadcast Music Incorporated), and played only the music of these artists. Unfortunately, the new organization didn't represent the cream of the American popular song but was made up of songwriters who had been denied membership in ASCAP. Blues, country, jazz, and western writers joined the new company, and in later years, rock writers would gravitate toward BMI.

For a year no ASCAP songs were broadcast. The networks, intent on making sure that no ASCAP melodies snuck their way into songs through jazz improvisations, ruled that all solos be submitted in writing prior to the broadcast. Not surprisingly, this hobbled the spirit of much of the music broadcast live. During that dark period, Stephen Foster's "Jeanie with the Light Brown Hair" was the apotheosis of music on the airwaves. In 1942, the ban was lifted, just in time for the final fatal blow to the big bands.

James J. Petrillo, president of the American Federation of Musicians, ordered a strike of its members, proclaiming that no mechanical recordings of any kind be made as of August 1, 1942, save Hollywood movies and "Soundies," short films played on jukebox-type machines in bars. (The only other exception was the recording of "V-Discs" or Victory Discs, made for soldiers fighting overseas.)

At first record companies and radio stations were defiant. WNEW in New York proclaimed, "With twenty thousand records in our collection, we aren't too worried about the extra twelve a week that are coming out now." But audiences wanted new recordings, so record companies held marathon sessions hoping to stock up on releasable sides before the clock struck midnight on July 31. When the strike when into effect, listeners were regaled with a cappella recordings, singers with choral backup, and people imitating instruments—hey, it worked for the Mills Brothers.

Though U.S. Attorney General Francis Biddle, threatened an injunction under anti-trust laws, the musicians won the fight. Decca made its own agreement with the union in September, 1943; Capitol followed in October; and a full year later, in November 1944, Victor and Columbia signed a new contract.

By the time the musicians returned to work, the public had discovered the glories of the singer. Men returned from the war and moved their families to the suburbs, away from nightspots, and television became the favored entertainment medium. In December 1946 eight of the greatest big bands announced they were folding: Les Brown, Benny Carter, Tommy Dorsey, Benny Goodman, Woody Herman, Ina Rae Hutton, Harry James, and Jack Teagarden. Big bands were relegated to nostalgia tours, often under the leadership of one-time members, and an era was at an end. ◆

The Glenn Miller Orchestra existed for less than five years, yet it remains the most identifiable band of all time, as well as one of the most popular. Its great success was due to more than just its unique sound. Miller may not have been the greatest trombonist in the country, nor was it his conducting that distinguished him—rather, it was his talent for arranging and organizing and his excellent sense of what the public wanted that put his ensemble over the top.

Miller positioned his band strictly in the center. Never avant-garde like Artie Shaw's group could be, and never as square and sweet as Kay Kyser or Lawrence Welk, Miller was strictly in the swing band category. His singers, including Ray Eberle (brother of Bob), Marion Hutton (sister of Betty), Paula Kelly, Skip Nelson, and the Modernaires, never overwhelmed the music with anything like emotion or an original sound (and that's not a criticism). His band members, including such greats as Al Klink, Tex Beneke, and Bobby Hackett, weren't known for their solos. Improvisation was never the strong suit of the Miller band. His arrangers, Bill Finegan, Billy May, and Jerry Gray, wrote in the Miller manner, as dictated by the boss. Listening to Finegan's arrangements for the Sauter-Finegan group or Billy May's flights of fancy for Sinatra and others, it's hard to imagine them bound by the Miller sound. As the bandleader explained in *Metronome* magazine in May 1939, "We're fortunate in that our style

One of Miller's favorite songwriters was Harry Warren who, fortuitously, was signed to Twentieth Century-Fox at the same time Miller was. Warren and his lyricist, Mack Gordon, clicked with Miller and "got it." For their films together, *Sun Valley Serenade* in 1941 and *Orchestra Wives* in 1942, Warren and Gordon wrote scores filled with future standards.

## THE GREAT SONGS

**1938** By the Waters of Minnetonka (Indian Love Song); My Reverie

**1939** In the Mood; Little Brown Jug; Moonlight Serenade; Sunrise Serenade

**1940** Blueberry Hill; Bugle Call Rag; The Call of the Canyon; Crosstown; Danny Boy (Londonderry Air); Fools Rush In; Handful of Stars; Imagination; The Nearness of You; Our Love Affair; A Nightingale Sang in Berkeley Square; Pensylvania 6-5000; Tuxedo Junction; When the Swallows Come Back to Capistrano

**1941** Along the Santa Fe Trail; Anvil Chorus; The Booglie Wooglie Piggy; Chattanooga Choo Choo; Elmer's Tune; Five O'Clock Whistle; I Dreamt I Dwelt in Harlem; I Know Why; It Happened in Sun Valley; Jingle Bells; Song of the Volga Boatman; A String of Pearls; The White Cliffs of Dover; You and I

**1942** Always in My Heart; American Patrol; At Last; Dearly Beloved; Don't Sit Under the Apple Tree; Dearly Beloved; Everything I Love; Juke Box Saturday Night; (I Got a Gal in) Kalamazoo; The Lamplighter's Serenade; Moonlight Becomes You; Moonlight Cocktail; Serenade in Blue; Skylark; Sweet Eloise; That's Sabotage

**1943** Blue Rain; That Old Black Magic

**BELOW:** Paula Kelly and the Modernaires.

doesn't limit us to stereotyped intros, modulations, first choruses, endings, or even trick rhythms. The fifth sax, playing clarinet most of the time, lets you know whose band you're listening to. And that's about all there is to it."

Actually, that isn't remotely "all there is to it." Miller was a master at picking material for his band, and racked up an unusually high number of hits in the short period of the band's existence. Miller didn't go in for the overly lachrymose ballads of the period, though he was thought of as a "sweet" band. He did record some of the novelty songs of the day, including "Three Little Fishes." Miller concentrated on good-natured songs with an upbeat attitude and simple, declarative lyrics, avoiding anything resembling a tone poem or a high falutin' lyrical exercise. He had a penchant for raiding the back catalog for (very) old favorites, updating them with his patented arrangements. Such chestnuts as "Little Brown Jug," "The Anvil Chorus," "Song of the Volga Boatman," and "Don't Sit Under the Apple Tree" found their way into the band's repertoire. Miller also had a soft spot for songs with "moon" in the title, including "Moonlight Serenade," "Moon Love," "Oh, You Crazy Moon," "Blue Moonlight," "Bluebirds in the Moonlight," "Moments in the Moonlight," "The Man in the Moon," "Moonlight Sonata," "Moonlight Mood," "Moonlight Becomes You," and "Moonlight Cocktail." Why? Why not?

It all began back in 1936, with the formation of the first Glenn Miller band. The congregation had five reed men and Miller suggested that Irv Fazola, a good sax player but a great clarinetist, double the tenor-sax lead on his clarinet instead of just sitting there waiting for his sax part to come in. Boing! The band wasn't a hit but Miller, who got his start as an arranger as well as a trombonist, took notice when he started up his next band in March 1938.

Miller was respected by most of his players because he got results—but that doesn't mean he was liked. He could be strict but never mean, just serious about making a success of his band. He was described as cold-blooded, at least when it came to firing band members. He'd always trade up, though, slowly building a top-notch unit that would follow him unquestioningly. If you wanted to shine individually or swing too hard or show up a little under the weather, well, you weren't in the Miller band for long. It's not that Miller wasn't a regular guy, it's just that he was never prone to showing his emotions. A child of a poor upbringing traveling from Iowa to Nebraska to Missouri and finally to Colorado, Miller never forgot the hardship of his early years. Money was important to him and success meant more money. Like many Americans who grew up during the Depression, he never forgot the tough times. Al Klink, the great reed player, recalled, "I guess the best one-word description I've heard, and it isn't mine though I'd agree with it, was that Glenn was 'G.I.'—and that was even before he was in the service."

Miller told his friend and later, biographer, George Simon, "I'm not the kind of guy I really want to be." He was aware of his shortcomings but the pressure of having a successful band drove him to be more of disciplinarian than he might have wanted to be. He could be kind and even generous, but preferred to keep his largesse a secret.

Personality quirks aside, it's important to keep in mind that Miller's music still lives on, remembered and played at least as much as any other music from the '40s. There's still a Glenn Miller tribute band touring the country and several international Glenn Miller appreciation societies meeting regularly. Miller and his music have always made a lot of people very happy, and continue to do so some six decades later. Again, considering they were together for less than five years, the Miller band has had a remarkable impact on American popular song. ❖

## Song and Story

### I GOT A GAL IN KALAMAZOO
Harry Warren: I had a dum-dum-dum-dum rhythm going in my head, which was why Johnny Mack [Mack Gordon] and I decided to spell out the name. And I had been in Kalamazoo when I was very young and had carved my name on the wall of the railroad station there. I guess maybe that was the basis for the lyric. It wasn't the first song to spell out its title, but it was an angle that worked.

### MOONLIGHT SERENADE
In 1935, while a student of Joseph Schillinger, Glenn Miller wrote a simple composition as a mathematical exercise. Miller picked up the piece years later when he was a member of Ray Noble's Orchestra and Edward Heyman supplied a lyric titled, "Now I Lay Me Down to Weep." A new lyric was subsequently written by historian George T. Simon titled "Gone with the Dawn," and yet another was tossed on the pile by Mitchell Parish (who specialized in new lyrics to old songs) called "Wind on the Trees." He finally came up with the winner, "Moonlight Serenade." That title was inspired by Miller's recording of Frankie Carle's "Sunrise Serenade." Who said songwriting was easy?

### THE ANVIL CHORUS
Glenn Miller: The trend seems to be to jazz up the classics. I don't have any objection to doing this if there is no sentimental value attached to them. So while the "Anvil Chorus" from *Il Trovatore* lends itself every inch of the way to an adaptation, the symphonies of Beethoven don't, because people think of them as sacred.

### SONG OF THE VOLGA BOATMEN
Feodor Chaliapin popularized this traditional Russian song in his concerts and recitals throughout the United States. When he heard the Bill Finegan swing arrangement played by the Miller band, his comment was, "The boatmen's song is tortured for American ears."

### PENNSYLVANIA 6-5000
The title of this tune was the actual phone number of New York's Hotel Pennsylvania, where Miller's band often played. Originally, the band didn't shout out the title—but once the short vocal was added, the song became a big hit and the hotel was mighty pleased.

### A HANDFUL OF STARS
Arranger Bill Finegan sometimes wrote wilder arrangements than Miller wanted and the leader would cut down the more egregious excesses. Miller did appreciate Finegan's work and when he first heard the arrangement of "A Handful of Stars" he cried.

### TUXEDO JUNCTION
This song was written by bandleader Erskine Hawkins, Julius Dash, and William Johnson. The latter two were saxophone players with Hawkins. The title of the song comes from an actual railroad junction in Alabama. Miller and Hawkins both appeared at the Savoy Ballroom in Harlem on Christmas Eve 1939. Hawkins played the tune and members of the Miller band took notice. Jerry Gray wrote up an arrangement a few days later and the Miller band recorded the song in 1940, to great success.

## Asides

The Miller band was so well rehearsed that they often played only one take in the studio. Sometimes two but almost never.

Miller made the band pay for their own uniforms, unheard of at the time. And he forbade them from wearing them off the bandstand.

Occasionally when Marion Hutton was singing, Al Klink would joke, "The mike is out of tune tonight."

Miller's rendition of "Chattanooga Choo Choo" was the first gold record, an honor that is still bestowed on commercially successful recordings today.

When the band appeared on a Chesterfield-sponsored radio show, they could smoke only Chesterfields and had to wear maroon socks (the color on the cigarette pack)—even though it was radio!

Tommy Dorsey lent Miller $5,000 to get started and was miffed when he was paid back without an interest in the band. For this, he dubbed Miller "Old Klondike."

## First Person

Harry Warren: I knew Glenn could play anything I could put on paper and that he could arrange it in a way that could only make it sound marvelous. He was a master—more than people realized. His influence was enormous. Glenn was more responsible for the sound of the big band era than anybody. I wish I could have written more music for him but he went into the army right after *Orchestra Wives* and two years later he was dead.

# War Songs

One good thing that has come out of the many tragic wars in our nation's history is the war song, that patriotic ditty meant to stir men's hearts, bring tears to the eyes of the girls they left behind, commemorate great battles, inspire patriotic frenzy, and in some cases, stir us to protest. Over the course of time, American war songs have run the gamut of messages and of popular genres.

The Civil War brought forth a great number of songs. "The Battle Hymn of the Republic," "Dixie's Land," "When Johnny Comes Marching Home Again," and "Tenting Tonight on the Old Camp Ground" are still sung today. Stephen Foster wrote a few Civil War tunes, including "Was My Brother in the Battle?" and "Willie Has Gone to the War."

Once Tin Pan Alley entered the picture, publishers realized there was big money to be made from war songs. The first war to bear the stamp of the Alley was the 1885 Spanish-American War. "Our Country, May She Always Be Right," is a title that could be used today. But that war was just a dress rehearsal for the big one and Tin Pan Alley was ready and willing to make a buck, er, to give voice to those pro and con.

The mother of all wars, musically speaking, was World War I. The song titles tell us all we need to know about the feelings of the songwriters:

"I Didn't Raise My Boy to Be a Soldier," "Wake Up America," "The Meaning of Our Flag," "America, Here's My Boy," "Goodbye Broadway, Hello France." The most popular song of the war was George M. Cohan's "Over There."

World War II continued to feed the coffers of music publishers. By that time, Tin Pan Alley was well-established nationally and the major songwriters of the day joined in commenting on the war, in such offerings as Rodgers and Hart's "The Bombardier Song," Hoagy Carmichael's "The Cranky Old Yank (In a Clanky Old Tank)," Frank Loesser's "Praise the Lord and Pass the Ammunition"—the most popular of all

Second World War songs, Johnny Mercer's "G.I. Jive," and Jule Styne and Sammy Cahn's "Vic'try Polka." These and many other songs filled jukeboxes and quickened hearts at the movies and on Broadway.

To skip ahead a few decades, the war in Vietnam gave rise to the protest song. Rock musicians wrote with their hearts and came up with the "I-Feel-Like-I'm-Fixin'-to-Die-Rag," "It Better End Soon," "Ohio," "I Ain't A-Marchin' Anymore," and perhaps the most famous, John Lennon and Yoko Ono's "Give Peace a Chance." There was one notable pro-war song, Barry Sadler's "Ballad of the Green Berets," but it was vastly outnumbered by antiwar songs.

Today's war in Iraq has spawned a lot of dissent but very few antiwar songs, as today's songwriters and singers seem more interested in speaking out than singing out. Perhaps national events have robbed us of the naive notion that patriotism can be captured in a song, or that protest songs can change the course of history. Or maybe it's just that Tin Pan Alley isn't as ready, willing, or able to rock the political boat. ❖

# Artie Shaw

Shaw or Goodman? Goodman or Shaw? The big debate rages on even fifty years after Shaw retired from playing the clarinet. It's an argument that can't be won. Shaw appreciated Goodman but saw himself as a better interpreter. "The distance between me and Benny," Shaw proclaimed, "was that I was trying to play a musical thing, and Benny was trying to swing. Benny had great fingers; I'd never deny that. But listen to our two versions of 'Star Dust.' I was playing; he was swinging." Most admit that Shaw was the more progressive musician.

Shaw certainly had the more interesting life. Married eight times, he was constantly torn between playing music and becoming a writer. His intelligence, high standards, and outspokenness made him a fascinating figure. And then he disappeared and, like Garbo, became even more fascinating. Few actually believed that Shaw would keep his word when he set down his clarinet for the last time in the mid '50s, since he had already quit and returned to music repeatedly. But he had finally had enough, and moved on to apply his intellect to a wide variety of other endeavors.

Shaw had first walked off the bandstand in December 1939, when he left his post at the Café Rouge in New York's Hotel Pennsylvania and anonymously retired to Acapulco, Mexico, then a sleepy coastal town. Unfortunately for Shaw, after three months he saved a woman from drowning and the world discovered him again. After the bombing at Pearl Harbor, Shaw quit music again to join the struggle, but the navy had other ideas. After a stint as a minesweeper, he was assigned to create a service band. In 1943, after almost getting blown up at Guadalcanal, they were sent home—many, including Shaw, with a medical discharge due to stress and fatigue.

He set up another band, this one featuring jazz great Roy Eldridge, but gave it up again in 1947. He spent the next few years recording and performing classical music with the country's top symphony orchestras. In 1949, he returned to the big band business and quit again in 1951, this time buying a dairy farm and working on his autobiography. Over the next few years he dabbled in music now and then, with new groups. In March 1954, Shaw put down his clarinet and vowed never to pick it up again. It was a promise he kept.

Shaw spent the rest of his life on a variety of interesting pursuits. He moved to Spain in 1955, following harassment by the infamous House Un-American Activities Committee. He returned to the States in 1960. His wide-ranging intellect led him to mini-careers in cattle ranching, writing, film distribution and production (he produced the 1964 hit movie *Séance on a Wet Afternoon*), and even acting (in the 1978 disaster film, *Crash*). He wrote three books and was working on an autobiographical novel in which, at the end of ninety chapters, the protagonist was still only twenty-five! At the time of his death, his library contained more than fifteen thousand books.

Shaw traveled the nation delivering lectures to college students on such subjects as "The Artist in a Material Society," "The Swingers of the Big Band Era," "Psychotherapy and the Creative Artist," and "Consecutive Monogamy and Ideal Divorce." He became an expert marksman, a champion fly fisherman, and opened a rifle range.

Perhaps the only person who could really sum up the life and work of this restless, uncompromising artist is the man himself, so read on, and marvel at Artie Shaw ❖

> **"You play the clarinet. I play music."**
> **—Artie Shaw to Benny Goodman**

## Shaw on Music

The big problem for some people—and unfortunately I'm one of them—is that you eventually reach a point where you're never satisfied with what you're doing, You finally get to where good enough ain't good enough.

Sure it stinks, but it pays good dough, so the hell with it.

I could never understand why people wanted to dance to my music. I made it good enough to listen to.

I am compulsive, I sought perfection. I was constantly miserable. I was seeking a constantly receding horizon. So I quit. It was like cutting off an arm that had gangrene. I had to cut it off to live. I'd be dead if I didn't stop. The better I got, the higher I aimed. People loved what I did, but I had grown past it. I got to the point where I was walking in my own footsteps.

Swing was a publicist's word. When they talk about "swing music" that was jazz music, and there were big bands playing it and small bands playing it. But jazz must swing and if it doesn't swing, it isn't jazz. That's why swing is, as far as I'm concerned, a verb and not an adjective and not a noun.

"Begin the Beguine" is a pretty nice tune. But after you've played it five hundred times in a row it gets a little dull. If you are reduced to packaging what you do as a commodity, and involved in selling it to a vast audience, you are in serious trouble.

It's time to debunk swing. Let's take all the nonsense, the ballyhoo and jive jargon out of it. The two outstanding types of swing that are now being played often merit the ridicule and somewhat harsh criticism directed from more erudite circles. The first type of swing is that which attempts to blast off the roof. Here is what I consider grating music. Offensive to most ears and definitely of the musically punch-drunk variety, it is an out-and-out menace. The second classification bears the alliterative titles of "smooth" or "sophisticated" swing. For sheer monotony, I don't think that this type of music can be surpassed. There is no attempt at color or ingenuity.

Swing—and I mean real swing—is an idiom designed to make songs more listenable and more danceable than they are in their original form. It is, in sum, the creation and sustenance of a mood.

In it, there are blasting, purring, subtlety, obviousness—each in its proper place. That is what swing means and it will remain only if it continues to explore all the potentialities of a composition, whether it be by Bach or Duke Ellington. The only difference between swing and all other forms of music is that in swing an instrumentalist uses improvisations to improve the melody.

What the swing musician says to the composer is this: "See here! I've got something to say, too. Let me express my own musical ideas. I'll take your melody but let me see if I can create something artistic around it. Let me invent something new."

## Shaw on Women

People ask what those women saw in me, Let's face it, I wasn't a bad-looking stud. But that's not it. It's the music; it's standing up there under the lights. A lot of women just flip; looks have nothing to do with it. You call Mick Jagger good-looking? I know nothing about marriage, but I'm an expert on divorce…. None of them were real marriages. They were legalized affairs. In those days you couldn't get a lease on an apartment if you were living in sin.

These love goddesses are not what they seem, especially if you're married to one. They all think they want a traditional marriage, but they aren't married for that sort of thing. Somebody's got to get the coffee in the morning, and an Ava Gardner is not going to do that. So you get up and get it, and then you find you're doing everything.

## Song and Story

### STAR DUST
Shaw to Sam Litzinger of CBS Radio: If I had to say something was perfect musically, the solo I did on "Star Dust" is as close to being perfect as I would have wanted.

### BEGIN THE BEGUINE
Songwriter Cole Porter and librettist Moss Hart took an around-the-world cruise on the *Franconia* in order to write the musical *Jubilee*. While in the Dutch East Indies, Porter heard a native dance and was taken by its unique rhythm. He wrote "Begin the Beguine" and played it for Hart who later admitted, "I had reservations about the length of the song. Indeed, I am somewhat ashamed to record that I thought it had ended when he was only halfway through playing it."

When Artie Shaw recorded the Jerry Gray arrangement at his first session for Victor, it got a similarly tepid response. Shaw explained, "I just happened to like it so I insisted on recording it at this first session, in spite of the recording manager, who thought it a complete waste of time, and only let me make it after I had argued it would make a least a nice quiet contrast to the 'Indian Love Call' [on the B side]. That recording of that one little tune…was the real turning point in my life."

### FRENESI
While traveling through Mexico on vacation, Shaw discovered the tune "Frenesi" by Alberto Dominguez, and recorded it in 1940 to great success. Ray Charles and Bob Russell supplied an English lyric.

## Asides

Shaw's eight wives included actresses Lana Turner, Ava Gardner, and Evelyn Keyes.

Shaw was born Arthur Arshawsky. He changed it to Art Shaw but people told him his name sounded like a sneeze. So he altered it slightly to Artie Shaw.

## THE GREAT SONGS

1936  Interlude in B-Flat
1938  Begin the Beguine
1939  Back Bay Shuffle; Traffic Jam
1940  Concerto for Clarinet; Frenesi; Moonglow; Star Dust; Summit Ridge Drive
1941  Blues in the Night; Dancing in the Dark O
1945  Ac-cent-tchu-ate the Positive; Little Jazz

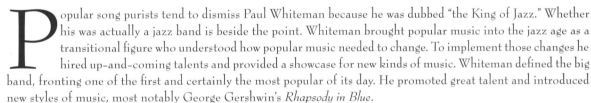

Popular song purists tend to dismiss Paul Whiteman because he was dubbed "the King of Jazz." Whether his was actually a jazz band is beside the point. Whiteman brought popular music into the jazz age as a transitional figure who understood how popular music needed to change. To implement those changes he hired up-and-coming talents and provided a showcase for new kinds of music. Whiteman defined the big band, fronting one of the first and certainly the most popular of its day. He promoted great talent and introduced new styles of music, most notably George Gershwin's *Rhapsody in Blue*.

The Whiteman band set the standard for future bands as well as the format for performance. It was the first band to feature a female vocalist, when Mildred Bailey stepped out in 1929. Later, Whiteman hired Bailey's brother, Al Rinker, along with Harry Barris and Bing Crosby, and introduced the idea of a vocal trio. With Ferde Grofe and later Don Redman and Bill Challis on payroll, it was only natural that Whiteman's band would be the first to use written arrangements. Grofe and Whiteman introduced the full reed and brass sections to the big band, another milestone. When he booked the band into vaudeville and led it on a European tour, he racked up two more firsts.

Whiteman had played violin and viola with the Denver Symphony, which instilled in him a respect for the classics and an interest in promoting new classical works in a modern idiom. During World War I he served as a bandsman and, upon being mustered out of the service in 1919, he started his own big band on the West Coast. Arranger and pianist Ferde Grofe, who would later write the *Grand Canyon Suite*, worked with Whiteman on that early band.

In 1920, Whiteman moved the band to New York, where he continued in the dance band tradition but with a slight difference. He employed jazz musicians and, as the decade progressed, they became more and more integral to Whiteman's music. Whiteman signed with Victor in 1920 and his fame grew outside New York. He soon toured throughout America and Europe, his popularity growing all the while.

In 1924, Whiteman commissioned a number of new works which he presented at the Aeolian Hall under the title, "Experiment in Modern Music." Chief among these works was George Gershwin's "Rhapsody in Blue," billed as a study in jazz—but it was actually a thrilling hybrid of jazz, classical, and popular music. The impact of that concert and the stunning reception to "Rhapsody" boosted Whiteman's reputation. He was encouraged to expand his repertoire and bring more jazz instrumentalists and singers into the fold.

The success of the Aeolian Hall concert encouraged Whiteman to commission additional works for the band. Some of the better compositions include Rube Bloom's "Soliloquy," "Metropolis" by Matt Malneck and Harry Barris, pianist Dana Suesse's "Blue Moonlight," and Peter De Rose's "Deep Purple".

Bix Beiderbecke, Red Nichols, Frankie Trumbauer, Henry Busse, Jack and Charlie Teagarden, Jimmy and Tommy Dorsey, Eddie Lang, and Joe Venuti all played for Whiteman. Mildred Bailey and Ramona and Joan Edwards supplied the distaff singing, and future lyric great Johnny Mercer also sang with the Whiteman ensemble. Each and every member of the Whiteman band loved their leader because he supported them wholeheartedly. Whiteman wasn't afraid to share the spotlight with a singer or player—or give it to them entirely.

When the 1930s rolled around, Whiteman was more popular than ever on stage, in concert, and in films. The 1930 showcase film *The King of Jazz*, produced by Universal Pictures, was an immediate sensation. Whiteman, the Rhythm Boys (with Bing Crosby making his film debut), Joe Venuti, Eddie Lang, Roy Bargy, and Wilbur Hall (playing "The Stars and Stripes Forever" on a bicycle pump!) were among the featured band members along with the Brox Sisters (an ür-Boswell Sisters group) and John Boles. Universal considered the film so promising that it paid for early Technicolor sequences including a cartoon, the first ever in Technicolor, directed by Walter Lantz, later the creator of Woody Woodpecker.

As the 1930s dawned, Whiteman turned to radio as a chief means of reaching ever greater audiences. In 1932, he began coast-to-coast broadcasts and decided to bring in new talent by holding local contests. It was in this way that he discovered Johnny Mercer, who was hired to sing and write special material at a princely $75 a week.

With the rise of the big bands in the '40s, Whiteman's productivity slowed. In the face of other more modern bands, he reformed his organization three times but couldn't shake off the dust of the past. Just as he began to gain some momentum, the draft decimated his roster and, by the time the war was over, so was the era of the big band, of which he was the consummate pioneer.

In 1942, Whiteman was repaid by Mercer by being one of the first artists signed by the new Capitol Records, but, though he was highly regarded historically, he just wasn't in vogue. He enjoyed the occasional television appearance and briefly led a band in Las Vegas in the early 1960s, but by the mid-'50s Whiteman was essentially retired.

Paul Whiteman's legacy is not necessarily musical, though he did produce some excellent sides in the "symphonic jazz" style. He is remembered more for his vision and enthusiasm, as well as his good heart. As such, both professionally and personally, he served as a model for all who came afterward. ◈

## Asides

When Bix Beiderbecke was too much of an alcoholic to play, Whiteman sent him home to Indiana to dry out and kept him on full salary.

In a first for the radio industry, Paul Whiteman's orchestra played "Ramona" over the airwaves from a studio in New York while Dolores Del Rio sang along from the Los Angeles living room of producer Joseph M. Schenck.

**OPPOSITE PAGE BOTTOM:** The Paul Whiteman Orchestra, augmented for the historic 1924 Aeolian Hall concert in which George Gershwin's *Rhapsody in Blue* premiered. **BELOW:** Way back in the distance is Whiteman, leading the orchestra in the 1930 musical, *The King of Jazz*. They don't make movies like that anymore.

## THE GREAT SONGS

| | |
|---|---|
| 1920 | The Japanese Sandman; Whispering |
| 1921 | Bright Eyes; Everybody Step; Song of India |
| 1922 | Do It Again; Hot Lips; I'll Build a Stairway to Paradise; I'm Just Wild About Harry; Pack Up Your Sins; Stumbling; Three O'Clock in the Morning |
| 1923 | Along the Old Lake Trail; An Orange Grove in California; Lady of the Evening |
| 1924 | Alabamy Bound; All Alone; Learn to Do the Strut; What'll I Do? |
| 1926 | The Birth of the Blues |
| 1927 | Broken-Hearted; Changes (with the Rhythm Boys); Washboard Blues; When Day Is Done |
| 1928 | American Tune; Because My Baby Don't Mean "Maybe" Now; Dardenella; From Monday On; I'm Bringing a Red, Red Rose; Louisiana (with Bing Crosby); Love Nest; Mississippi (with the Rhythm Boys); My Pet; Ol' Man River (with Bing Crosby); Poor Butterfly |
| 1929 | After You've Gone; I'm a Dreamer—Aren't We All?; Nola; Rhapsody in Blue; Waiting at the End of the Road |
| 1930 | A Bench in the Park; Happy Feet; It Happened in Monterey; Ragamuffin Romeo; Ramona |
| 1931 | When It's Sleepy Time Down South (with Mildred Bailey and the King's Jesters) |
| 1932 | I'll Never Be the Same (with Mildred Bailey) |
| 1933 | Ah! But Is It Love?; Are You Makin' Any Money? (with Ramona) |
| 1934 | All Through the Night (with Bob Lawrence); Fare-Thee-Well to Harlem (with Johnny Mercer and Jack Teagarden); I'm Counting on You (with Ramona); Pardon My Southern Accent |
| 1935 | Ain't Misbehavin' (with Jack Teagarden); A Picture of Me Without You (with Ramona and Ken Darby) |
| 1936 | On Your Toes (with Ramona) |

# AMERICAN SONG
# YEAR BY YEAR

One hundred years of American popular song:
Victor Herbert, Irving Berlin, and John Philip Sousa.

# THE 19TH CENTURY

Popular songs in the first half of the nineteenth century came from the church and political rallies. The beginning of the second half of the century was marked by the Civil War, and popular music grew out of the conflict. Religious songs evolved into inspirational marching songs used to rally the troops. The men in the field sang to express their homesickness and nostalgia for the old ways of life. As the soldiers sang about the old folks at home and beloved Southern rivers, their families stood around the parlor piano singing songs about their loved ones on the battlefields. Negro spirituals crossed racial barriers and were adopted and sung by whites. Regiments traveled with their own bands, which played as they engaged in battle. The predominant instruments of choice were drums—to keep the soldiers in line; fifes—which could be heard above the cannons' roar; and bugles—for announcing commands. Songs were composed to take advantage of the power of these martial instruments. After the war, minstrel shows swept the country and the Civil War songs were adapted to be sung by white performers in blackface.

As the century rolled on, the industrial revolution transformed the country. The profusion of inventions began with Eli Whitney's cotton gin and entertainment inventions quickly followed those of more utilitarian purposes. Thomas Edison invented the phonograph in 1877 and a decade later Emile Berliner perfected the gramophone and the first recorded discs. A year after that, in 1888, the Columbia Phonograph Company released the first commercial recordings, not discs but wax-covered cylinders. Flat discs, in seven- and ten-inch sizes, were issued by Columbia around 1891.

The year 1895 was an important one in musical history. That year, Scott Joplin, the premier ragtime composer, sold his first two songs, "Please Say You Will" and "A Picture of Her Face." Four years later, his "Maple Leaf Rag" exploded onto the American musical scene. The military band soon evolved into larger aggregations led but such bandleaders as Patrick Gilmore and Giuseppe Creatore. Also in 1895, John Philip Sousa's first successful operetta, *El Capitan*, opened on Broadway. The following year, Sousa composed "The Stars and Stripes Forever." He composed 70 songs in his lifetime but he is best known for his 135 marches. That same year, in Pontecchio, Italy, Guglielmo Marconi began experimenting with wireless telegraphy, sending a signal for over a mile and a half. By 1899 he had set up elaborate wireless broadcasting centers, and in 1900 received a patent for "tuned or syntonic telegraphy." The next year he sent a signal across the Atlantic Ocean, over 2,100 miles, and the radio was on its way to becoming the first mass medium.

By the turn of the century, American entertainment had become an industry and all the pieces were in place for the widespread dissemination of the popular arts. ◈

## Song and Story

### THE STARS AND STRIPES FOREVER

John Philip Sousa: Here came one of the most vivid incidents of my career. As the vessel [the *Teutonic*] steamed out of the harbor I was pacing on the deck, absorbed in thoughts of my manager's death and the many duties and decisions which awaited me in New York. Suddenly, I began to sense a rhythmic beat of a band playing within my brain. Throughout the whole tense voyage, that imaginary band continued to unfold the same themes, echoing and re-echoing the most distinct melody. I did not transfer a note of that music to paper while

## GREAT SONGS OF THE DECADES

**1860** Annie Lisle; The Glendy Bark; Lincoln And Liberty; Old Black Joe; Rock Me to Sleep, Mother; 'Tis but a Little Faded Flower; All Quiet Along the Potomac; Aura Lee; John Brown's Body; Maryland! My Maryland! ; Ole Shady: the Song of the Contraband; The Vacant Chair; Battle Hymn of the Republic; The Bonnie Blue Flag; Evangeline; Grafted into the Army; Kingdom Coming; That's What's the Matter; Was My Brother in the Battle? ; We Are Coming, Father Abraham, 300,000 More ; We've a Million in the Field ; Babylon Is Fallen!; The Battle-Cry of Freedom; Cousin Jedediah; Daisy Deane; Folks That Put on Airs; Just Before the Battle, Mother; The President's Proclamation; Rally Round the Cause, Boys; Tenting Tonight on the Old Camp Ground; Weeping, Sad and Lonely, or, When This Cruel War Is Over; When Johnny Comes Marching Home; Willie Has Gone to the War;All Quiet Along the Potomac Tonight; Beautiful Dreamer; Come Home, Father!; Rally for Old Abe; Tenting on the Old Camp Ground; Tramp! Tramp! Tramp!; Wake Nicodemus!; When the War Is Over, Mary; Beautiful Isle of the Sea; Beware; Ellie Rhee, or Carry Me Back to Tennessee; The Little Brown Church; Marching Through Georgia; Captain Jinks

of the Horse Marines; The Flying Trapeze; The Little Brown Jug; O Little Town of Bethlehem; Shew! Fly, Don't Bother Me; Sweet By and By; When You and I Were Young Maggie

**1870s** The Babies on Our Block; Carry Me Back to Old Virginny; Eileen Allana; Goodbye Liza Jane; I'll Take You Home Again, Kathleen; The Mulligan Guard; Oh! Dem Golden Slippers; Reuben and Rachel; Rose of Killarney; Silver Threads Among the Gold; The Skidmore Fancy Ball; The Skidmore Guard; Where Was Moses When the Light Went Out?

**1880s** Always Take Mother's Advice; Away in a Manger; The Convict and the Bird; Darkest the Hour; De Golden Wedding; Dear Mother, in Dreams I See Her; Down Went McGinty; Drill, Ye Tarriers, Drill; I Never Drank Behind the Bar; If the Waters Could Speak as They Flow; If You Love Me Darling, Tell Me with Your Eyes; I'll Be Ready When the Great Day Comes; Maggie, the Cows Are in the Clover; McNally's Row of Flats; Never Take the Horse The Outcast Unknown; Shoe from the Door; Oh Promise Me; Rock-a-Bye-Baby; Semper Fidelis; Sleep, Baby, Sleep; Strolling on the Brooklyn Bridge; There's a Tavern in the Town; Wait Till the Clouds Roll By; The Washington Post; Where Did You Get That Hat?; The Whistling Coon; Why Did They Dig Ma's Grave So Deep?

I was on the steamer, but when we reached shore, I set down the measures that my brain-band had been playing for me, and not a note of it has ever changed.

## NEW COON IN TOWN/ALL COONS LOOK ALIKE TO ME

The "coon song," or, as it was originally called, "coon shout," is a mostly forgotten genre of American popular song. Written by blacks as well as whites, coon songs used Southern clichés as their lyric motifs, and early syncopation marked much of the music. The lyrics weren't usually racist but the word "coon" consigned them to oblivion as we entered a more enlightened era. The first coon song was "New Coon in Town," written by Paul Allen in 1883. Ernest Hogan, the author and performer of "All Coons Look Alike to Me" (1896), was black himself and later concluded that the song was demeaning. It was recorded in 1897 and its success led to a spate of imitations.

## DAISY BELL

Songwriter Harry Dacre came from England to the United States with a bicycle in his possession. Customs agents levied a duty on the bicycle. When he heard about this, songwriter William Jerome quipped, "It's lucky you didn't bring a bicycle built for two, otherwise you'd have to pay double duty." Dacre picked up on the phrase and quickly wrote the song which was introduced in the English music hall by Kate Lawrence. It made its American debut by Tony Pastor at his Music Hall. In 1892, Jennie Lindsay sang it at the Atlantic Gardens on the Bowery, the same year bicycles were redesigned for women.

**1890s**   After the Ball Is Over; All Coons Look Alike to Me; America, the Beautiful; American Patrol; Annie Rooney; The Armorer's Song; Ask the Man in the Moon; Asleep in the Deep; The Band Played On; Because; The Bowery; Break the News to Mother; Brown October Ale; Daisy Bell; El Capitan; Gypsy Love Song; The Hand That Rocks the Cradle; Hats Off to Me; Hello! Ma Baby; A Hot Time in the Old Town Tonight; I Don't Want to Play in Your Yard; Kiss and Let's Make Up; Little Boy Blue; Love Will Find a Way; Mammy's Little Pumpkin Colored Coon; The Man Who Broke the Bank at Monte Carlo; Maple Leaf Rag; The Moth and the Flame; My Sweetheart's the Man in the Moon; My Wild Irish Rose; On the Banks of the Wabash Far Away; The Pardon Came Too Late; See-Saw, Margery Daw; She Is the Belle of New York; The Sidewalks of New York; The Stars and Stripes Forever; Sweet Rosie O'Grady; Ta-ra-ra-bom-der-e; Throw Him Down, McCloskey; When You Were Sweet Sixteen

## AT A GEORGIA CAMP MEETING

Kerry Mills wrote this 1899 coon song, set at a religious meeting, as a response to what he considered the degrading lyrics of many songs in the genre. When it came to publishing the piece, however, no one was interested—so Mills created F. A. Mills music publishers (his real name was Frederick Allen Mills). He convinced the song-and-dance team Genaro and Bailey to put the song into their vaudeville act and it soon became an immense success.

## THE BAND PLAYED ON

John Palmer was sitting in his apartment listening to a German brass band play under his window. Palmer's sister went to close the window and Palmer remarked, "Let the band play on." Boing! He wrote the song and peddled it around, to no success. He happened to be singing the song one day when vaudevillian Charles B. Ward heard it and offered to buy the rights outright. Since no publisher seemed to be interested, Palmer sold the rights to Ward who promptly put his name on the song. Ward created the New York Music Company to publish it and pushed to get the song covered by as many of his vaudeville friends as possible. Ward introduced the song at Hammerstein's Harlem Opera House, and subsequently, the *New York World* printed it in their rotogravure section and plugged it in their paper, marking the first time a newspaper promoted a song. The song became a smash hit and sales of the sheet music surpassed 1 million copies. Poor John Palmer never received a penny beyond Ward's initial payment.

## DIXIE

Dan Emmett's classic was probably the first true popular song. Emmett, a member of Bryant's Minstrels, then playing Mechanics Hall in New York City, recalled how he came to write the song: "One Saturday night in 1859, as I was leaving Bryant's theatre where I was playing, Bryant called after me, 'I want a walk-around for Monday, Dan.' The next day it rained and I stayed indoors."

With the weather so bad, Emmett remarked to his wife, "I wish I was in Dixie." Ding! "Suddenly, I jumped up and sat down at the table to work. In less than an hour I had the first verse and chorus. After that it was easy. When my wife returned I sang it to her."

Emmett premiered the song and it was an immediate hit. Peters Publishers bought it outright from Emmett for $500. Minstrel companies adopted it and it became the most popular song of its time. Its debut in "the land of cotton" came when it was performed by the minstrel troupe Rumsey and Newcomb in Charleston, South Carolina, in 1860. In March 1861, in New Orleans, Susan Denim led a group of Zouaves performing the song in a production of Pocahontas. Confederate soldiers soon appropriated it, new martial lyrics were added, and General Pickett ordered that "Dixie" be played to boost morale just prior to his charge at Gettysburg. Lincoln, too, favored the song, considering it among his spoils of war and asking that Northern bands take it up.

## ON THE BANKS OF THE WABASH FARAWAY

Novelist Theodore Dreiser, well-known anti-Semite and the brother of Paul Dresser, claimed to have given Dresser the idea to write about the river they knew so well as children. But Max Hoffman, a well-known orchestrator for Witmark Publishing claimed, "I went to his room in the Auditorium Hotel, where instead of a piano there was a small camp organ Paul always carried with him. It was summer. All the windows were open and Paul was mulling over a melody that was practically in finished form. But he did not have the words. So he had me play the full chorus over and over again at least for two or three hours, while he was writing the words, changing a line here and a phrase there, until the lyric suited him…. During the whole evening we spent together, Paul made no mention of anyone's having helped him with the song."

# THE 1900s & TEENS

The first two decades of the twentieth century were transitional years in the history of popular music. Technical advances were setting the stage for the burgeoning radio and recording industries. Blues, musical theater, and jazz enjoyed their first successes. Authors and politicians had been the stars of their day but with the advent of the talking machine, performers gained widespread fame around the world.

Musical comedy was born, in a way, when *Floradora* opened on November 10, 1900, at the Casino Theater. Combining a ballet company and theatrical company, *Floradora* spawned the famous *Floradora* Sextette, which elevated the chorus girl to star status. The show was in trouble in its first months, until publicist Anna Marble made sure the Sextette was touted across the nation, and pushed the show's hit song, "Tell Me Pretty Maiden," written by Leslie Stuart and Owen Hall.

In 1901, Guglielmo Marconi broadcast wireless signals across the Atlantic, a total of 2,100 miles, later winning the Nobel Prize for Physics for his invention. Radio would soon become the first medium for mass communication.

On April 11, 1902, Enrico Caruso, soon to be the world's leading tenor, recorded ten songs in Milan, and was paid 100 pounds for the day's work. In November and December of the same year, he recorded another ten cylinders and the next year ten more records, this time for the International Zonophone Company. In 1904, Victor signed Caruso to an exclusive contract and released 245 sides prior to his death in 1921. All of Caruso's recordings are still in print on CD, over one hundred years after they were recorded. Caruso was the first superstar in recorded history.

The blues gained popularity when W. C. Handy wrote the political campaign song "Boss Crump" for Edward Crump in 1909. He later renamed it "The Memphis Blues" and self-published it in 1912. Two years later, it was recorded and became a huge hit. Handy's "St. Louis Blues" made him even richer, and in 1917, he recorded for Columbia Records. The next year, he moved his Handy and Pace music publishing operation to New York City.

Irving Berlin penned "Alexander's Ragtime Band" in 1911, the first hit song to incorporate syncopation into popular music. Though it wasn't a true rag by any means, it opened the door to the public's acceptance of rhythms other than the waltz, fox-trot, and polka.

ASCAP, the American Society of Composers, Authors, and Publishers, was formed in 1914 for the licensing and collection of royalties for public performances. ASCAP started by collecting on live performances in cafes and restaurants, and moved on to radio performances and even Muzak. ❖

## Song and Story

### AFTER THE BALL

Charles K. Harris was an established songwriter by 1892, when he attended a ball in Chicago. While at the dance he saw a couple quarrel and split up. The lyric "Many a heart is aching after the ball" immediately flashed in his mind. He quickly wrote the rest of the song and convinced vaudevillian Sam Doctor to introduce it during an engagement in Milwaukee. Doctor forgot the lyrics and the song was a failure. Harris then gave the song to J. Aldrich Lilley, a performer in a road company of the musical *A Trip to Chinatown*. Harris paid Lilley $500 and a cut of the royalties to interpolate the song during the Milwaukee engagement. Harris remembered the audience's stunned silence

# GREAT SONGS OF THE DECADES

**1900**   Absence Makes the Heart Grow Fonder; A Bird in a Gilded Cage; Every Race Has a Flag but the Coon; Good-bye, Dolly Gray; Ma Blushin' Rosie; Tell Me Pretty Maiden

**1901**   Coon! Coon! Coon; Hello, Central, Give Me Heaven; Mighty Lak' a Rose; My Castle on the Nile

**1902**   Bill Bailey, Won't You Please Come Home?; In the Sweet Bye and Bye; Mister Dooley; Under the Bamboo Tree

**1903**   Bedelia; Ida! Sweet As Apple Cider!; You're the Flower of My Heart, Sweet Adeline; I Can't Do the Sum; The March of the Toys; Toyland

**1904**   Absinthe Frappe; Give My Regards to Broadway; The Yankee Doodle Boy; Meet Me in St. Louis, Louis

**1905**   Forty-Five Minutes from Broadway; Mary's a Grand Old Name; I Want What I Want When I Want It; Kiss Me Again; In My Merry Oldsmobile; In the Shade of the Old Apple Tree; My Gal Sal; Wait 'Til the Sun Shines, Nellie

**1906**   Anchors Aweigh; Chinatown, My Chinatown; Keep in the Sunny Side; Every Day Is Ladies' Day with Me; The Streets of New York; Waltz Me Around Again Willie—'Round, You're a Grand Old Flag

**1907**   Budweiser's a Friend of Mine; Harrigan; It's Delightful to Be Married; School Days

**1908**   Cuddle Up a Little Closer; Shine On, Harvest Moon; Take Me Out to the Ball Game

**1909**   By the Light of the Silvery Moon; Casey Jones; Heaven Will Protect the Working Girl; I Wonder Who's Kissing Her Now; Meet Me Tonight in Dreamland; Put on Your Old Gray Bonnet

**1910**   Come, Josephine, in My Flying Machine; Every Little Movement; Ah! Sweet Mystery of Life; I'm Falling in Love with Someone; Let Me Call You Sweetheart; Mother Machree; Put Your Arms Around Me Honey

after the number was introduced: "I was ready to sink through the floor. He then went through the second verse and chorus, and again complete silence reigned. I was making ready to bolt, but my friends…held me tightly by the arm. Then came the third verse and chorus. For a full minute the audience again remained quiet, and then broke loose with applause…The entire audience arose and, standing, applauded wildly for five minutes."

### ALEXANDER, DON'T YOU LOVE YOUR BABY NO MORE?

The vaudeville and musical comedy team of McIntyre and Heath used the name "Alexander" as a running gag in their blackface comedy routines. One day in 1904, Harry von Tilzer overheard a black woman in the theater's lobby remark, "Don't you love your baby no more?" He added the name "Alexander" to the comment and had his lyricist, Andrew Sterling, write a "coon song" with that title. The name became associated with black characters and Irving Berlin used it in his 1910 song "Alexander and His Clarinet." Berlin used that song's lyrics as the basis for "Alexander's Ragtime Band," written a year later.

### A BIRD IN A GILDED CAGE

Sentimental ballads were the rage in the 1890s, and this popular narrative ballad became one of the biggest hits in the first decade of the new century. When Arthur J. Lamb asked Harry von Tilzer to write the lyrics, von Tilzer assented on the understanding that the heroine of the song was the millionaire's wife, not mistress. Von Tilzer may have been looking out for his reputation because--in an early example of test marketing—he had

tried the song out in a brothel. When the women cried over the poor heroine's plight, von Tilzer explained, "Now I know I have a hit, if even these ladies can weep over my song." The team later wrote a sequel, "The Mansion of Aching Hearts" and had another hit on their hands.

### BREAK THE NEWS TO MOTHER

Songwriter Charles K. Harris was sitting in the theater one evening in 1897, watching the great actor William Gillette in the play *Secret Service*. Toward the end, a wounded Confederate drummer boy whispered to a black butler, "Break the news to mother." Harris couldn't wait to get home and write a lyric based on that line. The next morning he had most of the song finished but was stuck on the ending. As he recalled it, "Try as I might, I could not think of a second verse or a climax for the song. How to end the song with a punch puzzled me. While in a barber's chair a thought came to my mind in a flash and I cried out, 'I have it! I'm going to kill him!' The barber who was shaving me at the time became very much startled when he heard this remark and thought I had lost my reason."

## First Person

Victor Herbert, 1911: We need an American School of Music in order to give our young composers a chance to develop and drive out the

quacks. Our young composers are too prone to get their ideas from the old world, and their work naturally will fall into the style of foreign composition. They do not get into their music that freshness and vitality so characteristic of this country. And yet on the other hand American musical taste has developed to a point where it demands something that is native.

**ABOVE:** Before she conquered Hollywood, Ina Claire, pictured here on the cover of *The Theatre* magazine, appeared in the *Ziegfeld Follies of 1915* on Broadway.

**1911** Alexander's Ragtime Band; Everybody's Doing It Now; Good-Night Ladies; I Want a Girl—Just Like the Girl That Married Dear Old Dad; Oh You Beautiful Doll

**1912** Do It Again; It's a Long, Long Way to Tipperary; The Memphis Blues; Moonlight Bay; My Melancholy Baby; Row, Row, Row; Waiting for the Robert E. Lee; When Irish Eyes Are Smiling

**1913** Ballin' the Jack; Peg o' My Heart; Sweethearts; The Trail of the Lonesome Pine; You Made Me Love You—I Didn't Want to Do It

**1914** By the Beautiful Sea; I Want to Go Back to Michigan—Down on the Farm; Play a Simple Melody; St. Louis Blues; They Didn't Believe Me; When You Wore a Tulip and I Wore a Big Red Rose

**1915** Down Among the Sheltering Palms; Hello, Frisco!; It's Tulip Time in Holland; Memories; M-O-T-H-E-R, a Word That Means the World to Me; The Old Grey Mare

**1916** Beale Street; Bugle Call Rag; I Ain't Got Nobody; I've a Shooting Box in Scotland; Ireland Must Be Heaven, for My Mother Came from There; M-i-s-s-i-s-s-i-p-p-i; Poor Butterfly; Pretty Baby; Yacka Hula Hickey Dula

**1917** The Darktown Strutters' Ball; For Me and My Gal; Indiana; Leave It to Jane; Over There; Smiles; They Go Wild Simply Wild Over Me; Thine Alone; 'Till the Clouds Roll By; We're Going Over; Will You Remember

**1918** After You've Gone; The Daughter of Rosie O'Grady; Hello, Central! Give Me No Man's Land; Hinky-Dinky Parlez-vous; I'm Always Chasing Rainbows; Ja-Da; K-K-K-Katy; Oh! How I Hate to Get Up in the Morning; Rock-a-bye Your Baby with a Dixie Melody

**1919** Dardanella; How Ya Gonna Keep 'Em Down on the Farm?; I'm Forever Blowing Bubbles; In My Sweet Little Alice Blue Gown; Mandy; A Pretty Girl Is Like a Melody; Swanee

# THE 1920s

The decade really did roar—in spite of (or perhaps because of) Prohibition. On January 16, 1920, the Eighteenth Amendment took effect and all importing, exporting, transporting, selling, and manufacturing of alcoholic beverages was banned by law. Shortly thereafter, the National Prohibition Act took effect and drinking went underground, confined to speakeasies where intoxicants were sipped from coffee cups. Prohibition is said to have paved the way for the rise of organized crime organizations, which stood to profit handsomely from the trafficking of the illegal substances. And of course they had to have some way to launder the money they made. The entertainment field was the perfect outlet, and crime bosses were soon investing in nightclubs and Broadway shows—and making the proverbial "killing" here and there.

The phonograph was becoming ubiquitous in American parlors, inevitably replacing the parlor piano. The first record companies emerged and, in 1921, and the British His Master's Voice Company opened the first HMV shop on Oxford Street in London. (It was HMV that first used the logo of the terrier listening to "his master's voice" on the gramophone. It was designed by British artist Francis Barraud, modeled on his own dog, Nipper, now immortal.)

In 1923, Louis Armstrong made his recording debut, playing a cornet solo on King Oliver's Creole Jazz Band recording of "Chimes Blues." The following year, George Gershwin's "Rhapsody in Blue" debuted at New York's Aeolian Hall in New York, in a concert commissioned by Paul Whiteman and subtitled, "An Experiment in Modern Music." Country music hit the airwaves in 1925 when WSM radio began broadcasting in Nashville. Among their shows was the "WSM Barn Dance," which would soon be renamed the "Grand Ole Opry."

Nineteen twenty-seven was a milestone year in popular music. King Oliver's Dixie Syncopaters' argument over salary at Harlem's Cotton Club made room for Duke Ellington and his Jungle Band's historic engagement. Live broadcasts from the club spread Ellington's fame throughout America. That same year, Ralph Peer, A&R man and field-recording engineer for the Victor Company, arrived in Bristol, Tennessee, and recorded both Jimmie Carter and the Carter family, thus introducing the world to modern country music. Florenz Ziegfeld's production of Jerome Kern and Oscar Hammerstein II's musical *Show Boat* opened at the Ziegfeld Theater and became one of the most influential shows in Broadway history. The Automatic Music Company put the first electric coin-operated phonographs, or "jukeboxes," in bars.

Also in 1927, *The Jazz Singer*, the first popular talking picture, premiered and changed the motion picture industry forever. By 1928, sound pictures had replaced silents. In small towns, a pianist or organist had always accompanied screenings of silent pictures, and in many big-city movie palaces, a full orchestra was employed. When sound films took hold, those musicians had to seek other work. The studios were forced to hire their own orchestras to record film soundtracks and, to get the most from all of the musicians now on the payroll, studios turned their energies to the movie musical. To fill the talent gap, Hollywood raided Broadway—most of the great songwriters and arrangers (the white ones, anyway) decamped for the coast, some permanently.

In 1929, RCA bought the Victor Talking Machine Company of Camden, New Jersey, and RCA-Victor was born. Victor was itself a merger of the Consolidated Talking Machine Company, owned by Eldridge R. Johnson, and Emile Berliner's Berliner Gramophone Company. Rudy Vallee, one of the day's most popular

# GREAT SONGS OF THE DECADE

**1920**   All She'd Say was "Umh Hum"; Avalon; Bright Eyes; Daddy, You've Been a Mother to Me; I'll Be with You in Apple Blossom Time; The Japanese Sandman; Look for the Silver Lining; The Love Nest; Margie; My Mammy; Rose of Washington Square; So Long! Oo-Long; When My Baby Smiles at Me; Whispering; Wild Rose

**1921**   Ain't We Got Fun?; April Showers; Bandana Days; Dapper Dan; I'm Just Wild About Harry; I'm Nobody's Baby; Kitten on the Keys; Ma—He's Makin' Eyes at Me; My Man; Sally; Say It with Music; Second Hand Rose; The Sheik of Araby; Shuffle Along; When Buddha Smiles; When Francis Dances with Me; Whip-poor-will

**1922**   Carolina in the Morning; "Chicago" That Toddlin' Town; Do It Again; I Wish I Could Shimmy Like My Sister Kate; A Kiss in the Dark; Mister Gallagher and Mister Sheen; My Buddy; Nellie Kelly, I Love You; Rose of the Rio Grande; Runnin' Wild!; Some Sunny Day; Stumbling; Three O'Clock in the Morning; Toot, Toot, Tootsie; 'Way Down Yonder in New Orleans; Who Cares

**1923**   Bambalina; Barney Google; Bugle Call Rag; Charleston; I Cried for You; I Love You; I Won't Say I Will but I Won't Say I Won't; It Ain't Gonna Rain No Mo'; Last Night on the Back Porch—I Loved Her Best of All; Oh! Gee, Oh! Gosh, Oh! Golly, I'm in Love; Some Sweet Day; That Old Gang of Mine; Who's Sorry Now?; Who'll Buy My Violets?; Wild Flower; Yes! We Have No Bananas;

**1924**   All Alone; Amapola—Pretty Little Poppy; California, Here I Come; Charley, My Boy; Deep in My Heart, Dear; Does the Spearmint Lose Its Flavor on the Bedpost Overnight?; Everybody Loves My Baby, but My Baby Don't Love Nobody but Me; Fascinating Rhythm; Hinky Dinky Parlay Voo; I Want to Be Happy; I'll See You in My Dreams; Indian Love Call; June Night; Keep Smiling at Trouble; The Man I Love; My Best Girl; Rose Marie; S-h-i-n-e; Somebody Loves Me; Tea for Two; What'll I Do?

**1925**   Alabamy Bound; Always; Collegiate; A Cup of Coffee, a Sandwich and You; Dinah; Don't Bring Lulu; D'Ye Love Me; Five Foot Two, Eyes of Blue; I'm Sitting on Top of the World; I Love My Baby—My Baby Loves Me; If You Knew Susie—Like I Know Susie; If You Were the Only Girl; Manhattan; Remember; Show Me the Way to Go Home; Sleepy Time Gal; Some Day; Sunny; Sweet and Low Down; Sweet Georgia Brown; That Certain Feeling; Ukulele Lady; Who; Yearning—Just for You; Yes Sir, That's My Baby

singers, made his first motion picture, *The Vagabond Lover*, in 1929 and became the host of the *Fleischmann's Yeast Musical Variety Hour* radio show.

The twenties were also the decade of such novelty songs as "Barney Google" by Billy Rose and Con Conrad, "Does the Spearmint Lose Its Flavor on the Bedpost Overnight?," Frank Silver and Irving Conn's "Yes! We Have No Bananas." Flapper-influenced songs became the rage as the twenties roared on, the most famous being "Five Foot Two, Eyes of Blue (Has Anybody Seen My Gal)" and "Yes Sir, That's My Baby" by Walter Donaldson and Gus Kahn.

Dance crazes were all the rage in the 1920s, and none was bigger than the Charleston. The song of the same name was written in 1923 by Cecil Mack (a pseudonym for R. C. McPherson) and James P. Johnson, and was introduced by Elisabeth Welch in the musical comedy *Runnin' Wild*. The masters of the dance craze song were De Sylva, Brown, and Henderson. In 1925, they came up with the "Black Bottom," named for the mud at the bottom of the Mississippi. Alberta Hunter invented (or at least codified) the dance. While few remember the actual steps, the song is still sung today. The dance was later dubbed "The Dance of Death" when the floor of the Hotel Pickwick in Boston collapsed, killing fifty people. Attempts to create popular dances in the thirties with such songs as "The Continental" and "Carioca" were doomed to failure. With the Depression going full force, people just didn't feel like dancing. ◆

## Song and Story

### YES SIR, THAT'S MY BABY
The rhythm of the opening lyric to this Walter Donaldson and Gus Kahn song was inspired by a toy wind-up pig belonging to Eddie Cantor's daughters. Kahn was over Cantor's house one day and he absent-mindedly wound up the pig. The rhythm immediately suggested the first line of the song.

### ALABAMY BOUND
Nora Bayes sang this song in 1928 during a benefit at the Bowery Mission House in New York. It would be the last song she would sing: she died four days later.

**1926** After I Say I'm Sorry; All Alone Monday; Are You Lonesome Tonight?; Baby Face; The Birth of the Blues; Black Bottom; The Blue Room; Breezin' Along with the Breeze; Bye Bye Blackbird; Charmaine; Clap Yo' Hands; Do-Do-Do; "Gimmie" a Little Kiss, Will "Ya" Huh?; The Girl Friend; Horses; I Know That You Know; If I Could Be with You One Hour To-Night; In a Little Spanish Town; It All Depends on You; Looking at the World Thru Rose Colored Glasses; Lucky Day; Moonlight on the Ganges; Mountain Greenery; One Alone; The Ranger's Song; The Riff Song; Rio Rita; Someone to Watch Over Me; Sunny Disposish; A Tree in the Park; When Day Is Done; When the Red, Red Robin Comes Bob, Bob Bobbin' Along

**1927** Among My Souvenirs; At Sundown; Back in Your Own Back Yard; The Best Things in Life Are Free; Bill; Blue Skies; Can't Help Lovin' Dat Man; Chloe; Funny Face; Hallelujah!; I'm Looking Over a Four Leaf Clover; Keep Sweeping the Cobwebs Off the Moon; Let a Smile Be Your Umbrella on a Rainy Day; Lucky in Love; Make Believe; Me and My Shadow; Miss Annabelle Lee; Mississippi Mud; My Blue Heaven; My Heart Stood Still; My One and Only; Ol' Man River; Ramona; Sam, the Old Accordian Man; Shaking the Blues Away; Side by Side; Sometimes I'm Happy; The Song Is Ended—But the Melody Lingers On; Soon; Strike Up the Band; 'Swonderful; Thou Swell; The Varsity Drag; Why Do I Love You?;

**1928** Button Up Your Overcoat; Constantinople; Crazy Rhythm; Diga Diga Do; Feeling I'm Falling; I Can't Give You Anything but Love; I Wanna Be Loved By You; I'll Get By— As Long As I Have You; In a Mist; Let's Do It; Let's Misbehave; The Lonesome Road; Love Me or Leave Me; Lover, Come Back to Me; Makin' Whoopee!; Manhattan Serenade; March of the Musketeers; Marie; My Lucky Star; Nagasaki; She's Funny That Way; Short'nin' Bread; Softly, As in a Morning Sunrise; Sonny Boy; Stout Hearted Men; Sweet Lorraine; Sweet Sue—Just You; That's My Weakness Now; There's a Rainbow Round My Shoulder; Watching the Clouds Roll By; When You're Smiling—the Whole World Smiles with You; You're the Cream in My Coffee; You Took Advantage of Me

**1929** Ain't Misbehavin'; Am I Blue?; Aren't We All; Broadway Melody; Can't We Be Friends?; Don't Ever Leave Me; Dream Lover; Great Day; Happy Days Are Here Again; Here Am I; Honeysuckle Rose; I've Got a Feeling I'm Falling; I Kiss Your Hand, Madame; If I Had a Talking Picture of You; June Moon; Liza; Louise; Love, Your Magic Spell Is Everywhere; Moanin' Low; More Than Your Know; Pagan Love Song; Ship Without a Sail; Singin' in the Rain; S'posin'; Star Dust; Sunny Side Up; Tip Toe Thru the Tulips with Me; True Blue Lou; Wedding Bells Are Breaking Up That Old Gang of Mine; The Wedding of the Painted Doll; Why Can't I?; With a Song in My Heart; Without a Song; You Do Something to Me

# THE 1930s

The '30s, the last decade before America's involvement in World War II, would mark the beginning of the big-band era. The fox-trot, the 1920s dance of choice, and which had replaced the previous century's waltz, was passé and newer dances took its place. Music changed, with swing gaining millions of fans, though it had its detractors, too, who believed that when swing came in the music went out. Playwright George S. Kaufman was among the naysayers when he opined, "The unbelievable invention known as 'swing' is strictly for mental defectives."

In 1931, EMI (Electric and Musical Industries Ltd.) was formed when the English Columbia Gramophone Company and the Gramophone Company/HMV merged, forming the largest record company in the world. The new company wouldn't have an impact on American music for another twenty years. The EMI Studios at Abbey Road opened that same year and became the world's largest recording studio.

Country music grew in popularity when radio station WSM upgraded to a 50,000-watt, clear-channel signal with the potential to reach far beyond its home in Nashville. By the end of the decade, NBC Radio was broadcasting the *Grand Ole Opry* to a nationwide audience.

More opportunities arose for black artists in the 1930s and, though they were far from being accepted generally in the still white-dominated media, significant strides were made. Ethel Waters, the most popular black singer of the '30s, led the way on a number of fronts. In 1933, she became the first black to host her own radio program. That same year she appeared at the Cotton Club singing "Stormy Weather" and opened in *As Thousands Cheer* on Broadway, becoming the first black performer to share equal billing with white performers. In 1938, she appeared at Carnegie Hall and,

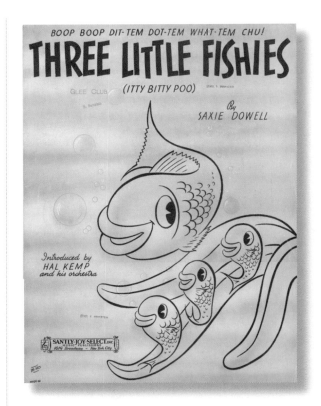

the next year, became the first black person on television, when NBC broadcast the Broadway hit *Mamba's Daughters* (starring Waters) and a variety show, *The Ethel Waters Show,* as early experiments in transmission. Also in 1933, Benny Goodman recorded "Your Mother's Son-in-Law" with vocals by Billie Holiday. It was Goodman's first step toward integrating his all-white band.

It was in 1935 that Benny Goodman hired pianist Teddy Wilson, a black man, to play with him and Gene Krupa, forming the interracial Benny Goodman Trio. They were well enough respected that they were booked at Carnegie Hall in 1938. In 1936, Rudy Vallee hired

# GREAT SONGS OF THE DECADE

I Take My Sugar to Tea; Where the Blue of the Night Meets the Gold of the Day; You're My Everything

**1930** A Bench in the Park; Beyond the Blue Horizon; Bidin' My Time; Body and Soul; Dancing with Tears in My Eyes; Embraceable You; Exactly Like You; Fine and Dandy; Georgia on My Mind; Get Happy; I Got Rhythm; Just a Gigolo; Love for Sale; On the Sunny Side of the Street; Rockin' Chair; Sing Something Simple; Something to Remember You By; Them There Eyes; Three Little Words; Time on My Hands; Walkin' My Baby Back Home; What Is This Thing Called Love?; You're Driving Me Crazy!—What Did I Do?

**1931** All of Me; Between the Devil and the Deep Blue Sea; Dancing in the Dark; Delishious; Dream a Little Dream of Me; Goodnight, Sweetheart; Heartaches; I Found a Million Dollar Baby—In a Five and Ten Cent Store; I've Got Five Dollars; I Love a Parade; Lady of Spain; Life Is Just a Bowl of Cherries; Love Is Sweeping the Country; Minnie the Moocher—The Ho Do Ho Song; Mood Indigo; Nevertheless; New Sun in the Sky; The Night Was Made for Love; Of Thee I Sing; Out of Nowhere; The Peanut Vendor; Penthouse Serenade; Prisoner of Love; River, Stay 'Way from My Door; Shadrack; Smile, Darnya, Smile; The Thrill Is Gone; Till the Real Thing Comes Along; Try to Forget; When

**1932** Alone Together; April in Paris; Brother, Can You Spare a Dime?; Eadie Was a Lady; Forty-Second Street; How Deep Is the Ocean?; I'm Gettin' Sentimental Over You; I Gotta Right to Sing the Blues; I've Told Ev'ry Little Star; If I Love Again; It Don't Mean a Thing; Let's Have Another Cup o' Coffee; Let's Put Out the Lights; Mimi; Night and Day; Shuffle Off to Buffalo; Soft Lights and Sweet Music; The Song Is You; Willow Weep for Me; You're an Old Smoothie; You're Getting to Be a Habit with Me; Young and Healthy

**1933** Annie Doesn't Live Here Anymore; The Boulevard of Broken Dreams; By a Waterfall; Carioca; Did You Ever See a Dream Walking?; Don't Blame Me; Easter Parade; Everything I Have Is Yours; Flying Down to Rio; The Gold Diggers' Song—We're in the Money; Heat Wave; I Cover the Waterfront; It's Only a Paper Moon; It's the Talk of the Town; Lazybones; Let's Fall in Love; Lover; Orchids in the Moonlight; Shadow Waltz; Smoke Gets in Your Eyes; Sophisticated Lady; Stormy Weather; Temptation; Who's Afraid of the Big Bad Wolf?; Yesterdays; You're Devastating

Louis Armstrong to take over his radio show while he was on vacation.

*Billboard* printed its first chart in 1938, as a benefit for jukebox owners. The chart's importance would soon reach far beyond that industry. ◆

## Song and Story

### TEMPTATION

Bing Crosby sang this Arthur Freed and Nacio Herb Brown standard to Marion Davies in *Going Hollywood* (seen right). He remembered it as "my first attempt at presenting a song dramatically." It became a huge hit and allowed him to expand his repertoire.

### I FOUND A MILLION DOLLAR BABY IN A FIVE-AND-TEN-CENT STORE

It was the midst of the Depression—and that's the whole point of this Billy Rose, Mort Dixon, and Harry Warren song. On the same lyrical wavelength as "The Best Things in Life Are Free," this 1931 hit put the highest value on love, and it was more than anyone in America had to his name (save Rockefeller and Ford). The song was introduced by Ted Healy, Fanny Brice, and Phil Baker in top hats, white ties, and tails. Hmmm. Reminds us of another Depression-era song.

**1934** All I Do Is Dream of You; All Through the Night; Anything Goes; Blow, Gabriel, Blow; Blue Moon; The Continental; Cocktails for Two; Deep Purple; Easy Come, Easy Go; For All We Know; Fun to Be Fooled; I Get a Kick Out of You; I Only Have Eyes for You; If There Is Someone Lovelier Than You; June in January; Let's Take a Walk Around the Block; Love in Bloom; Love Thy Neighbor; Moonglow; The Object of My Affection; On the Good Ship Lollipop; One Night of Love; P.S. I Love You; Solitude; Stars Fell on Alabama; Tumbling Tumbleweeds; Two Cigarettes in the Dark; The Very Thought of You; What a Diff'rence a Day Made; Winter Wonderland; You and the Night and the Music; You're the Top; You Oughta Be in Pictures

**1935** Alone; Begin the Beguine; Bess, You Is My Woman Now; Broadway Rhythm; Cheek to Cheek; I'm Building Up to an Awful Let-Down; I'm Gonna Sit Right Down and Write Myself a Letter; I'm in the Mood for Love; I Feel a Song Comin' On; I Got Plenty o' Nuttin'; Isn't This a Lovely Day—To Be Caught in the Rain?; It Ain't Necessarily So; Just One of Those Things; Lovely to Look At; Lullaby of Broadway; Lulu's Back in Town; Moon Over Miami; Stairway to the Stars; Summertime; Top Hat, White Tie and Tails; You Are My Lucky Star; Zing! Went the Strings of My Heart

**1936** Bojangles of Harlem; I've Got You Under My Skin; It's De-Lovely; Let's Face the Music and Dance; Let Yourself Go; Pennies from Heaven; Picture Me without You; Shoe Shine Boy; Stompin' at the Savoy; There's a Small Hotel; Until the Real Thing Comes Along; The Way You Look Tonight; Where Are You; You Turned the Tables on Me

**1937** Bei Mir Bist du Schön; Bob White—Whatcha Gonna Swing Tonight?; The Donkey Serenade; A Foggy Day; I Can Dream, Can't I?; I've Got My Love to Keep Me Warm; In the Still of the Night; Johnny One Note; The Lady Is a Tramp; Let's Call the Whole Thing Off; My Funny Valentine; Nice Work If You Can Get It; September in the Rain; Slumming on Park Avenue; Thanks for the Memory; That Old Feeling; Too Marvelous for Words; Where or When; Whistle While You Work

**1938** A-Tisket A-Tasket; Change Partners; Falling in Love with Love; Get Out of Town; I'll Be Seeing You; Jeepers Creepers; Love Walked In; September Song; This Can't Be Love; Two Sleepy People; You Go to My Head; You Must Have Been a Beautiful Baby

**1939** All the Things You Are; Beer Barrel Polka; Frenesi; God Bless America; I Concentrate on You; I Didn't Know What Time It Was; I Poured My Heart into a Song; I'll Never Smile Again; Over the Rainbow; Three Little Fishes

# THE 1940s

The war brought an end to the Depression and the popular arts began to flourish, but there was a shortage of the raw materials needed for production. Wood and metal were in short supply, necessitating certain compromises, both in Hollywood and on Broadway. When Rodgers and Hammerstein's *Oklahoma!* opened on Broadway, it featured painted drops rather than the elaborately built sets that had become the norm. Critics embraced the simplicity and artistry of the sets and, for the next decade or so, Broadway shows featured painted drops. Similarly, record companies had trouble finding enough shellac to press their records, as the substance was made from the resin secreted by insects in Japanese-controlled Southeast Asia. But somehow, they made do.

With the war separating husbands from wives, boyfriends from girlfriends, and mothers from sons, songs with a rich nostalgia quotient struck a chord. Sometimes even an old song could be spruced up and reissued to great success, as in the case of Neville Fleeson and Albert Von Tilzer's "I'll Be with You in Apple Blossom Time." The song was originally introduced by Nora Bayes, a very successful entertainer (and cowriter of "Take Me Out to the Ball Game," with her husband, Jack Norworth). It was a waltz—but when the Andrews Sisters got hold of it in 1941, they changed it to a 4/4 rhythm and the song hit the charts. Fleeson's lyric was ahead of its time, with its use of false rhymes such as "time" and "mine." The 1939 song "I'll Never Smile Again," by Ruth Lowe, was written by the Ina Rae Hutton band pianist to celebrate the memory of her late husband, but wartime audiences embraced it as a poignant expression of their own loneliness. Cole Porter's 1943 standard "You'd Be So Nice to Come Home To" was also interpreted as an expression of

longing for distant loved ones, as was Mack Gordon and Harry Warren's "You'll Never Know," from the 1943 film *Hello, Frisco, Hello.*

Kicking off the decade in 1940 was the formation of the music licensing organization Broadcast Music Incorporated (BMI), an alternative to ASCAP. As country and folk music began to enter the public consciousness, many songwriters in these emerging fields joined BMI.

Also in 1940, Pete Seeger, Lee Hays, and Millard Lampell formed the Almanac Singers, a left-leaning folk group. Woody Guthrie joined the next year, and folk music became associated with liberal and socialist causes. After two albums, *Songs for John Doe* and *Taking Union,* the group's members were blacklisted and the group broke up—but their music influenced a new generation of singer/songwriters. Each member continued the good fight, often against great opposition. Earl Robinson and John Latouche had penned "Ballad for Americans," a popular cantata, in 1939, but it came to fame in 1940, when it was performed at both the Republican and Communist parties' conventions.

In 1941, the solid-body electric guitar came into being through the efforts of Leo Fender and Les Paul, and changed the sound and history of music. Paul recorded and was the sole player on the Rodgers and Hart tune "Lover" in 1947, featuring eight individual electric guitar tracks. A decade later, in 1952, Paul's guitar, sold by the Gibson company, became a best seller just in time for the emergence of rock–and-roll. Slowly, the piano was replaced by the guitar as the solo performer's instrument of choice.

In 1942, Johnny Mercer, B. G. De Sylva, and Glenn Wallichs founded Captiol RecordThat same year, Bing Crosby first sang Irving Berlin's "White Christmas"

## GREAT SONGS OF THE DECADE

**1940**     All or Nothing at All; Ballad for Americans; Cabin in the Sky; Fools Rush In; How High the Moon; Imagination; It's a Big, Wide, Wonderful World; It's a Lovely Day Tomorrow; The Last Time I Saw Paris; The Nearness of You; Taking a Chance of Love; This Is My Country; When You Wish Upon a Star; You Are My Sunshine; You Stepped Out of a Dream

**1941**     The Anniversary Waltz; Bewitched; Blues in the Night; Chattanooga Choo Choo; Deep in the Heart of Texas; Dolores; Flamingo; How About You?; I Don't Want to Walk without You; I Don't Want to Set the World on Fire; I Got It Bad and That Ain't Good; I'll Remember April; It's Always You; Jersey Bounce; Music Makers; There! I've Said It Again; This Is New; Tonight We Love; The White Cliffs of Dover

**1942**     Be Careful! It's My Heart; Dearly Beloved; Don't Get Around Much Anymore; I'm Old Fashioned; I Had the Craziest Dream; I Left My Heart at the Stage Door Canteen; Jingle, Jangle, Jingle; The Lamplighter's Serenade; Paper Doll; Praise the Lord and Pass the Ammunition; Serenade in Blue; That Old Black Magic; This Is the Army, Mr. Jones; White Christmas; You Were Never Lovelier; You'd Be So Nice to Come Home To

**1943**     Besame Mucho; Comin' in on a Wing and a Prayer; Do Nothin' Till You Hear from Me; Holiday for Strings; I Couldn't Sleep a Wink Last Night; I've Heard That Song Before; In My Arms; A Lovely Way to Spend an Evening; Mairzy Doats; My Heart Tells Me; Oh What a Beautiful Mornin'; Oklahoma!; People Will Say We're in Love; Pistol Packin' Mama; Shoo-Shoo Baby; Speak Low; Star Eyes; Sunday, Monday, or Always; The Surrey with the Fringe on Top; They're Either Too Young or Too Old; Tico-Tico; What Do You Do in the Infrantry?; You Keep Coming Back Like a Song; You'll Never Know

**1944**     Ac-cent-tchu-ate the Positive; Candy; Close as Pages in a Book; Don't Fence Me In; Dream; Going My Way; How Blue the Night; I'm Making Believe; I Should Care; I'll Walk Alone; Irresistible You; It Could Happen to You; Long Ago and Far Away; More and More; Right As the Rain; Rum and Coca-Cola; Sentimental Journey; Spring Will Be a Little Late This Year; Strange Music; Swinging on a Star

The Andrews Sisters

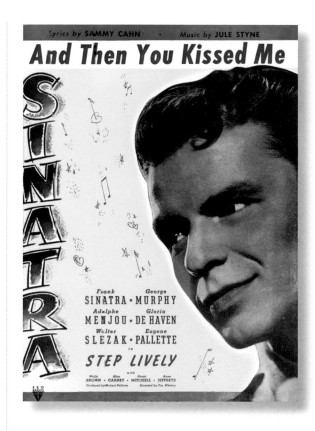

In 1944, Aaron Copland's "Appalachian Spring," first performed by Martha Graham's dance troupe, became a favorite of orchestras throughout the country. Along with Copland, composer Marc Blitzstein of *The Cradle Will Rock* fame, Charlie Seeger, musicologist, composer, and Pete Seeger's father, and others formed the Composers Collective in order to create music that would support the causes of the working class.

Also in 1944, Norman Granz presented a jazz concert at Philharmonic Auditorium in Los Angeles with a borrowed $300. Nat King Cole, Les Paul, and Illinois Jacquet were among the performers featured in this, the first of Granz's series of concerts eventually known as Jazz at the Philharmonic.

Earl Robinson wrote "The House I Live In" with lyricist Lewis Allan, a pseudonym for Abel Meeropol, a high school teacher who wrote "Strange Fruit." "The House I Live In" was used as the basis for a film short starring Frank Sinatra, produced to combat bigotry. The song went out of favor after McCarthy branded its writers communists, but ultimately the song triumphed when Sinatra himself sang it in 1986 at the commemoration of the centenary of the Statue of Liberty. (Former commie-hunter President Ronald Reagan was in proud attendance.)

In a further triumph of the little man, in 1948 Ahmet Ertegun borrowed $10,000 from his dentist to found Atlantic Records with Herb Abramson of National Records. At the same time, Columbia Records issued the first mass-produced 12-inch 33 ⅓ record. Not to be outdone, RCA-Victor issued the first 45

in the Paramount Pictures film *Holiday Inn*. Crosby's recording of the song becomes the biggest selling recording of all time. On August 1, 1942, James Caesar Petrillo, the despotic head of the American Federation of Musicians, forbade commercial recordings by musicians (though they could still make V-discs for the troops). Singers weren't members of the musician's union so they could make records either a cappella or with choral backup. Because of the ban, several Broadway shows were never recorded and their runs and future popularity suffered. The public began to value singers above the big bands, spelling the beginning of the end of the big band era.

America was feeling its oats and, on March 31, 1943, when that most American of musicals, *Oklahoma!* premiered at the St. James Theater in New York. Decca Records recorded most of the original score sung by the original cast, and that recording, though not really the first original-cast recording, became the most popular one ever, opening the door for Broadway cast recordings to become a major category of most labels' catalogues.

rpm discs to the public in 1949 and, although they had better fidelity than the 33 ⅓ discs, they were used mainly for singles. Miles Davis's "The Birth of the Cool" was released by Blue Note, beginning the cool jazz movement. And at the opposite end of the musical spectrum, Hank Williams debuted at the Grand Ole Opry, singing "Lovesick Blues." ◆

---

**1945** Aren't You Glad You're You; Cruising Down the River; Dig You Later—A Hubba-Hubba-Hubba; Doctor, Lawyer, Indian Chief; For Sentimental Reasons; Give Me the Simple Life; I Can't Begin to Tell You; If I Loved You; It's a Grand Night for Singing; It's Been a Long, Long, Time; It Might As Well Be Spring; June Is Bustin' Out All Over; Laura; Let It Snow! Let It Snow! Let It Snow!; The More I See You; On the Atchison, Topeka and the Santa Fe; Rodger Young; Some Sunday Morning; That's For Me; Till the End of Time; Waitin' for the Train to Come In; You Came Along—Out of Nowhere

**1946** All Through the Day; Along with Me; Anniversary Song; Chiquita Banana; Come Rain or Come Shine; Doin' What Comes Natur'lly; Five Minutes More; For You, for Me, For Evermore; Full Moon and Empty Arms; The Girl That I Marry; Golden Earrings; How Are Things in Glocca Morra; I Got the Sun in the Morning; If This Isn't Love; In Love in Vain; It's a Good Day; Linda; Ol' Devil Moon; The Old Lamp-Lighter; Ole Buttermilk Sky; Shoofly Pie and Apple Pan Dowdy; South America, Take It Away; Tenderly; There's No Business Like Show Business; They Say It's Wonderful; To Each His Own; When I'm Not Near the Girl I Love; Zip-a-Dee-Do-Dah

**1947** Almost Like Being in Love; Ballerina; Beyond the Sea; But Beautiful; Chi-Baba Chi-Baba; Civilization; A Fellow Needs a Girl; Feudin' and Fightin'; The Gentleman Is a Dope; I'll Dance at Your Wedding; I Wish I Didn't Love You So; Mam'selle; Open the Door, Richard; Papa, Won't You Dance with Me?; So Far; The Stanley Steamer; There but for You Go I; Too Fat Polka; Woody Woodpecker

**1948** "A"—You're Adorable; Baby, It's Cold Outside; Buttons and Bows; Enjoy Yourself—It's Later Than You Think; A Fella with an Umbrella; Haunted Heart; Here I'll Stay; It's a Most Unusual Day; It's Magic; Manana—Is Soon Enough for Me; My Darling, My Darling; Nature Boy; The Night Has a Thousand Eyes; On a Slow Boat to China; Once in Love with Amy; So in Love; Tennessee Waltz; A Tree in the Meadow; You're Breaking My Heart; You Say the Nicest Things

**1949** Bali Ha'i; Bibbidi-Bobbidi-Boo; Copper Canyon; Dear Hearts and Gentle People; Diamonds Are a Girl's Best Friend; Don't Cry, Joe; A Dreamer's Holiday; Huckle-buck; I've Got a Lovely Bunch of Cocoanuts; Let's Take an Old-Fashioned Walk; Mona Lisa; Mule Train; My Foolish Heart; Some Enchanted Evening; The Old Master Painter; Rudolph the Red-Nosed Reindeer

# THE 1950s

The postwar years saw cataclysmic changes in the music business sociologically, technologically, sociologically, and artistically. Servicemen returning to their families put an emphasis on home life, getting married, and having children—they definitely were *not* going out to dance or listen to music. The suburbs were growing and the younger generation was busy buying homes and raising their 2.5 children. The latest invention, television, provided ready entertainment for the whole family.

Radio gave up the ghost as the networks turned their attention to the new medium, there were few actual radio shows produced, and the networks' place on the audiowaves was taken by independent stations. Dave Dexter, writing in *Billboard*, explained the transition: "By the 1950s there were no more radio announcers. Now there were disc jockeys. Guys who didn't know a tenor sax from a tuba were spinning discs on three speeds and telling listeners what to buy. They were receiving hundreds of records a week from scores of companies. Payola became evident. More stress was being made on promoting, merchandising, and selling. The 'little' record shops began to fold."

In 1951 Alan Freed, then a DJ with WJW in Cleveland, Ohio, hosted the *Moondog Rock and Roll Party*. His influence grew as he promoted the music he liked, and as rock-and-roll began to supplant the old standards, record companies put their resources behind rock, abandoning traditional artists. Jo Stafford told Michael Feinstein, "Rock was sold to the kids. The name of the game is peer pressure. It started in 1954. I was there; I saw it happening. The record companies took their cue from the automotive industry; they began a program of planned obsolescence. When I came up, the idea was that when you made a record, it was supposed to last forever. Now it was the opposite. The new

god was called 'turnover.' Put one rocker on and then shove in another and another. A hit in the morning, a golden oldie in the afternoon. Quality was out. It took a few years to set in, but it started in 1954."

That was the year that Bill Haley and the Comets made "Rock Around the Clock." On July 5, 1954, Elvis Presley strolled into the Memphis Recording Service to record "That's All Right (Mama)" with Arthur "Big Boy" Crudup. During a break, Presley improvised around the song and came up with the single, "Blue Moon of Kentucky."

If one had to point to a single watershed year in rock history, it would certainly be 1955. Hollywood jumped on the rock bandwagon that year with *The Blackboard Jungle* Featuring the Bill Haley and the Comets' recording of "Rock Around the Clock" on the soundtrack, by July the song hit number one on the *Billboard* Best Sellers in Stores chart. That same year, Capitol Records, a company formed to provide artistic freedom to the likes of Peggy Lee, Nat King Cole, and Frank Sinatra, was sold to EMI, a British company. Capitol's pop singers were let go as their contracts expired. Chuck Berry played a demo he made of the hillbilly song "Ida Mae" for Leonard Chess of Chess records, and Chess agreed to release the song, retitled "Maybelline." The lyrics established two of the main themes of rock, hot girls and fast cars. Berry's recordings influenced would-be rockers throughout the world, including the Beach Boys, the Beatles, and the Rolling Stones. Ray Charles merged blues and gospel when he recorded "I Got a Woman" that same groundbreaking year. On the Latin front, Perez Prado's mambo song "Cherry Pink and Apple Blossom White" earned the number one spot on *Billboard*'s pop singles chart, the first Latin tune to do so.

# GREAT SONGS OF THE DECADE

Pittsburgh, Pennsylvania; Takes Two to Tango; Thumbelina; Wheel of Fortune; Wish You Were Here; Your Cheatin' Heart; Zing a Little Zong

**1950**  Autmun Leaves; A Bushel and a Peck; C'est Si Bon; Chattanoogie Shoe Shine Boy; Dearie; Hoop-Dee-Doo; If I Knew You Were Comin' I'd 'Ave Baked a Cake; It's a Lovely Day Today; It's So Nice to Have a Man Around the House; Music! Music! Music!; My Heart Cries for You; Rag Mop; Sam's Song; You Wonderful You

**1951**  Be My Love; Because of You; Cold, Cold Heart; Come on-a My House; Cry; Hello, Young Lovers; I'm in Love Again; I Get Ideas; I Talk to the Trees; I Whistle a Happy Tune; In the Cool, Cool, Cool of the Evening; Kisses Sweeter than Wine; The Little White Cloud That Cried; Make the Man Love Me; Marshmallow Moon; Mister and Mississippi; Shrimp Boats; Sparrow in the Tree Tops; Tennessee Waltz; Too Young; Unforgettable; We Kiss in a Shadow

**1952**  Anywhere I Wander; Because You're Mine; Botch-a-Me; Count Your Blessings Instead of Sheep; Glow-Worm; High Noon—Do Not Forsake Me; How Do You Speak to an Angel; I Saw Mommy Kissing Santa Claus; Jambalaya—On the Bayou; Kiss of Fire;

**1953**  Allez-Vous-En, Go Away; And This Is My Beloved; Baubles, Bangles and Beads; C'est Magnifique; Crying in the Chapel; Ebb Tide; Hi-Lilli, Hi-Lo; I Am in Love; I Believe; I Love Paris; Istanbul; It's All Right with Me; Make Love to Me!; No Other Love; Oh! My Pa-pa; Rags to Riches; Rock Around the Clock; Ruby; Secret Love; The Song from Moulin Rouge—Where Is Your Heart; Stranger in Paradise; That Doggie in the Window; That's Amore

**1954**  All of You; Fanny; Hernando's Hideaway; Hey There; If I Give My Heart to You; Let Me Go, Lover!; Little Things Mean a Lot; Lost in Loveliness; Make Yourself Comfortable; Mambo Italiano; That Man That Got Away; Mister Sandman; The Naughty Lady of Shady Lane; Papa Loves Mambo; Shake, Rattle, and Roll; Sh-Boom; Somebody Bad Stole de Wedding Bell; Steam Heat; Teach Me Tonight; This Ole House; Three Coins in the Fountain; Young and Foolish; Young at Heart

Stafford, the biggest selling female singer of the decade, recalled, "To compare music in the '40s to music that came out after '55 it's pitiful. I just think it's too bad. The American popular song was truly one of America's greatest contributions. No other country was ever able to match the output of the pop music form that America brought out. And most of the people who wrote it were of European descent. That came to a halt. Are there any standards in the making? There are talented writers but they don't have the opportunity to be heard. In the heyday of the really good popular song you had some pretty heavy teachers teaching you. You had Tommy and Jimmy Dorsey and Benny Goodman and Woody Herman. You had a whole bunch of people telling you what was good, playing what was good.

"After that passed, you had DJs that were very nice men but not musically smart. I think economics had something to do with it. 'Cause suddenly kids of eleven, twelve, thirteen, or fourteen had enough money to influence the market. Irving Caesar described it as brainwashing. Basically what they put on the airwaves, if they play it enough, people think it's good—especially if they play it over and over again."

In 1957, the year that Buddy Holly's "That'll Be the Day" hit number one, Dick Clark's *American Bandstand* was broadcast nationally for the first time on August 5. *Bandstand* was, amazingly, a daily offering until 1964, when it moved from Philadelphia to Los Angeles and became a weekly program. It finally left the air in 1987. Also in 1957, Chet Atkins and Owen Bradley gave a pop sheen to country with strings-heavy arrangements that became known as the "Nashville Sound."

Traditional Tin Pan Alley was driving on fumes, but there were a few highlights. The original Broadway cast recording of Lerner and Loewe's *My Fair Lady* became one of the most popular recordings of all time, selling more than 5 million copies following its release in 1956. It hit number one on the charts and stayed in the top forty for 311 weeks. In 1958, Perry Como's "Catch a Falling Star" became the first gold single as certified by the RIAA (Recording Industry Association of America), signifying that it had shipped 1 million copies to stores in the United States. The first gold album was the original soundtrack to Rodgers and Hammerstein's *Oklahoma!*

By 1959, when Berry Gordy started Motown Records, American popular song was officially outside the mainstream for good. ❖

## Song and Story

### QUE SERA SERA

Paramount wanted Doris Day to sing a song in Alfred Hitchcock's *The Man Who Knew Too Much*, figuring that audiences would expect it. Hitchcock concocted a way to make "Que Sera Sera" integral to the plot. Day sings the song in the lair of her child's kidnappers, hoping the kid will hear it and respond. Paramount liked the song but insisted that the title be listed as "Whatever Will Be, Will Be," because the Academy wouldn't allow a non-English title to be submitted for an Oscar! At first hearing, Day considered the song too simple and childlike. Marty Melcher, her husband and manager, talked her into singing it, and it went on to win an Oscar and be her biggest hit. She would sing it twice more in films (*Please Don't Eat the Daisies* and *The Glass Bottom Boat*) and make it the theme of her television series.

## Asides

The earliest experiments with stereo recording took place in 1876! Alexander Graham Bell was the first to use the term "stereophonic," but the idea of left and right channel grooves on a disc was that of W. Bartlett Jones in the late 1920s. Unfortunately, his design called for two needles, one for each side of the groove wall. He later patented a single-groove, single-stylus system. In 1933 EMI actually made stereo 78s and, reportedly, the stereo effect was perfect. After much more innovation, RCA became the first company to record in stereo. They laid down the Boston Symphony playing *The Damnation of Faust* in February 1954. The recordings were issued in mono until stereo recordings were generally available a few years later.

**1955** Ain't That a Shame!; All at Once You Love Her; Ballad of Davy Crockett; The Bible Tells Me So; Cherry Pink and Apple Blossom White; Cry Me a River; Dance with Me Henry; Dungaree Doll; Heart; I'll Never Stop Loving You; Impatient Years; Learnin' the Blues; Love and Marriage; Love is a Many-Splendored Thing; Maybellene; Melody of Love; Only You; Pete Kelly's Blues; The Rock and Roll Waltz; Seventeen; Sincerely; Sixteen Tons; Something's Gotta Give; The Tender Trap; Two Lost Souls; Unchained Melody; Wake the Town and Tell the People; Whatever Lola Wants; The Yellow Rose of Texas

**1956** Allegheny Moon; Around the World; Band of Gold; Blue Suede Shoes; Blueberry Hill; Canadian Sunset; Don't Be Cruel; Friendly Persuasion; The Great Pretender; Heartbreak Hotel; Hey, Jealous Lover; Hot Diggity; Hound Dog; I Could Have Danced All Night; Joey, Joey, Joey; Juke Box Baby; Just in Time; Just Walkin' in the Rain; Love Me Tender; Memories Are Made of This; Mr. Wonderful; Moonglow; More; On the Street Where You Live; The Party's Over; Picnic; The Poor People of Paris; The Rain in Spain; See You Later, Alligator; Singing the Blues; Standing on the Corner; Too Close for Comfort; True Love; Whatever Will Be, Will Be; Why Do Fools Fall in Love?; You're Sensational

**1957** All Shook Up!; An Affair to Remember; All the Way; April Love; The Banana Boat Song; Be-Bop Baby; Bye-Bye Love; Ça, C'est l'Amour; Chances Are; Fascination; Honeycomb; I Feel Pretty; In the Middle of an Island; It's Not for Me to Say; Jailhouse Rock; Love Letters in the Sand; Maria; Marianne; Old Cape Cod; Party Doll; Round and Round; Send for Me; Seventy-Six Trombones; Tammy; (Let Me Be Your) Teddy Bear; Tonight; Whole Lot-ta Shakin' Goin' On; Wonderful! Wonderful!

**1958** Catch a Falling Star; A Certain Smile; The Chipmunk Song—Christmas Don't Be Late; Everybody Loves a Lover; Firefly; For the First time; Gigi; The Hawaiian Wedding Song; I Enjoy Being a Girl; It's All in the Game; Left Right Out of Your Heart; Lollipop; Love, Look Away; Pink Shoe Laces; The Purple People Eater; Stagger Lee; Tears on My Pillow; To Know Him Is to Love Him; Twilight Time; Who's Sorry Now; Witch Doctor; Yakkety Yak; You Are Beautiful; Young and Warm and Wonderful

**1959** Alvin's Harmonica; The Battle of New Orleans; Charlie Brown; The Children's Marching Song; Climb Ev'ry Mountain; Do-Re-Mi; Dream Lover; Everything's Coming Up Roses; High Hopes; I'm Just a Lonely Boy; Kookie, Kookie; Once Knew a Fella; Personality; La Plume de Ma Tante; Put Your Head on My Shoulder; Sixteen Going on Seventeen; Small World; Some People; The Sound of Music; Staying Young; Take Me Along; A Teenager in Love; While the Angelus Was Ringing

# THE 1960s

It's fairly safe to assume that the majority of song hits in 1961 will be based on the same old 32-bar chorus formula, will still have a verse which nobody ever uses, and will still have the second and last eight-bar strains similar to the first eight. That's the way at least half the hits of 1921 and 1941 were made. And similarly they'll still be playing and singing the blues in 1961, with its traditional 12-bar chorus which seems to have been handed down at least two generations already." So proclaimed Leonard Feather in *Song Hits* magazine in September 1941.

Feather was an accomplished critic, historian, and sometime songwriter, but his crystal ball was definitely cracked. The 1960s saw the last gasp of the traditional Tin Pan Alley, whose repertoire was permanently relegated to what was laughingly called the "back catalog."

The Hollywood musical was all but dead and the Broadway musical entered its own decade-long slump. There was some life here and there on Broadway but, as Burton Lane noted, the song "On a Clear Day You Can See Forever" was just about the last hit song to come from a Broadway musical. The only songs being written for films were title songs and exploitation numbers. In fairness, many of these, usually penned by Henry Mancini, became hits. The one place that the popular song remained alive and well in the sixties was on television, for it was the last decade of the television variety show.

One could still hear live performances of American popular songs, at least until the urban riots of 1968 killed the inner cities and many clubs were forced to close. But there was still one desert outpost. Vegas was going strong and many of the singers who recorded for Reprise and Capitol appeared in its clubs and lounges.

The LP was king and music could be purchased in two formats, mono and stereo. The latter cost $1 more,

and since you couldn't play a stereo record with a mono stylus, many consumers were content not to upgrade their hi-fis. Capitol and Decca put many of their mono recordings through bizarre echo chambers and issued them as Duophonic or Simulated Stereo recordings. Later in the decade, advances in technology allowed stereo recordings to be played on mono machinery. In the early seventies Columbia issued some quadraphonic recordings, but these never really caught on.

In 1963, Philips introduced the tape cassette format and many titles were released on cassette as well as LP. Cars were fitted with cassette players in addition to radios. In 1964, Robert Moog invented the music synthesizer and the ear of electronic music was born. Live musicians quaked in their boots and science fiction scorers retired their Theremins for good. The Moog synthesizer and its future brethren would be instrumental (perhaps a bad choice of words) in the 1970s, with the advent of disco (and later techno) music.

There came a piece of good news for the record industry in 1967, when Russ Solomon opened the first Tower Records store in Sacramento, California. Other chains existed, but Tower, with its knowledgeable staff and all-inclusive stock policy, would change the course of music retailing.

In February 1964, the United States was once again invaded by the British—in the form of four good-natured, long-haired band mates who called themselves the Beatles. If anyone doubted that rock-and-roll was here to stay, they were horribly, horribly mistaken.

Surprisingly, there were a few new singers who were able to muscle their way through the rock wall to achieve popular success, and the record companies supported them with marketing dollars. Jazz was definitely out—but crooning, as heard in the lounges of Las Vegas, was in. Sweet and mellow ruled the day

## GREAT SONGS OF THE DECADE

**1960**    The Best of Everything; Camelot; Chain Gang; Dolce Far Niente; I Ain't Down Yet; I'm Sorry; If Ever I Would Leave You; It's Now or Never; Itsy, Bitsy, Teenie, Weenie, Yellow Polka Dot Bikini, Mr. Lucky; Never on Sunday; Only the Lonely Know the Way I Feel; Puppy Love; Save the Last Dance for Me; Sink the Bismarck; Stuck on You; The Twist; The Unforgiven—The Need for Love

**1961**    Big Bad John; Hey, Look Me Over; I Believe in You; Love Makes the World Go 'Round; Exodus; Moon River; Pocketful of Miracles; Runaround Sue; Travelin' Man; Where the Boys Are; Wonderland by Night; Yellow Bird; You Don't Have to Be a Tower of Strength

**1962**    All Over the World; Any Day Now; Ballad of Jed Clampett; Be a Performer; Be My Host; Big Girls Don't Cry; Blame It on the Bossa Nova; Blowin' in the Wind; Breaking Up Is Hard to Do; Bye Bye Birdie; Call Me Irresponsible; Can't Get Used to Losing You; Days of Wine and Roses; El Watusi; The End of the World; Follow the Boys; Go Away,

Little Girl; A Holly Jolly Christmas; How Does the Wine Taste?; How the West Was Won; I Want You to Be the First One to Know; If and When; (Hey There) Lonely Boy; Make It Easy on Yourself; The Man Who Shot Liberty Valance; My Coloring Book; On Broadway; Once Upon a Time; Our Day with Come; Ramblin' Rose; Return to Sender; Sherry; The Sweetest Sounds; Turn! Turn! Turn!; Up on the Roof; Walking Happy

**1963**    Before I Kiss the World Goodbye; Before the Parade Passes By; Charade; Chim Chim Cher-ee; Don't Think Twice, It's All Right; Flipper; Hello, Dolly!; Hello Muddah, Hello Fadduh; I Could Go on Singing; I Don't Care Much; It Only Takes a Moment; It's a Mad, Mad, Mad, Mad World; Look for Small Pleasures; Love with the Proper Stranger; Puff (The Magic Dragon); Ribbons Down My Back; A Room without Windows; She Loves Me; The Times They Are A-Changin'; Walk on By; Wishin' and Hopin'; Wives and Lovers

**1964**    Always Something There to Remind Me; Anyone Can Whistle; Baby, the Rain Must Fall; The Ballad of Gilligan's Island; Barry's Boy; Dear Heart; Don't Rain on My Parade; Emily; Goin' Out of My Head; Golden Boy; I Get Around; I Want to Be with You; If I Were a Rich Man; I'm All Smiles; King of the Road; Leader of the Pack; Mr. Tambourine Man; My Kind of Town; Pass Me By; People; The Sounds of Silence; Sunshine, Lollipops

and handsome, white, clean-cut male vocalists like Andy Williams, Jack Jones, Matt Monro, and Ed Ames climbed the charts.

Ah, the sixties. Free love and the Osmond Brothers. The age of Aquarius and assassinations. The New Christy Minstrels and riots in the streets. The music business and the American popular song would never be the same. ◆

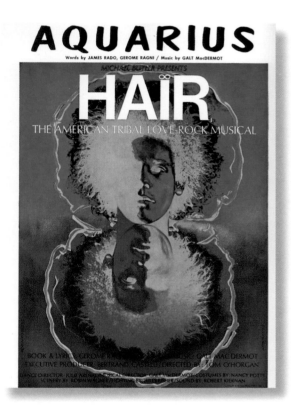

**ABOVE:** Middle America's fears of rock-and-roll were sent up in 1960's satirical musical *Bye Bye Birdie* by Charles Strouse, Lee Adams, and Michael Stewart. Here Conrad Birdie, an Elvis-style teen idol about to be drafted into the army, advises the citizens of Sweet Apple, Ohio, that they have to be "Honestly Sincere."

**LEFT:** Real rock music came to Broadway in 1968's *Hair* and caused a lot of controversy. Conservatives were shocked at the invasion of the sacred turf on Times Square while liberals saw a new path for the Broadway musical. Other shows with pseudo-rock scores followed but most were failures.

and Rainbows; When in Rome (I Do As the Romans Do); Who Are You Now?; With So Little to Be Sure Of; You've Lost That Lovin' Feelin'

**1965**    The Ballad of Cat Ballou; Big Spender; California Dreaming; Come Back to Me; Do I Hear a Waltz?; England Swings; Eve of Destruction; For Once in My Life; Green, Green Grass of Home; Help Me, Rhonda; On a Clear Day (You Can See Forever); Papa's Got a Brand New Bag; The September of My Years; The Shadow of Your Smile; She Touched Me; Stop! In the Name of Love; Sunny; The Sweetheart Tree; Tell Her (You Love Her Each Day); What the World Needs Now Is Love; What's New Pussycat?; Where Am I Going?; Workin' My Way Back to You; You Can't Hurry Love

**1966**    Alice's Restaurant; The Beat Goes On; Born Free; The 59th Street Bridge Song (Feelin' Groovy); Good Vibrations; I Heard It Through the Grapevine; If He Walked Into My Life; I'm a Believer; Is That All There Is?; Last Train to Clarksville; Mame; Monday, Monday; My Cup Runneth Over; Somewhere My Love (Lara's Theme); Strangers in the Night; Summer in the City; These Boots Are Made for Walking; This Is My Song; A Time for Love; Wedding Bell Blues

**1967**    Ain't No Mountain High Enough; Aquarius; Both Sides Now; By the Time I Get to Phoenix; Can't Take My Eyes Off of You; Didn't We?; Do You Know the Way to San Jose?; Everybody's Talkin'; Let Me Light Your Fire; Frank Mills; Gentle on My Mind; Good Morning Starshine; I Say a Little Prayer; I've Gotta Be Me; Let the Sunshine In (The Flesh Failures); Light My Fire; The Look of Love; Music to Watch Girls By; Sherry!; Somethin' Stupid; Soul Man; Star!; Talk to the Animals; Thoroughly Modern Millie; Up—Up and Away; What a Wonderful World

**1968**    Chitty Chitty Bang Bang; (Sittin' On) The Dock of the Bay; For Love of Ivy; I'll Never Fall in Love Again; Little Green Apples; Mrs. Robinson; Ma Cherie Amour; Promises, Promises; Proud Mary; Seattle; This Guy's in Love with You; The Windmills of Your Mind

**1969**    The April Fools; Bridge Over Troubled Water; Come Saturday Morning; He Ain't Heavy…He's My Brother; Jean; Oh Happy Day; Put a Little Love in Your Heart; Raindrops Keep Fallin' on My Head; Sweet Caroline (Good Times Never Seemed So Good); What Are You Doing the Rest of Your Life?

# THE
# SONGWRITERS

Equally at home writing for Broadway, Hollywood, and the Cotton Club, Harold Arlen is perhaps the greatest underappreciated songwriter in the history of American popular song. While Arlen's total output doesn't equal that of Irving Berlin, Richard Rodgers, or Jule Styne—and except for *Bloomer Girl*, he never had a hit show—the quality of his work was consistently brilliant. And if his role as one of America's finest composers is unknown, so too is his expert singing.

Arlen's unique singing style, influenced by liturgical singing and the techniques of black vocalists, led to jobs in vaudeville. He appeared on the Loew's vaudeville circuit and on Broadway at the Palace Theater, the ultimate vaudeville venue. In fact, Arlen would continue singing throughout his career though he preferred to put his energies into recording. He eventually cut sides with the Red Nichols Orchestra and others, on the Capitol, Columbia, and Walden labels.

Arlen got his start in his hometown of Buffalo, New York, in the choir of a synagogue where his father was a cantor. But as the young Hyman Arluck he was more interested in secular music than in the hymns and prayers he sang. (Does this remind anyone of *The Jazz Singer*?) While in his teens he founded the Snappy Trio, a group that soon evolved into the equally well-named Southbound Shufflers. Arlen and his fellow musicians played at local functions and on the excursion boats that plied Lake Erie. His first real success was with the Buffalodians, for which he sang and arranged the music. When they earned a recording contract Arlen's self-confidence grew, and in 1925 he decided to try his luck in New York City.

He worked as a singer, arranger, and pianist in several dance bands before landing the job that would lead his career in a new direction, playing in the pit orchestra of the Broadway revue *George White's Scandals of 1928*.

**PREVIOUS PAGE:** Harold Arlen and Tory Bennett.

While Arlen was working as a rehearsal pianist for the Vincent Youmans show, *Great Day*, Harry Warren, then a Broadway composer, overheard a musical riff Arlen used to call the performers back from their breaks. Warren was impressed enough to encourage Arlen to start composing music in earnest. The little ditty turned into "Get Happy," written in collaboration with Arlen's first great songwriting partner, Ted Koehler.

Their success led to a job writing the scores for a series of Cotton Club revues, and it was there that Arlen became acquainted with black singing styles and adapted many of the techniques into his vocals and compositions. During this period, Arlen and Koehler wrote tremendous hits including "Kickin' the Gong Around," "Between the Devil and the Deep Blue Sea," "I Love a Parade," "I've Got the World on a String," "Minnie the Moocher's Wedding Day," "Ill Wind," "As Long As I Live," and, in 1933, their greatest hit, "Stormy Weather." And it was at the Cotton Club that Arlen cemented his relationships with such black performers as Cab Calloway, Lena Horne, and Ethel Waters. He continued writing nonstereotypical scores for black artists throughout his career. In fact, Lena Horne called Arlen the blackest white man she had ever met.

The success of the Cotton Club shows led Arlen and Koehler back to Broadway and a series of great revues, including *The Nine Fifteen Revue* (1930; "Get Happy"), *Earl Carroll's Vanities* (1930; "Hittin' the Bottle"), *Earl Carroll's Vanities of 1932* ("I Gotta Right to Sing the Blues," "Rockin' in Rhythm"), *Americana* (1932; "Satan's Li'l Lamb"), *George White's Music Hall Varieties* (1932), *Life Begins at 8:40* (1934, lyrics by Ira Gershwin and E. Y. Harburg, "Fun to Be Fooled," "Let's Take a Walk Around the Block," "You're a Builder Upper"), and *The Show Is On* (1936).

Success in the revue format led to book shows, many of which prominently featured black performers. These included *You Said It* (1931; "Sweet and Hot," "You Said It"), *Hooray for What!* (1937; "Down with Love"), *Bloomer Girl* (1944; "The Eagle and Me," "Right As the Rain"), *St. Louis Woman* (1946; "Any Place I Hang My Hat Is Home," "Come Rain or Come Shine"), *House of Flowers* (1954; "I Never Has Seen Snow," "A Sleepin' Bee"), *Jamaica* (1957; "Push the Button," "Napoleon"), and *Saratoga* (1959; "Love Held Lightly").

While these shows were rarely commercially successful, the scores Arlen wrote, mainly in collaboration with E. Y. Harburg or Johnny Mercer, were as rich as any on Broadway. In addition to Lena Horne, among the great stars who appeared in Arlen shows were Pearl Bailey, Diahann Carroll, Ricardo Montalban, Celeste Holm, Dooley Wilson, Ed Wynn, Bert Lahr, Ray Bolger, the Nicholas Brothers, Ray Walston, Geoffrey Holder, Josephine Premice, Carol Lawrence, Ossie Davis, and Howard Keel.

Arlen also enjoyed a long career in Hollywood, writing for such films as *The Wizard of Oz* ("Over the

## THE GREAT SONGS

| | |
|---|---|
| 1930 | Get Happy (Ted Koehler) |
| 1931 | Between the Devil and the Deep Blue Sea); I Love a Parade (both Ted Koehler) |
| 1932 | I Gotta Right to Sing the Blues; I've Got the World on a String (Ted Koehler); It's Only a Paper Moon (E.Y. Harburg, Billy Rose) |
| 1933 | Stormy Weather (Ted Koehler) |
| 1934 | Ill Wind (Ted Koehler); Fun to Be Fooled; Let's Take a Walk Around the Block (both Ira Gershwin, E. Y. Harburg) |
| 1936 | I Love to Sing-A (E. Y. Harburg) |
| 1937 | Buds Won't Bud (E. Y. Harburg) |
| 1939 | Ding-Dong! The Witch Is Dead; Lydia the Tattooed Lady; Over the Rainbow (all E. Y. Harburg) |
| 1941 | Blues in the Night (Johnny Mercer); This Time the Dream's on Me (both Johnny Mercer) |
| 1942 | Hit the Road to Dreamland; That Old Black Magic (both Johnny Mercer); Poor You (E. Y. Harburg) |
| 1943 | Happiness Is a Thing Called Joe (E. Y. Harburg); My Shining Hour; One for My Baby (And One More for the Road) (both Johnny Mercer) |
| 1944 | Ac-cent-tchu-ate the Positive (Johnny Mercer); Now I Know (Ted Koehler); Right As the Rain (E. Y. Harburg) |
| 1945 | Out of This World (Johnny Mercer) |
| 1946 | Any Place I Hang My Hat Is Home; Come Rain or Come Shine (both Johnny Mercer) |
| 1948 | Hooray for Love (Leo Robin) |
| 1953 | Today I Love Ev'rybody (Dorothy Fields) |
| 1954 | I Never Has Seen Snow; A Sleepin' Bee (both Harold Arlen, Truman Capote); The Man That Got Away (Ira Gershwin) |
| 1963 | I Could Go on Singing (E. Y. Harburg) |

Three great singers: Harold Arlen (a truly magnificent singer), Peggy Lee, and Vic Damone.

Rainbow"), *At the Circus* ("Lydia the Tattooed Lady"), *Blues in the Night* ("Blues in the Night," "This Time the Dream's on Me"), *Star Spangled Rhythm* ("That Old Black Magic," "Hit the Road to Dreamland"), *Cabin in the Sky* ("Happiness Is a Thing Called Joe"), *The Sky's the Limit* ("My Shining Hour," "One for My Baby"), *Up in Arms* ("Now I Know"), *Here Come the Waves* ("Ac-cent-tchu-ate the Positive"), *Out of This World* ("Out of This World"), *Casbah* ("For Every Man There's a Woman," "Hooray for Love"), *Mr. Imperium* ("Let Me Look at You"), *The Farmer Takes a Wife* ("To-day I Love Everybody"), *A Star Is Born* ("The Man That Got Away"), and *The Country Girl* ("Dissertation on the State of Bliss").

Arlen's gentle nature, dapper good looks, and quick sense of humor were the hallmarks of a remarkable man. He always wrote with a complete belief in and understanding of his characters, never letting the audience see, as so many composers do, a glimpse of the composer behind the character. Even his revue songs were never simply pop songs—and, although Harold Arlen's name remains unknown to many who fancy themselves aficionados of American song, his compositions have become mainstays of the canon. He is undisputedly one of our masters. ◆

**BELOW:** Three vastly underrated talents: lyricist Ted Koehler, singer Ruth Etting, and composer Harold Arlen.

# Song and Story

### I LOVE A PARADE

Ted Koehler: Harold liked to walk. I didn't. However, he used to talk me into walking and I remember one day it was cold out and to pep me he started to hum an ad-lib marching tune. I guess I started to fall into step and got warmed up. By the end of the walk, the song was written.

### COME RAIN OR COME SHINE

Arlen was noodling around on the piano looking for a tune when a phrase caught Johnny Mercer's ear. Mercer exclaimed, "I'm gonna love you like nobody loved you…" and Arlen jokingly replied, "Come hell or high water." The proverbial light bulb went off over Mercer's head and he answered, "Of course, why didn't I think of that? 'Come rain or come shine.'" The song was finished before the night was over.

### LAST NIGHT WHEN WE WERE YOUNG

Arlen considered this song one of his top two compositions; his other personal favorite was "One for My Baby."

### ONE FOR MY BABY

Harold Arlen called this song one of his "tapeworms," because the melody sort of wanders along. Arlen credited Mercer with much of the success of the song: "[It's] a wandering song. Johnny took it and wrote it exactly the way it fell. Not only is it long—forty-eight bars—but it also changes key. Johnny made it work."

## Asides

It's the lucky song and lucky performer who are joined forever in musical matrimony. Judy Garland was forever bonded to Arlen and Harburg's "Over the Rainbow." Ethel Waters owed him a great debt for "Stormy Weather," a song with which she was associated until Lena Horne came along and sang it in the film of the same name.

## First Person

Irving Berlin, November 20, 1986: Harold Arlen was one of my oldest and best friends. We would talk on the telephone for hours. Never about songs. Music by Harold Arlen is "Stormy Weather," "Over the Rainbow," "That Old Black Magic," "Blues in the Night," and many other songs that will stay around for a long time. He wasn't as well known as some of us, but he was a better songwriter than most of us and he will be missed by all of us.

OPPOSITE PAGE TOP LEFT: Arlen and E.Y. Harburg's longest-running Broadway show, *Bloomer Girl*. OPPOSITE PAGE RIGHT: Arlen and Harburg's flop, *Jamaica*. Now, wouldn't you give up any current Broadway show to see Lena Horne in this "flop?"

THIS PAGE LEFT: Another failure for Arlen, this time with Johnny Mercer. Ruby Elzy and Harold Nicholas in *St. Louis Woman*. The score contains "Come Rain or Come Shine" and "Any Place I Hang My Hat Is Home." So what if the book stunk? In these days of lower standards, it would be a smash hit.

TOP RIGHT: A mutual admiration society, Ella and Harold.

> "Harold was a great singer. Everybody wanted Harold to sing. Harold could perform a song better than anybody and he got all kinds of offers to go on the air and to go on stage and so on, but he refused to do it. Harold is really a purist in every sense of the word, as an artist who would not compromise his talent by being half singer and half writer, as others do." —E. Y. Harburg

# ASCAP & BMI

Herbert called a meeting of composers at Luchow's Restaurant near Union Square, then the center of the New York theater. It wasn't an auspicious start as only five people came to meet the four men. On February 13, 1914, another meeting was convened, and this time over one hundred people showed up and ASCAP was established.

Widespread opposition to ASCAP continued through a series of lawsuits, several of which resulted in decisions against ASCAP. Herbert appealed to the Supreme Court and, ultimately, they ruled in the organization's favor. ASCAP's first payments to composers came in 1916.

A decade passed before ASCAP began distributing significant monies to artists. The reason for the windfall? Technology. Movies and radio generated millions in payments to the organization through the thirties. In 1940, with the radio agreements expiring, ASCAP decided that, as a monopoly, it could call the shots. It doubled its rates and the radio stations rebelled. Program directors decided to cease broadcasting all ASCAP music on their stations, which still left them with classical music, country-and-western tunes, music by non-ASCAP members, R & B songs, and folk music.

At that point, nobody was happy—neither the composers, the radio stations, nor the public. ASCAP had always been highly restrictive in its membership policies, shunning anyone outside of the mainstream and mainly representing film and Broadway composers and pop songwriters. So the broadcasters decided to start their own music-licensing agency, Broadcast Music Incorporated, BMI.

The new organization threw open its doors to all songwriters, regardless of genre. BMI also created a system that paid out royalties almost immediately, while ASCAP continued to employ a baroque ranking system of payments. With the drastic changes in the music industry in the 1950s and '60s, BMI's power increased. ASCAP was forced to play catch up as BMI signed the majority of contemporary songwriters. Today, BMI represents the majority of rock, R & B, and rap music, while ASCAP represents more traditional genres. ◇

The American Society of Composers, Authors and Publishers (ASCAP) and Broadcast Music Incorporated (BMI) license the right to publicly perform the nondramatic, copyrighted musical compositions of their members. In other words, if you're a band, cabaret, radio station, television station, concert hall, or any other entity that offers the performance of music, you have to pay ASCAP or BMI for the right to do so.

ASCAP had its beginnings in 1910, when the famous opera composer Giacomo Puccini, on a visit to the United States, asked George Maxwell, the American representative for an Italian publishing company called Ricordi, why he wasn't seeing any money from the performance of his compositions in hotels and restaurants. The United States copyright law of 1909 guaranteed the owners of musical copyrights the exclusive right "to perform the copyrighted work publicly for profit if it be a musical composition" but businesses ignored the rule since there was no enforcement of it.

In 1913, composer Raymond Hubbell, author of "Poor Butterfly," met with lawyer Nathan Burkan and George Maxwell. The three men approached the most famous American composer of the time, Victor Herbert, and asked him to help their cause.

# Harold Adamson

Harold Adamson, whose career as a lyricist spanned almost fifty years, was a graduate of the University of Kansas and Harvard University. His first Broadway show song was "Say, Young Man of Manhattan," written with Vincent Youmans and placed into the 1929 show *Great Day!* Youmans and Adamson followed it up the next year with a complete score for *Smiles*, and the hit of that show was "Time on Your Hands." In 1931, Adamson teamed with Burton Lane to write "Heigh Ho, the Gang's All Here" for *Earl Carroll's Vanities*. The song was later placed in the film *Dancing Lady* (1933) when Adamson and Lane ventured to Hollywood. They had another hit that same year with "Tony's Wife," placed in the film *Turn Back the Clock*. In 1935 Adamson collaborated with Walter Donaldson on the hit song "Tender Is the Night" (*Here Comes the Band*—1935). Adamson also wrote the pop hits "The Little Things Mean So Much" (1939—Teddy Wilson), "The Woodpecker Song" (1939—Bruno Di

Lazzaro, Eldo Di Lazzaro), "Comin' in on a Wing and a Prayer" (1942—Jimmy McHugh), and "Manhattan Serenade" (1942—Louis Alter).

In 1941, Adamson and Vernon Duke supplied a score for Eddie Cantor's Broadway show *Banjo Eyes* and also wrote the song "We're Having a Baby, My Baby and Me." Then it was back to Hollywood for Adamson, and a fruitful collaboration with Jimmy McHugh on such songs as "I Couldn't Sleep a Wink Last Night" and "A Lovely Way to Spend an Evening"(*Higher and Higher*—1943); "Dig You Later, A-Hubba, Hubba, Hubba" (*Doll Face*—1945); "You Say the Nicest Things Baby" (the show *As the Girls Go*—1948); and "It's a Most Unusual Day" (*A Date with Judy*—1948). Adamson scored two big hits in 1951, with the theme song for *I Love Lucy*, written with Eliot Daniels; and "My Resistance Is Low," written with Hoagy Carmichael and put into *The Las Vegas Story.* Carmichael and Adamson wrote several songs for the film *Gentlemen*

*Prefer Blondes* (1953), including "Ain't There Anyone Here for Love" and "When Love Goes Wrong (Nothin' Goes Right)." His last hit, written with Victor Young, was the title tune for the 1956 film *Around the World in 80 Days.* ◆

---

# Milton Ager

Born in Chicago on October 6, 1893, Milton Ager enjoyed a double career as both a pop songsmith and a contributor of special material for a variety of performers, especially Sophie Tucker. Ager began as a song-plugger for Watson, Berlin, and Snyder in 1910. He moved from Chicago to New York for the publishing company in 1914 to arrange songs. In the early 1920s Ager met lyricist Jack Yellen and a great team was born.

Ager's early hits included "Everything Is Peaches Down in Georgia" (1918) and "Anything Is Nice If It Comes from Dixieland" (1919—both Grant Clarke). Sophie Tucker introduced several Ager/Yellen songs including "Lovin' Sam (The Sheik of Alabam')" (1922), "Louisville Lou" (1923), and "Mamma Goes Where Papa Goes" (1923). In 1924, they hit their stride with "I Wonder What's Become of Sally," "Big Boy," "Hard-Hearted Hannah" and "Big Bad Bill Is Sweet William Now." In 1927 they surpassed themselves with "Ain't That a Grand and Glorious Feeling," "Crazy Words, Crazy Tune," "Is She Still My Girlfriend," "Forgive Me," and "Ain't She Sweet?," the biggest hit of their career.

Eddie Cantor introduced "Hungry Women" in Florenz Ziegfeld's production of *Whoopee* (1928), the same year as their quintessentially twenties number, "My Pet." In 1929, Ager and Yellen joined the vast exodus to Hollywood, writing "I'm the Last of the Red Hot Mamas" for Sophie Tucker to sing in the film *Honky Tonk* (1929). Thus, a theme song and lifelong nickname were born. The team's last successes were the title song for the film *Glad Rag Doll* and "Happy Days Are Here Again," composed for *Chasing Rainbows*.

Yellen and Ager split up in 1930 and Ager wrote few hits after that, retiring in 1944. ◆

## Song and Story

### HAPPY DAYS ARE HERE AGAIN

Jack Yellen described the writing of this classic to David Ewen: In the last week of production, the producer of *Chasing Rainbows* phoned me and said he wanted a song for a scene in which a group of World War I soldiers receive news of the armistice. I relayed the message to Ager, whom I hadn't seen in weeks. He said he would stop in at my house next morning, on his way to the golf course. He came in, sat down at the piano, and lighted a cigar. "Got a title?" he asked finally. I didn't have any, but blurted out, "Happy days are here again."The first tune he played was good enough. He kept playing the melody and I scribbled off the first words that came to me and handed him the corny lyrics. His only comment was that he didn't think the lyric should start with the title. I said I thought it should, and the conversation ended.

### LOVIN' SAM, THE SHEIK OF ALABAM'

Jack Yellen remembered: Milton Ager and I finally became our own publishers because we couldn't get a break with other publishers. We scraped together a few thousand dollars and rented a couple of rooms in a dilapidated building on Broadway. We were almost broke when Max Winslow, professional manager for Waterson, Berlin, and Snyder, phoned me to send over a copy of "Lovin' Sam" to his office. He wouldn't tell me what he wanted it for. About two weeks later we heard that Grace Hayes had gone into *The Bunch and Judy*, an Otto Harbach-Jerome Kern show, and was a riot with "Lovin' Sam" in a cabaret scene. We paid off the sheriff and were in business.

# Bacharach & David

## CAREER HIGHLIGHTS

**1921** Hal David born May 25.

**1928** Burt Bacharach born May 12.

**1932** Bacharach's family moves to Queens, New York.

**1940** Marie Dionne Warwick born December 12.

**1947** David writes his first song for bandleader Sammy Kaye.

**1953** Bacharach marries Paula Stewart.

**1957** Bacharach and David meet in the Brill Building offices of Famous Paramount Music, they have their first hit: "The Story of My Life."

**1958** Perry Como records "Magic Moments"; Bacharach divorces Paula Stewart; he begins European tour with Marlene Dietrich.

**1961** Bacharach returns to U.S. and resumes writing career; he discovers Dionne Warwick, a member of the Gospelaires.

**1966** Television musical *On the Flip Side* broadcast with Ricky Nelson.

**1968** *Promises, Promises* opens on Broadway.

**1969** Bacharach and David win Oscar for "Raindrops Keep Fallin' on My Head" from *Butch Cassidy and the Sundance Kid.*

**1970** Bacharach splits romantically with Angie Dickinson, then professionally with Hal David; Bacharach sues David, who sues him right back; Bacharach and David split with Dionne Warwick, who sues them both.

**1974** David's musical, *Brainchild*, written with Michel Legrand, closes out of town.

**1982** Bacharach marries Carole Bayer Sager.

**1997** Bacharach and David win Trustees Award from NARAS.

**1991** Bacharach splits with Carole Bayer Sager.

**1993** Bacharach, David, and Warwick collaborate on an album: *Sunny Weather Lover.*

**1995** Bacharach begins collaborating with Elvis Costello.

**1999** Bacharach and David (with Warwick) reunite on songs for *Isn't She Great?*, the film bio of Jacqueline Susann.

**2000** Bacharach named one of the sexiest men alive by *People* magazine.

There are three kinds of songs: those in which the music and lyric are equal in importance (think Gershwin), those in which the lyric is more important than the music (think Sylvia Fine), and those in which the music far overshadows the lyric (think Bacharach and David). In the new world of pop music in the sixties, the great success of Bacharach and David owed little to Broadway and the movies. Rather, the inventive rhythms and tempi of Bacharach's music, paired with David's inoffensive, simple lyrics and catchy titles, kept their songs at the top of the charts.

Bacharach, like George Gershwin, was influenced by a variety of sources both highbrow and low, classical and pop, American and foreign. He showed an early predilection for music, studying piano, cello, and drums. His knowledge of music expanded when his family moved to New York from Kansas City in the 1940s, just in time for cool jazz and the ascendance of Charlie Parker, Dizzy Gillespie, and other hepcats around Fifty-second Street. Bacharach's classical training took place at the Mannes School, the New School for Social Research (under Henry Cowell and Darius Milhaud), McGill University, and the Berkshire Music Center. Lyricists tend to be untrained. Experience and practice, plus a born affinity for words, make them good or sometimes even great lyricists. Hal David, brother of lyricist Mack David, has stated that he follows no formula when writing lyrics, often starting with a title and letting inspiration flow—and that's exactly how his lyrics sound. The title is by far the most important element of his songs, and the rest of the lyrics spill out in a sort of everyman's stream of consciousness. David's strength is the straight-ahead ballad, but without the wordplay associated with Harburg, the wittiness of Porter, or the emotional pull of Berlin.

Bacharach and David are resolutely popular writers whose attempts at character songs in such shows as *Promises, Promises* and the film *Lost Horizon* were mostly unsuccessful (though both of these projects launched successful pop songs).

It's telling that Bacharach and David's number one interpreter, Dionne Warwick, possessed a powerful voice and strong sense of rhythmic drive but, like most singers of her time, paid little attention to specific lyrics.

Warwick would become a key element in the remarkable pop success of Bacharach and David. In fact, when the team broke up, Warwick sued, maintaining that they owed her songs. She clearly understood that her pop career, no matter how great her talents, depended in part on her association with the songwriters.

Separately, Warwick and Bacharach went on to have busy, distinguished careers in recording and performing, but neither ever quite regained the fame of those years together at the top of the charts. Bacharach did enjoy a slight renaissance in the late nineties, due to the retro appeal of the Austin Powers movies, which used his work liberally on their soundtracks. But it wasn't quite clear whether he was being celebrated or parodied—probably a mixture of both. David, for his part, has become primarily an administrator, representing ASCAP and the Songwriters Hall of Fame and sitting on several boards. ◆

## THE GREAT SONGS

| | |
|---|---|
| **1957** | The Story of My Life |
| **1958** | Magic Moments; (Theme from) *The Blob* |
| **1961** | Baby It's You (lyric by Mack David and Barney Williams); The Man Who Shot Liberty Valance; Mexican Divorce (lyric by Bob Hilliard); Please Stay; Tower of Strength (lyric by Bob Hilliard) |
| **1962** | Any Day Now (lyric by Bob Hilliard); Don't Make Me Over; Make It Easy on Yourself; Only Love Can Break a Heart |
| **1963** | Anyone Who Had a Heart; Be True to Yourself; Blue on Blue; They Long to Be Close to You; True Love Never Runs Smooth; Twenty Four Hours from Tulsa; Wives and Lovers |
| **1964** | A House Is Not a Home; (There's) Always Something There to Remind Me; Walk on By; Wishin' and Hopin'; You'll Never Get to Heaven (If You Break My Heart) |
| **1965** | Are You There (With Another Girl); Don't Go Breaking My Heart; What the World Needs Now Is Love; What's New, Pussycat? |
| **1966** | Alfie; I Just Don't Know What to Do with Myself; A Message to Michael; Trains and Boats and Planes |
| **1967** | I Say a Little Prayer; The Look of Love; The Windows of the World |
| **1968** | Do You Know the Way to San Jose?; Let Me Be Lonely; Promises, Promises; This Girl's in Love with You; I'll Never Fall in Love Again |
| **1969** | I'm a Better Man; Raindrops Keep Fallin' on My Head |
| **1970** | (They Long to Be) Close to You; One Last Bell to Answer |
| **1973** | Living Together, Growing Together; The World Is a Circle |
| **1981** | Arthur's Theme (music and lyric by Peter Allen, Burt Bacharach, Christopher Cross, Carole Bayer Sager); Stronger Than Before (lyric by Carole Bayer Sager) |
| **1982** | Heartlight (lyric by Neil Diamond, Carole Bayer Sager); Making Love (lyric by Bruce Roberts, Carole Bayer Sager); That's What Friends Are For (lyric by Carole Bayer Sager) |
| **1984** | To All the Girls I Loved Before (music by Albert Hammond) |
| **1986** | On My Own |
| **1995** | God Give Me Strength (lyric by Elvis Costello) |
| **1998** | I Still Have That Other Girl (lyric by Elvis Costello) |
| **1999** | Walkin' Tall (lyric by Tim Rice) |

## Song and Story

### MAKE IT EASY ON YOURSELF
When Dionne Warwick recorded the song, she thought it was for commercial release. When she found out the song was a demo only and that Bacharach and David had given it to Jerry Butler, Warwick yelled out, "Don't make me over, man!" meaning, "Don't lie to me!" "Don't Make Me Over" became the title of Warwick's 1962 hit.

### I'LL NEVER FALL IN LOVE AGAIN
"I'll Never Fall in Love Again" was a late addition to *Promises, Promises*, added because the producers felt the show lacked a breakout hit. When Bacharach and David discovered that Jill O'Hara could play the guitar, the number was quickly completed and staged.

## First Person
John Zorn, composer: Bacharach's songs explode the expectations of what a popular song is supposed to be. Advanced harmonies and chord changes with unexpected turnarounds and modulations, unusual changing time signatures, and rhythmic twists, often in uneven numbers of bars...but he makes it all sound so natural you can't get it out of your head or stop whistling it. Maddeningly complex, sometimes deceptively simple, these are more than just great pop songs: these are deep explorations of the materials of music and should be studied and treasured with as much care and diligence as we accord any great works of art.

**OPPOSITE PAGE:** Bacharach, Paul Anka, and Lena Horne.

**ABOVE:** (left to right) David, Warwick, and Bacharach.

**BELOW:** Jerry Orbach and Jill O'Hara in *Promises, Promises*.

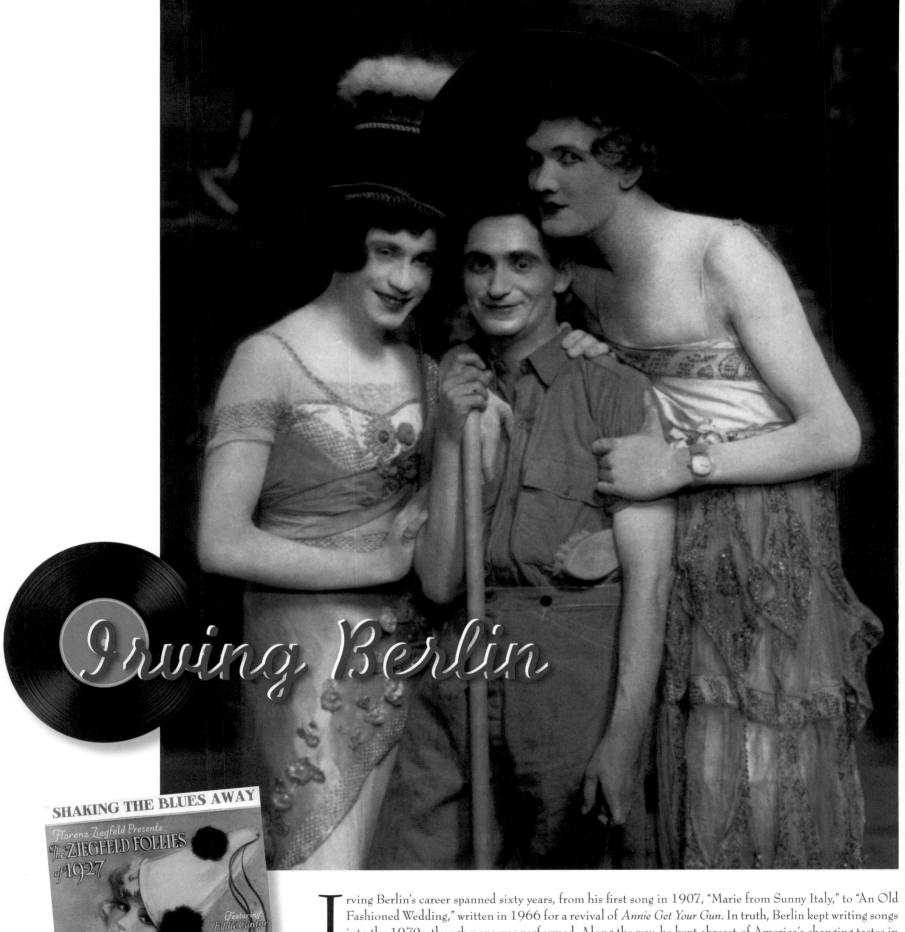

# Irving Berlin

SHAKING THE BLUES AWAY

*Florenz Ziegfeld Presents*
THE ZIEGFELD FOLLIES of 1927

*Featuring
Eddie Cantor
Words & Music by
Irving Berlin
Dances by
Sammy Lee*

OOH, MAYBE IT'S YOU
SHAKING THE BLUES AWAY
IT ALL BELONGS TO ME
LEARN TO SING A LOVE SONG
WHAT MAKES ME LOVE YOU
RIBBONS AND BOWS
IT'S UP TO THE BAND
RAINBOW OF GIRLS
JIMMY
JUNGLE JINGLE

MADE IN
USA

I rving Berlin's career spanned sixty years, from his first song in 1907, "Marie from Sunny Italy," to "An Old Fashioned Wedding," written in 1966 for a revival of *Annie Get Your Gun*. In truth, Berlin kept writing songs into the 1970s, though none was performed. Along the way, he kept abreast of America's changing tastes in popular song. We are so familiar with the giant careers of our greatest songwriters, Berlin, Gershwin, Arlen, Porter, and so on, that we forget what a monumental achievement it is to sustain a career through decades of change. This ability to connect with the common man over many years requires a special talent that the great songwriters themselves are very likely unaware of.

A 1910 newspaper article quotes Berlin about staying in favor: "Songwriting all depends on the public. The thing it likes one minute, it tires of the next. Just now for some reason the public wants to have some fun with the marriage relation. Get up a song panning the husband or the wife, roast them, have some fun with them, show up some of the little funny streaks in domestic life and your fortune is made, at least for the moment. Pretty soon the public will tire of these and then you must be able to switch your lyre to something else. If not a new writer will take your place and your star which rose so suddenly will set as rapidly as it came up."

The one period during which the great songwriters attempted to appropriate foreign (to them) musical styles was when the rock era arrived—and the experiment was an abject failure. In the sixties, Berlin wrote "The Washington Twist" for his last show, *Mr. President*; Cole Porter gave us "The Ritz Roll and Rock" for the film version of *Silk Stockings*; Jule Styne, Betty Comden, and Adolph Green parodied stupid pop songs with *Do Re Mi*'s "What's New at the Zoo." Or was it a parody?

Berlin was the Elvis of American popular song, in that he borrowed black musical idioms and transformed them into music that the average white guy could accept. His use of black ragtime syncopations caused a sensation—but he was just doing what came natur'lly as he had been exposed to a variety of nontraditional musical forms during his childhood. When Berlin was five, his family left Russia and settled on the Lower East Side of New York. After the death of his father, when he was eight, he left school and by his teens was singing in Bowery saloons and restaurants. Songwriting was just becoming a big business, and he began writing lyrics for others' tunes and plugging songs for publishers. His first song, "Marie from Sunny Italy," had music by Mike Nicholson.

Although he never learned to read music, Berlin was on the way to becoming a professional songwriter. In 1909, he was hired as a staff lyricist by the Ted Snyder Company, and soon Berlin was matching his words to his own music. The next year he performed in vaudeville, quickly moving on to musical comedy in *Up and Down Broadway*. His first success, "Alexander's Ragtime Band," catapulted Berlin to the top of his field. Some would argue that he never lost his perch as the greatest American songwriter. ❖

## THE GREAT SONGS

1907 Marie from Sunny Italy (music by Mike Nicholson)
1909 Sadie Salome (Go Home) (music and lyric by Irving Berlin and Edgar Leslie); My Wife's Gone to the Country (Hurrah! Hurrah!) (music by Ted Snyder, lyric by George Whiting and Irving Berlin); That Mesmerizing Mendelssohn Tune
1910 Grizzly Bear (The Dance of the Grizzly Bear)
1911 Everybody's Doing It Now
1912 I Want to Be in Dixie; When the Midnight Choo-Choo Leaves for Alabam'
1913 Snooky Ookums
The International Rag
1914 I Want to Go Back to Michigan (Down on the Farm)
1915 I Love a Piano
1918 Oh! How I Hate to Get Up in the Morning
1919 I've Got My Captain Working for Me Now; Mandy; A Pretty Girl Is Like a Melody; You'd Be Surprised
1921 All By Myself; Everybody Step; Say It with Music
1924 All Alone; Lazy; What'll I Do?
1925 Always; Remember
1927 Shaking the Blues Away; The Song Is Ended (But the Melody Lingers On)
1929 Let Me Sing and I'm Happy; Puttin' on the Ritz (written in 1927); Waiting at the End of the Road
1932 How Deep Is the Ocean (How High Is the Sky); Let's Have Another Cup of Coffee; Say It Isn't So; Soft Lights and Sweet Music
1933 Easter Parade; Harlem on My Mind; Heat Wave; How's Chances; Maybe It's Because I Love You Too Much; Supper Time
1934 Say It with Music
1935 Cheek to Cheek; Isn't This a Lovely Day (To Be Caught in the Rain)?; No Strings (I'm Fancy Freed); Top Hat, White Tie and Tails
1936 Get Thee Behind Me, Satan; I'm Putting All My Eggs in One Basket; Let Yourself Go; Let's Face the Music and Dance
1937 He Ain't Got Rhythm; I've Got My Love to Keep Me Warm; Slumming on Park Avenue
1938 Change Partners; I Used to Be Color Blind; Now It Can Be Told
1939 God Bless America
1940 Fools Fall in Love; It's a Lovely Day Tomorrow
1942 White Christmas
1945 You Keep Coming Back Like a Song
1946 Anything You Can Do; Doin' What Comes Natur'lly; The Girl That I Marry; I Got Lost in His Arms; I Got the Sun in the Morning; There's No Business Like Show Business; They Say It's Wonderful; You Can't Get a Man with a Gun
1948 A Couple of Swells
1949 Let's Take an Old-Fashioned Walk; You Can Have Him
1950 The Best Thing for You; You're Just in Love
1954 Count Your Blessings Instead of Sheep

**OPPOSITE PAGE:** Irving Berlin and two rather masculine chorus girls in *Yip, Yip Yaphank*.

**LEFT:** A salute to the most expensive statue in the world in *Miss Liberty*.

# Song and Story

### ALL ALONE

When faced with the death of his first wife, Dorothy Goetz, and his mother, Irving Berlin decamped to the Ritz Hotel in Atlantic City. He wrote "All Alone" as an expression of his sadness.

### WHAT'LL I DO

"What'll I Do" came to Berlin when he was slightly drunk on champagne and feeling sorry for himself at a birthday party. It seems Berlin wasn't good enough for Clarence Mackay, the industrialist father of Ellin Mackay, Berlin's intended. Eventually, Berlin got the girl and a hit song in the bargain.

### ALEXANDER'S RAGTIME BAND

Though it is considered a ragtime song, "Alexander's Ragtime Band" bears little relationship to traditional ragtime. After the huge success of Scott Joplin's "Maple Leaf Rag" in 1899, the first white songwriter to capitalize on the new rhythms and counterpoint was Joseph E. Howard, in the song "Hello, Ma Baby," which he wrote that very same year. In 1902, Hughie Cannon wrote the ragtime tune "Bill Bailey, Won't You Please Come Home." It took Berlin longer to absorb the rag influences but when he finally did he was generally accepted as the first white songwriter to incorporate ragtime. Songs like "Play Some Ragtime," (1910), "Stop That Rag," and "Yiddle on Your Fiddle" helped establish his reputation.

### BLUE SKIES

One of the most famous songs to come from a Rodgers and Hart show wasn't even written by them. Berlin's "Blue Skies" was interpolated into the show *Betsy* and sung by Belle Baker. The opening-night reception was tumultuous, with Baker enjoying twenty-four encores—the last with composer Irving Berlin, who was summoned up from the audience. Talk about stopping the show!

### REMEMBER

Never has a romance resulted in more great standards than that of Irving Berlin and Ellin Mackay. His three greatest songs were written at the beginning of the affair, when Berlin was trying desperately to overcome the objections of Ellin's powerful father. Mackay decided to send his daughter on a cruise, figuring that a long ocean voyage and crisp salt air would drive that skinny Jewish songwriter right out of her heart.

### GOD BLESS AMERICA

Mary Ellin Barrett, daughter of Irving Berlin, recalls: I was eleven years old when I first heard "God Bless America." Now, to me, this was a very strange Irving Berlin song because I knew my father as this jazzy, sophisticated or earthy vernacular writer of songs like "Alexander's Ragtime Band" and "Cheek to Cheek." And then

it began creeping up on me. I came to understand that it wasn't "God bless America, land that we love." It was "God bless America, land that *I* love." It was an incredibly personal statement that my father was making, that anybody singing that song makes as they sing it. And I understood that that song was his thank-you to the country that had taken him in. It was the song of the immigrant boy who made good.

### MY WIFE'S GONE TO THE COUNTRY (HURRAH! HURRAH!)

Irving Berlin: "My Wife's Gone to the Country" was my first big hit and I got the idea of that from a Chicago fellow: He and I were having a little drink and chat near dinner time and, noting the clock, I said to him, "Almost suppertime. Suppose you've got to be beating it home?" He said, "Oh, no! My wife's not in the city." Now you'll probably laugh, but right then and there it occurred to me that "My Wife's Gone to the Country" would be a capital name for a popular song. The music buzzed into my head. I got somebody to write it and there I was.

### MARIE FROM SUNNY ITALY

Irving Berlin to Ed Sullivan: I never wanted to be a songwriter. All I wanted in those days was a job in which I could earn twenty-five dollars a week. That was my idea of heaven. But a bartender in another Bowery saloon, Al Piantadosi, had written a song, an Italian type of tune, and "Nigger Mike" sneered at us and asked us why we didn't write something. So Mike Nicholson and myself wrote "Marie from Sunny Italy," and split it thirty-three cents apiece. That was in 1907, Joe Schenck, the drug clerk around the corner, bought a copy. I think he was the only one.

### CHEEK TO CHEEK

One of the rejected songs from *As Thousands Cheer* took only a day to write, but it was one of Berlin's most infectious songs. Fred Astaire sang in to Ginger Rogers later, in *Top Hat*. The song was "Cheek to Cheek."

### ALWAYS

Berlin's musical secretary, Arthur Johnston (who would later become a successful songwriter in his own right), had a girlfriend named Mona. She asked Berlin to write a song for her and Berlin obliged with a song titled, "I'll Be Loving You, Mona." Years later, in 1925, Berlin amended the song for the Marx Brothers stage vehicle *The Cocoanuts*, substituting the word "always" for "Mona." The rest of the lyrics were inspired by Berlin's love for Ellin Mackay, soon to be his wife.

The music to "Easter Parade" was born as "Smile and Show Your Dimple" in 1917. Berlin took out the saccharine and slowed down the tempo to create "Easter Parade" for the show *As Thousands Cheer*.

## Asides

Since Berlin could neither read nor write music fluently, he employed several musical secretaries. Many of these turned out to be excellent songwriters, including Harry Akst, Cliff Hess, Milton Ager, Harry Ruby, Arthur Johnston, and, for one song only, George Gershwin.

Berlin could be incredibly stingy and also incredibly generous. Most people know that all of his royalties for "God Bless America" go to the Girl Scouts of America and that the royalties for *This Is the Army* go to Army Emergency Relief. Few know that, during the Second World War, he donated proceeds of "Angels of Mercy" to the American Red Cross, "Any Bonds Today" to the Treasury Department, and "Arms for the Love of America" to the Ordinance Department. What's more, Berlin donated all proceeds from *This Is the Army*, over $10 million, to the war effort.

**OPPOSITE PAGE TOP:**
Nanette Fabray and Robert Ryan in the white elephant musical, *Mr. President*.

**OPPOSITE PAGE BOTTOM:**
George Gershwin and Irving Berlin.

**TOP:** Irving Berlin and wife, Ellin Mackay Berlin.

If you were going to whip up a Johnny Burke, the recipe would consist of the down-home values of Johnny Mercer, the romanticism of E. Y. Harburg, and the gentle humor of Frank Loesser—plus a dash of impish whimsy and a dollop of self-deprecation.

Burke was born in Antioch, California, on October 3, 1908. He spent his adolescence in Chicago, then moved to New York and got a job peddling pianos. Perhaps as a result of being in such close proximity to those eighty-eight keys, Burke turned to writing songs. He was called to California in the great song rush of 1929, at the advent of sound pictures, when the studios were intent on making millions on movie musicals. Burke wasn't quite ready for his first professional job as a songwriter. As he recalled, "Getting that Fox contract was really a 'freak.' I went to the coast and, of course, wrote a couple of things. But I'll admit they were very mediocre. The Fox people let me out at the end of the six months.

"I returned to New York and had to start all over again. The publishers didn't take to my lyrics at all, and I knew no melody-writer with whom I could work. I wanted to write like Gilbert of 'Gilbert and Sullivan' fame. Wanted to write with my tongue in my cheek—not too sentimentally."

His first hit, with Joe Young and Harold Spina, was "Annie Doesn't Live Here Anymore" in 1933. Burke described Spina as "fiery. He is musicianly. Very daring in his work." The new team started without a dime but they were determined to write songs that departed from the usual Tin Pan Alley 32-bar AABB tunes. Today, songs like "Annie Doesn't Live Here Anymore" and "The Beat of My Heart" don't seem groundbreaking, but at the time they were oddities and considered very forward-looking. In fact, "Annie…" was given an ASCAP award in 1933. Publishers were doubtful about the songs' chances. Remembered Burke, "The publishers kept turning us down. They accused us of writing over everybody's head. They complained that the songs were too *tricky*."

In 1935, Burke made another stab at Hollywood stardom, this time at Paramount Pictures. He was teamed with veteran songwriter James V. Monaco. Monaco was much older than Burke, born in Fornia, Italy, on January 13, 1885. He arrived in America at age six and taught himself to play the piano. After working in clubs in Chicago, Monaco moved to New York in 1910, trying to find work as a pianist. The next year he had his first song published, "Oh, Mr. Dream Man." He wrote both the music and lyrics, which may explain why the song is forgotten today.

Monaco would have a smash hit the very next year when Lilliane Lorraine sang "Row, Row, Row" in the *Ziegfeld Follies of 1912.* The song is the very definition of a standard, still sung almost one hundred years since its first hearing. In 1913, Monaco and Joseph McCarthy were lucky enough to have Al Jolson introduce the song "You Made Me Love You." Jolson put all his tremulous heart-tugging into his interpretation and the song was set to become one of the greatest hits of the century. It was revived in 1941 by Harry James and his orchestra and became a smash all over again.

Jolson picked up "You're a Dog Gone Dangerous Girl" in 1916 and interpolated it into his hit show, *Robinson Crusoe, Jr.* Then came the Monaco hit "What Do You Want to Make Those Eyes at Me For?" After a few unmemorable tunes, Monaco and Jolson teamed up again in 1921 for a smash, "Dirty Hands, Dirty Face," with lyrics by Edgar Leslie and Grant Clarke (and Jolson listed as colyricist too). Jolson sang it again in the first popular talking picture, *The Jazz Singer,* in 1928.

Monaco moved to Hollywood in 1930, around the time Burke hit the Golden State, but the composer was more successful than the lyricist. He worked on no fewer than twelve films in 1930 though none of the songs became hits. He stayed in Hollywood, working steadily, and, in 1936, signed with Paramount Pictures and met Johnny Burke.

Monaco and Burke were assigned to write songs for Bing Crosby pictures and they quickly became Crosby's favorite songwriting team. Their first hit for Der Bingle was "I've Got a Pocketful of Dreams," for 1938's *Sing You Sinners.* They wrote "Six Lessons from Madame La Zonga" in 1940 and Jimmy Dorsey made it into a big hit with Helen O'Connell on vocals. The team wrote for the first of the Hope and Crosby road pictures, *Road to Singapore* (1940), and scored a hit with "Too Romantic."

Monaco moved to Fox where he contributed a series of hit songs for films like *Stage Door Canteen* (1943), *Pin-Up Girl* (1944), *Irish Eyes Are Smiling* (1944), and *The Dolly Sisters* (1945—"I Can't Begin to Tell You"). James V. Monaco died of a heart attack on October 16, 1945.

When Monaco left Paramount, Burke was left without a songwriting partner, so he was quickly paired with James Van Heusen. Van Heusen was born Edward Chester Babcock (a name that shows up in the road pictures) in Syracuse, New York, on January 26, 1913. He started writing songs in high school and even broadcasted them on a local radio station. His outgoing, gregarious personality made him well suited to a radio career but his given name didn't exactly sing—so he took a new moniker from a famous shirt manufacturer and the rest is history.

**OPPOSITE PAGE TOP:** A match made in Tin Pan Alley heaven: Jimmy Van Heusen and Johnny Burke. **OPPOSITE PAGE BOTTOM:** Another match made in Tin Pan Alley heaven: Jimmy Van Heusen and Sammy Cahn. **RIGHT:** Two more matches: Jimmy Van Heusen joins Eddie Fisher and Debbie Reynolds and Doris Day and Nat King Cole in musical matrimony.

Following high school, Van Heusen became a staff pianist for the Santly Brothers and Remick publishing companies in New York. He began writing songs in 1933, though he fancied himself a lyricist. He first began composing songs in 1938 with Jimmy Dorsey, among others, scoring two hits that year with "Deep in a Dream" and "Shake Down the Stars," both written with Eddie De Lange. He and DeLange wrote the score for the 1939 Broadway show, *Swingin' the Dream,* which proved to be a songwriters' dream come true. In the cast of this jazzy retelling of Shakespeare's *A Midsummer Night's Dream* were Louis Armstrong and Maxine Sullivan, ably abetted by Butterfly McQueen; Dorothy, Etta, and Vivian Dandridge; the Deep River Boys; Jackie "Moms" Mabley; Dorothy McGuire; Nicodemus; Warren Coleman; and Oscar Polk—a veritable who's who of black talent. In the pit were both the Benny Goodman Sextette and Bud Freeman's Summa Cum Laude Band. Van Heusen and DeLange were inspired to write a big hit for the show, "Darn That Dream," which Goodman recorded with Mildred Bailey.

In 1940 Van Heusen moved to Hollywood and teamed with Burke on the film *Road to Zanzibar* (1941). The two instantly clicked and came up with the first of their many standards for Crosby, "It's Always You." Tommy Dorsey made a hit recording of the song, sung by the young Frank Sinatra. The singer never forgot the song, and a decade later Van Heusen would become Sinatra's composer of choice. In fact, in 1944 Van Heusen and comedian Phil Silvers would write a song commemorating the birth of Sinatra's daughter, the hit "Nancy with the Laughing Face."

The "road" pictures rolled on with *Morocco* (1942), *Utopia* (1945), *Rio* (1947), and *Bali* (1952), and so did the Burke and Van Heusen songs. The two spent practically their entire partnership at Paramount writing for Crosby, though there were notable exceptions such as *Lady in the Dark* (1944), and, well, that's about it.

They did try their luck on Broadway with the show *Nellie Bly* in 1946. It was a flop. Another Broadway attempt, *Carnival in Flanders* (1953), starring John Raitt and Dolores Gray, was a failure too—though it did contain a standard, "Here's That Rainy Day." That

## THE GREAT SONGS

All songs by Burke and Van Heusen, unless otherwise indicated.

| | |
|---|---|
| 1933 | Annie Doesn't Live Here Anymore (music by Harold Spina, lyric by Johnny Burke and Joe Young) |
| 1935 | My Very Good Friend the Milkman (music by Harold Spina) |
| 1936 | Pennies From Heaven (music by Arthur Johnston) |
| 1938 | On the Sentimental Side (music by James V. Monaco); Deep in a Dream; Shake Down the Stars (both music by Eddie DeLange) |
| 1939 | Darn That Dream; Heaven Can Wait (both lyrics by Eddie DeLange); I Thought About You (lyric by Johnny Mercer); Imagination; Oh! You Crazy Moon; Polka Dots and Moonbeams |
| 1940 | Ain't It a Shame about Mame; April Played the Fiddle (both music by James V. Monaco); Isn't That Just Like Love |
| 1941 | It's Always You; What's New (music by Bob Haggart); You Lucky People You |
| 1942 | Ain't Got a Dime to My Name (Ho Ho Hum); Moonlight Becomes You; The Road to Morocco |
| 1943 | Sunday, Monday or Always |
| 1944 | Going My Way; It Could Happen to You; Like Someone in Love; Nancy with the Laughing Face (lyric by Phil Silvers); Suddenly, It's Spring; Swinging on a Star |
| 1945 | Aren't You Glad You're You?; It's Anybody's Spring; Personality; Welcome to My Dream; Yah-ta-ta, Yah-ta-ta (Talk, Talk, Talk) |
| 1947 | As Long As I'm Dreaming; But Beautiful; My Heart Is a Hobo; Smile Right Back at the Sun; You Don't Have to Know the Language |
| 1949 | Busy Doing Nothing; If You Stub Your Toe on the Moon; Once and for Always |
| 1950 | Life Is So Peculiar |
| 1952 | The Merry-Go-Runaround; To See You |
| 1953 | Here's That Rainy Day |
| 1954 | Misty (music by Erroll Garner) |
| 1958 | There's a Flaw in My Flue |
| 1961 | He Makes Me Feel I'm Lovely (music and lyric by Johnny Burke) |

basically marked the end of Burke and Van Heusen's collaboration (they reteamed a couple of times, in 1954 and '58). With the exception of Dubin and Warren, no team wrote as many great songs for Hollywood as Burke and Van Heusen.

Burke's last hit was his lyrics to Erroll Garner's "Misty" in 1954. He made another attempt at Broadway in 1961 with the show *Donnybrook,* for which he wrote music and lyrics, but the show, despite a marvelous score, was another failure. Johnny Burke died on February 25, 1964, in New York City.

Jimmy Van Heusen stayed in California after the breakup of the team, and in 1955 he teamed up with Sammy Cahn. They started their collaboration with a bang, working on a television musical version of *Our Town* (1955) starring Paul Newman, Eva Marie Saint, and Frank Sinatra. The score is tender and charming, and "Love and Marriage" emerged a standard.

By the mid-fifties Hollywood had changed and movie musicals were less in demand. So, between scores, Cahn and Van Heusen wrote title tunes for a variety of films. As Sinatra's team of choice, they also wrote pop tunes for him to record, including the album *Come Fly with Me* (1957), with its swinging title tune and "It's Nice to Go Travellin'." The team perfectly captured Sinatra's new ring-a-ding-ding persona—in fact, they helped to define it.

Cahn and Van Heusen also dreamed of Broadway success as a team. They first struck out with 1965's *Skyscraper,* starring the unlikely Broadway musical star, Julie Harris. The score wasn't bad, though, and "Ev'rybody Has the Right to Be Wrong" was a pop hit from the score. The next year, Cahn and Van Heusen took a few trunk songs they had written for the 1956 unproduced Paramount musical, *Papa's Delicate Condition,* added a few more songs, and came up with the Norman Wisdom vehicle, *Walking Happy.* It, too, was a failure. The only song to achieve some success was the title song. (Another song from *Papa's Delicate Condition* achieved pop success later, "Call Me Irresponsible.")

Van Heusen retired to enjoy his boat, his weekly poker games, and his alcoholic refreshment. He died on February 7, 1990. ◆

**WHAT'S NEW?**

Bob Haggart, the great bass player, wrote an instrumental piece for the trumpeter Billy Butterfield, called "I'm Free." Johnny Burke came up with a lyric, and it became "What's New?"

**ALL THE WAY**

James Van Heusen explained to author David Ewen: The song was written to dramatize Joe E. Lewis's loss of his voice [in the film *The Joker Is Wild*] and the big jump musically at the end of the second bar to the middle of the third bar was specifically designed to be difficult for him to sing, and he was supposed to break down dramatically.

. . . . . . . . . . . . . . . . . . . . . . . . . . . . . . . . .

"One of the best things that ever happened to me was a 145-pound leprechaun named Johnny Burke." —Bing Crosby

. . . . . . . . . . . . . . . . . . . . . . . . . . . . . . . . .

# Sammy on Sammy

I had a marvelous, marvelous mother. Typical Jewish mother. Instead of the typical Jewish family, which has four sons and one daughter, I had four sisters and me, an only son. And at a very, very early age I started to go bad. By bad, I meant that I got acquainted with musicians. My mother insisted that I play the violin. Had she insisted that I play the piano it might have made all the difference in the world. I adored my mother because my mother was the kind of lady you could make a deal with. And I made a deal with her that I would play the violin up to and until my Bar Mitzvah, my thirteenth birthday.

And there was a twist of fate. On my thirteenth birthday, we had the usual typical party. And we had a little orchestra playing there, I think it was a six piece orchestra, and about one o'clock in the morning my mother said to me, "Let us pay the orchestra." And we paid the orchestra from the presents I received, the envelopes with the checks.

And that was the most astonishing thing I ever heard. I never realized that these six fellows that were playing and having such a great time all night got paid. And as I was paying them I instinctively said, "Do you do a lot of this?"

They answered, "Oh yes, we play all kinds of affairs, parties, weddings, engagements."

I said, "Well, gee, how do I get to do that?"

"Would you like to do that?"

I said, "I'd love to do that."

Have fun and get paid, I guess you could call that the slogan of my life, because ever since that time, I've had fun and they paid me for it. Writing songs is the most fun I've ever had in my life to this day. And if I couldn't write lyrics I would be a very, very unhappy fella. I love writing songs and if they don't let me write songs for money I write 'em for free and that's ninety percent of the songs I write.

Cahn and Van Heusen wrote two Broadway musicals, both flops. **ABOVE:** Leading lady who couldn't sing, Julie Harris, and, just hanging around, Peter Marshall, in *Skyscraper*. **RIGHT:** Norman Wisdom making his Broadway debut (and farewell) in *Walking Happy*. **OPPOSITE PAGE:** Der Bingle, Old Ski-nose, and, well, Sammy Cahn.

## SAMMY CAHN SONGS, CONT'D

**1942** I've Heard That Song Before (music by Jule Styne)

**1944** Come Out, Come Out Wherever You Are; I Guess I'll Hang My Tears Out to Dry; I'll Walk Alone; Saturday Night Is the Loneliest Night of the Week; There Goes That Song Again (all music by Jule Styne)

**1945** Day By Day; I Should Care (both music by Axel Stordahl and Paul Weston); I Begged Her; I Fall in Love Too Easily; It's Been a Long, Long Time; Let It Snow, Let It Snow, Let It Snow; Tonight and Every Night; You Excite Me (all music by Jule Styne)

**1946** Five Minutes More; The Things We Did Last Summer (both music by Jule Styne)

**1947** I Still Get Jealous (music by Jule Styne); Papa Won't You Dance with Me (music by Jule Styne); The Song's Gotta Come from the Heart (music by Jule Styne); Time After Time (all music by Jule Styne)

**1948** It's Magic; It's You or No One; Put 'Em in a Box, Tie 'Em with a Ribbon and Throw 'Em in the Deep Blue Sea (all music by Jule Styne)

**1950** Be My Love (music by Nicholas Brodszky); Go to Sleep, Go to Sleep, Go to Sleep (music by Fred Spielman)

**1952** Because You're Mine (music by Nicholas Brodszky); Good Little Girls (music by Vernon Duke); The Second Star to the Right (music by Sammy Fain)

**1954** Teach Me Tonight (music by Gene DePaul); Three Coins in the Fountain (music by Jule Styne)

**1955** Love and Marriage; Our Town; (Love Is) The Tender Trap (all music by James Van Heusen)

**1956** Call Me Irresponsible; Walking Happy (both music by James Van Heusen); Hey, Jealous Lover (by Sammy Cahn, Kay Twomey, Bee Walker);

**1957** All the Way (music by James Van Heusen)

**1958** Come Fly with Me; Fancy Meeting You Here To Love and Be Loved (both music by James Van Heusen)

**1959** High Hopes (music by James Van Heusen)

**1960** The Second Time; Ain't That a Kick in the Head (both music by James Van Heusen)

**1961** Pocketful of Miracles (music by James Van Heusen)

**1964** My Kind of Town (music by James Van Heusen)

**1965** The September of My Year; Ev'rybody Has the Right to Be Wrong (both music by James Van Heusen)

**1967** Thoroughly Modern Millie (music by James Van Heusen)

**1968** Star! (music by James Van Heusen)

**1954** Teach Me Tonight (music by Gene DePaul); Three Coins in the Fountain (music by Jule Styne)

**1955** Love and Marriage (music by James Van Heusen); Our Town (music by James Van Heusen); (Love Is) The Tender Trap (music by James Van Heusen)

**1956** Call Me Irresponsible (music by James Van Heusen); Hey, Jealous Lover (by Sammy Cahn, Kay Twomey, Bee Walker); Walking Happy (music by James Van Heusen)

**1957** All the Way (music by James Van Heusen)

**1958** Come Fly with Me; Fancy Meeting You Here To Love and Be Loved (all music by James Van Heusen)

**1959** High Hopes (music by James Van Heusen)

**1960** The Second Time; Ain't That a Kick in the Head (all music by James Van Heusen)

**1961** Pocketful of Miracles (music by James Van Heusen)

**1964** My Kind of Town (music by James Van Heusen)

**1965** The September of My Year; Ev'rybody Has the Right to Be Wrong (all music by James Van Heusen)

**1967** Thoroughly Modern Millie (music by James Van Heusen)

**1968** Star! (music by James Van Heusen)

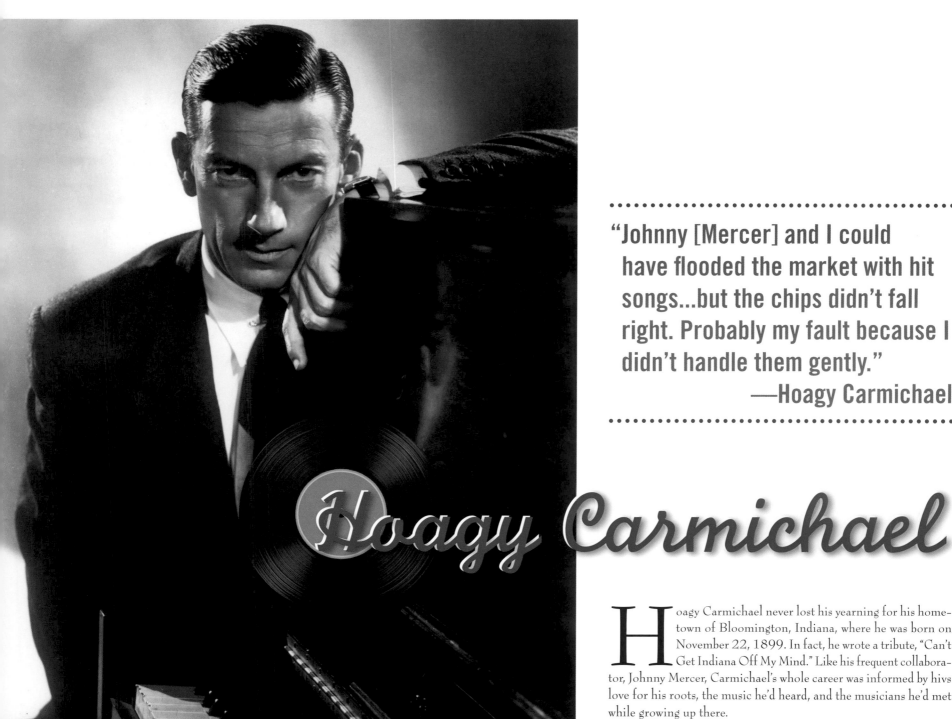

"Johnny [Mercer] and I could have flooded the market with hit songs...but the chips didn't fall right. Probably my fault because I didn't handle them gently."

—Hoagy Carmichael

# Hoagy Carmichael

Hoagy Carmichael never lost his yearning for his hometown of Bloomington, Indiana, where he was born on November 22, 1899. In fact, he wrote a tribute, "Can't Get Indiana Off My Mind." Like his frequent collaborator, Johnny Mercer, Carmichael's whole career was informed by hivs love for his roots, the music he'd heard, and the musicians he'd met while growing up there.

In 1916, Carmichael's father, an itinerant electrician, and his mother, a pianist in a silent-movie house who also played the occasional dance, and their son moved to Indianapolis. Carmichael developed an interest in the piano and took lessons from his mother and from black pianist (and barber) Reggie Duval (sometimes spelled DuValle). In 1919, back in Bloomington, he heard Howard Jordan's ensemble who, as Carmichael put it, "exploded in me almost more music than I could consume." When Carmichael was studying law at Indiana University (what is it with composers and law school?), he founded his first band, the curiously named Carmichael Syringe Band (later renamed Carmichael's Collegians). In 1924, he met Bix Beiderbecke, then leader of the Wolverines. Cornetist Beiderbecke would prove to be the most important influence on Carmichael's life both personally and professionally.

Carmichael was urged by Beiderbecke to try his hand at composition, and his first piece, "Riverboat Shuffle," was performed and then recorded by the Wolverines in 1924. It was Carmichael's first composition, first recording, and first published piece of music. In the last category he was not to receive his due, however, in that Jack Mills credited the song to the Wolverines' pianist, Dick Voynow, along with Mills's brother, the king of the cut-in, Irving Mills. (Strange, since Irving Mills was usually credited with lyrics he didn't write—but the "Riverboat Shuffle" didn't even *have* lyrics until Mitchell Parish added them in 1939).

Beiderbecke went on to join Paul Whiteman's aggregation but didn't forget his friend Hoagy. In November 1927, Whiteman recorded "Washboard Blues," with Carmichael handling the piano chores and singing Fred B. Callahan's lyric. That same year marked the debut of Carmichael's most successful composition ever, "Star Dust." The first recording was made with Emil Seidel's band, performing under the name Hoagy Carmichael and His Pals. The recording session took place on October 31, 1927, and the piece was published by Mills Music in January 1929 as an instrumental. Mitchell Paris was called in to supply a lyric in May of that year.

Meanwhile, Carmichael was barely making ends meet as a lawyer in West Palm Beach. The gig was short-lived. In 1929, he finally moved to New York City to make his fortune in songwriting. Things were bound to be slow in New York, of course, as the Depression was in full force, so it took until 1930 for "Star Dust" to become well known, largely because of the Isham Jones recording on the Brunswick label, at the tempo at which it is now conventionally played.

As the thirties rolled in, the hits came fast and furious, including "Rockin' Chair" recorded with Louis Armstrong and Mildred Bailey, "Georgia on My Mind" with a lyric by Stuart Gorell (the guy who named "Star Dust"), and "Lazy River."

In 1931 Beiderbecke died and Carmichael moved further toward mainstream, Tin Pan Alley writing and away from his jazz roots. In 1936, he married Ruth Meinardi and left New York for a Hollywood screen career. Most of Carmichael's appearances are no more than glorified cameos, much like Dooley Wilson's in *Casablanca*. His most famous appearance is in *To Have and Have Not* (1944), where he sang "How Little We Know." He also appeared in *The Best Years of Our Lives* (1946) in a straight role (he played it even straighter as a regular on the TV western *Laramie* in 1959). Carmichael made one stab at success on the Great White Way, 1939's *Walk with Music*, which, though it had a marvelous score, failed.

Carmichael's somewhat monotone singing voice had a county twang and a wry quality, and he became a noted performer of his own work as well as others'. His recordings for Decca, along with his film, radio, and television appearances, made him probably the most recognizable songwriter in the country. But as the 1950s progressed, popular music left the great craftsmen behind, and Carmichael's opportunities diminished. He died on December 27, 1981. ◈

· · · · · · · · · · · · · · · · · · · · · · · · · · · ·

## "Hoagy was a very big talent but a very small man." —Johnny Mercer

· · · · · · · · · · · · · · · · · · · · · · · · · · · ·

## *Song and Story*

### LAZY BONES

Hoagy Carmichael: [Johnny Mercer] walked in one day and I was sitting in the chair, the door was open, summertime. He knocked, and I said, "Come in!" And I'm sitting in the chair, half-dozing. This is the absolute truth. I said, "What's on your mind?" He said, "Well, I thought we might try to write a song." I said, "Have you got any idea?" He said, "I thought I'd like to write a song called 'Lazy Bones.' What do you think of that title?" I said, "With this kind of summer we're having in New York, and what with the Depression, and nobody working, it sounds mighty logical."

### IN THE COOL, COOL, COOL OF THE EVENING

Hoagy Carmichael: As I was driving down the highway, coming into Palm Springs to join Johnny [Mercer] to write this score, I happened to think of an old old joke, not a very funny joke. But it was about a jackass. And it seemed that the king of the jungle, the lion, sent an emissary to the jackass to say, "Jackass, are you coming to the king's big party?" And the jackass, sitting with a pipe in his mouth and his legs crossed, said, "Tell the king in the cool, cool, cool of the evening, I'll be there." Well, I told this joke to Johnny Mercer and in two days we had the song.

### STAR DUST

In 1927, the story goes, Hoagy Carmichael was sitting on the "spooning wall" at Indiana University, pining for a girl named Dorothy. He ran to an old upright piano in the Book Nook and finished the song. A great story but apparently not true. Carmichael had actually been working on the song since 1926. He had even written a lyric including the words "stardust melody." However and wherever it happened, Carmichael recorded "Star Dust" in 1927 for Gannett Records. Publisher Irving Mills took the song to Mitchell Parish and, after slowing down the melody, wrote new lyrics for the tune. Carmichael's friend (and lyricist for "Georgia on My Mind") Stuart Gorrell, came up with the title "Star Dust," as the melody reminded him of "dust from stars drifting down through the summer sky."

In 1936, RCA pressed what must certainly be one of the most unique records of all time—"Star Dust" on both the A and B sides of a 78, with Benny Goodman's Orchestra on one side and Tommy Dorsey's on the flip.

## *Asides*

Hoagy Carmichael was caricatured by puppeteer Bil Baird as Slugger Ryan, a gangly upright piano player with his fedora perched back on his head and cigarette poised perilously between his lips.

## THE GREAT SONGS

1924 Riverboat Shuffle

1925 Washboard Blues

1929 Star Dust (lyric by Mitchell Parish)

1930 Georgia on My Mind (lyric by Stuart Gorrell); Rockin' Chair

1931 Come Easy Go Easy Love (lyric by Sunny Clapp); Lazy River (lyric by Sidney Arodin)

1932 In The Still of the Night (lyric by Jo Trent)

1933 Lazybones (lyric by Johnny Mercer)

1936 Little Old Lady; Lyin' to Myself (both lyrics by Stanley Adams); Moonburn (lyric by Edward Heyman)

1937 The Nearness of You (lyric by Ned Washington)

1938 Heart and Soul; Small Fry; Two Sleepy People (all lyrics by Frank Loesser); I Get Along Without You Very Well

1939 Hong Kong Blues; Riverboat Shuffle (lyric by Mitchell Paris and Dick Voynow)

1940 Can't Get Indiana Off My Mind (lyric by Robert De Leon); I Walk with Music (lyric by Johnny Mercer); Way Back in 1939 A.D.

1941 Skylark (lyric by Johnny Mercer)

1942 Baltimore Oriole; The Lamplighter's Serenade (both lyrics by Paul Francis Webster)

1943 Old Music Master (lyric by Johnny Mercer)

1945 Billy-A-Dik; Doctor, Lawyer, Indian Chief; Memphis in June (all lyrics by Paul Francis Webster); How Little We Know (lyric by Johnny Mercer)

1946 Ole Buttermilk Sky (lyric by Jack Brooks)

1950 In the Cool, Cool, Cool of the Evening (lyric by Johnny Mercer)

1951 My Resistance Is Low (lyric by Harold Adamson)

1952 Watermelon Weather (lyric by Paul Francis Webster)

1953 Ain't There Anyone Here for Love? (lyric by Harold Adamson); When Love Goes Wrong (Nothin' Goes Right)

Coleman & Leigh

Cy Coleman was the jazziest of Broadway composers. A child prodigy born to Russian emigrant parents on June 14, 1929, he began picking out tunes on the family piano at age four. His father, a carpenter, grew so annoyed that he nailed the cover down over the keys. Coleman gave his first recital at age six, at Steinway Hall; made his Carnegie Hall debut at seven; and for the next few years was a regular at New York's Town Hall and other concert venues. It was jazz that he really loved, and while still in his teens he played many clubs. Though his career took him in another direction, Coleman never forgot his love of jazz. In fact, just before his sudden death in 2004, he had completed an engagement at Feinstein's at the Regency.

Coleman's Broadway career began in 1953, when he placed songs in the revue *John Murray Anderson's Almanac*. His collaborator was Joseph McCarthy, Jr., the son of a famed Tin Pan Alley composer.

Carolyn Leigh was born in New York on April 21, 1926. Leigh was minding her own business, working at an advertising agency one day, when she tried to reach a magazine editor by phone but dialed the wrong number. In a stroke of fate, she got the music publisher Buddy Morris on the phone. He asked to see some of her writing. After looking over her material, he assigned her the task of writing a lyric to a Johnny Richards tune. She came up with "Young at Heart." Mary Martin, then preparing a new musical version of *Peter Pan*, heard the song and insisted on Leigh for the lyrics. She wrote some wonderful songs for the show in collaboration with another Morris composer, Moose Charlap. The show was a hit, both on Broadway and on television screens for years to come.

In 1956, Buddy Morris made the professional match of a lifetime when he paired Leigh with Coleman. They wrote their first song, "One Day," in 1956.

In 1960, their perseverance paid off and the result was the score to *Wildcat*. The show starred Lucille Ball, fresh from her divorce from Desi Arnaz and ready to conquer the Great White Way. Ball silently put up money for the show, which opened to kind reviews including good notices for the Coleman and Leigh score. The hit song was "Hey, Look Me Over" and the show was poised for success—but Ball had underestimated the energy needed for an extended run on Broadway and the show closed.

The Leigh-Coleman collaboration was tempestuous—each possessed a healthy temper—but the songs they wrote together made all the ups and downs worthwhile, at least for a few more years. *Little*

Dubbed in Hollywood but singing for herself in her Broadway musical theater debut (and farewell), Lucille Ball and Dom Tomkins in *Wildcat*.

*Me* was their next Broadway outing, it just may be the funniest score in Broadway history. Sid Caesar starred in the 1962 production, and biggest hit among many worthy songs was "Real Live Girl." After writing a few more pop tunes the team broke up.

The year was 1965 and Coleman chose Dorothy Fields as his next collaborator. The result was *Sweet Charity* (1966), the jazziest of all Broadway scores. "Big Spender" was the hit, though the score contains many other brilliant songs that have entered the Broadway canon. Leigh next wrote one excellent song with Harold Arlen, "Bad for Each Other," but their personalities didn't mesh and Arlen was at the end of his composing career. She went on to collaborate with Elmer Bernstein on the musical *How Now Dow Jones* (1967)—not a success, though it contained many wonderful songs including the briefly popular "Step to the Rear."

Coleman and Leigh worked on one last song, "Feathers," in 1971, and, though they shared a mutual respect, they knew that further collaboration would kill at least one of them, possibly both. Leigh teamed with Lee Pockriss, a fine composer, but the three shows they worked on were never produced and their pop tunes couldn't withstand the rock-and-roll juggernaut that did in so many great tunesmiths of the time. In the late 1970s, Leigh wrote a show with Morton Gould based on Fellini's *Juliet of the Spirits* but it was a no-go.

In 1981, against their better judgment, Coleman and Leigh got back together and in 1982 wrote a couple of numbers for a revival of *Little Me*. At the same time Leigh teamed with Marvin Hamlisch on a musical version of the film *Smile*. Carolyn Leigh died of a heart attack on November 19, 1983, and her words were replaced with inferior lyrics by Howard Ashman.

Coleman reteamed with Dorothy Fields for what would be their last show, *Seesaw* (1973). Alas, she died soon thereafter.

Coleman was the king of the unproduced musical, often working on three or four projects at the same time though he had a success with the tiny musical *I Love My Wife* (1977), featuring lyrics by Michael Stewart. In 1978, Coleman teamed with Betty Comden and Adolph Green for the operetta/farce/satire *On the Twentieth Century* (1978), considered by some to be the last great Broadway musical.

Coleman scored one of his biggest hits with *Barnum* (1980). Michael Stewart provided the libretto and lyrics. Coleman's next success came in 1989 with the intricately scripted *City of Angels,* featuring equally intricate lyrics by David Zippel. In 1991, Coleman again teamed up with Comden and Green, and the result was *The Will Rogers Follies* (1991), the team's last Broadway show.

*The Life* (1996), with lyrics by Ira Gasman, was a colorful tour through the world of Times Square prostitutes. In 2001, *Grace* opened in Amsterdam, produced by a fan of Grace Kelly. Coleman's final project, with lyrics by Alan and Marilyn Bergman, was called *Like Jazz*.

Coleman suffered a massive heart attack and died on November 18, 2004, to the shock of fans and friends who had come to think of him as a hardy perennial on the musical scene. ◆

## Song and Story

### HEY, LOOK ME OVER

Carolyn Leigh: I must confess, shamefacedly, the second half of the song was not written with any craft, any experience, any forethought, or anything at all except desperation.

When we played it down at the office, the publisher said, "I guarantee you I will break every contract I have with you and I will not publish that score [*Wildcat*] unless you put that song in it." Of course I had to finish it. Simple song. But the simple songs are the hardest usually for lyric writers. I thought, "Okay, since I think Buddy Morris is the greatest man I know at this stage in my life, why don't I just use his name for good luck?" Hence, "don't thumb your nose, bud." The moral of this story is never pick a publisher named Irving.

### I'VE GOT YOUR NUMBER

Carolyn Leigh: We had written a song for [*Little Me*] that between the time we had started to write the show and auditions seemed to be slipping out of the show altogether. Songs get written out shows quite a lot—but Swen [Swenson] implored us to let him have a go at this one number before we made the final [casting] decision. And out came this guy with the most incredible version of a song I've ever seen. And Cy Feuer said, "Well, damn it all, he's gotta be in it and its gotta stay

in." So back to the drawing board. And that song stopped that show every night.

## Asides

They didn't get the job—but the two fine songs that Coleman and Leigh wrote as an audition for the privilege of writing the score to *Gypsy* were "Firefly," recorded by Tony Bennett, and "To Be a Performer," which landed in the score of *Little Me*.

## THE GREAT SONGS

Music by Cy Coleman and lyrics by Carolyn Leigh unless otherwise indicated.

1952 Why Try to Change Me Now? (lyric by Joseph McCarthy, Jr.)

1953 The Riviera (lyric by Joseph McCarthy, Jr.); Young at Heart (music by Johnny Richards)

1954 I Won't Grow Up; I'm Flying; I've Gotta Crow (all music by Moose Charlap)

1956 How Little It Matters, How Little We Know (music by Phil Springer)

1957 Witchcraft

1958 A Doodlin' Song; Firefly; I Walk a Little Faster; It Amazes Me; You Fascinate Me So

1959 The Best Is Yet to Come

1960 Give a Little Whistle (And I'll Be There); Hey, Look Me Over; The Rules of the Road

1962 Here's to Us; I've Got Your Number; Real Live Girl

1963 When In Rome

1965 I'm in Love Again (lyric by Peggy Lee); Pass Me By; Sweet Talk (lyric by Floyd Huddleston)

1966 Bad Is for Other People (lyric by Bob Wells); Big Spender; If My Friends Could See Me Now; There's Gotta Be Something Better than This (all lyrics by Dorothy Fields)

1967 Everyone Here Kindly Step to the Rear (music by Elmer Bernstein)

1968 My Personal Property (lyric by Dorothy Fields)

1973 It's Not Where You Start; Nobody Does It Like Me (both lyrics by Dorothy Fields)

1978 Our Private World (lyric by Betty Comden and Adolph Green)

1980 The Colors of My Life; Come Follow the Band (both lyrics by Michael Stewart)

1983 Killing Time (music by Jule Styne)

1985 Night Life in Santa Rosa

1989 You're Nothin' Without Me (lyric by David Zippel)

Possibly no medium has affected the course of popular music more than television. At the turn of the century, sheet music was the medium of choice for disseminating new tunes, but one had to be able to play the piano in order to take advantage of it. Though some sheets sold over a million copies, the only people listening were those in the immediate vicinity of the piano. Radio and recordings brought music to millions but without images. Some popular singing stars and big bands showed up in the movies, but there was never a generalized movement to feature these performers. On the whole, movie stars sang in films but seldom made records and recording stars sang on record but seldom ventured into the movies.

When television came along in the early '50s, the variety show, based on Broadway's revues and the vaudeville tradition, was a mainstay of the networks. Suddenly, thousands and then millions of people could hear new songs and see their favorite stars performing them. The granddaddy of all variety shows was Ed Sullivan's *Toast of the Town* (later, simply *The Ed Sullivan Show*). Each week, Sullivan, a noted reporter (though a very stiff host), would introduce a veritable who's who from the world of international entertainment. The original casts of current Broadway shows performed fully staged and costumed numbers, singers sang their latest singles, opera stars came by to lend a touch of class to the proceedings, all within an hour that included plate spinners, acrobats, and Topo Gigio, the Italian marionette mouse. The *Hollywood Palace* on ABC tried to clone the Sullivan formula but featured a guest host on every episode. Other notable variety shows were hosted by Garry Moore, Perry Como, Dinah Shore, Milton Berle, Jerry Lester and Dagmar, Danny Kaye, the Smothers Brothers, Andy Williams, Tennessee Ernie Ford, and Carol Burnett.

Television also featured the amateur contest, an idea picked up from radio's *Major Bowes and the Original Amateur Hour*. Bowes's producer, Ted Mack, took over the show on radio and then transferred the proceedings to television, where the show became a smash hit. *Arthur Godfrey's Talent Scouts* was a reworking of the *Amateur Hour* idea, but

**ABOVE LEFT:** Lena Horne and Dean Martin. **ABOVE:** Tony Bennett. **RIGHT:** Ella Fitzgerald; **BELOW RIGHT:** Bing Crosby, Carol Lawrence, and Maurice Chevalier.

so-called "talent scouts" were sent out to "discover" unsung performers and bring them before a national audience.

In the 1970s television rediscovered the talent show format when former Johnny Carson sidekick Ed McMahon hosted *Star Search*. It was still the same old showcase for up-and-coming or down-and-out wannabes, but with added production values and big prizes for the winners in each entertainment category. And for minorities there was the syndicated *Show-*

# Television

*time at the Apollo*. On these shows you could hear pop singers, comedians, musicians, opera singers, and every other permutation of performer.

You could say that all of this has led up to today's craze for "reality television," showcasing real people (whatever *they* are) competing for high stakes. *American Idol* is the most successful of them all, and it has

relegated the search for talent to a search for young, attractive clones who belt out bland pop, rock-and-roll, or country-western tunes in a kind of pseudo-gospel style, complete with sliding notes, "soul endings," grimacing faces, and lounge-singer microphone tossing. It used to be that performers tried to make it all look easy—but on *Idol* and its clones, it is a virtue to work *hard*. Would Frank Sinatra and the Hoboken Four made it on *American Idol* like they did on *Major Bowes*? Heck, even future rockers Johnny and Edgar Winters and Gladys Knight appeared on Ted Mack. *Idol*, with its emphasis on "text-messaging your vote as soon as the show is over," is really more an exercise in marketing than in talent-mining, with the complicity of the networks, record labels, Internet providers, and personality magazines. The winners get a lot of press and airtime—and that all-precious recording contract—but where will they be in a few years? We can only wait and see.

The early talent shows really did work. To take but one example, Godfrey's show was instrumental in helping along the careers of Pat Boone, Tony Bennett, Eddie Fisher, Steve Lawrence, Connie Francis, Leslie Uggams, Lenny Bruce, Connie Francis, Roy Clark, and Patsy Cline. Godfrey's eye for talent wasn't perfect, though. He refused to showcase either Buddy Holly or Elvis Presley.

We were taught in school that every action has an equal and opposite reaction and so it is in television: Ted Mack begot Chuck Barris, whose brainchild *The Gong Show* featured the worst performers, and the more excruciating the better. It all goes to show that in television, either end of the talent spectrum can be wildly entertaining to the masses.

Remember that physics theory above? Need we say more than *The Lawrence Welk Show*? Bubbles, ragtime piano, clean-scrubbed singers, barber shop quartets, and an accordion. Let's just move on.

Rock-and-roll got exposure on television through the ministrations of Dick Clark and his *American Band-stand*. The hottest acts of the 1950s and '60s appeared on *Bandstand*, lip-synching their way into the hearts of America as freshly scrubbed teens danced in the background. *Bandstand* was basically your high school hop in a television studio, that is, if some big-time talent happened to drop by your school gymnasium. In the 1960s production values were deployed and rock lite tunes were featured on NBC's *Hullabaloo* and its ABC clone, *Shindig*.

One last bastion of music on television is the musical game show. Among the earliest was ABC's *Juke Box Jury*, which premiered in 1953 and was later syndicated. ABC also featured the 1954 game show *So You Want to Lead a Band?* and the next year, NBC broadcast *Musical Chairs*. But the greatest musical game show of them all was *Name That Tune*. It began production in 1953 and ran for six years, first on NBC and then on CBS, with a later syndicated version appearing in the 1970s. If you could name a tune in one note and run down and ring a bell, you could win a lot of stuff you didn't need.

With the exception of an occasional spot on talk shows or *Saturday Night Live*, there isn't a lot of music performed on network television. Call us old-fashioned, but we'd settle for some great reruns of those variety shows of the past. ◆

# Comden & Green

**B**etty Comden and Adolph Green contributed to the development of the art of the musical both in the theater and on the screen. They were the longest-running writing team in Broadway history, and yet, because their subjects tended to be comedic rather than dramatic, they have not always received their due from critics and historians.

They both began their careers as members of the Revuers, a nightclub troupe that also included Judy Holliday (then named Judith Tuvim), for which they both wrote and performed. Their early collaborations for the Revuers proved popular in Greenwich Village club Village Vanguard, but less so in the swankier environs of the Rainbow Room uptown. Comden and Green then went to Hollywood to star in the movie *Greenwich Village*, but were mostly cut from the picture.

Leonard Bernstein, a former campmate and roommate of Adolph Green, caught their new act at the Blue Angel in 1944; he convinced them to write the book and lyrics for a new musical adaptation of his ballet *Fancy Free*, to be titled *On the Town*. The show was a smash, featuring such standards as "New York, New York" and "Lucky to Be Me." After the failure of *Billion Dollar Baby* (1945) and *Bonanza Bound* (1947), Comden and Green went to Hollywood, where they joined MGM for a series of successful film musicals. They wrote the screenplay for *Good News* (1947), lyrics for *Take Me Out to the Ball Game* (1949), adapted *On the Town* for the screen that same year and wrote an additional song with Andre Previn, and wrote the screenplay for *The Barkleys of Broadway* (1949), the last pairing of Fred Astaire and Ginger Rogers.

In 1951, the team made another attempt at Broadway, meeting their next great partner, Jule Styne. Their initial collaboration was the musical revue *Two on the Aisle* (1951). Following that success, Comden and Green returned to Hollywood to write the screenplay for perhaps the greatest movie musical of all time, *Singin' in the Rain* (1952). They followed that with another classic MGM film, *The Band Wagon* (1953), which was released after their next Broadway hit, *Wonderful Town*, with a score by Bernstein. They worked again with Styne on their next musical, *Peter Pan*, starring Mary Martin, which was followed by the film *It's Always Fair Weather* (1955).

In 1956, in collaboration with Styne, the team wrote *Bells Are Ringing* for their old Revuers partner, Judy Holliday. The score yielded such gems as "Just in Time" and "The Party's Over." *Say, Darling* (1958) was a roman à clef about the making of the Broadway musical *The Pajama Game*. While Jule Styne was occupied with *Gypsy*, Comden and Green worked on the film adaptation of *Bells Are Ringing*, and then the threesome returned to Broadway with *Do Re Mi* (1960), containing another hit song, "Make Someone Happy." David Merrick, producer of *Do Re Mi*, also presented the Styne/Comden and Green musical *Subways Are for Sleeping* (1961), featuring the hit song "Comes Once in a Lifetime."

Styne went on to write *Funny Girl* while Comden and Green wrote the film *What a Way to Go* (1964). That same year Broadway saw the debut of *Fade Out-Fade In*, starring Carol Burnett. Comden and Green's *Hallelujah, Baby!* (1968) had an excellent score, though the days of pop hits arising from Broadway shows were virtually over.

Comden and Green, hardy perennials, wrote the libretto to Strouse and Adams's *Applause* (1970), starring the unlikely musical comedy star, Lauren Bacall. Then it was a long eight years before Comden and Green's next Broadway show, *On the Twentieth Century* (1978), with music by Cy Coleman. This classic—and classy—farce is considered by many to be the last great Broadway musical. Their next Broadway assignment was the score for *A Doll's Life* (1982). Between Broadway gigs, Comden and Green themselves starred in a two-person retrospective called *A Party with Comden and Green*. Their last Broadway show was a reteaming with Cy Coleman for *The Will Rogers Follies* in 1991.

Green called their collaboration "an unconscious give-and-take"; Comden called it "mental radar." Whatever it was, it resulted in some of the most joyfully enthusiastic moments of musical theater. Their shows, especially when they contributed librettos, too, are marked by a smart, urbane innocence perfectly captured in the personality of Judy Holliday. Their characters are plain people who express their feelings with an exuberance and joie de vivre. Comden and Green's wit, humor, and slightly wry look at the world have resulted in one of the finest catalogue of productions in Broadway and Hollywood musical history. ◆

## THE GREAT SONGS

**(ALL MUSIC BY JULE STYNE UNLESS INDICATED OTHERWISE)**

**1944** I Can Cook Too (music by Bernstein, lyric by Bernstein, Comden, and Green); Come Up to My Place; New York, New York; Some Other Time (all music by Leonard Bernstein)

**1951** If; There Never Was a Baby Like My Baby

**1953** Conversation Piece; A Little Bit in Love (both music by Leonard Bernstein)

**1955** I Like Myself (music by Andre Previn)

**1956** Just in Time; Long Before I Knew You; The Party's Over

**1958** Dance Only with Me

**1960** Adventure; Make Someone Happy

**1961** Comes Once in a Lifetime

**1964** Fade Out-Fade In; The Usher from the Mezzanine

**1967** Being Good Isn't Good Enough; I Wanted to Change Him

**1978** On the 20th Century

**1991** Give a Man Enough Rope; Never Met a Man I Didn't Like

## Song and Story

### JUST IN TIME

Jule Styne: I wrote the tune. I said [to Comden and Green], "I'm just gonna write a top tune." Find a title to this, "da da da." You could call the tune anything. "da, da, da." It sings by itself. For three months it was called "da da da." No title, they couldn't write the song. So I said, "I'm gonna help you. I'm gonna see my friend Frank Loesser." This is done. Many lyric writers [have helped each other]—Leo Robin has helped Ira Gershwin—you need someone to talk to. So, I went to Frank, I said, "Frank, I'm writing with Comden and Green." He said, "They don't understand what a popular song is. What it consists of. It's something that you remember melodically, not lyrically but melodically. You don't remember the melody, you ain't remembering the song. They don't understand that." So I played it for him. He said, "It has to have a rolling title." I played it over and over. I came back and he said, "I have the title to the song, it goes, 'Just in Time.'" All he said was, "Just in Time." And they wrote a very good lyric to it. It's a very good lyric. They're very nice people. They're very sophisticated people. They're well learned and well read.

## First Person

Jule Styne: I thought in on *On the Town*, Lenny's songs prevailed over the lyrics. Melodically he prevailed. I said [to Comden and Green], "Look, you've never written with anyone who gave you songs that people sing on the streets. That's what we like to do. Don't be afraid to write songs—not *ungepachke*, special material—you've written a show but I call that writing special material. Because, no one can get up in the café and sing those songs because people don't know what you're talking about. You write wonderful if there's a story in the book, while you're in the theater they're fine." The first song we wrote was for Bert Lahr [*Two on the Aisle*]. It had some material in it, "Catch Our Act at the Met" and "If." I accommodate them, they can't accommodate me, but it was solid. The ballads didn't make it; I was hearing their failings and I knew exactly what was wrong, they were setting words to my notes instead of setting ideas, thoughts. Good lyric writers don't try to rhyme your notes. They write thoughts, big thoughts, lyric writers like Oscar Hammerstein, Ira Gershwin, Johnny Mercer, Frank Loesser, and now Stephen Sondheim.

Betty Comden: Adolph is a man who reads while crossing streets. It is no uncommon sight to see him weaving his way across Broadway at Forty-Fifth Street in the crush of matinee traffic, all the daily papers bunched under one arm, the *Saturday Review*, *Atlantic Monthly*, *Life*, and *Paris-Match* slipping from under the other, an ash-trailing cigarette drooping from his lips, head deep in some book or periodical as brakes screech and drivers swear. Oblivious, he shuffles across, engaged in leisurely perusal of anything from *A Skeleton Key to Finnegan's Wake* to this week's grosses in *Variety*.

**TOP:** Bernie West and Judy Holliday in *Bells Are Ringing*.
**ABOVE:** Comden and Green as the title characters in *A Party with Comden and Green*.

## De Sylva, Brown, & Henderson

The upbeat numbers of lyricists B. G. De Sylva and Lew Brown and composer Ray Henderson define the bubbly insouciance of the 1920s. Though none of their shows has lasted, they wrote some of the most endearing songs in the American popular canon. They were most famous as a trio, though each member also worked with others. De Sylva collaborated with George Gershwin, Victor Herbert, Jerome Kern, Emmerich Kalman, and Lewis Gensler; Brown wrote with Harry Akst, Charles Tobias, and Sam Stept; Henderson teamed with lyricists Ted Koehler, Jack Yellen, and Irving Caesar.

Lew Brown was born on December 10, 1893, in Odessa, Russia. His parents traveled to New Haven and then to New York, where Brown began his songwriting career. He was lucky enough to meet up with successful composer Albert Von Tilzer, and the pair had some early successes in both New York and London. Among their hits were "Give Me the Moonlight, Give Me the Girl," "Oh, By Jingo, Oh by Gee," and "Dapper Dan." Brown hooked up with Ray Henderson but continued to produce hits with a variety of other composers, including "Last Night on the Back Porch" (with Carl Schraubstader), "Shine" (with Cecil Mack and Ford Dabney), "Then I'll Be Happy" (with Cliff Friend), and "Collegiate" (with Moe Jaffe and Nathan A. Bonx). Friend was a frequent collaborator with Brown, including on Brown's first complete musical comedy score, *Piggy*, which opened in 1927.

B. G. De Sylva's parents were vaudevillians, and his early songs were incorporated into Al Jolson's Broadway shows (often with Jolson taking a cut-in, or credit without work). De Sylva found himself writing for the prestigious Remick music publishing company, the leading publisher of Broadway scores at the time. Remick paired De Sylva with the young George Gershwin and lyricist Arthur Jackson, and the result was 1919's *La, La, Lucille*, the team's first full Broadway score. (De Sylva had already had a show close out of town, *Dodo*).

De Sylva was then paired with veteran composer Jerome Kern and the result was a mixed blessing. Though *Zip Goes a Million* never made it to Broadway, it did contain "Look for the Silver Lining," which became a standard when interpolated into their next show, *Sally* (1920). That show also included the hit song "Whip-poor-will." Jolson incorporated two more De Sylva numbers into his hit show *Bombo* (1921), and both "April Showers" and "California, Here I Come" were smash hits. Jolson and De Sylva had another hit show with *Big Boy* (1925), featuring "If You Knew Susie" and "Keep Smilin' at Trouble."

De Sylva was now an important force in songwriting, and his next show, *Orange Blossoms* (1922), was written with the great Victor Herbert. The hit song from that show was "A Kiss in the Dark." He was then hired, along with Gershwin, to supply the scores for three editions of the *George White Scandals*, and the result was "I'll Build a Stairway to Paradise" and "Somebody Loves Me." When Gershwin moved on to write with his brother Ira, De Sylva continued to contribute to George White's shows as a part of the new team of De Sylva, Brown, and Henderson.

Ray Henderson was the son of a musician who played several instruments. He composed his first songs at age eight and held several jobs in the music industry, including church organist, piano teacher, vaudeville accompanist, pianist in a dance band, and arranger for a music publisher. His first published song was "Humming," written in collaboration with lyricist Louis Breau. The song found its way into the Broadway show *Tip Top*, starring the Duncan sisters. With Lew Brown he wrote "Georgette," which was put into the *Greenwich Village Follies*. The team of Brown and Henderson wrote several songs that would come to be standards, the best known of which is "Don't Bring Lulu."

Brown continued to collaborate with others as well, and found success with "That Old Gang of Mine," "Five Foot Two, Eyes of Blue," and "I'm Sitting on Top of the World." Brown first collaborated with B. G. De Sylva in 1925, on the song "Alabamy Bound" (also written with Bud Green). Since he'd worked with both De Sylva and Henderson, it was only natural that the three writers would team up to make Broadway's most successful songwriting trio.

The threesome's music exemplified the Roaring Twenties with its emphasis on speed and rhythm. Their songs incorporated jazz and blues into the Broadway idiom. Optimistic and energetic, the team produced a remarkable number of standards in only five years together.

De Sylva, Brown, and Henderson were responsible for the following revues and musicals: *George White's Scandals* (1925); *George White's Scandals* (1926), "Birth of the Blues," "The Black Bottom," "This Is My Lucky Day"; *Good News!* (1927), "The Best Things in Life Are Free," "Good News," "Just Imagine," "Lucky in Love"; *Manhattan Mary* (1927); *George White's Scandals* (1928) "I'm on the Crest of a Wave"; *Hold Everything!* (1928) "You're the Cream in My Coffee"; *Follow Thru* (1929) "Button Up Your Overcoat," "Then I'll Have Time for You"; and *Flying High* (1930).

The team started an eponymous publishing company to handle their Broadway scores, but sold it in 1929. That same year they signed a contract with Fox pictures and traveled to Hollywood. Their first

film, on which De Sylva was producer, was *Sunny Side Up*, starring Janet Gaynor. The next year they worked on their last film with Fox, *Just Imagine*.

After De Sylva's left the team, Brown and Henderson wrote the score to *George White's Scandals* (1931) and the songs "Ladies and Gentlemen, That's Love," "Life Is Just a Bowl of Cherries," "That's Why Darkies Were Born," "This is the Missus," and "The Thrill Is Gone." Their next show was *Hot-Cha!* (1932) with Henderson as colibrettist, and *Strike Me Pink* (1933) with Brown and Henderson also producing, directing, and furnishing the libretto.

Ray Henderson went on to his own career, and on *Say When* (1934), written in collaboration with Ted Koehler, he also acted as coproducer. He went on to contribute to *George White's Scandals* (1935) and the *Ziegfeld Follies of 1043*.

Lew Brown, along with Harry Akst, wrote *Calling All Stars* (1934), for which he was also colibrettist, producer, and codirector, and *Yokel Boy*, on which he was librettist, producer, and director. He worked in Hollywood before retiring.

De Sylva stayed in Hollywood, producing a number of films including the Shirley Temple vehicles *The Little Colonel* (1935), *The Littlest Rebel* (1935), *Captain January*, *Poor Little Rich Girl*, and *Stowaway*, all in 1936.

He also worked on Broadway as colibrettist and lyricist on the hit *Take a Chance* (1932). Its score contained "Eadie Was a Lady," "Rise and Shine," and "You're an Old Smoothie." De Sylva produced and cowrote the libretto to Cole Porter's *Du Barry Was a Lady* (1939) and produced Irving Berlin's *Louisiana Purchase* (1940), on which he was colibrettist. From 1941 to 1945 he was a producer at Paramount Studios.

De Sylva made a vitally important contribution to American popular song when he cofounded Capitol Records with Glenn Wallichs and Johnny Mercer. In 1955, Capitol was sold to EMI and De Sylva's share of the take was $1.75 million dollars. Be that as it may, his film biography was titled after one of his biggest hits, "The Best Things in Life Are Free." ❖

## THE GREAT SONGS (CONTINUED)

**1925** Collegiate (music and lyrics by Nat Bonx, Lew Brown, Moe Jaffe); Don't Bring Lulu (music by Ray Henderson, lyric by Lew Brown, Billy Rose); Five Foot Two, Eyes of Blue (Has Anybody Seen My Girl) (music by Ray Henderson, lyric by Sam M. Lewis, Joe Young); Hello 'Tucky; It All Depends on You (both music by Ray Henderson, lyric by Lew Brown, B. G. De Sylva); If You Knew Susie (music by Joseph Meyer); Keep Smiling at Trouble (Trouble's a Bubble) (music by Lewis E. Gensler, lyric by B. G. De Sylva, Al Jolson)

**1926** The Birth of the Blues; The Black Bottom; (The Girl Is You) The Boy Is Me; Lucky Day (all music by Ray Henderson, lyrics by Lew Brown, B. G. De Sylva); (You Must Have Been a) Beautiful Baby (music by James F. Hanley); Bye Bye Blackbird (music by Ray Henderson, lyric by Mort Dixon); When Day Is Done (music by Robert Katscher)

**1927** The Best Things in Life Are Free; Good News; Here Am I Broken Hearted; Just Imagine; Lucky in Love; The Varsity Drag (all music by Ray Henderson, lyrics by Lew Brown, B. G. De Sylva)

**1928** I'm on the Crest of a Wave; I'm Sitting on Top of the World; If I Had a Talking Picture of You; Sonny Boy; You're the Cream in My Coffee (all music by Ray Henderson, lyrics by Lew Brown, B. G. De Sylva)

**1929** Back In Your Own Back Yard (music by Dave Dreyer, lyric by B. G. De Sylva, Al Jolson); Button Up Your Overcoat; I'm a Dreamer, Aren't We All; If I Had a Talking Picture of You; Sunny Side Up (all music by Ray Henderson, lyrics by Lew Brown, B. G. De Sylva)

**1931** Ladies and Gentlemen That's Love; Life Is Just a Bowl of Cherries; That's Why Darkies Were Born; This Is the Missus; The Thrill Is Gone (all music by Ray Henderson, lyrics by Lew Brown)

**1932** Eadie Was a Lady, You're An Old Smoothie (both music by Nacio Herb Brown, Richard A. Whiting)

**1934** Baby, Take a Bow (music by Jay Gorney and Lew Brown, lyric by Lew Brown), Nasty Man (music by Ray Henderson, lyric by Irving Caesar, Jack Yellen)

**1935** Animal Crackers in My Soup (music by Ray Henderson, lyric by Ted Koehler)

**1938** That Old Feeling (music by Sammy Fain, lyric by Lew Brown)

**1939** The Beer Barrel Polka (music by Jaromir Vejvoda, lyric by Lew Brown)

**1939** Wishing (Will Make It So) (music and lyrics by B. G. De Sylva)

**1942** Don't Sit Under the Apple Tree with Anyone Else but Me (music by Sam H. Stept, lyric by Lew Brown, Charles Tobias)

**ABOVE:** Alice Faye making her Broadway debut (and farewell) in the 1974 revival of *Good News*.

## *Song and Story*

### IF YOU KNEW SUSIE, LIKE I KNOW SUSIE

Al Jolson, in a rare fit of generosity, gave this song to Eddie Cantor after his own performance of it in the musical *Big Boy* failed to make an impression. After Cantor had a smash hit with the song, Jolson remarked to him, "If I'd known that the song was *that* good, you dirty dog, you'd never have gotten it."

## *Asides*

"Lucky Day" became the theme song for radio's *Your Hit Parade.*

On April 10, 1970, Ray Henderson wrote in a letter to Irving Brown at Chappell Music, "Learned yesterday the 'Beatles' have new album on Apple Records, 'Sentimental Journey' (*Songs My Mom Sang to Me*), a group of old standards which includes 'Bye Bye Blackbird,' to be released in this country in May. Finally made the Beatles circle. Also, last nite on Dean Martin Show, Tom Jones (guest) sang B.B. Blackbird & later Martin sang it. Good plug . . . hey what?"

# Parodists

As long as there have been popular songs, there have been parodies of them. Early on, the parody song became a tidy little genre of its own, making money for sheet music publishers, performers, and record companies. And occasionally, an accomplished and witty performer comes along who makes his mark by parodying other performers or performance styles.

The greatest of all musical satirists was Spike Jones. The red-headed bandleader started his career as a drummer on radio and soon added sound effects to his performances. In 1942, he formed the City Slickers and they had an immediate success with "Der Fuehrer's Face." Other hits followed: "Cocktails for Two," "Chloe," and "You Always Hurt the One You Love," among many others. Trumpeter George Rock was the baby voice behind the bestseller "All I Want for Christmas (Is My Two Front Teeth)." Being funny was hard work and Jones was a no-nonsense guy, making sure that his band's mayhem was tightly rehearsed. The result was a series of recordings that are still beloved today, even after much of what they parodied has lapsed into relative obscurity.

Stan Freberg also parodied popular songs of his day, but in a slyer, less anarchic way than Jones had done. Freberg simply took the basic song and exaggerated its weaknesses. His hits from the early 1950s include treatments of "I've Got You Under My Skin," "The World Is Waiting for the Sunrise," "Sh-Boom," "C'est Si Bon," "The Great Pretender," "Heartbreak Hotel," "Rock Island Line," and "Wun'erful, Wun'erful," a send-up of Lawrence Welk. Today, Weird Al Yankovic is the parodist of note, producing records as well as music videos.

Others made fun of songs either by performing them dreadfully or adapting them to unlikely genres. The master and mistress of mistakes had to be Jonathan and Darlene Edwards, a most incompetent pianist married to the worst singer ever recorded—a perfect(ly awful) match. Jo Stafford (who had nothing to do with Darlene Edwards, we're absolutely, positively sure of it) was certainly not the voice behind Cinderella G. Stump, a singer with Red Ingle and His Natural Seven. They would perform popular songs in a country-music fashion. "Tim-tayshun" was Ms. Stump's best known recording.

Singers were also known to parody each other. In *Here Come the Waves* (1945), Bing Crosby performed "That Old Black Magic" à la Frank Sinatra. Crosby got his comeuppance constantly, as every impressionist and singer on the planet took a turn making fun of Bing's "Buh buh buh boo."

Irving Berlin was among the first songwriters to write parodies of opera and popular songs. For 1912's *Hanky Panky* he contributed an "Opera Burlesque on the Sextette from *Lucia*." *Watch Your Step* (1914) featured his "Ragtime Opera Melody." Berlin also reversed the gag, placing popular songs into operatic settings, as he did in *The Cocoanuts* (1925).

Among the first of the parody songs was 1903's "Under the Anhauser Bush," a parody of "Under the Mulberry Tree." Both were written by Harry Von Tilzer and Andrew Sterling. "Sam, You Made the Pants too Long" by Fred Whitehouse, was a parody of a serious song, "Lord, You Made the Night Too Long" by Sam M. Lewis and Victor Young. Joe E. Lewis, famed for the film, *The Joker Is Wild*, performed the parody and it launched his career as a comic. Harold Arlen and Johnny Mercer parodied themselves when they wrote a joke chorus of "My Shining Hour" for the film *The Sky's the Limit* (1943).

We think it's safe to say that, as long as there are songwriters, there will be parodists nipping at their heels, deflating, commenting upon—and sometimes bettering their best efforts. ◆

**TOP:** Spike Jones and His City Slickers. **ABOVE:** Our son the folk singer, Allan Sherman.

Dubin & Warren

ABOVE: The greatest Hollywood songwriting team of all time! Al Dubin and Harry Warren. RIGHT: Hear the beat of tapping feet on *42nd Street*.

Harry Warren (born December 24, 1893, died September 22, 1981) was the most successful and prolific composer for motion picture musicals of his day, and probably second only to Berlin in number of hit songs. After racking up a few hit Broadway shows, Warren went to Hollywood and enjoyed long relationships with each of the major studios, where he wrote hits for almost every film score. Most of all, he was a character. Beloved but rough around the edges like many of his Lower East Side brethren (including Berlin and Cantor), he was street smart and knew how to pick and win a fight.

Warren spoke about growing up on the streets of New York and his early career as a songwriter in an extended interview with Michael Feinstein. Most of the quotes included here are from that interview.

Like Harold Arlen, but unlike his contemporaries Gershwin, Berlin, Porter, et al., Warren was hardly a household name. Very few had heard of him and no one knew what he looked like, in part because of the studio system. Since he wasn't considered a great Broadway composing star like Porter or Berlin, the studios took him for granted and didn't hype his pictures. You'd never see, "Harry Warren's *42nd Street*" in the credits or on the marquee. And Warren didn't act the part of the artist. He looked like any number of first-generation Italian Americans and never participated in the Hollywood party scene.

He insisted that his relative obscurity didn't bother him, but perhaps he protested too much. He did speak of it an awful lot: "I'm a Capricorn. They call the Capricorn the hard-way guy, you know, you have to go the hard way. Well, a lot of things happened to me where—if I go to a hot dog stand and there's a lot of people standing around, and I keep saying 'Give me a hot dog,' he probably waits on everybody but me, and finally when it gets to me he says, 'Wait your turn.' That's what happens to me all the time.

"Even on the lot the cops used to stop me in the beginning, you know; they knew Al Dubin because he was big and fat and kind of lurched a little bit. And Mack Gordon they knew. He always had a big heater in his mouth. But I look like a *nudnick*, like the average guy, so they'd always stop me.

"Even when we had the ASCAP show in New York at Lincoln Center. I arrived in a tuxedo at the door—the fellow stopped me. He didn't stop the other people. He stopped me. He said to me, 'Where are you going?' I said, 'Where the hell do you think I'm going?' That's the story of my life."

Warren was even stopped at the entrance to the 1935 Academy Awards—and then proceeded to win an Oscar for "Lullaby of Broadway"! The famous 1924 Aeolian Hall concert that introduced Gershwin's "Rhapsody in Blue" also featured an early Warren effort titled "So This Is Venice," but his name was left off the program. He professed not to mind it, saying, "Michelangelo didn't sign his paintings. If they don't know my work then the hell with them."

Born Salvatore Guaragna, Warren was the last of eleven children (or possibly the eleventh of twelve), born to Italian immigrants. He got his love for Italian opera, especially Puccini, from his family. (Harry wasn't the only Warren in show business, his brother "Mousy"

"Some of the cafés and saloons for instance where I used to play in back rooms we had singing waiters. They had a great repertoire—they sang, 'In the Heart of the City That Has No Heart' or 'By the Sea.'

"I finally got a job at the Vitagraph Movie Company in Brooklyn because I could sing, and I sang in the Vitagraph quartet. From that I got to be an assistant director of some pictures. I picked up the piano in the meantime. I had a little training in church, where I used to sing in a choir. But I was inquisitive about music, how to write a song down, and of course my worst subject in school was mathematics. That's all music is when you write it down, it's mathematics. But I finally got the idea of it, how to write the notes in a bar and how to divide it, you know.

"I was assistant director for a fellow named Webster Campbell who was married to Corinne Griffith, who was a big star at the time. Well, I used to play the piano for her on the sets. I used to make up tunes, and she liked for me to play for her. I also played for dance

I'd get on a trolley car with one side lopsided.

"I also wanted to write songs, and at Vitagraph the casting director had a friend who was a lyric writer, a fellow named Howard Johnson. I came to New York and played him some songs. He said, 'Well you have a pretty good idea of the tunes, but the words and titles are not so hot.' Then the war came on, and I went into the navy—that's the First World War, not the Civil War. In the navy I played piano and we had a little band. I was stationed out at Montauk Point Naval Air Station. I was a flying piano player.

"After the war, I got this job with Stark and Cowan Music Publishers, and I had a song called 'I Learned to Love You When I Learned My ABC's' which I had written words and music for. Just as they'd decided to take the song and publish it, Woolworth—a big outlet for sheet music—decided to take all the music off the counters. So the song was never published.

"I had another song that they liked very much, and that was the first tune I ever had published—'Rose of

---

# "They bombed the wrong Berlin."
# —Harry Warren on hearing of the Allied air strikes in Germany

---

was a well-known song plugger.) "My sister was a dancer with Broadway shows. But she wasn't a star or anything. I was always interested in music as a child. I don't know why, I never had a formal musical education at all, but I had a terrific thirst for music. I started playing the harmonica but I was always musical, I don't know why. My two sisters and my brother loved to sing four-part harmony. Old time songs, of course. That's my earliest recollection of music, until I got to be an altar boy. My mother was very religious, I had to go to church. Being an altar boy listening to the choir was just fantastic to me. I couldn't get to church fast enough. Finally, when I got old enough, I got into the choir and I think that started my whole musical education. We sang some wonderful masses.

"But I guess my parents didn't understand that, you know. In those days, your father—mine was a handcraft boot maker—felt you should have a trade. Despite all of that, I got into the music business. As I got to be about fourteen, I was a drummer with a band. My godfather was a band leader. He had a band that went on the road with a carnival show, and I started with him.

"We toured the East, these little towns up the Hudson in the summer time. I learned all the marches that they used to play in those days. Then I got to fooling around with the piano. I was a lousy piano player, too. Never a good piano player. In fact, a producer told me I was the lousiest piano player he ever heard. I said, 'If I was a good piano player would I be a songwriter? I'd be playing with an orchestra.'

"Later on I started playing weddings and christenings and things like that and learned all the overtures. I never had a formal musical education, you know. But I learned how to write music just by being so interested in it, I guess.

scenes. And they would look off the screen to an imaginary orchestra and applaud. You had to have something to give them the rhythm to dance to, you see.

"From that I worked in the old time movie theaters, the open-air houses where I used to play the piano for the silent movies. At night, out in East New York, there was an open air movie where I got $12 a week, and they paid me off in nickels and dimes. It used to weigh a ton.

the Rio Grande.' They still play it today, and that's how I started. I got $20 a week as a song plugger. No raise. And I never collected the royalties on that song. They gave me a promissory note and then they sold the company and I never collected the money from the bank. The bank moved and then went out of business.

"Lots of times I did the music first, but I also wrote to lyrics or titles. That's harder, because you're confined

to the cadence and the lyric, you know, and how are you going to change it? But I loved to write; to me it wasn't work. I enjoyed it. That was the great thing. I didn't care what the hours were. I used to play piano in saloons on Saturday night too. Don't forget when I got $20 a week as a song plugger I was still taking side jobs, playing weddings and bar mitzvahs. Trying to make a buck, you know, because you couldn't live on twenty bucks a week even then.

"First I wrote some pop songs with Young and Lewis, who were very big at that time. And I started with Bud Green; we wrote some songs together. We had one hit called 'I Love My Baby, My Baby Loves Me.' The first

over here and we suddenly break out...." He keeps on doing this double talk and the next time one of them waltz through they ask, "How much is it gonna cost?" That's all they thought about. Was it any good? Will it look good? They never asked that question. Everything was the budget, what's it gonna cost. That's the whole history of making pictures. What's it gonna cost.

"Don't forget, when you did a show in New York, if you made two or three hundred a week you made a lot of money. I was getting about $1,500 a week in Hollywood.

"Al Dubin was already there under contract with them. Al was six foot three or four, big husky fella,

---

## "Honey, they're not Brazilian—they're Italian. But don't tell anybody." —Harry Warren to Carmen Miranda in answer to how he wrote all those Brazillian tunes for her

---

show, I think, was with Billy Rose; it was called *Sweet and Low*. And in that show I had 'Would You Like to Take a Walk?' and 'Cheerful Little Earful'—with Ira Gershwin lyrics. That show was a big success, and then we did another show called *Crazy Quilt* and I had 'Million Dollar Baby in the Five and Ten Cent Store' in that one. Then I did a show for Ed Wynn called *The Laugh Parade*, and that had 'You're My Everything' in it.

"After that I got to California. I hated it. Oh, I thought it was the most awful place in the world. It was some change from being in the city and Lindy's every day for lunch. All of a sudden I was out in what was almost a desert; the Warner Studios in those days in Burbank was really in a desert. No air conditioning at that time. The time I went there to write *42ⁿᵈ Street*—with Al Dubin—there were no writers on the lot. It was summertime and the lot was practically closed.

"The songwriters were absolutely ignored on the lot. But if a guy came from New York that had just done a show he was supposed to be somebody. Some of these producers were impressed by fellas who went to college, you know who spoke very good English and analyzed a script in double talk and they thought it was great.

"Buzz Berkeley used to do that to the head of the studio when he asked him "How you gonna do this number, Buzz?" He'd give him a double talk, "You see we're gonna go in this way and have the girls go over there, and we zoom over there, then we move

weighed 360 some pounds. And he ate like Henry VIII. He loved to eat. He'd eat two steaks at one sitting; while he was eating a steak he'd ask the chef to make him another one. He could drink a whole case of Coca-Cola. Loved to eat and loved to drink too. He loved far away places too.

"I was under contract with Warner's too. You see, I happened to be with Remick Music Company when Warner's bought it. And I had a contract; they had to honor the contract. So, Dubin was out there writing some lyrics, rewriting some German lyrics because he knew German—not even translating but getting an idea for writing in English from the German.

"The only recollection I have [of *42ⁿᵈ Street*] is that Al Dubin usually disappeared. I would give him a tune and write a lead sheet for him, and I'd never hear from him. All of a sudden he'd come back and he'd have a lyric. He brought in the lyric of 'Shuffle

Off to Buffalo'—he wrote it down on a menu up in San Francisco.

"We'd meet at the studio every day we'd work a few hours and maybe go back at night. Dubin used to chew cigars, he'd bite cigars. He'd have a cuspidor in the corner but he'd always miss it. I used to smoke ten or fifteen cigars a day. And all those cigar butts and cigarette butts and Dubin's chewing tobacco, it was really awful. You couldn't do that in your own house.

"Half the time it's hard to explain why I write a song. They come to me subconsciously. I think that if you're in the business of trying to write songs, I wouldn't call it a business—a craft—that you think about it incessantly. I know I did when I worked a lot on pictures. I often wondered what would happen on the next picture if I didn't get anything but it always came. And I think that's it, the secret of it subconsciously thinking about what you want to write or put yourself in the mood or sometimes it's the artist himself or a woman, or a band. You fit 'em like a tailor.

"Some tunes [came quickly], some didn't. But it was never hard for me, because I liked it. I think the more you write the better you get. The problem is the layoff in between—which I never had. Don't forget, I worked for almost twenty-five years in the studios without stopping. Warner's, Fox, Metro, and Paramount.

"I've always written music the way I felt it. I write for the public because I feel like the public, the way they would write if they could. You don't have to know anything about music to understand what I write.

"No, it wasn't difficult at all. I liked it a lot."◆

## Song and Story

### CHATTANOOGA CHOO-CHOO
### SHUFFLE OFF TO BUFFALO
### I'VE GOT A GAL IN KALAMAZOO

Harry Warren: I've had a lot of titles about places that I've never been to. I think everybody around those days was writing about far-off places they'd never been to. A lot of fellas wrote Southern songs about Dixie and they didn't know anything about it. But they wrote them just the same. I've written songs like 'Shuffle Off to Buffalo.' I've gone through Buffalo but I never stayed in Buffalo. Like Kalamazoo. The city of Chattanooga, I'm an honorary citizen, but I've never been there.

### SEPTEMBER IN THE RAIN

Harry Warren: You're playing for people that don't know much about music. The most important thing depends on the demonstration. Not the contents of the song. What they're mostly impressed by is a good demonstration. James Melton was at the Metropolitan Opera House when they brought him out for a picture, and we wrote "September in the Rain." When I played and sang it to Jack Warner

he didn't like it. I got Jack Elfeld and I got a hold of Jimmy Melton who was crazy about the song. Jimmy sang the song. Jack said, "That's a wonderful song." I didn't say, "I played it for you and you didn't like it." That's how you get around those corners.

### YOU'RE GETTING TO BE A HABIT WITH ME

Harry Warren: We had a gal on the Warner lot and we used to kid her a lot about some guy she was going with. And she was real Southern, she had a Southern accent. And Al Dubin said to her, "Why are you going around with that guy all the time?" And she said, "I don't know, I guess he's getting to be a habit." And that's how we wrote, 'You're Getting to Be a Habit with Me.'

### ON THE ATCHISON, TOPEKA, AND THE SANTA FE

Harry Warren: I didn't know where to put that title in the melody. I was trying all ways of starting off with the line. Then I finally got it the other way, with the title at the end, which worked out better.

### YOU MUST HAVE BEEN A BEAUTIFUL BABY

Harry Warren: Johnny Mercer is a very clever fellow. We wrote some nice songs like "You Must Have Been a Beautiful Baby"—he gave me that title. I wrote that from the title. And he wrote "Jeepers Creepers" to the music.

### FEUDIN' AND FUSSIN' AND A-FIGHTIN'

It was up to Frank Loesser and composer Burton Lane to write the lyrics for "Feudin' and Fussin' and A-Fightin'"—though the credit went to Al Dubin who was off on one of his many benders. On the other hand, Dubin ghostwrote lyrics for others. Dubin himself wrote the lyrics to "Among My Souvenirs," accepting twenty-five dollars from Edgar Leslie for the credit. Just to complicate matters, the music is by Horatio Nicholls, a pseudonym for British publisher Lawrence Wright.

# Dixon & Wrubel

M ort Dixon was a New Yorker through and through, born in the city on March 20, 1892. After performing in vaude-ville while still in his teens, Dixon joined the army and was sent to France at the beginning of World War I, where he directed the army show *Whiz Bang* (named after a German bomb). He turned to lyric writing in 1923, collaborating with composer Ray Henderson on a series of songs including "That Old Gang of Mine" (with co-lyricist Billy Rose). In 1924, he had a mild success with "Follow the Swallow," written with Henderson and Rose and interpolated into the *Ziegfeld Follies of 1924*. "Bam Bam Bammy Shore" was a hit in 1925 with music by Henderson.

Dixon and Henderson's next hit was "Bye Bye Blackbird" (1926), made famous by Nick Lucas and Gene Austin. He had another success that same year with "I Wish't I Was in Peoria," written with Harry Woods and Rose. In 1927, Dixon and Woods came up with the deathless "I'm Looking Over a Four-Leaf Clover" and "Just Like a Butterfly That's Lost in the Rain." Keep in mind that the decade of the '20s was devoted to silly, upbeat songs (come to think of it, so were the '30s, '40s, '50s...) well, you get the idea. When Dixon teamed with Harry Warren in 1928, the result was a huge hit, "Nagasaki."

Dixon wrote a couple of songs for films in 1928, including "If You Want the Rainbow (You Must Have the Rain)" for the film *My Man*. Oscar Levant supplied the music and Billy Rose—the husband of Fanny Brice, who introduced the song in the film—was the co-lyricist. Dixon placed only one song in a film in 1929, but it was the hit, "River, Stay 'Way from My Door." Harry Woods supplied the music.

Harry Warren teamed with Dixon for the 1930 Broadway revue *Sweet and Low* in 1930, and the hit "Would You Like to Take a Walk (Sumpin' Good'll Come from That)" with Billy Rose taking co-lyricist credit. Another hit from the show, "They're Dancing with Tears in Their Eyes," was written by Dixon, Rose, and Will Irwin. *Sweet and Low* was rejiggered and renamed *Billy Rose's Crazy Quilt* and, in it, Warren, Dixon, and Rose had another big hit with "I Found a Million Dollar Baby in a Five-and-Ten-Cent Store." Warren, Dixon, and Joe Young hit pay dirt again in 1931 with the *Laugh Parade*'s "You're My Everything" and "Ooh That Kiss."

Warren's successes on Broadway led him to Hollywood, and Dixon followed in 1934, but the two didn't work together in California even though they were both working for Warner Brothers. Warren was teamed with Al Dubin and Dixon was paired with Allie Wrubel.

Allie Wrubel was born in Middletown, Connecticut, on January 15, 1905. After studying medicine at Columbia University, he played saxophone for Paul Whiteman's band for a year and later became a theater manager. He started writing music and lyrics in 1924. We should mention two interesting titles from Wrubel's prior catalog, 1931's "I've Got a Communistic Feeling for You" and 1933's "Rasputin (That Highfalutin' Lovin' Man)." Both had music and lyrics by Wrubel—and wouldn't you love to hear them right now?

Fame eluded Wrubel until 1934, when he went to California and Warner Brothers and met Dixon. The two started off with a hit, "Try to See It My Way (Baby)" from the film *Dames*. The next year, the film *In Caliente* featured their successful tune "The Lady in Red." Wrubel and Herb Magidson came up with a huge jazz standard in 1937, "Gone with the Wind," and followed it with three more hits in 1938: "How Long Has This Been Going On?" (not to be confused with the much better known Gershwin song), "(I'm Afraid) The Masquerade Is Over," and "Music, Maestro, Please."

Wrubel's last hit song was "Zip-a-dee Doo-dah" written with Ray Gilbert for the 1946 Disney film *Song of the South*. By this time Dixon had retired from songwriting, and he died in Bronxville, New York, on March 23, 1956. Wrubel went on to write the score to the film *Never Steal Anything Small*, with Maxwell Anderson, and retired. He died in Twentynine Palms, California on December 13, 1973. ◆

## Song and Story

### I'M LOOKING OVER A FOUR-LEAF CLOVER

Some songs are smash hits when first written—and this is one of them. The upbeat tune was first performed by Nick Lucas and Gene Austin, and then covered by Ben Bernie, Eddie Cantor, and, most notably, Al Jolson. Some songs become hits all over again years later and this is one of those, too. In 1948 Art Mooney and His Orchestra recorded it on the MGM label, prominently featuring Mike Pingatore on the banjo. It sold over a million copies and stayed on *Your Hit Parade* for almost four months.

### GONE WITH THE WIND

The title of this huge jazz standard was inspired by Margaret Mitchell's novel, though the sheet music reads, "Based upon the greatest of all Motion Pictures, by arrangement with Selznick International Pictures, Inc." Of course, the film wasn't released until two years later.

# Song Pluggers

Johnny Mercer on song pluggers: "They used to be as close to an entertainer as those small birds on rhinos or elephants or the pilot fish that accompany whales, but their original function was entertaining also. They would demonstrate a new song to whomever would listen, much in the manner of the buskers outside London theaters, and try to get the public to buy or sing the song they were promoting....All over the country, not only at the side show in the Savannah Park extension, men were working—on the boardwalk at Atlantic City, at vaudeville houses in Chillicothe, in basements, at the music counters in dime stores—all plugging away at new songs each one hoped would sweep the country and make him rich."

By the 1890s, selling songs had become a big business. At first publishers made deals with newspapers to promote their songs in the color rotogravure sections. Shapiro-Bernstein joined with the Hearst chain of newspapers to promote six of its songs, but after a year the top seller had moved only 50,000 copies. Most minor sales were 250,000 or above. Bernstein commented, "Songs must be heard by the people who pay to buy them."

As a result, real live humans were hired to plug songs and sell sheet music. Among the leading song pluggers at the turn of the century were Johnny Nestor, Sammy Levy, Joseph Santley, Ben Bloom, Jimmie Flynn, Harry Tenney, Harry Bishop, and Mose Gumble.

Hired by the likes of George M. Cohan, Nora Bayes, and Weber and Fields, Gumble was paid fifteen dollars a week to play the piano and plug songs throughout Manhattan and into Coney Island. He visited vaudevillians, dance halls, conductors, and restaurants, cajoling musicians, singers, and band leaders into performing the songs he brought them. He was responsible for the success of such current standards as "In the Shade of the Old Apple Tree," Oh, You Beautiful Doll," and "I'm Forever Blowing Bubbles." It was Gumble who convinced Eva Tanguay to introduce, "I Don't Care." When sound was joined with film, Gumble went out to the coast to place old songs into films. And, in May of 1914, it was Gumble who hired then fifteen-year-old George Gershwin at Remick's music publishers.

Other pluggers, including Joseph Santley and Johnny Nestor, concentrated on plugging songs at the hundreds of nickelodeons cropping up throughout the city, supplying nickelodeon owners with magic lantern slides illustrating the songs' lyrics. As silent films unspooled on the screen, the piano accompaniment would feature songs of the day. Between films the pluggers would often entertain audiences by teaching them the newest songs. Sammy Smither, a famed song plugger and ex-professional baseball player, bragged that he could plug one song fifty times in a single evening.

During the day, pluggers haunted music stores, department stores, and five and dimes promoting the latest sheets. They even frequented penny arcades, where mechanical pianos could pump out the latest tunes on their rolls and early coin-operated cylinder players featured such stars as May Irwin and Clarice Vance (who was married to Gumble for a brief period).

Of course, the most important people to reach were the vaudeville performers and band leaders who had the most influence over popular taste. In return for adopting a particular song, the performer would have his or her name and face put on the music. If a performer wasn't quite sure of the lyrics or music during an early performance, the plugger could be depended upon to stand up in the auditorium and sing along with the star. Pluggers sometimes arranged for big performers like Al Jolson to be cut in on royalties (and even credits) on numbers they featured in their acts or interpolated into their Broadway shows.

These energetic, self-reliant, and charismatic men also had good ears. They picked the songs they plugged and worked hard to make them successful. In that way, they can be viewed as among the most influential figures in the history of popular song. ◈

**TOP:** Hillman's sheet music store in 1906. Notice the song demonstrator at the far right, seated at the piano. **INSET:** Song plugger extraordinaire, Mickey Addy.

# Walter Donaldson

W alter Donaldson was another of the premier songwriters of the 1920s. Like the teams of De Sylva, Brown, and Henderson and Arthur Freed and Nacio Herb Brown, Donaldson and Gus Kahn helped to define the flapper era with their catchy melodies and bright lyrics.

Donaldson was born on February 15, 1893, in Brooklyn, New York. His mother was a piano teacher and gave him some lessons but he was largely self-taught. While in high school he was already writing shows for his fellow students, and these were dutifully reviewed by the local newspapers. Donaldson and his sister Jane augmented their allowances by singing on street corners and nothing could stop them except for the local policemen, who chased them away for disturbing the peace. After graduation, Donaldson worked plugging songs at local five-and-dimes, demonstrating sheet music, playing piano at a Brighton Beach hotel, and accompanying silent films in neighborhood nickelodeons. He did his best to help support his family—but he was one of eleven children—so he took a job as a Wall Street broker for awhile, quitting to return to song plugging for $15 a week. The job didn't last long, as Donaldson was fired when his bosses found him writing his own songs at the piano instead of demonstrating theirs.

Donaldson enlisted in World War I and spent the war years playing piano at bond rallies and entertaining the troops. During his time in the army, he met Irving Berlin, then at Camp Upton. When the war was over, Donaldson and the team of Sam M. Lewis and Joe Young wrote the hit song "How Ya Gonna Keep 'Em Down on the Farm After They've Seen Paree?" Donaldson joined Irving Berlin, Inc. in 1919, and stayed there for ten years.

He really came into his own in the 1920s with hit after hit. When he gave "My Mammy" to Al Jolson (after it was introduced by William Frawley), Donaldson was surprised that the song went over so well. He had thought that both his music and the lyrics by Sam M. Lewis and Joe Young were overly sentimental, but apparent the song was just what war-

weary audiences needed. Another Donaldson song that perfectly captured the American mood at the time was "My Buddy." With its melancholy lyric by Gus Kahn, the song resonated with the many people who had lost friends and family in the war. In fact, Donaldson wrote the song to commemorate the death of his fiancée.

In 1928, Donaldson set up his own music publishing firm, Donaldson, Douglas and Gumble, just in time to capitalize on the success of his smash musical comedy, *Whoopee*. The Eddie Cantor vehicle opened to rave reviews, especially for its hit-laden score. When the stock market crashed a year later, Donaldson, an inveterate horse player, remarked, "My God. A racetrack is safer."

Samuel Goldwyn called Donaldson and Kahn out to Hollywood to adapt *Whoopee* for the movies, and it became one of the earliest Technicolor films, with Cantor reprising his role. That was the end of Donaldson's connection with Broadway. He remained in Hollywood with Kahn and they wrote another Goldwyn musical for Eddie Cantor, *Kid Millions* (1934), featuring the song "When My Ship Comes In," a minor hit for Cantor.

Donaldson signed with MGM in 1933 and went on to write music for films until the 1940s. In 1941, Gus Kahn died and Donaldson began to collaborate with newer, younger writers, including Johnny Mercer, Mort Greene, Johnny Lange, and the team of Robert Wright and George Forrest. During the Second World War he entertained troops at the USO but his creative output waned due to ill health.

Donaldson was sick from 1945 until his death on July 15, 1947. He was only fifty-four years old. ❖

## Song and Story

### CAROLINA IN THE MORNING
William Frawley, later known as Fred Mertz in the popular television show, *I Love Lucy*, introduced this song, as well as "My Melancholy Baby" and "My Mammy."

### MY BLUE HEAVEN
Walter Donaldson composed this song in 1927 at the Friars Club while waiting for a billiards game to begin. Donaldson played the song for vaudeville star George Whiting, who was so enthusiastic that he begged to write the lyric. Whiting performed the number but it would not catch on. In 1927, Tommy Lyman sang it on radio and then Gene Austin recorded the song for Victor. That recording and Austin's covers of the song sold more than 5 million copies.

### LOVE ME OR LEAVE ME
Gus Kahn's son, Donald, told Cantor biographer Herbert Goldman, "Walter Donaldson told my dad that he didn't like The Gimp [Ruth Etting's gangster husband and manager] and that he wasn't going to write Ruth Etting a decent song. So he wrote her what he thought was this God-awful thing that went 'Dada-Da-Dada, Da-Dada, Da-Dada,' and my dad wrote a lyric to it." Despite Donaldson's worst efforts, the song became a huge success and Etting's theme song.

### HOW YA GONNA KEEP 'EM DOWN ON THE FARM AFTER THEY'VE SEEN PAREE?
This humorous take on the end of the fighting overseas was introduced in the February 1919, Victory Parade that welcomed President Wilson home from Paris and the signing of the Treaty of Versailles. Lt. James Reese Europe, the band leader of the legendary "Hellfighters' Regiment" of black recruits, led his band as they marched through the streets of New York City.

## Asides

When George Olsen's orchestra left Whoopee, they were replaced by Paul Whiteman's Orchestra. Among Whiteman's players were the Rhythm Boys, marking Bing Crosby's only Broadway appearance

## THE GREAT SONGS

**ALL MUSIC AND LYRICS BY WALTER DONALDSON UNLESS OTHERWISE INDICATED.**

**1915** (Just Try to Picture Me) Back Home in Tennessee (lyric by William Jerome); We'll Have a Jubilee in My Old Kentucky Home (lyric by Coleman Goetz)

**1918** The Daughter of Rosie O'Grady (lyric by Monty C. Brice); My Mammy (lyric by Sam M. Lewis and Joe Young)

**1919** Don't Cry Frenchy, Don't Cry; How Ya Gonna Keep 'Em Down on the Farm, After They've Seen Paree?; I'll Be Happy When the Preacher Makes You Mine; You're a Million Miles from Nowhere (When You're One Little Mile from Home) (all lyrics by Sam M. Lewis and Joe Young); Some Sunny Day (lyric by Arthur Jackson)

**1920** My Little Bimbo Down on a Bamboo Isle (lyric by Grant Clarke)

**1921** Down South (lyric by B. G. De Sylva); On the 'Gin, 'Gin, 'Ginny Shore (lyric by Edgar Leslie)

**1922** Carolina in the Morning; My Buddy (both lyrics by Gus Kahn)

**1923** Beside a Babbling Brook (lyric by Gus Kahn)

**1924** My Best Girl; Sioux City Sue (music by Phil Napoleon, Al Siegel, and Frank Signorelli)

**1925** Isn't She the Sweetest Thing? (lyric by Ernie Erdman and Gus Kahn); My Sweetie Turned Me Down; That Certain Party; Ukulele Lady; Yes Sir! That's My Baby (all lyrics by Gus Kahn)

**1926** (What Can I Say, Dear) After I Say I'm Sorry (lyric by Abe Lyman); There Ain't No Maybe in My Baby's Eyes (lyric by Raymond B. Egan and Gus Kahn)

**1927** At Sundown; My Blue Heaven (lyric by George Whiting); Sam the Old Accordion Man

**1928** I'm Bringing a Red, Red Rose; Love Me or Leave Me; Makin' Whoopee; My Baby Just Cares for Me (all lyrics by Gus Kahn); Because My Baby Don't Mean Maybe Now

**1929** Kansas City Kitty (lyric be Edgar Leslie); Georgia (lyric by Howard Johnson); In the Middle of the Night (lyric by Billy Rose); Let It Rain, Let It Pour (lyric by Cliff Friend)

**1930** Little White Lies; 'Tain't No Sin to Dance Around in Your Bones (lyric by Edgar Leslie); You're Driving Me Crazy

**1936** San Francisco

**1940** Mister Meadowlark; On Behalf of the Visiting Firemen (both lyrics by Johnny Mercer)

**1942** (Did I Get Stinking) At the Club Savoy

# Vernon Duke

**ABOVE:** Vernon Duke attempts the impossible—teaching Bette Davis to sing—in the revue Two's Company.

**OPPOSITE PAGE BOTTOM:** Duke writing his score for the Coast Guard show, Tars and Spars.

One of Broadway's master songwriters as well as a classically trained musician, Vernon Duke was born Vladimir Dukelsky in Parfianovka, Russia. Duke and his mother escaped from Russia during the revolution, on the last boat to leave St. Petersburg. They went to Europe, where Duke composed ballets for Diaghilev's Ballets Russes. Although his training under such greats as Reinhold Gliere and Marian Dombrovsky seemed to foreshadow a distinguished classical career, Duke achieved his greatest success as a musical theater composer.

He arrived in New York in 1929 after trying his hand at several musicals in London, including *Yvonne* (dubbed *Yvonne the Terrible* by Noel Coward) in 1926, *The Yellow Mask* (1928), and *Open Your Eyes* (1930). Clearly, his London lyricists, Percy Greenbank, Desmond Carter, and Collie Knox, didn't sufficiently inspire him. In New York, Duke contributed songs to *The Garrick Gaieties* (1930) before attempting a complete score. His first American score, *Walk a Little Faster* (1932), written with E. Y. Harburg, included his first hit, "April in Paris." Duke and Harburg next collaborated on a number for the *Ziegfeld Follies of 1934* and came up with another hit, "I Like the Likes of You." Duke soon wrote the standard "Autumn in New York"—both music and lyrics—for the revue *Thumbs Up!* (1934). For the 1936 edition of the *Follies*, Duke teamed up with Ira Gershwin to write another standard, "I Can't Get Started." Duke and Ted Fetter contributed some songs to the musical revue *The Show Is On*, which opened on Christmas Day 1936.

Duke's success in the revue field inspired him to try his hand at book shows, and his first was the classic *Cabin in the Sky* (1940), with lyrics by John Latouche and starring Ethel Waters. The superior score featured three huge hits:

the title song, "Honey in the Honeycomb," and "Taking a Chance on Love," the last with lyrics by Latouche and Ted Fetter. Sadly, though he did a lot of excellent work later in his career, *Cabin in the Sky* was to be Duke's last successful Broadway show.

*Banjo Eyes* (1941), an Eddie Cantor vehicle, received excellent reviews and spawned a hit song, "We're Having a Baby (My Baby and Me)," but Cantor soon abandoned the show and it closed prematurely. The unlikely project *It Happens on Ice* (1941) didn't make much of a splash—and Duke's next show, *The Lady Comes Across* (1942), lasted only three nights on Broadway.

Howard Dietz supplied the lyrics to two of Duke's shows in 1944, *Jackpot* and *Sadie Thompson*, neither of which was a success. Duke's last Broadway show, *Two's Company* (1952), boasted lyrics by Ogden Nash and introduced Bette Davis to musical theater audiences. No matter—it closed quickly.

Perhaps getting the hint, the composer looked to Off Broadway for his next assignment. Impressario Ben Bagley, a fan of Duke's, hired him and Nash for the Phoenix Theatre's *The Littlest Revue* (1956). Duke's last show, *Zenda*, closed in Los Angeles in 1963.

Duke never enjoyed a Hollywood career of note. He went to the West Coast in 1930 and supplied songs for eight films, none of them hits. That was the extent of his film career until 1952's *April in Paris* and *She's Working Her Way Through College*, both with lyrics by Sammy Cahn. He fared better in the world of classical music, composing the ballets *Zephyr and Flora* and *Lady Blue*; three symphonies, Violin Concerto, Cello Concerto, Sonata in D for Violin, Piano; Parisian Suite; Surrealist Suite; Six Songs from a Shropshire Lad; Souvenirs de Monte Carlo; and Ode to the Milky Way.

Duke's songs are models of cohesive melody and deep emotion. Superficially, they seem simple, but when studied they reveal their intricacies and are difficult to sing and play. Thanks in large part to Ben Bagley and Bobby Short, Duke's songs have lived on and are being rediscovered and appreciated by new generations. ◆

## Song and Story

### TAKING A CHANCE ON LOVE

Vernon Duke wrote in his autobiography that while working on *Cabin in the Sky*, "We needed a heart-warming song to put the first act over. I reached for the trunk—three days before the opening—and stumbled on 'Fooling Around with Love,' a song Ted Fetter and I had written for an unproduced Abbott show. I tried it out on Latouche; he fell for the tune, but thought the title not sufficiently 'on the nose' for the dramatic situation. An afternoon's work, with an assist from Fetter, followed, and what emerged was 'Taking a Chance on Love,' one of my better-known songs."

### APRIL IN PARIS

Vernon Duke and friends were eating at Tony Roma's restaurant in New York City. A guest exclaimed, "Oh, to be in Paris now that April's here." Lightbulb! Duke rushed upstairs to an old upright piano and proceeded to write the music.

### I CAN'T GET STARTED

"I Can't Get Started" began life as "Face the Music with Me," with lyrics by Duke. A few years later Ira Gershwin swapped in his lyrics and the song was featured in *The Ziegfeld Follies of 1936*. Trumpeter Bunny Berigan's vocal on his famous 1937 recording of the tune for Victor remains the definitive version and one of the milestones in recorded jazz. Ira Gershwin hated that Berigan changed his lyric to sing a grammatically improper double negative in one line.

## Asides

Duke never had much luck on Broadway, even when he scored a hit. *Cabin in the Sky*, his greatest success, was a black show, which limited the possibilities for future productions. *Banjo Eyes*, starring Eddie Cantor, got great reviews, but when Cantor's wife Ida found out that her husband was having an affair with a member of the company, she threatened to divorce him unless he quit the show. That was the end of both the affair and *Banjo Eyes*.

The pseudonym "Vernon Duke" was given to Vladimir Dukelsky by George Gershwin. Duke created the published solo piano arrangement for "Rhapsody in Blue" in 1927 but did not receive credit.

## THE GREAT SONGS

**1930** I Am Only Human After All (lyric by Ira Gershwin and E. Y. Harburg)

**1932** April in Paris (lyric by E. Y. Harburg)

**1934** I Like the Likes of You; What Is There to Say? (both lyrics by E. Y. Harburg)

**1935** Autumn in New York

**1936** I Can't Get Started; That Moment of Moments (both lyrics by Ira Gershwin)

**1940** Cabin in the Sky; Honey in the Honeycomb; Love Turned the Light Out; Not a Care in the World (all lyrics by John Latouche); Taking a Chance on Love (lyric by Ted Fetter and John Latouche)

**1941** We're Having a Baby My Baby and Me (lyric by Harold Adamson)

**1944** If You Can't Get the Love You Want; Life's a Funny Present from Someone; The Love I Long For; When You Live on an Island (all lyrics by Howard Dietz)

**1952** That's What Makes Paris Paree; The Theatre Is a Lady; Turn Me Loose on Broadway (all lyrics by Sammy Cahn)

**1956** Born Too Late; Madly in Love (both lyrics by Ogden Nash)

Duke Ellington

Duke Ellington's may have been the greatest of the big bands and had the longest reign, but it was never the most popular. Ellington had exactly the band he wanted and refused to kowtow to popular taste. If other bands offered sweet pablum or high energy swing without depth, that was fine with Ellington. His wasn't a band that featured the latest songs from Broadway and Hollywood. He didn't follow the trends of Tin Pan Alley. His audiences didn't come to hear the great hits of Berlin or Gershwin. If they wanted standards, Ellington would write them himself.

He turned out to be an extremely successful writer of both instrumentals and songs. One reason for his success as a composer was the fact that he had a great band to play his tunes to his own captive audience, and from those performances he could gauge the success of his compositions. His audiences were savvy and, as he said to George T. Simon, he learned from them. "When out somewhere in the provinces a doctor or a car washer or a farmer may travel two hundred miles just to hear you. And then they start talking to you, and usually one of them says, 'I like that last record of yours, but you know the one that really knocked me out….' And he mentions something you haven't even thought about in a long time but you've always liked."

Ellington had planned to retire at a certain point and devote himself to composing—after all, the band was a great responsibility both financially and personally—but he realized he'd lose that great advantage. "I could keep on composing," Ellington told Simon, "something I always intended to do, but then I'd have nobody to play the things I write so that I can hear what they sound like."

Of all the big bands, Ellington's was an especially loyal group. Several of his musicians stayed with him for over forty years, and the group became like an organism. They knew him and he knew them, and they performed as a single unit. Miller or Goodman, by contrast, had to rehearse their bands constantly because the personnel kept changing. Their play book seldom changed and each appearance sounded much like another. But Ellington played fast and loose with his band, often writing and sketching out an arrangement hours or minutes before the band was set to perform live in front of an audience or on radio. He would have no qualms about putting fresh charts in front of them, sometimes only sketches, and with minimum instruction let them find their own way.

It was a matter of trust—between Ellington and his musicians and between the band and the audience. That mutual admiration society formed the foundation for Ellington's success as a composer. He also found a kindred spirit in Billy Strayhorn, composer, arranger, and muse. Ellington adored Strayhorn as a person and for his talents. He was impressed with the young man's remarkable facility with music and found the perfect partner—separate but not quite equal. Sometimes credit would go to Strayhorn alone and sometimes the two collaborated. And, apparently, sometimes Ellington would take sole credit for work on which Strayhorn collaborated or wrote by himself. It was a shifting, undefined arrangement, both personally and professionally, but it seemed to suit the two.

It's not surprising that Strayhorn and Ellington never had a written agreement between them, and as time wore on, the ebb and flow of their long relationship grew murky. They were credited as co-composers late in their collaboration but they mainly wrote separately, knowing each other so well as to make the final product sound as if written by one person.

How or by whom the great songs were written is, perhaps, irrelevant. What does matter is their excellence, their perfect melding of the blues, jazz, and Tin Pan Alley traditions, and their effect on audiences. Duke Ellington is among the most neglected composers of popular songs, so important are his other contributions to music, but a glance through the great songs he wrote show him to be among the greatest of all composers. ◆

# Song and Story

### MOOD INDIGO
Ellington was sitting at his mother's house while she was cooking dinner, thinking about a recording session that evening. In fifteen minutes he wrote "Mood Indigo," then went out and recorded it, and performed it that night at the Cotton Club.

### IN A SENTIMENTAL MOOD
Ellington was in Durham, North Carolina, at a party where two women were fighting. Ellington put one girl at each end of the piano and told them he had written a new song dedicated to them. He improvised a tune while the girls cooled off. It was later published as "In a Sentimental Mood."

### SOLITUDE
Ellington was at a recording session in Chicago with three tunes ready but still needing a fourth to round out the side of a 78. As he waited for another recording session to finish and free up the studio, he leaned against the studio's glass wall and wrote out a new tune in about twenty minutes. When the band recorded it everyone in the band and in the booth got choked up. When someone asked what the title was, musician Artie Whetsol answered, "Solitude." The name stuck.

Duke Ellington, Ella Fitzgerald, and a friend.

> "I want you to notice one thing and that's the huge expanse of red carpeting that covers the ground floor. That's Duke's blood."
> —A friend of George Simon, describing Irving Mills's home

### DON'T GET AROUND MUCH ANYMORE

Duke Ellington wrote "I Let a Song Go Out of My Heart" for the *Cotton Club Revue*. It was dropped from that production and replaced by "Swingtime in Honolulu." Still, he liked the song and played "I Let a Song" on the radio. Benny Goodman even made a recording of it. After some time away from New York, Ellington decided to rearrange the song, adding a counter melody, but audiences preferred the version they knew, and Ellington was forced to dig up the old arrangement. Never wanting to let anything good go to waste, Ellington took the counter melody and, in 1939, recorded it as "Never No Lament." Lyricist Bob Russell took that instrumental, added lyrics, and called it "Don't Get Around Much Anymore."

### SOPHISTICATED LADY

George Gershwin told Oscar Levant that he wished he had written the bridge to this song.

**BELOW:** Mitch Miller asks Duke Ellington and Billy Strayhorn who really wrote what already.

### FLAMINGO

Duke Ellington: A good friend of mine named Edmund Anderson came over with Ted Grouya and their new song entitled "Flamingo." I listened and like it, and gave it to Strayhorn right away so that he could prepare it for Herb Jeffries to sing. The orchestration he did on "Flamingo" was, in my opinion, a turning point in vocal background orchestration, a renaissance in elaborate ornamentation for the accompaniment of singers. It soon caught on and became a big hit. Since then, other arrangers have become more and more daring, but Billy Strayhorn really started it all with "Flamingo."

**ABOVE:** Avon Long in the Ellington's Broadway flop Beggar's Holiiday.

**BBELOW:** Duke constantly publicized the band and himself.

# Sammy Fain

S ammy Fain was born in New York on June 17, 1902. Like Harold Arlen, Fain's father was a cantor. Fain began working as a staff pianist with Mills Music right out of high school. His first published song, "Nobody Knows What a Red Head Mamma Can Do," was written with Al Dubin and, supposedly, Irving Mills. Fain formed a partnership with Irving Kahal and together they went to Hollywood and worked at Paramount Pictures and Warner Brothers on such early film musicals as *The Big Pond* (1930), *Footlight Parade* (1933), and *Dames* (1934) sometimes with Pierre Norman, a pseudonym for Father O'Connor.

Fain and Bob Hilliard wrote a jazzy score to Disney's *Alice in Wonderland* (1951) and, with Sammy Cahn, for Disney's *Peter Pan* (1952). Later, Fain teamed with Paul Francis Webster for a series of memorable title songs as well as the film *Calamity Jane* (1953) and the Oscar-winning "Secret Love."

Frank Fain: Mostly he worked at home or in a car. He would be driving along and humming and not watching the road. While at the races, betting on horses, he wrote between races. He wrote twenty-four hours a day, whether he had an assignment or not. He was always writing on a scrap of paper.

Fain also tried his hand on Broadway, beginning with *Everybody's Welcome* (1931). He and Jack Yellen had a big hit in "Are You Havin' Any Fun?" introduced by Ella Logan in the *Ziegfeld Follies of 1936*. *Hellzapoppin'* was a huge hit in 1938, but it was Olsen and Johnson's hijinks, not the score by Fain and Charles Tobias, that made the show run and run. That same year, *Right This Way* featured a score by Fain and Kahal, including the standards "I Can Dream Can't I?" and "I'll Be Seeing You"—two remarkable songs from a less-than-successful show.

*George White's Scandals* (1939) put Fain back on top. After 1941's *Sons o' Fun*, a sequel of sorts to *Hellzapoppin'*, Fain returned to the movies, until the 1946 show, *Toplitzky of Notre Dame*, with lyrics by the vastly underrated George Marion Jr.

In 1951 *Flahooley* sported an excellent score by Fain and E. Y. Harburg, especially the songs "Here's to Your Illusions," "The Spring-time Cometh," and "The World Is Your Balloon." *Ankles Aweigh* (1955) had a guilty-pleasure score by Fain and Dan Shapiro and 1960's *Christine* featured some good songs with lyrics by Paul Francis Webster. Fain's last Broadway show was *Something More!* with lyrics by Alan and Marilyn Bergman.

His film career ended on a high note with the wonderful score to the Disney animated film *The Rescuers* in 1977. He died on December 6, 1989. ❖

## THE GREAT SONGS

**1927** I Left My Sugar Standing In The Rain (Lyric By Irving Kahal); Let A Smile Be Your Umbrella (Lyric By Irving Kahal And Francis Wheeler)

**1929** Wedding Bells Are Breaking Up that Old Gang of Mine (lyric by Irving Kahal and William Raskin); You Brought a New Kind of Love to Me (Sammy Fain, Irving Kahal, and Pierre Norman)

**1931** Was That the Human Thing to Do? (lyric by Joe Young); When I Take My Sugar to Tea (Sammy Fain, Irving Kahal, Pierre Norman)

**1933** By a Waterfall (lyric by Irving Kahal)

**1936** Are You Havin' Any Fun? (lyric by Jack Yellen)

**1938** I Can Dream, Can't I?; I'll Be Seeing You (both lyrics by Irving Kahal); That Old Feeling (lyric by Lew Brown)

**1939** The Mexiconga; Something I Dreamed Last Night (both lyrics by Herb Magidson and Jack Yellen)

**1950** Dear Hearts and Gentle People (lyric by Bob Hilliard)

**1951** Alice in Wonderland; I'm Late (both lyrics by Bob Hilliard); Here's to Your Illusions; The Springtime Cometh; The World Is Your Balloon (all lyrics by E. Y. Harburg)

**1952** The Second Star to the Right (lyric by Sammy Cahn)

**1953** Secret Love; A Woman's Touch (both lyrics by Paul Francis Webster)

**1955** Love Is a Many Splendored Thing (lyric by Paul Francis Webster)

**1957** April Love; Clover in the Meadow (both lyrics by Paul Francis Webster)

**1958** Once Upon a Dream (lyric by Jack Lawrence); A Very Precious Love (lyric by Paul Francis Webster)

**1977** Someone's Waiting for You (lyric by Carol Connors and Ayn Robbins)

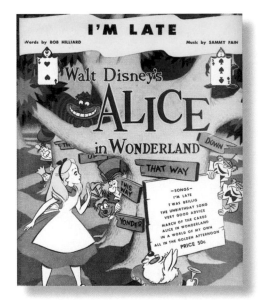

Rodgers and Hammerstein were Broadway's most successful composers. Here's a raucous wedding from their modest hit, *Flower Drum Song.*

# Broadway Songwriters

From the beginning of Tin Pan Alley, Broadway songwriters have been considered among the great contributors to the art form. After all, the demands of writing for Broadway are stringent indeed. A good show song must advance the plot, define the characters, illuminate the setting—and be a damn great song. Just below the Broadway writers on the evolutionary scale are the Hollywood songwriters (generally a breed unto themselves, though some crossed over). The Hollywood writers inhabit a netherworld between Broadway and writers of individual popular songs.

The earliest Broadway songwriters came out of the European operetta tradition of lush, romantic melodies scored for orchestras with large string sections. Many of these writers were, in fact, born in Europe and came to Broadway around the turn of the century. Victor Herbert, Rudolf Friml, Sigmund Romberg, and others carried on the traditions of the Viennese operettas. One of the earliest home-grown writers of musicals was John Philip Sousa, whose first show, *Chris and the Wonderful Lamp*, premiered in 1900 and featured the dominant rhythm of the day, the march. The two-step and the waltz formed the basis of most early scores.

With the emergence of jazz and ragtime, popular music evolved and native-born composers like George M. Cohan and Jerome Kern incorporated the four-step rhythm of the fox trot into a series of jazzy tunes while still utilizing the traditional waltzes and two-steps as well.

The fox-trot rhythm gave tunes a momentum and excitement that was perfectly suited to the demands of the Broadway musical. Instead of the lush strings of the orchestra, new instruments like the saxophone were introduced, and orchestrations began to favor the piano, drums, and bass. Tunes were still hummable, the melody remained king, but there was a new electricity to the beat.

With these new rhythms and syncopations at his command, the Broadway musical composer had new ways to express character, situation, and locale. The lyricist, too, had the means to write increasingly complex verses.

Until the 1950s, the Broadway songwriter and popular songwriter were somewhat synonymous, as the Great White Way provided many of the top tunes for bands and singers. As popular tastes in music changed, with the onslaught of rock-and-roll and the disappearance of popular song from radio, television, and recordings, the Broadway musical lost its influence. Although there have been the occasional breakout hits, few standards have come out of Broadway in the past fifty years.

Attempts to recreate the musical in a contemporary idiom have been inconsistent, running from the sublime (*Hair*) to the ridiculous (*Aida*). Even scores by such rock masters as Elton John have failed to produce memorable or lasting songs. Sir Andrew Lloyd Webber has enjoyed a modicum of success off the stage with three or four songs, but considering that his shows enjoy endless runs in New York, London, and around the world, he isn't doing so hot on radio and records. Such consummate theater artists as Charles Strouse and Lee Adams, Jerry Bock and Sheldon Harnick, John Kander and Fred Ebb, Tom Jones and Harvey Schmidt find that their superlative work is seldom appreciated outside of the legitimate theater.

In the fifties and early sixties, singers and instrumentalists regularly covered the latest songs from Broadway, each hoping that his recording of would break out. There were a few hits: Ed Ames's "My Cup Runneth Over" from Jones and Schmidt's *I Do! I Do!*; the great and underappreciated (and still performing) Marilyn Maye's recordings of the title songs from *Cabaret* and *Sherry* (even though the latter show was a failure). Eydie Gorme had hits with two songs from *Mame:* "If He Walked into My Life" and the title number. Robert Goulet's Rogo Productions was one of the producers of the Burton Lane and Alan Jay Lerner musical *On a Clear Day You Can See Forever* and he recorded a number of the songs from the show, to some acclaim.

When Strouse and Adams wrote *Bye Bye Birdie* back in 1960, they could still count on hit songs coming from their shows. The songwriters hated the staging of the title song while *Birdie* was in its out-of-town tryout, and asked director/choreographer Gower Champion to change the choreography. Champion agreed but said he had other things to accomplish first. Meanwhile, Buddy Greco's recording of the song became a big hit and, as the show found its audience, the number got a better and better response from audiences, even though the staging never changed. By the time the show premiered in New York, Strouse still thought the staging stank but audiences loved it. That's the power of a hit tune. Viewers knew the song from radio and recordings, so they loved it no matter what the staging.

In 1977, Strouse and Martin Charnin enjoyed a mega-popular hit with "Tomorrow" from *Annie*. It was to be the last smash hit from a Broadway show, with the possible exception of "Memories" from *Cats*.

Even Stephen Sondheim, considered the greatest Broadway songwriter of the second half of the twentieth century, had few recorded hits until Judy Collins recorded "Send in the Clowns" two years after the close of *A Little Night Music*. The success of Collins's recording led to Sinatra covering the song on one of his albums.

Bob Merrill went from really stupid pop songs in the 1950s to some of Broadway's finest scores. Here's Jackie Gleason in Merrill's *Take Me Along*.

The Broadway song will never again have the influence it once did. Writers today count on making their money from successive professional and amateur productions of their shows; ASCAP and BMI contribute less and less to the songwriters' income; and most of the population is unaware of Broadway as anything but an occasional tourist treat. The era of the Broadway hit may be over, but the great Broadway songs of the past endure. ◆

GEORGE GERSHWIN'S "PORGY AND BESS" AT THE MAJESTIC THEATRE
*"The town's bargain—with best seats at $2.75"*—Walter Winchell

## *Song and Story*

### I TALK TO THE TREES

During the writing of *Paint Your Wagon* Lerner came up with the title of this song and gave it to Loewe, who wrote a marvelous melody. As was his wont, Lerner wrote version after version of a lyric but none seemed to work. Then he tried one with no rhymes at all, and the song came to life.

### OVER THERE

The morning papers of April 6, 1917, announced that America was going to join the war against Germany. George M. Cohan, that most patriotic of songwriters, read about it at his Great Neck, Long Island, home and was inspired. "I read those war headlines," Cohan later wrote, "and I got to thinking and humming to myself—and for a minute I thought I was going to dance. I was all finished with the chorus and the verse by the time I got to town, and I also had a title." The first line, "Johnny get your gun," was taken from a popular song of 1886. The melody took off from a three-note bugle call.

Nora Bayes is the person who put it across with the public. She sang it in vaudeville and recorded it for the Victor Talking Machine Company on July 13, 1917. Over two million copies of sheet music were sold and the song became an anthem for World War I. In 1940, with war raging in Europe, Cohan wrote "This Is Our Side of the Ocean." It didn't catch on. Nor did 1942's, "For the Flag, for the Home, for the Family (For the Future of All Mankind)." It would be his last song.

"Over There" was first performed publicly in the fall of 1917 by Charles King at a Red Cross benefit in New York. But it was the popular singer and comedienne Nora Bayes who made the song famous. Cohan, it is said, personally chose her to premiere his song on stage. Bayes also recorded "Over There" for the Victor Talking Machine Company on July 13, 1917 (in a 78-rpm format). Other contemporaries of Bayes who recorded the song included the operatic tenor Enrico Caruso and recording artist Billy Murray. By the end of the war more than 2 million copies of the sheet music had been sold.

## YOU'RE A GRAND OLD FLAG

George M. Cohan was always interested in things patriotic and one day he was having a conversation with a GAR veteran who told Cohan that he had been a color-bearer at Pickett's charge at Gettysburg. The man remarked, "She's a grand old rag." That's what Cohan used as the title for his new song. Patriotic groups, perhaps at the urging of a disgruntled drama critic (and aren't they all), objected to the use of the word "rag." Cohan changed it to "flag" and the song became a smash hit.

## SOMETHING I DREAMED LAST NIGHT

Another rediscovered song. Jack Yellen relates what happened after Ella Logan introduced it in George White's Scandals of 1939, "the show died, and so did the song. But somehow or other the bistro torch singers managed to get copies, and every now and then I would hear it in the wee hours in some dive. Then somebody made a record, and somebody else, of no importance. Finally Peggy Lee caome out with hers, and Julie London, and Johnny Mathis. And so another standard came to life."

**TOP:** Elliott Gould and Lillian Roth in Harold Rome's *I Can Get It for You Wholesale*. **CENTER:** Tony Randall and Abbe Lane in Livingston and Evans's *Oh, Captain!* **BOTTOM:** Johnny Mercer and Gene De Paul musical success *Li'l Abner*. Edith Adams's Daisy Mae, Peter Palmer's Li'l Abner, Tina Louise's Appassionata Von Climax, and Al Nesor's Evil Eye Fleagle.

## MONOTONOUS

Producer Leonard Sillman described Kitt's performance in New Faces of 1952: "Just before the Philadelphia closing we held one last rehearsal. When Eartha Kitt came on with 'Monotonous' I stood down in the front row of the orchestra screaming at her, 'For God's sake, be a cat…. Spit the damned song out! When you say 'Monotonous' say it between your teeth and open your eyes wide. Be a cat! She sang the song sullenly that night, hissing most of it in an absolute paralysis of boredom until the very end when she really let loose—and killed the customers."

## BEFORE THE PARADE PASSES BY

Jerry Herman: "My proudest moment. It was written during a blizzard on a tinny upright in my Detroit hotel room inte middle of the night, under unbelievable pressure from David Merrick. It became the perfect prelude to Dolly's return to the human race, and because it was written specifically for Carol Channing, her comfort level allowed her to belt the song to the last row of the St. James's balcony.

## MAME

Jerry Herman: "I didn't want to write another big title song. And I told my producesr that lightning doesn't strike twice. Bobby Fryer, one of the producers, came to visit me and practically begged me to try writing one. I was on my way to St. Thomas with Don Pippin, my new musical director, to work on choral arrangements. The combination of Bobby's plea and beautiful tropical weather made my homage to the old South pour out of me on a beach in the Caribbean."

## LOOK WHAT HAPPENED TO MABEL

Jerry Herman: "All the songs in the show are totally different in style, and together they make the score into a bouquet of mixed colors, that I think is my best work. I've always been disappointed that Mack and Mabel never found its true place. But I think there's still a chance for it."

## ON THE STREET WHERE YOU LIVE

The number died after the first performance out of town. Everybody, including Moss Hart and Frederick Loewe, wanted to drop the song having always hated it. Lerner was sure that the song could be a hit and didn't want to cut it. So, he thought about why the audience hadn't responded at all to the song and he realized that the character who was singing it, the audience had seen one scene previously. And Freddy was wearing the same pearl grey Ascot costume as everyone else and the audience didn't know who he was when he came on stage to sing the song. So, Lerner wrote a short little scene with a new verse to the song, where the parlor maid comes to the door and actually announces to the audience who the character is. The number practially stopped the show at the next performance. Loewe said to Lerner, "How dare you give me an inferiority complex."

S tephen Foster was America's first superstar songwriter, though his name was little known to the general public—people assumed that his compositions were traditional folk songs.

Foster was the ninth of ten children born in Lawrenceville, Pennsylvania, on July 4, 1826. His parents indulged his early interest in music by paying for lessons from Henry Kleber, a major figure on the Pittsburgh music scene. Foster moved to Cincinnati in 1846 and began to sell songs to a local music publisher. In 1850, with twelve songs published and looking forward to what he hoped was a successful career, Foster felt he could afford to ask Jane Denny MacDowell to marry him.

Foster wrote many songs about the South, but he seldom strayed far from Pittsburgh until he moved to New York in 1860. He paid particularly close attention to the music of America's immigrants, thinking of himself as a "people's composer" and believing that by adapting the music of his diverse countrymen, he could make his work widely accessible and thus more popular. He was a disciplined, diligent writer who often took many months to finish a song, worrying over every word and comma.

A humanist, Foster endeavored to write positive, uplifting songs. Even in his depictions of the common practice of slavery, he treated blacks with the same respect as other Americans. Contrary to what some latter-day listeners assume, he wrote in dialect to convey his characters realistically and insisted that white performers present his songs with compassion for all. His goal, he said, was to "build up taste…among refined people by making words suitable to their taste, instead of the trashy and really offensive words which belong to some songs of that order." To that end, he refrained from using especially virulent words or lyrics that might inflame an already politically and socially charged situation.

In 1848, Foster's "Oh! Susanna" was performed by the Christy Minstrels troupe. Although the sheet music earned tens of thousands of dollars, Foster received only $100 from his music publisher. He vowed to improve his lot as a songwriter and became a pioneer in the early music business. He led the way on many important fronts, paying close attention to contracts (the first ever written between a songwriter and music publisher) and keeping accurate accounts of his royalties and other payments. Still, Foster was often cheated.

He signed with the New York publishing firm of Firth, Pond & Company on December 3, 1849. That year he wrote, "Nelly Was a Lady," the first song to depict two blacks in a loving relationship. The use of the word "lady," which up to that point had been reserved for highborn white women, was a bold move on his part. "Ring, Ring de Banjo!" written in 1851, seems to be a jolly slave song but the lyric, which concerns a man leaving the plantation when the "ribber's running high," is really about an escape. "The Old Folks at Home" (1851), a song about blacks that has been adopted universally, was Foster's next huge hit and was among the first American popular songs. It was followed by "My Old Kentucky Home, Good Night" (1853) and "Jeanie with the Light Brown Hair" (1854), by which time Foster had given up using dialect altogether, preferring to label his songs "American melodies."

In 1853, Foster separated from his wife, and two years later his parents died. Depressed and deep in debt, Foster finally managed to pen some new plantation songs, the most famous of which was "Old Black Joe" (1860).

Foster took his wife and daughter back to Pennsylvania, where they lived in a series of boarding houses and cheap hotels. He tried his hand at musical theater–style songs and, for the first time, took on a lyricist partner, the young poet George Cooper. Foster also tried his hand at "Sunday school songs" but without much success.

Foster never managed to improve his situation significantly. In all, he earned only $15,000 for his compositions and, at the time he died on January 13, 1864, had only thirty-eight cents in his pocket. ◆

## Song and Story

### [I DREAM OF] JEANIE WITH THE LIGHT BROWN HAIR

Stephen Foster wrote this number as a tribute to his wife Jane, from whom he was temporarily separated. The song had a remarkable resurgence in popularity in 1941, when ASCAP and the radio broadcasters entered a feud resulting in a ban on playing all ASCAP-controlled recordings. Program directors were forced to spin the classics and "Jeanie" became one of the most frequently played numbers.

### MY OLD KENTUCKY HOME, GOOD NIGHT

Stephen Foster wrote this song one morning while at his cousin's mansion in Bardstown, Kentucky. He heard mockingbirds outside the window and young black children playing. The mansion was bought by the State of Kentucky in 1922 and made into a shrine, and the song became the official state song of Kentucky.

# Dorothy Fields

The baby of a famed theatrical family, Dorothy Fields was born in Allenhurst, New Jersey, on July 15, 1901. Her father was Lew Fields, half of the vaudeville and musical comedy team of Weber and Fields. Dorothy's brother Joseph became a well-known playwright in collaboration with Jerome Chodorov; brother Herbert was one of Broadway's top librettists. Dorothy overcame much sexism to become one of Broadway's top lyricists. One of her great strengths was her ability to incorporate current slang into her lyrics, creating colloquial, up-to-the-moment songs. Throughout her long career she remained in the vanguard of the musical theater, always able to keep up with popular taste. She was the only member of her family to make a successful transition to film, with scores with such great composers as Jerome Kern and Harold Arlen.

Fields made a splash on Broadway in Lew Leslie's *Blackbirds of 1928,* in collaboration with composer Jimmy McHugh. Their hit tune was "I Can't Give You Anything but Love." The aptly titled *Hello, Daddy!* (1928) came next, produced by and starring father Lew in his last Broadway appearance, and with a libretto by brother Herbert. Fields and Jimmy McHugh provided a few songs for the show. Her final Broadway collaboration with McHugh was on *The International Revue* (1930). They contributed one smash hit, "On the Sunny Side of the Street." Their *Clowns in Clover* closed out of town in 1933 but it did contain the future standard "Don't Blame Me."

Fields and McHugh joined many of their fellow composers and lyricists in Hollywood for most of the 1930s, placing a number of individual songs in mostly dramatic films. By 1935 they were writing complete film scores, and that year was a banner one for Fields. She and McHugh wrote "I Feel a Song Coming On" with a title by George Oppenheimer, and Fields collaborated with Jerome Kern on *I Dream Too Much.* She also provided some additional songs for the film version of *Roberta,* including "Lovely to Look At" and "I Won't Dance," the latter with Oscar Hammerstein II. In 1936, she and Kern wrote songs for Fred Astaire and Ginger Rogers to sing in *Swing Time.* That exceptional score included "Bojangles of Harlem," "A Fine Romance," "Never Gonna Dance," "Pick Yourself Up," and "The Way You Look Tonight." Kern and Fields wrote *The Joy of Living* (1938), with wonderful songs including "You Couldn't Be Cuter" and "What's Good About Good-Night?," and *One Night in the Tropics* (1940), with the marvelous "Remind Me."

Fields returned to Broadway in 1939 with *Stars in Your Eyes,* music by Arthur Schwartz. The score was excellent although no standards emerged (very strange, considering that the great Ethel Merman starred). Dorothy and brother Herbert's first project as a team was Cole Porter's *Let's Face It!* (1941). The siblings supplied a mischievous script to match Porter's equally sassy music and lyrics. Another Porter show, *Something for the Boys,* followed in 1943. Herbert and Dorothy again wrote lines for Merman in the Michael Todd production. Herbert, Dorothy, Porter, and Todd next collaborated on *Mexican Hayride* in 1944.

European-style operetta, pronounced dead at the end of the 1920s, made a surprisingly successful return to Broadway with *Up in Central Park* (1945). Sigmund Romberg wrote the music and Dorothy returned to lyric writing for the occasion, also collaborating with Herbert on the book. To everyone's surprise, the Mike Todd production enjoyed a long run. The songwriters had come up with a lovely, melodious score including the breakout hit "Close as Pages in a Book."

Herbert and Dorothy's entertaining but minor efforts on Porter musicals didn't prepare Broadwayites for the genius of their next show, *Annie Get Your Gun*. Originally, Dorothy was to write lyrics to the melodies of Jerome Kern. She went so far as to title some of the songs. When Kern died unexpectedly, he and Dorothy were replaced by Irving Berlin, who kept some of Dorothy's song titles.

She returned to Hollywood in 1951 and worked on a few pictures including *Mr. Imperium*, *Texas Carnival*, and, with Arthur Schwartz, *Excuse My Dust*. Fields and Schwartz collaborated again on *A Tree Grows in Brooklyn*, a vehicle for Shirley Booth. The 1951 production boasted a charming score with real emotional power. "Make the Man Love Me" became a hit and has remained a favorite of pop singers.

The next year she wrote *Lovely to Look At*. It was a remake of *Roberta*. In 1953, Fields paired up with Harold Arlen for the Betty Grable film, *The Farmer Takes a Wife*. Fields and Schwartz brought out the best in each other, and they next collaborated on *By the Beautiful Sea* (1954), also starring Shirley Booth. This time Herbert joined Dorothy on the script, but the results were weak. The brother and sister then wrote the libretto to the first murder-mystery musical, *Redhead* (1959), with a score by Dorothy and Albert Hague. Gwen Verdon starred and the hit this time was "Merely Marvelous."

Upon Herbert's death in 1958, Dorothy took a seven-year break from the theater, returning in top form with the 1966 smash hit, *Sweet Charity*. Dorothy's lyrics perfectly matched Cy Coleman's jazzy rhythms, providing exactly the right tone for the alternately romantic, salty, and sentimental score. "Big Spender" emerged as the big hit, but the rest of the score is much more sophisticated and praiseworthy. Fields's last Broadway show, *Seesaw* (1973), was another Coleman collaboration, but the result wasn't nearly as satisfying as *Sweet Charity*.

Of all the Broadway lyricists, Dorothy Fields was the most able to keep up with her times, using contemporary idiomatic phrases without sounding forced or trendy. Her more poetic lyrics never become cloying and her imagery remains sharp, fresh, and hip. It's to her credit that she could collaborate with composers as wildly diverse in style as Arthur Schwartz, Jerome Kern, and Cy Coleman. And, perhaps most noteworthy of all, in a field largely dominated by men, she always held her own and defied categorization as a "female" songwriter. ◆

## Asides

Dorothy Fields often titled songs in the negative, as in "I Can't Give You Anything But Love," "You Couldn't Be Cuter," and "Nobody Does It Like Me."

Jimmy McHugh was a song plugger at Mills Music. When he and Fields teamed up, they wrote instant songs based on headlines of the day. She later called herself "Mills Music's fifty-dollars-a-night-girl."

## Song and Story

### I CAN'T GIVE YOU ANYTHING BUT LOVE

Jimmy McHugh and Dorothy Fields were reportedly outside Tiffany's jewelry store when they heard a swain tell his girlfriend, "I Can't Give You Anything but Love." They took the phrase, added "Lindy" (referring to Charles Lindbergh), and wrote a song. Perhaps realizing that the addition would date the song, they replaced the name with "baby." Or maybe not. Fats Waller claimed he wrote the tune and sold it to Jimmy McHugh, along with "On the Sunny Side of the Street." We do know that later, when Fields wrote additional lyrics for the film remake of *Roberta*, titled *Lovely to Look At*, she kept McHugh's name as co-author on the songs although he had nothing to do with writing them.

### I WON'T DANCE

"I Won't Dance" was written by Jerome Kern, Otto Harbach, and Oscar Hammerstein II for the 1934 London musical *Three Sisters*. The show was not a hit but Fred Astaire happened to see it and admired the song. When it came time to film *Roberta* at RKO, he suggested that the song be used in the film. Dorothy Fields amended the lyrics for the 1935 Hollywood version.

Lew Fields: Ladies don't write lyrics.
Dorothy Fields: I'm no lady, I'm your daughter.

# Star Turns

## NANCY WILSON

More a pop singer than a traditional jazz vocalist, Nancy Wilson nevertheless surrounded herself with the best jazz backing, fooling a lot of listeners into thinking she was singing jazz. From George Shearing on 1960's *The Swinging's Mutual* to her acclaimed 1962 pairing with Cannonball Adderley, Wilson, glamorous of form, has always used her acting skills, superb phrasing, and fine voice to create a series of beautifully produced recordings. She herself eschewed the term "jazz singer." In her heyday, from 1962 to 1971, Wilson enjoyed twenty-nine charting LPs and nine *Billboard* Hot 100 singles. She also employed excellent arrangers, such as Billy May, Oliver Nelson, and Sid Feller on 1967's *Lush Life* and Gerald Wilson on *Yesterday's Love Songs, Today's Blues* (1963). As

Nancy Wilson

time went by her singing sometimes got a little pushy, as if she'd spent too much time in Vegas. She came back big in the 1980s, again with fine jazz accompaniment, on such albums as *The Two of Us* with Ramsey Lewis (1984).

## MARGARET WHITING

One of the best-loved singers ever, both professionally and personally, Margaret Whiting has always exhibited a refreshing mixture of class and naughty fun. She is an excellent pop singer with a wonder-

Margaret Whiting

fully warm tone and a caressing way with words—not surprising as she came from great stock: her father was the superb composer Richard A. Whiting. As a young girl, she was immersed in music and knew all the great songwriters, it seemed to be her destiny to become a singer. In 1942, Whiting began her recording career at Capitol Records, the brainchild of her father's sometime collaborator, Johnny Mercer. She was backed by noted bands on her early hits, including Freddie Slack on "That Old Black Magic," Billy Butterfield on "Moonlight in Vermont," and Paul Weston on "It Might As Well Be Spring." Touchingly, her father's "My Ideal" became a sort of theme song for Whiting. Between 1946 and 1954, she recorded more than forty hit songs for Capitol. Some of her better-known recordings are "Oh, But I Do," "A Tree in the Meadow," "Slippin' Around" with Jimmy Wakely, "Baby, It's Cold Outside" with Johnny Mercer, and "Blind Date" with Bob Hope. When the bottom fell out of the market for pop standards in the mid-'60s, she continued to perform in cabarets and concerts, and administered the Johnny Mercer Foundation that has helped hundreds of aspiring cabaret and jazz singers. Recent injuries and ill health have not slowed her down one iota. As late as 1997, she appeared on Broadway in the Johnny Mercer musical revue, *Dream*. The show was a failure but Whiting's appearance was nothing short of remarkable. She can still be seen around New York, attending seminars, supporting young artists, and singing with all her grace and charm intact.

## JOE WILLIAMS

Joe Williams's pleasingly creamy, deep voice enveloped listeners with a warmth that sprang from his heart. He enjoyed a special rapport with audiences even though he never felt the need to indulge in vocal gymnastics. His was an easy-go-

ing style, even when he was singing blues songs such as 1951's "Every Day I Have the Blues." Williams graduated from the Basie band with a self-assurance and dapper gentility. He never shouted the blues or pushed his ballads, but he got their essence across as deeply as anyone, and both his ballads and his up-tempo songs were delivered with an underlying wit. Whether singing hot licks with Ella Fitzgerald on "Party Blues" or his hit "Alright, Okay, You Win," Williams put across a song unlike anyone else. His voice improved with age, gaining a fine patina of extra richness. He classed up any song he sang—and when he joined television's *Bill Cosby Show*, Williams lent an air of authenticity, soul, style, and humor—the very same attributes he'd always exhibited in his finest performances. Williams passed away on March 29, 1999.

Joe Williams

## JACK JONES

Son of the superior singer Allan Jones, Jack Jones has enjoyed a long career singing the swinging songs of the '60s. His first and only album on Capitol was a bomb, but he moved over to Kapp Records and found success. Jones's albums featured superior songs sung in his inimitably confident style. In the '60s he was a sort of second-tier hip singer, recording such songs as "Lollipops and Roses" and "Wives and Lovers." Composer Henry Mancini was good to singers of his generation, and Jones had his Mancini hit with "Dear Heart." He swung but he never connected emotionally with audiences. Still, his confidence, good looks, and pleasing voice were enough to sustain a long career on records and in clubs. Following in his father's footsteps, Jones has starred in productions of

*Man of La Mancha* (recording a hit version of "The Impossible Dream") as well as other musicals. He still sounds terrific, so it is a little sad that most of the country has turned its back on popular singers of the 1960s. Still, the man who sang the theme to *The Love Boat* has a busy performing schedule in the United States and Great Britain. His hair has turned a distinguished gray along with that of his audiences, but for them, the love affair continues.

### ANDY WILLIAMS

Genial, clean-cut Andy Williams, with his mellow, unobjectionable voice, was a favorite of suburban audiences in the 1950s and '60s. He learned his craft at the knee of the indomitable Kay Thompson, as a member of her backup group, the Williams Brothers. Discovered by Steve Allen (who did the same for Steve and Eydie, among others) in 1951, Williams was squarely in the Perry Como mold (with an emphasis on square), the perfect guest to invite into rec rooms and dens through the magic of television. He subbed for Dinah Shore and for Garry Moore during their summer breaks. After a successful partnership with Cadence Records, in 1962 Columbia signed him and put the impressive strength of their A&R and marketing departments behind him. "Can't Get Used to Losing You" was a huge hit, and then Williams met Henry

Mancini and a musical match was made. "Moon River" and "The Days of Wine and Roses" were their two first pop smashes. NBC signed Williams for his own variety show, which premiered on September 13, 1962. During the next nine years, his show was constantly at the top of the ratings. When he finally left the air in 1972, Williams practically dropped out of sight. His style of singing fell out of favor and Mancini and the movies weren't producing the kind of songs at which he excelled. There was only one place for him, the town where all pop careers go to die—Las Vegas. Williams became a regular at Caesar's Palace. In 1992, he built his own theater in Branson, Missouri, a town devoted to the talents of singers whose nostalgia quotient is higher than a coon up a tree. Every day busloads of polyester-clad tourists shuffle into the eponymous theaters to see their favorite stars of the past in the cosmetically enhanced flesh. Though his voice may have dropped a little from his younger days, Williams sings as well as ever.

### TEDDI KING

The term "singer's singer" is meant to describe someone who might be unappreciated by the mainstream public but is highly regarded by fellow artists. Our favorite is Teddi King.

Theodora King was born in Revere, Massachusetts, on September 18, 1929 and grew into a jazz singer of modest ambition, preferring to stick to her spot-on jazz phrasings rather than pandering to pop tastes of the 1950s. She wasn't a show-off like O'Day, McRae, and their ilk, but kept her ego strictly in check, preferring to tell a story in song. She employed warm vocals and a swinging style in the tradition of other uncelebrated jazz singers such as Lee Wiley, Helen Ward, Jackie Cain and her sister-in-law Irene Kral, Dardenelle, and Maxine Sullivan. Not that King couldn't swing with the best of them, but she chose to keep her power in check until it was needed. She was the bopping girl next door. Teddi King had great taste

in material and trusted it. Her honesty was refreshing in an era of singers who tended to put their own twists on the rhythm and timing. King was the kind of a singer who would come by a club and informally join the pianist for a few vocals.

Teddi King began singing in the late forties, at the tail end of the dance band era, with such local bands as Roy Dorey, George Graham, Jack Edwards, and Nat Pierce. George Shearing saw her potential and rescued her from New England, taking her on tour for a couple of years. Shearing remained devoted to King, performing with her until 1959 though they recorded only six sides together. The great George Wein became her manager and King recorded a few albums on Storyville before signing with RCA. Her contract ended in 1958 (she had a chart hit with "Mr. Wonderful" in 1956) and the next year she recorded an album on Coral. That company tried to make her into a straight pop singer, which so depressed her that she never recorded for a major label again.

In 1962, King opened the Playboy Club in New York City. She was a Playboy Club exclusive—no radio, television, or recordings—until 1970. She didn't mind, she got to perform jazz as she liked it and she got to see the world, too. Just as her contract with Playboy was ending, King was diagnosed with lupus, a degenerative autoimmune disease. She worked only occasionally, when her health permitted.

In 1977, after an appearance in North Carolina, an enthusiastic fan kissed her. He was suffering from meningitis and the kiss literally killed King. She died two days later, on November 18, at the age of forty-eight.

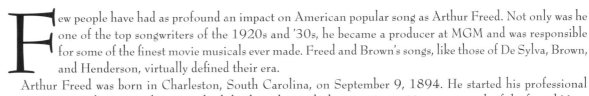

## Freed & Brown

Arthur freed, Gene Kelly, and Frederick loewe on the set of *Brigadoon.*.

Few people have had as profound an impact on American popular song as Arthur Freed. Not only was he one of the top songwriters of the 1920s and '30s, he became a producer at MGM and was responsible for some of the finest movie musicals ever made. Freed and Brown's songs, like those of De Sylva, Brown, and Henderson, virtually defined their era.

Arthur Freed was born in Charleston, South Carolina, on September 9, 1894. He started his professional career as a song plugger in Chicago and, while plying his trade, he met Minnie Marx, matriarch of the famed Marx Brothers. Soon, he'd embarked on a career in vaudeville, singing while the Marxes cavorted. From there he teamed up with songwriter Gus Edwards. He then joined songwriter Louis Silvers and they wrote their first songs in 1917. Soon, one was interpolated into a Broadway show, *Jim-Jam Revue*.

Freed's ultimate songwriting partner, Nacio Herb Brown, spent his early years in Deming, New Mexico, where he was born on February 22, 1896. The family eventually moved to Los Angeles, where Brown attended the Musical Arts High School. Brown began his professional career as accompanist to vaudevillian Alice Doll, spending a year or so on the Orpheum circuit. He had stars in his eyes—movie stars, that is—so he quit vaudeville and moved back to LA, where he opened a custom tailor shop. His wish to rub elbows with the stars came true when the likes of Rudolph Valentino, Charles Chaplin, and Wallace Reid started coming to the shop. He then went into real estate but, through it all, Brown yearned to write songs—so in 1919 he started collaborating with King Zany.

They had their first hits in 1921 with "When Buddha Smiles" and "Take Me in Your Arms." In 1927, one of Brown's instrumental pieces, "The Doll Dance," was interpolated into the *Hollywood Music Box Revue*. For that same show Brown teamed up with the young lyricist, Arthur Freed, to write the song "Singing in the Rain." It didn't receive much attention.

Freed and Brown were well situated, living in Los Angeles just as the talkies brought movie screens to life. MGM production chief Irving Thalberg convinced the pair to write for the studio and their first picture was the all-talking, all-singing, all-dancing extravaganza, *The Broadway Melody* (1929). There was no stopping them after that. They became the most successful songwriters in the early years of the talkies. In 1931, the team temporarily broke up and, in 1932, Brown, along with composer Richard A. Whiting and lyricist B. G. De Sylva, wrote the Ethel Merman stage vehicle, *Take a Chance*. The show was a big Broadway hit that yielded not one but two standards, "Eadie Was a Lady" and "You're an Old Smoothie."

Then it was back to Hollywood and Arthur Freed in 1933, for a series of pictures. Brown and Freed continued to churn out hit after hit until 1939, when Freed was promoted to the production office at MGM. They would write a few more songs over the years, the last of which was "Make 'Em Laugh" for *Singin' in the Rain*. Brown occasionally wrote songs until 1961. He died in San Francisco on September 28, 1964.

Freed, meanwhile, was made a full-fledged producer, responsible for musicals and dramas alike, but it's for the musicals that he's best remembered. As head of the now legendary Freed unit, he cut his teeth as associate producer of *The Wizard of Oz* in 1939. He went on to produce such classic musicals as the Judy Garland/Mickey Rooney vehicles *Babes in Arms*, *Strike Up the Band*, *Babes on Broadway*, and *Girl Crazy*; Broadway transfers (often with new scores) of *Panama Hattie*, *Cabin in the Sky*, *Best Foot Forward*, *DuBarry Was a Lady*, *Brigadoon*, *Silk Stockings*; *Bells Are Ringing*; *Meet Me in St. Louis*, *The Harvey Girls*, *The Pirate*, and *Easter Parade*; composer biopics *Words and Music* and *Till the Clouds Roll By*; Fred Astaire vehicles *The Barkleys of Broadway*, *Royal Wedding*, and *The Belle of New York*; and four pictures considered to be among the greatest movie musicals of all time, *An American in Paris*, *Singin' in the Rain*, *The Band Wagon*, and *Gigi*. Quite an impressive list and not a clunker among them.

Freed's last picture was *Light in the Piazza* in 1962, for which he wrote the lyrics to Mario Nascimbene's title song, an apt conclusion to a remarkable career. Freed died in Los Angeles on April 12, 1973. ❖

## *Song and Story*

### SINGIN' IN THE RAIN
Brown and Freed actually wrote this song for the 1927 *Hollywood Music Box Revue*. It was later put into the film *Hollywood Revue of 1929*, where it achieved great success as sung by Cliff Edwards.

### YOU WERE MEANT FOR ME
Standards are songs that transcend the years and remain active in the publishers' catalogs. This song was introduced in *The Broadway Melody*, sung by Charles King. King sang it again in *The Hollywood Revue of 1929*—but it was Conrad Nagel's lips that were moving on the screen, in one of the earliest cases of dubbing. The song was also featured that year in *The Show of Shows*, where Winnie

Lightner and Bull Montana sang it. In 1940, it was featured in two films. Frank Morgan sang it in *Hullabaloo* and an off-screen chorus sang it in *Forty Little Mothers*. In 1948, a movie was named for it and Dan Dailey sang and danced to it. And finally (and perhaps most memorably), Gene Kelly sang it to Debbie Reynolds in the 1953 classic, *Singin' in the Rain*.

### MAKE 'EM LAUGH
Among the compendium of tunes Freed and Brown wrote in 1952 for *Singin' in the Rain*, the tune of "Make 'Em Laugh" was remarkably similar to Cole Porter's "Be a Clown," written a few years earlier for MGM's *The Pirate*. When Irving Berlin visited the MGM lot he was invited to have a look at the filming of "Make 'Em Laugh." He was appalled at the appropriation, and immediately called Porter, who brushed Berlin off. His regard for Freed was so great that he decided never to refer to the similarities, considering the plagiarism unintentional.

Fun at MGM. **OPPOSITE PAGE:** Arthur Freed and Nacio Herb Brown sitting around with Eleanor Powell. **LEFT:** Brown shows Frank Sinatra how to sell a song. **BELOW:** Freed, Judy Garland, and Fred Astaire during filming of *Easter Parade*.

Born in Cologne, Germany, on September 30, 1875, composer/lyricist Fred Fisher was an early pioneer of Tin Pan Alley. Fisher ran away from home at the age of thirteen and joined the German navy. In 1900, following a stint in the French Foreign Legion, he landed in the United States, quickly making his way to Chicago, where he took piano lessons from a black saloon pianist. He learned to put syncopation into his compositions, giving him a leg up on the usual foursquare European composers. In fact, Fisher was known for incorporating quirky rhythms into his tunes. These gave his songs a wonderful momentum and set them apart from the usual Tin Pan Alley fodder.

Fisher moved to New York and took a management position with Harms & Co. and later Leo Feist and Co. In 1905, he founded his own music publishing firm in anticipation of future hits. He didn't have to wait long: the next year he enjoyed his first success with "If the Man in the Moon Was a Coon," for which he wrote both music and lyrics.

He hit it big with several more songs, each selling over 2 million copies of sheet music. Although he published hundreds of songs, Fisher wrote hundreds more. If he decided he didn't like the results, he'd have trucks back up to his office and he'd literally dump them. Fisher was a nervous man who'd pull dollar bills from his pocket and tear them up.

In 1929, Fisher traveled to Hollywood to work on the new sound films. His first movie song was 1928's "I'd Rather Be Blue (Over You Than Be Happy with Somebody Else)," written for Fanny Brice to sing in the film *My Man*. Fisher wrote a few scores for silent movies and when MGM producer asked him if he could write a symphony, the composer answered, "When you buy me, you're buying Chopin, Liszt, and Mozart. You're getting the very best!" Despite Fisher's self-confidence, he stayed in Hollywood for only two years, giving up the business in 1930 without ever producing any big hits. A few of Fisher's songs were placed in Broadway shows, beginning in 1914, but they made little splash. He never wrote a complete score for film or stage.

Fisher's daughter, Doris, became a minor songwriter under contract to Columbia Pictures. In collaboration with her partner, Allan Roberts, she wrote "Put the Blame on Mame" for the film *Gilda*, and "You Always Hurt the One You Love." In 1941, she collaborated with her father on the song "Whispering Grass," which became a hit in England.

Fred Fisher died in New York City on January 14, 1942. In 1949, Hollywood treated America to a highly fictionalized biopic titled *Oh, You Beautiful Doll*. ◈

## Song and Story

### DARDANELLA

Vaudevillian Johnny S. Black bought the music to the piano rag "Turkish Tom Tom" from composer Felix Bernard for $100. In 1919, Fisher added a lyric and, with Black, amended the music. The song, now titled "Dardanella," sold over two million copies of sheet music and over 6 million recordings. Bernard sued, claiming that he should share in the royalties of "Dardanella," but the judge ruled the sale fair and square. This wouldn't be the only lawsuit surrounding "Dardanella." Fisher, already a syncopater, put what would later be called a boogie-woogie bass line into the song. In 1921, Jerome Kern used a similar bass line for "Ka-lu-a" and Fisher sued. The judge found on behalf of Fisher and fined Kern $250, though he commented that the lawsuit was "a trivial pother of scarcely more than irritation and a waste of time for everyone."

## THE GREAT SONGS

1906 **If the Man in the Moon Was a Coon; I've Said My Last Farewell** (lyric by Ed Rose)

1910 **Any Little Girl That's a Nice Little Girl Is the Right Little Girl for Me** (lyric by Thomas J. Gray); **Come Josephine in My Flying Machine** (lyric by Alfred Bryan)

1912 **Peg o' My Heart** (lyric by Alfred Bryan)

1914 **There's a Little Spark of Love Still Burning** (lyric by Joseph McCarthy); **Who Paid the Rent for Mrs. Rip Van Winkle (When Rip Van Winkle Went Away** (lyric by Alfred Bryan)

1915 **There's a Broken Heart for Every Light on Broadway** (lyric by Howard E. Johnson)

1916 **Ireland Must Be Heaven for My Mother Came from There** (lyric by Howard E. Johnson and Joseph McCarthy); **There's a Little Bit of Bad in Every Good Little Girl; You Can't Get Along with 'Em or without 'Em** (both lyrics by Grant Clarke)

1917 **They Go Wild Simply Wild Over Me** (lyric by Joseph McCarthy)

1918 **Would You Rather Be a Colonel with an Eagle on Your Arm than a Private with a Chicken on Your Knee?** (lyric by Leo Edwards)

1919 **Dardenella** (music by Felix Bernard; lyric by Fred Fisher and Johnny Black)

1920 **Daddy You've Been a Mother to Me**

1921 **I Found a Rose in the Devil's Garden** (lyric by William Raskin)

1922 **Chicago—That Toddlin' Town**

1923 **Barney Google** (by Fred Fisher and Billy Rose)

1924 **And the Band Played On; Savannah, That Georgiana Blues**

1925 **Phoebe Snow the Anthracite Mama** (by Fred Fisher and Al Kay)

1927 **When the Morning Glories Wake Up in the Morning then I'll Kiss Your Two Lips Goodnight** (lyric by Billy Rose)

1928 **I'd Rather Be Blue (Over You Than Be Happy with Somebody Else)** (lyric by Billy Rose)

1929 **I Don't Want Your Kisses If I Can't Have Your Love; There Ain't No Sweet Man That's Worth the Salt of My Tears**

1930 **Happy Days and Lonely Nights** (lyric by Billy Rose)

1936 **Your Feet's Too Big** (by Fred Fisher and Aba Benson)

# Christmas Songs

There's not much to say about Christmas songs except to note that a high percentage of them were written by Jews. Irving Berlin, Jule Styne, Mel Torme, Jerry Herman, and Johnny Marks all wrote Christmas songs and all were Jewish (though we suspect that one or more them had a "Hanukkah bush" in his house growing up). But seriously, Christmas songs, at least the more secular, "holiday" ones, have become a mainstay American culture, crossing religious barriers to become true pop standards. Though some school districts restrict the singing of Christmas songs out of respect for their diverse constituencies, most of us harbor a sentimental attachment to those tunes about Rudolph, silver bells, and chestnuts roasting on an open fire.

King of the Christmas songs, Johnny Marks, composes another standard.

## Song and Story

### SANTA CLAUS IS COMING TO TOWN

"Santa Claus Is Coming to Town" (J. Fred Coots) and "Winter Wonderland" (Felix Bernard and Dick Smith) were both written in 1934. No publisher was interested in the former, as they considered it a mere children's song. Coots was a writer for the Eddie Cantor radio show and gave the song to Cantor, who wasn't interested in singing it. But his wife, Ida, convinced him to do it and it made its debut one week before Thanksgiving. The song became a huge hit, though Cantor insisted that he still didn't like it.

### RUDOLPH, THE RED-NOSED REINDEER

In 1939, the Montgomery Ward department stores asked employee Robert L. May to write a story that could be given away to Ward's customers as a present. May came up with "Rudolph, the Red-Nosed Reindeer," and got Denver Gillen from Ward's art department to illustrate it. The little book was so popular that more than 6 million copies had been given away by 1949. More might have been printed but for wartime paper shortages. Montgomery Ward owned the copyright but, in a remarkable example of corporate "Christmas spirit," he gave ownership to May in January of 1947. May immediately asked songwriter Johnny Marks, who happened to be his brother-in-law, to turn his story into a song. Gene Autry recorded the result in 1949 and it sold more than 30 million copies, making it second in popularity only to "White Christmas."

The leading Christmas composer by far (he never had a single hit that wasn't a Christmas song) was Johnny Marks. Once he hit with "Rudolph, the Red-Nosed Reindeer" in 1949, Marks spent a good deal of the rest of his career trying to equal that success. He never quite matched it but he came pretty close with such perennials as "I Heard the Bells on Christmas Day" (1956), "Rockin' Around the Christmas Tree" (1958), "A Holly, Jolly Christmas" (1964), and that favorite of Johnny Mathis impersonators, "The Most Wonderful Day of the Year" (1964).

Of course the most successful Christmas song of all time is Irving Berlin's "White Christmas," written in 1942 for the Paramount Picture *Holiday Inn*. Bing Crosby performed the song in the film and his recording sold more than 30 million copies. On March 19, 1947, Decca Records had Crosby record an exact duplicate of the previous recording because the original master was simply worn out! When Paramount produced the 1954 film *White Christmas* (now, where did they get that name?), Crosby was again on hand to deliver the song. "White Christmas" remained the best-selling single of all time until 1998, when Elton John's special version of "Candle in the Wind," commemorating the death of Princess Diana (that spinning sound you hear is Irving Berlin), overtook it. We can only assume that "White Christmas" will have more legs than John's song, since Christmas comes every year and princesses die only once. It's just a matter of time before the holiday favorite once again achieves supremacy.

Crosby was also largely responsible for the 1943 hit, "I'll Be Home for Christmas" by Walter Kent and Kim Gannon, a song that touched American hearts during wartime. The movies also brought forth Hugh Martin's "Have Yourself a Merry Little Christmas," first sung by Judy Garland in *Meet Me in St. Louis*. Mel Torme and Bob Wells wrote a little ditty simply called "The Christmas Song," which has become better-known as "Chestnuts Roasting on an Open Fire." Meredith Willson penned "It's Beginning to Look a Lot Like Christmas," along with a countermelody, "Pine Cones and Holly Berries," for the musical *Here's Love*. The latter tune never caught on, though Willson's "May the Good Lord Bless You and Keep You" did. It's a sort of Christmas song—sort of. Another song that premiered on the Great White Way was Jerry Herman's "We Need a Little Christmas," from *Mame*. The granddaddy of all Broadway Christmas songs has to be Victor Herbert and Glen MacDonough's "Toyland," from the 1903 musical *Babes in Toyland*. The instrumental "March of the Toys" from that show is another Christmas favorite that has endured for over a century.

Christmas has also inspired funny songs, not just nostalgic paeans to snow and presents. "I Saw Mommy Kissing Santa Claus" and "All I Want for Christmas Is My Two Front Teeth" had their moments to shine, though Spike Jones's send-up of the latter made it impossible to hear the original version without snickering. And, lest you think that nobody writes songs like those anymore, keep in mind the 1979 hit "Grandma Got Run Over by a Reindeer," written and performed by Elmo (Shropshire) and Patsy (Trigg). As long as there's a Christmas, there'll be Christmas standards in the air from Halloween till New Year's. ◆

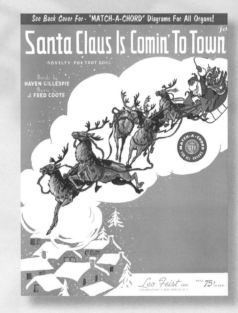

## The Gershwins

BIDIN' MY TIME
Music by GEORGE GERSHWIN · Lyrics by IRA GERSHWIN

From the WARNER BROS. Picture
"RHAPSODY IN BLUE"

LIZA
SWANEE
DELISHIOUS
'S WONDERFUL
I GOT RHYTHM
BIDIN' MY TIME
CLAP YO' HANDS
THE MAN I LOVE
EMBRACEABLE YOU
OH, LADY BE GOOD!
SOMEBODY LOVES ME
FASCINATING RHYTHM
SOMEONE TO WATCH OVER ME

Price 60¢

NEW WORLD MUSIC CORPORATION · HARMS, INC.
NEW YORK

Perhaps the most popular songwriters of the "Golden Age" of Broadway were the Gershwins. George's gregarious personality, as much as his brilliance, made his death at such a young age a shock to millions of Americans.

George was born in 1898 into a poor family of first-generation immigrants. In 1910 his parents purchased a piano so that his brother Ira, two years his senior, could take lessons (Yip Harburg later claimed to be on the street watching it hoisted through the Gershwin's parlor window—but Harburg claimed a lot of things that weren't necessarily so). But it was George who amazed his family when he sat down at the new piano and played simple tunes. In fact, George had already taught himself the basics at a neighbor's house. He went on to study in a more structured way with Charles Hambitzer, who in turn urged George to study theory, orchestration, and harmony with Edward Kilenyi.

George had ambitions to become a concert pianist, but his teachers convinced him that this was impractical. Luckily, he had an interest in the burgeoning field of American popular song. Like most of his contemporaries, he idolized Jerome Kern and Irving Berlin, who, along with George M. Cohan, were most responsible for bringing an American sensibility to what had been a predominantly European art.

George was most interested in the new sounds and syncopations that jazz was bringing to American song. Once blacks had invented ragtime (a sophisticated form in its own right), white pop writers appropriated its rhythms, smoothing out the rougher edges and merging it with the European art forms with which they were familiar. Berlin

made ragtime acceptable to white, middle-class ears (the middle class was another new American institution) with "Everybody's Doing It Now" and "Alexander's Ragtime Band." But it was George who really integrated jazz into his popular songs (and his symphonic works, too) and so became the most influential writer of the twentieth century. Ira's playful, slangy lyrics matched George's rhythms perfectly.

George's first published song, copyrighted in 1916 with lyrics by Murray Roth, carried the intriguingly tricky title, "When You Want 'Em, You Can't Get 'Em (When You Got 'Em, You Don't Want 'Em)." The remarkable success of that song led to George's earliest Broadway assignments. His first Broadway song, "The Making of a Girl," was written for *The Passing Show of 1916* in collaboration with Sigmund Romberg, with lyrics by Harold Atteridge. George created his first important song (and the biggest seller of his career), "Swanee," in 1919 for the Capitol Theater's revue *Demi-Tasse* and it was later incorporated into the tour of the Al Jolson show, *Sinbad*.

Ira followed in George's footsteps, collaborating on his first show with George. Alas, *A Dangerous Mind* closed out of town, in Pittsburgh. Ira, concerned that it would appear he had been hired out of nepotism, assumed the pen name Arthur Francis, combining the first names of the other Gershwin siblings. Ira had always been interested in language, and had written light verse all through school. He had successfully submitted his early work to Franklin P. Adams for publication in Adams's newspaper column, "The Conning Tower," a showcase for many young talents, including Howard Dietz and E. Y. Harburg.

The brothers were quite opposite in personality and habit. George was a born raconteur who couldn't be pried away from the keyboard of any party he happened to be attending. Ira preferred curling up at home with a dictionary and leftovers. George adamantly avoided marriage, preferring a series of affairs, most notably with fellow composer Kay Swift. Ira got married relatively young and for good. George's music is an ideal reflection of his personality: quixotic, hard to pin down, and constantly surprising. Everything and everyone interested George. He painted, experimented with photography, played tennis, and drew inspiration from everyday life. *Rhapsody in Blue* was inspired by the sound of a train clickety-clacking up the rails from New York to Boston. He explained, "I heard it as a sort of musical kaleidoscope of

America—of our vast melting pot, of our unduplicated national pep, of our metropolitan madness."

Ira played games with words. His erudition informed his lyrics, but he was equally at home with slang: just think of "I Got Rhythm" and "'S Wonderful." His lyrics were a perfect match for George's music and together they encompassed a wide variety of influences. Ira insisted that his lyrics weren't poetry: "Since most of the lyrics in this lodgment were arrived at by fitting words mosaically to music already composed, any resemblance to actual poetry, living or dead, is highly improbable."

Of course, George and Ira didn't arrive as full-blown expert songwriters. However, they were born in an era of opportunity, when live theater was the popular entertainment of choice. The brothers started out, in humble fashion, supplying a song here and there to be interpolated into a wide range of early musicals and operettas. The first Gershwin brothers song to appear in a Broadway show that actually reached Broadway was "The Real American Folk Song Is a Rag." It was put into *Ladies First*, where it received little notice and wasn't published until years later. Their first published song as a team was "Waiting for the Sun to Come Out," written for *The Sweetheart Shop*. With such pieces, George and Ira seemed destined to become merely adequate composers who created minor songs for minor musicals.

What seemed to change the tide—for George in particular—was not a Broadway production but the premiere of *Rhapsody in Blue* in 1924, a turning point year for the young composer. In June, he wrote his first real standard (excepting "Swanee"), "Somebody Loves Me," in collaboration with B. G. De Sylva and Ballard Macdonald. The success of that song, along with the *Rhapsody*, reinforced George's self-confidence. His and Ira's next Broadway show was *Lady, Be Good!*, a huge hit and the first of a series of playful musical successes with fine scores. *Oh, Kay!*, *Strike Up the Band* (a flop out of town but revised into a hit a few years later), *Funny Face*, *Girl Crazy*, and a host of others featured Gershwin's jazz-influenced rhythms and Ira's playful yet heartfelt lyrics.

George's classical aspirations were well served by such masterworks as his *Concerto in F*, *Cuban Overture*, and *An American in Paris*. With sojourns in Hollywood, a Pulitzer Prize (for Ira only) for *Of Thee I Sing*, and even a radio show (George), their fame grew and grew. While George worked on *Porgy and Bess*, Ira proved he could write with other composers: *Life Begins at 8:40* featured Harold Arlen's music along

## THE GREAT SONGS

**1918** Swanee (lyrics by Irving Caesar)

**1922** I'll Build a Stairway to Paradise (lyrics by Ira and B. G. De Sylva)

**1923** Somebody Loves Me (lyrics by B. G. De Sylva and Ballard Macdonald); Fascinating Rhythm; The Man I Love; Oh, Lady Be Good

**1925** Looking for a Boy; That Certain Feeling

**1926** Do, Do, Do; Maybe; Someone to Watch Over Me

**1927** 'S Wonderful; Funny Face; He Loves and She Loves; How Long Has This Been Going On?; My One and Only (What Am I Gonna Do); Strike Up the Band

**1928** Feeling I'm Falling; I Don't Think I'll Fall in Love Today; I've Got a Crush on You

**1929** Soon

**1930** Bidin' My Time; Boy! What Love Has Done to Me!; Embraceable You (written in 1929) I Got Rhythm

**1931** Blah, Blah, Blah; Love Is Sweeping the Country; Of Thee I Sing (Baby)

**1932** Isn't It a Pity?

**1933** Mine

**1934** Fun to Be Fooled; Let's Take a Walk Around the Block (both music by Harold Arlen)

**1935** I Got Plenty o' Nuthin' (lyric by Ira Gershwin and DuBose Heyward); It Ain't Necessarily So; Summertime (lyrics by DuBose Heyward)

**1936** I Can't Get Started (music by Vernon Duke)

**1937** (I've Got) Beginner's Luck; A Foggy Day in London Town; Let's Call the Whole Thing Off; Nice Work If You Can Get It; Slap That Bass; They All Laughed; They Can't Take That Away from Me; I Can't Be Bothered Now

**1938** Love Is Here to Stay; Love Walked In

**1940** (The Saga of) Jenny; My Ship; Tschaikowsky (And Other Russians) (all music by Kurt Weill)

**1944** Long Ago (And Far Away); Put Me to the Test (both music by Jerome Kern)

**1947** Aren't You Kinda Glad We Did?

**1954** The Man That Got Away (music by Harold Arlen)

**OPPOSITE PAGE:** Two hands too many for "Heart and Soul"—Fred Astaire, George Gershwin, and Ira Gershwin.

## CAREER HIGHLIGHTS

**1896** Ira is born.

**1898** George is born.

**1910** The Gershwins purchase a piano; George immediately starts playing it, self-taught at a neighbor's.

**1913** George writes his first songs, "Since I Found You" and "Ragging the Traumerei," with Leonard Praskins.

**1914** George quits high school and takes a job at Remick's, a music publisher.

**1915** George records piano rolls.

**1916** George publishes his first song, "When You Want 'Em, You Can't Get 'Em, When You Got 'Em, You Don't Want 'Em."

**1917** George begins work as rehearsal pianist for the Victor Herbert/Jerome Kern show, *Miss 1917*; the brothers' first collaboration, "You Are Not the Girl."

**1918** George signs a contract with T. B. Harms; *Hitchy-Koo of 1918* opens with "You-oo Just You" in the score, George's first song in a Broadway show; the Gershwins' first song for a show.

**1919** *La, La, Lucille* opens, the first show with a complete score by George.

**1920** Al Jolson puts "Swanee" into his show *Sinbad* while on the road.

**1921** The brothers' first complete score, *A Dangerous Maid*, opens.

**1924** *Rhapsody in Blue* premieres at Aeolian Hall; *Lady, Be Good!* opens on Broadway.

**1925** Concerto in F premieres at Carnegie Hall.

**1927** *Funny Face* opens at the Alvin Theater.

**1928** *An American in Paris* premieres at Carnegie Hall.

**1930** *Girl Crazy* opens at the Alvin Theater.

**1931** *Delicious*, the brothers' first film score, is released; *Of Thee I Sing* opens on Broadway.

**1932** George's Second Rhapsody premieres at Symphony Hall in Boston; Ira, George S. Kaufman, and Morrie Ryskind win the Pulitzer Prize for *Of Thee I Sing*; *Rhumba* (Cuban Overture) premieres in New York's Lewisohn Stadium; film version of *Girl Crazy* is released.

**1935** *Porgy and Bess* opens.

**1937** Film *Shall We Dance*, with Astaire and Rogers, opens; George has a dizzy spell but the doctors find nothing wrong; one month later, he dies of a brain tumor.

**1938** Film *Goldwyn Follies* opens.

**1941** Ira returns to Broadway, collaborating with Kurt Weill on *Lady in the Dark*.

**1944** *Cover Girl* opens with a score by Ira Gershwin and Jerome Kern.

**1945** Film bio *Rhapsody in Blue* opens.

**1946** *Park Avenue* opens. It will be Ira's last solo Broadway score.

**1947** Film *The Shocking Miss Pilgrim*, with posthumous score, opens.

**1954** *A Star Is Born* premieres with music by Harold Arlen; *The Country Girl*, Ira's last collaboration (with Harold Arlen), opens.

**1959** Film version of *Porgy and Bess* is released.

**1964** Film *Kiss Me, Stupid* premieres. It contains three previously unpublished Gershwin brothers songs.

**1972** Broadway's Uris Theater is renamed the Gershwin Theater.

**1983** Ira Gershwin dies.

with lyrics by Ira in collaboration with E. Y. Harburg. "Fun to Be Fooled," and "Let's Take a Walk Around the Block" are the standards that came out of that score.

*Porgy and Bess* opened on Broadway to, shall we say, confused reviews. Opera lovers considered it a musical; and Broadway fans, an opera. The work was clearly ahead of its time. This may sound like a cliché, but in the case of *Porgy and Bess* it was true. Finally, in 1943, the world caught up with *Porgy and Bess* and it received the acclaim it so richly deserved. Unfortunately, George didn't live to see the folk opera's worldwide success.

George's death in 1937 was devastating to Ira and, apart from completing the film score of *The Goldwyn Follies* with the help of Vernon Duke and Kay Swift, Ira went into a creative hiatus for years. He returned to writing in 1941, collaborating with Kurt Weill on *Lady in the Dark*, then went on to pen a series of hits: the film *Cover Girl* (with Jerome Kern), *The Barkleys of Broadway* (with Harry Warren), *A Star Is Born* (with Harold Arlen). He was also responsible for some misses, including *The Firebrand of Florence* (with Weill) and *Give a Girl a Break* (with Burton Lane). But even Ira's failures were marked by excellence of idea and craft.

The Gershwins' songs have become an integral part of the American songbook. Their work has been recorded continually, their shows revived endlessly, and new shows continue to crop up based on their catalog. Even with the rise of rock-and-roll and a host of other new musical idioms, the Gershwins continue to hold their own with no end in sight. ◆

**ABOVE:** There are only two color photos of George Gershwin and this is one of them. Here he is on a trip to Mexico with Frieda Kahlo and Diego Rivera.

## *Song and Story*

### THE MAN I LOVE

"The Man I Love" is that rare Gershwin brothers song that achieved fame away from the lights of Broadway. Not that there wasn't a concerted effort to use the song in a show. It was written for the Fred and Adele Astaire vehicle *Lady, Be Good!*, but cut in Philadelphia. In 1927, it was inserted into the score of *Strike Up the Band* (as "The Girl I Love") but that show closed out of town. Its final stage appearance was in *Rosalie* (1928), where it was sung by Marilyn Miller, but again it was cut before the show reached Broadway. Lady Mountbatten introduced the song, by then published, to the haut monde in England and it soon conquered the continent, too. Finally, America woke up to the song and it became a hit in the States in the thirties.

### LET'S CALL THE WHOLE THING OFF

One day in 1937, Ira Gershwin was speaking to his brother-in-law, English Strunsky, who was telling him that the local New Jersey farms didn't understand when Strunsky said "to-mah-to" rather than "to-may-to." Ira complained in turn that Strunsky's sister, Leonore, insisted that the proper pronunciation was "eye-ther" while Ira said "ee-ther." Pretentious or not, the Strunskys' affected pronunciation led to one of the greatest songs in the popular repertoire.

# Asides

George Gershwin was always ashamed that he couldn't write hits of the magnitude of Harry Warren.

Vincent Youmans and Ira Gershwin asked producer E. Ray Goetz for $15 a week for both writers for the songs in *Piccadilly to Broadway*. Goetz told Youmans, "Get the hell out."

The lyrics to "Do, Do, Do" from *Oh, Kay!* were written in half an hour by Ira before going out to dinner with his fiancée and his brother, George.

The Theatre Guild, producers of *Porgy and Bess*, wanted Kern and Hammerstein to write the score and Al Jolson to star.

George was a mentor to the young Burton Lane and encouraged his entry into songwriting.

## THE GREAT SONGS

**1926** I've Got the Girl; Wistful and Blue; Pretty Lips

**1927** I'm Coming Virginia; My Blue Heaven

**1928** Ol' Man River; You Took Advantage of Me; Let's Do It; Makin' Whoopee; I'll Get By

**1929** Great Day; My Kinda Love; Can't We Be Friends; If I Had a Talking Picture of You; S'posin

**1930** A Bench in the Park; Three Little Words; Happy Feet; Them There Eyes; Song of the Dawn; You Brought a New Kind of Love to Me

**1931** I Surrender Dear; Just One More Chance; Out of Nowhere; Temptation; Sweet and Lovely; Where the Blue of the Night; Just a Gigolo

**1932** Dinah (with the Mills Brothers); Here Lies Love; St. Louis Blues; Lawd, You Made the Night Too Long (with the Boswell Sisters); Please; Shine (with the Mills Brothers); Sweet Georgia Brown; Some of These Days; Just an Echo in the Valley; Sweet Sue; Just You

**1933** Learn to Croon; Shadow Waltz; Moonstruck; Did You Ever See a Dream Walking?; Thanks; I've Got the World on a String; Temptation

**1934** June in January; Little Dutch Mill; With Every Breath I Take; Someday Sweetheart; Love Is Just Around the Corner; Love in Bloom

**1935** It's Easy to Remember; Red Sails in the Sunset; Soon; I Wished on the Moon; Moonburn

**1936** I'm an Old Cowhand; Pennies from Heaven; The Way You Look Tonight; A Fine Romance

**1937** Bob White; It's the Natural Thing to Do; The Moon Got in My Eyes; Basin Street Blues; Too Marvelous for Words; Sweet Leilani

**1938** Alexander's Ragtime Band Small Fry; I've Got a Pocketful of Dreams; I Cried For You; Mr. Gallagher and Mr. Shean (with Johnny Mercer); Moon of Manakoora; You Must Have Been a Beautiful Baby (with Bob Crosby)

**1939** Ciribiribin (with the Andrews Sisters); Home on the Range; Stardust; Wrap Your Trouble in Dreams; What's New; Alla En El Rancho Grande; Deep Purple

**1940** Devil May Care; Mister Meadowlark (with Johnny Mercer); Sierra Sue; On Behalf of the Visiting Firemen (with Johnny Mercer); Only Forever; When Day Is Done; Tumbling Tumbleweeds

**1941** White Christmas; Danny Boy; You Are My Sunshine

**1942** Deep in the Heart of Texas; Skylark; Moonlight Becomes You; Silent Night; Be Careful It's My Heart; Blues in the Night; Wait 'Til the Sun Shines, Nellie (with Mary Martin); Nellie

**1943** I'll Be Home for Christmas; Pistol Packin' Mama (with the Andrews Sisters); Sunday, Monday or Always; Poinciana; Sanat Claus is Comin' to Town; September Song; People Will Say We're in Love

**1944** A Hot Time in the Town of Berlin (with the Andrews Sisters); Amor; Don't Fence Me In; I Love You; I'll Be Seeing You; Put It There Pal (with Bob Hope); The Road to Morocco (with Bob Hope); San Fernando Valley; Too-Ra-Loo-Ra-Loo-Ral; Swingin' on a Star; Accentuate the Positive

**1945** I Can't Begin to Tell You; MacNamara's Band; It's Been a Long, Long Time; Siboney; All of My Life; Sioux City Sue; You Belong to My Heart

**1946** Route 66; South America; Take It Away (with the Andrews Sisters); Blue Skies; All By Myself; A Gal in Calico

**1947** The Whiffenpoof Song; But Beautiful; Imagination; Now Is the Hour; Galaway Bay; If I Loved You

# Tin Pan Alley

Tin Pan Alley has always been as much a state of mind as an actual location, encompassing the universe of American music publishers, songwriters, performers, vaudeville chains, Broadway producers, sheet music sellers, song pluggers, piano roll makers, minstrel performers, and those in the recording industry. Of course there was an actual area of New York dubbed Tin Pan Alley, a few square blocks of midtown Manhattan where most of the key players in the music business had their offices and studios. But the name came to include publishers based in Milwaukee, Chicago, Boston, and St. Louis, and even came to refer to "the road," a series of theaters across the country where shows and artists tried out. The music itself was an amalgam of jazz influences from New Orleans, Kansas City, and Chicago; the blues of Memphis; the plaintive ballads of the Old South; and more. The musical traditions of blacks, Jews, the Irish, and the church all fed Tin Pan Alley.

As for the geographic Tin Pan Alley: New York, like most world capitals, has always had neighborhoods devoted to specific businesses. There is the financial district, the theatrical district, the garment district, the flower district, and so on. Its many entertainment districts have moved up Broadway decade by decade, along with the population. The first center was near City Hall, on Park Row. It was there, at the corner of Ann Street, that Barnum built his great museum. Lower Manhattan and the Bowery were alive with theaters, bawdy houses, bars, and other temptations. By the last decades of the nineteenth century, Union Square was the focal point of entertainment, with theaters such as Tony Pastor's Music Hall on 14th Street and Third Avenue, drawing customers in to see and hear the latest shows.

By the turn of the century, there were a few theaters around 23rd Street and Sixth Avenue, but most of the district had progressed as far as 34th Street and Herald Square. The old Metropolitan Opera House, the Empire Theater, and other halls brought in the patrons. Theatrical organizations, such as the Lamb's Club, followed, occupying a site next to Keen's Chop House, a restaurant that still features hundreds of theatrical broadsides on its walls.

The *New York Herald*, housed in the square that bears its name, assigned songwriter Monroe Rosenfeld to write a series of articles on the music business then taking root in the neighborhood. Rosenfeld began his odyssey at the music publishing office of Harry Von Tilzer at West 28th Street between Fifth and Sixth Avenues, proceeding  vdown 28th Street, and as he walked he heard hundreds of pianos through open windows, pounding out the hits of the day, future hits, and songs that would never be heard again. This cacophony reminded Rosenfeld of tin pans clattering together—so he dubbed the street Tin Pan Alley.

Once Oscar Hammerstein had built his first theater, the Olympia, in Longacre Square and the subway opened in 1904, Tin Pan Alley came along, too. The northern end of Times Square, from West 46th to W. 52nd Street, housed most of the music publishers. At the southern end, on the southwestern corner of 47th and Broadway, was the Gaiety Building (still standing today), home to black music publishers. The Exchange Building on West 45th Street was home to many of the top music publishers.

Though there were a few theaters built around Columbus Circle at Broadway and West 59th Street, for all intents and purposes the theatrical district has remained centered in Times Square up to the present day.

With so many publishers in the neighborhood, it made sense that songwriters should have their own building and so, in 1930, the Brill Building opened at the corner of West 49th Street and Broadway. Twenty years later, when young songwriters like Ellie Greenwich, Lesley Gore, and the team of Barry Mann and Cynthia Weil were working out of the building, writing the next big song for the next young star, the building was dubbed, Teen Pan Alley.

Today, many publishing companies are owned by movie studios or big conglomerates, and their offices are all over New York and the world. But Tin Pan Alley still exists as an idea, if not an actual location. ◇

# Asides

*George Washington, Jr.*, a patriotic musical by George M. Cohan with guess-who in the title role, had its New York premiere at the Herald Square Theater, where it ran for only ninety performances but left an enduring impression with its hit song, "You're a Grand Old Flag." This was the first number written specifically for a stage musical, to sell more than a million copies of sheet music.

**ABOVE:** The Witmark Building at 144–146 37th Street was the first building owned by a Tin Pan Alley publisher.

**OPPOSITE PAGE:** The T.B. Harms building at Broadway and 42nd Street in 1910. Note the first Broadway Theater down the block.

# Gordon & Revel

## THE GREAT SONGS

**ABOVE:** Mack Gordon and Harry Revel at work and at play.

**LEFT:** Enjoying the fruits of their labor! Note that the cigar was left back at the office!

Composer and lyricist Mack Gordon racked up one of the most impressive Hollywood songwriting careers ever, earning nine Oscar nominations including six in a row from 1940 to 1945. He finally won for "You'll Never Know."

He was born Morris Gittler in Warsaw, Poland, on June 21, 1904, and his family soon immigrated to the United States, settling first in Brooklyn and then the Bronx. Gordon joined a minstrel show as a boy soprano and later played in vaudeville as a comedian and singer, before giving it all up for songwriting.

He wrote his first stage scores in 1925, finally hitting the jackpot with the song "Time on My Hands" for the 1930 show, *Smiles*. Gordon got a preview of his future collaborator Harry Warren when they wrote the song "There Will Be a Girl (There Will Be a Girl)" for the 1931 show, *Meet My Sister*. But then Gordon teamed up with English émigré Harry Revel in 1931, and they followed the westward exodus to Hollywood in 1933.

Gordon and Revel became an instant sensation in Hollywood, writing scores that included 1933's *Broadway Thru a Keyhole* and *Sitting Pretty*. The latter contained their first Hollywood hit, "Did You Ever See a Dream Walking?" They stayed with Paramount Pictures until 1936, when they began writing for Twentieth Century-Fox, most notably on Shirley Temple's pictures. Once in a while Gordon would supply his own music, but mostly he collaborated with Revel.

The team broke up in 1939 and Gordon found a new writing partner almost immediately, his old acquaintance, Harry Warren. They worked on a series of pictures starring the Glenn Miller Orchestra and these films, including *Sun Valley Serenade* (1941) and *Orchestra Wives* (1942), provided both the band and the songwriters with some of their greatest hits. Among the film scores Warren and Gordon wrote for Fox were *Tin Pan Alley* (1940), *The Great American Broadcast* (1941), *Weekend in Havana* (1941), *Iceland* and *Springtime in the Rockies*, both in 1942, *Hello, Frisco, Hello* (1943), *Pin-Up Girl* (1944), and *Billy Rose's Diamond Horseshoe* and *The Dolly Sisters* (both 1945).

In 1946 Gordon worked with Josef Myrow on the score for *Three Little Girls in Blue* and for *Mother Wore Tights*. He rejoined Warren at MGM for Judy Garland's last film with the studio, 1950's *Summer Stock*. Beyond that, his work failed to make much of an impression on the Hit Parade. His final score was for the Eddie Fisher and Debbie Reynolds songfest *Bundle of Joy* (1956—Josef Myrow).

Gordon died in New York City on March 1, 1959. ◈

E. Y. "Yip" Harburg was Broadway's most complex lyricist. At once outspoken, liberal, and uncompromising, Harburg was also sentimental, romantic, and humorous. He was a man of strong moral and political beliefs who exhibited great tolerance toward those whose politics differed from his own. He believed in the power of lyrics, and used that power to move audiences both emotionally and artistically.

Harburg was born in New York City on April 8, 1898. He began writing lyrics while still at New York City's Townsend Harris High School, where he toiled on the school newspaper alongside schoolmate Ira Gershwin. While he was at City College, Harburg's work was published in Franklin P. Adams's influential column, "The Conning Tower." After graduating, Harburg opened an electrical supply store, which failed at the onset of the Depression. He then followed in the footsteps of Gershwin and became a lyricist. Harburg's first partner was composer Jay Gorney. After contributing songs to a succession of musical revues, the team struck gold with "Brother Can You Spare a Dime?," written for a show called *Americana* (1932). The song became the unofficial anthem of the Depression.

Harburg scored hits in three early revues: *Walk a Little Faster* (1932), featured Vernon Duke and Harburg's "April in Paris," and people couldn't believe that Harburg had never actually visited Paris but that his inspiration had come from a travel brochure; The *Ziegfeld Follies of 1934* is credited with a Harburg and Duke score, including the successful "What Is There to Say?," although it also included the songs of many other writers; and for *Life Begins at 8:40* (1934), Harburg teamed with his old friend Ira Gershwin. Along with Harold Arlen, they came up with such hits as "Let's Take a Walk Around the Block," "You're a Builder Upper," and "Fun to Be Fooled."

Beginning in 1935, Harburg devoted himself to film scores. He continued to collaborate with Harold Arlen in Hollywood while also working with Johnny Green, Walter Donaldson, Jerome Kern, Burton Lane, and Jay Gorney on occasion. The year 1939 turned out to be a banner one in which Harburg and Arlen scored the Marx Brothers extravaganza *At the Circus,* including "Lydia the Tattooed Lady," and what might be the finest score written for film, *The Wizard of Oz*. This was Harburg and Arlen's first work for Judy Garland. In 1943, the team wrote a new score for the film version of *Cabin in the Sky,* featuring "Happiness Is a Thing Called Joe," and "Ain't It de Truth." The latter, sung by Lena Horne, was cut from the film and recycled by the team for their Lena Horne Broadway vehicle, *Jamaica*.

*Hooray for What!* (1937), written in collaboration with Arlen, was Harburg's first book show. Songs included "Down with Love," "Moanin' in the Mornin'," and "In the Shade of the New Apple Tree." This antiwar musical gave Harburg ample opportunity to express his pacifist leanings. He then explored both race relations and women's rights in the brilliant *Bloomer Girl* (1944), which included such hits as "Right as the Rain," "The Eagle and Me," "T'morra T'morra," and "Evelina." Harburg was honing his ability to entertain even as he made social and political statements.

His greatest success was certainly *Finian's Rainbow* (1947), written in collaboration with Burton Lane (and Fred Saidy, with whom he wrote the libretto). *Finian* has one of theater's finest scores, including "How Are Things in Glocca Morra," "Look to the Rainbow," "Old Devil Moon," and "When I'm Not Near the Girl I Love." His associates felt that Harburg, who at times could be magical and mischievous himself, bore more than a passing resemblance to the character of Og the leprechaun.

When Harburg was blacklisted and couldn't find work in Hollywood, he turned his attention to Broadway, producing a rare failure in *Flahooley* (1951). However, the score, with music by Sammy Fain, does provide some excellent songs, including "He's Only Wonderful," "The World Is Your Balloon," and "Here's to Your Illusions." Artistically, *Jamaica* (1957) suffered because it was too much a vehicle for its star, Lena Horne, but the Arlen/Harburg score includes such fine songs as "I Don't Think I'll End It All Today," "Push de Button," and "Napoleon." Harburg tackled the Lysistrata legend for his Broadway show *The Happiest Girl in the World* (1961). The music was adapted from the works of Jacques Offenbach, to which Harburg added lyrics that perfectly reflected his view of the world. Although some thought Harburg's unofficial theme song was, "When I'm Not Near the Girl I Love (I Love the Girl I'm Near)" from *Finian's Rainbow*, those who knew him best felt his theme might be "Adrift on a Star."

In 1963, Harburg and Arlen wrote a new score for Judy Garland (Arlen had written the music for *A Star Is Born* in the meantime), for the 1962 animated film, *Gay Purr-ee*, and followed it with another song for her, the title song of 1963's *I Could Go on Singing.*

Harburg's last Broadway show, *Darling of the Day* (1968), was written with Jule Styne. The show starred Vincent Price and Patricia Routledge, whose singing voices did not serve the score well. Although it was a failure, Harburg and Styne considered it their *My Fair Lady*. And while it may not be as wonderful as the Lerner and Loewe show, it does have an excellent but sadly unappreciated score.

Harburg died on March 5, 1981, in Hollywood. ◆

## Song and Story

### BROTHER CAN YOU SPARE A DIME?

Harburg and composer Jay Gorney (then Paramount Pictures' East Coast music director) were strolling through Central Park when a beggar asked, "Buddy, can you spare a dime?" Substituting the word "brother" for "buddy," Harburg had a classic lyric—a symbol of the great Depression.

### ADRIFT ON A STAR

Harburg was working on the "Barcarolle" lyric and having trouble with it. His wife had stepped out of the house for a few hours, so when he came home, there was no dinner on the table, but she'd left him a note. She knew he was working on a very tough lyric and she wrote, "Don't worry, I know you're a man who's always valiant enough to always swim against the tide and keep your eyes on the universal stars and your hand on the eternal plow. It'll come to you and you will find one meatball in the icebox." So he thought, "Why can't the boat in the song, instead of being a gondola, be the earth—which is a universal boat that is roaming around in space?" From there, he wrote the lyric. He commented, "I know why I'm here. I'm here because I'm on a boat. I'm a little astronaut in a great big astronautic vehicle called the world. Here we are adrift on a star."

## First Person

Johnny Mercer on E. Y. Harburg: In making me a kind of assistant during the formation of the New Americana score, he taught me how to work at lyric writing. I had been a dilettante at it, trying hard but very undisciplined, waiting for the muse to smile. Yip taught me to go seeking her, never letting a day or a work session go by without something to show for it. Often the songs went unpublished, but there were songs. Finished. Complete. Work done.

Harburg on his treatment at MGM in Hollywood: Every lyric was fingerprinted and the history of it taken and the microscopes were applied to every word to see what hidden meanings there were and I lost many a job and people were afraid to write with me. They used to call you in at Metro and say, "Look it, we don't want any messages in the stuff you write. We like your stuff, we don't like your messages." They had one big cliché, "Messages are for Western Union." They would have kicked me out if it wasn't for the fact that I was able to write humorous stuff and things that made the thing work.

during that era, most of them just kept right on with parties at the Fitzgeralds and little puffy love plots. But I think I had a predisposition to feeling for the underdog. I grew up in the slums. I know what it is to work in a sweatshop. I know what it is to have your father come home from a sweatshop after working twelve hours a day and greeting him. I know what it is for a neighbor to come and ask for a piece of bread and what it is to have your rooms emptied by the sheriff and be put out because you can't pay the rent. When you know that, you also start thinking about causes, what is the cause of those things. Then you get interested in reading. Then you begin taking courses that will give you an insight into the reason for this poverty, for this kind of thing. When you come out, if you're an artist of any kind, then you're certainly going to apply the thing that impressed you most as a child. So that you make a hook-up between cause and effect. It will work inside you. Your creative juices will be working around the thing that either has aggravated you or made you hostile or made you philosophical and wise, that you want to educate others about it or that you want to laugh at it.

## Asides

Harold Arlen once called Burton Lane at home begging him to come down to the theater where *Jamaica* was previewing. When he arrived, Lane found Arlen crying, he was so frustrated at Harburg's megalomania.

Harburg on writing about causes: Harold Arlen met Oscar Hammerstein in the Astor Hotel while we were in rehearsal. Hammerstein said to Harold, "Yipper's such a good writer, why does he always have to get mixed up with such things as 'Hooray for What!' and war? The stage is not a place for proselytizing and propaganda. The stage should be used for entertainment." Now this was Oscar Hammerstein, a nice, human, decent, wonderful guy.

Everybody thought that I was spoiling the protocol or in some way hurting the theatre by representing social causes in my musicals. I really felt honestly that like Shaw, Gilbert and Sullivan, Swift, satirists, I was only doing an honest job of educating and getting people thinking about good things.

Always the political and social climate affect the writer. The writer is not ever living in a void. He's living in a live, vibrant, vigorous world and he tries to reflect that world around him. Of course, you must have some predisposition to react to that world. There were many chaps in 1930 who were still writing about castles in the air or palaces in Long Island. If you go through the list of songs and the list of shows that were done

**ABOVE LEFT:** Jack Haley shakes hands with Martha Raye while Harburg smiles at the camera.

# Foreign Influences

Ever since Erno Rapee became a leading composer of silent films in the 1920s, composers have been adapting foreign songs into American popular standards. Rapee used a waltz he had written in Hungary in 1913 as the basis for a theme in the 1926 motion picture *What Price Glory?* That very same year, lyricist Lew Pollack added English lyrics to the theme and called it "Charmaine." Maurice Yvain and Albert Willmetz's "Mon Homme" became "My Man" in 1921, with the addition of an American lyric by playwright Channing Pollock. In 1930, Irving Caesar put a lyric to Leonello Casucci's "Schöner Gigolo" (with German lyrics by Julius Brammer) to create "Just a Gigolo."

Latin rhythms have long been in favor up north. Nilo Menendez's 1931 hit "Aquellos Ojos Verdes," with a lyric by E. Rivera and E. Woods, became 1941's "Green Eyes" when Jimmy Dorsey recorded it with Bob Eberly and Helen O'Connell. Another Cuban melody became a Tin Pan Alley hit in 1930 when Marion Sunshine and L. Wolfe Gilbert put English words to Moises Simons' "El Manisero" and called it "The Peanut Vendor." Maria Grever was a favorite of American lyricists. Her "Cuando Vuelva a Tu Lado" (1934) was transformed into "What a Difference a Day Makes" by lyricist Stanley Adams. It didn't take much imagination for Vera Bloom to transform Jacob Gade's 1915 tune "Jalousie" into "Jealousy." Dick Manning adapted the 1912 "Valse Tsigane" by F. D. Marchetti, into the 1932 easy-listening favorite, "Fascination."

Charles Trenet and Albert Lasry's "La Mer" (1947) became the hit "Beyond the Sea" with the addition of Jack Lawrence's now-classic lyrics. Lawrence also wrote hits with American composers including "All or Nothing at All" (1939—Arthur Altman), "Sleepy Lagoon" (1940—Eric Coates), "Yes My Darling Daughter (1941), "Tenderly" (1947—Walter Gross) . He also adapted A. Pestalozza's "Ciribiribin" in 1939 with the help of Harry James, "Play Fiddle Play" (1941—Emory Deutsch, Arthur Altman), "Overnight" (1955—Erwin Halletz, Karl Parkes), and "The Poor People of Paris" (1956—Margarite Monnot).

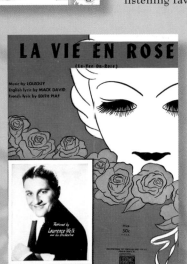

The talented songwriter Ervin Drake scored a hit with "A Room without Windows," from the 1964 musical, *What Makes Sammy Run?* Drake wrote other big hits including "I Believe" (1952—Irvin Graham, Jimmy Shirl, Al Stillman), "Good Morning, Heartache" (1946—Dan Fisher, Irene Higginbotham), and "It Was a Very Good Year (1961)—but many of his most successful songs were based on foreign melodies or instrumentals, including "Perdido" (1942—Juan Tizol, Hans J. Lengfelder), "Tico-Tico" (1943—Zequinha Abreu, A. Oliviera), "Al-Di-La" (1962—Carlo Donada), and "Quando, Quando, Quando" (Elio Cesare, Alberto Testa).

Bob Russell wrote popular hits from scratch as well as adapting instrumentals and foreign tunes. Right off the bat, in 1940, he wrote a hit in each genre. "Busy As a Bee, I'm Buzz, Buzz, Buzzin'" with Joseph Meyer and Carl Sigman and "Frenesi" with Alberto Dominguez and Ray Charles. In 1941, he continued in a South American vein with "Babalu" (Margarita Lecuona) and "Maria Elena" (Lorenzo Barcelata). Russell wrote lyrics to a couple of tunes by Ellington, 1942's "Don't Get Around Much Anymore" and, in 1943, "Do Nothin' Till You Hear from Me." "Dance Ballerina Dance" was a 1947 hit with music by Carl Sigman. With John Brooks Benton, he wrote "You Came a Long Way from St. Louis" (1948). The next year saw "Circus" (Louis Alter) and "Crazy He Calls Me" (Carl Sigman). In 1951, Russell collaborated with Illinois Jacquet and Sir C. Thomas on "Just When We're Falling in Love." Russell surprised everyone with his 1969 hit, "He Ain't Heavy…He's My Brother," written with Bobby Scott.

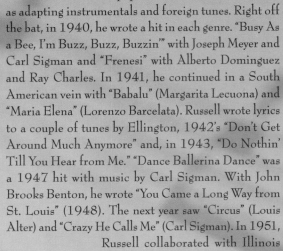

Mitchell Parish

Mitchell Parish also specialized in writing lyrics to established instrumentals and foreign hits. His first hit was "Sweet Lorraine" in 1928, based on an instrumental by Cliff Burwell. Parish at first rejected a 1929 tune by Hoagy Carmichael but then relented and wrote "Star Dust," once the most recorded song of all time. Though Irving Mills (who never wrote a lyric in his life) and Duke Ellington put their names on the 1931 hit, "Mood Indigo," it was Barney Bigard and Parish who actually wrote the song. The Boswell Sisters had a 1932 hit with "Sentimental Gentleman from Georgia" with music by Frank Perkins. That same year Perkins and Parish wrote the Cab Calloway hit "The Scat Song." The next year, Parish and Hoagy Carmichael wrote "One Morning in May." Ellington had a piece of band material for which Parish added lyrics and the result was 1933's "Sophisticated Lady." 1934's "Hands Across the Table" was written with Jean Delettre for the film, *Continental Varieties*. Perkins and Parish reteamed for 1934's "Stars Fell on Alabama." Matty Malneck and Frank Signorelli's 1935 tune "Park Avenue Fantasy" became "Stairway to the Stars" when Parish added lyrics in 1939. Another instrumental, 1925's "Riverboat Shuffle," this time by Hoagy Carmichael, became a hit all over again in 1939 with Parish's lyric. Peter De Rose wrote a lovely tune in 1934 that became a bigger hit five years later as "Deep Purple." "Moonlight Serenade" (1939) was a Glenn Miller hit with Parish lyrics. In 1950, Parish got on a Leroy Anderson jag with "The Syncopated Clock," "Serenata," and "Sleigh Ride" but the instrumentals prevailed. ❖

# Victor Herbert

The most important and prolific of the early composers of musical comedy and operetta, Victor Herbert was a major influence on an entire generation of musicians and composers. His thirty-year career included many triumphs, including forty-four complete scores for the musical and operetta stage and two operas, *Natoma* in 1911 and *Madeleine* in 1913. The operas were not successful, although their music has won some admirers today. Herbert also wrote many orchestral works, including "A Suite of Serenades" for the Paul Whiteman Aeolian Hall concert, at which George Gershwin's "Rhapsody in Blue" also premiered.

Herbert was a portly figure known for his generosity, business sense, appreciation of fine food and drink, and love for Ireland. His 1892 orchestral work "Irish Rhapsody" contains some of his most heartfelt melodies. He was also a staunch supporter of composers' rights. His suit against Shanley's Restaurant set the stage for the establishment of the American Society for Composers, Authors and Publishers (ASCAP).

Herbert was born in Dublin on February 1, 1859. When his father died, his mother remarried and the family moved to Stuttgart, where he attended Stuttgart Conservatory and studied with Bernhard Cossman and Max Seifrz. He spent many years as a cellist with German and Austrian symphony orchestras, including five years with the Court Orchestra of Stuttgart.

After immigrating to the United States in October 1886, Herbert became a cello soloist at the Metropolitan Opera and played in the symphony orchestras of Anton Seidl and Theodore Thomas. He soon graduated to conductor, first with the 22nd National Guard Band, and then, from 1898 to 1904, with the Pittsburgh Symphony. In 1898 he performed his own work, Concerto No. 2 for Cello and Orchestra, Op.30, with the New York Philharmonic.

The group known as the Bostonians had been founded in 1879 as the Boston Ideal Opera Company, dedicated to presenting Gilbert and Sullivan operettas. In 1894, they commissioned Herbert to compose the score for the operetta, *Prince Ananias*. After its success Herbert collaborated with Harry B. Smith on the hit *The Wizard of the Nile*. Herbert would write thirteen scores in all with Smith, who matched Herbert's prodigious output but not his talent. Many critics felt that Herbert never had a collaborator worthy of his talents. Although many of his scores are famous today, their libretti and lyrics are nearly all dated or second-rate.

Herbert's shows include *The Gold Bug* (1896—Glen MacDonough), *The Serenade* (1897—Harry B. Smith), *The Idol's Eye* (1897—Harry B. Smith), and *The Fortune Teller* (1898—Harry B. Smith). The following year, three Herbert shows debuted: *Cyrano de Bergerac* (Harry B. Smith), *The Singing Girl* (Harry B. Smith), and *The Ameer* (Frederic Rankin and Kirke La Shelle). In 1900, Herbert and Smith's *The Viceroy* followed.

In 1903, the first of Herbert's masterpieces opened. *Babes in Toyland*, with book and lyrics by Glen MacDonough, remains a favorite more than one hundred years after its premiere. Herbert followed that triumph with *Babette* (1903—Harry B. Smith). MacDonough and Herbert reteamed for *It Happened in Nordland* (1904). Other hits in Herbert's repertoire, many of which are often revived, include the classics *Mlle. Modiste* (1905—Henry Blossom), *The Red Mill* (1906—Henry Blossom), *Naughty Marietta* (1910—Rida Johnson Young), *The Lady and the Slipper* (1912—James O'Dea), *Sweethearts* (1913—Robert B. Smith), and *The Princess Pat* (1915—Henry Blossom).

On the day after Herbert's *The Debutante* opened in 1914, Irving Berlin's modern musical comedy, *Watch Your Step*, opened around the corner. The operetta's days were numbered. Producers Charles Dillingham and Florenz Ziegfeld joined forces to produce *The Century Girl* (1916), which contained songs by both Herbert and Berlin. In one scene entitled "The Music Lesson," both Herbert and Berlin were portrayed onstage. Herbert's hit, "Kiss Me Again," was featured in the scene and Berlin wrote a countermelody to the tune.

*Miss 1917* contained a few Herbert tunes but the majority of the score was by Jerome Kern. Herbert's next shows were less successful and he was eventually relegated to writing incidental music for the *Ziegfeld Follies*.

Herbert died on May 26, 1924, but he would have one more standard to his name. In 1939 a contest was held for a lyric to go with a newly discovered Herbert tune. The winner was Al Dubin and the song was "Indian Summer," today a jazz staple. ◆

## GREAT SONGS

**1898** Always Do As People Say You Should; The Gypsy Love Song; Romany Life (all lyrics by Harry B. Smith)

**1903** Don't Cry Bo-Peep; I Can't Do the Sum; March of the Toys; My Castle in Spain; Toyland (all lyrics by Glen MacDonough)

**1904** Absinthe Frappe; Al Fresco (both lyrics by Glen MacDonough)

**1905** I Want What I Want When I Want It; Kiss Me Again (If I Were on the Stage); A Woman Is Only a Woman but a Good Cigar Is a Smoke (all lyrics by Harry B. Smith)

**1906** Every Day Is Ladies Day with Me; Mignonette; In Old New York (The Streets of New York); The Isle of My Dreams; Moonbeams; When You're Pretty and the World Is Fair (all lyrics by Henry Blossom)

**1910** Ah, Sweet Mystery of Life; I'm Falling in Love with Someone; Italian Street Song; 'Neath the Southern Moon; Tramp! Tramp! Tramp! (all lyrics by Rida Johnson Young)

**1913** The Angelus; Game of Love; I Might Be Your Once-in-a-While; Pretty As a Picture; Sweethearts; Wooden Shoes (all lyrics by Robert B. Smith)

**1914** When You're Away (lyric by Henry Blossom)

**1915** Neopolitan Love Song (Sweet One How My Heart Is Yearning); Two Laughing Irish Eyes (both lyrics by Henry Blossom)

**1916** Eileen, Allan Asthore (lyric by Henry Blossom)

**1922** A Kiss in the Dark (lyric by B. G. De Sylva)

**1939** Indian Summer (lyric by Al Dubin)

# Jerry Herman

A tunesmith in the old-fashioned sense, whose smash hits are the definition of American musical comedy Jerry Herman is the most famous and successful songwriter never to fully receive his critical due as a master composer and lyricist. With the possible exception of Sir Andrew Lloyd Webber, Herman may be the only contemporary Broadway songwriter whose name is recognized by the general public, due to the success of a mere three shows: *Hello, Dolly!*, *Mame*, and *La Cage aux Folles*. His works are glitzy, upbeat extravaganzas, long on energy and the kind of catchy tunes that the audience is sure to hum on the way out. That is what is expected of a Jerry Herman show—and that expectation has both helped and hurt him as he has bravely attempted to write deeper, more psychologically acute works that extend the boundaries of musical theater.

Herman was born at the Polyclinic Hospital on 50th Street in Manhattan, and his mother's room looked out at Broadway's Winter Garden Theater. She once told Herman that she considered it a sign that one day he would have a hit there. Tragically, his mother died just as his career was taking off, so she never had the chance to share his great success. Still, she implanted in Herman a zest for life and an optimism that pervades his work.

He was educated at the University of Miami and the Parsons School of Design. His first score was for the off-Broadway revue, *I Feel Wonderful* (1954), which started life at the University of Miami before moving to New York. He followed it with another revue, *Nightcap* (1958), which employed the talents of Charles Nelson Reilly, Dody Goodman, and Phyllis Newman. Another off-Broadway revue, *Parade*, followed in 1960.

The modest success that Herman had thus far enjoyed didn't portend the enormous impact of his Broadway book shows. The first was *Milk and Honey* (1960), starring Robert Weede and Molly Picon. He followed the Off-Broadway misstep, *Madame Aphrodite* (1961), with the blockbuster *Hello, Dolly!* (1964), which became one of the most successful musicals in Broadway history, racking up 2,844 performances and spawning many revivals.

Herman's next show proved almost as popular. *Mame* opened on May 24, 1966, to extraordinary acclaim. Herman's score is first-rate, ably assisted by the fine orchestrations of Philip J. Lang; and in the lead role, Angela Lansbury proved she could make a successful transition from Hollywood to the musical stage. Lansbury, Herman, and librettists Lawrence and Lee

teamed up again for *Dear World*, a musical version of Jean Giraudoux's *The Madwoman of Chaillot*. Audiences expected another razzmatazz Herman show, but *Dear World* was a more delicate, serious piece (albeit blown out of proportion in producer Alexander Cohen's lavish production).

*Mack and Mabel* (1974) followed, and, despite having what some consider to be Herman's most mature score as well as the talents of Bernadette Peters and Robert Preston, the show played only sixty-five performances—a particularly sad failure. Herman's next show fared even worse: *The Grand Tour* (1979) was an ill-conceived vehicle for Joel Grey, and to his credit, Herman had to be talked into the undertaking.

After three failures in a row, critics proclaimed Jerry Herman's career finished. Skeptics pointed to the success of *Hello, Dolly!* and *Mame* as flukes and suggested that Herman's style wasn't suited to the supposedly more sophisticated Broadway of the 1980s. But on August 21, 1983, Herman burst back onto Broadway with *La Cage Aux Folles*, a huge hit in the style of his previous masterworks, but with a powerful message embedded beneath the farcical elements of the story. Herman had achieved his goal of working serious themes into popular entertainment, and he'd gotten the recipe just right. After the triumphant opening night, he walked out onto Times Square and proclaimed that he would never again write a Broadway musical. Unfortunately for his fans and musical theater history, he has so far kept his promise. ◆

**ABOVE:** What makes you think this is a staged photo? Just because Jerry Herman is holding the sheet music upside down?

**INSET:** Angela Lansbury and Frankie Michaels in the magnificent, memorable *Mame*.

## THE GREAT SONGS

**1960** Jolly Theatrical Season; Two a Day

**1961** Let's Not Waste a Moment; Shalom; There's No Reason in the World

**1964** Before the Parade Passes By; Hello, Dolly!; It Only Takes a Moment; It Takes a Woman; Ribbons Down My Back; To Be Alone with You; Too Charming

**1966** Bosom Buddies; If He Walked Into My Life; It's Today; Mame; My Best Girl; Open a New Window

**1969** And I Was Beautiful; I Don't Want to Know; A Sensible Woman; The Tea Party

**1974** I Won't Send Roses; Tap Your Troubles Away; Time Heals Everything; Wherever He Ain't

**1979** I'll Be Here Tomorrow; One Extraordinary Thing

**1980** Just Go to the Movies

**1983** The Best of Times; I Am What I Am; A Little More Mascara; Song on the Sand

**1996** Almost Young; We Don't Go Together at All

# W. C. Handy

orn in Florence, Alabama, on November 16, 1873, W. C. Handy brought blues to the mainstream in one stroke, with his immortal composition, "St. Louis Blues." Handy played in a series of bands as a child, trooped around the South with Mahara's Minstrels, and played at the Chicago World's Fair in 1893.

In 1912, he wrote "The Memphis Blues." Realizing that he could greatly benefit by becoming his own publisher, he joined with his friend, Harry Pace, to form Pace and Handy Music Company. In 1914, he published "St. Louis Blues," partially based on a section of his "Jogo Blues," written the year before. The song was not an instant success; it was first recorded in 1916 by Prince's Band and the first vocal recording was by Marion Harris in 1920. When the Original Dixieland Jazz Band recorded it 1921, the song became a smash hit, bringing the blues into the popular song tradition for the first time.

Handy's other compositions included "Yellow Dog Blues" (1914), "Joe Turner Blues" and "Hesitating Blues" (both 1915), "Ole Miss Rag" and "Beale Street," (both 1916), and "The Kaiser's Got the Blues" (1917). In 1921, Handy wrote another blues standard, "Aunt Hagar's Blues," and a beautiful ballad first known as "Loveless Love" and later changed to "Careless Love."

Handy died in New York on March 29, 1958, the same year as the release of a somewhat fictionalized Hollywood biopic of his life, *St. Louis Blues*, starring Nat King Cole.◆

## Song and Story

### THE MEMPHIS BLUES

Handy supported candidate Edward H. Crump in the 1909 Memphis mayoral race and, to help inspire black voters, he wrote a campaign song in the blues style while seated at Pee Wee's Saloon on Beale Street. The song and the campaign were both successful. In 1912, Handy returned to the tune and rewrote it as a piano blues number, calling it "The Memphis Blues" and publishing it himself, making it the first published blues piece.

Later that year the Theron A. Bennett Company in New York purchased all rights to the song for $50. They hired George A. Norton to write a lyric and, in 1913, the sheet music was a big success. In 1931, the new copyright holder, the Joe Rose Music Company, hired Peter De Rose and Charles Tobias to write a new lyric.

### ST. LOUIS BLUES

Having made only $50 from the successful "Memphis Blues," Handy looked around for a suitable subject for another blues song. He remembered a time a few years earlier, when he was "unshaven, wanting even a decent meal, and standing before the lighted saloon in St. Louis, without a shirt under my frayed coat." He also recalled a "woman whose pain seemed even greater. She had tried to take the edge off her grief by heavy drinking, but it hadn't worked. Stumbling along the poorly lighted street, she muttered as she walked, 'My man's got a heart like a rock cast in the sea.' By the time I had finished all this heavy thinking and remembering, I figured it was time to get something down on paper, so I wrote, 'I hate to see de evenin' sun go down.' If you ever had to sleep on the cobbles down by the river in St. Louis, you'll understand the complaint."

# Joe Howard

oe Howard was born in New York City on February 12, 1867. A precocious lad, he ran away from home when he was only eight years old. Somehow, he was able to support himself by selling papers and doing odd jobs. After a short career singing in saloons, Howard went into vaudeville at age eleven, as a boy soprano, and later joined a theatrical stock company. At seventeen, he and Ida Emerson, the second of his nine wives, teamed up to form a song and dance act, appearing at Tony Pastor's Music Hall singing a song they wrote, "Hello, Ma Baby." Five years later Howard wrote the sequel, "Goodbye My Lady Love," which Ida introduced. Howard, Frank R. Adams, and Will M. Hough became a songwriting team, creating many musicals for the Chicago market. Their biggest hit was "I Wonder Who's Kissing Her Now," which premiered in 1909's *A Prince of Tonight*. It turns out, however, that Harold Orlob actually wrote the music to the tune, not Howard. Howard died in Chicago on May 19, 1961. ◆

**Today, most people know Joseph E. Howard, if at all, from the Warner Brothers cartoon, "One Froggy Night" where the vaudevillian frog sings and dances to "Hello, Ma Baby!" A fine legacy!**

# Jerome Kern

Along with George M. Cohan, Jerome Kern was one of the first Broadway composers to give the musical an American feeling. Cohan brought vaudeville and music hall influences to the musical, while Kern was more in touch with its European roots, infusing the European operetta form with a real American sound. Though eventually overshadowed by the likes of George Gershwin and Richard Rodgers, Kern was the favorite composer of the generation that directly succeeded him: Gershwin and Rodgers themselves were in awe of Kern's talents and worked to emulate his success.

Born in New York City, the young Jerome Kern attended the New York College of Music. At the turn of the century he traveled to England and Germany, where he discovered the great operetta traditions. Upon his return to the United States in 1904, Kern found work at the T. B. Harms music publishing firm.

As he was the transitional figure between European operetta and American musical comedy, it is telling that Kern's first jobs on Broadway were interpolating songs into the American versions of foreign musicals. As an American, Kern was influenced by the harmonies and rhythms of America's classical and popular writers, and those influences provided a springboard for his own talents. In 1904, with the help of T. B. Harms, Kern provided his first interpolations, into an English show called *Mr. Wix of Wickham*, starring famed female impersonator Julian Eltinge. His next interpolation, "How'd You Like to Spoon with Me?" with a lyric by Edward Laska, was written for *The Earl and the Girl,* and it became his first hit. Kern finally had a shot at a full score when he was commis-

**DEARLY BELOVED**

Music by JEROME KERN
Lyric by JOHNNY MERCER

FRED ASTAIRE AND RITA HAYWORTH
IN THE NEW COLUMBIA MUSICAL PRODUCTION
"YOU WERE NEVER LOVELIER"
WITH
ADOLPHE MENJOU
AND
XAVIER CUGAT
AND HIS ORCHESTRA

DEARLY BELOVED
I'M OLD FASHIONED
YOU WERE NEVER LOVELIER
WEDDING IN THE SPRING
THE SHORTY GEORGE
ON THE BEAM

CHAPPELL

**OPPOSITE PAGE:** Kern, Jean Harlow, and director Victor Fleming on the set of *Reckless.*

sioned to write *The Red Petticoat* in 1905. In 1914, Kern and lyricist Harry B. Smith wrote the lyrics for *The Laughing Husband,* featuring the song "You're Here and I'm Here," another success. Another great early hit was "They Didn't Believe Me," with a lyric by Herbert Reynolds, written for *The Girl from Utah.*

In 1915, Kern opened five shows on Broadway, including one of his most enduring hits, *Very Good Eddie,* with lyrics by Harry B. Smith and a libretto by Guy Bolton, who would continue to figure prominently in Kern's career. *Very Good Eddie* was the second of what became known as the Princess Theater shows, intimate musical comedies with American locales and simple settings. The shows were less overtly romantic than the typical operetta or musical comedy, and they were more in tune with current trends and feelings.

The producer of the Princess shows was Elisabeth Marbury, a well-known literary agent of the day. She believed that a kind of permanent company devoted to the American musical should be established, and when producer F. Ray Comstock had difficulty filling his 299-seat Princess Theater, she seized the opportunity to try out the idea.

*Have a Heart,* one of five Kern musicals to open in 1917, was the first to have lyrics by P. G. Wodehouse. Another Kern, Wodehouse, and Bolton show of 1917 was *Oh, Boy!,* a great success that introduced the enduring classic "Till the Clouds Roll By." *Leave It to Jane,* also from 1917, was the third show by the successful trio, and enjoyed hundreds of subsequent productions up through the 1960s.

The 1920s was Kern's greatest decade, starting in 1920 with the lavish Ziegfeld production of *Sally,* featuring Marilyn Miller. Its score contained many of Kern's greatest melodies, including the title song, "Wild Rose," and "Whip-Poor-Will," but its best song became one of Kern's most enduring standards; "Look for the Silver Lining," in which the B. G. De Sylva lyric is perfectly married to Kern's simple melody. Kern and Marilyn Miller were reunited for 1925's *Sunny* with lyrics by Otto Harbach and Oscar Hammerstein II. That score included such big hits as "Who?," "D'Ye Love Me?," and the title song.

Kern's masterwork came at the end of the decade. The Florenz Ziegfeld production of *Show Boat* opened on December 27, 1927, at the Ziegfeld Theater with a cast that included Charles Winninger, Howard Marsh, Norma Terris, Helen Morgan, Edna Mae Oliver, and Jules Bledsoe, all perfectly personifying Edna Ferber's

fascinating characters. The score was equally brilliant, comprising such standards as "Can't Help Lovin' Dat Man," "Life Upon the Wicked Stage," "You Are Love," "Why Do I Love You?," and "Bill." The show continues to be a favorite around the world to this day. Helen Morgan returned in Kern's final show of the decade, *Sweet Adeline* (1929). Two of the great torch singer's numbers, "Why Was I Born?" and "Don't Ever Leave Me," are among Kern and Hammerstein's finest numbers. Otto Harbach supplied the book and lyrics for Kern's next triumph, *The Cat and the Fiddle,* with such songs as "The Night Was Made for Love," "She Didn't Say Yes," "Try to Forget," and "One Moment Alone."

*Roberta* began the 1930s on a successful note with its cherished score by Kern and Harbach. "The Touch of Your Hand," "You're Devastating," "Yesterdays," "Let's Begin," and "I'll Be Hard to Handle" all became standards, but the breakout ballad is the exquisite "Smoke Gets in Your Eyes." Kern's last Broadway musical, *Very Warm for May,* opened in 1939. Its "All the Things You Are" is considered by many to be the one perfect song written for the American musical theater, and is certainly among Kern and Hammerstein's greatest achievements.

Kern turned his attention to Hollywood musicals. *Show Boat, Sweet Adeline, Sunny, Sally, The Cat and the Fiddle, Music in the Air,* and *Roberta* all transferred to the screen with varying success. During the filming of *Roberta,* Kern and Dorothy Fields wrote two new numbers, "Lovely to Look At" and "I Won't Dance." *I Dream Too Much,* with Lily Pons (1935), was his first original screen score. It was followed by the Astaire/Rogers musical *Swing Time* whose superior score (lyrics by Fields) included "A Fine Romance," "Never Gonna Dance," and "The Way You Look Tonight." After three more films, *High, Wide and Handsome* (1937), *When You're in Love* (1937), and *The Joy of Living* (1938), Kern returned to New York and composed music for the show *Very Warm for May.*

Back to Hollywood: *Cover Girl* (1944), with lyrics by Ira Gershwin and starring Gene Kelly and Rita Hayworth, featured the hit song "Long Ago and Far Away." The Deanna Durbin vehicle *Can't Help Singing* (1944) had a Kern's hit, "More and More," with lyrics by E. Y. Harburg. Kern's last film score, *Centennial Summer* (1946), written in conjunction with Leo Robin, included the hits "In Love in Vain" and (with Oscar Hammerstein II) "All Through the Day."

## THE GREAT SONGS

**1905** How'd You Like to Spoon with Me? (lyric by Edward Laska)

**1914** They Didn't Believe Me (lyric by Herbert Reynolds)

**1915** Babes in the Wood (lyric by Schuyler Greene, Jerome Kern); Isn't It Great to Be Married? (lyric by Schuyler Greene)

**1917** And I Am All Alone (lyric by Jerome Kern, P. G. Wodehouse); Cleopatterer; The Crickets Are Calling; The Land Where the Good Songs Go; Leave It to Jane; Sir Galahad; Till the Clouds Roll By (all lyrics by P. G. Wodehouse)

**1918** Bill; Go Little Boat (both lyrics by P. G. Wodehouse)

**1919** Whip-Poor-Will (lyric by B. G. De Sylva)

**1920** Look for the Silver Lining (lyric by B. G. De Sylva); Whose Baby Are You? (lyric by Anne Caldwell)

**1921** Blue Danube Blues (lyric by Anne Caldwell)

**1923** Once in a Blue Moon (lyric by Anne Caldwell)

**1925** D'Ye Love Me ; Sunny; Who? (all lyrics by Otto Harbach, Oscar Hammerstein II)

**1927** Bill (lyric by Oscar Hammerstein II, P. G. Wodehouse); 'Til Good Luck Comes My Way; Can't Help Lovin' Dat Man; Life upon the Wicked Stage; Make Believe; Ol' Man River; Why Do I Love You?; You Are Love (all lyrics by Oscar Hammerstein II)

**1929** Don't Ever Leave Me; Here Am I; Why Was I Born? (all lyrics by Oscar Hammerstein II)

**1930** Don't Ask Me Not to Sing; I Watch the Love Parade; The Night Was Made for Love; Poor Pierrot; She Didn't Say Yes; Try to Forget (all lyrics by Otto Harbach)

**1932** And Love Was Born (I'm Alone); I've Told Ev'ry Little Star; The Song Is You; We Belong Together (all lyrics by Oscar Hammerstein II)

**1933** I'll Be Hard to Handle (lyric by Bernard Dougall); Let's Begin; Smoke Gets in Your Eyes; The Touch of Your Hand; Yesterdays; You're Devastating (all lyrics by Otto Harbach)

**1935** I Dream Too Much; ; Lovely to Look At (both lyrics by Dorothy Fields); I Won't Dance (lyric by Dorothy Fields, Oscar Hammerstein II)

**1936** Bojangles of Harlem; A Fine Romance; Never Gonna Dance; Pick Yourself Up; The Way You Look Tonight (all lyrics by Dorothy Fields); Waltz in Swing Time (instrumental)

**1937** Can I Forget You; The Folks Who Live on the Hill (both lyrics by Oscar Hammerstein II)

**1938** Just Let Me Look at You (lyric by Dorothy Fields)

**1939** All in Fun; All the Things You Are; In the Heart of the Dark; That Lucky Fellow (all lyrics by Oscar Hammerstein II)

**1940** The Last Time I Saw Paris (lyric by Oscar Hammerstein II); Remind Me (lyric by Dorothy Fields)

**1942** Dearly Beloved; I'm Old Fashioned; You Were Never Lovelier (all lyrics by Johnny Mercer)

**1944** Any Moment Now; Long Ago (and Far Away); Put Me to the Test; Sure Thing (all lyrics by Ira Gershwin); Make Way for Tomorrow (lyric by Ira Gershwin, E. Y. Harburg)

**1945** All Through the Day (lyric by Oscar Hammerstein II); In Love in Vain; Up with the Lark (both lyrics by Leo Robin); Two Hearts Are Better Than One (lyric Johnny Mercer)

**1956** April Fooled Me (lyric by Dorothy Fields)

Once again in New York, Kern set to work on a new musical produced by Rodgers and Hammerstein, based on the life of Annie Oakley. Dorothy Fields was signed to provide the lyrics. On November 5, 1945, Kern collapsed on Park Avenue at 57th Street. Because he had no identification on him, he was taken to City Hospital on Welfare Island. Hospital personnel found his ASCAP card and Oscar Hammerstein II was contacted by the organization. Kern was moved to Doctor's Hospital on November 7 having suffered a cerebral hemorrhage. On the last day of Kern's life, Hammerstein sat at his bedside and gently sang, "I've Told Every Little Star," hoping to rouse him. After finishing the song, Hammerstein looked down at his friend and realized Kern had died.

Deems Taylor, then president of ASCAP, said, "I know that my own sorrow at his passing must be shared by the millions who for many years have derived so much pleasure from his lovely tunes. I think that no composer in his field since Victor Herbert has inspired so much real affection from countless hearers who never saw him face to face." ◆

> "I'm a musical clothier—nothing more or less. I write music to both the situations and the lyrics in plays." —Jerome Kern

## Song and Story

### COVER GIRL

Ira Gershwin: I got along very well with him. He liked me. But I wasn't used to working with anyone like that, you know. We started first on *Cover Girl*. He would say, "Here"—and hand me tunes. He'd say, "We have to use this," and he played me a sixteen-bar schottische. Rather monotonous. I said, "Very nice, Jerry, but I'll have to find a spot for it, you know." And every time we'd keep on working—we worked a long time on that thing—every time he'd say, "Have you done that schottische yet?" And I'd say, "No, I'm waiting for a spot." Finally, at the very end, we had to write a title song and I said, "Jerry I think I can find that!" It was that schottische! And that was the last thing I wrote in the picture—the thing he had given me so many months back to write up!

### WHY DO I LOVE YOU?

When *Show Boat* was trying out in Pittsburgh, star Norma Terris asked for a song she could sing in Act II. Kern and Hammerstein stayed up all night writing "Why Do I Love You?"

### OL' MAN RIVER

"Ol' Man River" originally began with the words, "Niggers all work on the Mississippi." (The lyric of Irving Berlin's "Puttin' on the Ritz" was also adapted to change the locale from Harlem to Park Avenue.) As the twentieth century rolled on, the regularly revived *Show Boat* sometimes found itself in conflict with an evolving civil rights movement, much to the puzzlement of those who knew the original show as being highly sympathetic to the struggles of blacks. The song's opening lyric was changed from "niggers all work" to "darkies all work," "colored folks work," and finally to "here we all work." Edna Ferber's reaction upon hearing "Ol' Man River" was as follows: "The music mounted, mounted, and I give you my word my hair stood on end, the tears came to my eyes, and I breathed like a heroine in a melodrama. This was great music. It was music that would outlast Jerome Kern's day and mine."

### I'VE TOLD EV'RY LITTLE STAR

One evening while on vacation on Nantucket in 1932, Jerome Kern heard a bird's whistle and immediately thought it would make a fine start of a song. He couldn't quite remember the tune or the type of bird, so he stayed awake until the bird sang again. This time Kern was ready with pen and paper. Later, an ornithologist friend identified the bird as a finch. Oscar Hammerstein II sang "I've Told Ev'ry Little Star" to Jerome Kern as the composer lay dying in a New York hospital, because Kern had told him that the song was his favorite.

ABOVE: Robert Alton, Kay Thompson, Lennie Hayton, Lucille Bremer, Arthur Freed, and Jerome Kern on the set of *Till the Clouds Roll By*.

### SMOKE GETS IN YOUR EYES

When *Show Boat* was trying out, Jerome Kern wrote a quick little melody to cover a scene change. In 1932, Kern expanded the idea into the title theme for an NBC radio program. The next year, while working on what would become the musical *Roberta*, Kern returned to the little tune. Though it was originally written in march tempo, lyricist Otto Harbach suggested that Kern slow it down and elongate some of the notes to make the music more romantic. Kern resisted but finally took Harbach's advice. The result was "Smoke Gets in Your Eyes."

### DEARLY BELOVED

Even as great an egotist as Jerome Kern was unsure of his songs. He had the teenage Margaret Whiting sing this song for him at his home in Beverly Hills. Cowed by the great man's talents, Whiting was speechless when she finished. Kern responded, "I guess you like it, even though you don't say so. If you didn't like it, you would not have been able to sing it so well."

### LOVELY TO LOOK AT

RKO bigwigs groused that the song was too short. Kern replied, "That's all I had to say."

### BILL

Wodehouse and Kern had written "Bill" for Vivienne Segal to sing in *Oh, Lady! Lady!* but it was cut before the show opened. Oscar Hammerstein II revised the lyrics for interpolation into *Show Boat*.

Gus Kahn

**I'M BRINGING A RED RED ROSE**

ZIEGFELD *production*
EDDIE CANTOR

*in*
Whoopee

Book Written and Staged by
Wm. ANTHONY McGUIRE
Music by
WALTER DONALDSON
Lyrics by
GUS KAHN
Dances Staged by
SEYMOUR FELIX

Gypsy Joe
Makin' Whoopee
Love Me or Leave Me
Song of the Setting Sun
(Love is the Mountain)
Until You Get Somebody Else
I'm Bringing A Red Red Rose
Come West Little Girl Come West
The Gypsy Song
(Where Sunset Meets the Sea)
Here's to The Girl of My Heart

WALTER DONALDSON
Music Publishers
New York

RED RED ROSE

Gustave Kahn from Koblenz, Germany, became one of America's top lyricists by using American slang to better effect than most of his contemporaries, whatever their backgrounds. Perhaps he was more attuned to English and its idiosyncrasies, as it was his second language. Just as E. Y. Harburg had never been to Paris when he wrote "April in Paris," Kahn had never been to Carolina when he wrote "Carolina in the Morning." His career can be roughly divided into two parts, Tin Pan Alley, for which he wrote almost exclusively until 1933, and his Hollywood period, which began that year and ran until his death in 1941.

Kahn came to Chicago approximately five years after his birth on November 6, 1886, and he began his songwriting career in 1908, collaborating with composer Grace LeBoy. They soon married and continued working together, writing for vaudeville and Tin Pan Alley for the next six years and sporadically thereafter. Kahn's next collaborator was fellow Chicagoan Egbert Van Alstyne, who had previously written hits with Harry Williams, including the standard "In the Shade of the New Apple Tree." Van Alstyne wrote the music to Kahn's first standard, "Memories," in 1915. The following year Van Alstyne wrote the verse and Tony Jackson the chorus to a hit that presaged the 1920s jazz era, "Pretty Baby," which was interpolated into the score of *The Passing Show of 1916*.

Making friends with Al Jolson was a lucky break for Kahn—getting Jolson to sing your song was the goal of every songwriter, who knew that it was considered a seal of approval for sheet music and record buyers. Even better, Jolson would often interpolate songs into his Winter Garden shows, if for only one performance. Thereafter, the sheet music would read, "As performed at the Winter Garden Theatre by Al Jolson."

## The title "Makin' Whoopee" was taken from Walter Winchell's *New York Daily Mirror* column.

Jolson put two Gus Kahn songs, "'N' Everything," and "I'll Say She Does," into *Sinbad*. In 1921, the singer interpolated "Toot, Toot, Tootsie" into his musical comedy *Bombo*. It was lucky for songwriters Kahn, Ernie Erdman, and Dan Russo that Jolson didn't demand to be cut-in on the royalties and songwriting credits, as he often did. He liked the song so much it made a reappearance in *The Jazz Singer* (1927), *Rose of Washington Square* (1939), *The Jolson Story* (1946) and *Jolson Sings Again* (1949).

Jolie also sang the Kahn and Donaldson song "My Buddy," his voice wavering with emotion. This 1922 salute to a fallen soldier of World War I struck a nerve in a country that was hurtling into the jazz age while still smarting from the loss of loved ones overseas only a few years earlier.

"Ain't We Got Fun?" (1921) appears at first glance to be the epitome of a '20s jazz song, Its short lines contributing to the momentum of a song that never runs out of steam. Pay attention to the lyrics: Kahn writes, the "rich get richer and the poor get children," a reference to the post–World War I depression.

Ted Fiorito gave 1924's "Charley My Boy" a typical '20s beat, but Kahn's next three hits that year, "It Had to Be You," "I'll See You in My Dreams," and "The One I Love," boasted surprisingly sophisticated music by popular bandleader Isham Jones. The songs are often thought to have been written in the 1940s, as they had a kind of '40s feeling and slang-free lyrics, and enjoyed a renewed popularity that decade.

"The One I Love Belongs to Somebody Else" started out as a beautiful torch song but, like so many, it was picked up by jazz bands who drove the tempo up, and these renditions bore no relation to the song as it was written. Another of Kahn's songs, 1925's "I Never Knew," with music by Ted Fiorito (or Fio Rito as he spelled it then), was also played at a fast tempo, the meaning of the lyric often getting lost in the shuffle.

Two Donaldson and Kahn songs with the word "baby" in their titles came out in 1925: "Yes Sir! That's My Baby" and "I Wonder Where My Baby Is Tonight." The word "baby" was originally used in songs (especially coon songs and early Southern ballads) to denote young black women, but it soon became a term of endearment for women of all races.

Kahn had written two full Broadway scores, *Holka-Polka* in 1925 and *Kitty's Kisses* in 1926, to no acclaim whatsoever. It was third-time lucky for Kahn in 1928 when, in collaboration with Walter Donaldson, he wrote the songs for *Whoopee*. Eddie Cantor, a favorite of Kahn's (he had a hit with "Charley My Boy" in 1924), starred and Florenz Ziegfeld produced. The film version of the show opened in 1930, in two-strip Technicolor, and featured the choreography of Busby Berkeley, making his film debut.

The success of *Whoopee* brought Kahn to the attention of Hollywood's bosses and he wrote his first film

scores in 1933, starting with *Flying Down to Rio*, which marked the film debut of the team of Fred Astaire and Ginger Rogers. (Astaire's partner was supposed to have been Dorothy Jordan but she chose to get married instead. The rest, as they say, is film history.) Kahn and composer Vincent Youmans supplied a score laden with hits, including the title song, "Music Makes Me," "Orchids in the Moonlight," and "Carioca." Unfortunately, it would be Youmans's last score. He retired to Arizona suffering from tuberculosis.

Kahn moved from RKO to MGM and worked on a series of films for the next eight years. He was used to punching up lyrics for MGM operettas (usually starring Jeanette MacDonald), including *The Merry Widow* (1934—lyrics also by Lorenz Hart!), *Naughty Marietta* (1935), *Rose Marie* (1936), *Maytime* (1937), *Balalaika* (1938), and *Girl of the Golden West* (1938).

Kahn worked until his death on October 8, 1941. He went out with a bang, though, collaborating with Nacio Herb Brown on the hit song "You Stepped Out of a Dream" for Tony Martin to sing in 1941's *Ziegfeld Girl*. ◆

# Song and Story

### CAROLINA IN THE MORNING
William ("Fred Mertz") Frawley introduced this song in vaudeville, to great acclaim. Gus Kahn was a master of the internal rhyme as in, "No one could be sweeter than my sweetie when I meet her" and "Strolling with my girlie where the dew is pearly early in the morning."

### DREAM A LITTLE DREAM OF ME
This song received little notice when it was first issued on sheet music in 1930. Fast forward to 1968 when it became a hit standard because of a beautiful rendition by Cass Elliot and the Mamas and the Papas—which only goes to prove what we've said before: a true standard can be rediscovered in any era.

### LIZA (ALL THE CLOUDS'LL ROLL AWAY)
Producer Florenz Ziegfeld wanted a score for *Show Girl* in only two weeks so Gus Kahn was called in to help out on the lyrics. Ruby Keeler, not even twenty years old, was the star of the show and she got mighty nervous at the dress rehearsal. When it came to singing "Liza," she froze. From the audience, Jolson got up and sang the song to her to steady her nerves. Apparently Ziegfeld thought it was a great gimmick and got Jolson to repeat the bit for the whole of the Boston engagement, on opening night in New York, and for a few performances afterward. As soon as he stopped, the box office plummeted.

## THE GREAT SONGS

**1915** Memories (music by Egbert Van Alstyne)

**1916** Pretty Baby (music by Tony Jackson and Egbert Van Alstyne)

**1921** Ain't We Got Fun? (music by Richard A. Whiting, lyric by Raymond B. Egan and Gus Kahn); Toot Toot Tootsie (music and lyric by Ernie Erdman, Ted Fiorito, Gus Kahn)

**1922** Carolina in the Morning; My Buddy (both music by Walter Donaldson)

**1923** Nobody's Sweetheart (music and lyric by Ernie Erdman, Gus Kahn, Billy Meyers, Elmer Schoebel); When Lights Are Low (music by Ted Fiorito, lyric by Gus Kahn and Ted Koehler)

**1924** I'll See You in My Dreams; It Had to Be You; The One I Love Belongs to Somebody Else (all music by Isham Jones); Charley My Boy (music by Ted Fiorito)

**1925** Alone at Last; I Never Knew (both music by Ted Fiorito); Ukelele Lady (music by Richard A. Whiting); I Wonder Where My Baby Is Tonight; Yes Sir! That's My Baby (both music by Walter Donaldson)

**1926** That Certain Party (music by Walter Donaldson); There Ain't No Maybe in My Baby's Eyes (music by Walter Donaldson, lyric by Raymond B. Egan and Gus Kahn)

**1927** Chloe (music by Neil Moret)

**1928** Little Orphan Annie (music by Joe Sanders); I'm Bringing a Red, Red Rose; Love Me or Leave Me; My Baby Just Cares for Me (all music by Walter Donaldson)

**1929** Liza (All the Clouds'll Roll Away) (music by George Gershwin, lyric by Ira Gershwin and Gus Kahn)

**1930** Dream a Little Dream of Me (music by F. Andree and W. Schwandt)

**1932** I'll Never Be the Same (music by Matty Malneck and Frank Signorelli)

**1933** Flying Down to Rio; Music Makes Me; Orchids in the Moonlight (all music by Vincent Youmans, lyrics by Edward Eliscu and Gus Kahn)

**1934** One Night of Love (music by Victor Schertzinger); When My Ship Comes In (music by Walter Donaldson)

**1935** Thanks a Million (music by Arthur Johnston)

**1936** San Francisco (music by Bronislau Kaper and Walter Jurmann)

**1937** All God's Chillun Got Rhythm (music by Bronislau Kaper and Walter Jurmann); Sympathy (music by Rudolf Friml)

**1941** You Stepped Out of a Dream (music by Nacio Herb Brown)

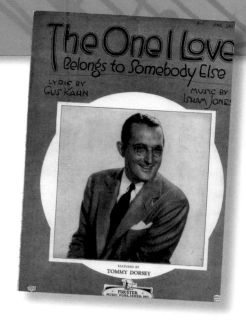

Lewis & Young

**ABOVE:** Joe Young. Lewis and Young are so unknown we couldn't find a photo of Sam M. Lewis. Got one? We'd gladly insert it here in future printings of this book.

Sam M. Lewis was born in New York City on October 25, 1885. He earned money by singing in cafés, sometimes his own songs. He wrote special material for others, including vaudeville favorites Van and Schenck, and minstrel Lew Dockstader. Lewis's first song, "Beside the Old Oak Tree," was written in 1906, with music by Ted S. Brown, but he began writing in earnest in 1910, averaging twenty or thirty songs a year until he began slowing down in the late 1930s.

In 1916, Lewis began collaborating on lyrics with Joe Young, who became his lifelong writing partner. Young was also born in New York City (on the Fourth of July, 1899)—which brings us to an interesting genre of songs for which they wrote the lyrics. Many Lewis and Young songs celebrated the American South, a region and sensibility that these two nice boys from New York City knew absolutely nothing about. But songwriting is not about facts, and let's face it, with the right sentiment and some catchwords, anyone with talent can write about anything. Among their better known Southern songs are "Dinah," "My Mammy," "Cryin' for the Carolines," "I'm All Bound 'Round with the Mason-Dixon Line," Rock-a-bye Your Baby with a Dixie Melody," "I'd Love to Fall Asleep and Wake Up in My Mammy's Arms," "Tuck Me to Sleep in My Old 'Tucky Home"—and that's just the hits. Many of these songs were sung by fellow Jewish non-Southerner, Al Jolson. And that folks, is the glory of American popular song.

Young wrote for various publishing houses in New York and toured Europe during the First World War, entertaining troops. Lewis and Young began writing together exclusively in 1917, and every year or so they would come up with a big hit. Considering the success of their songs and the various numbers they had interpolated into Broadway shows, it's interesting that they tried their hands on only a few complete Broadway shows: *Sinbad* (1918); three shows the next year—*Monte Cristo, Jr.* (music by Maurice Abrahams), *The Water's Fine* (music by Ted Snyder), and *Ziegfeld Follies of 1919* (various composers); and 1927's *Lady Do* (music by Abel Baer).

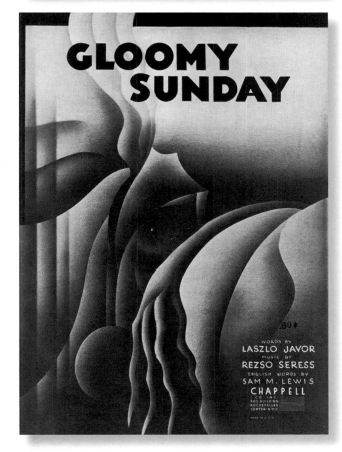

Lewis and Young had a only a brief, two-year career in Hollywood, in 1929 and '30. They wrote exactly one full score, for *Spring Is Here* (1930) with Harry Warren, and one hit came from it, "Cryin' for the Carolines."

Perhaps the pair realized that writing complete scores was a complex proposition, involving more than just coming up with a catchy title and writing a song around it. Writing for the stage requires character and plot development through the lyric, and Lewis and Young just didn't have it in them. In fact, looking through their list of hits, one is struck by how the titles are the best parts of the songs. Yes, they were good craftsmen, all the words rhyme correctly, the lyrics sit correctly on the music, and there are some okay ideas here and there. But their works were virtually devoid of interesting turns of phrase or surprises. The title and the music propelled the song, and the rest was just coasting. To be fair, anyone writing that many songs a year with a variety of composing partners doesn't have a lot of time for polish.

When Lewis and Young broke up in 1930, they both pursued careers apart. Lewis wrote until around 1955. Young, fourteen years younger than Lewis, continued to write at breakneck pace. In 1932, he wrote just under one hundred songs! Young supplied the English lyrics to a

German musical, *Zwei Herzen Im ¾ Takt*, with music by Robert Stolz, in 1930. The next year he wrote complete scores for two more German shows, a couple of songs for two more, and a song for a German film. History has not recorded how or why his career took this peculiar turn.

Young finally slowed down in 1936—he only wrote twenty or so songs that year and fewer each succeeding year until his death on April 21, 1939. Sam M. Lewis died in New York City on November 22, 1959. ◆

## THE GREAT SONGS, CONT'D

1934 For All We Know (music by J. Fred Coots, lyric by Sam M. Lewis); I Believe in Miracles (music by George W. Meyer and Pete Wendling, lyric by Sam M. Lewis); I'm Growing Fonder of You (music by George W. Meyer and Pete Wendling)

1935 I'm Gonna Sit Right Down and Write Myself a Letter (music by Fred E. Ahlert, lyric by Joe Young); You're a Heavenly Thing (music by Little Jack Little, lyric by Joe Young)

1936 There's Frost on the Moon, Spring in My Heart (music by Fred E. Ahlert, lyric by Joe Young)

# *Song and Story*

### DINAH

"Dinah" was written for Ethel Waters to sing at the Plantation Club, a nightclub at 50th Street in Broadway, and it was one of the first hit songs to come out of a nightclub show. Songwriters Harry Akst and Joe Young approached Waters with the number. The singer recalled, "They sang it themselves for me, doing it fast and corny. 'Is that the way you want me to sing it?' I asked. Akst and Young looked at each other. 'Why not sing it your own way?' they said." She took it home, slowed it down, and sang it straight. And the song was a huge success.

### FIVE FOOT TWO, EYES OF BLUE (HAS ANYBODY SEEN MY GAL?)

This song so clearly evoked its 1925 origins that it has become a sort of shorthand for the roaring twenties.

### LAWD, YOU MADE THE NIGHT TOO LONG

This song was parodied by Sam M. Lewis himself in 1940 as "Sam, You Made the Pants Too Long" (with music by Victor Young).

### IN A SHANTY IN OLD SHANTY TOWN

This is an unusual song, an upbeat number about living in a shack. It was written in the Depression, when people were actually living in shacks and welcomed an optimistic take on their reduced means. It was originally conceived as a waltz, but after Rudy Vallee, Ted Lewis, and Johnny Long and his Orchestra each weighed in with their various versions of it, the song swung.

# Kalmar & Ruby

**B**ert Kalmar and Harry Ruby enjoyed success on Broadway and in Hollywood, but they are best known as writers of some of the Marx Brothers' zaniest material. Harry Ruby was born in New York on January 27, 1895. He had no interest in his studies, preferring to memorize baseball statistics. He was kicked out of two high schools before starting his professional career as a staff pianist (along with Walter Winchell) at Gus Edwards's music publishing company. Ruby's job was to plug songs at the F. W. Woolworth five and dime stores and the Harry Von Tilzer company. Ruby tried his luck in vaudeville, as half of the team of Edwards and Ruby. "Edwards" would grow up to be Harry Cohn, the founder of Columbia Pictures. Ruby then played piano for the Messenger Boys Trio, and the stint led Ruby to his future partner, Bert Kalmar, who was attempting to be a dancer.

Kalmar was born on February 16, 1884, and ran away from home at age ten, determined to become a magician. By the time he met Ruby, he already had a publishing company in partnership with composer Harry Puck. Kalmar and Puck had racked up a few successes on Tin Pan Alley, starting with the 1913 hit "Where Did You Get That Girl?" Kalmar hired Ruby as a staff pianist at Waterson, Berlin, and Snyder. Ruby's first hit, for which he wrote both music and lyrics, was "What'll We Do on a Saturday Night When the Town Grows Dry?" (1919)

In 1920, Kalmar and Ruby collaborated on the hit "Where Do They Go When They Row, Row, Row?" That same year they wrote a big hit, "My Sunny Tennessee." Eddie Cantor made it a hit when he sang it in his show, *The Midnight Rounders.*

Kalmar and Ruby exhibited their off-kilter sense of humor with a piece of material written for two of those comics, Van and Schenck. "The Sheik of Avenue B," a satire on "The Sheik of Araby." The latter song's music was written by Ted Snyder who mustn't have minded the parody, because he supplied the music for Kalmar and Ruby's next hit, "Who's Sorry Now?" (Clearly, they experienced much luck with "question" songs.)

The team came up with successful Broadway scores, including *The Ramblers* (1926—"All Alone Monday"), *The 5 O'Clock Girl* (1927—"Thinking of You"), and *Good Boy* (1928—"I Wanna Be Loved by You"). Kalmar and Ruby's lives and career changed with their next show, *Animal Crackers* (1928), written for the four Marx Brothers. For the occasion, they came up with "Hooray for Captain Spaulding."

Hollywood beckoned when sound films came on the scene. Kalmar and Ruby's huge hit "Three Little Words" was interpolated into the score of the film. The team wrote many screenplays, including *Look for the Silver Lining*, *The Kid from Spain*, *Bright Lights*, and *Duck Soup*. Bert Kalmar died on September 17, 1947.

In 1950, the team of Kalmar and Ruby was saluted by the movies with their own biopic, *Three Little Words*. Red Skelton played Ruby and Fred Astaire played Kalmar. For Ruby, the picture was a bittersweet experience. He wrote, "Kalmar signed the contract for the movie just two days before he passed away. My father, who waited for the movie of his son, counted the days and minutes for its release. He died the morning the picture opened in New York." The story was, like all of Hollywood's biographies, largely made up, but they got some things right, like Ruby's love of baseball."

Ruby retired shortly after the film came out and died on February 23, 1974. ◆

## THE GREAT SONGS

**ALL SONGS BY KALMAR AND RUBY UNLESS OTHERWISE INDICATED.**

**1913** Where Did You Get That Girl? (Kalmar and Harry Puck)

**1916** Since Maggie Dooley Learned the Hooley Hooley (music by George W. Meyer, lyric by Kalmar and Edgar Leslie)

**1919** All the Quakers are Shoulder Shakers Down in Quaker Town; Oh, What a Pal Was Mary (both music by Pete Wendling, lyrics by Kalmar and Edgar Leslie)

**1920** I'm a Vamp from East Broadway (Kalmar and Ruby and Irving Berlin); Snoops the Lawyer; So Long Oolong; Timbuctoo

**1921** My Sunny Tennessee (Kalmar, Ruby and Herman Ruby); She's Mine All Mine; The Sheik of Avenue B (Kalmar and Ruby, Sam J. Downing, and A. Friend)

**1922** I Gave You Up Just Before You Threw Me Down (music by Fred Ahlert); Who's Sorry Now? (music by Ted Snyder)

**1923** I Like a Big Town; It Was Meant to Be; What Makes a Business Man Tired?

**1926** All Alone Monday

**1927** Happy Go Lucky; Thinking of You; Up in the Clouds

**1928** Good Boy; Hooray for Captain Spaulding; I Wanna Be Loved By You; Watching the Clouds Roll By; Who's Been List'ning to My Heart

**1930** Three Little Words

**1932** Ev'ryone Says, I Love You

**1935** A Kiss to Build a Dream On (lyrics by Oscar Hammerstein II, Bert Kalmar)

**1936** Show Me a Rose (Or Leave Me Alone); A Tulip Told a Tale

**1947** Go West, Young Man

Frank Sinatra and Jimmy Durante in 1947's *It Happened in Brooklyn.*

# Hollywood Songwriters

In black-and-white mode, Twentieth Century-Fox produced a series of period musicals in the 1930s with Ameche, Alice Faye, Tyrone Power, and Ethel Merman. Sure, the plots were all the same, but audiences didn't seem to mind. Irving Berlin was associated with much of the Fox output in the thirties. The forties belonged to Fox and their series of lush, Technicolor musicals featuring the likes of Carmen Miranda, Don Ameche, Betty Grable, and Charlotte Greenwood.

Paramount Pictures' musicals were looser affairs including the *Big Broadcasts* and the Hope-and-Crosby Road pictures. Crosby was the big musical star on the Paramount lot and his musicals, mostly with scores by Burke and Monaco and then Burke and Van Heusen, were small productions compared to the lavish spectacles of Fox and Warner.

MGM's Freed Unit was launched with *The Wizard of Oz* in 1939—and the movie musical entered its golden age. In a series of musicals with screenplays by the likes of Comden and Green and Alan Jay Lerner, boasting scores by such greats as Berlin, Porter, and Burton Lane and direction by Vincente Minnelli, the MGM musical became the sine qua non of the genre. Also on the lot was Joseph Pasternak, who had graduated from directing Deanna Durbin musicals at Universal to command his own unit at MGM. His stable of stars included Jane Powell and that singing and splashing sensation, Esther Williams.

When the MGM musical died in the late 1950s, musicals were only sporadically being produced. Some—*Grease, Saturday Night Fever,* and *Oliver!*—were quite successful, but the end of the studio system and the rise of the television variety show marked the end of the era of film musicals. Despite the occasional *Chicago* or *Rent,* (both movie versions of shows already successful on Broadway), the genre is only a sideline to the once great Hollywood tradition. ❖

**W**hen sound came into the movies at the end of the 1920s, Broadway composers packed their bags and headed west with dreams of fortune dancing in their heads. Everyone went out to Hollywood, that is, everyone except black writers like Thomas "Fats" Waller and the team of Noble Sissle and Eubie Blake. They weren't asked to the party. Some of the Broadwayites, like Rodgers and Hart, preferred the autonomy of Broadway despite their success in Hollywood and soon returned east making only occasional forays back to the land of orange groves. Others, like Harry Warren, established long careers in Hollywood with only the occasional dabble on Broadway, professing all the while to miss New York.

MGM and Paramount were the leaders in producing early film musicals and revues. In the '30s these studios began to believe that the public had grown tired of movie musicals, and that's when Warner Brothers came along, launching the talents of Busby Berkeley, the songwriting team of Harry Warren and Al Dubin, and stars Ruby Keeler and Dick Powell. Suddenly the genre was transformed.

A few years after Warner's success, RKO pictures stepped into the breach with a musical stock company that included Fred Astaire, Ginger Rogers, Eric Blore, Eric Rhodes, Helen Broderick, and Edward Everett Horton. RKO hired the best Broadway composers, Irving Berlin, Jerome Kern and the Gershwin brothers, to write for their witty, sophisticated musicals.

> ## "In those days the studio was some combination of Nirvana, Shangri-la, the Taj Mahal, and the great teat in the sky from which the dollars would keep flowing." —Fred Myrow

# Song and Story

### SILVER BELLS

The song was originally titled "Tinkle Bell." Jay Livingston told Michael Feinstein why the name was changed. "My wife said, 'What'd you do at school?' as she usually said, and I said, 'I wrote a song called 'Tinkle Bell.' She said, 'Do you know what 'tinkle' means to most people? I don't know if that's an English expression or not, but it has a bathroom connotation. You can't have a song called 'Tinkle Bell.'" The song became a Christmas perennial, and Ray Evans ascribed its success to the fact that it is the only Christmas song written about the city. The truth is, the urban setting was derived from the fact that it was written for a specific scene in *The Lemon Drop Kid*.

### QUE SERA SERA

Paramount wanted Doris Day sing a song in Alfred Hitchcock's *The Man Who Knew Too Much*, figuring that audiences would expect it. Hitchcock concocted a way to make "Que Sera Sera" integral to the plot. Day sings the song in the lair of her child's kidnappers, hoping the kid will hear it and respond. Paramount liked the song but insisted that the title be listed as "Whatever Will Be, Will Be," because the Academy wouldn't allow a non-English title to be submitted for an Oscar! At first hearing, Day considered the song too simple and vchildlike. Marty Melcher, her husband and manager, talked her into singing it, and it went on to win an Oscar and be her biggest hit. She would sing it twice more in films (*Please Don't Eat the Daisies* and *The Glass Bottom Boat*) and make it the theme of her television series.

### MR. ED

Filmways took note of the success of the *Bonanza* theme and asked Livingston and Evans to write one for their new comedy, *Mr. Ed*. Jay Livingston recalls, "Raoul Kraushaar, who scored all of Filmways's pictures, went to Rome to record it. They got an Italian opera singer to sing 'Mr. Ed.' I'd like to have heard that!" Producer Al Simon was aghast at the Italian version and asked Livingston if he would lay down a temporary track until another singer could be found and recorded. "I said okay," recalls Livingston. "I had a lot of trouble with it because there's no place to breathe... My wife coached me; otherwise, I would never have gotten through it." Livingston's recording became the permanent one.

# First Person

Richard Rodgers to Max Wilk: One of their pet procedures was to assign four or five different songwriters to the same spot in the same picture and then to take the song they liked the best. So you found youself working in competition with other writers. They did it to Larry Hart and to me, to everybody, even to Jerry Kern—and if they would do that to Kern, for God's sake... This was sheer suicide for a composer.

**RIGHT:** Billy Eckstine romances a costar in 1947's *Rhythm in a Riff*.

Fred Myrow, composer Joseph Myrow's son, remembers the glory days on the Fox lot: What an extraordinary community of writers it was. They all knew each other, they played for each other, they helped each other, they called each other. The whole concept of the studio being sold or executives changing once they were in there was inconceivable. You developed a relationship with someone, it went on forever, the studio went on forever.

The composers' contracts were long and they were well paid. There was never a thought of the composer as an entrepreneur. Music didn't count for movies the same way it did for Broadway shows. The movies still existed as literature plus direction, and the music was an afterthought; that's why music was "for-hire," why composers didn't participate in profits.

The composers lived very lavishly, they mixed constantly, but at people's houses; there were no clubs in LA like in New York. Those were the good old days—it was a great time.

Pianist Roy Mace remembers working with Marilyn Monroe: The Fox studio assigned pianists to the Dance School which was in a bungalow on the lot. There they trained and worked out the dancers for the musicals, or actors who had to dance in a film. I was assigned to accompany the dancers. I rehearsed Marilyn Monroe for dancing and singing parts Monroe would complain that Lionel Newman never would play in her key, but I would, because I could transpose on the keyboard. She worked hard. She also loved to change the lyric to make it sexier. I was like her security blanket; she had me come in to accompany her on her screen tests.

Mack Gordon and Harry Revel wrote most of Shirley Temple's songs at Fox. She saved the studio while singing their songs.

**ABOVE:** Al Dubin and Harry Warren were the songwriters of choice at Warner Brothers. Busby Berkeley staged their songs with his usual understatement, as evinced here in 1933's *Footlight Parade*. **RIGHT:** Johnny Burke and Jimmy Van Heusen were the favorite songwriters of Hope and Crosby, shown here with Judith Barrett and Dorothy Lamour in 1940's *Road to Singapore*.

> "We wrote every day until rock came in. If George Gershwin were alive today, he'd be standing on the corner with a tin cup."
> —Jay Livingston

# Livingston & Evans

Jay Livingston was born in McDonald, Pennsylvania, on March 28, 1915. Ray Evans was born in Salamanca, New York, on February 4 of the same year. Livingston took piano lessons from composer Harry Archer in Pittsburgh before entering the University of Pennsylvania. Ray Evans took statistics courses at the Wharton School of Business and played clarinet and alto saxophone in the college band. Jay became the pianist in the band and then bandleader—in 1937, it was hired by Cunard Lines. On one of their last voyages that year, Evans said to Livingston, "Let's stay in New York and write songs."

Livingston found work as a pianist and arranger at NBC and as a rehearsal pianist for Olsen and Johnson's Broadway show *Hellzapoppin'*. The team convinced the secretary of music publisher Jack Mills to pester her boss into seeing the duo. He agreed to publish their song "Monday Mourning on Saturday Night." They went on to write some special material for Olsen and Johnson and contribute songs to the comedy team's Broadway show *Sons o' Fun*. Olsen asked them to drive his car across country. When they got to Hollywood, he put them up in his house.

That same year, 1944, Livingston and Evans went to work for PRC studio. The pair wrote a score for *Swing Hostess*, starring Martha Tilton, who was recording for Capitol Records. She introduced them team to Johnny Mercer, and he performed their songs on the *Johnny Mercer Chesterfield Music Shop* radio show.

B. G. De Sylva, Mercer's partner at Capitol and the Executive Producer at Paramount Pictures, asked the team to submit material for the Betty Hutton feature, *Stork Club*. They wrote three songs on spec, from which De Sylva picked "I'm Just a Square in the Social Circle." That got them a contract with Paramount for the munificent sum of $200 a week (each). They began work in August 1946.

Paramount had a picture titled *To Each His Own* and nobody was willing to write a title song, so Livingston and Evans came up a little something—and surprised everyone when recordings by the Ink Spots, Eddy Howard, Freddy Martin, Tony Martin, and the Modernaires all hit the top ten of the *Billboard* charts at the same time!

In 1958, they wrote their first complete Broadway score, *Oh, Captain*. In 1961, they tried their luck again with *Let It Ride!*, which included one very good song, "My Own Little Island."

It's worth noting that they received three Academy Awards and four other nominations. They won with "Que Sera Sera," "Mona Lisa," and "Buttons and Bows."

Jay's brother, Alan Livingston, vice president of programming at NBC, spotted a new western on the network's schedule and suggested that it needed a theme song. So Livingston and Evans came up with the title song for *Bonanza*—perhaps the catchiest theme ever to grace the small screen. They went on to pen other classic television themes, including *Mr. Ed* and, with Henry Mancini, *Mr. Lucky*.

Jay Livingston died on October 19, 2001. ◆

## THE GREAT SONGS

| | |
|---|---|
| 1938 | G'Bye Now |
| 1945 | Cat and Canary; A Square in the Social Circle; Stuff Like That There |
| 1946 | To Each His Own; Warm As Wine |
| 1947 | Golden Earrings (music by Victor Young) |
| 1950 | Baby, Obey Me!; Mona Lisa |
| 1951 | It Doesn't Cost a Dime to Dream; Mister Christofo Columbo; Silver Bells |
| 1954 | You're So Right for Me |
| 1956 | Que Sera Sera (Whatever Will Be, Will Be) |
| 1957 | Never Let Me Go; Tammy |
| 1958 | Almost in Your Arms; Life Does a Man a Favor (When It Gives Him Simple Joys); The Morning Music of Montmartre |
| 1959 | Bonanza; Dreamsville (music by Henry Mancini) |
| 1960 | Mr. Ed |
| 1961 | His Own Little Island |
| 1965 | Dear Heart (music by Henry Mancini); Never Too Late (music by David Rose) |
| 1966 | In the Arms of Love (music by Henry Mancini); Paris Smiles (music by Maurice Jarre) |

# Lerner & Loewe

## THE GREAT SONGS

All music by Frederick Loewe and lyrics by Alan Jay Lerner unless otherwise indicated.

**1947** Almost Like Being in Love; The Heather on the Hill; I'll Go Home with Bonnie Jean

**1948** Green-Up Time (music by Kurt Weill); Here I'll Stay (music by Kurt Weill)

**1951** How Could You Believe Me When I Said I Loved You When You Know I've Been a Liar All My Life? (music by Burton Lane); I Still See Elisa; I Talk to the Trees; They Call the Wind Maria; Too Late Now (music by Burton Lane); Wand'rin Star

**1956** Get Me to the Church on Time; Hymn to Him; I Could Have Danced All Night; I've Grown Accustomed to Her Face; On the Street Where You Live; The Rain in Spain; Show Me, With a Little Bit of Luck; Wouldn't It Be Loverly?

**1958** Gigi; I Remember It Well; The Night They Invented Champagne; Thank Heaven for Little Girls

**1960** Camelot; Follow Me; How to Handle a Woman; If Ever I Would Leave You

**1965** Come Back to Me; Hurry! It's Lovely Up Here; On a Clear Day You Can See Forever; What Did I Have that I Don't Have? (all music by Burton Lane)

**1979** One More Walk Around the Garden; Why Him? (all music by Burton Lane)

Alan Jay Lerner was born on August 31, 1918, in New York, a scion of the family whose fortune had been built on the Lerner Shops chain of women's clothing stores. At Choate prep school, Lerner was caught smoking and dismissed. He went on to Harvard, where he took up boxing and lost the sight in his left eye from a wild punch. The accident exempted him from having to serve in World War II, at which point he began to pursue a writing career. For two years he wrote for a variety of radio shows, but then caught the theater bug as a contributor to Harvard's Hasty Pudding shows. One day, he was having lunch at the Lambs Club when a man, looking for the men's room, recognized him and sat down. "Would you like to write lyrics with me?" he asked. "My partner just went into the navy." The man was Frederick Loewe.

Loewe was born in Berlin on June 10, 1904, to Austrian parents. His father, Edmund, was a leading vocalist and encouraged his son in music. Frederick became a child prodigy on the piano and studied with such well-known composers as Eugen d'Albert and Ferruccio Busoni. At the age of thirteen, he became the youngest soloist to appear with the Berlin Symphony. When only fifteen, he wrote the song "Katrina," which became a huge hit in Europe. The family emigrated to the United States in 1924 so that the elder Loewe could appear in operetta. Unfortunately, he died soon after the family arrived in New York, leaving his wife and son virtually penniless.

Loewe worked as a busboy in a cafeteria and as a riding instructor in New Hampshire. He tried his luck as a boxer in Brooklyn. The unfortunate loss of several teeth to an opponent (better than an eye, at least) led to another change in career. This time, Loewe traveled out west and briefly became a cowboy. He then worked on a ferry, plying the international waters between Miami and Cuba, where thirsty customers could sidestep the strictures of Prohibition. He played piano on the ship, returning to New York at the end of Prohibition and taking a job in a beer garden.

Loewe broke into the theater as a rehearsal pianist for one of the last operettas, *Champagne Sec* (1933). He joined the Lambs Club, like Lerner, hoping to make contacts in the theatrical world. At the Lambs in 1935, Loewe became friends with actor Dennis King, who was about to appear in the play *Petticoat Fever* at the Ritz Theater. King liked a song Loewe had written with lyricist Irene Alexander, "Love Tiptoed Through My Heart," and interpolated it into the show, thus providing Loewe with his Broadway debut. After another interpolation, his first complete score, written with Earle Crooker, was *Salute to Spring* (1937), a big hit in St. Louis that never transferred to Broadway. Producer

Dwight Deere Wiman liked the team's work and hired them to compose the 1938 Broadway operetta *Great Lady*. The show was a fast flop, closing after only twenty performances. In 1942, Detroit producer Henry Duffy asked Loewe about *Salute to Spring* and Loewe said he needed to find a new lyricist. Which takes us back to that fateful meeting at the Lambs Club.

Lerner agreed to the collaboration and two days later, the new team was on a train to Detroit. The show, now titled *Life of the Party,* opened and closed in Detroit—but a team was born.

Although not the best of friends, the two men got on well enough. Lerner was notoriously unreliable although remarkably talented, and Loewe was universally disliked for his meanness. But somehow their talents seemed to mesh. Alas, their next show, *What's Up?* (1943), was another failure. Then came *The Day Before Spring* (1945), which ran a mediocre 165 performances in spite of good reviews and a fine score. It was to be the team's last failure.

*Brigadoon* (1947), a commercial and artistic triumph, tells a story of the power of love and faith, and its score is a lyrical evocation of the Scottish Highlands. It ran for 581 performances and has been revived continuously ever since.

Lerner next undertook a project with Kurt Weill, *Love Life* (1948). He returned to his partnership with Loewe for *Paint Your Wagon* (1951), a lighthearted adventure set during the California gold rush. The score was, according to reviewers, much more entertaining than the book. Also that year, Lerner wrote the screenplay and lyrics to the Astaire film, *Royal Wedding*, with music by Burton Lane and an excellent score.

Lerner and Loewe's next Broadway offering was their biggest success, but it took six years to reach the stage. *My Fair Lady* (1956), based on Shaw's *Pygmalion,* was turned down by most of Broadway's veteran

songwriters. E. Y. Harburg, Dietz and Schwartz, Noel Coward, Cole Porter, and Rodgers and Hammerstein all passed on the project. Lerner and Loewe tried their hand, but were unable to get a handle on the story of a young flower seller's social transformation by an arrogant professor of linguistics. They walked away, only to return after other projects failed to materialize. The illustrious score contains what is considered by many to be Broadway's finest score.

The team then went to Hollywood and MGM to write one of the last classic film musicals, *Gigi* (1958). After the success of *My Fair Lady* and *Gigi*, there was tremendous pressure on Lerner and Loewe. *Camelot* (1960) was considered just that by many critics, though no one questioned the superior score

The difficulties of getting *Camelot* to the stage, and its reception, led to Frederick Loewe's retirement. He didn't return to writing until the 1975 motion picture musical, *The Little Prince*. Lerner, however, was not ready for retirement. He worked with Burton Lane on *On a Clear Day You Can See Forever,* (1965), proving that he was still at the top of his game. Lerner then turned to Andre Previn for *Coco* (1969), which marked Katharine Hepburn's musical theater debut. Perhaps Lerner should have quit while he was ahead; a number of flops followed, including *1600 Pennsylvania Avenue* (1976), written with Leonard Bernstein. That remarkable score has never gotten its due. Lerner reteamed with Lane for *Carmelina* (1979) which, although a failure, has a marvelous score. Lerner's last show, *Dance a Little Closer*, written with Charles Strouse, opened and closed on May 11, 1983. Lerner died on June 14, 1986. Loewe died on February 14, 1988.

During their heyday, the team of Lerner and Loewe produced some of the most enduring of all American musicals. The Lerner and Loewe hallmark was witty, sophisticated, and emotionally complex lyrics married to lively, passionate music, and their work continues to enchant new generations of theatergoers. ◆

# Song and Story

### BEFORE I GAZE AT YOU AGAIN

Lerner felt that the character of Guinevere needed a number in the second act. He talked it over with Loewe, and they realized they had very little time until the *Camelot*'s opening night. Loewe wrote the melody and sent it off for orchestration before the lyric was even written. Lerner finished the lyric the morning of opening night and slid the lyric under Julie Andrews's hotel room door with a note saying, "Learn this by this evening," which she did.

### I TALK TO THE TREES

Lerner came up with the title of this song and gave it to Loewe, who wrote a marvelous melody. As was his bent, Lerner wrote version after version of a lyric but none seemed to work. Then he realized it should have no rhymes at all. When he took out the rhymes, the song came to life.

### WHAT DID I HAVE THAT I DON'T HAVE

For this tune, Lerner decided that words of one syllable were called for, and those words would have to be hard sounding with strong consonants.

### GIGI

This song was written for what Maxwell Anderson called "the recognition scene," in which the lead character realizes what he has been missing all along. In the course of it, Gaston realizes, slowly, that he loves Gigi. Lerner has stated that he was most proud of this song.

### THE SIMPLE JOYS OF MAIDENHOOD

Lerner didn't want this song rushed in performance, so he purposely made the last few words of the lyric difficult to sing, thus assuring that the performer would take her time.

**ABOVE:** Julie Andrews in Lerner and Loewe's last show, *Camelot.* **RIGHT:** Lerner and Loewe run through the score of *4* with Leslie Caron.

# Burton Lane

Composer Burton Lane may not have had as many Broadway shows produced as did his contemporaries, but they all had superior scores, full of rich, inventive melodies. When not writing for Broadway, Lane pursued a successful career in Hollywood.

Born on February 2, 1912, in New York City, Lane showed an early aptitude for music; he took his first piano lessons at age three but then his parents imposed a six-year break so that he would concentrate on his school work. When he returned to piano, he was soon considered so talented a young composer that he was given an audience with J. J. Shubert, one of the most powerful men on Broadway. Lane, only fourteen at the time, was assigned the score for a new Shubert show. The show was never produced because the intended star was not available, but had it premiered, Lane would have been the youngest songwriter in Broadway history. Later, the Shuberts appropriated some of Lane's melodies, ascribing them to one of their staff writers. Lane's father found out and sued the Shuberts, forcing them to drop the songs from their show.

Lane's father knew his son had a gift and wanted him to meet the great George Gershwin. The elder Lane heard that Gershwin stayed in a certain hotel in Atlantic City and booked a room there. He positioned Burton at the lobby piano, playing his own compositions, hoping that Gershwin would come by and recognize the young man's talents. The plan worked! Gershwin became Lane's mentor. At the tender age of fifteen, Lane landed a job plugging songs at Remick Publishing Company. It was at that time that he met lyricist Howard Dietz, who was working on the revue *Three's a Crowd* (1930). When the show opened it contained two Dietz and Lane songs, "Out in the Open Air" and "Forget All Your Books."

A few more interpolations followed, including nine songs with lyrics by Harold Adamson for *Earl Carroll's Vanities* in 1931. That job led to Hollywood, and Lane and Adamson's first film score, for MGM's *Dancing Lady*, in 1933. The movie contained the twenty-one-year-old composer's first hit song, "Everything I Have Is Yours." Lane remained in Hollywood for the next seven years, working on songs for film musicals. Most of Lane's Hollywood output during the 1930s consisted of single songs for nonmusicals, but he did write a few full scores while achieving great success on the hit parade.

In 1940, Lane returned to Broadway and wrote the score for *Hold On to Your Hats*, starring Al Jolson and Martha Raye. Although it received excellent reviews, Jolson left the show, claiming he had pneumonia (doubtful), and it quickly closed. Lane's score, written with E. Y. Harburg, contained the hits "The World Is in My Arms" and "There's a Great Day Comin' Mañana."

Then it was back to Hollywood and another series of fine songs placed in nonmusical films. *Laffing Room Only* (1944) was a vehicle for Olsen and Johnson of *Hellzapoppin'* fame. Lane tried his hand at lyric-writing for that one, which included one big hit, "Feudin' and Fightin'."

Lane's next score was written with Harburg, and it remains one of the great Broadway musicals, *Finian's Rainbow* (1947). The remarkable score features a large number of hit songs, including "How Are Things in Glocca Morra?," "When I'm Not Near the Girl I Love," "If This Isn't Love," "Old Devil Moon," and "Look to the Rainbow."

**ABOVE:** Mickey and Judy in *Babes on Broadway*.

In 1951, Lane joined Alan Jay Lerner to work on the MGM musical *Royal Wedding*, starring Fred Astaire, who had made his film debut in Lane's first movie score, *Dancing Lady*. The score contained a big hit, "Too Late Now." Lane worked with Ira Gershwin on the 1952 film *Give a Girl a Break*. He was so nervous about collaborating with his friend Ira that he took a sedative to calm his nerves on the day they were to begin. When he arrived at Gershwin's house, Lane admitted that he took the pill. Gershwin laughed, reached into his pocket to reveal his own stash of medication, and said to Lane, "Me, too!" Their collaboration was a happy one, yielding a score that reflects their mutual admiration and ease at working together. The 1955 flop *Jupiter's Darling*, with lyrics by Adamson, with whom Lane had fulfilled his first film assignment, was also his last live-action musical. (He wrote a score for the animated film *Heidi* in 1976.)

Almost twenty years after *Finian's Rainbow*, Lane's next show opened on Broadway. *On a Clear Day You Can See Forever*, with lyrics by Alan Jay Lerner, proved that Lane hadn't lost his touch. The title song and "Come Back to Me" received their due, though the rest of the score is equally excellent. Lane and Lerner reteamed for *Carmelina* (1979), a failure that contained the some of the songwriters' best work.

Lane's songs are not just pop tunes. They are true theatrical songs written for characters in dramatic situations. Like the best theatrical songs, though, they transcend their original context; many have become standards in their own right, enjoying continued vibrancy through interpretations of the masters of American song. ◆

- - - - - - - - - - - - - - - - - - - - - - - - - - -

# "He was as great as Gershwin or Berlin."
# —Michael Feinstein

- - - - - - - - - - - - - - - - - - - - - - - - - - -

## Song and Story

### HOW COULD YOU BELIEVE ME WHEN I SAID I LOVED YOU WHEN YOU KNOW I'VE BEEN A LIAR ALL MY LIFE
Reportedly the longest title in Tin Pan Alley history.

### HOW'DJA LIKE TO LOVE ME?
This song was written for the film *College Swing*, to be sung by the heavily accented Lyda Roberti—hence the "how'dja." When Roberti died before filming began, the song was handed to Martha Raye and Bob Hope and became one of the funniest sequences ever put on celluloid.

### ON A CLEAR DAY YOU CAN SEE FOREVER
At a point when Burton Lane had only the first eight measures of the song in mind and no idea where it would go, he and Lerner did an interview with David Susskind, in which the interviewer asked Lane to play something from the show. Lane went to the piano and played the first eight measures of the song and continued playing, making up the rest on the spot. At the end, Lane looked at Lerner, who nodded his approval. It still took Lerner over six months to write the lyric. He wrote twenty drafts and Lane rejected each one as worse than the one before it, despairing that Lerner would never finish. But one day Lerner came in with the perfect lyric and it never changed. Lane put up with Lerner's mercurial personality and odd work habits because he knew that, ultimately, he could put words to music brilliantly.

### FEUDIN' AND FIGHTIN'
This song traveled a rough road on its way to becoming a hit. Lyricist Al Dubin wrote only the title before he disappeared on one of his legendary binges. Lane called in his friend Frank Loesser to help write the lyric. The song was a hit in the show but the producers of *Laffing Room Only* were having a dispute with ASCAP and refused to allow it to be broadcast. Finally, in 1947, Lane bought the rights, and the song was sung on Bing Crosby's radio show and recorded by Dorothy Shay to great acclaim.

### HOW ARE THINGS IN GLOCCA MORRA?
Burton Lane couldn't get a handle on "the Irish song" for Sharon. Yip Harburg had given him the dummy title "There's a Glen in Glocca Morra." Burton wrote fifty opening phrases but couldn't get a handle on the song. Burton described the moment to Michael Feinstein: "One day, Harburg came over and asked how the song was going. Yip said, 'Well, let's hear something.' And very sarcastically I picked up my manuscript book and I said, 'Okay, I'm going to start with the first one.' And I started to play, 'da da dee da da da dee dum….' Yip was sitting across the room from me, and when I looked at his face I knew he was hearing something he liked! He said, 'Play it again.' I started to play and he stopped me and said, 'No,

start it. How are things in Glocca Morra?' And the minute he said, 'How are things…' it became personal. I knew we were home. Who cares if there's a glen in Glocca Morra? But the minute he said, 'How are things in Glocca Morra?' I said, 'Well, Yip, don't you want to hear the other 49?' He said, 'We've got it! Forget it!'"

## Asides

Lane wanted to commit to writing only with Harburg after the success of *Finian's Rainbow*, but Harburg refused. Lane wouldn't write another Broadway show for almost twenty years.

Lane always said he would have like to collaborate with Jerry Herman, whom he greatly admired.

Lane's writing exhibited his great sense of humor and fun. When he met Yip Harburg, he played him both musical comedy- and operetta-style tunes. Harburg asked him, "When you listen to George Gershwin, what impresses you in his music?" Lane responded, "Well, his originality, his humor." Harburg replied, "That's it—the humor. You must try to get humor in your melodies."

# Frank Loesser

One of the great writers of Hollywood and Broadway, Frank Loesser was as much a character as those he musicalized in *Guys and Dolls*. He was also extremely loyal to those who helped him and tried to help those who came after him.

Burton Lane was responsible for Loesser's success in Hollywood. In July 1937, Lane heard some of Loesser and Manning Sherwin's songs. Lane was impressed and recommended the team to Paramount, where they were given a ten-week contract. This was a typical tryout at the studio: at the end of ten weeks, anybody who had managed to get some good songs into films got to stay. Manning Sherwin was an Englishman, who had great success as the composer of "These Foolish Things," but in 1937, Paramount wasn't impressed with his work.

Sherwin and Loesser had written songs for the film *Cocoanut Grove* and the executives liked the lyrics but not the music—so they asked Burton Lane to write a new tune immediately. They stuck him in a piano room and waited while he pounded out a song. The result was "Says My Heart," a big hit (which surprised Lane, who didn't find out the song was in the picture until he heard it played on the radio!). The success of that song led to a long-term contract for Loesser at Paramount.

Prior to the success of "Says My Heart," Lane would always pick up Loesser at his house, as the newcomer couldn't afford a car. One day, Lane and Loesser were invited to a party and Lane dutifully arrived at Loesser's to drive him to it. "Frank and his wife were having dinner. I looked down and there on the two plates were baked beans and a half an apple each. Frank said to me, 'Oh, we're having dinner, did you want to join us?' It was a very embarrassing situation. They were so broke that Frank only had one suit that he had to keep cleaning.

"Then, 'Says My Heart' went through the ceiling. A few weeks later I went to pick up Frank again, who still didn't have a car, and when I walked in this time, there's a tailor there who's measuring Frank for custom-made suits. He knew he was well on his way."

When Jule Styne, entombed at Republic Studios, asked that Loesser be loaned from Paramount, the lyricist was incensed to be working at a B studio. Loesser told Styne that he'd work for a week to finish writing the lyrics and then take a couple of weeks off. He instructed Styne not to hand in the songs to the studio until the three weeks were up. There was no reason to let the brass know they could turn out songs so quickly.

At age thirty-two, Loesser soon got a hankering to supply his own music to his lyrics—and the tunes were good, really good. Loesser joined the pantheon of George M. Cohan, Irving Berlin, Cole Porter, and Noel Coward as a guy who could write both music and lyrics.

**RIGHT:** Frank and Lynn Loesser pictured on the sheet music of their party song, "Baby, It's Cold Outside."

**OPPOSITE PAGE TOP:** Loesser and Fran Warren.

He was arguably the most versatile of all musical theater writers, each of his shows entirely unique. His first show, *Where's Charley?*, was a farcical drawing-room comedy. He then did an about-face with the raucous *Guys and Dolls*, based on Damon Runyon's short stories about the colorful denizens of Times Square. *The Most Happy Fella* followed, a sung-through musical (almost an opera) based on the serio-comic play, *They Knew What They Wanted*. Then to something completely different, a sweet, bucolic look at small-town life, *Greenwillow*. For his next show, Loesser tackled the world of big business with the playfully satirical musical, *How to Succeed in Business without Really Trying*. *Pleasures and Palaces*, a Russia-based tuner, closed out-of-town. His last show, *Señor Discretion Himself*, which took place in a small Mexican town, was another departure from his previous work; however, Loesser died without completing it.. His remarkable versatility was the product of an active intellect, as well as the need to stretch his own talents and the art form in which he worked.

But Loesser will be remembered for more than his songwriting or shows. As the owner of Frank Music, a highly regarded music publisher, he encouraged the careers of Robert Wright and George Forrest (writers of *Kismet* and *Grand Hotel*), Richard Adler and Jerry Ross (*The Pajama Game* and *Damn Yankees*), Meredith Willson (*The Music Man*), Moose Charlap (*Peter Pan*), and Jerry Herman (*Hello, Dolly!*). Loesser put many of these composers on salary knowing that the security would enable them to do their best work. Unhappy with the sorry state of dramatic licensing, Loesser started Music Theatre International. He arranged for Stephen Sondheim's first lawyer.

Loesser was quite a guy—a brilliant songwriter, astute businessman, faithful friend and colleague. His faith in his own talents gave him the courage to tackle a remarkable variety of subjects for his musicals; his songs are paeans to the regular guy, be it a winegrower in the Napa Valley, a crapshooter in the sewers of New York, or an ambitious office worker. Frank Loesser thought of himself as one of those regular guys—talented, to be sure, but in the end just a guy trying to do his best at a job. ◆

## Song and Story

### ADELAIDE'S LAMENT

Loesser first thought he'd write a song about a stripper who constantly caught cold, but he realized that the idea of a psychosomatic illness would be funnier, and would make the character of Miss Adelaide more sympathetic.

### ONCE IN LOVE WITH AMY

In *Where's Charley?*, Ray Bolger led the audience in a rousing chorus of "Once in Love with Amy." Producer Cy Feuer told the story of how the idea came to Bolger: "My son, Robert, seven years old at the time, and a friend of his, were taken to one of the first matinees by my wife, who arranged to have them seated down front by themselves. She waited for them in the back of the house. Bobby, of course, knew Ray Bolger from having met him at home, and Bobby also knew the song. When Ray came to 'Once in Love with Amy' in the second act, he either forgot the lyrics or pretended to forget them, and as a result, stopped the music and said to himself something to the effect of 'I forgot the words' or 'What were the lyrics again?' Bobby stood up and unselfconsciously reminded Ray of the lyric. The audience laughed, and Ray, of course, didn't know it was Bobby. In order to recover, Ray asked the little boy whether he would join him in singing. Bobby said he would, whereupon the two of them began to sing. Ray then urged the rest of the audience to join them, and so was born the community-sing spot, which over a period of a couple of years evolved to about a fifteen-minute number, depending upon how long Ray felt like keeping it running."

### BABY IT'S COLD OUTSIDE

Richard Rodgers to Frank Loesser: I listened to it, and jumped up from my chair to phone Frank in California and say I thought it was one of the finest pieces of songwriting I had ever heard. Today, I don't care why I thought so; I just know what it did for me and millions of others. Perhaps this sort of emotional response is all any piece needs to become a valid work of art.

**RIGHT:** Frank Loesser shows members of the service his stirring war song "Rodger Young."

ABOVE: Marlene Dietrich, Loesser, and Fran Warren.

## A BUSHEL AND A PECK

Lynn Loesser explained to radio host Ezio Petersen the genesis of this song: This was written before *Guys and Dolls* was even thought of. It had come about because I had read a book from Truman Capote called *Other Voices, Other Rooms*, a collection of short stories that came out as he was just breaking on the literary scene. I insisted that Frank read it. I was getting ready for bed one evening and Frank came tearing upstairs hollering, "You've got to come down, I've just found something." So I went down to the piano and he'd found a passage in Capote's book that quoted an old nursery rhyme that went, "I love you a bushel and a peck and a hug around the neck." He quickly wrote the whole song based on that line. After he'd written it, I asked him if maybe he should talk to Capote and ask if it was all right to use the line. Frank brushed it off as being obviously in the public domain, since it was quoted as a nursery rhyme or saying.

When *Guys and Dolls* came along, Frank pulled it out of the trunk and that was that. I met Capote a year or so later and he said he'd almost sued Frank, but decided at the last minute that it wasn't worth it

## I DON'T WANT TO WALK WITHOUT YOU

While Jule Styne and Loesser were writing at Republic Studios, Styne played a new melody. Loesser told him to save it for Paramount, not to waste it on Republic's B pictures. Styne did as he was told, and after Loesser arranged for Styne to come to Paramount, they handed in the song and it was put in *Sweater Girl* and became a huge hit for Helen Forrest and Harry James.

## CAREER HIGHLIGHTS

| | |
|---|---|
| 1910 | Frank Loesser born in New York City, June 29. |
| 1914 | Loesser already playing piano. |
| 1926 | Father dies. |
| 1928 | Signs contract with Leo Feist for song lyrics—none are published. |
| 1931 | First published song, "In Love with a Memory of You," music by William Schuman. |
| 1934 | First hit song, "I Wish I Were Twins," with music by Joseph Meyer. |
| 1936 | First Broadway show, *The Illustrator's Show*, with music by Irving Actman, opens January 20 and closes after five performances; Loesser and Actman sign with Universal; Universal contract expires; marries Lynn Garland. |
| 1937 | First Hollywood song hit, "The Moon of Manakoora," with music by Alfred Newman. |
| 1939 | "Seventeen," first published song, music and lyrics by Loesser. |
| 1944 | Susan Loesser born. |
| 1948 | Loesser creates Susan Publications, Inc.; *Where's Charley?*, first full Broadway score, opens on October 11. |
| 1950 | John Loesser born; *Guys and Dolls* opens on November 24. |
| 1952 | Film *Hans Christian Andersen* opens. |
| 1957 | Divorces Lynn Loesser. |
| 1959 | Marries Jo Sullivan on April 29. |
| 1962 | Hannah Loesser born on October 22. |
| 1965 | Emily Loesser born on June 2. |
| 1969 | Begins work on *Señor Discretion Himself*; dies on July 28. |

## Asides

When writing a new lyric, Oscar Hammerstein II often took a popular song of the day and fit his lyric to the existing music. Frank Loesser, a composer in his own right, would often compose a dummy score for his lyric and then send the lyric to a composer. When he wrote "Praise the Lord and Pass the Ammunition," Loesser was encouraged to keep his dummy music rather than passing the lyric to another composer. He agreed and it became a huge hit.

Sometimes songs were written in roundabout ways. Dorothy Lamour needed a song for an appearance at the Palladium in London. She leaned on Loesser to supply her with a song because he owed her. She told songwriter Barry Kleinbort that she used to regularly give Loesser $2 for whorehouses in Los Angeles. It was a good exchange all the way around: Lamour got her song for the London engagement and was able to sing it on screen in the United Artists picture, *On Our Merry Way*. Loesser eventually got paid for the song.

Loesser believed in himself most of all. He assumed that anything he undertook would be a success, and he was usually correct. One day he sang "The Best Things in Life Are Free" to Burton Lane and told Lane that it would be a snap to write a melody like that. Lane said, "You could? Well go ahead and write one, you don't need me." As Lane then recalled, "Well, the son of a gun went off and did it."

## First Person

Composer Burton Lane appreciated talent and certainly recognized Loesser's genius. He also experienced the Loesser temper firsthand: "I had to sit at the piano and play the tune constantly until he remembered it well enough to write a lyric to it…. Now Frank was very secretive. He would sit across the room from me, a pad held very high so that all I could see was his eyes. He would write very small, and then he would suddenly start to smile, and I'm dying to know what he's writing. I would say, 'Frank, what is it, what did you get, what made you laugh, what's tickling you?' And he'd go on writing till he'd finished, and then he'd put what he'd written up on the piano. His handwriting was terrible and I'm supposed to sing the song and read his handwriting at the same time. Now I really adored Frank, but if I blew a line because I couldn't understand his writing, he'd say, 'God damn it, what's the matter with you, can't you read?' and he'd get upset. But finally he would settle down and I would ask him to type it out." Lane understood Loesser's frustrations since Lane was known to have a short fuse himself. They'd both get frustrated because they cared so much about their craft, and sometimes they'd lose patience as much with themselves as with their collaborators.

Hoagy Carmichael on first being teamed with Frank Loesser: You can well understand my enthusiasm when the head of the music department deposited Frank in my crib. But he shook me up a little bit on first meeting. His exuberance and zany talk were too much for an older man who took composing seriously. All of a sudden, I felt as if I wasn't adequate in spite of the hits I'd written. He just didn't seem serious enough about this serious matter of writing songs.

Abe Burrows: The public Loesser was a cerebral, tough, sharp man with wit and charm. In a working relationship, he was a demanding perfectionist with a short fuse…his anger directed against himself as much as anyone else. But all these qualities were surface. Somewhere, buried very deep, was a gentle something that wanted to "make them cry."

BELOW: Loesser and wife, Lynn Loesser, during rehearsals for *The Most Happy Fella*.

# Mitchell & Pollack

Lyricist Sidney D. Mitchell and his frequent collaborator, Lew Pollack, were members of an elite Hollywood group: staff writers who could write terrific Tin Pan Alley tunes on assignment, frequently under tight deadlines. Their movies didn't yield sheet music sales by the millions or a reliable catalog of standards, though Mitchell did write "You Turned the Tables on Me" and Pollack had success with "Charmaine" (1926—Erno Rapee), "Diane" (1927—Erno Rapee), and "Two Cigarettes in the Dark." They did, however, provide wonderful musical moments in dozens of films.

Mitchell was born in Baltimore, Maryland, on June 15, 1888. After a stint as a journalist, he moved to New York and became a staff writer for music publishers. An early success was the catch World War I hit, "Would You Rather Be a Colonel with an Eagle on Your Shoulder or a Private with a Chicken on Your Knee?"

He enjoyed a successful career on Tin Pan Alley with songs featured in Broadway musicals. Among those shows were *Hitchy-Koo of 1918*, *Her Family Tree* (1910), *The Midnight Rounders of 1920*, *The Whirl of New York* (1921—with Lew Pollack), *Snapshots of 1921*, *Greenwich Village Follies* (1921), *Spice of 1922*, and the *Ziegfeld Follies* (1918 and 1920 editions). Though none of these shows was especially memorable, they provided an excellent education in popular songwriting and afforded Mitchell many contacts in the entertainment industry.

Answering the call of sound pictures, Mitchell moved to Hollywood along with many of his Tin Pan Alley brethren, writing mainly with Lew Pollack.

Composer and lyricist Lew Pollack was born in New York City on June 16, 1895. He began his career as a singer/pianist in vaudeville. Through his contacts, he was hired by Fox Pictures to score such landmark silent films as *What Price Glory?* (1926) and *Seventh Heaven* (1927). He wrote the hit "(Who's Wonderful, Who's Marvelous?) Miss Annabelle Lee" with Sidney Clare in 1927. Harry Richman made a hit recording of the song. He and lyricist Jack Yellen supplied Sophie Tucker with a standard, "My Yiddische Mama" which was issued on a 78-rpm disc with the song sung in both Yiddish and English. Pollack had many songs featured in Broadway musicals, such as

*The Passing Show of 1918*, *Luckee Girl* (1928), and *Sweet and Low* (1930). Pollack and Paul Francis Webster had a hit with "Two Cigarettes in the Dark" in the play *Kill That Story* (1934).

Mitchell and Pollack collaborated on such films as *Pigskin Parade*, *One in a Million* (1936), *Life Begins in College* (1937), *In Old Chicago* (1938—"I've Taken a Fancy to You"), and *Rebecca of Sunnybrook Farm* (1938—"Happy Ending"), as well as songs for *Captain January* (1936—"At the Codfish Ball").

Mitchell died in Los Angeles on February 25, 1942. Lew Pollack died in Los Angeles on January 18, 1946. ◆

## Song and Story

### CHARMAINE

This was written as the theme song for the silent film, *What Price Glory?* Pollack, though he had no hits to this time, was embarrassed by the lyric and insisted that the 1926 printing of the sheet music credit Louis Leazer. The song became a smash hit and when it was republished by Sherman, Clay, Pollack agreed to have his name on the sheet.

### YOU DO THE DARN'DEST THINGS, BABY

*Pigskin Parade* (1936) is set on a college campus with a big football game providing the tension-filled climax. (This popular formula was also used in *The Freshman*, *Good News*, *Sunny Side Up*, *So This is College*, *Sunny Skies*, *Sweetie*, and countless other films.). A Fox Pictures scout heard the young Judy Garland on the *Jack Oakie Radio Hour* and arranged for her to be loaned out from MGM (who didn't know what to do with the little girl with the big voice) for their film *Pigskin Parade*. MGM agreed to the loanout since they had no plans for Garland. They had a liberal loanout policy with Fox since Louis B. Mayer's son-in-law was Darryl Zanuck's executive assistant.

Fox knew exactly what to do with Garland: they gave her Mitchell and Pollack songs tailored to her voice. She made quite an impression in the film, but MGM held her contract and Fox had to let her go.

Johnny Mercer was born on November 8, 1909, in Savannah, Georgia. His early life in the South would influence his writing throughout his career. Mercer wrote an astonishing number of hit tunes, including many for which he supplied the music and lyrics, and he also became a successful singer and a founder of Capitol Records. Mercer's lyrics are lightly poetic, flavored with slang, casual, conversational, and best sung with a slow Southern drawl.

When he was three years old, Mercer began to develop a fascination with music, listening to the family's cylinder player. By fifteen he had written his first song, titled, "Sister Susie, Strut Your Stuff." Three years later, his life would change when his father's real estate business collapsed, leaving the family heavily in debt. Mercer's father promised to repay the almost 1 million dollars he owed, a promise that Mercer himself fulfilled. With no money for college, Mercer planned to stow away on a ship headed for New York City. When his father informed the captain, he ended up working for his passage.

In New York, Mercer tried his luck as an actor, auditioning for the *Garrick Gaieties*. He ended up supplying a song for the revue, "Out of Breath and Scared to Death of You." He fell head-over-heels in love with one of the chorus girls, Elizabeth "Ginger" Meehan. She didn't encourage the youngster, but didn't put him off, either. He took a day job in a Wall Street brokerage office but continued to place a few songs in Broadway revues, and in 1932 he collaborated with Harold Arlen on "Satan's Li'l Lamb." This became Mercer's first recorded song, committed to posterity by Ethel Merman. Mercer, Arlen, and lyricist E. Y. Harburg became fast friends.

Paul Whiteman held a contest for a new band singer, needing to fill a gap in his roster that was caused by the departure of the Rhythm Boys, Al Rinker, Harry Barris, and Bing Crosby. (Crosby, by the way, was having his own tempestuous affair with Ginger Meehan.) Mercer won the contest and the job and joined Whiteman's organization.

Mercer met Hoagy Carmichael through Whiteman and the two teamed up to write Mercer's first hit, "Lazy Bones." In addition to singing and emceeing with Whiteman, Mercer supplied songs for Whiteman's Kraft Music Hall radio appearances. He and Whiteman trombonist Jack Teagarden became something of a team on the broadcasts. He also wrote for Benny Goodman and sang with Bob Crosby's band.

Mercer placed a few songs in Hollywood pictures, beginning when "Lazy Bones" was interpolated into the 1933 film *Bombshell*. So he decided to try his luck in Hollywood, and made a minor splash as a performer in two 1935 films, *Old Man Rhythm* and *To Beat the Band*, both of which also featured his lyrics. He acquitted himself gracefully, but that was the end of his acting career. Mercer continued working for RKO until 1940, with occasional loan outs to other studios. On a trip back to Georgia, Mercer and Ginger, now his wife, passed through Texas and had their first look at a mechanical bull. It inspired the lyric to "I'm an Old Cowhand," with uncredited music by Harry Warren, which became a huge hit for Bing Crosby in the 1936 film, *Rhythm on the Range*. In 1938, Mercer recorded duets with Bing Crosby for Decca Records.

While working on the 1937 film *Hollywood Hotel*, Mercer reacquainted himself with Benny Goodman, and in 1939 he became a regular on Goodman's *Camel Caravan* radio show. Mercer had his own radio show, *The Johnny Mercer Chesterfield Music Shop*, for twenty-six weeks in 1944. He made another stab at Broadway with the show *Walk with Music* (1940), collaborating with Hoagy Carmichael, but despite a fine score, the show was not a success.

On April 8, 1942, Mercer, technician/businessman Glenn Wallichs, and songwriter/producer B. G. De Sylva established a company they intended to call Liberty Records, but the name was already in use. Ginger Mercer supplied a substitute: Capitol Records. There were a few hurdles to overcome for the fledgling company. Shellac was in short supply during the war years, but Wallichs discovered a young bandleader whose father had a large stash of it. The bandleader was signed to Capitol, where he recorded four sides, and Capitol had its shellac. Wallichs also advertised in local newspapers for people to "trade unwanted records for new," and collected over twenty thousand pounds of shellac. Capitol's next crisis had a salutary ending. The musicians went on strike on August 1, 1942. Capitol and Decca

resolved their differences in November 1943, but Columbia and RCA held out for another year, giving Capitol a jump on the larger labels.

Mercer's first act at Capitol was to sign Paul Whiteman, and he was featured on the label's first release, which included "I Found a New Baby" and "The General Jumped at Dawn." Mercer also signed Martha Tilton, and he himself recorded numerous hits. By 1946, Capitol could boast one-sixth of the total record sales in the United States.

In 1947, Mercer resigned as president of Capitol, and in 1955 he sold his interest to EMI, Ltd. for $8.5 million. He insisted that the company's success was dependent on full-time stewardship and he didn't find it fun anymore. He used part of the money to finish paying off his father's debts.

Mercer continued writing pop tunes and songs for films, publishing more than 250 songs in the 1940s, more than sixty of them bona fide hits. His efforts as a vocalist paid off as well, and he racked up twenty-seven hit records.

Mercer's Hollywood assignments included *You'll Find Out* and *Second Chorus* (both 1940); *Blues in the Night* (1941); 1942's *The Fleet's In*, *You Were Never Lovelier*, and *Star Spangled Rhythm*; *The Sky's the Limit* (1943); *Here Come the Waves* (1944); 1945's *Out of This World*; *The Harvey Girls* in 1946; *The Belle of New York* in 1952; *Seven Brides for Seven Brothers* (1954); and *Daddy Long Legs* (1955). He also wrote for Broadway but didn't find much success there. *St. Louis Woman* 1946), written with Harold Arlen, contained one of Broadway's finest scores but the libretto brought the production down. In 1949, Mercer and Robert Emmett Dolan wrote the lighthearted *Texas, Li'l Darlin'*, which did enjoy a respectable run. *Top Banana* (1951)

**RIGHT:** Bob Crosby shooting the breeze with pal Johnny Mercer.

starred Phil Silvers, and this time Mercer wrote the songs himself. Mercer's biggest Broadway success was *Li'l Abner* (1956), which he wrote with Gene de Paul. Mercer and Arlen teamed up for the unfortunate failure *Saratoga* (1959), again with an under-appreciated score. His last Broadway show was the Bert Lahr vehicle *Foxy*, with music by Robert Emmett Dolan. The show closed prematurely in 1964. Mercer's last stage score was for the London production of *Good Companions* (1974), for which Andre Previn wrote the music. Mercer's lyrics revealed an artist still at the top of his form. Though he claimed never to have had a Broadway hit, it isn't quite true, and his songs remain top-notch musical theater works.

With each succeeding decade Mercer's output fell, mirroring that of other masters of the American popular song whose opportunities waned as rock–and–roll captured the public's imagination. Johnny Mercer died on June 26, 1976. ❖

## THE GREAT SONGS, CONT'D

**1949** The Big Movie Show in the Sky; It's Great to Be Alive(both music by Robert Emmett Dolan)

**1950** Autumn Leaves (music by Joseph Kosma); In the Cool, Cool, Cool of the Evening (music by Hoagy Carmichael)

**1951** I Wanna Be a Dancin' Man (music by Harry Warren); When the World Was Young (Ah the Apple Tree) (music by M. Philippe-Gerard); You're So Beautiful—That

**1952** Early Autumn (music by Ralph Burns and Woody Herman); Glow Worm (music by Paul Lincke); I Got Out of Bed on the Right Side (music by Arthur Schwartz)

**1953** Satin Doll (music by Duke Ellington and Billy Strayhorn)

**1954** When You're in Love (music by Gene DePaul)

**1955** Something's Gotta Give

**1956** The Country's in the Very Best of Hands; If I Had My Druthers; Love in a Home; Namely You (all music by Gene DePaul)

**1959** Goose Never Be a Peacock (music by Harold Arlen); I Wanna Be Around (lyrics with Sadie Vimmerstadt); Love Held Lightly; The Man in My Life (both music by Harold Arlen)

**1961** Moon River (music by Henry Mancini)

**1963** The Days of Wine and Roses (music by Henry Mancini)

**1964** Charade (music by Henry Mancini); (This Is) My Night to Howl (music by Robert Emmett Dolan)

**1965** Emily (music by Johnny Mandel); Summer Wind (music by Henry Mayer); The Sweetheart Tree (music by Henry Mancini)

**1970** Whistling Away the Dark (music by Henry Mancini)

**1973** I'm Shadowing You (music by Blossom Dearie)

**1974** Dance of Life; Good Companions; The Pleasure of Your Company; Stage Struck (all music by Andre Previn)

# *Song and Story*

## BOB WHITE

This song was a favorite with B. G. De Sylva, so he hired Mercer to work at Paramount and later, De Sylva, Glen Wallichs, and Mercer started Capitol Records.

## THIS TIME THE DREAM'S ON ME

Johnny Mercer: It's one of Harold's nicest tunes. It's kind of a poor lyric, I think. Build on the thing about "the drink's on me." I think it's too flip for that melody. I think it should be nicer. I was in a hurry. I remember the director didn't like it. I could have improved it, too. I really could. I wish I had. But, you know, we had a lot of songs to get out in a short amount of time, and we had another picture to do.

## MOON RIVER

A preview of *Breakfast at Tiffany's* in San Francisco didn't go so well. At the meeting afterward, producer Marty Rakin said, "I don't know what you guys are gonna do but I'll tell you one thing, that damn song can go."

## P.S. I LOVE YOU

Johnny Mercer: I recall one time when my wife Ginger was away on a trip and I naturally desired to write to her. Taking pen in hand, ol' massa Mercer wrote a long letter dealing with just the sort of trivia that occurs to one lonely for another. There it was, completed. I'd written many a love song, and I read it over. I'd left out the real reason I started the letter. So below the great message, I scrawled "P.S. I Love You." Immediately, the thought of that phrase as a song title struck me and I dashed off what later, thanks to forgetful me and lucky fate, became a hit tune.

## I WANNA BE AROUND TO PICK UP THE PIECES

Johnny Mercer: A lady sent me this title, she worked at a cosmetic counter in Youngstown, Ohio. I told her we had a record by Tony Bennett and she was thrilled. She said, "You've changed my life, Mr. Mercer. People are coming in the store and asking for my autograph. Next week I have to go on the radio in Cleveland." Two weeks later she said, "I'm going to Cincinnati, I'm getting to be so famous." Finally, she came to New York and she was on *To Tell the Truth* and then she went to Europe. She said, "I'm tired, I'm going to get out of show business."

## LAURA

The song "Laura," so beautiful that both Cole Porter and Irving Berlin wished they'd written it, originally had a lyric by Irving Caesar. If David Raksin hadn't adamantly rejected Caesar's original lyric, Johnny Mercer's life might have been radically different.

Johnny Mercer: If a fellow plays me a melody that sounds like something, well, I try and fit the words to the sound of the melody. It has a mood, and if I can capture that mood, that's the way we go about it. *Laura* was that kind of picture. It was pre-designed, because *Laura* was a mystery. So I had to write "Laura" with kind of a *misterioso* theme. That's hard, because there are so few notes. And because the intervals are tough, the key changes are strange. And at the time it came out, it was most strange. But since it has become so popular, it's easier now. That kind of song is always difficult because you have to write a lyric that's going to be a hit, and you don't have many notes to work with.

## LAZY BONES

Johnny Mercer and Hoagy Carmichael won $1,250 each from ASCAP for the song. Red Norvo recalled, "Mildred [Bailey] and I were living in Queens at the time. Johnny phoned me on a Friday. He said he'd just got this check from ASCAP and couldn't cash it. We told him to come out to our apartment. When he got there, Mildred told him to call Ginger and tell her to take a cab. She said we'd pay for it. Ginger came and we spent the weekend with them and on Monday morning, Mildred went to her bank and got the check cashed for him."

## THAT OLD BLACK MAGIC

Harold Arlen: The words sustain your interest, make sense, contain memorable phrases and tell a story. Without the lyric, the song would be just another song.

## FOOLS RUSH IN (WHERE ANGELS FEAR TO TREAD)

The tune was adapted from Rube Bloom's instrumental, "Shangri-La." The title came from Alexander Pope's *An Essay on Criticism: Part II*.

## JEEPERS CREEPERS

Johnny Mercer: My wife and I went to see a movie one night at the Graumann's Chinese and Henry Fonda played a farm boy in it. And you know how he is, he's got that wonderful kind of slow delivery, genuine, real, homespun. And in the movie he saw something, something impressed him, and he said, "Jeepers creepers," and that just rang a little bell in my head, and I wrote it down when I got out of the movie. 'Cause you know, "jeepers creepers" in America in those days was kind of a polite way, I think, of saying "Jesus Christ."

## THE DAYS OF WINE AND ROSES

Johnny Mercer: I completed it in nine minutes. I had it all in my mind and couldn't get the words down fast enough. Gene Lees did an article about me in a magazine. He noticed that that song was written with only two sentences. Well, that's true. But I didn't do it on purpose. I mean, it wasn't like a crossword puzzle or anything. I just followed where the melody went. As a matter of fact, I don't feel too responsible about this song, although it's one of my very favorites. Because Ernest Dowson wrote, "They are not long, the days of wine and roses." And that's where the picture title comes from, and the television show, so I don't take too much credit for that.

### AC-CENT-CHU-ATE THE POSITIVE

Johnny Mercer to the BBC: When I was working with Benny Goodman back in '39, I had a publicity guy who told me he had been to hear Father Divine, and that was the subject of his sermon, "Accentuate the positive and eliminate the negative." Well, that amused me so, and it sounds so Southern and so funny that I wrote it down on a piece of paper. And this was, what, five years later? And Harold Arlen and I were riding home from the studio after a conference about getting a song for the sailors. … And Harold was singing me this little tune he had sung me before. Now, that's a strange thing about your subconscious, because here's a song that's kind of lying dormant in my subconscious for five years, and the minute he sang that tune, it jumped into my mind as if it dialed a phone number. Because it doesn't really fit. The accent is all different. I just think there's some kind of fate connected with it.

## First Person

Lillian Mercer: He disappeared one morning [when he was six] and was gone all day. I looked all over town for him. When he finally got home late in the evening, I found out that he had followed the town band, the Irish Jasper Greens, out to a picnic and stayed with them all day. He just couldn't resist the music.

Harold Arlen: Our working habits were strange. After we got a script and the posts for the songs were blocked out, we'd get together for an hour or so every day. While Johnny made himself comfortable on the couch, I'd play the tunes for him. He has a wonderfully retentive memory. After I would finish playing the songs, he'd just go away without a comment. I wouldn't hear from him for a couple of weeks, then he'd come around with the completed lyric.

Johnny Mercer on his collaborators: I like a guy who writes his way and his way is so high that it starts where everyone else leaves off. I've often had a lot of good lyrics loused up by writing them first because the guy doesn't understand the meter

that I want. I'd rather catch the mood of his tune."

Margaret Whiting: When John drank he was a mess. The best way to handle it was just to shun John when he was drinking. He was completely two different people when he was sober and when he was drinking. After chewing someone out something terrible the next morning he would send roses by way of apologizing. He never got out of line with me until one night he started and I could see the direction it was going and I just stopped him and said, "John I don't want any of your roses tomorrow morning." And he stopped. The fact is, he could do it all, write the most tender love lyrics and come out with "Ac-Cen-Chu-Ate the Positive" and "Blues in the Night," which is Americana. I don't know anybody who was any better.

Eubie Blake, in a letter to Mercer: I saw and heard you on the Steve Allen show last night. Well, first I want to tell you I am an old timer, and I've seen them all. Ophays, I mean. You are in my estimate the greatest Rhythm Singer of all Ophays I've ever heard.

Johnny Mercer, in the ASCAP magazine: I'm crazy about songwriters.…I can remember being terribly jealous of a few writers when I was a young man, but after I got a few hits of my own, I didn't mind them at all. I've never been jealous since, of any writer. I love to hear a good song, no matter where it comes from.

Songwriter Carl Sigman: I worshipped him because I was learning about writing. He really helped me a lot. There was real goodness in the man. We all worshipped him. He was, to me, the hippest, coolest person that I ever met.

## Asides

Mercer the singer charted with "Strip Polka," "G.I. Jive," "Ac-cent-Chu-ate the Positive," "Candy" (with Jo Stafford), "On the Atchison, Topeka, and the Santa Fe," "Personality," and "Sugar Blues."

When "Lazy Bones" became a hit, Paul Whiteman asked Mercer to put together a new singing trio à la the Rhythm Boys. Mercer got Jerry Arlen, Harold's brother, and Jack Thompson. They joined the band and were fired after only one week. Mercer, however, was kept on to sing duets with Jack Teagarden.

When Johnny Mercer went to audition as an actor for the 1930 edition of the *Garrick Gaieties*, assistant director Everett Miller shooed him away, stating, "We only need girls and songs." Miller was surprised when, a few days later, Mercer showed up with a song—"Out of Breath and Scared to Death of You"—and it went into the show.

· · · · · · · · · · · · · · · · · · · · · · · · · · · · · · · · · · · · · · · · · · · · · · · · · · · · · · · · · · · · · · · · · · · · · · · · · · · · · · · · · · · · · · · · ·

**"Johnny Mercer is the greatest of the folk poets. I think it has something to do with him being from the south. He has the descriptive flair of a Mark Twain and the melodies of Stephen Foster." —E.Y. Harburg**

· · · · · · · · · · · · · · · · · · · · · · · · · · · · · · · · · · · · · · · · · · · · · · · · · · · · · · · · · · · · · · · · · · · · · · · · · · · · · · · · · · · · · · · · ·

# Hugh Martin

Hugh Martin and Ralph Blane comprised one of the most successful songwriting teams of the 1940s. The secret, however, was that Martin and Blane never collaborated—they wrote separately and then put both names on the music. Martin was the more successful writer of the pair, though Blane had his share of hits.

Hugh Martin was born in Birmingham, Alabama, on August 11, 1914. Expecting to pursue a classical career, he studied music with Edna Gussen and Dorsey Whittington. After graduating from Birmingham Southern College, his love for popular music (George Gershwin's in particular) inspired him to become a songwriter. Martin moved to New York City in the mid-1930s and almost immediately found work as a vocal arranger on the Broadway shows *Hooray for What!* (1937), *The Boys from Syracuse* (1938), and five musicals in 1939: *One for the Money*, *The Streets of Paris*, *Too Many Girls*, *Very Warm for May* and *Du Barry Was a Lady*. Martin also founded the vocal group the Martins, and hired the young Ralph Blane as a member after they met in the cast of *Hooray for What!* The quartet appeared in Irving Berlin's musical *Louisiana Purchase* (1940). Even after composing his own scores, Martin continued to work as a leading vocal arranger on such shows as *High Button Shoes* (1947) and *Gentlemen Prefer Blondes* (1948).

Upon completing his vocal-arranging chores for 1940's *Cabin in the Sky*, Martin teamed with Blane on their first Broadway musical, *Best Foot Forward* (1941). They wrote their songs separately, with Blane coming up with the hit "Buckle Down Winsocki" and not much else. The duo collaborated on one song for the show, "What Do You Think I Am?", the only collaboration of their career.

MGM owned the film rights to *Best Foot Forward* and Martin and Blane went to Hollywood to work on the film. Their first, and perhaps best, film score was for the Judy Garland classic, *Meet Me in St. Louis* (1944). They also contributed songs to MGM's 1946 extravaganza *Ziegfeld Follies*. Two years later, Martin returned to Broadway to contribute a marvelous score to *Look Ma, I'm Dancin'!* In 1951, he wrote *Make a Wish*, another fine effort. In 1952, Martin went to London for *Love from Judy*, teaming with Timothy Gray. Three more films followed in quick succession, *Athena* (1954), *The Girl Rush* (1955), and *The Girl Most Likely*, all with Blane sharing credit.

In 1962, Martin and Marshall Barer collaborated on a stage vehicle for Jeanette MacDonald and Liza Minnelli, entitled *A Little Night Music*. MacDonald's health forced the cancellation of the project. Martin's last Broadway show was 1964's *High Spirits*, again Timothy Gray shared credit.

Martin served as Judy Garland's accompanist when she appeared at the Palace Theater on Broadway, and as Eddie Fisher's pianist at the London Palladium. He kept writing scores throughout the sixties and seventies though none was produced. ◆

## THE GREAT SONGS

| | |
|---|---|
| 1941 | Ev'ry Time; Just a Little Joint with a Juke Box; The Three B's |
| 1943 | Wish I May; Alive and Kicking |
| 1944 | The Boy Next Door; Have Yourself a Merry Little Christmas; The Trolley Song |
| 1945 | Pass That Peace Pipe (with Roger Edens) |
| 1946 | Love |
| 1948 | Gotta Dance, I'm the First Girl in the Second Row in the Third Scene of the Fourth Number; Little Boy Blues; Tiny Room |
| 1951 | I Wanna Be Good 'n' Bad; Suits Me Fine; What I Was Warned About |
| 1954 | Faster Than Sound; Love Can Change the Stars |
| 1955 | Birmin'ham; An Occasional Man |
| 1958 | I Happen to Love You |
| 1960 | You Are for Loving |
| 1962 | Here Come the Dreamers (lyric by Marshall Barer) |
| 1964 | Home Sweet Heaven (with Timothy Gray); I Know Your Heart (with Timothy Gray); You'd Better Love Me (with Timothy Gray) |

## Song and Story

### SING FOR YOUR SUPPER

Hugh Martin: I wrote a letter to Dick Rodgers whom I had never met and said, "Dear Mr. Rodgers, this is a very presumptuous letter, I know, but I've just got to get it out of my system. Why are there no vocal arrangements in Broadway shows? I go to the movies and I hear really interesting, exciting things with choruses and duets and inventive things. But I go to the Broadway shows and I hear the greatest music in the world, but they sing a verse and two choruses and that's it. I just don't understand." I didn't get a reply to the letter, but I did get a phone call. He didn't call me personally; Joe Moon, his rehearsal pianist, called me and said, "Dick wants you to come over to the Alvin Theater right away." So I went over. I was shaking like a leaf. He said, "We have a number called 'Sing for Your Supper,' and I thought your letter was very interesting. Maybe we should not just sing a verse and two choruses; maybe we should do something like the Boswell Sisters. I thought it might be fun to have our three principals do a girls trio in harmony. Would you like to try doing it?" I said, "Yes, sir. I really would like to try that."

### HAVE YOURSELF A MERRY LITTLE CHRISTMAS

Hugh Martin explained the original lyric of the song: "Have yourself a merry little Christmas. It may be your last. Next year we may all be living in the past. Have yourself a merry little Christmas. Pop that champagne cork. Next year we may all be living in New York…" I thought it was grand! We submitted it to the studio, and Judy refused to sing it, quite wisely, because it was terribly sad. She said, "They'll think I'm a monster if I sing that to that little Margaret O'Brien. They'll think I'm a sadist!"

# Joseph McCarthy

**N**ot THAT Joe McCarthy! The lyricist Joseph McCarthy was born just outside Boston on September 27, 1885. After a short period of singing in cabarets, he began writing lyrics, achieving his first hit with "You Made Me Love You" in 1913, in collaboration with James V. Monaco. Three years later, the team came up with "Why Do You Want to Make Those Eyes at Me For?" McCarthy soon graduated to Broadway shows and, in 1918, he and Harry Carroll combined forces on the score for *Oh, Look* and the song "I'm Always Chasing Rainbows." Once McCarthy hit Broadway, there was no stopping him. He and Harry Tierney had a number of successes, beginning with the 1919 hit show *Irene* and the enduring standard "Alice Blue Gown." They wrote a succession of shows, including *The Broadway Whirl*, *Up She Goes*, *Glory*, and 1923's Eddie Cantor showcase, *Kid Boots*.

*Rio Rita* was the smash hit of the 1927 Broadway season, and in addition to the title song, its Tierney and McCarthy hits included "The Rangers' Song," "You're Always in My Arms," "Following the Sun Around," "The Kinkajou," and "If You're in Love, You'll Waltz." Tierney and McCarthy's last show was the unsuccessful *Cross My Heart* in 1928.

McCarthy racked up some additional popular favorites, including "Ireland Must Be Heaven for My Mother Came from There" (1916—Fred Fisher), "I'm in the Market for You" (1930—James F. Hanley), and "Ten Pins in the Sky" (Milton Ager), which Judy Garland sang in the 1938 film *Listen Darling*.

McCarthy died on December 18, 1943. His son, Joseph McCarthy, Jr., was Cy Coleman's first collaborator. Among their better known songs are "Why Try to Change Me Now" and "The Riviera." ❖

## Song and Story

### I'M ALWAYS CHASING RAINBOWS
This was the first smash hit derived from a classical theme, in this case Chopin's Fantasie Impromptu in C-sharp minor.

### IN MY SWEET LITTLE ALICE BLUE GOWN
"Alice Blue" became the term for a shade favored by Theodore Roosevelt's daughter, Alice Roosevelt Longworth.

Debbie Reynolds and Patsy Kelly (for whom only the word "inimitable" will do) in the revival of *Irene*.

# Jimmy McHugh

A Touch Of Texas
Lyrics by FRANK LOESSER
Music by JIMMY McHUGH

from
7 Day's Leave

co-starring
VICTOR        LUCILLE
MATURE   ☆   BALL
GINNY SIMMS

The All
Musical featuring
the Sweet & Hot Bands
FREDDY
MARTIN  and
LES
BROWN

An RKO Radio Picture
A Tim Whelan
Production

CAN'T GET OUT OF THIS MOOD
I GET THE NECK OF THE CHICKEN
SOFT HEARTED
A TOUCH OF TEXAS
PLEASE, WON'T YOU LEAVE
MY GIRL ALONE
BABY
PUERTO RICO
YOU SPEAK MY LANGUAGE

MELODY LANE PUBLICATIONS,

Jimmy McHugh was born in Boston on July 10, 1895. After graduating from Staley College with a degree in music, McHugh tried several careers. As he recalled, "My father wanted me to be a plumber's helper and follow in his footsteps. When I was eighteen I put the tools on my shoulder and went to it. On a job where I carried four-inch pipes from one part of a house to another, one of the pipes fell *bang* on my feet. I said, 'That's the *end* of *plumbing!*'"

His next plan was to become a pilot. "In Squantum, Massachusetts, the Wright Brothers and other noted aviators were having a big meeting. I went there. About that time, an important aviator was killed. I said, 'No aviation for me.' Returning home, I applied for the position of office boy at the Boston Opera House. For three years, that was my place. Next, [in 1917] I worked for the Irving Berlin Company in Boston. I plugged songs and rehearsed acts for eight dollars a week. There were no regular hours, but I received seventeen raises in salary."

At Watson, Berlin, and Snyder, McHugh joined his fellow pluggers in biking around town. McHugh finally made it to New York in 1921 and took a job with Jack Mills at Mills Music. He had been writing songs since 1917 but the first one to be published was "Emaline" with lyrics by George A. Little. In 1924, McHugh had his first hit, "When My Sugar Walks Down the Street," written with Gene Austen and Irving Mills. McHugh composed with a number of lyricists including Jack Mills's brother Irving. In 1925, they wrote "Everything Is Hotsy Totsy Now" and began calling themselves the "Hotsy Totsy Boys." Mills would go on to be Duke Ellington's manager and to cut himself in on hundreds of songs, so it's strange to think that he might have actually written some lyrics. (McHugh himself very likely took credit for work he didn't do, but that was later.)

McHugh's "I Can't Believe That You're in Love with Me," with music by Clarence Gaskill, was interpolated into the show *Gay Paree* in 1925. In 1926, McHugh was introduced to Dorothy Fields and they joined forces, first on Lew Leslie's very successful *Blackbirds of 1928*. The score contained such great songs as "I Can't Give You Anything but Love," "I Must Have That Man," and "Diga Diga Do." And that's the problem. Years later, both Fats Waller and Andy Razaf claimed they had written "I Can't Give You Anything but Love" and had sold it to McHugh.

The song had been introduced in *Harry Delmar's Revels* the year before but hadn't received any notice. "I Can't Give You Anything but Love" was put into the *Blackbirds* score, where it became a smash. Fats Waller did make several recordings of the song and Andy Razaf, on the occasion of being inducted into the Songwriters Hall of Fame, told Don Redman's wife that it was the song of which he was the most proud. Short of any real proof, we'll never know who wrote the song, but many believe Waller and Razaf.

Fields and McHugh also began writing for the Cotton Club in 1927. In 1930, Lew Leslie produced *The International Revue* and the team supplied the show with another standard, "On the Sunny Side of the Street." Some have accused McHugh of buying that one from Waller and Razaf as well. The great hit "Exactly Like You" is also from the score, and both songs were introduced by Harry Richman.

The Broadway success of Fields and McHugh led to a contract in Hollywood. They arrived in 1930, along with many songwriting brethren from the East Coast. The first complete score by the team came in 1935 with *Every Night at Eight*. The hits were "I'm in the Mood for Love" and "I Feel a Song Comin' On," the latter with a lyric by Fields and George Oppenheimer. McHugh's name showed up, along with Dorothy Fields, as lyricist of additional songs for the film version of *Roberta*. Although he had nothing to do with it, McHugh's name was added to the music too. That year, Fields and McHugh decided to split up.

McHugh then teamed up with Harold Adamson though he occasionally worked with other lyricists. He returned to New York in 1939 for the Carmen Miranda vehicle, *Streets of Paris*. Al Dubin wrote the songs, including "South American Way," and they went on to collaborate again the following year, on *Keep Off the Grass*.

McHugh wrote for Hollywood with a number of other lyricists including Frank Loesser, Al Dubin, and Johnny Mercer. In 1942, he and Adamson wrote the wartime hit, "Comin' in on a Wing and a Prayer." They also wrote "I Couldn't Sleep a Wink Last Night" for the film *Higher and Higher* in 1943.

McHugh and Adamson continued to write regularly for the movies until 1948, the year of their last big success, "It's a Most Unusual Day," written for *A Date with Judy*. They continued writing pop tunes and the occasional Hollywood title song until 1958. McHugh continued writing until his death on May 23, 1969. ◆

## Song and Story

### CUBAN LOVE SONG

Jimmy McHugh claimed a first for this song: For the recording, I had Tibbett make a harmony record of himself (overdubbed), and on the screen it showed the real Tibbett as a soldier and his image as a ghost standing beside him. This was the first multiple recording in record history.

OPPOSITE PAGE: McHugh and Dorothy Fields.
ABOVE: With Dinah Shore and Dean Martin.
RIGHT: With Frank Sinatra.

## THE GREAT SONGS

**1924** When My Sugar Walks Down the Street (lyric by Gene Austin)

**1925** Everything Is Hotsy Totsy Now (lyric by Irving Mills); I Can't Believe That You're in Love with Me (lyric by Clarence Gaskill); The Lonesomest Girl in Town (lyric by Al Dubin and Irving Mills)

**1926** There's a New Star in Heaven Tonight (Lyric by J. Keirn Brennan and Irving Mills)

**1928** Dig Dig Do; Doin' the New Low-Down; I Can't Give You Anything but Love (all lyrics by Dorothy Fields)

**1930** Blue Again; Exactly Like You; On the Sunny Side of the Street (all lyrics by Dorothy Fields)

**1931** Cuban Love Song (lyric by Dorothy Fields)

**1933** Don't Blame Me (lyric by Dorothy Fields)

**1935** Hooray for Love (lyric by Dorothy Fields); I Feel a Song Comin' On (lyric by Dorothy Fields and George Oppenheimer); I'm in the Mood for Love (lyric by Dorothy Fields); I'm Shootin' High; I've Got My Fingers Crossed; Spreadin' Rhythm Around (all lyrics by Ted Koehler)

**1936** Picture Me Without You (lyric by Dorothy Fields)

**1939** South American Way (lyric by Al Dubin)

**1940** Say It (Over and Over Again) (lyric by Frank Loesser)

**1942** Can't Get Out of This Mood (lyric by Frank Loesser); Comin' in on a Wing and a Prayer (lyric by Frank Loesser)

**1943** Let's Get Lost (lyric by Frank Loesser); I Couldn't Sleep a Wink Last Night (lyric by Harold Adamson); Say a Pray'r for the Boys over There (lyric by Herb Magidson)

**1945** Can't Get Out of This Mood (lyric by Frank Loesser)

**1948** It's a Most Unusual Day (lyric by Harold Adamson)

**1955** Too Young to Go Steady (lyric by Harold Adamson)

EASY TO LOVE
BORN TO DANCE

WORDS AND MUSIC BY
COLE PORTER

STARRING
Eleanor
POWELL
AND HER MUSICAL COMEDY CAST

A
Metro-
Goldwyn-
Mayer
PICTURE

PRICE 75c IN U.S.A.

Cole Porter

There's a special camaraderie among songwriters and, not surprisingly, several of our most important ones were close friends. Irving Berlin spoke to Harold Arlen almost every day. Both Arlen and Burton Lane were great friends with E. Y. Harburg, even though they found collaborating with him to be an infuriating process. On the West Coast, Bob Russell was among a group including Al Hoffman, Al Stillman, and others who shared offices around Hollywood and Vine. Cole Porter, on the other hand, had little in common with most of his contemporaries. He wasn't Jewish and grew up wealthy. No matter. Cole was undisputedly a genius, and meeting him was one of the highlights of several lyricists' lives.

Sammy Cahn commented, "When I met Cole Porter for the first time in my life, it was one of the great thrills for me because I think that he, alongside Irving Berlin, are the two single most gifted men of American words and music—because they wrote both. Cole said to me, 'I've always wanted to meet you Mr. Cahn.' My jaws locked, which is not an easy thing for my jaws to do. And I couldn't comprehend what he meant and I finally managed to say, 'You wanted to meet me, why?' He said, 'Because I always envied you the fact that you were born on the Lower East Side. Had I been born on the Lower East Side I would have perhaps been a really true genius.'"

Of course, Porter *was* a genius and many of his lyrics concerned themselves with exactly the high society in which he lived and played. He might have been jealous of the rough-and-tumble of the Lower East Side, but had he been born there, we wouldn't have had what made Porter unique. Alan Jay Lerner, whose upbringing was closer to that of Porter, recalled meeting Porter during one of the latter's frequent hospital stays: "Well, I called up and said I'd like to see him. Two days later I received a phone call from his secretary, asking whether I would appear at five o'clock two days later. Of course, I did. It was like a command performance. I arrived at the ninth floor of the Harkness Pavilion exactly at five o'clock. His butler was waiting for me at the elevator landing. He took me to the conservatory at the end of the corridor where Cole sat in the corner with a cocktail shaker, some hors d'oeuvres, a little dish of fudge. All through that entire time hot hors d'oeuvres were served, because Cole had taken another room in the hospital and put a little stove in it to prepare them for his guests."

Lerner's story perfectly captures Porter's lifestyle. Even in the hospital he insisted on being the proper host. Luckily, he had the money to fulfill his ambitions. Although he was wealthy, he was never simply a playboy. In fact, few writers can claim the output of Porter. It's true that when he chose to write a show he might take a round-the-world ocean voyage (as he did when writing *Jubilee* with Moss Hart) or spend the summer at the Lido in Venice. So it's no surprise that Porter's wealth is reflected in his lyrics. No one else in the world could have written "You're the Top," with its references to the Louvre Museum, the Derby winner, and a Waldorf salad. What makes Porter more than just a snob with talent, though, is his appreciation of both the heady highs of café society and the delights of the common man: to wit (from the very same song) Mickey Mouse, Cellophane, and the nose of the great Durante. Not that we could ever forget where he was coming from, nor would we want to. His lyrics constantly refer to the likes of society designer Elsie de Wolfe and renowned party-giver Elsa Maxwell. Porter enjoyed juxtaposing polite convention with all-too-human feelings in such songs as "Miss Otis Regrets" and "Thank You So Much, Mrs. Lowsborough-Goodby." "Down in the Depths on the Ninetieth Floor" includes the immortal line, "Even the janitor's wife has a perfectly good love life…" as a favorite Porter theme was that money can't buy happiness. This theme resounds in "Make It Another Old-Fashioned, Please," which takes as its subject a favorite drink of the haut monde.

People have often confused Porter's insistence on the good life and his shunning of the spotlight as snobbery. Frank Sinatra recalled their first meeting: "Many, many years ago, when I was a young man, I was working in a roadhouse in Englewood, New Jersey, just across the river from New York. One Sunday evening, when there were about thirty or forty people present in the club, I was singing with the six-piece orchestra. I was also the head waiter, answered telephones, and made out the radio programs…. A party of people arrived. I recognized Mr. Porter. Of course, I was absolutely astounded that he'd be in the same room. I had been singing only about a year-and-a-half or two years and I always tried to do as much Cole Porter material as I could because, as I said, I enjoy his lyrics. Another reason: Mr. Porter, unlike Mr. Rodgers, let's say, didn't go out and get loaded because of an arrangement somebody else made of his music. Mr. Porter was a very liberal man in that sense. He really didn't care how you arranged it as long as you did the song in its entirety. Even if you changed the tempo from a slow four to a twelve-eight, it made no difference to him. I very bravely said, 'We have in our midst this evening, ladies and gentlemen, one of the great artists in our musical world in America, a man of great renown,' and I went on and on and on and gave him the greatest buildup since Charles Lindbergh. Asked him to take a bow and he did, and he stared daggers at me. That's when I found out he was a snob, by the way; that was the first time. He hated the whole idea of being introduced in a beaten-down nightclub. Then I began to sing 'Let's Do It' and forgot all the words, I was so nervous."

Sinatra's interpretation of Porter's reticence isn't quite on the money—as his close friend Ethel Merman explained, "Basically, he was shy rather than snobbish." After all, Porter wasn't slumming in that New Jersey club, he was going to hear an up-and-coming singer. Porter himself once explained his interest in the good things in life: "I'm not a snob. I just like the best of everything." ❖

## Song and Story

### WUNDERBAR

Kiss Me, Kate's "Wunderbar" was conceived as a spoof on nostalgic German drinking songs. In spite of the composer's intentions and the ridiculous lyric, the song became a success. Henry Sullivan and Harry Ruskin's "I May Be Wrong, But I Think You're Wonderful" was another purposely over-the-top song that was taken seriously, as was "Sonny Boy" by De Sylva, Brown, and Henderson.

### LOVE FOR SALE

"Love for Sale" was performed in the 1930 show The New Yorkers by Kathryn Crawford, who sang it under an awning of a smart club with a street sign identifying the location as Madison Avenue. The public and critics were aghast at the image of a prostitute on the Broadway stage—or maybe they were aghast at seeing a white woman playing a prostitute. Shortly after that, when it was sung by Elisabeth Welch under a street sign designating Harlem (with the name "The Cotton Club" painted on the awning), there were no further complaints. Nevertheless, the song was banned on the radio.

### IT'S DE-LOVELY

Sometimes there are conflicting stories surrounding Porter songs. "Night and Day" was written while

**BELOW:** Lilo and Peter Cookson in front of Jo Mielziner's magnificent backdrop for Can-Can. The drop was so stupendous, Cole Porter was inspired to write "I Love Paris" after seeing it.

## THE GREAT SONGS

Cole was on vacation in Morocco, after hearing a muezzin calling the faithful to worship. Or maybe he wrote it at the Ritz Carlton and finished the lyrics on the beach at Newport. Cole told both stories, so take your pick. Another double story concerns "De-Lovely." One story concerns the moment when Cole, his wife Linda, and Monty Woolley caught their first look at Rio de Janeiro. Porter said, "It's delightful!" Linda responded, "It's delicious!" and Wooley chimed in, "It's de-lovely!" Or perhaps Porter wrote the show while cruising to the South Seas with author Moss Hart, working on the show *Jubilee*. Either way, "It's De-Lovely" was rejected for the film *Born to Dance*, so Porter took it to Broadway, where it became a hit as sung by Ethel Merman and Bob Hope in the 1936 show *Red, Hot and Blue!*

## First Person

Fred Astaire, on first hearing "Night and Day": It had a long range, very low and kind of very high, and it was long, as they all said, and I was trying to figure out what kind of dance could be arranged for it. I asked him to play it again and again, and after four or five times I began to get with it…. It was a known fact that it made the show. had an awfully rough trip when it first opened on the road and later in New York. It was known, after it caught on, as "the *Night and Day* show."

Gene Kelly on the genesis of "Be a Clown": Roger Edens, who was the associate producer of the show [*The Pirate*], and the producer, Arthur Freed, decided a dance number was needed. Somehow they sent me to Cole's house and I had the temerity to go. He said, "What kind of a number do you really need?" I said, "Well, a gay number, I don't know." He said, "Well, what do you see?" I said, "Something fast." And he said, "Well, how about a lot of lyrics?" And I said, "That's good!" The more lyrics, you know, the better for us dancers. Anyway, the next afternoon he came in with three choruses of this song, "Be a Clown," and we used it as a reprise throughout the picture. Naturally, I think he's a genius.

Dr. Albert Sirmay, T. B. Harms's house arranger, on "Ev'ry Time We Say Goodbye": It chokes me whenever I hear it, it moves me to tears. This song

**ABOVE:** Cole and Dinah Shore.

is one of the greatest songs you ever wrote. It is a dithyramb to love, a hymn to youth, a heavenly, beautiful song. It is not less a gem than any immortal song of a Schubert or Schumann.

Alan Jay Lerner: That thing that was so unique about Cole, for us who are in his craft, is that he seemed to spring from nowhere. You see, when the musical theater started in this country about 1919 or '20, when Jerome Kern led the break from the European operetta and so on, you could follow a progression from Jerome Kern to Dick Rodgers to Gershwin, but Cole seemed to spring like Jupiter from Minerva's head—all made. What he did was so special and so unaccountable and unexplainable that he really, of them all, in a strange way, is the most irreplaceable.

Frank Sinatra: I particularly like Cole's lyrics to sing because he made it fun to sing a song. He gave it a freshness. When I first would see one of his songs, the surprise of the couplet or the inner rhyme was always exciting to me. Consequently, when I worked in clubs—particularly in clubs—the material was fun to do because it was sophisticated enough for a drunk audience.

# Robin & Rainger

Ralph Rainger was born in New York City on October 7, 1901. At the age of twenty-two, he had his first composition published. Like many of his songwriting contemporaries, Rainger tried law school but soon felt drawn to the musical field. In 1926, he joined the company of the Broadway musical *Queen High* as a rehearsal pianist. Soon he was playing in Broadway pit orchestras with fellow pianist Edgar Fairchild. The duo-piano team was successful on Broadway and in vaudeville. Rainger got a job in the pit orchestra of the musical revue, *The Little Show*, and contributed a hit song to the proceedings, "Moanin' Low," with lyrics by Howard Dietz.

Leo Robin was born in Pittsburgh, Pennsylvania, on April 6, 1900. He, too, went to law school but decided to pursue songwriting. His first hit came in 1926 with "My Cutey's Due at Two-to-Two Today," with music by Albert Von Tilzer. Robin and Clifford Grey wrote lyrics to Vincent Youmans's music for the Broadway show *Hit the Deck* (1927), and "Hallelujah" was the big hit from the show. Robin and Rainger first teamed up for the pre-code film *Station S.E.X.* in 1929. Robin and Richard A. Whiting wrote "Louise" for Maurice Chevalier to sing in *Innocents of Paris* (1929) and had another hit the next year with W. Frank Harling and Richard A. Whiting on "Beyond the Blue Horizon" from the film *Monte Carlo*.

In 1932, Robin and Rainger were put under long-term contract to Paramount, where they specialized in songs for Bing Crosby, including "Please" and "Here Lies Love" (1932—*The Big Broadcast*). That year also saw their next hit, the title number from *One Hour with You*, later Eddie Cantor's theme song. In 1933, the team's "I'll Take an Option on You" was interpolated into the Broadway revue *Tattle Tales*. They came up with more hits for Crosby in 1934, including "June in January" and "With Every Breath I Take," written for *Here Is My Heart*. Robin and Lewis Gensler had a hit with "Love Is Just Around the Corner," from the same movie. "Love in Bloom" was written for Crosby to sing in the 1934 film, *She Loves Me Not*.

"Whispers in the Dark" was a hit from *Artist and Models* with music by Frederick Hollander (1936). The title tune from *Easy Living* (1937) became a jazz standard, and "Blue Hawaii" (1937) also became famous years after it was introduced. The team had one of its biggest successes, "Thanks for the Memory," written for Bob Hope and Shirley Ross to sing in *The Big Broadcast of 1938*. It became Hope's theme song for the rest of his career. "You Took the Words Right Out of My Heart" was another hit from the film. "Love with a Capital 'You'" and "Mama, That Moon Is Here Tonight" were two fine songs written for Martha Raye to sing in the film. Rainger and Robin wrote other catchy tunes for Raye, including "I'm Havin' Myself a Time" (1938—*Tropic Holiday*) and "The Tra La La and the Oom Pah Pah" (1939—*Never Say Die*). Robin collaborated with Hoagy Carmichael and Sam Coslow on the hit "Kinda Lonesome" for 1939's *St. Louis Blues*.

The team of Rainger and Robin moved to Twentieth Century-Fox in 1939. Rainger died in a plane crash on October 24, 1942. The last films with music by Rainger were 1943's *Coney Island* and *Riding High* ("No Love, No Nothin'). Robin went on to write with Harry Warren for *The Gang's All Here* ("The Lady in the Tutti-Frutti Hat," "No Love, No Nothin'," and "Paducah.") In 1946 Robin paired with the great Jerome Kern for Universal Pictures' *Centennial Summer*. "In Love in Vain" and "Up with the Lark" were both hits from that score. Also in 1946, Robin teamed with Arthur Schwartz for *The Time, the Place and the Girl* and its hits, "A Gal in Calico," "Oh, But I Do," and "A Rainy Night in Rio." Robin and Harold Arlen got together in 1948 to write "For Every Man There's a Woman," "Hooray for Love," and "What's Good About Goodbye" for *Casbah*. That same year, Robin retuned to Broadway in a big way with the smash hit *Gentlemen Prefer Blondes*. Jule Styne supplied the music for "Bye Bye Baby," "Just a Kiss Apart" and the standard "Diamonds Are a Girl's Best Friend."

In 1952, Robin and Harry Warren wrote the score to the film *Just for You*, which contained "Zing a Little Zong." In 1954 came the premiere of *The Girl in Pink Tights*, Sigmund Romberg's final Broadway score (he died before it opened). Don Walker completed the score according to Romberg's notes, and the result is one of Broadway's great undiscovered treasures. "Lost in Loveliness" was its hit song. In 1955, after Jule Styne and Robin completed the film *My Sister Eileen*, Robin retired. He wrote one more score, with Styne, for the television musical *Ruggles of Red Gap* in 1957.

After his retirement, Robin was often offered assignments, including the lyrics for the stage musical *Funny Girl*, but he stuck to his guns and didn't take on any more projects. He remains one of our finest lyricists, with the ability to inject humor into a song while staying true to the nature of the character singing it. His lyrics never reveal the hand of the lyricist—they aren't showy or self-conscious, like the works of many of his contemporaries. A solid craftsman as well as an artist, Leo Robin is an unsung genius of American popular song. ◆

# Billy Rose

Billy Rose inspecting the troupes for his *Aquacade* at the New York World's Fair of 1940.

Noted producer and lyricist Billy Rose had many talents. He was a successful popular songwriter, noted producer of musicals and revues, and a whiz at Gregg shorthand—trained by John Robert Gregg himself. He got his start as a secretary to financier Bernard Baruch. When the *Titanic* sank, it was Rose who took down the first list of survivors.

Rose produced shows for several world's fairs, including the famous *Acquacade* at the 1939–40 New York World's Fair. He owned the Diamond Horseshoe nightclub in New York City, as well as the Ziegfeld and Billy Rose theaters, in which he produced many revues. He was married to famed "funny girl" Fanny Brice, but divorced her for *Aquacade* star Eleanor Holm. Rose's name appears on many songs, and while it's indisputable that he wrote the majority of them, rumors have persisted that he cut himself in on several.

Born in New York City on September 6, 1899, Rose's first standard was the 1923 hit "Barney Google," written with composer Con Conrad. There was nowhere to go but up. The same year he wrote "That Old Gang of Mine" with Ray Henderson and Mort Dixon and "You've Got to See Mamma Ev'ry Night (Or You Can't See Mamma at All) (Con Conrad). The following year Rose, Ernest Breuer, and Marty Bloom came up with the immortal "Does the Spearmint Lose Its Flavor on the Bed Post Overnight?" Jazz favorite "Clap Hands, Here Comes Charlie" (with Joseph Meyer and Ballard Macdonald) followed in 1925, along with "Don't Bring Lulu" (with Ray Henderson, Lew Brown), "Ukulele Baby" (with Marty Bloom, Al Sherman, Jack Meskill), and, for the *Charlot Revue of 1926*, "A Cup of Coffee, a Sandwich, and You," written with Joseph Meyer and Al Dubin.

Fred Fisher wrote the music to 1927's "And the Band Played On." That same year, Rose, Dave Dreyer, and Al Jolson wrote "Me and My Shadow," which became Ted Lewis's theme song. In the 1928 film *My Man*, Fanny Brice scored a hit with the Rose/Fred Fisher collaboration, "I'd Rather Be Blue Over You Than Be Happy with Somebody Else." Al Jolson's *The Singing Fool* featured "There's a Rainbow 'Round My Shoulder," credited to Dreyer, Jolson, and Rose. In 1929, Rose collaborated with Thomas "Fats" Waller and Harry Link on "I've Got a Feeling I'm Falling."

Rose's big Broadway show of that year was *Great Day!* with music by Vincent Youmans and lyrics by Rose and Edward Eliscu. The title tune was a big hit, along with "Happy Because I'm in Love," "More Than You Know," and "Without a Song." The 1930 film extravaganza *The King of Jazz* premiered his Mabel Wayne collaboration "It Happened in Monterey." Also that year, Rose produced the Broadway revue *Sweet and Low* and the hit songs "Cheerful Little Earful (with Harry Warren and Ira Gershwin), "Dancing with Tears in My Eyes" (with Will Irwin and Mort Dixon), and "Would You Like to Take a Walk (Sumpin' Good'll Come from That)," written with Warren and Dixon. The same trio came up with 1931's *Crazy Quilt*, produced by Rose, natch. The hit this time was "I Found a Million Dollar Baby in a Five and Ten Cent Store."

*The Great Magoo* (1932), a flop play, nevertheless spawned a classic song, "It's Only a Paper Moon (If You Believed in Me)," with music by Arlen and lyrics by Rose and E. Y. Harburg.

After 1940, Rose wrote few songs, concentrating his efforts on producing and his investments. He left a legacy of great songs (if in fact he wrote them), and on his death on February 10, 1966, he left behind a large bequest to the New York Public Library at Lincoln Center for the establishment of the Billy Rose Theater Collection. ◆

Richard Rodgers and Lorenz Hart were the premier collaborators of the early years of the American musical theater—and the first songwriting duo in which the lyricist received equal billing with the composer. They were the perfect songwriting team, and their enduring fame is well deserved. Their music and lyrics are superbly integrated into a sophisticated whole and, although their personal relationship was somewhat stormy, their songs never reflect their conflict.

Lorenz "Larry" Hart's parents, Max and Frieda Hart, were immigrants who instilled in their son a love of language and literature. He attended his first play when he was seven and was permanently hooked on theater. Richard Rodgers showed an early gift for music and could play the piano at age four. At that time, composing for the Broadway theater was considered the top of the art form and, like most aspiring songwriters of his generation, the young Rodgers hoped for a career in musical comedy. There were no movies or radio, and most popular songs were introduced first on the Broadway stage.

A friend, Philip Leavitt, introduced Rodgers to the young Lorenz Hart. Rodgers wrote in *Theatre Arts* of their first meeting, "Neither of us mentioned it, but we evidently knew we'd work together, and I left Hart's house having acquired in one afternoon a career, a partner, a best friend, and a source of permanent irritation." Leavitt believed that the two would make a good songwriting team and was pleased with the way the two boys got along. He convinced Lew Fields to listen to their songs, and the producer decided to interpolate a Rodgers and Hart number, "Any Old Place with You," in his Broadway show *A Lonely Romeo* (1919). The team then contributed songs to *You'd Be Surprised* (1920), an Akron Club show, on which they collaborated with many young professionals with whom they would subsequently work, including Herbert Fields and Oscar Hammerstein II (in the cast was Dorothy Fields, later to become a famous lyricist in her own right).

Lew Fields hired the boys to write their first complete Broadway score, *Poor Little Ritz Girl,* but by the time the show opened, Fields had gotten cold feet and replaced most of their score with music by Sigmund Romberg and Alex Gerber. Rodgers and Hart's big break came in 1925, with a revue, *The Garrick Gaieties,* produced as a two-performance benefit for the Theatre Guild. Featuring a cast of unknowns, including Sterling Holloway, Libby Holman, Romney Brent, and future acting coach Lee Strasberg, the show was an immediate smash hit. Six performances were added, which sold out almost immediately, and the Guild decided to give the show an indefinite run. For the show, Rodgers and Hart contributed one of their best tunes, "Manhattan."

Rodgers and Hart wrote a number of musicals in collaboration with librettist Herbert Fields, starting with *Dearest Enemy* in 1925—the top ticket price was $3.30! Critic Frank Vreeland, writing in the *New York Telegram,* wrote, "We have a glimmering notion that someday they will form the American counterpart of the once great triumvirate of Bolton, Wodehouse, and Kern." The trio went on to write, among other shows, *The Girl Friend* (1926), *Peggy-Ann* (1926), and *A Connecticut Yankee* (1927).

Like many of their Broadway contemporaries, Rodgers and Hart were wooed to Hollywood in the early 1930s, where they scored a series of films, including *The Hot Heiress* (1931); the brilliant *Love Me Tonight* (1932); the *Phantom President* (1932), starring George M. Cohan; *Hallelujah, I'm a Bum* (1933), starring Al Jolson; *Hollywood Party* (1934); and *Mississippi* (1935).

The duo then returned to New York and wrote *Jumbo* (1935), one of the biggest extravaganzas ever seen in New York. Producer Billy Rose rented Manhattan's enormous Hippodrome Theater and employed an entire circus. The production opened three months late, but most critics felt that it was worth the wait. After *Jumbo,* Rodgers and Hart entered their most productive and successful period, beginning with *On Your Toes* (1936). It tells the story of a vaudeville family that gets mixed up with gangsters and a Russian ballet company, and the score features such great songs as "There's a Small Hotel," "Glad to Be Unhappy," and the title song, along with two landmark dance numbers, "La Princess Zenobia" and the classic "Slaughter on Tenth Avenue."

Following a largely unsuccessful return to Hollywood for the film *Dancing Pirate* (1936), Rodgers and Hart presented Broadway with one of their most exuberant hits, *Babes in Arms,* on which they also contributed the libretto. Almost every song in the score became a standard, including "Where or When," "I Wish I Were in Love Again," "My Funny Valentine," "Johnny One-Note," and "The Lady Is a Tramp." Their next show, "I'd Rather Be Right" (1937), marked the first time that a living president was depicted in a musical comedy. For the role of President Franklin Roosevelt, they chose George M. Cohan, known for his patriotism and for his ability to turn in a respectful interpretation even when dancing and singing. "Have You Met Miss Jones?," "Off the Record," and the title song were its hits.

The excellent score of the team's next show, *I Married an Angel* (1938), included the great standard "Spring Is Here." One of their most memorable collaborations followed, *The Boys from Syracuse* (1938), the first musical based on a work by Shakespeare. The songwriters were obviously inspired by the material and wrote such wonders as "Falling in Love with Love" and "This Can't Be Love." The remainder of the score was equally well crafted. The show that followed *The Boys from Syracuse* ran longer but is almost forgotten today: *Too Many Girls* (1939). Its score includes inspired moments, but only one standout song: "I Didn't Know What Time It Was."

*Higher and Higher* followed in 1940, featuring "It Never Entered My Mind," and then came *Pal Joey,* not a typical musical comedy in any way. For one thing, the lead character, the unscrupulous Joey, is a scoundrel. The score is among the team's most sophisticated and adult. In fact, the racy lyric of "Bewitched, Bothered, and Bewildered" had to be softened before radio stations would play it. The film *They Met in Argentina* (1941) was released prior to the opening of the team's last Broadway show, *By Jupiter* (1942), for which they supplied the book, music, and lyrics. Unfortunately, it was the last full-scale collaboration between Rodgers and Hart.

Rodgers was a disciplined man, used to working regular hours with great determination and single-mindedness. Larry Hart was exactly the opposite. Insecure and unstable, he became increasingly difficult to work with over time. He would disappear for days at a time, forcing Rodgers to halt production or write lyrics himself. Hart's insecurities led to heavy drinking and missed deadlines. Rodgers reached the end of his patience during *By Jupiter* and began quietly to inquire about other partnerships.

Lorenz Hart (left) and Richard Rodgers in the 1929 Vitaphone short, *Makers of Melody.*

Theresa Helburn of the Theatre Guild wanted Rodgers to adapt the play *Green Grow the Lilacs* into a musical comedy. Rodgers reluctantly approached Hart, but both of them knew he wasn't up to the task, either mentally or physically. Rodgers then turned to his old friend, and sometimes collaborator from his early days at Columbia University, Oscar Hammerstein II. The result was *Oklahoma!* (1943). Hart was present at the opening of the milestone musical and congratulated Rodgers on his success, but the success of the show must have been a terrible blow to Hart's already damaged self-esteem.

Rodgers felt that a new project might help Hart straighten out his life, so he agreed to work on a revival of *A Connecticut Yankee*. Hart did stop drinking during the process but, following the opening-night performance on November 17, 1943, he disappeared. He went missing for two days and was finally found unconscious in a hotel room. He was taken to Doctors' Hospital, where it was determined he had pneumonia. He died a few days later.

Rodgers went on to have an entire second career teaming with Oscar Hammerstein, as well as working on a few projects with other lyricists (including himself). However, his personality seemed to change, and while his work with Hart was often playful and funny, his collaborations with Hammerstein were weightier. He is justifiably remembered as a great man of the theater. ◆

## *Song and Story*

### MY HEART STOOD STILL
Lorenz Hart: Charles Cochran asked us to do a sophisticated show for London, like the *Garrick Gaieties*. But first we went to Paris to rest for two weeks. On a drive from Paris to Versailles with two girls, we were nearly hit by a cab. One of the girls said: "My God! My heart stood still!" I said to Dick, "That's a good title." Before long, Dick came to me with "My Heart Stood Still" for our new Cochran show, *One Dam Thing After Another*.

### BEWITCHED, BOTHERED, AND BEWILDERED
This song first became a hit in France under the title "Perdu dans un Rêve Immense d'Amour." Why in France? Because of the ASCAP broadcasting ban in the U.S. It wasn't until 1950 that the song achieved widespread success in this country.

### BLUE MOON
Was it galling to Richard Rodgers that his most often performed song was the only pop song in his catalogue? It's not that he and lyricist Lorenz Hart didn't try to make it a product on song. The tune started out as the music to "Prayer," written for the 1933 musical film *Hollywood Party*. It was cut from the film, and the melody was used as the title song for *Manhattan Melodrama* in 1934. The lyric wasn't used and a new lyric was written for Shirley Ross in the same picture, under the title "The Bad in Ev'ry Man." The song didn't catch on,

and in 1934 Hart wrote yet another lyric, the last, and titled it "Blue Moon." It wasn't attached to any show or movie, but became a hit anyway.

### THERE'S A SMALL HOTEL
While out of town with the show *On Your Toes*, Lorenz Hart went down to the men's room of New Haven's Shubert Theater and wrote the lyrics to "There's a Small Hotel."


## *First Person*

Larry Hart: I'd been out of the Columbia School of Journalism for a year or two. Of course, we decided to write the college varsity show, *Fly with Me* — a great success. . . . After our Columbia show, Dick met Herbert Fields, a son of Lew Fields of the famous Weber and Fields Minstrels. Lew Fields was putting on *Poor Little Ritz Girl*, so Herbert

## "Larry Hart can rhyme anything . . . and does!" —Howard Dietz

asked his father to use some of our songs. By the time the show opened all the songs were ours.

*Poor Little Ritz Girl* ran twenty-two weeks on Broadway. Rodgers was then only seventeen. Of course we felt that we had arrived. We expected the managers to make us some offers but no offers came. We put on amateur shows, benefits, and did anything we could to make a few dollars. Finally with Herbert Fields writing the book, Dick and I sat down and wrote a musical comedy. Some managers liked the music and hated the lyrics, some loved the lyrics but couldn't hear the melodies. Nobody took it. Then we all three wrote *The Melody Man* for Lew Fields. He took it on the road. Yes, it was a colossal—failure. We showed *Dearest Enemy* to Max Dreyfus. He liked it, and now signed us up on his staff. This was in the month of March. The show could not open until fall. We were unknown—and now very, very broke.

We wrote *Garrick Gaieties* in a week. We used two or three numbers that we had been peddling around. One of them was "Manhattan." At the opening matinee I stood in the back of the theater with a young writer about town, Walter Winchell. Three boys came before the curtain and recited that polysyllabic lyric! I felt like the thing was doomed. But that matinee, because of the long applause, lasted until seven o'clock.

## Asides

When writing with Hart, Rodgers wrote the music first, but when collaborating with Hammerstein, the lyrics were the starting point. Whenever he was asked about which came first, the music or the lyrics, Rodgers—always the businessman—replied, "The advance."

**OPPOSITE PAGE:** Marcy Westcott and Larry's brother, Teddy Hart, in *The Boys from Syracuse.*

**LEFT:** Mickey Rooney and Judy Garland in the MGM Rodgers and Hart biopic, *Words and Music.*

**ABOVE:** Three of *South Pacific*'s Nellie Forbushes: Rodgers and Hammerstein assisting Mary Martn, Janet Blair, and Martha Wright in washing their men right out of their hair. **INSET:** Mary Martin explains to Lauri Peters that she is sixteen in *The Sound of Music*. **OPPOSITE PAGE:** Julie Andrews and her prince, John Cryer, in *Cinderella*.

R ichard Rodgers and Oscar Hammerstein II are considered by many to be the greatest of all Broadway musical theater teams. Their formula consisted of crafting well-integrated songs woven into a full-blooded book, the songs propelling the story and carefully reflecting the characters' personalities in both the words and music. This method of constructing a musical has been emulated for all of the years since the team's first hit show, *Oklahoma!*

The success of that show came at a crucial point in the careers of both collaborators, and at a crucial point in the history of its producer, the Theater Guild. Rodgers had already enjoyed a successful career with his longtime partner, Lorenz Hart, with whom he had created a number of sophisticated, witty, and for the most part lighthearted shows. When Hart's personal problems stood in the way of further collaboration, Rodgers was forced to seek another partner, and he turned to Oscar Hammerstein II, the scion of a great theatrical family.

At the time, Hammerstein had his own problems. Although he had already enjoyed a distinguished career that included such successes as *Show Boat*, *Rose-Marie*, and *The Desert Song*, his recent productions had been failures and it was whispered along Broadway that he was washed up. He, too, was looking for a new partner to challenge him and revive his talents.

The Theater Guild was also suffering. Its recent productions had proved unsuccessful at the box office and it was close to bankruptcy. Theresa Helburn, codirector of the Guild, recalled an earlier Guild-produced play, *Green Grow the Lilacs*, and thought that it might work as the basis for a successful musical. She approached Rodgers, whose Guild-produced musical *The Garrick Gaieties*, written with Hart, had proved to be a great success, putting the early Guild on a firm financial footing. Rodgers in turn approached Hammerstein.

In transforming *Green Grow the Lilacs* into *Oklahoma!* Rodgers and Hammerstein took many liberties with the musical comedy tradition. They dispensed with the usual opening chorus sung by a bevy of leggy chorines, opening instead with a lone figure singing "Oh, What a Beautiful Morning." The villain, Jud, was a truly menacing figure, not the kind of two-dimensional moustache twirler audiences were accustomed to hissing. And Jud was killed at the end, an uncommon twist in the musical comedy of the day. But its timing couldn't have been better: *Oklahoma!* opened on May 31, 1943, just as the nation was embracing homespun values as a reaction to the war.

Any doubts as to the potential of the new songwriting team were laid to rest when the curtain rose. The show became a smash hit and the score was recorded by Decca Records. It was the first original-cast recording to achieve popular success, opening the door to the modern era of theatrical recordings.

Questions as to whether Rodgers and Hammerstein could repeat their success were answered when *Carousel* opened in 1945. The Theater Guild again produced, and again Rodgers and Hammerstein broke new ground. Their lead character, Billy Bigelow, is a bully and crook who is killed but reappears as a spirit. The show dealt with serious subjects, and the means of telling the story were as groundbreaking as the story itself. Many critics and audience members considered the score superior to that of *Oklahoma!*

The team then wrote their first and only original film musical, *State Fair*. The Twentieth Century-Fox film was a great success. It was on their next show, *Allegro* (1947), that the pair hit a rare artistic snag. They attempted to break more musical theater conventions by using the chorus act as a kind of Greek chorus, but this and other ideas simply did not work. The show did contain a minor hit, "The Gentleman Is a Dope." RCA paid a lot for the rights, spiriting the team away from Decca Records, but they lost their gamble when the show ran for less than a year.

Rodgers and Hammerstein redeemed themselves with *South Pacific* (1949), an immensely successful show starring Mary Martin and Ezio Pinza. The score remains one of Broadway's finest, including many enduring standards. *South Pacific* ran until the beginning of 1954, earning its writers and producers (one and the same, as Rodgers and Hammerstein had opened their own production office by this time) a good deal of money. Columbia Records made the original cast recording twice, on vinyl and, in an early experiment, on magnetic tape.

Their next hit, *The King and I* (1951) made a star out of Yul Brynner and was Gertrude Lawrence's last and perhaps best performance. The score measured up to Rodgers and Hammerstein's high standards and was recorded by Decca Records. Hobe Morrison, writing in *Variety*, exclaimed, "Hammerstein's lyrics are another of his characteristic blends of apparently effortless grace, pictorial beauty and irresistible sentiment." The songs were perfectly suited to the idiom of the script and clearly

defined each character's personality and point of view. As in all of their best work, the songs propelled the plot forward instead of providing entertaining stopgaps or commenting on general themes.

RCA took another stab at a Rodgers and Hammerstein cast album with their next show, *Me and Juliet* (1953). Again, no dice. The story concerned two backstage romances, and the score, except for the hit "No Other Love," was not up to their usual standards. On April 5, 1954, a dubious milestone was reached when, for the first time since March 31, 1943, there was no Rodgers and Hammerstein production on Broadway. During the eleven years since the opening of *Oklahoma!*, sometimes as many as four of their shows were playing, in addition to others on with their names attached as authors or producers.

RCA came back to record the team's next show, *Pipe Dream* (1955). Again the critics were disappointed and the show folded after only 246 performances. R & H turned to a new medium, television, for their next project, an original musical version of "Cinderella." The eponymous show was broadcast on March 31, 1957, with a young Julie Andrews starring, and it was a great success.

Gene Kelly directed Rodgers and Hammerstein's next outing, *Flower Drum Song* (1958). The show and score received modest praise, enabling a 600-performance run. The one hit was "I Enjoy Being a Girl." Though not a smash, it fared better than had *Allegro*, *Pipe Dream*, or *Me and Juliet*. Columbia Records took charge of the cast album duties. John Chapman commented in the *Daily News* that the show was "thoroughly sentimental," but he hadn't seen nothin' yet. The R & H penchant for sentimentality reached its zenith with *The Sound of Music* (1959), their last show as a team. The score was in their own great tradition, and yielded no fewer than five hit songs. The critics noted its sweetness but audiences flocked to the Lunt-Fontanne theatre for 1,443 performances.

Oscar Hammerstein II died on August 23, 1960, leaving Richard Rodgers without a partner for the first time in his nearly fifty-year career. For his first outing without Hammerstein, *No Strings* (1962), he wrote his own lyrics. The show was a moderate success, running 580 performances, and yielding one oft-recorded song, "The Sweetest Sounds." Rodgers's surprisingly adept lyrics had more in common with Hart's work than Hammerstein's. The job of writing both music and lyrics was tough, though, and Rodgers decided to join up with a new partner for his next show, *Do I Hear a Waltz?* (1965). He chose Hammerstein's protégé, Stephen Sondheim. The two didn't see eye to eye, and the collaboration was stormy, but they did produce a good score. Rodgers next show, *Two by Two* (1970), was a collaboration with Martin Charnin and marked Danny Kaye's return to Broadway. It fared better than its predecessor, though the score was nowhere near as good. Sheldon Harnick was Rodgers's next collaborator, on *Rex* (1976). Based on an unlikely subject, the court of King Henry VIII, it was a fast failure. Rodgers's last show, *I Remember Mama* (1979), featured lyrics by both Martin Charnin and Raymond Jessel. Starring the unlikely musical comedy choice, Liv Ullmann, the show received devastating reviews.

Richard Rodgers died in New York on December 30, 1979. ❖

# Song and Story

## I'M IN LOVE WITH A WONDERFUL GUY

Mary Martin first heard this song at two o'clock in the morning in Joshua Logan's apartment. "I almost passed out. I was so excited. I fell off the piano bench and I remember that the management had to call up to complain of the noise."

## SOME ENCHANTED EVENING

In this lyric Hammerstein emphasizes the sensory aspects of love. In the first verse he write about seeing a stranger, in the second about hearing her laughing, and in the third about feeling her call.

## THIS IS A REAL NICE CLAMBAKE

Hammerstein asked his daughter to research a real clambake and find as many recipes as possible at the local library. He incorporated all of the dishes into his final lyric.

# Asides

Josh Logan had an apartment overlooking the East River. When he was working on *South Pacific* with Richard Rodgers, he used to tease him by pointing out the tugboats going by and saying, "There's another boat taking money up to Irving Berlin."

There are three motifs that run through all of Hammerstein's songs, subjects about which he felt deeply: nature, love, and music. He repeatedly wrote of the sounds and beauty of nature, the songs people sing, and the ways in which they express love. Look no further than the lyrics to "Oh, What a Beautiful Morning," "Younger Than Springtime," and "It's a Grand Night for Singing."

# First Person

Oscar Hammerstein to his wife, just prior to the opening of *Oklahoma!*: I don't know what to do if they don't like this. I don't know what to do because this is the only kind of show I can write.

Richard Rodgers to Max Wilk: When we started to do *Oklahoma!* Oscar meant to be helpful. I'd never been to Oklahoma. And I certainly wasn't in the Southwest in 1906; I was only four years old at the time. So he sent me a book about the subject. And I opened it up, took one look at it, and then closed it and never opened it again. The only thing I could do was what any self-respecting artist would do: I put on music paper my idea of how Oklahoma sounded in 1906. The way Indian Territory sounded at the beginning of the century. Did it again in *The King and I*. I certainly hadn't been to Siam before I wrote that, but I wanted to express my feeling about the way Siam sounded.

Orchestrator Richard Rodney Bennett on the otherwise difficult Richard Rodgers: The only way I can define it is that down deep somewhere in that soul of his there must be a warm, beautiful thing…to come out with all these melodies.

# Special Event Songs

Songs have been used to commemorate festive occasions for as long as humans have enjoyed music and rhythm. But it wasn't until the turn of the twentieth century that celebratory music became a lucrative field in itself for songwriters and music publishers.

Before 1900, Mendelssohn's "Wedding March" from *Lohengrin* (as in "Here Comes the Bride") and Bach's "Wedding Cantata" were nuptial staples, and at the end of the century, Reginald De Koven and Harry B. Smith's "Oh, Promise Me," from the 1891 musical comedy *Robin Hood,* joined them. As we entered the twentieth century, the concept of couples having "their song" began to take hold.

Sometimes the betrothed would pick a popular romantic song of the day, often something from a movie. *West Side Story's* "One Hand, One Heart" (Stephen Sondheim and Leonard Bernstein) was popular starting in 1961, when the film version was released, but was supplanted by 1968's "A Time for Us" (Nino Rota, Larry Kusick, and Eddie Snyder), the love theme from the film version of *Romeo and Juliet.* Two years later, "Where Do I Begin?" with music and lyrics by Francis Lai and Carl Sigman, from *Love Story,* made mothers weep with joy (although the marriage in the film happened to have ended, just as those of its predecessors, in premature death). *Ghost* (1990), another love story with a hearty dose of death in the plot, featured Alex North and Hy Zaret's "Unchained Melody," and soon that topped the list of favorite wedding tunes, only to be replaced by *Titanic's* "My Heart Will Go On" (James Horner and Wilbur H. Jennings). Death again—but who really listens to the lyrics?

Jerry Bock and Sheldon Harnick's "Sunrise, Sunset" from *Fiddler on the Roof* is a popular song for the bride's dance with her father. And what anniversary would be complete without a song made famous by Al Jolson, "The Anniversary Waltz" by Jolson himself and Saul Chaplin? No matter what the occasion, when it's time for the band or DJ to start up the action on the dance floor, in addition to whatever ethnic dances are de rigueur, the "Hokey Pokey" (Roland Lawrence LaPrise), the "Bunny Hop" (Ray Anthony and Leonard Auletti) and the ubiquitous "Chicken Dance" by Werner Thomas and Louis Julien Van Rijmenant cross cultural boundaries (and those of taste) to inspire even the tipsiest bridesmaids to kick off their silk shoes and shake a leg (or at least put one in and shake it all about).

Speaking of DJs, as opposed to live bands, a friend of ours tells us that during a Bar Mitzvah he attended there was a candle-lighting ceremony where each member of the boy's family got up and lit a candle and bussed him on the cheek. Everyone had his or her own theme song, played by the DJ as he or she came forward. When it came to Grandma, the DJ was supposed to play the beautiful "Family," by Barry and Neil Kleinbort. But he hit the wrong button and Grandma was accompanied by Eric Michael Gillett singing "When I See an Elephant Fly," a song written by Ned Washington and Oliver Wallace for the score of *Dumbo.*

The three most popular English-language songs of all time are "Happy Birthday to You," "For He's a Jolly Good Fellow," and Guy Lombardo's favorite, "Auld Lang Syne." The last, of course, is the go-to song for New Year's Eve and no other song comes close. We can only think of one other New Year's song, Frank Loesser's "What Are You Doing New Year's Eve?" and we only know that one because our minds are filled with such things. Don't think about it for a second—"Auld Lang Syne" is the ticket, even though most of us have no clue what it means. ("Old long ago," if you must know.) ◆

## Song and Story

### AULD LANG SYNE

Robert Burns transcribed this song and sent a copy along to the British Museum. His note read, "The following song, an old song, of the olden times, and which has never been in print, nor even in manuscript until I took it down from an old man's singing, is enough to recommend any air." It's suspected that Burns himself wrote the lyrics based on the originals.

### OH, PROMISE ME

This song, sung at almost every wedding until the mid-1960s, was originally interpolated into the musical, *Robin Hood.* Its publisher, Isadore Witmark, wrote in his autobiography about the first success of the song, "It had been found that *Robin Hood* needed another song; [Reginald] De Koven, for some reason, did not relish composing a new tune, so he brought this old one to rehearsal. He could not interest any of the singers in the song! Finally it was offered to Jessie Bartlett Davis, the contralto playing Alan-a-Dale. Miss Davis, annoyed because she had not been offered the song at first, hummed it over, then disdained it. Something in the melody, however, remained. She found herself singing it an octave lower. MacDonald [the show's producer] happened to pass by her dressing room; all who heard Jessie sing will understand why he stopped. He could not contain himself until the song was finished. 'Jessie!' he cried, bursting into her room. 'If you ever sing that song as you're singing it now, on the low octave, it will make your reputation.' She sang it, and the prophecy came true."

### HAPPY BIRTHDAY TO YOU

Know another birthday song? We don't. This one seems to have cornered the market. It was composed on June 27, 1859, by Mildred J. Hill, a Louisville schoolteacher. Her sister, Dr. Patty Smith-Hill, who taught at Columbia University, added lyrics in 1893. She titled the song "Good Morning to All."

Here's the beauty part. The song was first copyrighted in 1935 and renewed in 1963. It earns approximately 2 million dollars a year in licenses!

Don't Be Left Out... Join The
## FUN
### Dance Instructions

**After Intro:**

**1.** Couples face each other–open and close hands (like a bird's bill) in time to the music. One-two-three-four!

**2.** Flap arms like the wings of a bird to the same beat of the music–one-two-three-four!

**3.** Wiggle your tail like a bird to the same tempo–one-two-three-four!

**4.** Clap hands four times with the beat of the music–one-two-three-four!

**5.** Lock arms and circle to the right for 16 counts. Reverse and circle to the left for 16 counts. Repeat entire dance from the beginning.

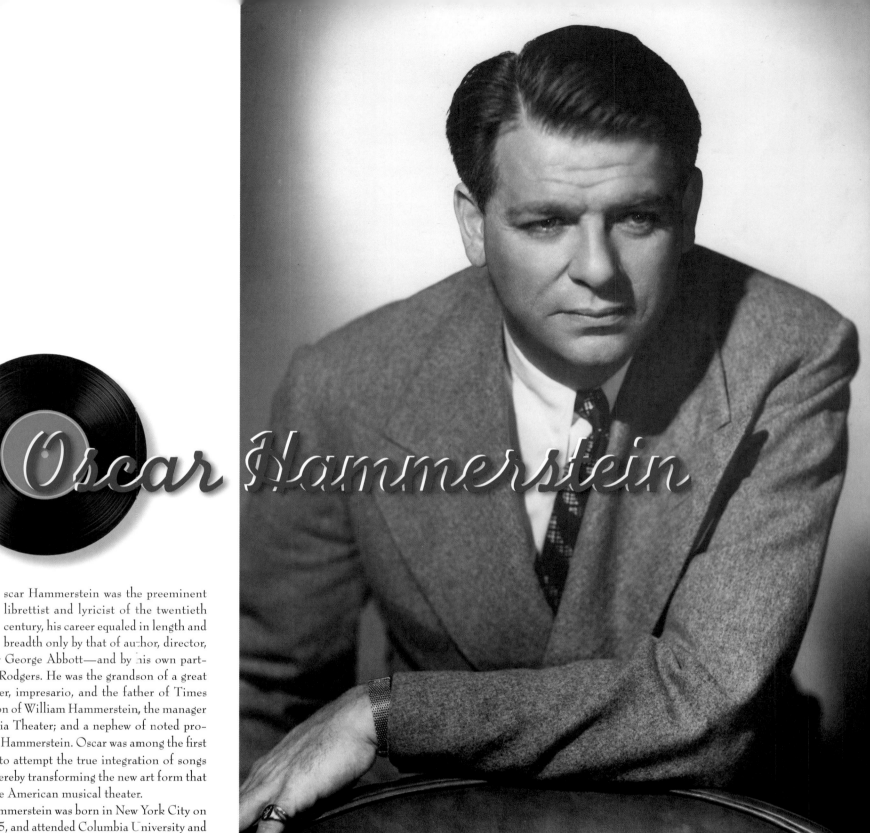

Oscar Hammerstein was the preeminent librettist and lyricist of the twentieth century, his career equaled in length and breadth only by that of author, director, and producer George Abbott—and by his own partner, Richard Rodgers. He was the grandson of a great theater builder, impresario, and the father of Times Square; the son of William Hammerstein, the manager of the Victoria Theater; and a nephew of noted producer Arthur Hammerstein. Oscar was among the first authors ever to attempt the true integration of songs and script, thereby transforming the new art form that would become American musical theater.

Oscar Hammerstein was born in New York City on July 12, 1895, and attended Columbia University and Law School. It was at Columbia that he began writing books and lyrics for his first musicals. In fact, his first collaboration with Richard Rodgers was for a Columbia University show, *Up Stage and Down* in 1916. A year later Hammerstein's "Make Yourself at Home," with music by Silvio Hein, was interpolated into the Broadway show *Furs and Frills*. His first full score was a collaboration with Herbert Stothart, *Always You* (1920). Reviewers were quick to note the young Mr. Hammerstein's talents. The *New York Times* said, "The lyrics are more clever than those of the average musical comedy." Stothart and Hammerstein next had a success with *Tickle Me* (1921). Hammerstein wrote a play, *Pop*, but it closed in Atlantic City. A series of flops followed, until he teamed up with Stothart and Vincent Youmans on *Wildflower* (1923), which contained the hit song "Bambalina." The same team wrote *Mary Jane McKane* that same year and had another success.

However, Hammerstein's greatest early successes were on a series of now classic operettas, usually with lyrics coauthored by Otto Harbach. These include *Rose-Marie* (1924), with its lush score by Rudolf Friml, *Desert Song* (1927), and *The New Moon* (1928), both with Sigmund Romberg. In between, Hammerstein collaborated with

Jerome Kern on the Marilyn Miller musical comedy *Sunny* (1925).

Hammerstein's greatest achievement was 1927's *Show Boat*. This legendary musical opened at the Ziegfeld Theater to deserved acclaim, and was the first show in which Hammerstein deals with social issues. (The plot deals with, among other things, interracial marriage and the consequences of racism.) The score is still considered by many to be the finest in the musical theater canon. After a hit run, *Show Boat* embarked on a long national tour, then returned to New York in 1932 for another successful engagement. It was presented in London to equal acclaim, especially for Paul Robeson in the role of Joe. *Show Boat* was revived on Broadway in 1946, 1954, 1961, 1966, 1976, 1983, and 1994. It was filmed in 1929, 1936, and 1951.

*Show Boat* featured Helen Morgan, and Hammerstein and Kern's next show did, too. *Sweet Adeline* (1929) had a lovely score and today is held in high regard by musical theater aficionados. In 1931, three Hammerstein shows were produced on Broadway, none lasting more than twenty-three performances. Then he collaborated again with Jerome Kern on *Music in the Air* (1932) and scored a major hit. After two London premieres, *Ball at the Savoy* and *Three Sisters*, Hammerstein ventured to Hollywood for the film *The Night Is Young*. The film got little attention and Hammerstein quickly returned to New York. His Hollywood output remained insignificant, including such films as *Give Us This Night* (music by Erich Wolfgang Korngold); *Swing High, Swing Low*; *High, Wide, and Handsome* (with Jerome Kern); *The Lady Objects* (music by Ben Oakland); and *The Great Waltz*.

On Broadway, the Kern and Hammerstein musical satire *Very Warm for May* (1939), despite a fine score (including what many consider to be the greatest song ever written, "All the Things You Are"), was a failure. That same year, *American Jubilee*, with a score by Arthur Schwartz, was produced at the New York World's Fair. In 1941, the Romberg operetta *Sunny River* played only thirty-six performances, becoming the last nail in the coffin of operetta.

Hammerstein was generally thought to be washed up. Aware of the talk along Broadway, he needed a hit to revive his career. Desperate as he felt for renewal, Hammerstein was nonetheless unprepared for the amazing turnaround he was to enjoy as the lyricist and librettist in the team of Rodgers and Hammerstein—the most successful songwriting partnership in the history of musical theatre. The Theatre Guild approached Hammerstein to collaborate on a new show with Richard Rodgers, whose longtime partner, Lorenz Hart, was having personal problems. The new team's first production changed the course of musical theater and broke most of the commonly held conventions of the art form. *Oklahoma!* began a second chapter in Hammerstein's career.

As a retort to all those who said he was washed up artistically, he took out an ad in *Variety*, which read:
SUNNY RIVER (6 weeks at the St. James)
VERY WARM FOR MAY (7 weeks at the Alvin)

THREE SISTERS (7 weeks at the Drury Lane)
FREE FOR ALL (3 weeks at the Manhattan)
"I've Done It Before and I Can Do It Again"

For his next production, Hammerstein chose to adapt Georges Bizet's opera *Carmen* (1943). The all-black show, *Carmen Jones*, earned rave reviews and was a great success.

Although the team of Rodgers and Hammerstein had their occasional failures, their great successes made an indelible mark on American theater. Rodgers's melodies to Hammerstein's lyrics were more expansive and soaring than those he'd written with Hart. Hammerstein's lyrics and libretti were warm and humane, and touched on themes of tolerance and understanding. Critics have accused Hammerstein of being saccharine or overly earnest, but his collaborations with Rodgers, as well as those with Kern, Friml, and Romberg, cannot possibly be overestimated for both their importance to the art form and their artistry.

Oscar Hammerstein died on August 23, 1960. As a tribute, the lights were dimmed on Broadway and "Taps" was played in Times Square. ◆

## *Song and Story*

### THE LAST TIME I SAW PARIS

Oscar Hammerstein was so distraught when the Germans entered Paris on June 14, 1940, that he wrote the lyric to "The Last Time I Saw Paris." Jerome Kern set it to music and it was introduced by Kate Smith. The song became so popular that MGM put it into the film *Lady, Be Good*. It went on to win the Academy Award, although it wasn't specifically written for the film. Hammerstein realized the injustice and insisted that the Academy change the rules for songs, which they did.

## *Asides*

Oscar Hammerstein would often write lyrics to existing songs, using them as a metric pattern.

Occasionally a pop tune will find acceptance in the jazz world, and soon the jazz version overshadows the original. A case in point is Friml, Harbach, and Hammerstein's "Indian Love Call." Artie Shaw made the tune swing, to the delight of bobby soxers in 1938, fourteen years after the song premiered as part of the score of the operetta *Rose-Marie*. Another great swinging hit made from a stalwart ballad is "Lover Come Back to Me." "Oh! Lady Be Good!," by the Gershwins, is another example, as is Isham Jones and Gus Kahn's "The One I Love Belongs to Somebody Else." Irving Berlin's "Marie" was written for the 1928 silent film *The Awckening*, but in 1937, Tommy Dorsey's band upped the tempo and the song became a hit. Porter's 1929 favorite, "You Do Something to Me," became a hit all over again at jazz tempo. Once in a great while, slowing down a tune yields a hit, as in the Gershwins' "Someone to Watch Over Me" and "I've Got a Crush on You."

## THE GREAT SONGS

**1923** Bambalina; Wildflower (both music by Vincent Youmans, lyrics with Otto Harbach)

**1924** Indian Love Call; Rose-Marie (both music by Rudolf Friml, lyrics with Otto Harbach)

**1925** D'Ye Love Me?; Sunny; Who? (all music by Jerome Kern, lyrics with Otto Harbach)

**1926** The Desert Song; One Alone; Romance (all music by Sigmund Romberg, lyrics with Otto Harbach)

**1927** Bill (music by Jerome Kern, lyric with P. G. Wodehouse); Can't Help Lovin' Dat Man; Make Believe; Ol' Man River; Why Do I Love You?; You Are Love (all music by Jerome Kern)

**1928** The Girl on the Prow; Lover, Come Back to Me; Marianne; Softly as in a Morning Sunrise; Stouthearted Men (all music by Sigmund Romberg)

**1929** Don't Ever Leave Me; Here Am I; Why Was I Born? (all music by Jerome Kern)

**1930** I Was Alone (music by Jerome Kern)

**1932** And Love Was Born; I've Told Ev'ry Little Star; The Song Is You (all music by Jerome Kern)

**1935** A Kiss to Build a Dream On (music by Harry Ruby, lyric with Bert Kalmar); When I Grow Too Old to Dream (music by Sigmund Romberg); I Won't Dance (music by Jerome Kern, lyric with Dorothy Fields)

**1936** I Have the Room Above Her (music by Jerome Kern)

**1937** Can I Forget You?; The Folks Who Live on the Hill (both music by Jerome Kern); I'll Take Romance (music by Ben Oakland)

**1939** All in Fun; All the Things You Are; In the Heart of the Dark; That Lucky Fellow (all music by Jerome Kern)

**1940** The Last Time I Saw Paris (music by Jerome Kern)

**1946** All Through the Day; Nobody Else but Me (both music by Jerome Kern)

SEE "RODGERS AND HAMMERSTEIN" FOR ADDITIONAL SONGS WITH LYRICS BY OSCAR HAMMERSTEIN II.

Eveyln Laye and Ramon Novarro filming 1935's *The Night Is Young*.

# Jule Styne

I n the 1970s, Jule Styne announced that he was the most talented composer living. He was right. No one else could write a hit tune tailored to a talent or dramatic situation the way that he could. No one could sit down and write a tune on any subject at all the way that he could. Jule Styne's ego made him fearless; he was a theater man, a collaborator, self-confident, yes, but not what we call today "a diva." He may have been a little crazy, but he was crazy like a fox. (Have you not noticed by now that most artistic geniuses have at least one screw loose?)

Many consider Styne the ultimate composer when it comes to writing to suit the talents of specific stars. He tailored *Gentlemen Prefer Blondes* for Carol Channing, *Gypsy* for Ethel Merman, *Funny Girl* for Barbra Streisand, and *Bells Are Ringing* for Judy Holiday. In fact, some feel that when he was faced with writing a show that didn't have a star in the lead, say, *Hazel Flagg*, which featured Helen Gallagher, his scores suffered. Although his best shows remain indelibly associated with their original stars, they are also cohesive, well-integrated scores that stand the test of time and the inevitable succession of interpreters. It is Styne's versatility and superb artistry that have led many to dub him our greatest living composer.

Jule Styne was born in London on December 31, 1905. His family emigrated from England in 1913 and settled in Chicago. By the time he was a teenager, Chicago was already on its way to becoming one of the capitals of jazz. The early jazz groups, known as the Chicagoans, did not escape the notice of the young prodigy. Despite a solid classical background (he made his debut at the age of nine as a solo pianist with the Chicago Symphony), Styne felt more and more drawn to the music of the backroom bars and nightclubs.

A scholarship to the Chicago College of Music enabled Styne to perfect his technique and to study composition, theory, and harmony. He formed his own dance band, for which he played the piano and contributed arrangements. He then joined some of the smaller bands touring the country, most notably that of Art Jarrett. Styne's early days in Chicago, and all of the great musicians playing there, influenced him greatly. He later referred to the time as "a feast."

In 1934, Styne moved to New York, where he earned his living as a vocal coach and then an accompanist for Harry Richman, a top Broadway and nightclub performer. A year later, Styne received an offer from Twentieth Century-Fox to come to Hollywood to coach Alice Faye, Tony Martin, Shirley Temple, and other Fox stars.

Styne had already had a big hit with his first song, "Sunday," written in 1927, and it didn't take the studio long to move him into the composers' stable. Styne moved from Fox to Republic and then to Paramount and Columbia.

Jule Styne plays the score to *Funny Girl* while Barbra Streisand and Sidney Chaplin listen.

His principal collaborators during his Hollywood years were Frank Loesser and Sammy Cahn. Styne wrote no smash-hit film musicals, but he did write many standards, especially for the early career of Frank Sinatra. Among his films are *Anchors Aweigh, Tonight and Every Night, The Kid from Brooklyn, Romance on the High Seas, The West Point Story, Two Tickets to Broadway, My Sister Eileen,* and *Meet Me After the Show.*

After experiencing some success in Hollywood, Styne, along with Cahn, attempted to write a Broadway musical. The result, *Glad to See Ya* (1944), was planned as a vehicle for Phil Silvers. His unavailability and other problems forced the show to close out of town, but a standard did emerge from the score, "Guess I'll Hang My Tears Out to Dry." The team had much better luck with their next offering, *High Button Shoes* (1947). This time they got their man, Phil Silvers. The Styne and Cahn score contained at least one song destined for the Hit Parade, "Poppa, Won't You Dance with Me?" Other standouts were "Can't You Just See Yourself?" and "I Still Get Jealous."

Two years later, Styne collaborated with lyricist Leo Robin on *Gentlemen Prefer Blondes* (1949), an adaptation of Anita Loos's popular novel. It was noteworthy as Carol Channing's Broadway debut as Lorelei Lee, singing a song that would become her trademark, "Diamonds Are a Girl's Best Friend." The show also featured such hits as "Bye Bye Baby," "A Little Girl from Little Rock," and "You Say You Care."

Styne's next show wasn't as successful, but it marked the first meeting between Styne and his longtime collaborators Betty Comden and Adolph Green. *Two on the*

*Aisle* (1951) was one of Broadway's last great revues before the television variety show sounded the death knell for the form, and it featured Bert Lahr and Dolores Gray. Styne's next important collaborator was Bob Hilliard, with whom he worked on *Hazel Flagg* (1953). The hit from the show was "Every Street's a Boulevard (in Old New York)."

Director/choreographer Jerome Robbins was working on a musical version of *Peter Pan*, starring Mary Martin, and the show was in trouble out of town. He called in the writing team of Styne, Comden, and Green to bolster the score by Moose Charlap and Carolyn Leigh, and the dynamic trio added "Never Never Land," "Distant Melody," and "Captain Hook's Waltz." After its hit Broadway run, the show became a perennial favorite on NBC television.

Next, Styne, Comden, and Green collaborated on the Judy Holliday vehicle *Bells Are Ringing* (1956). Comden and Green had cut their teeth writing for and performing with Holliday, as members of the Revuers. For the new show, they gave their star two great hits, "The Party's Over" and "Just in Time." *Say, Darling* (1958), the trio's next Broadway outing, was a play about a musical, a roman à clef on the making of *The Pajama Game*. Alas, it never received its due, probably because it was more of a play with songs than a full-fledged musical. Its one hit was "Dance Only with Me."

Styne then collaborated with Stephen Sondheim on what some consider the greatest musical of all time, *Gypsy* (1959). Styne and Sondheim perfectly tailored their bravura score to Merman's talents with such songs as "Some People," "Together," and "Everything's

## THE GREAT SONGS

**1926** Sunday (music and lyric by C. Cohn, Ned Miller and Jule Styne)

**1942** I Don't Want to Walk Without You (lyric by Frank Loesser) I've Heard that Song Before (lyric by Sammy Cahn)

**1944** I Guess I'll Hang My Tears Out to Dry; I'll Walk Alone; Saturday Night is the Loneliest Night in the Week (all lyrics by Sammy Cahn)

**1945** I Fall in Love Too Easily; It's Been a Long, Long Time; Let It Snow, Let It Snow, Let It Snow (all lyrics by Sammy Cahn)

**1946** Five Minutes More; The Things We Did Last Summer (both lyrics by Sammy Cahn)

**1947** I Still Get Jealous; Papa, Won't You Dance with Me?; Time After Time (all lyrics by Sammy Cahn)

**1948** Bye Bye Baby; Diamonds Are a Girl's Best Friend (both lyrics by Leo Robin); It's Magic (lyric by Sammy Cahn)

**1953** Every Street's a Boulevard in Old New York; How Do You Speak to an Angel? (both lyrics by Bob Hilliard)

**1954** The Christmas Waltz; Three Coins in the Fountain (both lyrics by Sammy Cahn); Never Never Land (lyric by Betty Comden and Adolph Green)

**1956** Just in Time; Long Before I Knew You; The Party's Over (all lyrics by Betty Comden and Adolph Green)

**1959** All I Need Is the Girl; Everything's Coming Up Roses; Let Me Entertain You; Small World; Together, Wherever We Go; You'll Never Get Away From Me (all lyrics by Stephen Sondheim)

**1960** Make Someone Happy (lyric by Betty Comden and Adolph Green)

**1961** Comes Once in a Lifetime (lyric by Betty Comden and Adolph Green)

**1964** Don't Rain on My Parade; I'm the Greatest Star; The Music that Makes Me Dance; People (all lyrics by Bob Merrill)

**1967** My Own Morning (lyric by Betty Comden and Adolph Green)

Styne loved beautiful women. Here he is with Yvonne Hover, wife of Ciro's owner H.D. Hover, and Rita Moreno.

Coming Up Roses." All the elements of the production came together and climaxed with one of the most brilliant songs in Broadway history, "Rose's Turn." Styne next collaborated with Comden and Green on *Do Re Mi* (1960), whose big hit was "Make Someone Happy," introduced by Nancy Dussault. *Subways Are for Sleeping* (1961) was the threesome's next offering, and although the score was better received than the show, one song, "Comes Once in a Lifetime," got noticed.

The composer's biggest hit, *Funny Girl*, opened in 1964 starring Barbra Streisand. She clearly inspired Styne and lyricist Bob Merrill to write a series of brilliant songs, including "People," "Don't Rain on My Parade," and "Who Are You Now." Carol Burnett was hoping to make as big a splash as Streisand had in Styne's next show, *Fade Out-Fade In* (1964), but, although the score was up to the team's usual standards, it was not to be. The writers returned to Broadway with *Hallelujah, Baby!* (1966), featuring an exceptional score married to a problematic libretto by Arthur Laurents. *Darling of the Day* (1968) was an especially heartbreaking production for Styne. He and E. Y. Harburg collaborated on a superior score, but the inability of leads Vincent Price and Patricia Routledge to do justice to the songs hurt the proceedings. Styne's next show, *Look to the Lilies* (1970), would fare even worse. A vehicle for the great Shirley Booth, the score, written in collaboration with Sammy Cahn, never achieved its potential. Things went from bad to worse for Styne with his next show, *Prettybelle*. It had the elements of a hit, star Angela Lansbury and lyricist Bob Merrill, but it closed out of town. Merrill and Styne reteamed for *Sugar*, a musical version of *Some Like It Hot*, that ran for over a year following its 1972 opening. Styne collaborated with playwright Herb Gardner on the score for *One Night Stand* (1980), which didn't even live up to its title, closing in previews.

In the fitful Broadway seasons of the eighties and nineties, Styne was relegated to the wings. His attempt at musicalizing *Treasure Island* with Susan Birkenhead got no further than Edmonton, Canada. She also collaborated on Styne's final score, *The Red Shoes* (1993) with additional lyrics by Bob Merrill. It closed after only five performances.

Styne died on September 20, 1994 and, though his late work may not have been as memorable, he left us with an astonishing legacy of great shows including *Gypsy, Funny Girl,* and *Do Re Mi.* ◆

**ABOVE:** Styne with David Wayne and Vivian Blaine, rehearsing for *Say, Darling.*

**LEFT:** With Barbra Streisand.

> ## "I have so many ideas that I can't wait till I say them all so I backtrack on them. It's all enthusiasm and great interest in what I'm doing." —Jule Styne

"I said to Arthur Laurents and Stephen and Jerome Robbins, 'What does Ethel sing at 11:00, where's that 11 o'clock number? You're gonna tell me she sings "Together" and that's the end of the act? Gentlemen, you're missing the boat.' Robbins says to Arthur, 'Jule's right. Arthur, I want you to tell me what would she sing about dramatically, what would she say. I guess she would review her life.' So I went home, I'm thinking, 'I gotta be on third base when I write this song.' You gotta be there. You can't start from the beginning. You've gotta be on the way. So I sat down and said, 'I know what I'm gonna do. I'm gonna take bits of the entire score, not head on but recalling. Like someone's trying to remember a song.'"

"Everything's an influence. As long as you live and your brain is working, if you hear everything… Most people don't hear everything because they're thinking what they're going to say. I don't think what I'm going to say. That's why I have to talk so much. Because there's so much I want to say."

"Writing for the theater is my first love. It's the only freedom I have, being able to write for the theater. Because no one can change it unless I allow them to change it. In Hollywood, you just write it, and they put it on a treadmill, and the orchestra changes notes."

"I don't sit at a piano and compose a song. I sit in my chair and I write a song. I hear the whole thing. After I've sketched it out, I go to the piano to hear what this thing I sat and wrote sounds like. I alter it then and make harmonic changes. The brain is like a computer: what you put into it, it will give you back."

## Styne on Styne

"In a meeting about *Gypsy*, I had just put over a big idea. The show was 25 minutes too long. I said, 'You know fellas, you can't cut words, you can't sentences. That won't give you 25 minutes; you gotta to take out two scenes. That takes out 25 minutes.'"

"Jerry Robbins, speaking to Sondheim and Arthur Laurents, said, 'We mustn't interrupt Jule—he'll say 100 things that are not right but wait for that 101.' I'm trying to get to the core of it. It's very difficult when you're working with the superb book writer like Arthur Laurents, and the most brilliant lyric writer of our time, Stephen Sondheim. You have to pull back a little bit; you're not speaking to the common man. These are creators. Trying to pull back, I throw in more. It's a habit of mine all my life."

"Steve [Sondheim] is the best lyric writer of my time and I'll tell you why. He's a great musician. And he knows why I wrote that note. He examines it."

"When I write for a man, I write girl songs. When I write for a girl, I write man songs. Each of them need a little of each other to make the words sound differently."

# Song and Story

## SUNDAY

Jule Styne: I go to Florida for the Arnold Johnson big band to arrange and play the piano. And while I'm there, I went walking on the beach down in Hollywood, Florida with this very pretty seventeen-year-old girl. I was seventeen, too. I just walk around humming parts of "Sunday." She said, "What is that? I bet you made that up" (What an expression, "made that up"). She said, "I'll give you a date tomorrow night if you play this song in the club tonight." Adolph Deutsch was the other arranger and he helped me finish it up for that night.

It was the first song of its time ever written with a 2/4, 1/8, 1/4 and 1/8 note tied over to the next bar. That's a two-beat Dixieland song. It's almost my biggest standard to this day. Someone every year plays it. Then I was playing at the club that night. In the audience is Jolson and Irving Caesar, they're down in Florida playing golf. Irving Caesar comes up to me and says, "I'm a lyric writer. What's that song you're playing?" I said, "I wrote it. I want to put lyrics to it. I'll get back to you."

## JUST IN TIME

Styne: One day I was writing *Bells Are Ringing* with Comden and Green. We needed a song. I said, "We need a simple song here, like we're speaking, 'good evening, hello,' easy.'" I said, "Vincent Youmans wrote on three notes. I'm going to write half steps. A whole song on half steps." I played it through, "Just in Time," from beginning to end —I played the whole song through spontaneously. "Liebestraum" it is, isn't it? I had classical background. I played Bach for morning, noon and night and that's the greatest bass line. Like in "Time After Time."

Cole Porter was my biggest fan. Told me, ["Just in Time"] is the most beautiful, attractive, pleasant, feel good song. You know when you walk into a room at a party, there's a band, and they quickly play one of your songs when you walk in? I have a going order with the bands in California and New York, when I walk in a room play "Just in Time." It makes me feel good.

## I DON'T WANT TO WALK WITHOUT YOU

Styne: Frank Loesser was the one who recognized I had great talent, and he told me how it goes. He said, "When you write songs, it's a horrendous thing for a composer who writes a tune and has to wait till the lyric's finished. Have patience, don't nudge a lyric writer, you'll have less." For five weeks I went to his house every day after the studio, we're both at Paramount, he got me to Paramount. He asked for me to be his lyric writer. I was at Republic. I asked for him first at Republic. And he hated me [for bringing him to a lesser studio]. He said to me, "You don't understand, all the big movies they have, they give to Johnny Mercer, and I get loaned out to Republic and stuff. But I like you. I'm gonna write [*Sis Hopkins*] in four days, but you won't hand it in for three weeks 'cause I'll be in Florida. You have to learn to fake it. Its part of the game, you just make up excuses." He says, "Play me something." I play, [what would become "I Don't Want to Walk Without You."] He says, "Shhh! Quiet! Never play that song anyplace. I'm taking it

to Paramount and we'll write it there." Every day I went to his house. This was the day before cassettes, the piano player sat at the piano and played it over and over, must have played it 24 times every day. One day he called me up and said, "You want to meet me someplace for lunch? 'Cause at lunch I'm gonna tell you the lyrics of your song." A pancake place on Hollywood Boulevard. No dummy lyrics. He doesn't write dummy lyrics. He writes in his mind. He sang me the whole song by memory.

## TIME AFTER TIME

Styne: "Time After Time' is a man's song. It loses all its power if a woman sings it. It's nice, but it loses all its power. It's a strong song. Even when he sings pianissimo, it has strength to it. Girls overphrase. Girls phrase the music instead of phrasing the lyrics, for the most part.

# Asides

"When the Weather's Better" was Harold Arlen's favorite Jule Styne song.

"Music That Makes Me Dance" is a Gershwin-influenced song.

"I Fall in Love Too Easily" is a tenor saxophone song solo.

# First Person

Stephen Sondheim: The rhythms of his speech will tell you everything you need to know about Jule Styne's character. In the middle of every sentence he has another thought and then another. You ask him a question and five minutes later he'll come out of the tunnel and he's talking about Ethel Merman. A tumble of ideas.

**ABOVE LEFT:** With Carol Channing.
**LEFT:** With Judy Garland.

# Schwartz & Dietz

**ABOVE:** Schwartz, Dietz, and Cyd Charisse in a publicity shot for 1953's *The Band Wagon*.

**OPPOSITE PAGE TOP:** Jack Haley and Bea Lillie look over the songs to *Inside USA* while Dietz and Schwartz ook on.

The greatest songwriters of Broadway revue, Dietz and Schwartz (we refer to them as Schwartz and Dietz in the heading of this chapter since it worked out better alphabetically but they were always known as Dietz and Schwartz) enjoyed a thirty-year collaboration. They are responsible for what is considered the greatest of all revues, *The Band Wagon*, and their many ballads are simply the epitome of the form. Their comedy and upbeat songs are equally well constructed.

Howard Dietz was born in New York City on September 8, 1896, and attended Townsend Harris Hall and Columbia University. While at Columbia, he frequently contributed to Franklin P. Adams's column, "The Conning Tower," writing under a pseudonym, Freckles. Dietz won a contest by writing an advertisement for Fatima Cigarettes, which led to a job at the Philip Goodman advertising agency. One of Goodman's clients was Samuel Goldwyn, of the emerging Metro-Goldwyn-Mayer film studio, and Dietz created the "Leo the Lion" logo that still roars from screens today. After a stint in the navy, Dietz went to work for Goldwyn as a film publicist, writing for the stage on the side. It seems ironic in retrospect that he was counting on his MGM pension to provide for him in his retirement. In fact, he was more than comfortable living out his life on his ASCAP royalties.

Dietz's first Broadway lyric (along with some uncredited dialogue) was for the W. C. Fields vehicle, *Poppy* (1923). The lyrics and light verse Dietz had contributed to "The Conning Tower" had not gone unnoticed, and Philip Goodman suggested to Jerome Kern that Dietz might make a good lyricist partner. The result was *Dear Sir* (1924), a rare failure for the master composer. Though inauspicious, this early work brought Dietz to the attention of Arthur Schwartz.

Like Irving Berlin and others, Schwartz was self-taught on the piano. He was born in Brooklyn on November 25, 1900, and attended New York University and Columbia University. He taught English in the New York City public school system, then entered legal practice in 1924, having already published his first song, "Baltimore M.D., You're the Only Doctor for Me" (lyrics by Eli Dawson). Bennett Cerf suggested to Schwartz that he contact Dietz about collaborating, as he felt that his style was most like Lorenz Hart's. Dietz wasn't interested, and responded by suggesting that Schwartz team up with an established lyric writer to gain from the education, as Dietz had done with Kern. Then, when they both became famous, they could write together.

The musical *Queen High* (1926) provided Schwartz with his first job. Schwartz collaborated on two songs with fellow composer Ralph Rainger and lyricist E. Y. Harburg. Unfortunately, by the time the show opened on Broadway, the Schwartz songs had been cut.

Meanwhile, Dietz's next score was for *Hoop-La* (1927), probably the first show to close out of town after only one act! He was experiencing more success as a publicist than as a writer, soon he was the director of advertising and publicity for Metro-Goldwyn-Mayer.

*The Little Show* (1929) was conceived as an answer to such big revues as the *Ziegfeld Follies*, the *Passing Shows*, and the *Earl Carroll Vanities*. Producer Tom Weatherly hired Dietz to write lyrics, and asked the writer if he had heard of Arthur Schwartz. Dietz showed the producer the correspondence between them, and Weatherly declared that it was fated they work together. Dietz and Schwartz's first joint effort was a satire on movie title songs, called "Hammacher Schlemmer, I Love You," a paean to the noted New York hardware store. The show was a smash, and "I Guess I'll Have to Change My Plan" was its big hit.

While Dietz was attending to his duties at the studio, Schwartz collaborated with other lyricists. He wrote songs for the revue *The Grand Street Follies* (1929) and the London musicals *Here Comes the Bride* and *The Co-Optimist* (1930). Then Dietz and Schwartz reunited for *The Second Little Show* (1930), which featured the now-classic ballad, "Something to Remember You By." The show also produce another standard, "Body and Soul" by John Green, Edward Heyman, Robert Sour, and Frank Eyton (with an assist by Dietz).

*The Band Wagon* (1931), starring Fred and Adele Astaire, Helen Broderick, Frank Morgan, and dancer Tilly Losch, was the first American revue with real sophistication. It was Dietz's great idea to integrate a revolving stage into the show. (Prior to that time, revolves had been used only to facilitate changes of scenery.) The score contained the team's greatest song,

"Dancing in the Dark." More fine Dietz and Schwartz revues followed: *Flying Colors* (1932), *At Home Abroad* (1935), and *Between the Devil* (1937). They also wrote their first book musical, *Revenge with Music* (1934), which was not a great success though it featured two exceptional ballads, "You and the Night and the Music" and "If There Is Someone Lovelier Than You."

Schwartz collaborated with Dorothy Fields on three shows: the Ethel Merman vehicle *Stars in Your Eyes* (1939), and two starring Shirley Booth—*A Tree Grows in Brooklyn* (1951) and *By the Beautiful Sea* (1954). Dietz wrote two shows with Vernon Duke: *Jackpot* and *Sadie Thompson*, both in 1944 and both failures. In 1948, Dietz and Schwartz reteamed for *Inside U.S.A.*, a revue starring Beatrice Lillie. It was their last great score. Their last two shows included fine material, though neither was a critical success. *The Gay Life* (1961) starred Barbara Cook and Walter Chiari, and included the classic "Magic Moment." *Jennie* (1963) starred Mary Martin, and she and her husband, producer Richard Halliday, turned it into a bad experience for all concerned, riding roughshod over the proceedings.

Dietz's battle with Parkinson's disease sent him into retirement. Schwartz attempted new projects (including a musical version of *Mrs. Arris Goes to Paris*, with Dietz) but none of them were produced. The two died a year apart, Howard Dietz in New York City on July 30, 1983, and Arthur Schwartz in London on September 3, 1984. ❖

Arthur Schwartz (seated at piano) and Howard Dietz (standing at piano) play the score of *Inside USA* for sketch writer Arnold Auerbach (left) and John Gunther (center left), the author of the book *Inside USA*.

In the preface to Dietz's autobiography, *Dancing in the Dark*, Alan Jay Lerner recalled that when he was a schoolboy, he already knew Dietz's songs: I sang them to myself as I walked down the street (which, incidentally, is what good popular music is supposed to make you do). Aside from their obvious wit, rhyming legerdemain, style, and at times philosophic tenderness, they were the most charming lyrics in the world. They had that special grace, that warm, elegant glow that hung a smile around you…. Howard is the Fred Astaire, the Chevalier, the Colman, the Lubitsch of lyric writers.

Howard Dietz on his collaboration with Arthur Schwartz: After about 500 lyrics, you get to know the composer. If you can stand it that long, you must like him.

Vernon Duke: Howard shone at everything he undertook; he never "dabbled" in a new hobby, but applied himself to it with ferocious energy…. A brilliant executive, generally considered the best publicist in the film industry, he was also an inventive and facile lyric writer. We should have been a great team, for we had many traits in common, such as facility, adaptability, and a sophisticated outlook; but we just didn't pan-out as a combination, probably because we had too much in common.

> "I don't like composers who think. It gets in the way of their plagiarism." —Howard Dietz

# Song and Story

### I GUESS I'LL HAVE TO CHANGE MY PLAN

The music to "I Guess I'll Have to Change My Plan" was written in 1924 as a camp song, "I Love to Lie Awake in Bed," with lyrics by Schwartz's bunkmate, Lorenz Hart. It was appropriated for *The Little Show* as "I Guess I'll Have to Change My Plan." The song was not a hit but, when Howard Dietz was in London, the Prince of Wales asked h m for "the blue pajama song." Dietz had no idea what the prince was referring to, until he recalled that the phrase came from "I Guess I'll Have to Change My Plan." The prince repeatedly requested the song at nightclubs and formal events, and it became a hit in Europe, finally being rediscovered by American audiences. When Arthur Schwartz heard the song performed in London, by the cabaret act De Lys and Carter, he asked who wrote it. "I don't know," replied De Lys, "someone like Noel Coward." Schwartz countered, "I think it's the best song someone like Noel Coward ever wrote." When Schwartz returned home, he said to his music publisher, "Dietz and I wrote it, you published it three years later, and I want to congratulate you on the effortless way you go about making a song hit."

### MOANIN' LOW

Schwartz was having difficulty finding a tune for Libby Holman to perform in *The Little Show*. Dietz heard pit pianist Ralph Rainger improvising and quickly wrote a lyric with the hitherto unknown composer.

### SOMETHING TO REMEMBER YOU BY

"Something to Remember You By" was conceived by Schwartz and Desmond Carter as a foxtrot titled "I Have No Way to Say How Much I Love You." Howard Dietz wrote a new lyric and Schwartz slowed down the tempo.

### IF THERE IS SOMEONE LOVELIER THAN YOU

The title to this song originally included the words, "Then I Am Blind" at the end, but Schwartz asked Dietz to shorten it. It became Schwartz's favorite song.

# Asides

Howard Dietz suggested the title to the Gershwin brothers' hit, "Someone to Watch Over Me."

Howard Dietz and Arthur Schwartz watch as Kay Kendall, Howard Morris, and Polly Bergen look through the sheet music to "Triplets" in preparation for a television version of *The Band Wagon*.

The television version of *Your Hit Parade* was doomed when the arrival of rock music made it seem more and more out of touch with the musical scene. In 1957, the cast was replaced with Tommy Leonetti, Jill Corey, Alan Copeland, and Virginia Gibson, but cast changes didn't help—the replacements were as square as the originals—and the show was canceled by NBC in 1958. *Your Hit Parade* enjoyed one last gasp when CBS picked it up, bringing back Dorothy Collins and adding Johnny Desmond and the Peter Gennaro Dancers. But, with rock-and-roll in the ascendancy, there was no saving it and the show was cancelled for good on April 24, 1959, after only one season. ❖

## First Person

Hugh Martin: It was September 1944, and I was in the army by then. I was standing at attention out in the Texas sun when somebody came running up to me with a telegram from Arthur Freed that said, "'The Trolley Song' is going to be on the *Hit Parade* tonight." Boy, I almost dropped my rifle! I could not believe it! I didn't have a radio, but there was one in the mess hall, so I got a couple of my buddies, and we gathered around the radio in the mess hall, and Frank Sinatra sang "The Trolley Song." He got about halfway through it, and he evidently dropped a lyric or something, and he said, "There are too many lyrics in this song!" On the air! And that was my debut on the *Hit Parade!*

# Your Hit Parade

Snooky Lanson—no, he's not just a joke in *Mad* magazine. Actually, Snooky, along with Dorothy Collins, Russell Arms, Eileen Wilson, and Gisele MacKenzie, was part of the cast of the longest running series ever devoted to American popular song, *Your Hit Parade*. The show was sponsored by Lucky Strike cigarettes, and each week announcer Andre Baruch (on television, anyway) intoned, "*Your Hit Parade* survey checks the best sellers on sheet music and phonograph records—the songs most heard on the air and most played on the automatic coin machines—an accurate, authentic tabulation of America's taste in popular music."

The show began on radio on April 20, 1935, with the top song countdown. Heading the list that week was "Lovely to Look At," followed by "Lullaby of Broadway" and "Soon." Some songs refused to vacate the top ten spots week after week. "White Christmas" held the record of thirty-two weeks on the list, two more weeks than "People Will Say We're in Love." They were closely followed by "Harbor Lights" (twenty-nine weeks), "I'll Be Seeing You" (twenty-four), and "You'll Never Know" which hung around for twenty-two weeks.

The top ten songs were followed by a Lucky Strike Extra, an older song that was an audience favorite. The show ran on either NBC or CBS until January 16, 1953. From 1950 until 1953, the show was broadcast on television and simulcast on NBC Radio.

The cast of the radio show included more than fifty singers at one time or another, but among the more prominent were Frank Sinatra (1943–45, 1947–49), Joan Edwards (1941–46), Dick Haymes, Wee Bonnie Baker, Johnny Mercer, Dinah Shore, Buddy Clark, Bea Wain, and Andy Russell.

After the switch to television in 1950, Wilson, Lanson, and Collins sang the top tunes assisted by the "Hit Parade Dancers and Singers." Each week, the seven top tunes would be performed in dramatic settings—and some of the especially long-running songs taxed the writers' and singers' ingenuity. In order to vary the show's lineup, there was also a three-song grouping sung by the Lucky Strike Extras.

Frank Sinatra and Dorothy Collins, two great stars from *Your Hit Parade*.

The team of Thomas "Fats" Waller and Andy Razaf wrote some of the finest songs in the history of American popular music. Despite their great talents, neither received his due, either financially or artistically, in his lifetime, partially due to the racism that pervaded the music industry in the first half of the last century. Razaf, in particular, was taken advantage of by white publishers and others. Neither was called upon to write Broadway or Hollywood musicals (save Waller's collaboration with George Marion, Jr. on *Early to Bed*).

Razaf was born Andreamenentania Razafinkeriefo (you don't pronounce the second "en" in his first name or the "in" in his last name — that makes it simple, no?) in Washington, D.C., although he was conceived in Madagascar, where his father was a royal prince and his mother was the daughter of an American diplomatic consul. When the French decided to claim Madagascar as a colony, Razaf's pregnant, sixteen-year-old mother escaped to the United States. After the family moved to New York, Razaf worked as an elevator operator, supporting his mother, while writing lyrics on the side. No music publisher was interested in his work, so he turned to poetry, having some of his work published in Harlem newspapers.

Waller, meanwhile, began playing piano at age six. His parents, lay preachers, gave sermons on the sidewalks of New York, accompanied by their son on a portable harmonium. He was entering and winning amateur contests in his teens and was coached by the great stride pianist, James P. Johnson. At the time of his mother's death, sixteen-year-old Waller was earning money recording piano rolls and accompanying silent movies at the Lincoln Theater. He began making records in 1922 for the Okeh label, and supplemented his income

Andy Razaf

Waller & Razaf

Fats Waller

by playing at parties and giving piano lessons (to Count Basie among others). That same year, Waller got married and had a child (not necessarily in that order). He divorced the next year.

Razaf had married a couple of years before Waller, but when he moved back to New York from Cleveland, he split with his wife, though not quite legally.

The old saw claims opposites attract, and so it was with the free-spirited Waller and the more conservative Razaf—though Waller tried his best to lure Razaf into the world of wine, women, and song. He succeeded little on the first, more so on the second, and was triumphant concerning the third.

Still, the team was perpetually hard up for money, and created many songs that were sold outright to others. Rumors persist that they wrote the Jimmy McHugh and Dorothy Fields hits "On the Sunny Side of the Street" and "I Can't Give You Anything but Love, Baby." Waller probably did write the music for both, and Razaf the lyric to the latter, but there is no concrete proof.

Waller sold arrangements to Don Redman and Fletcher Henderson for peanuts or, to be exact, hamburgers. Publisher Irving Mills, king of the cut-in, bought all of Waller's rights to the songs from *Connie's Hot Chocolates* for only $500—and that score included "Ain't Misbehavin'."

Razaf himself claimed the lyric to "Squeeze Me," though composer/publisher Clarence Williams (who had written very few lyrics) is officially credited. In 1927, Razaf's share of the song "Louisiana" was cut in by Bob Schafer, a friend of publisher Joe Davis, who owned the Triangle Music Publishing Company. Davis managed to cheat Razaf out of royalties to the great hit "S'posin'," which was written to Paul Denniker's music.

Razaf's last hit song, for which he wrote both music and lyrics, was "That's What I Like 'Bout the South." Phil Harris appropriated it, even copyrighting it in his name.

When Razaf objected, Harris changed a few lines of the lyrics, slightly altered the title to "That's What I Like About the South" and claimed authorship.

Both Waller and Razaf were in financial straits through most of their careers, even though, in the late 1930s, Waller earned what today would be a million dollars a year in songwriting, radio, and recording royalties. Clearly, his profligate ways, nascent alcoholism, and bad health drained his coffers. Razaf simply never made that much money. Proceeds from his revue work were split fifty-fifty with the shows' producers; for the lyric to "In the Mood," a big hit for Glenn Miller, Razaf got a flat $200.

By 1932, the team's collaborative years were practically over, and Waller was concentrating on performing rather than writing. In 1943, he appeared in the film *Stormy Weather*, an all-black musical for Twentieth Century-Fox. In that period, he did write an excellent score for a Broadway show, *Early to Bed*. In 1943, Waller died while traveling by train from Los Angeles to New York.

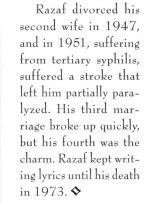

Razaf divorced his second wife in 1947, and in 1951, suffering from tertiary syphilis, suffered a stroke that left him partially paralyzed. His third marriage broke up quickly, but his fourth was the charm. Razaf kept writing lyrics until his death in 1973. ◆

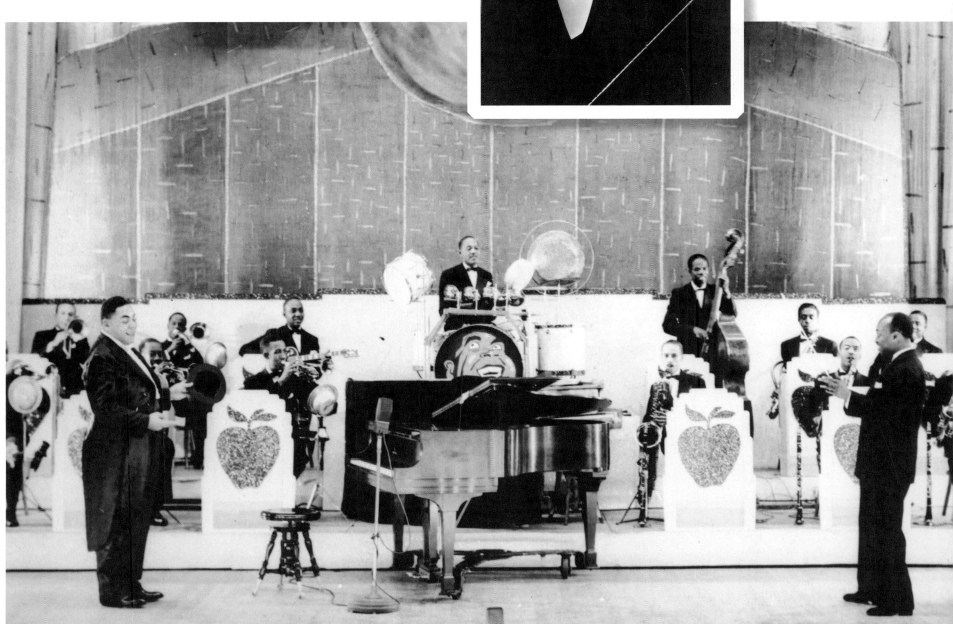

## Song and Story

### AIN'T MISBEHAVIN'

Andy Razaf described how the song was written: I remember one day going to Fats's house on 133rd Street to finish up a number based on a little strain he'd thought up. The whole show was complete, but they needed an extra number for a theme, and this had to be it. He worked on it for about forty-five minutes and there it was.

Razaf's memory doesn't include Harry Brooks, who is credited with co-writing "Ain't Misbehavin'" and other songs for the show *Connie's Hot Chocolates*. He might have been a cut-in or he might have written the verses. Brooks once recalled that, "Ain't Misbehavin'" was "an attempt to copy the successful formula Gershwin used for 'The Man I Love.' We imitated the opening phrase that began just after the first beat and the minor part of the bridge, too."

### I'M JUST WILD ABOUT HARRY

Noble Sissle and Eubie Blake's "I'm Just Wild About Harry" was another old standard that was revived for political purposes—this time for Harry Truman. Jack Yellen and Milton Ager's song "Happy Days Are Here Again" was written for the movie musical, *Chasing Rainbows*. It had a new lease on life as the campaign song of Franklin Delano Roosevelt in 1932.

### HONEYSUCKLE ROSE

Andy Razaf recalled trying to get Waller to sit down and write this song: "It was hard to tie Fats down to a job; my mother used to make all the finest food and special cookies for him, just to keep him out at our home in Asbury Park, New Jersey. We were working on a show called *Load of Coal* for Connie, and had just done half the chorus of a number, when Fats remembered a date and announced, 'I gotta go.' I finished up the verse and gave it to him later over the telephone."

### IN THE MOOD

Joe Garland and Wingy Manone's 1937 tune "Tar Paper Stomp" was adapted by Garland for "In the Mood." Andy Razaf added a fine (if often ignored) lyric. Garland offered the song to Artie Shaw, but the bandleader though it too long. Miller picked it up, made a few cuts—and it became his theme song.

# Paul Francis Webster

Lyricist Paul Francis Webster was born in New York City on December 20, 1907. After growing bored with his studies and dropping out of New York University, he worked on various ships throughout Asia, and in the late 1920s, found a job as a dance instructor at Arthur Murray Studios—which must have made his parents very proud. Though he has remained off the radar of most Tin Pan Alley aficionados, Webster penned many standards and won three Academy Awards out of sixteen nominations.

Webster's first chart success was 1932's "Masquerade," written with John Jacob Loeb. They also wrote the classic song "Virgins Wrapped in Cellophane," the basis of a production number in the show *Murder at the Vanities*. Actually, the number is forgotten now (and no one was paying much attention at the time, either), but the title is enough to make it endure. Several minor hits followed, and then Webster hit the big time with "Two Cigarettes in the Dark" (1934), featured in the film *Kill That Story*. Lew Pollack was the collaborator on that song and a number of others, all written for Hollywood beginning in 1934. In 1941, Webster enjoyed an especially fruitful collaboration on the musical *Jump for Joy*. The hit was "I Got It Bad and That Ain't Good" but the score also included "The Brown-Skin Gal in the Calico Gown," "Chocolate Shake," and the title number, which Webster coauthored with Sid Kuller. The following year, 1942, Webster and Hoagy Carmichael wrote "The Lamplighter's Serenade." He and Carmichael also wrote "Baltimore Oriole" (*To Have and Have Not*), "Billy-a-Dik," "Doctor, Lawyer and Indian Chief" (*The Stork Club*), and "Memphis in June" (*Johnny Angel*), all in 1945.

The 1950s were especially good for Webster. Peggy Lee made a hit out of the Sonny Burke collaboration "Black Coffee." In 1953, Webster and Sammy Fain wrote the score for the Doris Day film *Calamity Jane*. "Secret Love" was the hit of that fine score, which also included "Just Blew in from the Windy City" and "A Woman's Touch." Webster spent much of the early fifties updating lyrics for filmed versions of operettas, including *The Merry Widow* (1952) and *Rose Marie* and *The Student Prince* (both 1954). In the latter half of the fifties, Webster found his real niche—he began writing a string of very successful movie theme songs, including "Love Is a Many Splendored Thing" (1955—Sammy Fain), "Friendly Persuasion" (1956—Dimitri Tiomkin), "Giant" (1956—Tiomkin), "April Love" (1957—Fain), "The Heart Is a Lonely Hunter" (1957—Fain), "A Certain Smile" (1958—Fain), "Raintree Country" (1958—Johnny Green), "Song of Green Mansions" (1959—Bronislau Kaper), "Imitation of Life" (1959—Fain), and "Tender Is the Night" (1961—Fain), the last a hit for Tony Bennett. Bennett also scored hits with "A Time for Love" (1966—Johnny Mandel) from *An American Dream* and "Days of Love" from *Hombre* (David Rose).

Having become one of the primo progenitors of movie themes, Webster went on to write three more enduring ones: "Somewhere My Love" (1966), written with Maurice Jarre for *Doctor Zhivago;* "The Shadow of Your Smile" (1965), written with Johnny Mandel for *The Sandpiper;* and what is probably now his biggest moneymaker—the theme to *Spider-Man*, written in 1967 with Bob Harris. He continued writing through 1983 and died on March 22, 1984. ❖

# Richard A. Whiting

Richard A. Whiting was born in Peoria, Illinois, on November 12, 1891. He started writing songs while in high school, and after graduation from military academy, he played piano for vaudeville shows.

In 1913, Whiting began his professional writing career when publisher James H. Remick published his first songs and hired the young man as the manager of his Detroit office for which he was paid $25 per week. In the evenings, Whiting worked as a member of a local hotel's Hawaiian band, wearing light blackface for an additional $10 a week. In 1914, Whiting had his first successes, "I Wonder Where My Lovin' Man Has Gone" (lyric by Earle C. Jones) and "It's Tulip Time in Holland" with a lyric by Dave Radford. His pay for the rights to the latter song was a Steinway grand piano. This turned out to be a bad deal—the song sold over 1.5 million copies of sheet music, roughly equal to $50,000 in royalties.

Whiting then teamed up with bank clerk Raymond B. Egan to write a succession of hits including, "Mammy's Little Coal Black Rose" (1916), "They Made It Twice as Nice as Paradise and They Called It Dixieland" (1916), "Where the Black-Eyed Susans Grow" (1917), and his biggest seller, "Till We Meet Again (Auf Wiedersehen)." In 1919, Whiting wrote three stage scores, *Toot-Sweet, Overseas Revue,* and *George White's Scandals.*

Whiting and Egan's success continued unabated in the 1920s with "Japanese Sandman" (1920), "Bimini Bay" (1921), "Sleepy Time Gal" (1925), and "Ukelele Lady", "Breezin' Along with the Breeze," "Horses" (1926), "Honey" (all 1928), and "My Future Just Passed (1929) . Whiting wrote lyrics to "She's Funny That Way." Whiting supplied both music and lyric for 1921's "Ain't We Got Fun?"

When talkies came in, Whiting was summoned to Paramount Pictures and teamed with lyricist Leo Robin. Their output was extraordinary: they contributed to *Innocents of Paris* (1929—"Louise"), *Dance of Life* (1929—"True Blue Lou"), *Safety in Numbers* (1929—"My Sweeter Than Sweet"), *Monte Carlo* (1930—"Beyond the Blue Horizon"), *Playboy of Paris* (1930—"My Ideal,"), *One Hour with You* (1932—title song) and others.

Whiting returned to Broadway for *Free for All* (1931) and the Ethel Merman vehicle *Take a Chance*, on which he, Nacio Herb Brown, and B. G. De Sylva teamed to write a spiffy score including You're an Old Smoothie" and "Eadie Was a Lady."

In 1933, Whiting and Ted Koehler wrote "On the Good Ship Lollipop" as part of their score for the Shirley Temple film, *Bright Eyes.* He stayed at the studio until 1935, when he moved to Warner Brothers. He and Walter Bullock wrote a good score for *Sing, Baby, Sing* (1936—"When Did You Leave Heaven?"), and then began a partnership with Johnny Mercer. *Ready, Willing and Able* (1937—"Too Marvelous for Words"), the exceptionally fine score for *Varsity Show* (1937—"Have You Got Any Castles," "We're Working Our Way Through College," "You've Got Something There"), *Hollywood Hotel* (1937—"Hooray for Hollywood," "I'm Like a Fish Out of Water," "Let That Be a Lesson to You"), and *The Cowboy from Brooklyn* (1938—"Ride, Tenderfoot, Ride") were the films they wrote for the studio. During production of the last film, Whiting suffered a heart attack and died on February 10, 1938. ◆

**LEFT:** Richard Whiting teaches "You're My First Love" to Janet Gaynor and Henry Carat, stars of the Fox film, *Adorable.*

## Song and Story

### LOUISE

When Whiting and Robin were hired to write the songs for *Innocents of Paris,* Chevalier told them that when writing for him they should keep in mind his strong French accent. They tried out many women's names on Chevalier before choosing "Louise."

### ON THE GOOD SHIP LOLLIPOP

Whiting was struggling to find a song for Shirley Temple when one day his daughter Margaret came into his room with a big, sticky lollipop. She managed to get her father, his piano, and his music sticky. As she tells it, he said, "Get away from me, where did you get that lollip…." He stopped mid-sentence. "That's it!" He rushed to the phone, called Sidney Clare, and said "I've got the title!"

### TILL WE MEET AGAIN

In 1918, a Detroit theater held a contest for a war song. Remick's Music asked its employee, Whiting, to enter the contest. He and lyricist Raymond B. Egan worked on a number but didn't think it good enough and threw it away. His canny secretary took the song out of the garbage and entered it into the contest—and of course it won. "'Til We Meet Again" went on to sell over 11 million copies of sheet music, the most of any song before or since.

Robert Wright and George "Chet" Forrest ruled a particular subgenre of Tin Pan Alley songwriting, the adaptation of classical themes into popular songs. A long-running team both on and off the Broadway boards, Wright and Forrest contributed a series of shows featuring music derived from the works of classical composers. Although the music, with its basis in the classics, is the focal point of most critics' assessment of the team's career, their lyrics are among the best of Broadway, sometimes equaling the wit and complexity of Stephen Sondheim. Wright and Forrest's lyrics reveal a particular propensity for internal rhyme and sophisticated wordsmithery.

George Forrest Chichester was born in Brooklyn on July 31, 1915. He was a piano prodigy at age three. After his family moved to Miami, he found work in local nightclubs while still in high school. At school he was a member of the glee club, which is where he met Robert Wright. Wright was born on September 25, 1914, in Daytona, Florida. While he was in high school he also conducted a local radio show.

They began their collaboration working with drag artist Rae Bourbon, who hired the team to write special material and took them on a tour of the States, eventually landing in Los Angeles. Bourbon used his connections in the film industry on Wright and Forrest's behalf. They auditioned for MGM, playing some of the eighty songs they had written for Bourbon's tour.

MGM signed the team and in 1937, at the behest of producer Hunt Stromberg, they adapted melodies of Tchaikovsky for the film *Maytime* with Jeanette Mac-Donald and Nelson Eddy. That same year they fashioned Rudolf Friml's music into new songs for the film version of Friml's operetta, *The Firefly*. That film contained their first pop hit, "Donkey Serenade," sung wonderfully in the picture by Allan Jones. Victor Herbert's melodies became the basis of songs for 1938's *Sweethearts* ("Pretty As a Picture") and 1939's *Balalaika*. Three of their songs were nominated for Academy Awards: "Always and Always" from 1938's *Mannequin*, "It's a Blue World" from 1940's *Music in My Heart,* and "Pennies for Peppino" (1942—*Flying with Music*). In 1942 their contract with MGM expired following a polish on Lorenz Hart's lyrics for *I Married an Angel* and the team decided to pursue a theatrical career.

They had already written two shows, *Thank You Columbus* (1940) and *Fun for the Money* (1941), which were produced on the West Coast. They began a long association with the Los Angeles Civic Light Opera, through the artistic director/producer Edwin Lester. Their biggest hit shows, *Song of Norway* (1944—based on the works of Edvard Grieg) and *Kismet* (1953—derived from music of Alexander Borodin), also began

life at the behest of Lester, and contained the standards "Strange Music," "Freddie and His Fiddle," "Stranger in Paradise," and "Baubles, Bangles and Beads." *Kismet* contained one song with music by the team that was based on a 1943 song from the *Copacabana Revue*, "I'm Going Moroccan for Jimmy." Their other Broadway shows, *Gypsy Lady* (1946—based on Victor Herbert's melodies) and *Anya* (1965—Rachmaninoff), were unsuccessful, though the scores contained much to admire.

They actually collaborated with a famous living composer, Heitor Villa-Lobos, on 1948's *Magdalena*, but the results were sadly unappreciated. Along the way they also wrote two scores without the help of dead composers—*The Love Doctor* (aka *The Carefree Heart*—1959) and *Kean* (1961). The latter contains some of the most felicitous music and would have been a major success but for Alfred Drake's health problems at the time. The album on Columbia Records has become a cult favorite.

In 1971 *Kismet* was adapted into the all-black musical *Timbuktu*, starring Eartha Kitt, and scored a modest success. In 1989, Wright and Forrest's perseverance paid off when *Grand Hotel* opened on Broadway to great acclaim. Based on a 1959 Los Angeles musical titled *At the Grand*, starring Paul Muni of all people, the show closed but was resurrected by director/choreographer Tommy Tune with additional songs by Maury Yeston. ◆

**INSET ABOVE:** Wright and Forrest's 1961 production, *Kean.* Here, Joan Weldon is begging Alfred Drake to get her out of this failure. Actually, the score is quite lovely.

*Wright & Forrest*

wrote a smash hit, "When the Red, Red Robin Comes Bob, Bob, Bobbin' Along" as well as the lesser hits, "Poor Papa (He's Got Nothin' at All)," with a lyric by Billy Rose, and "Me Too," written with Al Sherman and Charles Tobias. His next monster hit was 1927's "I'm Looking Over a Four Leaf Clover," with a lyric by Mort Dixon. That same year, Dixon also supplied the lyric to "Just Like a Butterfly That's Caught in the Rain." Another 1927 Woods standard was "Side By Side."

As sound films came into vogue, Woods contributed a plethora of songs to movies. In 1929, the film *Swanee River* boasted "River Stay Way from My Door" (Mort Dixon) and the film *The Vagabond Lover*, starring Rudy Vallee, premiered "Heigh-ho, Ev'rybody, Heigh-ho," which would become Vallee's theme song. Kate Smith found her theme song in "When the Moon Comes Over the Mountain" (written in 1930 with Howard Johnson), which she first sang in the film *Hello, Everybody*. "Just an Echo in the Valley," (1932) was written with Englishmen Jimmy Campbell and Reg Connelly, and provided a hit for Bing Crosby. That same year, the trio also composed "A Little Street where Old Friends Meet" and "Try a Little Tenderness." Woods didn't need a collaborator for "We Just Couldn't Say Goodbye" (1932).

The 1934 film *Roadhouse* featured Woods's "What a Little Moonlight Can Do." By that time, Woods was living in London practically full time and he wrote songs for a variety of English motion pictures, most notably the 1935 Jessie Mathews vehicle, *Ever Green*. It would be the songwriter's last hit, though he continued writing until his death in an automobile accident on January 14, 1970. ❖

## Song and Story

### TRY A LITTLE TENDERNESS

Harry Woods was known for his virulent temper as well as his fondness for all things alcoholic. One day he was at a bar beating a man's head against the counter with the stump of his arm, when the police arrived. They pulled Woods off the unfortunate victim and someone asked, "Who is that man?" Woods's drinking partner explained, "That's Harry Woods. He wrote 'Try a Little Tenderness.'"

## First Person

Jule Styne: One day my band was playing at the College Inn in Chicago that was in the Sherman Hotel. A fellow walks up to the band after the set and says, "You have a wonderful band and you play very well. One day soon you'll be writing songs." I said, "I already started that, that's for older people." He says, "No, you'll go back. But I'll tell you what you have to do. You have to write simple. I write on three notes. Anybody can write all over the place you have to keep it simple but harmonically attractive." (I loved that "harmonically attractive.") And we became great friends.

**B**orn in North Chelmsford, Massachusetts, on November 4, 1896, songwriter Harry Woods began his career as a lark, preferring to live as a farmer on Cape Cod. When the hits began coming, he left the farm and decided to pursue songwriting full time.

Woods was missing one hand, and would play the piano by pounding the keys with his stump. He wrote a remarkable series of hit tunes, beginning with 1921's "I'm Goin' South"(with Abner Silver), which Al Jolson interpolated into the score of Bombo. Not all of Woods's hits have stood the test of time. "Long Lost Mamma (Daddy Misses You)" was a hit in 1923 for Lanin's Arcadians but is never sung today. More lasting is "Paddlin' Madelin' Home," interpolated into the 1925 Broadway musical *Sunny*. The next year, Woods

Most people who care about American popular song are familiar with the giants of the field, but many worthy composers and lyricists remain completely unknown. Many of these were fine craftsmen as well as artists, and Ned Washington is a case in point. A winner of numerous Academy Awards for film lyrics, Washington wrote enduring standards that have stood the test of time, even as his name remains largely unknown.

Washington was born in Scranton, Pennsylvania, on August 15, 1901, and like many of his contemporaries, he started his career in vaudeville, first as an emcee and agent and then a writer of special material. He came to New York in the late 1920s but managed to place only one song into a show, "My Arms Are Open," written with his first major collaborator, Michael Cleary. It appeared in *Earl Carroll's Vanities of 1928*. The next year, Washington began supplying a steady stream of songs to the emerging musical film industry. Cleary supplied the music and Herb Magidson collaborated with Washington on the lyrics. In 1929, the trio had a hit with "Singin' in the Bathtub," featured in the film *Show of Shows*. When musical films briefly fell out of fashion in the early 1930s, Washington concentrated on popular songs and then Broadway scores.

The year 1932 was a banner one for Washington. His big hit was "(I Don't Stand a) Ghost of a Chance," written by Victor Young, Washington, and Bing Crosby. Naturally, Crosby made the song a hit, but whether he actually contributed to the writing or was simply cut in is unknown. Another famous singer, Lee Wiley, collaborated with Victor Young on the music to Washington's next hit in 1932, "Got the South in My Soul." Wiley was having an affair with Young at the time, and wasn't known for her songwriting, so her exact contribution is a matter of conjecture (though Wiley, Young, and Washington did write the 1933 hit, "Any Time, Any Place, Anywhere"). Then it was on to a collaboration with composer George Bassman on "I'm Getting Sentimental Over You."

Young and Washington contributed the hit "A Hundred Years from Today" to their score for *Lew Leslie's Blackbirds of 1934* (which actually opened in 1933). In 1935, Washington finally moved to Hollywood and spent the remainder of his career writing for pictures. That year, he collaborated with composers Bronislau Kaper and Walter Jurmann on "Cosi Cosa," featured in the madcap Marx Brothers picture, *A Night at the Opera*. The satiric song was so effective that to this day, most listeners assume it is a real Neopolitan song. Two years later, Hoagy Carmichael and Washington came up with one of the decade's finest songs, "The Nearness of You," featured in the now forgotten film, *Romance in the Rough*.

Washington surpassed himself in 1940 with the score to the animated classic *Pinocchio*, written with Leigh Harline. "When You Wish Upon a Star" is the standard that comes to mind, but the rest of the score, including "Give a Little Whistle," "I've Got No Strings," and "Hi-Diddle-Dee-Dee (An Actor's Life for Me)," is also excellent, the songs serving the story brilliantly while transcending it to stand beautifully on their own. Washington then took on another animated Disney feature, *Dumbo* (1941). He and composer Frank E. Churchill were again able to both serve and transcend the story with a remarkable score. "Baby Mine," is one of the most touching songs in the American songbook, and "When I See an Elephant Fly" (with music by Oliver Wallace) has also received its share of recordings.

Victor Young and Washington wrote the suitably haunting "Stella by Starlight" for the creepy 1944 film, *The Uninvited*. Washington seldom wrote complete scores for films in the late forties and fifties, concentrating on single songs and title numbers including *On Green Dolphin Street* (1947—Bronislau Kaper) and a bunch with music by Dimitri Tiomkin, including *High Noon* (1952), *Wild Is the Wind* (1957), *Rawhide* (for the television series in 1958), and *Town Without Pity* (1961). Washington's last hit was the title song to *Ship of Fools* (1965) written with Ernest Gold.

Ned Washington died on December 20, 1976. ◆

## Song and Story

### HIGH NOON (DO NOT FORSAKE ME)

This song wasn't originally planned for the picture High Noon but, after an early screening flopped, Tiomkin decided a theme song was needed. Recalled Tiomkin, "The rule book says that in movies you can't have singing while there's dialogue; but I convinced Stanley Kramer that it might be a good idea to have the song sung, whistled, and played by the orchestra. A melody came to me, I played it on the piano at home, and developed it until I thought it was right."

The next screening of the film was also a failure and Tiomkin took the opportunity to obtain all the publishing and recordings rights to the song. Tex Ritter, who sang on the soundtrack, refused to record it, so Tiomkin went to Frankie Laine at Columbia Records. Laine's version became an immense success and when the picture opened four months later, the interest in the song spurred ticket sales.

*Ned Washington*

## THE GREAT SONGS

Vincent Youmans shows dominated Broadway in the 1920s. His closest competitor was George Gershwin, who was born one day before Youmans. Jerome Kern also provided scores to many fine shows in the 1920s, but it was Youmans who imbued his music with a drive and rhythm that seemed to define the decade's spirit, speed, and humor. Zelda Fitzgerald even gave Youmans a nod in her novel, *Save Me the Waltz*. Although his shows were wonderfully popular, Youmans's career as a whole was not as impressive

as those of some of his contemporaries, for two reasons. First, with only ninety-three published songs to his credit, he wasn't that prolific. Gershwin was sometimes represented on Broadway by four shows in a single season, whereas there were only two occasions when Youmans had two or more shows running in the span of a year. Second, he was hampered by constant battles with tuberculosis and alcoholism.

Vincent Youmans was born in New York on September 27, 1898. He began writing songs while assigned to the Army's Great Lakes Training Station, and these camp shows whetted his appetite for show business. After his discharge he was committed to a composing career. Like many of his contemporaries, he broke into the business as a song plugger for Remick music publishers, his second choice, having been turned down by Max Dreyfus of T. B. Harms. Remick published Youmans's first popular song, "The Country Cousin," written with lyricist Al Bryan.

Youmans landed his first theater job as a rehearsal pianist for producer Alex Aarons's show, *Oui Madame*, composed by Victor Herbert. The first song he wrote specifically for the stage, "Maid-to-Order Maid," was interpolated into a Charlotte Greenwood vehicle, *Linger Longer Letty*, but it stayed in for only one performance in Stamford, Connecticut. Two more Youmans songs were interpolated into *Piccadilly to Broadway* in Atlantic City, New Jersey, but the show closed out of town.

Youmans decided to see Dreyfus again and ask for a job. The music publisher was a sort of father figure for his employees, and he took pains to give them every opportunity to develop their talents. Dreyfus finally hired Youmans as a song plugger. Alex Aarons paired Youmans with composer Paul Lannin and brought in George Gershwin's brother Ira to supply the lyrics. The resulting show was *Two Little Girls in Blue* (1921), marking the Broadway debuts of both Youmans and Ira Gershwin.

Although Youmans had passed his first test, he was not happy. He was unable to get another Broadway assignment and found himself again behind the piano working rehearsals of Victor Herbert's *Orange Blossoms*. Youmans's drinking increased, despite the fact that his second show, *Wildflower* (1923), proved a great success and solidified his place in the musical theater. Youmans and his collaborator, Herbert Stothart, must have been taken aback when they read in the *New York Times* that the show "contains the most tuneful score that Rudolf Friml has written in a number of seasons."

*Mary Jane McKane* (1923) was next, and it failed to make a splash. Youmans's first score without a co-composer was *Lollipop* (1924), on which he was teamed with lyricist Zelda Sears, one of the few women lyricists writing for Broadway. Youmans now had three shows running simultaneously.

His next assignment, *No, No, Nanette* (1925), proved to be an even bigger hit, although it did not run as long as *Wildflower*. It was produced and directed by H. H. Frazee, infamous one-time owner of the Boston Red Sox. Prior to its New York engagement Frazee ran the show for a year in Chicago, set up three national companies, and even sent a company to Europe. Youmans seemed made to compose up-to-the-minute tunes that perfectly captured the syncopation and drive of the era.

*A Night Out* was next and closed before coming to Broadway. Then Youmans paired up with lyricist Anne Caldwell for *Oh, Please!* (1926), starring Beatrice Lillie. The score was lackluster and, except for "Like He Loves Me," faded into oblivion.

Youmans was dissatisfied with the way his shows were produced, so he produced *Hit the Deck* himself, in collaboration with veteran producer Lew Fields (Dorothy's father). Commented the composer, "For the first time in my life I am able to select my own singers and my own cast to interpret my music and to play the parts as I would like to have them played. For the past six or seven years, I have been completely at the mercy of the managers and of the actors." Leo Robin and Clifford Grey provided the lyrics and Herbert Fields wrote the libretto. *Hit the Deck* contained two smash hit songs, "Hallelujah" and "Sometimes I'm Happy."

Although Youmans continued producing after the success of *Hit the Deck*, he provided only the score for his next show, *Rainbow*. Oscar Hammerstein II directed and collaborated on the libretto with Laurence Stallings. The enterprise plummeted Youmans from smash success to great failure. It had a particularly disasterous opening night, and critic Gilbert Gabriel commented, "One intermission was so long and lapsy that the orchestra played everything but 'Dixie' to fill it up."

Youmans bounced back, but a poor libretto, and history, would doom his next show, *Great Day* (1929). He was so sure of his producing talents that he bought the Cosmopolitan Theater, long considered a jinxed house. Edward Eliscu and Billy Rose wrote the lyrics for what was one of Youmans's best scores, featuring four big hits: "Happy Because I'm in Love," "More Than You Know," "Without a Song," and the title song. It suffered a particularly painful out-of-town tryout, leading Broadway wags to dub it *Great Delay*. A week after the show opened the stock market crashed, and Youmans, producer as well as composer, was forced to close *Great Day*.

Youmans fled New York for the more hospitable clime of Hollywood, overseeing the adaptation of several of his stage musicals for the screen. He also wrote an original movie musical, *What a Widow!* (1930) but, when it flopped, returned to New York. He had borrowed money from Florenz Ziegfeld for *Great Day*, and in return had promised the impressario a new score. The result, *Smiles* (1930), starred Fred and Adele Astaire but was a failure. Youmans and Ziegfeld fought incessantly, and Ziegfeld went so far as to get a court injunction barring Youmans from the out-of-town theater. One hit emerged from *Smile*, "Time on My Hands," with lyrics by Adamson and Mack Gordon.

Youmans's career was clearly on the skids. His work wasn't bad, but personal problems prevented him from realizing his potential. He had determined that his failures were due to bad management. He produced *Through the Years* (1931) but it was another huge failure, running only twenty performances. "Drums in My Heart" and the title song received the most notice. Youmans's last Broadway show was *Take a Chance*. He was asked to come in and bolster the show by Richard A. Whiting, Nacio Herb Brown, and B. G. De Sylva—and the show ended Youmans's Broadway career with a hit.

The composer's last assignment was for the Astaire/Rogers film *Flying Down to Rio* (1933). He tried to come to an agreement with RKO for more movies, but while the negotiations dragged on, he discovered he had tuberculosis. Although his health improved, his relationship with RKO did not. Youmans moved from location to location, trying vainly to settle down. He was nearly broke and unemployable on Broadway and in Hollywood. Inspired by George Gershwin, he took classical music lessons and occupied his last years readying a revue that would feature Latin rhythms. The show was titled *Vincent Youmans's Revue* though there were no Youmans songs in the show. It closed in Baltimore in 1944. Vincent Youmans died in Denver on April 5, 1946. ❖

## Song and Story

### TEA FOR TWO

While on a lunch break from working on *No, No, Nanette*, Vincent Youmans wrote this sprightly tune. He gave the music to lyricist Irving Caesar who set it to dummy lyrics so he'd remember the emphasis of the notes. That "dummy" version of the song became the standard we all know now.

### HALLELUJAH

Youmans wrote a march while stationed at the Great Lakes Naval Station in Illinois. The year was 1917 and the song became something of a success, and was even recorded by the March King himself, John Philip Sousa. In 1927, "Hallelujah" made its debut on a Broadway stage with lyrics by Clifford Grey and Leo Robin. Its name got it into trouble in England, where they considered it sacrilegious.

### TIME ON MY HANDS

Written for *Smiles*, this song didn't satisfy star Marilyn Miller. She insisted that Youmans write her something as good as "Wild Rose," a Jerome Kern song she'd sung in *Sally*. Nothing the composer came up with was good enough. Youmans wrote Ziegfeld, "This is the usual request for nearly every number I have written in the shows you have made. In other words, it has been 'Write me a number like so and so or so and so.'"

Do all lifeguards wear such tight shorts? Anyway, Susan Johnson and chorus in the fabulous revival of *No, No, Nanette*.

# Music Publishers

The Witmark building at 8 West 29th Street in New York. This was Witmark's first home of their own.

At the start of the Tin Pan Alley era, most sheet music was published by stationers and music stores, and newspapers printed song lyrics in their rotogravure sections. When Charles K. Harris published "After the Ball" in 1892, the sheet sold an amazing 2 million copies, due in large part to constant promotion, or what came to be known as "song plugging." The piano was the instrument of choice in turn-of-the-century America, and by 1899, manufactures were building more than 350,000 pianos a year for parlors, saloons, and theaters. Interest in making music transcended economic and racial divides and all those pianists wanted more than the usual Beethoven, Bach, and Brahms. Stoked with the optimism of the new century and inspired by the industrial revolution, everyone wanted to be up to date. The new musical forms, ragtime and later jazz, captivated the public imagination and the fox-trot replaced the waltz as the dance of choice. Tin Pan Alley publishers and writers sprang up to fill the need for the latest sounds and rhythms.

Soon, cylinder machines and record players became affordable for the growing middle class, and, with the growth of cities, the rural population dropped and American mores began to change. Dance halls, restaurants with dancing, and nightclubs sprang up in the new urban centers, and they demanded the newest, the latest, the most modern popular songs.

Vaudeville and musical comedy took hold, the former an excellent way to introduce new popular songs and the latter the art form of choice for songs that could cross over from the stage to the parlor. The popular standard was born.

The folk tradition that supported the likes of "Yankee Doodle," and "The Streets of Laredo" was codified by the music publishers. Regional publishers couldn't compete with the larger ones who did business through a vast retail network that included that monumental retailing innovation, Mr. Woolworth's five-and-dime. The department store was also in its infancy, and R. H. Macy and Company, and Siegel, Cooper and Company in New York began selling sheet music at discount prices. Song pluggers and song demonstrators across the country pushed the newest songs.

Many of the new music publishers had been songwriters who'd become disgruntled with their royalties and decided to set up their own houses. It wasn't easy getting a song heard amidst the cacophony of music pouring forth from Tin Pan Alley. By 1906, publisher T. B. Harms, whose founder died that same year, already had more than 25,000 songs in its catalogue.

The story of Harms reflects the history of many publishing houses. In 1901, arranger Max Dreyfus joined the firm and soon thereafter purchased a one-quarter interest. In 1904, he bought out the firm. Dreyfus began signing the younger generation of Broadway composers, betting on their continued productivity. One of these, Jerome Kern, himself bought a one-quarter interest in T. B. Harms in 1917. A new company, Harms, Inc., was formed to publish all songs not by Kern. In 1920, Dreyfus joined forces with the British publisher Chappell and Company, eventually merging the two companies.

When sound films became a reality, the movie studios set up their own companies to publish the songs from their pictures, and they also started buying up other catalogs. Warner Brothers Pictures bought the M. Witmark and Sons, Jerome Remick, and T. B. Harms catalogues, and later bought Advanced Music Corporation which owned the Ager, Yellen, and Bornstein holdings as well as other catalogs. Still, independent publishers such as Bourne, Helene Blue Music, and September Music continue to operate in the shadow of the huge conglomerates. Composers were regaining control of their copyrights and hiring the majors to administer their songs without giving up ownership.

Today there are no song pluggers or demonstrators, no vaudevillians to introduce songs on the Orpheum Circuit. But songs are still licensed by them for use on soundtracks, in commercials, theater productions, and even as telephone ring tones. Although ASCAP collects monies for such performances as broadcast, radio, Internet, and cabarets, and then sends the money to the publishers, the role of the publisher is still that of a salesman—and that is unlikely to change. ◆

## First Person

Pace and Handy Music Company, the first black-owned publishing house, located in the Gaiety Theater building at 47th and Broadway. The building is now the W Hotel.

vous butts of their half-consumed cigarettes; small, squeaky actresses of ten or twelve towed by their belligerent mothers—these are the unknowns who rub shoulders with the great folk of minstrelsy in the clamorous outer office. Probably the Al Jolson or the Nora Bayes of tomorrow is somewhere in the group....

Back of this, providing a kind of thorough-bass for the composition, is a strange, unending blurr of sound, bits of music seeping out from the supposedly sound-proof studios in which a new Berlin from Chinatown may be eagerly showing what melodies are in his sheaf or a new favorite from vaudeville may be having the latest ballad adjusted to her immovable voice. On the other hand, the voice you hear sifting through the keyhole may be one you recognize fondly as the voice of Grace La Rue. Or the deep boom-boom of Nora Bayes. And, as like as not, that plump and pleasing person elbowing his way through the crowded anteroom will be none other than the Lord of Jazz, Paul Whiteman. In summer time, when the doors and windows of Tin Pan Alley stand open all day long, the sidewalks underneath are clogged with stray listeners to the favorites of the coming season as they leak from the rooms where orchestras and pianos and quartettes are trying them.

# INDEX

Sophie Tucker

Anita Ellis, Red Skelton, and Danny Kaye

Frank & Nancy Sinatra

Frank & Nancy Sinatra

**Patti Page**

**Dean Martin & Rosemary Clooney**

Sammy Davis, Jr.

Jo Stafford

Margaret Whiting

Steve Lawrence & Eydie Gorme

## PHOTO CREDITS

We are grateful to the following individuals and institutions for permission to publish the photographs in this book. Every effort has been made to obtain appropriate permissions and clearances. The author and publisher apologize for any inadvertent oversight and, if made aware, will include an appropriate acknowledgment in all future printings.

PHOTOFEST: opposite title page, copyright page, acknowledgements page, 9–28, 29 (top), 30–32, 33 (top and bottom), 36, 37 (bottom left), 38–47, 49–51, 53, 54, 56–60 (bottom), 64, 65 (top right)–69, 71–73 (top), 74–90, 92–95 (top left & lower right), 96 (all but bottom left)–109 (top right), 112–144, 146–154, 156–159, 169, 171, 177–187, 189–192, 193 (top)–196 (top), 197–199 (left), 200, 201 (bottom), 202, 205–207, 208 (right), 209, 210, 214–219, 222 (top), 224–229, 231–233, 235, 238–239, 241–244, 245–250, 255–260, 261 (bottom right)–269, 271–273 (top), 274–277, 279–286 (top), 288, 290–300, 301 (bottom)–304 (bottom), 305 (bottom right), 306–308, 313–316 (top left), 317–320; BILLY ROSE THEATRE COLLECTION, THE NEW YORK PUBLIC LIBRARY FOR THE PERFORMING ARTS, ASTOR, LENOX, AND TILDEN FOUNDATIONS: contents page, 34, 35, 52 (bottom), 80, 108, 109 (bottom), 110, 111, 175 (top right), 185 (bottom), 188 (top), 193 (bottom), 196 (bottom), 201 (top), 204 (left), 221 (right), 222, 244 (bottom), 261 (top left), 273 (bottom), 286 (bottom), 305 (center left), 309 (bottom); MANOAH BOWMAN COLLECTION: 48; BEN CARBONETTO COLLECTION: 94 (top), 95 (bottom left and top right), 96 (bottom left); BARBARA CARROLL: 33 (right); ERIC COMSTOCK: 65 (bottom left); ELLEN DONALDSON: 212; MICHAEL FEINSTEIN: 8, 37 (top); IRA AND LENORE GERSHWIN TRUST: 234; DAVID JASEN COLLECTION: 52 (top), 160, 208 (left), 211, 223, 236, 237, 252, 280, 301 (top), 304 (top), 310, 312; STANLEY MILLS, SEPTEMBER MUSIC: 289; NICK PERITO COLLECTION: 29; DARYL SHERMAN: 65 (top left); DONALD SMITH, MABEL MERCER FOUNDATION: 91; GEORGE ZENO COLLECTION: 70, 73 (lower right).

Dionne Warwick